REVISED
SECOND EDITION

PSYCHOLOGY
A Way to Grow

Carl R. Green, Ph.D.   **William R. Sanford, Ph.D.**

AMSCO SCHOOL PUBLICATIONS, INC.,

a division of Perfection Learning®

Please visit our Web sites at **www.amscopub.com** and **www.perfectionlearning.com**

Text and Cover Design: Merrill Haber
Art: Hadel Studio
Composition: Sierra Graphics, Inc.

When ordering this book, please specify:
13507   *or* PSYCHOLOGY: A WAY TO GROW,
SECOND EDITION, REVISED, SOFTBOUND

ISBN 978-1-56765-666-4

PRINTED IN THE UNITED STATES OF AMERICA

4 5 6 7 8 9 10   14 13

PSYCHOLOGY
A Way to Grow

PREFACE

PSYCHOLOGY: A WAY TO GROW, Second Edition, Revised, is designed to introduce students to psychology in two ways. First, the book provides its readers with a foundation in the basic theories and principles of psychology. Second, it guides students toward a greater understanding of their own capacity for growth. Students who plan to take additional courses in psychology will thus have a solid basis on which to build. All students, however, will be able to benefit from the insights provided by a field that touches almost every aspect of their daily lives.

The book fits readily into most psychology courses. Traditional topics, such as personality, learning, and social psychology, are given proper attention. We have also included chapters on the brain and consciousness, child and adolescent development, and new frontiers in psychology. Special sections on research techniques, dreams, career opportunities, the troubled personality, and parapsychology add interest and depth.

Several major themes run through PSYCHOLOGY: A WAY TO GROW, Second Edition, Revised. First, students are led toward self-understanding. Principles of behavior are illustrated by real-life situations that lie within the range of adolescent and young-adult experiences. As self-understanding grows, the student moves toward greater understanding of others. Connections among individuals, family, community, and society are probed for useful insights. Then, as understanding of self and others develops, readers begin to recognize opportunities for growth. Students become aware of the self-defeating behaviors and counterproductive choices that keep them from making more positive decisions about their lives.

No single school of psychology dominates this book. Freud receives respectful attention, but we are not Freudians. Neither are we biased toward behaviorism, humanistic psychology, or existentialism. When we discuss strategies for coping with the problems of daily life in Chapter 16, our approach is totally pragmatic.

We have done our best to write a readable, easy-to-use text. Technical terms are defined in context, and the language is clear, direct, and personal. The layout is open and inviting. Each chapter starts with a lively "grabber" that sets the stage for the new material to come. Pro & Con features involve the reader in a series of debates on controversial issues. Similarly, BioBoxes introduce readers to outstanding figures in the field (but not always to the most predictable ones). Other special features describe important experiments, summarize key ideas, and illustrate the people and events that make psychology so dynamic. Finally, carefully written summaries lead to an extensive set of end-of-chapter materials. These study aids include key terms, objective and discussion questions, student activities, and a student-oriented reading list.

After all the theories, experiments, and debates are considered, what does psychology say to us? Perhaps Shakespeare put it best almost 400 years ago. In *Hamlet,* he has old Polonius say:

This above all, to thine own self be true;
And it must follow, as the night the day,
Thou canst not then be false to any man.

Psychology gives people the chance to know who they are and what they are. With that self-knowledge, they are free to become happy and productive individuals.

CARL R. GREEN
WILLIAM R. SANFORD

CONTENTS

UNIT I   THE MIND AT WORK   1

1 Psychology Is the Study of Human Behavior   2

1.1 What Is Psychology?   5
1.2 Why Should You Study Psychology?   8
1.3 How Can Psychology Help You Achieve Self-Actualization?   10
1.4 How Do Psychologists Learn About Human Behavior?   11
1.5 What Are the Basic Areas of Study in Psychology?   19
1.6 What Career Opportunities Does Psychology Offer?   23

PRO & CON THE PSYCHOTHERAPIST RESPONDS TO CRITICISM   12–13

2 Consciousness   30

2.1 How Does Consciousness Help You Deal With Reality?   32
2.2 What Role Do Sensory Experience and Perception Play
    in Bringing Order to a Confusing World?   35
2.3 What Role Do Sleep and Dreams Play in Your Life?   37
2.4 What Is Hypnosis?   45
2.5 What Effect Do Psychoactive Drugs Have on Behavior?   49

BIOBOX ANN FARADAY   41

PRO & CON SETTING THE RECORD STRAIGHT ABOUT HYPNOSIS   48

3 The Brain and Behavior   61

3.1 What Roles Do the Brain and Glands Play in Behavior?   63
3.2 What Effect Does Vision Have on Behavior?   73
3.3 How Does Your Sense of Hearing Affect Behavior?   77
3.4 How Do Your Senses of Smell and Taste Work?   80
3.5 What Effect Do the Skin Senses Have on Behavior?   83
3.6 Do You Have Any Senses Beyond the Basic Five?   86

PRO & CON IS PSYCHOSURGERY A PROPER TREATMENT
          FOR MENTAL PROBLEMS?   70

BIOBOX JOSÉ DELGADO   72

UNIT II   HOW PEOPLE GROW   93

4 The Child Grows Up   94

4.1 Why Is the Psychologist Interested in Child Growth and Development?   *96*

4.2 What Effect Does Heredity Have on Human Behavior?   *101*

4.3 What Factors Influence the Physical Development of the Child?   *108*

4.4 What Are the Stages of Intellectual Development?   *113*

4.5 How Does a Child Develop Emotionally?   *119*

4.6 What Can Parents Do to Ensure That Their Children Develop Physically, Intellectually, and Emotionally?   *122*

4.7 What Special Problems Do Parents and Children Face Today?   *127*

PRO & CON SHOULD GENETIC SCREENING BE MADE COMPULSORY FOR COUPLES WHO PLAN TO MARRY?   112

BIOBOX JEAN PIAGET   116–117

5 The Adolescent Searches for Identity   134

5.1 What Is Adolescence?   *136*

5.2 What Physical Changes Take Place During Adolescence?   *139*

5.3 What Emotional Challenges Does the Adolescent Face?   *144*

5.4 What Are the Developmental Tasks of Adolescence That Relate to the Self?   *150*

5.5 What Are the Developmental Tasks of Adolescence That Relate to Others?   *153*

5.6 What Special Problems Do Adolescents Face Today?   *157*

PRO & CON DO MANY OF THE PROBLEMS OF ADOLESCENCE RESULT FROM THE BREAKUP OF THE TRADITIONAL FAMILY?   158

UNIT III   PERSONALITY DEVELOPMENT   169

6 Freud's Theory of Personality   170

6.1 How Do Psychologists Define Personality?   *172*

6.2 How Have Philosophers and Scientists Tried to Explain Personality?   *174*

6.3 What Contributions Did Sigmund Freud Make to the Understanding of Personality? *181*

6.4 How Does Freud Explain the Defense Mechanisms That the Ego Uses to Protect the Personality? *187*

6.5 Why Does Freud's Theory of Psychosexual Development Arouse So Much Controversy? *191*

6.6 What Happens During Psychoanalysis? *194*

BIOBOX SIGMUND FREUD 180

PRO & CON HOW WOULD TODAY'S WOMEN DEBATE SIGMUND FREUD? 186

7 Personality Theory Since Freud   202

7.1 How Do the Behaviorists Describe the Development of Human Personality? *204*

7.2 What Have the Neo-Freudians Contributed to Personality Theory? *209*

7.3 What Contributions Did Carl Jung Make to Personality Theory? *219*

7.4 How Do the Humanist Psychologists Approach Personality Theory? *223*

7.5 What Have the Existentialists and Other Creative Thinkers Added to Personality Theory? *229*

PRO & CON IS BEHAVIOR MODIFICATION THE ANSWER TO SOCIAL PROBLEMS? 208

BIOBOX KAREN HORNEY 214

BIOBOX ROLLO MAY 227

UNIT IV   WHEN PERSONALITY IS DISTURBED   237

8 Understanding the Troubled Personality   238

8.1 What Is a Troubled Personality? *240*

8.2 What Are the Causes of Mental Illness? *244*

8.3 What Specific Abnormal Behaviors Does the Psychologist Label as Neurotic? *250*

8.4 How Does the Psychologist Classify Different Types of Psychotic Behavior? *256*

8.5 What Abnormal Behaviors Have Been Identified as Personality Disorders? *263*

8.6 What Personality Problems Can Be Traced to Brain Damage or Dysfunction? *268*

BIOBOX KARL A. MENNINGER 243

PRO & CON SHOULD DEPRESSED PATIENTS BE GIVEN ELECTROCONVULSIVE THERAPY? 264

9 Helping the Troubled Personality — 278

9.1 What Is Psychotherapy? *280*

9.2 What Types of Individual Psychotherapy Are Available? *286*

9.3 How Do Different Group Therapies Work? *294*

9.4 Where Can Troubled People Go for Help? *306*

PRO & CON DOES PSYCHOTHERAPY WORK? 293

BIOBOX FRITZ PERLS 301

UNIT V HOW PEOPLE LEARN — 317

10 Learning, Thinking, and Developing Creativity — 318

10.1 How Do People Learn? *320*

10.2 How Does Memory Work? *329*

10.3 How Do People Think? *337*

10.4 How Can You Improve Your Learning and Problem-Solving Abilities? *340*

10.5 How Can You Improve Your Creativity? *348*

BIOBOX EDWARD DE BONO 346

PRO & CON SHOULD SCHOOLS TEACH CREATIVE THOUGHT? 349

11 Psychological Testing 358

11.1 What Do Psychologists Mean by Intelligence and IQ? *359*
11.2 How Do Psychologists Measure a Person's Intelligence? *365*
11.3 Do Intelligence Tests Really Measure What They Claim
   to Measure? *374*
11.4 What Do Achievement and Aptitude Tests Reveal? *379*
11.5 What Can You Learn From Personality Tests? *383*

BIOBOX ALFRED BINET 367

PRO & CON SHOULD YOU BE GIVEN YOUR SCORES ON PSYCHOLOGICAL
   TESTS? 378

UNIT VI THE INDIVIDUAL AND SOCIETY 397

12 Behavior in Groups 398

12.1 How Do Groups Influence Your Behavior? *400*
12.2 What Effect Do Social Pressures Have on Behavior? *405*
12.3 What Causes Aggression? What Can Be Done About It? *410*
12.4 What Causes Prejudice? What Can Be Done About It? *417*
12.5 What Can Psychology Tell You About Suicide, Aging,
   and Death? *423*

PRO & CON IS THE UNITED STATES DECLINING OR ONLY CHANGING? 416

BIOBOX ELISABETH KÜBLER-ROSS 428–429

13 Sex Roles, Sexism, and Sexuality 435

13.1 How Do People Learn Masculine and Feminine Sex Roles? *438*
13.2 What Are the Effects of Sexism on Women? *442*
13.3 What Are the Goals of the Women's Movement? *450*
13.4 What Effect Is the Women's Movement Having on Men? *457*

13.5 How Do Changing Patterns of Sexuality Affect the
Individual? *461*

PRO & CON THE DEBATE NEVER SEEMS TO END 446–447

BIOBOX BETTY FRIEDAN 451

UNIT VII NEW DIRECTIONS IN PSYCHOLOGY 471

14 Exploring Unknown Worlds 472

14.1 Why Do People Believe in the Supernatural? *474*
14.2 Do the Pseudosciences Offer Any Useful Insights? *476*
14.3 What Do Eastern Religions Teach About the Powers of the
Mind? *484*
14.4 What Is Parapsychology? *487*
14.5 How Can Research in Parapsychology Be Controlled? *493*

PRO & CON DID YURI GELLER USE PSYCHIC POWERS TO BEND NITINOL
WIRE? 490–491

BIOBOX JAMES RANDI 495

15 Searching for New Ways to Grow 501

15.1 Why Are So Many People Searching for New Ways to
Grow? 503
15.2 How Do Bodywork Techniques Help People? *506*
15.3 Can People Attain Personal Growth Through Control of Their
Minds and Bodies? *510*
15.4 Which Therapies Combine Self-Realization Techniques With
Traditional Psychotherapy? *515*
15.5 How Can Transactional Analysis Help People Stay in the "OK"
Position? *520*

PRO & CON CAN SELF-REALIZATION BE LEARNED FROM A BOOK? 507

BIOBOX MICHAEL MURPHY 518–519

16 Strategies for Coping

Case History 1 Marjorie: Overcoming Loneliness *534*
Case History 2 Jim: Making Choices for the Future *536*
Case History 3 Rosa: Learning to Express Anger *539*
Case History 4 Martin: Adjusting to Change *542*
Case History 5 Tammy: Coping With Divorce *545*
Case History 6 Ralph: Resolving Problems With Parents *548*
Case History 7 Judy: Overcoming Shyness *551*
Case History 8 Eric: Finding Happiness *555*

Afterword

On Developing a Beautiful Soul 558

Index 561

ACKNOWLEDGMENTS

Grateful acknowledgment is made to the following sources for permission to use copyrighted materials in this book.

30–31 From THE SEARCH FOR BRIDEY MURPHY by Morey Bernstein. Copyright © 1956, 1965 by Morey Bernstein. Used by permission of Doubleday, a division of Bantam Doubleday Dell Publishing Group, Inc.

41–43 From pages 10–11, 69–83, adaptation of pages 39–48 in THE DREAM GAME by ANN FARADAY. Copyright © 1974 by AFAR Publishers, A.G. Reprinted by permission of HarperCollins Publishers, Inc. From "All You Have to Do Is Dream" by Ann Faraday in *The New York Times,* May 13, 1972. Copyright © 1972 by The New York Times. Reprinted by permission.

123 *Poem by Bradley* in *Born to Win* by Muriel James and Dorothy Jongeward (p. 44) © 1971 by Addison-Wesley Publishing Company, Inc. Reprinted by permission of the publisher.

135–136 From I'M OWEN HARRISON HARDING by J. W. Ellison, Doubleday, 1955. Reprinted by permission of Curtis Brown, Ltd. Copyright © 1955 by James Whitfield Ellison. Reprinted by permission of Curtis Brown, Ltd.

135 From A SKY FULL OF POEMS by Eve Merriam. Copyright © 1964, 1970, 1973, 1986 by Eve Merriam. Reprinted by permission of Marian Reiner.

137 Reprinted with the permission of Charles Scribner's Sons, an imprint of Macmillan Publishing Company from LOOK HOMEWARD ANGEL by Thomas Wolfe. Copyright 1929 by Charles Scribner's Sons, reviewed © 1957 by Edward C. Aswell, as Administrator C.T.A. of the Estate of Thomas Wolfe and/or Fred W. Wolfe.

148 From ANNE FRANK: THE DIARY OF A YOUNG GIRL by Anne Frank. Used by permission of Doubleday, a division of Bantam Doubleday Dell Publishing Group, Inc.

170–172 From EXPLORING THE MIND OF MAN by Lucy Freeman. Reprinted by permission of Grosset & Dunlap, Inc.

180, 181 Excerpt from page 164 from THE ORIGINS OF PSYCHO-ANALYSIS: LETTERS TO WILLIAM FLIESS BY SIGMUND FREUD. Edited by Marie Bonaparte, Anna Freud, and Ernst Kris. Authorized translation by Eric Mosbacher and James Strachey. Copyright 1954 by Basic Books, Inc. Reprinted by permission of BasicBooks, a division of HarperCollins Publishers, Inc.

180 From *An Autobiographical Study* by Sigmund Freud, translated by James Strachey. Copyright 1935 by Sigmund Freud. Copyright 1952 by W. W. Norton & Company, Inc. Copyright renewed 1963 by James Strachey. Quote used by permission of the publisher W. W. Norton & Company, Inc.

202–204 From THE SHAPING OF A BEHAVIORIST by B. F. Skinner. Copyright © 1979 by B. F. Skinner. Reprinted by permission of Alfred A. Knopf, Inc.

238 Excerpt from pages 142–143 from THE BELL JAR by Sylvia Plath. Copyright © 1971 by Harper & Row, Publishers, Inc. Reprinted by permission of HarperCollins Publishers, Inc.

239 Reprinted with the permission of Macmillan Publishing Company from LISA AND DAVID by Dr. Theodore I. Rubin. Copyright © 1961 by Theodore Isaac Rubin. Pages 1–3 from MANIA by L. M. Jayson. Copyright 1937 by Funk & Wagnalls Company. Copyright renewed. Reprinted by permission of HarperCollins Publishers, Inc.

243 From THE VITAL BALANCE by Karl Menninger. Copyright © 1963 by Karl Menninger, M.D. Used by permission of Viking Penguin, a division of Penguin Books USA Inc.

254, 278–279 From the *Making of a Psychiatrist* by David Viscott. Copyright © 1972 by David S. Viscott. Published by Arbor House Publishing Company.

286 From *A Psychiatrist's Head* by Martin Shepard. Reprinted by Permission of Wyden Books.

290, 547 From KNOTS by R. D. Laing. Copyright © 1970 by R. D. Laing. Reprinted by permission of Pantheon Books, a division of Random House, Inc.

291, 296–297 From *Basic Approaches to Group Psychotherapy and Group Counseling* (Second Edition) by Gazda. Copyright © 1975 by Charles C. Thomas. Courtesy of Charles C. Thomas, Publisher, Springfield, Illinois.

297 Poems from PSYCHOPOETRY by Gilbert A. Schloss, copyright © 1976 by Gilbert A. Schloss. Reprinted by permission of Grosset & Dunlap, Inc.

298–299 From *Own Your Own Life* by Richard G. Abell, MD., with Corliss W. Abell, Berkley Publishing, 1979. Reprinted courtesy of Quicksilver Books, Inc.

305 From *I'll Cry Tomorrow* by Lillian Roth with Gerold Frank and Mike Connolly, 1954. Used with the permission of Lifetime Books, Inc.

319–320 Used with the permission of The Gorilla Foundation.

338 From *Floundering in Fallacy: Seven Quick Ways to Kid Yourself* by Carol S. Offir, April 1975. Reprinted with permission from *Psychology Today Magazine.* Copyright © 1975. (Sussex Publishers, Inc.)

367 Excerpt from pages 463–464 from THE ROOTS OF PSYCHOLOGY by S. Diamond. Reprinted by permission of HarperCollins Publishers, Inc.

370 Reprinted by permission of The Putnam Publishing Group from THE IQ CULT by Evelyn Sharp. Copyright © 1972 by Evelyn Sharp.

381 From THE BRAIN WATCHERS by Martin L. Gross. Copyright © 1962 by Martin L. Gross. Reprinted by permission of Random House, Inc.

382–383 Differential Aptitude Tests: 4th Edition. Copyright © 1982, 1972 by The Psychological Corporation. Reproduced by permission. All rights reserved.

398–399 From BODY LANGUAGE by Julius Fast. Copyright © by Julius Fast. Reprinted by permission of M. Evans and Company, Inc.

409–410 From "Some Conditions of Obedience and Disobedience to Authority" by Stanley Milgram, Human Relations, Vol. 18, No. 1, 1965, pp. 57–76. With permission of Alexandra Milgram.

428–429 Reprinted with the permission of Macmillan Publishing Company from ON DEATH AND DYING by Elisabeth Kübler-Ross. Copyright © 1969 by Elisabeth Kübler-Ross.

429 Conversation with Daniel Coleman: "The Child Will Always Be There; Real Love Doesn't Die,"

Elisabeth Kübler-Ross, Sept. 1976. Reprinted with permission from *Psychology Today Magazine,* Copyright © 1976 (Sussex Publishers, Inc.) "We Are Breaking the Silence About Death," poem by Richard Allen, Sept. 1976. Reprinted with permission from *Psychology Today Magazine.* Copyright © 1976 (Sussex Publishers, Inc.)

448–449 Excerpt from A ROOM OF ONE'S OWN by Virginia Woolf, copyright 1929 by Harcourt Brace & Company and renewed 1957 by Leonard Woolf, reprinted by permission of the publisher.

451 From *The Feminine Mystique* by Betty Friedan. Reprinted with the permission of the publisher W. W. Norton & Company, Inc.

458 From THE MALE MACHINE by Marc Fasteau. Copyright © 1974 by Marc Fasteau. Used with permission of McGraw-Hill, Inc.

480 From POWERS OF THE MIND by Adam Smith. Copyright © 1975 by Adam Smith. Reprinted by permission of Random House, Inc.

483 Adapted from "Conduct Your Own Pyramid Experiments" by Marvin Grosswirth, *Science Digest,* February 1976. Reprinted with permission.

485 Adapted from *The Relaxation Response* by Herbert Benson, M.D., with Miriam Z. Klipper. Copyright © by William Morrow and Company, Inc.

496 Adapted from *Lectures in Psychical Research* by C. D. Broad. Copyright © 1962 by C. D. Broad. Used with the permission of Routledge & Kegan Paul, Ltd.

519 From "How to Have an Extraordinary Life" by George Leonard in *Psychology Today,* May/June 1992. Used with the permission of George Leonard.

534–535 Adapted with the permission of Macmillan Publishing Company from THE BOOK OF HOPE by Helen A. DeRosis and Victoria Y. Pelligrino. Copyright © 1976 by Helen A. DeRosis and Victoria Y. Pelligrino.

539 Reprinted from HOW TO DECIDE: A GUIDE FOR WOMEN by N. T. Scholz, J. S. Prince, and G. P. Miller. Copyright © 1975 and 1985 by College Entrance Examination Board. All rights reserved.

ILLUSTRATION CREDITS

ILLUSTRATION CREDITS

(Jeremy P. Tarcher, Inc.) **495** AP/Wide World **502** Joel Gordon **504** JIM BERRY reprinted by permission of UFS, Inc. **506** Joel Gordon **508** Bonnie Freer/ Photo Researchers **511** Menninger Foundation Photo **513** Single Slices by Peter Kohlsaat/Los Angeles Times Syndicate **515** Janov Primal Institute **517** (*left*) Mark Antman/The Image Works; (*right*) Hazel Hankin/Stock Boston **518** Joyce Lyke/Esalen Institute **523** Jules Feiffer/Universal Press Syndicate **533** Cathy by Cathy Guisewite/Universal Press Syndicate **534** Joseph Schuyler/Stock Boston **537** Jean-Claude Lejeune/Stock Boston **540** Diakopoulos/Stock Boston **543** Arlene Collins/The Image Works **546** Francois Hers/Woodfin Camp **549** Patricia H. Gross/Stock Boston **552** Sylvia Johnson/Woodfin Camp **556** Frank Siteman/Stock Boston **558** Russell Myers/Reprinted by permission of Tribune Media Services.

xviii

THE MIND AT WORK

- PSYCHOLOGY IS THE STUDY OF HUMAN BEHAVIOR
- CONSCIOUSNESS
- THE BRAIN AND BEHAVIOR

Chapter

1

Psychology Is the Study of Human Behavior

Does your life ever seem as though it's not working out the way you'd like? You'd give anything to be really happy, but fate keeps throwing you too many curve balls. Or just when things are going smoothly, you stumble over your own feet.

You're not alone. A lot of other people struggle with the same feelings. Take Bob and Susan, for example. You probably know a couple like them: sharp, talented people, the kind who get elected to class office and who wind up on the homecoming court. They show up at the best parties and always seem to wear the "in" clothes.

To look at Bob, you'd never know that his father is an alcoholic, would you? Or that Bob unconsciously fears that he might someday end up like his dad? No wonder he runs so hard. He's afraid something is gaining on him.

And Susan, honor student and part-time model—what torments her? Get to know her. You'll discover a lot of anxiety behind her easy manner and ready smile. Part of Susan wants to get married as soon as she finishes high school. But another part of her wants to go on to college and a career in the business world. Sometimes she feels torn in two.

OK, you say, so everyone's got problems. That's life. Can anything be done about it?

Anyone who looks for quick, easy solutions is going to be disappointed. But since

the late 1800s, specialists in human behavior known as psychologists have been searching for ways to help people live happier, more productive lives. Most psychologists are optimists. They believe that human beings can overcome the personal problems that fill too many lives with despair.

The following situations will give you some idea of what psychologists do.

At first glance, you might mistake the old stone building for an expensive resort hotel. If you look again, however, you'll see heavy steel mesh over the windows. A few solitary figures stroll across the lawn. In the distance you can hear the sounds of a spirited basketball game. Old movies to the contrary, in this mental hospital no one is wearing a straitjacket.

Stop for a moment outside a first-floor office. Through the window, you can see a white-coated doctor talking to a middle-aged woman.

The woman's eyes are smudged by recent tears. The doctor's voice reveals a warmth that you didn't expect.

"Cindy," he says to the woman, "that's a real breakthrough. Do you know that those are your first tears since you came here?"

A hesitant smile brightens the woman's face. "That means I'm getting better, doesn't

FIGURE 1.1 ▓ Every child begins life with hundreds of thousands of possibilities. Some children grow up to find joy; others find only despair. The job of psychology is to help troubled people find solutions to their life problems.

it? Dr. Browning, can I really start thinking about going home?"

The doctor leans over and pats her shoulder. "That's right, Cindy, you'll be going home soon. But we still have some work to do. Are you ready to talk about your husband and the time when . . . ?"

A thousand sharp-clawed feet scramble inside the banks of cages as you walk into the laboratory. Lights reflect from the white rats' watching eyes. You feel a little nervous. Where is Professor Peterson?

"Ah, you're right on time." As always, her voice is sharp and precise. "So you want to see what's going on in my lab, do you?"

You nod, wondering again what rats can possibly tell a researcher about the behavior of humans.

Professor Peterson motions you over to a special cage. Inside, you can see a single rat. Just as you start to touch the cage, you stop. Something's different about this rat. It seems to have a piece of metal embedded in its head!

In one swift motion, Professor Peterson scoops up the rat and attaches electrical wires to the metal strip. She returns the rat to its cage, the wires trailing behind. At first, the animal seems confused, but Professor Peterson turns to a control panel and flips several switches. A motor hums, and a lever moves slowly in and out of the cage. Instantly, the rat runs to press the lever. Every time the lever emerges, the rat repeats this behavior.

Professor Peterson reads the question on your face. "That electrode is planted in a special part of the rat's brain. We call it the pleasure center," she goes on. "Every time the rat

3

touches the lever, it receives a jolt of pure ecstasy.''

You look thoughtful, your eyes following the rat's frantic behavior. You wonder what this experiment tells us about human beings. Perhaps we also have a pleasure center, and if it were stimulated . . .

You have an extra period with nothing special to do, so you drift into the counseling office. The file of college catalogs catches your eye, and you sit down and start leafing through one of them. The thin partition between you and Ms. Logan's office doesn't block out voices, however. Without really meaning to, you find yourself listening to the conversation going on inside.

"Sam," Ms. Logan is saying, "let's look at your choices. Your grandfather wants what he thinks is best for you, and he's willing to pay half your college expenses to prove it. You've got the grades for a prelaw program, and you've been accepted at the university."

Sam breaks in. "I know, but this last year has been a drag. I want to get away from school for a while and earn some money. Do you know what I mean?"

Ms. Logan's voice is calm. "I hear what you're saying, Sam. That job offer from the fast-food restaurant over in the valley sounds pretty good. To be an assistant manager at your age is quite a compliment."

"Well, why shouldn't I take it?" Sam's angry tone reflects the conflict going on inside his head. "Decisions! It was easier when I was younger!"

You can almost visualize the counselor's friendly gaze as she leans forward. "Maybe you'll find it easier to make a decision if you think about it this way, Sam. The restaurant will give you a quick payoff. Law school means postponing a lot of luxuries for seven or eight years. But what do you see yourself doing 20 years from now . . . ?"

*　　*　　*

Marge looks happier than you've ever seen her. In fact, when you think about it, you realize that she hasn't been laughing much lately. "Hey, did you win the lottery?" you call to her.

"Would you believe it?" she cries. "My mother and I are actually talking to each other! And it's not one of those one-way conversations, either. She's really listening to me."

"Tell me about it," you urge her.

Marge doesn't need much encouragement. "You know how it used to be. Every time I'd ask her for something, she'd automatically say 'no.' I'd get upset, and we'd scream at each other. Before long, we'd both be in tears. Finally, I heard in psychology class about a different way to handle conflicts. It was tough at first, but after a while I learned how to stay in control."

"What's this magic method for handling parents?" you ask.

"There's no magic—just a little insight into human nature. Once I understood that Mom was reacting to my childish behavior, I just acted as adult as I could. I told her how much I love her and appreciate the things she does for me. And then I tried to help her see that I'm 18 now, not 8. Since I stayed calm and adult, she did, too. And before long we were *really* talking to each other. . . ."

Well, that gives you some brief glimpses of what psychology is all about. At one level, psychology is a science—the study of human behavior, whether it's trying out new drugs in a mental hospital or studying the behavior of white rats in a laboratory. But at another more important level, it's one of the helping professions. Thanks to psychology, people like Bob, Susan, Cindy, Sam, and Marge can learn to cope with the frustrations of living in today's high-pressure world.

Perhaps this introduction has made psychology seem relatively simple. Unfortunately, that is not the case. Since human behavior is complicated, psychology cannot be reduced to a few easy theories. This chapter will help you learn something about the basic organization and methods of this relatively young science. More important, you'll also learn more about how psychology applies to your own life. The topics are as follows:

1.1 What is psychology?

1.2 Why should you study psychology?

1.3 How can psychology help you achieve self-actualization?

1.4 How do psychologists learn about human behavior?

1.5 What are the basic areas of study in psychology?

1.6 What career opportunities does psychology offer?

1.1 ■ WHAT IS PSYCHOLOGY?

Sample a typical day's headlines: "War Breaks Out in the Middle East. Child Killed in Gang Shooting. Bribery Scandal Rocks City Hall. Stock Market Falls."

Once in a while a note of hope creeps in: "Doctors Conquer Fatal Illness. Neighbors Aid Homeless Family. Hero Risks Life to Rescue Fire Victim."

People, apparently, are capable of both great cruelty and great compassion. If so, you might wonder why humanity so often chooses violence over caring. After all, poets and artists have created great art to remind us of the heights to which our species can aspire. A play by Shakespeare or a painting by Rembrandt (see Figure 1.2) speaks to the human potential within everyone. Shakespeare and Rembrandt, however, don't tell us *how* to achieve inner peace. That's the task the psychologist has taken on.

PSYCHOLOGY DEFINED

The word *psychology* comes from the Greek *psyche*, which means "soul," and *logos*, which has come to mean "logic or science." In practice, however, this "science of the soul" has been given a modern definition: *Psychology is the study of human behavior.*

FIGURE 1.2 ■ In this self-portrait, the great painter Rembrandt provides a glimpse of the dignity and self-awareness to which humanity can aspire. Psychology's goal is to help more people move toward that same peak of inner strength and insight.

Psychologists use the scientific method to collect data about behavior. Using the insights gained through observation and experiment, they attempt to answer some of life's most important questions: Why do people act as they do? Can behavior be predicted or changed? Can people's lives be made happier and more productive? What can be done to help people who have lost touch with reality?

If human beings were simple creatures like dogs or horses, the answers to these questions would be relatively easy. But our lives are not controlled by the same instincts and drives that dominate other forms of animal life. Human beings are uniquely gifted with the power of reason and language and the ability to create a complex culture. Psychologists, therefore, have their work cut out for them. The study of behavior yields few easy answers.

PSYCHOLOGY—A YOUNG SCIENCE

In the beginning, no one thought too much about *why* people act the way they do.

Scene 1: A cave, 500,000 B.C.

OBLA: Why is Rad sitting there in the corner all by himself? It's nicer here by the fire with all the others.

KRIK: I don't know. Forget him. I'm ready to eat.

Later, people blamed demons or spirits for behavior they couldn't explain any other way. If Rad acts strangely, the wise ones said, it is because an evil spirit has invaded his body.

It remained for the ancient Greeks to study behavior more carefully. Their gifted philosophers understood that emotional states can affect the way a person feels.

Scene 2: Greece, Fourth century B.C.

PHIPIAS: Plato, you're a philosopher. Do you think there's any connection between the mind and the body?

PLATO: Whenever the soul within it is stronger than the body and is in a very passionate state, it shakes up the whole body from within and fills it with maladies.

Insights such as Plato's helped teach humanity that the mind can affect the behavior of the body. But until a little over a hundred years ago, psychology could not be called an organized science. A 19th-century French-American doctor, Edouard Séguin, set the stage when he wrote, "I look upon psychology as . . . a science of observation, where things are to be observed and put in their places, and nothing is to be created or imagined."

In 1879, Wilhelm Wundt, a German professor, established the first psychological laboratory at the University of Leipzig. Wundt believed that he could discover the nature of the mind by studying behavior "from the inside."

Scene 3: Leipzig, 1879

STUDENT: Tell me again, Herr Professor, exactly what it is I should do.

WUNDT: I call my method of self-observation *introspection*. While you take part in my experiments, you must keep careful records of your feelings, thoughts, emotions—everything that happens inside you. From these reports, we will learn about the structure of the mind and the nature of consciousness. We'll see how simple mental states are built up into complex experiences such as memory, creativity, and learning.

Wundt's methods put psychology on a firm footing as a science but gained little support in the United States. Americans were more interested in behavior that could be observed than in what the introspectionists claimed to feel. Philosophers such as William James and John Dewey studied the way individuals adjust to their environment. They emphasized the importance of experience and learning.

Their followers made studies of mental illness, animal behavior, normal and retarded children, and ways of measuring intelligence.

So complex is human behavior, however, that other schools of psychology also developed. At the beginning of the 20th century, Sigmund Freud developed his theory of *psychoanalysis*, a method of analyzing and treating mental disorders. Inspired by Freud's work, psychologists began to study the role of the unconscious in influencing our behavior.

Scene 4: Vienna, 1900

PATIENT: But, Doctor Freud, what does my relationship with my father have to do with my problem?

FREUD: Ah, everything. You must realize that the experiences of childhood, buried deep within your unconscious, still influence you. The child is father to the man.

Many psychologists weren't satisfied with Freud's emphasis on the role of the unconscious. Ivan Pavlov, a Russian physiologist who won the Nobel Prize in 1904 for his work on the digestive process, helped prepare the way for a new explanation of behavior. Pavlov discovered that dogs could be conditioned (trained) to salivate when they heard a musical tone. Normally, saliva is produced only when the animals see, smell, or taste food. Pavlov conditioned this automatic response by sounding the tone each time he fed the dogs a special meat powder. He repeated the process six to eight times. After that, the dogs salivated freely whenever they

FIGURE I.3 ▪ Ivan Pavlov performed one of psychology's most famous experiments with this apparatus. Pavlov began by sounding a musical tone whenever he presented food to the dog. In a short time, the dog salivated whenever it heard the tone.

heard the tone, even when no food was present (see Figure 1.3).

John Watson, an American psychologist, saw the value of Pavlov's work. Soon after World War I, Watson announced that psychology should deal only with behavior that can be observed and measured. The goal, Watson proclaimed, was to "predict and control behavior." This approach, known as *behaviorism,* now ranks as one of modern psychology's most important concepts.

Since the 1960s, *humanist psychology* has emerged as a contrasting school of thought to both psychoanalytic and behaviorist theories. Humanist psychologists emphasize the study of healthy, productive emotions. Carl Rogers, a leading American psychologist, summed up the humanist philosophy when he said, "The aim is . . . to assist the individual to *grow,* so that he can cope with the present problem and with later problems in a better integrated fashion."

In recent years, researchers have found that human behavior is strongly influenced by biology. In the *biological view,* mental illness is viewed as a malfunction of the brain and nervous system. Instead of using a traditional "talk" therapy, these psychologists rely on psychoactive drugs and other medical interventions. A severely depressed patient, for example, would be treated with mood-elevating drugs.

■ SECTION CHECKUP

1 Why has the study of human behavior attracted so much attention over the centuries?

2 How does Sigmund Freud's belief in the power of the unconscious differ from John Watson's behaviorist ideas?

3 What do the humanist psychologists see as the goal of psychology?

1.2 ▓ WHY SHOULD YOU STUDY PSYCHOLOGY?

In schools across the country, psychology ranks as one of the most popular of all courses. Can you think of a reason for this surge of interest? Perhaps the following comments by a high school senior will help put your own answer into perspective:

> I first became aware of my own problems with identity when I started my psych class. After I learned about identity problems, I realized that's what had been bothering me all along. I'm still working on my identity. When I find the "real" me, I know I'll be able to build a happier, better life for myself.

Research in physics has provided the know-how that industries need to build space stations and portable computers. Similarly, a knowledge of psychology enables people to apply principles of behavior to their own lives. In this course, you can start learning to understand yourself, the people around you, and the society you live in.

UNDERSTANDING YOURSELF

As you master the basic teachings of psychology, you will find them useful in a number of ways.

1. Psychology can help you understand why you act the way you do. Seen in the light of psychological theory, the inner forces that drive you take on new meaning. Once you understand how important your need to be loved is, for example, you'll be in a better position both to give love and accept love from others.

2. You will learn to recognize the nature and causes of personal difficulties. If the problem is a minor one (such as a reluctance to speak in public), you may be able to deal with it yourself. But you will also learn that it's no disgrace to seek the help of a professional therapist for more serious problems.

3. As a student, you'll understand the nature of the lifelong learning process and your own boundless potential. You'll probably discover interests and abilities that you would otherwise have overlooked. Aptitude tests, for example, can help you choose a career fitted to your particular talents.

4. You will learn that only one person can be responsible for your life—you. Some people have physical or mental handicaps; others have had difficult and troubled childhoods. But no one has to remain a victim. Whatever your background, you have the capacity to make a success of your life, if you choose to do so.

UNDERSTANDING OTHERS

Like it or not, you must share your life with other people. Some of us find it difficult to deal with parents, friends, lovers, co-workers, teachers, and employers. Psychology can help you develop better *interpersonal relationships*—productive, positive ways of dealing with others.

1. You will learn to recognize those emotional responses that keep people apart. As you break down the barriers to good relationships, you will get more done and experience more love in your life.

2. As a member of a particular age group, you will better understand what makes your friends and acquaintances tick. Once you realize why your friend Jason needs attention so badly, for example, you'll be in a position to help him resolve his self-doubts and insecurities.

3. At the same time, you'll be better equipped to cope with the different values and crises common to people both younger and older than yourself. Why, for example, do your parents find it so hard to let you grow up? Should you be worried about seven-year-old Tom's interest in violent war games? And as you grow older, you'll be better prepared to face each new challenge as it arrives.

UNDERSTANDING SOCIETY

Just as you wouldn't want to live apart from other people, you cannot divorce yourself from the larger society in which you live. You may not agree with every value or choice accepted by your culture. Nevertheless, psychology will help you understand how your personality has been affected by growing up in this particular country at this particular time.

1. You will appreciate how the freedom of choice guaranteed by American society affects each of us. As you learn more about your own aptitudes and interests, you will learn how to work within the system to find self-fulfillment.

2. You will understand why modern society has bred such a terrible increase in crime, hostility, and mental illness. With a better understanding of why these problems exist, you will become a more informed citizen and a potential force for helping solve these social ills.

■ SECTION CHECKUP

1 Why are so many more people interested in psychology nowadays?

2 How can psychology help you understand yourself better?

3 How can psychology help you enjoy better interpersonal relationships?

1.3 ▪ HOW CAN PSYCHOLOGY HELP YOU ACHIEVE SELF-ACTUALIZATION?

Many psychologists look forward to a revolution that will alter the society we all live in. The revolution they describe has nothing to do with guns or violence, however. Using their insights into the workings of the human personality, psychologists propose nothing less than freeing all of us from the chains of fear, anxiety, frustration, depression, and other self-defeating emotional states.

Let 15-year-old Patty explain their goal from her point of view:

A month ago, I had this big fight with my best friend. At first I cried about it,

Learning Is Growing

After a while you learn the subtle
    differences between holding a hand
    and chaining a soul,
And you learn that love doesn't
    mean leaning and company
    doesn't mean security,
And you begin to learn that kisses
    aren't contracts and presents
    aren't promises,
And you begin to accept your defeats
    with your head up and your eyes open,
    with the grace of an adult,
    not the grief of a child,
And you learn to build all your roads
    on today because tomorrow's ground
    is too uncertain for plans.
After a while you learn that even
    sunshine burns if you get too much.
So plant your own garden and decorate
    your own soul, instead of waiting
    for someone to bring you flowers.
And you learn that you really can
    endure . . . that you really are strong,
And you really do have worth.

ANONYMOUS

but after a while I began to realize what was happening. I began thinking, "What's wrong with me? What's wrong with my life? Where am I going? Who am I?" I felt so insecure. Then I realized that my friend was my crutch in life, that I liked her more than I liked myself. Well, I thank her very much for making me look at myself. Now I'm getting myself together. Oh, yes, our friendship now is better than ever.

A psychologist would describe Patty's insight as a step toward *self-actualization*, or *self-direction*. That means she's beginning to take responsibility for her own life and decisions, instead of leaning on others.

Many popular psychology books set self-actualization as an important goal. This idea comes from humanist psychology. The concept of self-actualization is based on the fact that the happiest, most productive people are those who have learned to satisfy their needs for personal esteem, accomplishment, and recognition. Like Patty, self-actualizing people understand their own psychological needs, and they take responsibility for their own mental health.

When you become a self-actualizing person, you gain realistic insights into what is possible. You don't frustrate yourself by working for impossible goals. You feel free to ask for help when it is needed, without feeling guilty or weak. You don't allow anyone or anything to dominate your life. Self-actualization frees you to start new projects, enter into new relationships, and seek new experiences. In fact, each experience becomes an opportunity for growth rather than a danger to be avoided.

Can you imagine a future in which self-actualization has become the rule instead of the exception? Problems wouldn't disappear overnight, of course. Society would still suffer from poverty, crime, pollution, and unemployment. But when men and women are no longer burdened by negative emotions, they will be free to rebuild society in a new, more humane way.

■ SECTION CHECKUP

1 How would you define *self-actualization?*

2 Why do the humanist psychologists believe that self-actualization is a worthwhile goal?

1.4 ▓ HOW DO PSYCHOLOGISTS LEARN ABOUT HUMAN BEHAVIOR?

For most of this chapter, you have been reading about psychology as the *science* that studies human behavior. But can something as unpredictable as human behavior be studied scientifically? The answer is "yes." Despite the complexity and inconsistency of human behavior, psychologists have collected a large body of knowledge that has been scientifically proven.

USING THE SCIENTIFIC METHOD

When psychologists investigate a theory relating to human behavior, they turn to the tool used by physicists and biologists—the scientific method. In fact, whether you are a research psychologist studying learning theory or a student trying to solve a personal problem, the four steps of the *scientific method* will help you find answers to complex problems. The four steps are (1) defining the problem, (2) forming a hypothesis, (3) testing the hypothesis, and (4) drawing a conclusion.

DEFINING THE PROBLEM.   Research in psychology usually starts with a question. Why, for instance, do people in an elevator look everywhere except at one another? A psychologist interested in this problem would begin by gathering as much data about the subject as possible. Information about eye contact in close quarters might be found in studies published in psychology books and journals. Further information might be gained from interviews with elevator riders or from personal observation of people's reactions while riding in elevators.

In time, the researcher can write a concise definition of the problem. This definition would include background data as well as the psychologist's own experiences, theories, and hunches. For example, the problem of avoiding eye contact in elevators might be defined as possibly relating to (1) social politeness, (2) fear of strangers, (3) a lack of interest in other people, or (4) a way of coping with enforced closeness.

FORMING A HYPOTHESIS.   Based on the definition of the problem, the psychologist can now form a *hypothesis*. Simply stated, a hypothesis is an educated guess about why certain things happen. In this case, the hypothesis would be a likely reason for the lack of eye contact in elevators. You may have already thought of a reason, but let's use this hypothesis: When people are forced to invade a stranger's private body space (the area around us that we don't want other people to enter without our permission), lack of eye contact makes the closeness bearable.

TESTING THE HYPOTHESIS.   How would you test this hypothesis? Like a psychologist, you would probably end up using any or all of four basic methods: life histories, surveys and questionnaires, observation, and experimen-

▓ **PRO & CON:**

The Psychotherapist Responds to Criticism

If you stopped the next ten persons you met on the street, you'd find at least four who have negative feelings about psychotherapy. *Negative,* in fact, may be too soft a word. Many people would rather have a tooth pulled than visit a psychotherapist for help with an emotional problem.

Like all arguments, however, that point of view has another side. In the Pro & Con, you will see how psychotherapists defend their profession against the criticisms they hear most often.

THE CRITICISM	THE RESPONSE
1 Going to a "shrink" usually does more harm than good. People can get well without a psychiatrist filling them full of drugs or shocking their brains.	**1** No one claims that psychotherapy is perfect. Some patients get better without therapy, and others don't respond to treatment. Some therapists do prescribe drugs or electroshock, and that scares people. The real point, however, is that countless men and women live happy and productive lives today because a psychotherapist helped them put their lives back in order.
2 Psychotherapists are just in it for the money. Even if they guaranteed results (which they never do), who can afford to spend $100 an hour or more for weeks and months of therapy?	**2** Like all professionals, psychotherapists expect to be paid for their long and expensive training. But no one need go without help. Free or low-cost therapy can be found in publicly supported mental health clinics and hospitals.

tation. To test the eye-contact hypothesis, for example, one researcher might rely mostly upon interviews with people found riding on elevators. Another might set up a series of experiments to test the hypothesis under controlled conditions.

DRAWING A CONCLUSION. Finally, the psychologist concludes the study by evaluating the data that has been collected, hoping that clear-cut results will prove the hypothesis true or false. Often, however, the data will not clearly confirm or deny the hypothesis. In that case, the researcher may use statistical techniques to decide whether any useful conclusions have been obtained.

Even after a conclusion has been reached,

it will be accepted as valid only if other researchers can duplicate the results. In the eye-contact study, the research verified the existence of private body space and the discomfort that comes when a stranger violates it. Check this out for yourself. Watch how uncomfortable other people become if you sit or stand too close to them.

THE PSYCHOLOGICAL EXPERIMENT

Everyone conducts simple experiments. For example, people are always trying to improve their appearance.

Hypothesis: A tube of Smile-Brite toothpaste will give you more sex appeal. *Experiment:* You buy a tube and try out your new

THE CRITICISM

3 For my money, most psychotherapists are just as mixed up as their patients.

4 Psychology calls itself a science, but few psychologists agree with one another. The whole field seems to be more a matter of opinion than of fact.

5 Psychotherapists will mess up your head before you know what's happening. They can't be trusted with the power to control people's behavior.

THE RESPONSE

3 Psychotherapists are people, just like everyone else. The profession has its share of poorly adjusted men and women—but so do medicine, education, and business. The majority of psychotherapists are concerned professionals who devote their lives to helping others.

4 Psychologists use the scientific method to gather data and to test theories. But human behavior is complex and varied; people can't be put into a test tube to insure that they remain constant. Because disturbed people need help *now*, psychologists cannot afford the luxury of waiting until all proofs are in before trying to apply the results of their research.

5 Psychotherapists don't have any magic power to make people do things they don't want to do. The best psychotherapy can do is to show people *how* to change. No one can be forced to change who doesn't want to do so.

Have you heard any of these criticisms? If the responses make sense to you, perhaps some day you can help someone understand that psychology may not be perfect but that it can give people a chance to live better, happier lives. In this day and age, that has to be worth something.

smile at a party. *Conclusion:* There's no magic shortcut to popularity.

Or faced by a family car that refuses to start, you try another *hypothesis:* It's out of gas. *Experiment:* Add a gallon of gas to the tank. *Conclusion:* It still won't start. So you try a new *hypothesis:* It's the ignition system. And so on, until you find the cause.

A scientist would call that the trial-and-error method of experimentation. Scientific experimentation differs in two ways. First, scientists attempt to control the *variables*, which are any aspects of an experimental situation that can change. Second, scientists keep careful records of everything that occurs during their experiments.

As an example, let's assume that a psychologist has come up with the following hypothesis: People are less likely to offer help to

someone in trouble when others are present at the scene. How can this hypothesis be tested? One psychologist chose to have a young woman drop an armload of books while waiting in an office. (Figure 1.4 illustrates the variables in this experiment.)

VARIABLES. Since the experimenter is looking for cause-and-effect relationships, all the variables in the situation that can be controlled are kept constant—except for the one being tested. The only factor allowed to change is called the *independent variable*. If the effect of the independent variable on the situation causes a measurable change, this result is known as the *dependent variable*. In the book-dropping experiment, a number of variables, called *controlled variables*, are kept constant: the location, the person who drops

FIGURE 1.4

The Variables Involved in a Psychological Experiment

Hypothesis: People are less likely to offer help to someone in trouble when others are present at the scene.

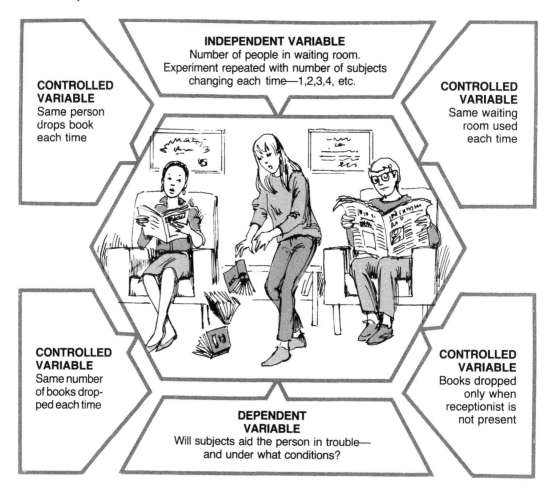

CONTROLLED VARIABLE
Same person drops book each time

INDEPENDENT VARIABLE
Number of people in waiting room. Experiment repeated with number of subjects changing each time—1,2,3,4, etc.

CONTROLLED VARIABLE
Same waiting room used each time

CONTROLLED VARIABLE
Same number of books dropped each time

CONTROLLED VARIABLE
Books dropped only when receptionist is not present

DEPENDENT VARIABLE
Will subjects aid the person in trouble— and under what conditions?

the books, the number of books, the reactions of the young woman who drops the books, and the absence of the receptionist. Only the independent variable—the number of people in the waiting room—is allowed to change. Will anyone offer to help the young woman? That is the *dependent variable* the researchers are waiting to measure.

In the actual experiment, the psychologists found that when only one other person was present, that person almost always offered to help. Neither the age nor the sex of the helper seemed to matter. As the number of people in the waiting room increased, however, the offers of help decreased. Thus, the data supported the hypothesis. People in groups apparently look at one another and say, "I will if you will." All too often, no one makes the first move.

CONTROL GROUPS. Not all experiments can be run as simply as the book-dropping study. In many types of experiments, the researcher must compare the presence of the independent variable on one group of subjects and the absence of the independent variable on another group. Groups of subjects who receive the independent variable are called *experimental groups*. Subjects who do not receive the independent variable are known as *control groups*.

For example, suppose that you hypothesize that learning how to meditate will improve a student's grade in a tough mathematics class. Since meditation is a rather simple technique for achieving relaxation, it can be taught to almost anyone. To conduct the experiment, divide your mathematics class into experimental and control groups. Each group should be matched to the other in as many factors as possible—age, sex, intelligence, previous mathematics experience, common interests, and the like.

Begin the experiment by teaching meditation techniques to the experimental group in addition to the standard work in mathematics. These students will be asked to meditate regularly for 20 minutes a day over a period of three weeks. At the same time, you will make sure that the control group receives identical mathematics instruction—but no training in meditation. At the end of the three weeks, give all students the same exam. Since the two groups are matched, they would normally score about the same. Any major improvement in the experimental group over the control group would validate your hypothesis.

SINGLE-BLIND AND DOUBLE-BLIND EXPERIMENTS. Many experiments cannot succeed if the subjects know what is going on. If you try out a new drug for the common cold, for example, your subjects' reactions might be influenced by their excitement at being asked to try a new "miracle" drug. To combat this, the researcher might design a *single-blind experiment*. In such an experiment, both experimental and control groups receive apparently identical pills; neither group knows the purpose of the pills. The experimental group, of course, receives the new drug. The control group, however, is given a *placebo* (an innocuous substance, usually a sugar pill, that cannot affect the subject in any way). If the experimental group reports 40 percent fewer colds over a winter season, you can assume that the new drug did its job.

Medical researchers have discovered another complication in running such experiments, however. The attitude of the scientists who conduct the tests can influence the results. First, researchers handing out the placebos might somehow project a different attitude from what they would when giving out the actual drug. Second, observations and record-keeping might be influenced by "insider" knowledge. Studies show that researchers smile more encouragingly at members of the experimental group, for instance. They also tend to overlook sniffles in the experimental group that would be recorded as full-fledged colds in the control group.

To avoid such problems, psychologists often turn to the *double-blind experiment*. In this procedure, a third party controls the distribution of the drugs and placebos. By adding this extra layer of control, neither researchers nor subjects can know who's in which group, or which pill is the drug and which the placebo. Such elaborate procedures add greatly to the cost of an experiment. Without them, no scientist would accept the result as scientifically valid.

USING STATISTICS

If you have a coin handy, flip it 20 times, counting the heads and tails. You might expect to get 10 heads and 10 tails. This ratio results from random chance. But suppose you obtained 16 heads and only 4 tails. Have you violated the laws of chance? Twenty flips is too few to tell. But if you try 10,000 flips and you still get four times as many heads as tails (a ratio of 4:1), you'll have discovered a significant variation from chance.

Psychologists evaluate their experiments in a similar way. They keep their judgments objective by looking for *statistically significant* results based on standardized mathematical techniques. In order for results to be significant, comparison of the experimental and control groups must show a difference beyond what could be expected through random chance.

Remember the experiment on meditation as a way of improving mathematics grades (page 15)? If all members of the experimental group (Group *A*) improved their scores but none of the control group (Group *B*) did, chance could be ruled out. In actual practice, however, an overlap will probably be found. Some students in Group *A* will not be helped, and some Group *B* students will show improvement. In that case, just looking at the numbers won't prove or disprove the hypothesis. Instead, a mathematical formula must be applied to the data. The researcher can then tell if the results of the experiment are unlikely to occur on the basis of chance. If the experimental group showed a statistically significant improvement in their grades, the researcher would conclude that training in meditation helps improve mathematics scores.

CORRELATIONS

Another statistical measure often used to show relationships between two sets of data is called a *correlation*. After gathering data on two types of behavior, the researcher uses a formula to obtain a numerical value for the degree of relationship.

A CORRELATION STUDY. Most people would automatically agree that hours of study time and high grades are positively correlated; that is, increased study time leads to higher grades. But to find out for sure, you'd have to collect data on a large number of student subjects. Although a thousand would be a good number, adequate results can be obtained if you use at least 30 subjects, selected at random from the total school population. If you find that each additional hour of study time *always* produces a higher grade-point average (GPA), you'll have a perfect +1.00 *positive correlation*. If that result is reversed, so that more study time always results in lower grades, you'll have identified a −1.00 *negative correlation*. As a third alternative, you might find that no relationship exists at all—a *zero correlation*. (On page 17, these three correlations are illustrated in the form of easily constructed scatterplots. Each dot on the scatterplot stands for one student's study time shown in relation to that student's grade-point average.)

MISUSE OF CORRELATIONS. Although a positive correlation may exist between two sets of data, this does not mean that one necessarily causes the other. For example, suppose that you surveyed students in your class and found that all the left-handed students made the honor roll last semester. Would you conclude from the evidence that left-handedness was the cause of their good grades? Probably not, just as you wouldn't conclude that all left-handers are certain to earn better grades than right-handed people.

In 1948, a group of scientists at Kalamazoo University (Michigan) thought they had discovered the cause of increased cancer among people in the developing countries. The cancer rate in several African and Asian nations increased after World War II—at a time when the people of those countries were drinking more milk. Using this apparent correlation, the scientists suggested that drinking milk-

FIGURE 1.5

Using the Scatterplot: A Way of Checking Correlations Between Two Sets of Data

If you collect data from 30 students on (1) the hours of study time they put in each week and (2) their grade-point averages (GPA), you can use a scatterplot to chart the degree of correlation. The three scatterplots on the right illustrate the possible extremes found in such a study. In reality, however, no scatterplot on human behavior ever turns out so exactly.

In these scatterplots, each dot equals one student's GPA (vertical axis) graphed against his or her hours of study per week (horizontal axis). Can you interpret each one? Scatterplot A tells us that hours of study correlates strongly with GPA—the longer you study, the better your grades. B says the opposite—the longer you study, the *lower* your grades. C reports no usable correlation—hours of study and GPA have no relationship.

Why not try your own scatterplot? Pick any two factors that might be related and that can be stated in numerical terms (ounces of orange juice consumed per week against number of colds in a year, for example). Use graph paper to construct a scatterplot similar to those shown here. If you survey a large number of people, you may discover some interesting relationships—but don't be surprised if the results don't verify your hypothesis.

SCATTERPLOT A: STRONG POSITIVE CORRELATION

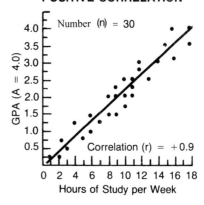

SCATTERPLOT B: STRONG NEGATIVE CORRELATION

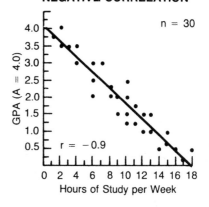

SCATTERPLOT C: ZERO CORRELATION

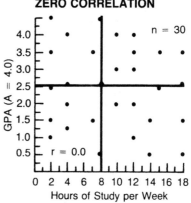

might be the cause of cancer. More careful study later revealed, however, that the increased cancer was related to the pollution of the air, water, and soil that comes with uncontrolled industrialization.

ETHICAL CONSIDERATIONS IN GATHERING DATA

At what point do the rights of animal and human subjects take priority over the need to increase scientific knowledge? Generally, researchers agree that human subjects must not be placed in a situation where lasting emotional or physical harm could result. Few such limits exist for the treatment of animal subjects, however.

DO ANIMALS HAVE RIGHTS? Studies have estimated that millions of mammals, reptiles, and birds are used in scientific research each year. Many of the animals are treated humanely, but others must endure painful surgical procedures and experimental drug treatments. Animal-rights groups have publicized this issue by taking their protests to the media and the courts. A few radical protesters have further disrupted research by "kidnapping" animals from the labs where they were being held. The federal government stepped into the debate in 1989 by issuing strict rules to regulate the use of animals in scientific research.

Supporters of experiments with animals point out that many people are alive today

FIGURE 1.6 ▓ Should this healthy chimpanzee undergo experimental brain surgery, which will probably cause its death? Experimenters say that human lives can be saved through such procedures, but animal-rights supporters claim that most such experiments are needlessly cruel.

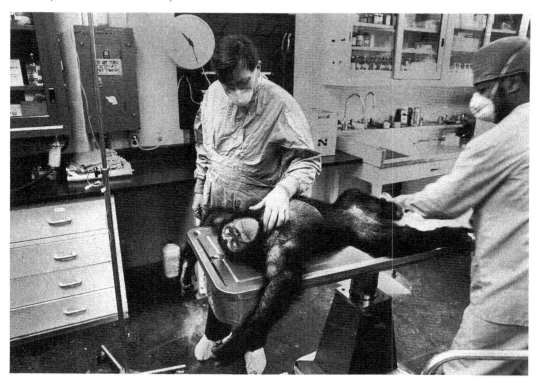

because of drug and surgical tests done with animals. Surgery for removal of brain tumors, for example, was perfected only after extensive experimentation on the brains of lower animals (see Figure 1.6). Many learning experiments could not be carried out if animal subjects couldn't be conditioned to pain, separated from their mothers, or otherwise treated in ways many people believe are inhumane. Experimenters feel that as long as the animals are well treated, except as required by the experiment, such tests must not stop just because some animals suffer.

Supporters of the rights of animals, however, feel differently. They believe that the human race's superior intelligence does not give it the right to exploit lower forms of life. Animal experiments that cause pain or mutilation, they believe, are not necessary. They point out that other procedures, such as the use of tissue cultures and computer simulations, often accomplish the same end. Instead of calling for a total end to animal studies, these animal-rights supporters ask that every new experiment be judged by a single question: Will the death or suffering of this animal truly benefit humanity?

MISLEADING HUMAN SUBJECTS. Another debate centers on the degree to which a researcher should mislead human subjects about the true purpose of an experiment. Most studies, psychologists point out, could

not obtain valid results if the subjects knew what behaviors were being observed. In the book-dropping experiment described earlier, for example, subjects who knew they were being watched would probably not react naturally when the young woman dropped her books.

American Psychological Association (APA) guidelines allow experimenters to mislead their subjects—but they must follow three rules. First, only volunteers should be used as subjects. Experiments that cannot be run if the subjects know they are being observed rate an exception. Second, experimenters must do their best to protect subjects from emotional and physical harm. Third, after the experiment wraps up, experimenters must tell the subjects about any deception practiced on them.

■ SECTION CHECKUP

1 What are the four steps in the scientific method as used by the psychologist?

2 Name the four methods a psychologist uses to gather data. Which method gives the most scientific results?

3 Describe the importance of the following terms used in a psychological experiment: (a) independent and dependent variables; (b) experimental and control groups; (c) single-blind and double-blind experiments.

4 Why does the psychologist use statistical methods to analyze experimental data?

1.5 ■ WHAT ARE THE BASIC AREAS OF STUDY IN PSYCHOLOGY?

Psychology has become such a broad and complex field that the psychologist can no longer be expert in every area. If you someday decide upon a career in psychology, your graduate school will expect you to concentrate on a narrow specialty, such as abnormal psychology or learning psychology. But even as a beginning student, you should know

how psychologists subdivide their subject. This section will introduce you to the major specialties (presented in alphabetical order).

ABNORMAL PSYCHOLOGY

Public health experts estimate that 30 percent of the people in this country need therapy for emotional problems. Their problems range from mild depression to complete breaks with reality (see Figure 1.7). If you became a clinical psychologist, psychiatrist, or psychiatric social worker, you would identify, diagnose, and care for people with emotional problems. On a typical day, you might help a man who believes the devil has tapped his phone; a woman who cannot stop beating her child; a drug addict who wants to kick his habit; a girl who cannot get out of bed to go to school; and an elderly man who has tried to commit suicide. Successful therapy can help these people return to productive lives free from their overwhelming feelings of depression, guilt, rage, and fear. Many psychologists, both in *abnormal psychology* and in the nine other specialties that follow, also spend part of their time teaching in colleges, clinics, and hospitals. (Chapters 8 and 9 take a closer look at the causes and treatment of emotional disturbances.)

COMPARATIVE PSYCHOLOGY

A few years ago, psychologists set up a large, enclosed colony of rats. While the population was small, the rats lived an orderly, peaceful life. But as their numbers grew, the rat society began to break down. Even though the rats still had enough food, the animals apparently could not cope with the lack of adequate living space. Can experiments like this give us insights into human behavior? *Comparative psychologists* believe that animal studies help us understand human problems such as those produced by life in crowded cities.

The field of comparative psychology is divided into two camps. One group believes that animals are worth studying for their own sake. For instance, these psychologists would try to find out why salmon return to the river of their birth to spawn without trying to relate that behavior to humans. The majority of comparative psychologists say that animal studies are worthwhile only if they help us learn more about our own species.

FIGURE 1.7 ■ You might be surprised if you could see what goes on in a psychotherapist's office. Instead of a black leather couch and electroshock apparatus, you'd likely see two people talking about the art of coping with everyday issues and problems.

DEVELOPMENTAL PSYCHOLOGY

If you were a *developmental psychologist*, your job would be to trace the behavior changes that occur as people grow and age. Since these changes take place most rapidly during the first years of life, children receive most of the developmental psychologist's attention. Along with other workers in this field, you would study specific behavior changes, such as how people acquire language, develop sex roles, and achieve a personal identity. Slow-motion photography of an infant, for example, reveals that language usage begins in the first few months of life.

Such films clearly show the baby responding to its parents' speech patterns with similar movements of its head and mouth. (Chapters 4 and 5, which deal with child and adolescent development, show how such research pays off in better understanding of these age groups.)

DIFFERENTIAL PSYCHOLOGY

Differential psychology (often called *personality theory*) attempts to analyze and understand all the individual differences that make up the human personality. Differential psychologists have learned that personality is shaped by an enormous number of hereditary and environmental factors—from the physical size and hair color you inherit from your parents to the effects of watching television and attending school. Sigmund Freud developed the first modern personality theory. Although a number of competing theories have been added since the early years of this century, no single theory has emerged that seems to satisfy all questions about behavior and personality. Differential psychologists believe that their studies will not only help us understand ourselves better but will also point the way toward better systems of therapy for the emotionally disturbed. (Chapters 6 and 7 explore a number of important personality theories.)

INDUSTRIAL PSYCHOLOGY

In recent years, business and industry have hired more and more *industrial psychologists.* If you were president of General Motors, for instance, you'd expect the industrial psychologists on your staff to help design cars with high sales appeal and safety features that people will be willing to use. In addition, industrial psychologists would advise you on how to select and train your employees, maintain their morale, increase their loyalty to the company, and decrease accidents on the assembly lines. Psychologists who understand why consumers choose one product over another have also found important jobs in advertising and television.

LEARNING PSYCHOLOGY

How do people and animals learn to cope with their environment? *Learning psychologists* try to answer that question by running experiments that measure the many factors affecting memory, creativity, and problem-solving ability. Researchers also study how learning is related to intelligence, motivation, and emotional states. Educational and school psychologists, meanwhile, focus on the special problems that face students in the years between enrollment in nursery school and graduation from college. Perhaps you've noticed how worry and tension can interfere with your performance on a test. Advances in learning theory may teach you how to relax before a test—or help your teachers design less stressful test situations. (See Chapter 10 for further discussion of learning theory.)

PHYSIOLOGICAL PSYCHOLOGY

The specialist in *physiological psychology* studies the way in which body processes relate to mental and emotional behavior. Many of the experiments in this field use animals because researchers cannot use human subjects for life-threatening experiments. A new surgical technique for treating epilepsy, for example, would most likely be tried out first on monkeys.

Much of the work in physiological psychology concentrates on the brain and the central nervous system. Researchers have begun to map the brain's control centers for body processes such as motor control, vision, pain, and sleep. Other studies are probing the biological bases for learning and memory. Physiological psychologists also study the glandular system because hormones directly affect behavior. Testing is now well advanced, for example, on so-called "learning" drugs, which help people perform better on problem-solving exercises. (Chapters 2 and 3 provide an overview of the close relationship between mind and body.)

RESEARCH PSYCHOLOGY

The role of the *research psychologist* overlaps all other work in psychology. Research psychologists design scientifically valid experiments to prove or disprove any new theory. You might wonder, does it make any sense to spend thousands of dollars to teach a rat to lower its heart rate on command? The researcher would point out that knowledge gained in such experiments has already been used to help people with high blood pressure control their problem without the use of drugs (see Figure 1.8).

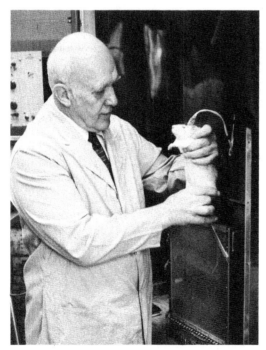

FIGURE 1.8 ■ Research psychologist Neal Miller trained rats to raise or lower their heart rate on command. Tiny jolts of electricity in the "pleasure center" of the brain rewarded the rats that responded by changing their heart rate.

SOCIAL PSYCHOLOGY

The next time you walk down a busy street, take a minute to study the behaviors of the people who share the sidewalk with you. Each person is an individual, but each is also a member of different ethnic, social, and religious groups. What would happen if you stopped one of these strangers and asked for help? Would you get assistance—or would the stranger brush on by, frightened or annoyed?

Such questions occupy the attention of *social psychologists*, who study the behavior of people in relation to their culture. They know that the society we live in exerts a powerful influence on both behavior and mental health. Typical research problems include changes in male and female roles; social pressures that force people to conform to group behavior; and causes of suicide. (Chapter 12 investigates the role of social pressures on behavior.)

SPORTS PSYCHOLOGY

No one is surprised today when well-known athletes turn to a *sports psychologist* to help them overcome a slump or fight an addiction. In this day of high-pressure, big-money competition, team owners and coaches no longer think of psychologists and psychiatrists as "shrinks" whose only value is in treating the troubled personality. They know that mental and emotional factors often make the difference between winning and losing. The primary job of sports psychologists is to apply sound psychological principles to the specialized problems of individual and team performance. They need not be athletes themselves, although a background in competitive sports may make it easier for their clients to relate to them.

■ SECTION CHECKUP

1 List the ten specialties in psychology. What work would a psychologist do in each specialty?

2 Which specialty (or specialties) would you

look to for assistance if you were (a) a politician anxious to be elected, (b) a doctor who needs help in testing a new drug, (c) a parent whose child is having difficulty learning to read, (d) a patient in a mental hospital, (e) a high school student curious about the effect of sexual maturation on behavior, (f) a factory manager who wants to increase worker output?

1.6 ■ WHAT CAREER OPPORTUNITIES DOES PSYCHOLOGY OFFER?

What do you plan to do with your life? Like many other Americans today, there's a good chance that you're probably as interested in the search for inner peace and happiness as you are in becoming wealthy or powerful.

No career can guarantee happiness, of course. But psychology does offer a wide variety of jobs with a number of positive benefits: (1) the chance of gaining insights that will improve your own life, (2) the opportunity of helping others, (3) the prestige of working at a useful and respected profession, and (4) the possibility of a better-than-average income.

Before you sign up for a career in psychology, however, you should also think about

Typical Undergraduate Course of Study For a Major in Psychology

	SEMESTER UNITS		SEMESTER UNITS
Freshman Year		*Junior Year*	
English Composition	9	Foreign Language	3
• Introductory Psychology	6	• Brain and Behavior	3
Mathematics, Statistics,		• Social Psychology	3
or Computer Science	3	• Personality	3
Physical Science	3	• Development in Infancy and	
Social Sciences	3	Childhood	3
Humanities elective	3	• Cognitive Processes	3
		Political Science or Economics	3
Sophomore Year		Literature, Philosophy, or	
• Psychological Methods:		Religious Studies	6
Statistical Procedures	3	Electives	9
Research Procedures	3		
Biology	3	*Senior Year*	
Science electives	6	• Psychology electives	12
Foreign Language	9	Electives	24
Social Science	6		
Fine Arts	3	• *Psychology courses*	
World History	3		

*Because colleges offer far more psych courses than even the most ambitious student can fit into a four-year program, each psych major will choose a slightly different mix of courses, depending on individual interests and goals.

the possible disadvantages: (1) a long and demanding period of preparation (four years of college as a minimum, with as many as five or more additional years for a graduate degree); (2) the strain of working with people suffering from mild to serious emotional problems; and (3) the knowledge that being a psychologist doesn't automatically guarantee that you'll be successful in solving your own personal problems.

THE SCOPE OF CAREERS IN PSYCHOLOGY

As in most professions, prestige and income in psychology are based roughly on the amount of training completed and the value society places on the service you perform. The chart on page 25 will give you a general outline of the most common job titles, along with training requirements, possible income, and job responsibilities.

HOW PSYCHOLOGISTS SPEND THEIR TIME

People who are thinking about careers in psychology usually assume they'll be working with severely disturbed people. As it turns out, only about four psychologists in ten do clinical work of that type. The others keep busy doing research, teaching, counseling, writing, and working in business or industry. A few move into administration and spend their time managing hospitals and clinics. The important point is that psychology is a growing, dynamic field with new opportunities opening up every year.

GETTING STARTED IN PSYCHOLOGY

Employment experts say that psychology will be one of the fastest growing of all occupations during the 2000s. The experts add two cautionary notes to this prediction, however.

First, cutbacks in government funding could eliminate some of these jobs. Second, the greatest demand will be for applicants who have earned their doctorates. Students who leave college with a Master of Arts degree will most likely find work as counselors in schools and mental health clinics. Psych majors who leave after four years with a Bachelor of Arts degree will be limited to lower-paying jobs in hospitals or rehabilitation centers. At any level, psychologists who are trained in quantitative research methods and computer science will be the first ones hired.

In order to begin practicing as a psychologist, you must meet state certification or licensing requirements. College catalogs usually list the course requirements for psychology majors. (See the table on page 23 for a typical undergraduate program.) If you want general information on career opportunities, certification requirements, approved schools, and financial assistance, write to:

American Psychological Association
Educational Affairs Office
1200 17th Street N.W.
Washington, D.C. 20036
<*http://www.apa.org*>

Your high school or college counselor can also help you find additional information. (Activity 5, page 29, will point you to a more immediate investigation of various careers in psychology.)

■ SECTION CHECKUP

1 What would you say are the advantages and disadvantages of a career in psychology?

2 Name some of the jobs a psychologist would be expected to do.

3 Describe the type of training you would need if you wanted to become a clinical psychologist.

Careers in Psychology

TITLE/AVERAGE SALARY*	TRAINING	JOB RESPONSIBILITIES
Psychoanalyst $180,000	M.D. degree, psychiatric residency, special training in Freud's psychoanalytic technique, plus a personal psychoanalysis.	Provides in-depth therapy for severely disturbed patients, using Freudian psychoanalytic techniques. Generally works in private practice. May also teach at a university or psychoanalytical institute.
Psychiatrist $160,000	M.D. degree, psychiatric residency.	Uses medical background as a basis for treating severely disturbed patients in public or private hospitals. Often opens a private practice or operates a clinic. May also teach at a college or university.
Clinical Psychologist $75,000	Ph.D. in clinical psychology, plus internship.	Works in a clinic, hospital, or private practice, diagnosing and treating disturbed patients. Frequently specializes in a particular type of practice—marriage counseling, children, elderly people, or group counseling. May teach at a college or university.
Educational or Industrial Psychologist $53,000	M.A. or Ph.D. with specialization in a particular field.	Applies psychological principles to problems of training, safety, efficiency, product design, testing, improvement of learning efficiency, and personal adjustment. Usually hired by public institutions and private businesses.
Counselor $45,000	B.A. or M.A. in an academic field plus graduate work in psychology.	Usually works in schools or clinics, assisting people who need help in making decisions about vocations, schooling, or personal problems.
Psychiatric Social Worker $48,000	M.S.W. includes advanced training in psychology and social work. M.S.W. prepares holder to give therapy to disturbed patients.	Helps people cope with economic, social, and marital problems. Often employed by public or charitable agencies to work with the poor or other people in need of assistance.
Psychiatric Technician $28,000	Two years of college training in a special program. Often has previous experience that can be applied to the work. Some on-the-job training is usually required.	Assists counselors, psychologists, and other professionals in treating and caring for patients. May conduct group therapy sessions, counsel the sick or dying, work with handicapped children, or give valuable assistance wherever fully trained psychologists are not available.
Lay Worker Income varies	Often college trained in own profession, but a degree is not required.	Anyone (often a teacher, doctor, pastor, or nurse) who is called upon to counsel people about personal problems in the course of his or her daily work.

*Salaries are average figures after five years on the job. Beginning wage scales will be lower, and experienced, talented people will often exceed the top figure. Inflation will also affect these salaries.

LOOKING BACK: A SUMMARY

1 Psychology deals with living, with the problems every person faces in trying to find happiness and cope with problems. Psychologists define their work as the study of human behavior. These scientists use observations and experimentation to collect data about behavior. Because people are complicated, psychology offers few easy answers.

2 As a science, psychology began in Europe in the late 1800s when Wilhelm Wundt attempted to study the mind and the nature of consciousness. Other psychologists took different directions. Both William James and John Dewey emphasized the ways in which individuals function in their environment. Sigmund Freud explored the role of the unconscious. John Watson used insights gained from Ivan Pavlov's work with conditioned reflexes and developed behaviorism. Behaviorists believe that only behavior that can be observed and measured has any meaning for the psychologist. Humanist psychologists emphasize the need for people to grow and take responsibility. The biological view takes a different tack, teaching that many so-called emotional disorders are actually caused by malfunctions in the brain and nervous system.

3 Psychology helps people understand themselves, others, and the society they live in. For the individual, psychology provides insights into the forces that make us unique. With increased understanding of themselves, people can live life to its fullest. By understanding others, they can improve interpersonal relations. A knowledge of culture gives people a chance to work within society to find self-fulfillment.

4 For the future, humanist psychologists hope to free people from the chains of fear, anxiety, frustration, depression, and other self-defeating emotions. According to humanist psychology, the ideal person is self-actualizing, someone who knows how to live a happy and productive life.

5 Psychology's claim to status as a science rests on the use of the scientific method. In order to gather valid information, the psychologist must (a) define the problem; (b) form a hypothesis; (c) test the hypothesis, usually through experimentation; and (d) draw a conclusion. Data sources include life histories, surveys and questionnaires, field observation, and experimentation.

6 Experimentation is the process of testing a hypothesis under controlled conditions. By keeping all variables unchanged except one (the independent variable), the researcher can be certain that any measurable change (the dependent variable) results from the single independent variable. Experimentation also requires that control groups (matched subjects who do not experience the influence of the independent variable) be used to ensure that changes in the behavior of the experimental group actually result from the action of the independent variable. Single-blind and double-blind experiments are used when the results would be biased if either subjects or experimenters knew the purpose of the experiment.

7 Researchers know that human behavior cannot be controlled like chemicals in a test tube. As a result, they often use statistical techniques to judge the results of an experiment. If the hypothesis is correct, the statistics will show that the subjects acted as predicted. Correlations are commonly used to show a relationship between two sets of data. Researchers must be careful not to assume that a cause-and-effect relationship exists whenever they find a positive correlation.

8 Experiments in psychology are governed by a number of ethical limits designed to ensure that subjects, particularly humans, are not harmed emotionally or physically. Similarly, subjects should be told the purpose of the experiment except when telling them would ruin the experiment. Use of animals in experiments that cause death or suffering has also attracted controversy. Many animal experiments have led to improvements in human health care, but animal-rights supporters believe that no animal should be sacrificed unless its death truly benefits humanity.

9 A number of specialized areas make up the general field of psychology. These include abnormal psychology (the study, diagnosis, and treatment of mental illness); comparative psychology (the study of behavior in the lower animals); developmental psychology (the study of human growth and development); differential psychology (the study of the development of the personality); industrial psychology (the application of psychology to industrial, business, and engineering problems); learning psychology (the study of how people learn and how to improve learning); physiological psychology (the study of body processes as they relate to

mental and emotional behavior); research psychology (the design and use of experiments to collect valid data about behavior); social psychology (the study of behavior in relation to the culture in which it occurs); and sports psychology (the application of psychological insights to the special needs of athletes and their teams).

10 Anyone planning a career in psychology must balance the advantages of income, prestige, and opportunities for service against the disadvantages of a long training period, the strain of working with disturbed people, and an uncertain job market. Jobs in psychology tend to pay in direct ratio to the length of the training required. The psychoanalyst, psychiatrist, and clinical psychologist require M.D. or Ph.D. degrees; counselors need a Master's degree; some paraprofessionals may be trained on the job after only two years of college. Most jobs in psychology involve treating patients, doing research, teaching, or counseling. Aside from work in private practice, psychologists are employed by hospitals and clinics, colleges, or by local, state, and federal governments.

PUTTING YOUR KNOWLEDGE TO WORK

■ TERMS YOU SHOULD KNOW

abnormal psychology	experimental group	psychoanalysis
behaviorism	humanist psychology	psychology
biological view	hypothesis	research psychology
comparative psychology	independent variable	scientific method
conditioning	industrial psychology	self-actualization
control group	interpersonal relationships	single-blind experiment
controlled variable	learning psychology	social psychology
correlation	negative correlation	sports psychology
dependent variable	personality theory	statistical significance
developmental psychology	physiological psychology	variables
differential psychology	placebo	zero correlation
double-blind experiment	positive correlation	

■ CHAPTER CHECKUP

I Which of these situations would *not* logically involve the use of psychology? (*a*) A father is trying to teach his daughter how to ride her first two-wheeled bicycle. (*b*) A doctor is examining her elderly patient, who is complaining of feeling tired and depressed. (*c*) A detective is attempting to analyze the motives that led to a baffling kidnapping. (*d*) A chemist develops a new form of plastic in the laboratory.

2 Wilhelm Wundt founded the first school of modern psychology, using a method he called (*a*) behaviorism (*b*) humanist psychology (*c*) introspection (*d*) comparative psychology.

3 The school of psychology that would be most concerned with the concept of self-actualization is (*a*) the humanist (*b*) the Freudian (*c*) the behaviorist (*d*) none of these.

4 Learning the principles of psychology will (*a*) guarantee that you will live a happy, productive life (*b*) give you control over the lives of others (*c*) lead to success in any career that you choose (*d*) help you understand your own behavior and how to change it if you want to do so.

5 Which example of behavior would you most likely find in a self-actualizing person? (*a*) When she's angry, Clara throws things at people. (*b*) When he's angry, Chester stays in his room and sulks. (*c*) When he has an argument with his wife, Clem goes out and gets drunk. (*d*) When Crissie received a grade on a paper she thought was unfair, she went directly to the teacher and asked for an explanation.

6 Which of the following data-gathering techniques used by the psychologist would have the greatest scientific validity? (*a*) collection of a life history (*b*) distribution and analysis of questionnaires (*c*) observation of people's behavior (*d*) controlled experimentation.

7 A social psychologist ran an experiment to find out which type of waiter receives the biggest tips—a smiling, friendly waiter or a less friendly waiter. The dependent variable in this experiment would be (*a*) whether the waiter smiled or not (*b*) the type of customer who eats in the restaurant (*c*) the amount of tips earned by each type of waiter (*d*) the quality and price of the food served to the customers.

8 A psychologist who is interested primarily in studying the changes that take place in children as they mature probably specializes in (*a*) physiological psychology (*b*) developmental psychology (*c*) social psychology (*d*) comparative psychology.

9 About four psychologists in ten are engaged in (*a*) research (*b*) educational psychology (*c*) clinical work (psychotherapy) (*d*) counseling and guidance.

10 Psychologists estimate that the approximate percentage of the population needing therapy for emotional problems is (*a*) 20 percent (*b*) 25 percent (*c*) 30 percent (*d*) 50 percent.

■ EXPLORING CONCEPTS

I What are the basic goals of psychology? If these goals can be achieved, what effect might that have on the future of the society you live in?

2 How would you explain the concept of self-actualization to someone?

3 Why is it so important that experiments in psychology use proper scientific methods? What role do control groups play in maintaining objectivity and validity in experimentation?

4 History records several instances in which rulers ordered that babies be raised in isolation in order to see what language they would speak. What ethical considerations would be involved in setting up such an experiment today?

5 If a good friend asked for advice on a career in psychology, what would you say? Describe the different fields within psychology from which your friend could choose.

■ HANDS-ON ACTIVITIES

I The odds are good that you know someone in your family or circle of friends who can be described as a "self-actualizing" person. Write a brief description of this person, concentrating on those traits, abilities, and ways of coping with problems that have impressed you. How does this person handle stress and the demands of school, job, and family? Do you spot any patterns of behavior that you could adopt for your own life?

2 Visit a local bookstore or library, and browse for a while in the psychology section. Many of the books will fall into the category that might be called applied psychology—the use of psychological principles and techniques to make a person's life happier. Read one or two of the books to see if they really can improve your life.

3 The yellow pages of your local phone book will list the names of practicing psychologists. In some cases, you will find that the local branch of the American Psychological Association maintains a speaker's bureau. Through that bureau, or through contacts with a local psychologist, invite someone to visit your class to discuss career opportunities in psychology. Ask the visitor to talk about training, job opportunities, personal experiences in the field, and the satisfaction of helping people.

4 Pick up any popular magazine and you're almost certain to find one or more articles about the uses of psychology in everyday life. If you have access to the Internet, give APA Online a try. Type in <*www.apa.org*> and use the search engine to find articles on "careers in psychology." The search is almost guaranteed to turn up several articles to share with your classmates.

5 If you are seriously interested in a career in psychology, try the following plan. (*a*) Check academic requirements by studying a number of college catalogs. (*b*) Do some extra reading about the work of a psychologist or a psychiatrist. (David Viscott's book in the reading list that follows would be a good start.) (*c*) Make appointments to talk to as many people involved in the field as possible. Start with school counselors or the school psychologist; then interview local psychologists. (*d*) Check on future job prospects in your chosen specialty. (*e*) Finally, draw up a balance sheet of the pros and cons as you see them—your goals, your abilities, your financial position, and your determination.

FOR FURTHER READING

Bernstein, Douglas A., and Astrid M. Stec, eds. *Psychology: Fields of Application.* Boston: Houghton Mifflin Co., 1999. If you're thinking that a college psychology major is only for people who plan careers as therapists, think again.

By the time you've finished this guided tour, you'll have learned that psychology can help you succeed in fields as diverse as animal training, business, education, law enforcement, mental health, and product design.

Carson, Richard D. *Never Get a Tattoo; Simple Advice on the Art of Enjoying Yourself.* New York: Harper & Row, 1990. Carson fills his pages with witty, common-sense lessons that can help you live a happier, more productive life. Unlike most self-help books, *Tattoo* also describes the psychological theories and insights that support the advice.

Fancher, Raymond E. *Pioneers of Psychology.* New York: W. W. Norton, 1996. Professor Fancher traces the evolution of psychology from its beginnings to the present day. The roll call of philosophers and scientists who helped create a modern science of human behavior includes names such as Gall, Wundt, Pavlov, Freud, Watson, Skinner, and Piaget. As is often the case in books of this type, the coverage of the early psychologists is stronger than that of today's leaders.

Restak, Richard M. *The Mind.* New York: Bantam Books, 1988. Written as a companion to a popular public television series, *The Mind* stands on its own as a fine overview of current trends in the science of human behavior. The reader can choose among topics such as "Search for Mind," "Addiction," "Pain and Healing," "Depression," and "The Violent Mind." Colorful illustrations back up the well-written text.

Viscott, David S. *The Making of a Psychiatrist.* New York: Arbor House, 1972. Viscott writes perceptively and honestly of the long years of training and growth that turned him into a psychiatrist. Particularly recommended for anyone thinking of making a career in psychology.

Woods, Paul J., ed. *Is Psychology the Major for You?* Washington, DC: American Psychological Assoc., 1997. This book is an invaluable aid to any student who's weighing the pros and cons of a college psychology major. Woods describes college entrance procedures, requirements of the major, graduate school entry, and employment prospects. A useful self-exploration exercise teaches decision-making strategies that can help lead to an appropriate choice of careers.

Chapter

2

Consciousness

Some people believe that they can take a guided tour of their past lives. That's right, their past *lives*, as they might have lived them in ancient Egypt, King Arthur's England, or even Kansas in the 1930s. Some subjects tell about living as far back as 4,000 years ago. One white teacher "remembers" an earlier life as a black slave. His wife reports that she was once rescued from a Civil War battle-field.

How do these people get in touch with their past lives? Their trip begins with a visit to a hypnotist who specializes in *age regressions* (*regress* means "to go backward") (see Figure 2.1). Psychologists have long used hypnotism for similar regressions. In the late 1800s, Sigmund Freud used hypnosis to help people in therapy remember events from their childhoods. But Freud did not report any experiences in which patients regressed beyond their own childhoods.

Modern interest in age regression was stimulated by a book written in 1956 by Morey Bernstein. Bernstein, a business executive and amateur hypnotist, had a favorite subject named Ruth Simmons. Today, most people who know this story think of Ruth Simmons as Bridey Murphy. Listen to Bernstein as he describes his "breakthrough":

> I decided that I would use an ordinary hypnotic age regression to take my subject back to the age of one year. And then I would suggest that her

memory could go even farther back. It seemed rather simple, but maybe it would do the job. . . .

This would be old stuff for Ruth Simmons; with me as hypnotist she had done the same thing twice before. On one occasion she had shown conclusively that she could, while hypnotized, recall events which had taken place when she was only one year old. But tonight I was going to attempt something more than an ordinary age regression. . . .

Farther and farther we went into memories stored deep, past the reach of the conscious mind, until Ruth remembered when she was only one year old. At the age of one year she had expressed her desire for water by saying, "Wa." But when she was asked to tell us how she had asked for a glass of milk, she replied, ". . . can't say that."

And now—now at last I was in a position to try something I had never before attempted. . . . In short, I was going to make an effort to determine whether human memory can be taken back to a period even before birth.

I instructed the entranced Mrs. Simmons, who was now breathing very deeply, that she should try to go still farther back in her memory . . . "back, back, back, and back . . . until, oddly enough, you find yourself in some other scene, in some other place, in some

FIGURE 2.1 ■ Can the mind recall events of lives earlier than the one you're living now? Age-regression hypnotists believe that it can. But despite the claims made for this process, most serious scientists strongly doubt its validity.

other time, and when I talk to you again, you will tell me about it." I finished, and then waited anxiously for a few long moments.

"Now you're going to tell me, . . ." I said. "What did you see? What did you see?"

". . . scratched the paint off all my bed!"

I didn't understand. I hesitated, and then asked the only question logical under the circumstances. "Why did you do that?"

Then we listened to that small, relaxed voice, so remote and so close, telling the logical touching story of a little girl who'd been spanked and who had taken her revenge against a grown-up world by picking the paint off her metal bed. She explained that they had just "painted it and made it pretty."

This little girl seemed part of another place, another time. And when I asked her name, the answer came from my subject: "Friday . . . Friday Murphy."

Bernstein hadn't heard the name clearly. Ruth Simmons was telling the story of Bridey Murphy, a woman who lived in Cork, Ireland, in the early 1800s. Her detailed life history became a minor sensation when it was published by Bernstein as *The Search for Bridey Murphy*. Some people believed in Bridey Murphy because they thought that Ruth Simmons couldn't possibly have made up so much accurate detail about a time and place far outside her own experience. Others believed in Bridey because the idea of multiple lives appealed to them on a philosophical or religious basis.

More skeptical observers pointed out, however, that Ruth Simmons could have been "remembering" a lifetime of information gathered through reading and listening to talk about Ireland. Other critics tried to find errors in Bridey Murphy's accounts of Irish life—not always successfully. Experts also pointed out that subjects under hypnotism often invent memories to please the hypnotist. Psychologist Martin Orne, for example, asked a group of college students to describe their sixth birthday while under hypnosis. His subjects responded with lengthy accounts of parties, presents, and other events. But Orne had researched each subject's actual sixth birthday—and the "memories" turned out to be largely inaccurate.

Thus, Pat M.'s age regression to a past life as a wealthy landowner in ancient China may be mostly wishful thinking. What do you believe? Even the most skeptical scientists are continually amazed by the power of the human mind to think, create, remember, analyze, and perform a thousand other feats of mental gymnastics.

This chapter will give you a chance to learn more about the behavior of the human mind, both awake and asleep. You'll also learn about the altered states of consciousness that the mind experiences while hypnotized or under the influence of drugs. The story of how you make contact with the world around you raises the following questions:

2.1 How does consciousness help you deal with reality?

2.2 What role do sensory experience and perception play in bringing order to a confusing world?

2.3 What role do sleep and dreams play in your life?

2.4 What is hypnosis?

2.5 What effect do psychoactive drugs have on behavior?

2.1 ▪ HOW DOES CONSCIOUSNESS HELP YOU DEAL WITH REALITY?

When you're through studying, lay this book aside and walk outdoors. Open yourself up to the world around you. Perhaps it's a clear, bright day. Sunlight warms your skin and you see shadows play across the sidewalk. You feel the cool touch of a breeze that also brings you the fumes of car exhaust. Rock music throbs from someone's radio. The smell of fried chicken cooking in a nearby kitchen makes your mouth water. You feel alive, alert to everything around you. It's a good feeling.

None of these experiences registered on your senses in the way people normally assume they do. Your eyes did not "see" the shadows, nor did your ears "hear" the music. Instead, your eyes and ears sent infor-mation to your brain. There, a network of nerve cells converted that data into "seeing" and "hearing." In other words, your brain processed the incoming data so that you could make sense of what was happening around you.

RESEARCH INTO BRAIN FUNCTION

Love, creativity, anger, sadness, memory—all occur inside your head. Even the most advanced computer can't begin to duplicate the brain's subtle abilities. But how can your brain—a complex of tissue, fluids, and electrochemical activity—produce human emotions and intellect? Centuries of research have only begun to unravel that mystery.

EARLY RESEARCH. As early as the fourth century B.C., the Greek physician Hippocrates studied the effects of brain damage. He concluded, "From the brain only arise our pleasures, joys, laughter, and jests as well as our sorrows, pains, griefs, and tears." In the 1600s, researchers began to map the brain, based on the belief that specific parts of the brain could be matched up with specific behaviors. In the 1860s, a French surgeon, Paul Broca, located the region that controls speech. About the same time, two German doctors, Eduard Hitzig and Gustav Fritsch, proved that electrical stimulation of the brain can cause movement of various parts of the body.

PENFIELD'S DISCOVERY. Muscle jerks and twitches clearly are not the same as thought, feeling, and memory. It remained for a Canadian brain surgeon, Dr. Wilder Penfield, to prove that those processes also can be located within the brain. Penfield's discovery came out of a treatment for epilepsy that he developed in the 1930s. Penfield reasoned that if he could find the exact bit of brain tissue that triggers an epileptic seizure, he could destroy it and end his patients' problems. For a search tool, Penfield used an electric probe that could stimulate the brain without injuring it.

Penfield's patients received only a local anesthetic because the brain itself cannot feel pain. When the surgeon exposed the brain and began to probe its responses, the patients were awake and could report what they felt. Like Hitzig and Fritsch, Penfield found that stimulation of certain brain areas caused a variety of physical sensations. Patients reported tingling feelings in their fingers and toes, their arms and legs jerked, and they "saw" flashes of brilliant light. During one operation in 1936, however, Penfield discovered a different response. As he probed a woman's brain, she suddenly cried out, "I hear my mother and my brother talking to each other." The patient reported that she felt as though she had actually relived the long-forgotten experience. When Penfield stimulated the spot a second time, the identical memory repeated itself, like a videotape being replayed.

Penfield reported that when their brains were directly stimulated, other patients heard orchestras play, relived the birth of a child, and revisited the circus. They described these memories as "real," undimmed by time. Old feelings of sadness, joy, anger, and other emotions also accompanied the experiences. Penfield concluded that the brain files experiences away, ready to be recalled whenever they are needed.*

Modern brain researchers have gone well beyond these early discoveries. As Chapter 3 will show you, the various parts of the brain control a number of specific behaviors. But no single area of the brain has been pinpointed as the location of conscious thought and feeling.

THE PROCESS OF CONSCIOUSNESS

Consciousness doesn't lend itself to easy definition. But if you're aware of what is going on around you right now and you're aware of yourself as a person, you're experiencing consciousness. Keep in mind, however, that consciousness is a process, not a "thing." So many individual events in the mind and body add up to consciousness that the best way to describe it is to experience it.

Imagine that you're walking home from school. Suddenly, you hear a dog barking. Lips laid back, fangs gleaming, the brute runs directly toward you (see Figure 2.2). Your senses instantly send data to the brain about the sight, sound, and smell of the onrushing animal. Your brain interprets the incoming

---

* Based on Irwin Lausch, *Manipulation, Dangers and Benefits of Brain Research* (New York: Viking Press, 1974), pp. 59–61.

FIGURE 2.2 ■ If you were faced with this unexpected danger, how would you react? Fortunately, you wouldn't have to spend a long time making up your mind. Your brain would take over and prepare your body to fight or flee.

data and triggers a flurry of mental and physical responses.

1. Your *conscious mind* calculates the danger: How best can I handle the situation? Should I run or stay and fight? Past experiences with other dogs, your chances of picking up a weapon, your position relative to safety—the brain instantly evaluates all these. Within split seconds, you're ready to make your decision.

2. At the same time, a part of your mind that lies outside your awareness, the *unconscious,* is also at work. Long-forgotten reactions to other dogs and other dangers remain in the unconscious and exert a powerful in-

fluence on the conscious mind. You won't be directly aware of the existence of these deeply buried memories. Nevertheless, practically all human behaviors are affected in some way by the experiences stored away in the unconscious.

3. Meanwhile, the brain has also alerted your *autonomic nervous system.* This network of nerves operates without your awareness. It regulates such vital activities as breathing, heart rate, blood pressure, digestion, and hormone production. When danger threatens, the autonomic nervous system prepares your body for the emergency by shutting down some systems and activating others. Digestion, for example, will stop, while your heartbeat will quicken and muscles will receive extra supplies of sugar. Once you've decided what to do, your body will be prepared to carry out your orders.

Luckily, your consciousness doesn't need to remain so intensely alert at all times. You've probably realized already that you can think about Friday's dance, chew gum, watch television, and pet your cat—all at the same time. For maximum efficiency, however, you must bring yourself to full alertness. This means that you concentrate your consciousness on the problem or activity at hand, whether it's pouring a glass of milk, reading a psychology book, or escaping from an angry dog.

■ SECTION CHECKUP

1 Imagine yourself walking through a forest. Just as you step over a log, you see a snake, coiled and ready to strike. Describe the reactions of your mind and body to this unexpected danger.

2 What is the basis for Wilder Penfield's conclusion that almost every life experience is filed away in the brain?

3 What does the psychologist mean by the term *consciousness*?

2.2 ▓ WHAT ROLE DO SENSORY EXPERIENCE AND PERCEPTION PLAY IN BRINGING ORDER TO A CONFUSING WORLD?

Imagine being bitten by a mosquito. Remember the sharp prick of pain and the itching that followed? Psychologists refer to any event from the outside world that affects your mind and body as a *stimulus* (plural *stimuli*). The sensation caused by a stimulus is known as a *sensory experience*. In this case, the mosquito bite is the stimulus; the itching is the sensory experience.

A particular stimulus does not always create the same sensory experience, however. Forget the mosquito bite and imagine that you're about to bite into a thick, juicy hamburger. The first bite (the stimulus) creates a wonderful sensory experience. Now, a friend challenges you to eat four more hamburgers. The fifth hamburger is just as fresh and flavorful as the first. But does it create the same sensory experience? Probably not. When your stomach is full, food doesn't have the same appeal. The stimulus remained the same, but your reaction to it changed dramatically.

By now you've probably looked at Figure 2.3, the unusual stimulus printed on this page. What did you see when you first looked at it? Some people see two black faces. Others see a white vase. Even as you study the drawing, the faces may abruptly change into the vase—and vice versa. The process of making sense out of a stimulus and your sensory experience of it (in this case, deciding between the figure and its background) is called *perception*. Psychologists use this illusion to show how the brain depends on visual clues to make sense out of confusing situations. But this drawing doesn't give you the clues you need to tell which is foreground and which is background. As a result, your perception of the figure varies.

FIGURE 2.3 ▓ Without clear-cut clues as to which is figure and which is background, you see either the vase—or the two faces. Now look steadily at this figure-ground illusion for a moment or two. Watch the two figures switch back and forth as your perception changes.

FORMING GESTALTS

When the brain makes a meaningful pattern out of many bits of sensation, the process is called a *gestalt* (from a German word that roughly translates as "good shapes" or "good figures"). If your brain "sees" a design made up of apparently random dots, for example, it immediately tries to organize the dots into a whole picture (see Figure 2.4). This need to make sense out of visual sensations probably explains why some people dislike abstract art. They look at the streaks, dribbles, and

FIGURE 2.4 ■ Can you make a pattern out of these apparently random dots? From the moment you began looking at them, your brain started trying to organize them into a meaningful pattern—a *gestalt*. Now step back a distance from the page, and the picture will take shape.

patches of color without finding a pattern they recognize. Their inability to perceive meaning upsets them; they prefer art that they can see and "understand."

PERCEPTUAL INFERENCE

By the time you are a few years old, your brain has a good idea of how the world should look and act. For that reason, your brain tends to build its gestalts on the basis of past experience. Psychologists call this process *perceptual inference*. Imagine yourself walking into a room. You look around for a place to sit down. There's a chair, but you can see only three of its legs. Would you hesitate to sit on it? Probably not. Perceptual inference tells you that chairs have four legs

and that the chair is probably safe to sit on. If you've ever mistaken a glass of buttermilk for regular milk, however, you know that perceptual inferences can't always be trusted.

Despite an occasional mishap, perceptual inference does help you handle situations that otherwise would confuse you. For example, you've learned that objects generally remain constant in size. For that reason, you don't feel surprised when a tiny dot on the horizon turns into a full-sized automobile as it speeds toward you. In fact, you don't even think of the car as growing in size. You know how distance affects the apparent size of everyday objects.

By contrast, the Mbuti of Africa often do not develop this form of perceptual inference. The Mbuti live in deep forest and may go a lifetime without seeing an open plain. A group of Mbuti hunters were once taken to a game preserve where they saw elephants grazing far away on the open plain. "Elephants the size of ants!" they marveled. Only as they moved toward the animals did the Mbuti realize how the unfamiliar perspective had fooled them.

FIGURE 2.5

EXPECTATIONS AFFECT WHAT YOU "SEE"

Perception can also be influenced by what you expect to see. Look at the drawing of the old woman in Figure 2.5. Can you see her? Now look at the picture again, but this time find the old woman's daughter. She's really there! If you have trouble finding her, note that the eye, nose, and chin of the old woman also form the ear, chin, and neck of the younger woman.

Did you see both women? If you tell your friends that they'll see the daughter first, they'll probably have trouble finding the old woman. Their expectations will affect what they see. Try this simple experiment and see what happens.

Now, see what tricks your expectations play on your perception when you look at the Roman arch in Figure 2.6. Is something wrong? Try to find the top of the middle column! You can see why this figure is called an "impossible figure" illusion. Your eye picks up information that conflicts with your expectations about the central column. As a result, your brain can't make any sense out of the data it receives.

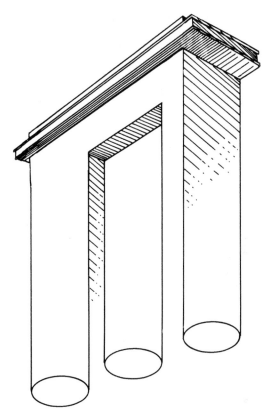

FIGURE 2.6 ▓ How can a Roman arch have three columns at the base and only two at the top? In reality it can't, of course. But in this drawing, the conflicting information given to the brain by the realistic perspective makes it seem possible—until you try to check it out!

▪ SECTION CHECKUP

1 Name some of the stimuli of which you are aware at this moment. Why do some of them seem stronger or more important than others?

2 Define the term *perception*. Why would two people have different perceptions of the same event?

3 How does perceptual inference affect your ability to interpret objects and events in the world around you?

2.3 ▓ WHAT ROLE DO SLEEP AND DREAMS PLAY IN YOUR LIFE?

Consciousness exists in forms other than your normal waking state. *Altered states of consciousness* (called *ASCs*) take you into a world where sensations and perceptions are no longer restricted by everyday reality. During dreams, for example, you might fly with eagles, meet a long-dead friend, or struggle to escape the grasp of a monster. Hypnosis and the state induced by certain drugs are also altered states of consciousness that "turn off" your normal waking consciousness.

DEFINING SLEEP AND DREAMS

Sleep and dreams provide by far your most common ASC experiences. Although much mystery still surrounds the role of sleep and dreams in your life, both are now being studied in great depth. A special device called an *electroencephalograph (EEG) machine* helps scientists carry on this research. The EEG machine translates your brain waves into visible patterns that can be seen on a screen or printed on a piece of paper.

SLEEP STAGES. When you fall asleep, your body shuts down some of its busy activities. You become less sensitive to outside stimuli, and your brain waves (measured in cycles per second, or cps) slow down from their usual 10–28 cps. Studies of the patterns of these brain waves on an EEG machine show that sleep is made up of four different levels, or stages (see Figure 2.7). About 75 percent of your sleep time is spent in Stages II, III, and IV. During Stage IV sleep, brain waves are reduced to about three cps. Sleepwalking and talking, if they occur at all, usually happen during this deep sleep.

REM SLEEP AND DREAMS. Stage I sleep, unlike the other three stages, is marked by brain-wave activity remarkably similar to normal consciousness. From time to time during

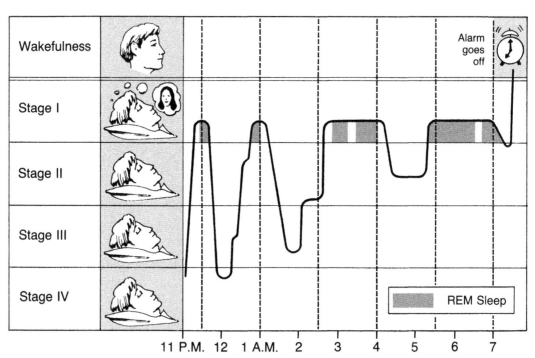

FIGURE 2.7 ▓ Each sleep cycle tends to last about 90 minutes. Dreaming, as shown by the shaded areas, takes place during Stage I sleep. Some REM (dreaming) sleep is possible during each cycle, but dream periods become longer during the early morning hours.

Stage I sleep, your eyes dart back and forth beneath your closed eyelids as if they are following some interesting event. These *rapid eye movements* give this type of sleep its name: *REM sleep.* If someone wakes you during a period of REM sleep, you'll probably remember that you've been dreaming, for dreams occur only during REM sleep. As Figure 2.7 shows, dream periods occur about every 90 minutes during the night but increase in length toward morning.

Dreams themselves are "stories" that your brain makes up during sleep. Like any good story, dreams include visual images, characters, and emotions. But like a badly edited film, dreams often ignore the rules of reality. They jump back and forth in time, invent new identities for old friends, and frequently defy common sense. Your body, however, moves very little during even the most active dreams. Hormone levels rise as if you were actually taking part in an emotional experience, but the brain "turns off" your muscles so you won't thrash around during those spectacular chase scenes.

Much of the data about dreams has come from special research laboratories. In these labs, volunteers sleep and dream while scientists observe and record their reactions. EEG machines record brain-wave patterns, and cameras record REM sleep and other physical movements. This research has enabled scientists to collect some useful information about dreams.

1. Everyone dreams, every night. You may not always remember your dreams, but dreams occupy about 18 to 33 percent of your total sleep time.

2. Most dreams run about the same length of time that the dreamed events would take in real life. This finding disproves an older belief that lengthy dreams are compressed into a few seconds of dream time.

3. Most dreams deal with common, everyday events. Toward morning, your dreams tend to become more exciting and easier to remember.

4. Most people do dream in color, but only about one third of the time.

5. Dreams of anxiety or anger occur more frequently than those of love or contentment. This suggests that dreams may be your mind's way of working out conflicts or of calling problems to your attention.

6. Every dream has a meaning. You may find it difficult to interpret your dreams, but they have useful things to tell you if you make the effort to understand them.

IMPORTANCE OF SLEEP AND DREAMS

Some years ago, a New York disc jockey set up a broadcasting studio in a store window on Times Square. With passersby looking on, the disc jockey stayed awake for eight straight days as a way of calling attention to his favorite charity. The stunt raised money all right, but it also showed that lack of sleep can interfere with normal behavior. As the days went by, the disc jockey became irritable. His behavior grew increasingly confused, and he suffered memory lapses. Even after catching up on his sleep, the disc jockey went through a three-month period of depression.

In another experiment, subjects linked to EEG machines were awakened whenever they fell into REM sleep. On the first night, the subjects' attempts to dream jumped from the usual four or five to ten or more. By the fifth night, their dream attempts had skyrocketed to 30 or more. During the daytime, the subjects all showed increased irritability, anxiety, tension, and lack of concentration.

Sleep and dreams are essential to your physical and mental well-being because they perform the following functions:

1. Sleep provides a time for the body to do its own housekeeping. Cells are replaced or repaired. Waste materials are cleaned out. The brain apparently also uses the time to repair (but not replace) individual cells and

FIGURE 2.8 ▪ Flight controllers work long, stressful shifts. When their work schedule disrupts normal sleep patterns, they find it even more difficult to stay alert. Some airports have tried to solve the problem by calling in sleep experts to design work schedules that fit each controller's natural sleep rhythms.

the networks of nerve cells that make human behavior possible.

2. Dreams serve as a safety valve. Buried emotions can be unearthed and examined—although the unconscious usually disguises these strong feelings. If you couldn't dream (as in the experiment mentioned earlier), these buried emotions would begin to intrude on your consciousness in the form of hallucinations and fantasies.

3. Both sleep and dreams give the brain time to sort out and store away the memories gathered during the day. In one study, researchers checked students taking an intensive language course. The students who were learning fastest showed an increase in REM sleep. The slower students didn't change their REM patterns. Perhaps the more you learn, the more you need dreams to lock the new information into long-term memory.

FREUD'S THEORY OF DREAMS

Ancient people viewed dreams as messages from the gods. Tribal leaders often based important decisions on the interpretation of dreams offered by priests or tribal elders. The modern interpretation of dreams, however, began with Sigmund Freud. Dr. Freud called dreams "the royal road to a knowledge of the unconscious activities of the mind." He believed that during sleep the unconscious calls attention to your deepest needs. Dreams permit people to satisfy wishes and desires they may not consciously know they have. Freud spoke of this as "wish fulfillment." But the wishes of the unconscious are so powerful and disturbing, he went on, that they would interfere with your sleep if they were not disguised in symbols. These symbols must be interpreted before the true meaning of a dream can be discovered.

Suppose you dream of getting a super report card. Freud would probably say it's your unconscious mind telling you that you need the praise your parents will give you for earning better grades. Freud also believed that many dreams are filled with sexual imagery. He said that jealousy, self-love, erotic desires, and the wish to hold onto one's parents show clearly in the symbols found in these dreams.

USING DREAMS CREATIVELY

Today's dream experts do not deny Freud's ideas, but they have gone beyond his emphasis on wish fulfillment. Properly interpreted, they say, dreams can add insight, beauty, and creative energy to your life. As an example, Roy T.'s dream shows the here-and-now aspect of dreams:

Roy T., a high-school senior, dreamed that he was playing basketball. In real life, Roy

■ BIOBOX

Ann Faraday:
Dreams Can Reveal Hidden Talents, Buried Beauty

Ann Faraday (1935–   ), a British psychologist, has made dream analysis more than a favorite tool of psychotherapy. With two successful books, *Dream Power* and *The Dream Game,* she awoke public interest in the use of dreams for personal insight and problem solving.

Dr. Faraday explains that she became interested in dreams early in life:

> My night life as a child was full of excitement, drama, and terror, but I could never get my parents or teachers to take my nocturnal adventures seriously. Just dreams, they said. But I knew better, and decided to become a psychologist in order to explore the mysteries of the other world which manifests during sleep.

In time, Dr. Faraday began to form her own dream study groups. These groups adopted the American Indian motto, "Respect your brothers' dreams." Her interest in dreams has also made Dr. Faraday into something of a crusader. She writes, "In truth, dreams are even more powerful revealers of hidden talents, buried beauty, and unsuspected creative energy. They urge us to recognize that we are actually a lot nicer than we have hitherto realized. . . ."

Dr. Faraday says that she is amazed at the inconsistency of dream psychologists who insist that dreams reveal a person's true colors only when the insight is a negative one:

> When the proverbial Plain Jane dreams of herself as beautiful and successful, her dreams are dismissed as mere wish fulfillment, attempts to compensate for the harsh realities of life. When George, the garage mechanic, dreams of winning the Grand Prix, he is told to come down to earth and stop indulging in Walter Mitty daydreams. But a dream is very different from a daydream . . . and my experience has shown time and time again that such dreams are actually *intimations* of what the dreamer might achieve if he made the effort in waking life. . . . Jane may never become a beauty queen, nor will George necessarily be a champion. But by enabling us to savor the sweet smell of success, as it were, dreams like these move us to realize our undeveloped potentialities.

Think of a recent dream of your own. Can you find any insights that might make your life healthier or happier, as Dr. Faraday suggests?

---

plays basketball poorly, but in the dream he dribbled like a pro and threw in baskets from all over the court. Soon, however, every move he made drew a whistle from the referee. He looked to see who was making these unfair traveling and double-dribble calls. To his surprise, the referee was his mother. The game went on, but now every time he moved he heard the shrill blast of his mother's whistle.

Can you see any meaning in Roy's dream? At first glance, it doesn't make much sense.

Roy doesn't play basketball very often, nor does his mother referee basketball games. So, on the surface, the dream seems empty of meaning. But as he thought about the dream, Roy remembered that he had been arguing with his mother about his plans for the summer. Roy planned to backpack through Canada with a friend, but his mother wanted him to stay home and work in the family business. As the dream illustrated so dramatically, she was "blowing the whistle" on his freedom to "score a basket" with his summer plans. After analyzing the dream, Roy decided that the conflict had to be resolved. He sat down with his mother and told her how important the trip was to him. Together they worked out a compromise work schedule. When June came, Roy was able to leave on his backpacking adventure.

A CONTRARY VIEW. Most dream researchers emphasize the value of dream analysis. Harvard psychiatrist J. Allan Hobson and his research team hold a far different view. Hobson is convinced that unconscious wishes have little to do with dreaming, nor are dream emotions censored. The dreams that accompany REM sleep, he says, are simply vivid hallucinations that most people forget upon waking up. Dreaming, therefore, is peripheral to the true role of REM sleep. The job of these nightly sleep periods, Hobson argues, is to support brain development, fortify the immune system, and help to lock in newly learned data.

MANIFEST AND LATENT DREAM CONTENT. Despite Hobson's warning, many people find that dream analysis enriches their lives. Most dreams can be studied at two levels, as in Roy's basketball dream. The obvious, surface level is called the *manifest content*. The underlying, symbolic meanings are referred to as the *latent content* of the dream. In Roy's case, the latent content related to his conflict over the trip.

A second example will illustrate this point.

Christie R. woke up from her dream feeling quite alarmed. In the dream, she had seen her garden flowers slowly wither and die from lack of water. She had rushed to water them, but it was too late.

To analyze that dream, Christie first looked at the manifest content. Were any of her plants dying because of lack of water, weeding, or fertilizer? If so, she could take the warning to heart and do whatever was necessary to save her flowers. But Christie's garden was doing fine. So she turned to the latent content. What could the garden symbolize? She decided that it must refer to some aspect of her life that she had been ignoring. As she looked over the possibilities, she realized that since she had started dating Bill, she had not been spending much time with her best friend, Gale. As the dream told her, the friendship would wither and die if she continued to neglect it. This analysis felt so right that Christie immediately picked up the phone and made plans to see Gale that afternoon.

STEPS IN ANALYZING YOUR DREAMS. As valuable as your dreams can be, you must "catch" them first. That takes patience and sometimes requires that you rearrange your sleeping habits (see box on page 43). Next, you must relate the dream to your own life. Dream dictionaries, which tell you that a gun equals power or a journey means a change in your life, simply can't substitute for your own insights. To analyze a dream, try the following five-step method. It should help you make sense of all but the most difficult dreams.

1. *Check for warnings*. Begin by examining the manifest content. Is the dream telling you about something that needs immediate attention? A dream about your brakes failing while you're speeding downhill could be a signal from your unconscious that your brakes really do need fixing before they fail and cause an accident.

Dream Catching: Ten Ways to Hold Onto Your Dreams

Some people remember their dreams without effort, but others must try every trick in the book. Ann Faraday suggests ten steps to catching your dreams for later analysis:

1 Always keep pen and paper or a tape recorder by your bedside. You may remember a dream clearly one minute, but if it's not written down, it will be gone the next.

2 Have a dim light or flashlight available that you can switch on without moving from your bed.

3 Tell yourself several times before falling asleep, "I will wake up from a dream tonight," or "I will remember one of my dreams tonight." The words aren't critical; the suggestion is.

4 If you're a heavy sleeper, arrange to be awakened several times during the night. A gentle alarm clock or a cooperative family member can do the job. Try this technique about every two hours, starting three or four hours after you've gone to sleep. It won't guarantee that you'll catch an REM period, but the odds are in your favor if you stick it out.

5 When you awaken with a dream in mind, sit up *very gently* and switch the dim light on. If you jolt yourself into wakefulness, you may lose the dream.

6 Write or record the dream immediately, in as much detail as possible. Try not to doze while you're doing this.

7 Also write down conscious associations that the dream triggers: events, feelings, insights as to the meaning of the dream symbols. These will be helpful when you begin analyzing the dream.

8 If you wake up in the morning with a dream in mind, write it down before you get out of bed. If you wait, you'll probably lose it.

9 As soon as possible, that day if you can, work on the analysis, using the five-step process described on pages 42–44.

10 Date your dreams along with your interpretations and keep them in a "dream diary" for later reference. As time goes by, this diary will provide useful data for working on new dreams and for clarifying your feelings about people and events in your life.

---

2. *Relate the dream to recent events.* Most dreams are triggered by something that's going on in your life right now. If you can match your dreams to those current happenings, your analysis will begin to make sense. For example, Pat dreamed about seeing a beautiful city far away, splendid on its high hill. As she tried to get there, she found obstacles in her path, but the beauty of the city drew her onward. Since Pat had been trying to choose between college and a good job offer, she guessed that her dream related to that decision. When she suddenly realized that the "city" resembled the college campus she had visited a week earlier, she understood the dream. Her unconscious was telling her that college was the best choice, despite the financial hardships it would cause.

3. *Interpret the people and symbols.* When your unconscious creates a dream, it often

conceals actual people and events in symbolic form. Your jealousy may become a green-eyed monster; your worry about grades may become a run-in with a traffic officer; guilt feelings about staying out too late can turn a parent into a prison warden. If the meaning of a person or object isn't obvious to you, think about possible symbolic meanings. A dream of falling, for example, could signify a feeling that you're "falling" in your personal life—falling in love, falling from grace, or whatever. Watch for puns as well. The unconscious apparently loves word games and riddles. If your dream shows you stuck in a giant honey jar, perhaps it means that your real-life "honey" is sticking too close to you.

4. *Examine the dream's feeling tone.* What feelings did the dream leave you with? Were you excited, depressed, uncaring, happy? This "feeling tone" can give you a useful clue in working out the dream's meaning. The heart-thumping fright that goes with a slow-motion chase in a typical nightmare, for example, suggests anxiety or fear about that unknown thing chasing you. A vivid dream of warfare, however, if accompanied by strong feelings of determination, may only reflect your desire to "fight through" some area of conflict in your life.

5. *Pull it all together.* Dreams don't come to waste your time. They bring fresh meanings, warnings, insights. You'll know that you've analyzed your dream properly when it makes sense in understanding or doing something constructive. Assume that in your dream you've been walking a dog on a leash. In your analysis, it becomes apparent that the dog is really a friend of yours. At the moment the symbol's meaning comes clear, you'll probably feel an "ah-so" reaction (as in, "Ah, so that's it!"). Now the dream has done its work. It's up to you to decide whether you're going to stop treating your friend like a dog. (See the box on page 45, which illustrates six common dream symbols. These meanings tend to be alike for everyone.)

LUCID DREAMING: TAKING CONTROL OF YOUR DREAMS

Dr. Patricia Garfield believes that you can choose and control the content of your dreams. This makes it easier, she says, to use your dreams to solve problems. Instead of waiting to catch a dream that deals with a particular problem, you can create your own *lucid dream.*

In a lucid dream, you're aware that you are dreaming. Instead of letting the dream run its own course, you take control of it. Perhaps there's a problem at work—you didn't get the same raise that everyone else did. Since no one will tell you why, tell yourself each night that you're going to dream about your job. After several fruitless nights, a lucid dream shows up in which you find yourself talking to the store manager.

"Anything's possible in a dream," you tell yourself. "I'll ask Ms. Barton to tell me what's wrong." You do—and to your surprise, Ms. Barton calls several customers forward. They all complain that you kept them waiting while you talked to a friend on the phone.

When you wake up the next morning you think about the dream. In your heart, you know it's telling the truth. Will you change your work habits? Lucid dreaming can give you useful insights—but you have to do the hard work of putting the lessons to work.

▪ SECTION CHECKUP

1 Why are sleep and dreams necessary to physical and mental health? What happens if you don't get enough sleep or have enough dreams?

2 What does the psychologist mean by REM sleep?

3 How can dreams be used to enrich your life?

4 Describe the five steps suggested for analyzing a dream.

Common Dream Symbols

Falling

People "fall" from grace or "fall" in the eyes of loved ones. Falling grades or a sense of falling out of touch with someone can trigger this type of dream.

Flying

The "feeling tone" of a flying dream is important. If you've sensed a feeling of power and freedom, the dream says you're "flying high" over some success in your life. Flying to escape something leaves you feeling upset and suggests a problem you can't "rise above."

Nudity

Dreams of nudity in public places often represent anxiety about a coming event where you might appear "naked" before others. If people don't notice your condition, your anxiety probably isn't necessary.

Examinations

Examination dreams in which you find yourself unprepared for the test can be warnings, particularly if you're in school. Otherwise, they tell you to get ready for the other "tests" that people face in everyday life.

Losing money

These are often warning dreams. Check your wallet, purse, or other valuables. Otherwise, think about what else you may be losing—a friend, a goal in life, a part of your identity. The loss may not be a bad thing, but the dream tells you it needs to be faced and resolved.

Finding money or valuables

Dreams of finding valuables usually mean that you should go ahead with some plan or purchase. Such dreams during a "down" period in your life can also be reassurance that you are really a person of value.

2.4 ▓ WHAT IS HYPNOSIS?

You've probably heard of the fakirs (magicians) of India who perform amazing tricks with a piece of rope. Andrija Puharich, a medical doctor and well-known researcher of psychic events, describes one such demonstration. According to the reports of several hundred onlookers, the fakir first threw a rope into the air. It stayed there, unsupported. Then a small boy climbed the rope and disappeared. Next, parts of the boy's cut-up body fell to the ground. The fakir put the pieces into a basket. Holding the basket, he climbed the rope. When he came down again, he had the boy with him, alive and well. The witnesses, including the scientists who arranged the demonstration, agreed with this description.

A motion picture of the event, however, showed that the fakir simply walked into the center of the crowd and threw his rope into the air. The rope dropped to the ground. The film then showed the magician and the boy standing quietly in the center of the crowd until the demonstration was over. Two hundred witnesses to the contrary, the rope did not stay suspended in the air, nor did the boy climb it!*

Since nothing magical took place, the scientists looked to hypnosis for an explanation. They knew that under the altered state of consciousness created by the hypnotic effect, the mind accepts the impossible without question. Stage hypnotists can convince you that Elvis Presley is in the audience or that little green Martians have just landed on your shoulder. But hypnosis has uses far beyond entertainment.

HYPNOTISM DEFINED

Hypnotism is an ASC in which the subject enters into a state of increased suggestibility. If you were hypnotized, you would focus your attention completely on the hypnotist. In this state you would accept almost any suggestion that the hypnotist gave you. In your condition of fixed attention, observers might think that you were asleep or in a trance. In actual fact, you would feel quite

* Andrija Puharich, *Beyond Telepathy* (Garden City, NY: Doubleday, 1973), pp. 33–34.

awake and in command of yourself. But if the hypnotist told you that you were playing baseball, you'd pick up an imaginary bat and swing lustily at an imaginary ball!

Achieving a hypnotic state is relatively simple. First, you must want to be hypnotized. Horror stories to the contrary, you normally cannot be hypnotized if you are not willing to cooperate with the hypnotist. If you agree to be hypnotized, the hypnotist will ask you to stare at an object (a swinging coin, perhaps) or a point in space. Then you will hear the hypnotist's soothing voice say over and over, "You are growing sleepy . . . you are feeling very relaxed. . . ." As your hypnotic state deepens, you will receive further instructions to obey the commands of the hypnotist. Even in a full hypnotic state, however, an EEG machine would not detect in your brain waves any great change from a normal state of consciousness.

USES OF HYPNOTISM

Hypnotism is an ancient art that has recently gained new attention from both medical doctors and psychologists. The "tricks" performed by fakirs and stage hypnotists have real-life applications that can improve both physical and mental health.

MEDICAL USES OF HYPNOTISM. One of the first medical uses of hypnotism was to block off pain during surgery or illness. Today, doctors are using hypnosis to reduce or eliminate pain in dentistry and childbirth, especially in cases where the usual painkilling drugs cannot be used. Hypnosis also seems to be helpful in treating problems that do not have a specific physical cause. Warts and allergies, for example, sometimes clear up "magically" when the patient is hypnotized and told that a simple medicine will make them disappear.

PSYCHOLOGICAL USES OF HYPNOTISM. Using hypnosis gives psychologists an effective technique for helping people. Under hypnosis, for example, a patient can talk about a serious emotional problem that is normally too painful to discuss. Phobic fears, stammering, and insomnia have all been successfully treated with hypnosis. Age regression can also be achieved under hypnosis, allowing patients to remember childhood events that contribute to adult difficulties.

POSTHYPNOTIC SUGGESTION. A hypnotist may plant an idea under hypnosis that stays with the subject afterward. This *posthypnotic suggestion* works well when subjects want to stop harmful habits such as overeating, drinking, or smoking. Smokers, for example, can be told under hypnosis that their cigarettes will have a bad taste. If that suggestion carries over into everyday life, the cigarettes really will taste bad. And if this posthypnotic suggestion is reinforced by a strong desire to quit, the smoking addiction can be broken.

FIGURE 2.9 ▓ Is fire walking a trick or a miracle? Neither, say scientists, who believe that fire walkers put themselves into a hypnotic state that prevents them from feeling the heat or pain. Equally amazing to those who witness one of these demonstrations is the fact that the fire walkers' feet are seldom burned by the hot coals.

Some psychologists also teach self-hypnosis as a means of improving performance in a given field. Subjects learn to relax, give themselves suggestions leading to greater self-confidence, and form a positive mental image of what they want to do. Baseball players, for example, have used self-hypnosis to raise their batting average by increasing self-confidence and concentration. You should remember, however, that hypnosis cannot give you abilities or skills you don't have. If you don't have the training, coordination, and experience, no amount of hypnosis will make you a .400 hitter. Self-hypnosis can also be used to relieve pain (see Figure 2.9).

HYPNOSIS IN THE COURTROOM. Law enforcement officers have long been interested in hypnosis. All too often people forget important information about a crime they have witnessed. Under hypnosis they can relive the experience and report details that may greatly aid the investigation. In 1976, for example, a California bus driver couldn't help police catch the men who kidnapped his busload of school children. Placed under hypnosis, the driver remembered all but one number of the license plate of the kidnappers' vehicle. That important clue led to the arrest of the criminals.

Despite successes of this type, the courts seldom admit testimony developed under hypnosis. The reason lies in the nature of the hypnotic state. Subjects try very hard to please the hypnotist, even to the extent of making up details they can't remember. Studies show that if two people witness a crime, the witness who undergoes hypnosis will recall twice as many details. Unfortunately, the hypnotized witness will also make three times as many mistakes. One Illinois man, for example, was hypnotized and told to "zoom in" on a suspect he had seen standing under a street lamp 273 feet away. The request led the man to make a positive identification of the suspect. Vision specialists, however, soon

▓ PRO & CON:

Setting the Record Straight About Hypnosis

Hypnosis seems to stand with one foot in its mysterious past and the other in modern science. Superstitions and misinformation about hypnotists and their seeming power to command people's minds alarm the uninformed. This Pro & Con matches up some of the most common false beliefs with the actual facts.

FALSE BELIEFS	FACTS
1 A hypnotist has special, mysterious powers that no one else can use. Hypnotism is probably a form of magic.	**1** Hypnotists do not possess any mystical powers. A hypnotist is merely someone who has learned to lead people into a state where they will accept almost any suggestion made by the hypnotist.
2 Only people with low intelligence or with little willpower can be hypnotized.	**2** Creative people with high intelligence make the best subjects for hypnosis.
3 The majority of people cannot be hypnotized.	**3** About nine out of ten people can be hypnotized. The best subjects are those who have a good reason to undergo hypnosis.
4 Being hypnotized means that the subject becomes unconscious or falls into a sleep-like trance.	**4** Even in a deep state of hypnosis, subjects remain aware of everything that goes on around them. What seems like a trance is their total concentration on the hypnotist.
5 Subjects always tell the truth while under hypnosis.	**5** People under hypnosis try to tell the truth. But they are so anxious to please the hypnotist that they will make up answers to fill in gaps in their memories.
6 It is almost impossible to wake up someone who is in a hypnotic state.	**6** Being hypnotized is similar to being totally absorbed in a book or movie. Either the hypnotist or the subject can end the hypnotic state at will.
7 Hypnotists can make their subjects do anything while under hypnosis, no matter how bizarre or dangerous the action.	**7** Except in special circumstances, people cannot be made to do anything under hypnosis that violates their morals. Hypnotized subjects will usually refuse orders that could cause mental or physical harm to themselves or to others.

Would you have answered "false" to all seven statements listed under *False beliefs?*

From the book *Helping Yourself With Self-Hypnosis* by Frank S. Caprio, M.D. and Joseph R. Berger. © 1963 by Prentice-Hall, Inc. Published by Prentice-Hall, Inc., Englewood Cliffs, N.J. 07632.

destroyed the man's testimony. They proved that no one can see facial details beyond a distance of around 30 feet under those particular conditions.

A WARNING ABOUT HYPNOSIS

Trained hypnotists know how to ensure the safety of their subjects. Amateur hypnotists, however, never know when they will stumble into some dark and painful area within their subject's mind. Such exploration can cause great harm to a person's emotional health. Hypnotists also must be careful not to pass on their own prejudices and ideas to their highly suggestible subjects.

Another precaution should be noted. Many people believe that hypnotic subjects won't do anything that they wouldn't do in real life. That block does exist, but a clever hypnotist can get around it. Put mild-mannered Joe under hypnosis, for example, and tell him to shoot the next person who walks into the room. Normally, Joe will resist that sugges-

tion to the point of ending his hypnotic state. But tell Joe that the person he's to shoot is a maniac who has just killed ten children—and Joe might very well pull the trigger.

■ SECTION CHECKUP

1 How would you define hypnosis? Why is it called an altered state of consciousness?

2 What uses can a doctor make of hypnotism? How do psychologists use hypnotism?

3 How would you convince a beginning hypnotist that "just-for-fun" hypnotism can be harmful?

2.5 ■ WHAT EFFECT DO PSYCHOACTIVE DRUGS HAVE ON BEHAVIOR?

Is this the Space Age . . . or the Spaced-Out Age? Never before have so many people swallowed, snorted, shot, smoked, or otherwise turned on to so many *psychoactive (mind-altering) drugs.*

From the president on down, more and more Americans have joined in the fight against drug abuse. The evidence shows clearly that drug abusers, both young and old, are hurting themselves and our society. Psychologists support this view. They remind young people that experimenting with psychoactive drugs involves psychological, medical, and legal risks. The social outlays are just as high. Substance abuse costs the economy some $276 billion a year in lost work time, accidents, health care fees, and crime.

That doesn't mean that you shouldn't take aspirin, antibiotics, or other drugs used to treat an illness. But what will you do the next time someone offers you a drink, snort, or joint? The following dialogue may help you make a healthy decision.

QUESTION: What effect do psychoactive drugs have on perception?

ANSWER: To a greater or lesser degree, all psychoactive drugs alter the user's perception of reality. Stimulants such as caffeine, cocaine, and amphetamines cause temporary feelings of alertness and well-being. That's why some athletes take "uppers" before a game. They believe the stimulant will improve their performance and reduce the pain of injuries. Hallucinogens such as LSD and PCP, however, lead users into a world beyond the reach of the ordinary senses. Tim G., for example, thought he'd achieved "a mystical sense of unity with the universe" the first time he tried LSD. A later "trip," however, ended in the hospital. While under the influence of the drug, Tim experienced the frightening illusion that his flesh was rotting off his bones. Even the artistic or religious insights gained through drug use fade as the drugs wear off. Artists often return from an ASC only to discover that their "great art" actually amounts to little more than scribbles.

QUESTION: Don't adults "turn on" with alcohol and nicotine, and "turn off" with sleeping pills and tranquilizers?

FIGURE 2.10

ANSWER: Public-health experts say that alcohol and tobacco are two of the biggest drug problems in the United States today. The real point is that *no recreational drug does your body any good!* The fact that adults use alcohol or sleeping pills doesn't make it logical for young people to try marijuana or PCP. Prolonged misuse of drugs can cause damage ranging from minor emotional problems to mental breakdowns and from addiction to incurable illness. In addition, possession of most recreational drugs can send you to jail. That gives you at least two practical replies to the argument that every generation has its own choice of how it will "turn on" (see Figure 2.10).

QUESTION: Did you say that tobacco is a *drug* problem? I've heard about lung cancer, but that's a medical matter. Next you'll be telling me that coffee is a dangerous drug!

ANSWER: Surely you've seen coffee drinkers tremble while they're waiting for their first cup in the morning? The caffeine in coffee, tea, and cola drinks causes a dependency habit similar to an addiction. Overuse of caffeine can also cause nervousness, heart damage, and illnesses of the digestive system.

Nicotine is a much more serious health problem. According to the surgeon general, about 1,200 Americans die every day from tobacco-related causes. Imagine the headlines if two fully loaded jumbo jets crashed each day, killing everyone aboard. That's how many people tobacco kills, but only the grieving families seem to notice. Even though cigarette smoking has been identified as the most easily preventable cause of death in the United States, thousands of children and teenagers start smoking every day. They replace the older smokers who have quit—or died.

In large doses, nicotine is a poison. In smaller amounts, it causes *psychological dependence;* that is, smokers become emotionally hooked on tobacco even though their bodies may not become physically addicted. People smoke because tobacco stimulates the central nervous system and helps distract their attention from their problems. Because of the life-threatening lung problems caused by smoking, the U.S. government has ordered cigarette companies to print warnings on every package. Many public places have been declared "no smoking" areas because second hand smoke poses a risk to nonsmokers. Even so, tobacco continues to tempt young people, who tend to see smoking as a sign of growing up. One in ten eighth graders smokes— and during the high school years, the number of smokers more than doubles.

If there's a plus side to this, it's the fact that people don't lose their grip on reality when they drink coffee or when they smoke a cigarette.

QUESTION: Well, maybe so, but what about the adults I see abusing alcohol? Are you saying that it's worse to smoke a few joints of marijuana than to have a couple of cocktails before dinner?

ANSWER: Psychologists hope you'll do some more thinking. They say that anyone who asks that question might as well be asking, "Which is better, having your hand burned or having your wrist broken?" The correct answer: *Neither choice makes sense!* Taking a drink is playing Russian roulette. Statistics show that one out of every ten persons who take that first drink will go on to have a problem with alcohol. Six million Americans are alcoholics, powerless to stop drinking without assistance. Drinking helps kill 18,000 people and injures 50 times that number on the highways each year. A substantial number of the people in prison committed their crimes while drunk. Excessive

use of alcohol by pregnant women can cause birth defects. And who can measure the suffering alcohol brings to the families of alcoholics?

QUESTION: I know a lot of people who drink. Are they in danger of becoming alcoholics?

ANSWER: There's a long road between social drinking and alcoholism. But as people continue drinking, their bodies require greater and greater amounts of alcohol to gain the results they desire. That's called building up a tolerance to the drug. Alcohol is a depressant. It relaxes the brain centers that normally control social behavior. If people seem happier and more active when they're drinking, that's because their inhibitions have been lowered. Long-term heavy drinking causes damage to the liver and the stomach. If alcoholics don't die in an accident, they usually die of medical problems brought on by their drinking.

QUESTION: By comparison, marijuana doesn't seem so terrible. Why do so many people get upset when someone smokes a little grass?

ANSWER: No matter what you hear on the streets, marijuana is not a harmless drug. For one thing, the marijuana sold today is much stronger than it was in the 1960s. A typical joint now contains five to ten times more THC (tetrahydrocannabinol), the chemical that creates marijuana's psychoactive effect. THC builds up in the body with repeated use. Research shows that it concentrates in the brain, lungs, and sex organs.

How harmful is this concentration? In the brain, marijuana causes a type of damage called ventricle enlargement. In the lungs, marijuana smoke causes more damage than smoking cigarettes. It contains 50 percent more cancer-causing hydrocarbons than tobacco smoke. In the sex organs, marijuana use has been connected with infertility and fetal deaths. The drug can also cause genetic damage

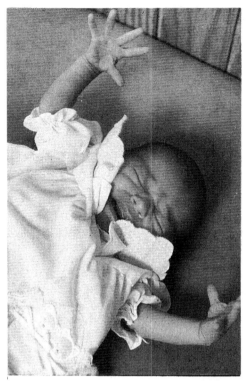

FIGURE 2.11 ▪ The tiniest victims of drugs can be found in the nurseries of the nation's hospitals. This baby girl was born to a mother who used crack cocaine during her pregnancy. At birth the baby displayed the typical symptoms of exposure to crack—tremors, irritability, and listlessness. If she survives, she will probably develop learning disabilities along with her physical disabilities. Even a single "hit" of crack can damage a developing fetus.

that results in the birth of babies who are deformed.

Behavioral changes have also been charged to marijuana. Evidence shows that regular use interferes with people's ability to concentrate, memorize, and solve problems.

QUESTION: What about the claims that marijuana is a "soft drug" that doesn't cause addiction?

ANSWER: Some evidence points to the possibility that marijuana is physically addictive. Whether that's true or not, many pot smokers quickly develop a psychological dependence. Even though they don't suffer the symptoms of physical withdrawal, these users do experience mood changes, insomnia, anxiety, appetite loss, and a general feeling of depression when they stop.

QUESTION: Does pot smoking always lead to the use of hard drugs?

ANSWER: A government-funded study surveyed 2,510 young drug abusers. Ninety percent of the heroin users and 96 percent of the cocaine users began their drug use with marijuana. On the other hand, many casual marijuana users never graduate to hard drugs. Unfortunately, people cannot know in advance whether or not they have an inherited tendency to abuse drugs. For those who do, smoking the first joint is just as dangerous as taking the first drink for a potential alcoholic.

QUESTION: I hear what you're saying—but I also hear about the medical uses of marijuana. What's the story?

ANSWER: The practice of using marijuana to treat sick and dying patients is a highly controversial issue. One side scoffs at the idea, and writes it off as a sneaky way of giving marijuana a veneer of legality. Supporters, however, point to research showing that marijuana and the related cannabinoid drugs relieve pain, control nausea and vomiting, and stimulate the appetite. The long-range goal, proponents say, is to develop medications that maximize the positive effects and at the same time minimize marijuana's harmful effects on the lungs and other organs.

QUESTION: Okay, it's clear that marijuana is much more than a funny looking cigarette. But what about the other psychoactive drugs? Every time I turn on the television I hear about a new type of drug abuse. Is there any way to make sense of this chemical jungle?

ANSWER: The chart on pages 54–55 gives basic data about the common psychoactive drugs. These drugs fall into four categories. The first class includes the *depressants* (downers) and *sedatives,* such as alcohol, tranquilizers, barbiturates, and GHB (the date rape drug). These drugs lower the level of activity in the brain and create a brief feeling of peaceful well-being. Combining depressants with alcohol multiples their effect. In too many cases, the end result of mixing pills and liquor has been a one-way trip to the morgue

Next come the *stimulants* (uppers), which create feelings of optimism and energy by triggering high levels of activity in the nervous system. They elevate blood pressure and decrease appetite. Typical stimulants include caffeine, nicotine, cocaine, the amphetamines, and Ecstasy.

The *hallucinogens,* or *psychedelics,* alter the user's perception of reality. Under the influence of one of these drugs, the senses play tricks, and emotions are also affected. The hallucinations alter reality according to the amount of the drug taken, plus the user's expectations. A dose that leaves one person only mildly affected can send another on a wild trip. Common hallucinogens include LSD, marijuana, peyote, and STP.

Finally, the *narcotics* lead directly to addiction. Opium, heroin, morphine, and codeine all reduce pain, depress the nervous system, and give users a temporary feeling of euphoria (intense feelings of well-being). As the user gains tolerance, the body demands greater and greater amounts of the drug. Drug addicts will do almost anything to get a "fix," including robbery and prostitution. Once addicted, a user must go through painful withdrawal symptoms before the habit can be broken. Narcotics users run the risk of arrest, as well as serious illnesses from dirty needles, impure drugs, and poor health habits. Addicts who "shoot up" with dirty needles or who sell their bodies for money to buy drugs are at high risk of being infected with the virus that causes AIDS.

QUESTION: When people talk about getting "hooked," they're only talking about narcotics, aren't they?

ANSWER: What you call "hooked," psychologists call dependence or addiction. Many drugs, including tobacco, cause both a physical dependence and a psychological dependence. People who have a physical dependence go through unpleasant withdrawal symptoms when they try to kick their habit. A psychological dependence doesn't cause the same physical withdrawal symptoms, but the mental craving for the drug can be equally overpowering.

Many well-meaning people once believed they could use cocaine without risk because "experts" said it wasn't physically addicting. They soon found out that psychological dependence is equally damaging. Today, crack (a crystallized form of cocaine) has emerged as the most highly addictive of all the non-narcotic drugs. The brief drug high the user experiences soon gives way to depression and paranoia. The only way to feel good again is to smoke more crack. Crack addicts often spend hundreds of dollars a day "chasing the high." With help, these addicts can kick their habits, but recovery is a slow process with no shortcuts.

QUESTION: With all these risks, why do people still use psychoactive drugs?

ANSWER: Some do it for a thrill. Others try them because they can't say "no" to their friends. To another group, it might be a way of saying, "Look at me. I'm grown up!" Far too many people use drugs as a way of escaping from problems that seem impossible to overcome. But no matter what the reason, people who use drugs regularly are gambling with their lives. Adult behavior means measuring the costs as well as the gains when making choices. The doctors, counselors, and therapists who work with drug abusers agree on one fact: The momentary pleasures of using drugs are never worth the cost.

(Text continues on page 56.)

Drug Identification Guide

(Note: Street names change with time and tend to be linked to a geographic region. To further confuse matters, the same street name may refer to one drug in the Midwest and to a different drug in the South or Northwest.)

Drug name (Street names)	Drowsiness	Excitability	Irritability/restlessness	Anxiety	Euphoria	Depression	Hallucinations	Panic	Irrational behavior	Confusion	Changed speech	Impaired coordination	Constricted pupils	Dilated pupils	Space/time distortion	Physical dependence	Psychological dependence	Tolerance	Unconsciousness	Hepatitis	Psychosis	Death from withdrawal	Death from overdose
DEPRESSANTS and SEDATIVES																							
Alcohol (beer, wine, booze, liquor, juice, suds, etc.)	●					●			●	●	●	●			●	●	●	●					●
Barbiturates (yellow jackets, downers, barbs, Nembutal, nebbies, etc.)	●				●				●	●	●	●			●	●	●	●			●		●
GHB (everclear, scoop, G, liquid X, etc.)	●	●				●			●	●	●	●		●	●	●	●	●			●		●
Rohypnol (roofies, R2, Roche, rope, etc.)	●		●						●	●	●	●		●	●	●	●	●			●		●
STIMULANTS																							
Amphetamines (pep pills, bennies, speed, uppers, bumblebees, dexies, etc.)		●	●	●		●	●	●					●			●	●		●	●		●	
Amyl nitrite, butyl nitrite (poppers, Locker Room, rush snappers, etc.)				●									●					●					
Caffeine (coffee, java, tea, cola, No-Doz, etc.)		●															●						
Cocaine (snow, coke, flake, C, nose candy, lady, etc.) *Crack* is a smokable form of cocaine	●		●			●					●				●	●	●					●	●
Methamphetamine (speed, meth, splash, crystal, etc.)		●	●			●					●				●	●	●						●

MDMA (Ecstasy, Adam, XTC)

Nicotine (cigarettes, cigs, tobacco, smokes, coffin nails, snuff, chewing tobacco, etc.)

HALLUCINOGENS

LSD (acid, sugar cubes, microdot, blue heaven, gooney birds, trippers, flash, etc.)

Marijuana (grass, pot, Acapulco gold, weed, reefer, Mary Jane, ganja, etc.)

Hashish (concentrated form of marijuana—hash, kif soles, Black Russian, etc.)

Peyote (buttons, beans, mescal, cactus, hikori, tops, topi, full moon, etc.)

Phencyclidine (PCP, angel dust, hog, killer weed, crazy coke, mad dog, gorilla tab, etc.)

STP (serenity, tranquility, peace, etc.)

NARCOTICS

Codeine (schoolboy, fours, Captain Cody, etc.)

Heroin (black tar, junk, horse, H, brown sugar, big H, mud, smack, chick, goof ball, etc.)

Meperidine (Demerol, Pethidine, Mepergan, peth, MPTP, etc.)

Methadone (dollies, amidone, Dolophine, fizzies, etc.)

Morphine (M, dreamer, Miss Emma, morf, C&M, mud, drugstore dope, etc.)

For those who still want to experience an ASC, drugless methods are available. Some people "get high" on yoga, meditation, or deeply felt religious beliefs. An isolation tank can also provide you with a drugless ASC (see the box on page 56), as can various self-awareness exercises (see Activities 1, 2, and 3, pages 59–60). The choice is up to you.

■ SECTION CHECKUP

1 What is a psychoactive drug?

2 Name the four categories of psychoactive drugs. Give one or two examples of each category.

3 Summarize the medical and psychological arguments against drug use.

John Lilly's Isolation Tanks: Creating a Drugless ASC Experience

Dr. John Lilly, a scientist famous for his work with dolphins, has designed a special isolation tank. There, cut off from contact with the usual stimuli, subjects float in a 94° solution of Epsom salts. No light enters the tank, and the only sound is that of a quiet pump. Under these conditions, Lilly finds, the mind is free to rest, solve problems, or explore its outermost limits.

Lilly has collected firsthand reports of experiences in the isolation tank. This one is by Tom Wilkes:

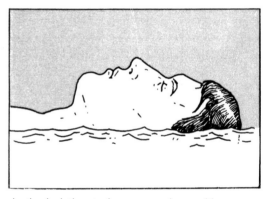

In the isolation tank, you are alone with your own mind.

My first sensation was one of stuffiness, humid warm . . . floating. This soon changed to a cool secure feeling accompanied by the overwhelming rhythm of my heart beat; . . . I heard fragments of messages, voices saying things I could not decipher. This continued for an undetermined length of time until colored visual images would pass by me. These images were nonobjective and seemed to pulsate as they passed. The colors were generally magenta, blue or whitish.

At some point, three female entities began questioning me. The feeling was warm and attracting. . . . I passed through them and there was a splash of golden light. At this point I became aware of three-dimensional spheres turning in several directions inside and outside of themselves, emitting a warm magenta glow. Their presence was awe-inspiring and produced a religious kind of emotional feeling. . . .

One woman, however, left after a few minutes, complaining of the "terrible noise" inside the tank. Lilly observed that the noise was inside her own head. Not everyone can take the tank. How do you think you would react?

John C. Lilly, *The Deep Self: Profound Relaxation and the Tank Isolation Technique* (New York: Simon & Schuster, 1977), pp. 252–253.

LOOKING BACK: A SUMMARY

1 Your eyes do not "see"; your ears do not "hear." Instead, the eyes and ears send data to the brain, where "seeing," "hearing," and other sensory experiences take place. Research shows that specific parts of the brain control specific behaviors. The brain, moreover, stores away all of your experiences, ready to be recalled when needed.

2 Consciousness is your normal waking state, when you're aware of yourself and the events around you. The unconscious contains stored experiences that you cannot readily remember, but it also exerts a powerful influence on your conscious behavior. When danger threatens, the autonomic nervous system prepares the body for emergency action. Consciousness operates during all your waking moments, but maximum efficiency comes only when you concentrate fully on the problem or activity at hand.

3 Physical events in the outside world that affect your mind or body are called *stimuli*. The feeling created by a stimulus is known as a *sensory experience*. The sense you make out of a stimulus and its accompanying sensory experience is called *perception*. Perceptual inference means that you interpret the world according to past experiences. Your expectations also affect your perception.

4 There are also altered states of consciousness, or ASCs. The most common ASC is sleep and dreams. Regular sleep and the dreams that come during sleep are apparently vital to your physical and emotional health. Sleep can be measured in four stages, according to the brain wave patterns typical of each stage. Stage I sleep, also called REM sleep because the eyes move rapidly under closed eyelids, coincides with dream periods.

5 Everyone dreams every night, and many psychologists are convinced that every dream also has a meaning. Freud thought of dreams as wish fulfillments, but many modern dream analysts believe that dreams bring useful messages from the unconscious about everyday problems. At the manifest level, a dream means exactly what it says. At the deeper, more complex latent level, the dream's meaning is concealed by symbols, puns, and disguises that make interpretation difficult.

6 Hypnosis is a state of heightened suggestibility in which a subject willingly accepts the direction of the hypnotist. Although the hypnotic state is considered an ASC, it does not involve sleep or a trance state. Once considered magical in nature, hypnosis today is used in medicine and in psychology. Doctors use it to block pain during medical procedures, and psychologists find it useful in helping people remember long-forgotten events or in overcoming fears and bad habits. Misuse of hypnosis can cause lasting harm to the subject.

7 Many people take psychoactive drugs to achieve an ASC. Doctors and psychologists agree that behavior-altering drugs harm the body. While narcotics, marijuana, amphetamines, PCP, and other drugs receive most of the headlines, health experts agree that alcohol and tobacco are the country's biggest drug problems. Psychoactive drugs can be put into one of four categories: (*a*) depressants lower the level of activity in the brain; (*b*) stimulants raise the level of activity in the nervous system; (*c*) hallucinogens alter the user's perception of reality; and (*d*) narcotics create a physical dependence on the drug. The regular use of any psychoactive drug almost always leads to physical or psychological dependence—and sometimes to both.

8 The marijuana sold on the street today contains more THC than it once did. Studies show that this psychoactive compound remains in the body far longer than once suspected. Although marijuana does have some valid medical applications, heavy recreational use can cause damage to the brain and lungs and has been linked to birth defects. Users develop a psychological dependence that is hard to overcome. Smoking pot also interferes with the user's ability to concentrate, memorize, and solve problems.

9 Despite the warnings against the use of psychoactive drugs, their use continues. Some people use them for thrills or as a means of rebellion. Others see in drugs a way of escaping from the problems of life. But one fact seems inescapable. No one uses drugs without taking the risk that the drug-induced ASC will become the most important thing in his or her life. Drugless ASCs can be obtained through meditation, religious experiences, and the use of isolation tanks.

PUTTING YOUR KNOWLEDGE TO WORK

■ TERMS YOU SHOULD KNOW

age regression
altered state of consciousness
    (ASC)
autonomic nervous system
conscious mind
consciousness
depressants
electroencephalograph (EEG)
    machine
gestalt

hallucinogens
hypnotism
latent content (of dreams)
lucid dream
manifest content (of dreams)
narcotics
perception
perceptual inference
posthypnotic suggestion

psychedelics
psychoactive drugs
psychological dependence
rapid eye movement
    (REM) sleep
sensory experience
stimulants
stimulus; stimuli
unconscious mind

■ CHAPTER CHECKUP

1 You would be experiencing a state of normal consciousness if you were (*a*) drunk on beer (*b*) having a nightmare (*c*) hypnotized by a psychologist (*d*) frightened by the sudden sound of a car horn.

2 If you are chased by a barking dog, your reaction might very well be affected by long-forgotten childhood experiences. Those memories are stored in your (*a*) conscious mind (*b*) unconscious mind (*c*) autonomic nervous system (*d*) sensory experiences.

3 The process of making sense out of a stimulus and its sensory experience is called (*a*) consciousness (*b*) an ASC (*c*) perception (*d*) an optical illusion.

4 You don't feel surprised when a distant airplane increases in size as it comes toward you because (*a*) you've seen the effect of distance on the size of objects many times (*b*) perceptual inference allows you to accept the increase in size without conscious thought (*c*) your brain automatically interprets the size of objects in relation to their distance (*d*) all of these are explanations for this phenomenon.

5 The most common altered state of consciousness (ASC) that people experience is (*a*) the hypnotic state (*b*) the dream state (*c*) being under the influence of psychoactive drugs (*d*) daydreaming.

6 Which is *not* a true statement about dreams? (*a*) People need sleep, but they could get by very well without dreams. (*b*) Everyone dreams every night. (*c*) Dreams don't come to waste your time; they always have something to tell you. (*d*) A dream event lasts about as long as the same event would in real life.

7 If you have a dream in which you forget to take an important paper to school with you, what is the proper *first* step in interpreting the dream? (*a*) Try to interpret the symbolism represented by forgetting a homework paper. (*b*) Look for the wish-fulfillment aspects of the dream. (*c*) Check it out as a warning not to forget something you'll need at school that day. (*d*) Examine the dream's feeling tone.

8 Which of the following is a *true* statement about hypnotism? (*a*) A good hypnotist can turn you into an instant championship tennis player even if you've never picked up a racket before. (*b*) Since hypnotized subjects don't actually go to sleep, no harm can be done to them while they're in a hypnotic state. (*c*) Hypnotized subjects never remember anything that happened while they were under hypnosis. (*d*) Under hypnosis, you will accept as true any suggestion given to you by the hypnotist that doesn't run counter to your moral values.

9 As a drug, marijuana fits into the category of the (*a*) depressants (*b*) stimulants (*c*) hallucinogens (*d*) narcotics.

10 People who regularly use psychoactive drugs to achieve an ASC (*a*) never risk injury to their bodies (*b*) can expect to overcome their emotional problems (*c*) don't have to worry about becoming addicted (*d*) almost always pay a heavy price for their involvement with substance abuse.

▪ EXPLORING CONCEPTS

1 How would you define the concept of "consciousness" to a ten-year-old? Since consciousness is so important, why is the psychologist also interested in the unconscious?

2 What is the difference between a stimulus and a sensory experience? Why would your perception of the taste of roast grasshopper be different from that of people who grow up eating grasshoppers as a regular part of their diet?

3 Imagine that you've just had a dream in which you were looking frantically through hundreds of drawers for something you'd lost. Every drawer you opened was empty. Then, just as you were about to give up, you found the lost object in your own pocket. What steps would you go through to interpret this dream?

4 How would you explain hypnotism to a friend whose doctor has suggested its use for a painful tooth extraction? What would you say to another friend who wants to hypnotize you for fun?

5 Why has the use of psychoactive drugs become so common in today's society? What would you say to a 12-year-old nephew who wants your advice on whether or not to experiment with drugs?

▪ HANDS-ON ACTIVITIES

1 Have you wondered what lies hidden in your unconscious? A simple experiment may put you in touch with your unconscious. Begin by finding a quiet place where you won't be disturbed. Place a single object on a table in front of you. A rock, a vase, or a figurine will do. Dim the light in the room and shine a lamp directly on the object. Sit comfortably and focus your attention on the object. Shut your mind to distractions while you study every detail of the object. In a little while, you may find that vivid, unexpected images are beginning to fill your mind. These images are probably emerging from your unconscious, set free by your concentration on the object. Break off the experience anytime you feel yourself becoming bored, anxious, or restless.

2 You can also expand your consciousness by making a deliberate effort to become more aware. If the weather permits, take off your shoes and walk outdoors. Forget about going anywhere. Close your eyes. For a little while, just *be*. Listen for your heartbeat; study the rhythm of your breathing; sense the miracle of your body at work. Now expand your awareness to the world around you. Feel the texture of concrete, grass, wood, asphalt under your feet. Feel the air moving delicately around your body. Feel the warmth of the sunlight. Hear the little sounds of life. Smell a leaf, taste a blade of grass. If you really let yourself get into this experience, you may discover a renewed sense of the sheer joy of being alive.

3 An altered state of consciousness can be induced without the aid of drugs or hypnosis. You might want to take some friends on a fantasy trip via a technique called *guided imagery*. Begin by helping everyone relax. Ask them to lie on the floor, eyes closed. Describe an imaginary "bubble" that surrounds each person, keeping its occupant safe, warm, and comfortable. Use these bubbles to transport everyone to a peaceful, natural spot of your choice. It could be a mountain meadow, a deserted beach, a quiet lake. Take everyone for a walk around your hidden place. Let them feel the breeze, listen to the sounds of wind or surf, sniff the flowers. In short, recreate all the lovely sensory experiences that the place has to offer. Take your time. Keep your voice low and calm. When it's time to return, gently bring everyone back to the room where you started. You'll find that most people can make the trip with you and that they'll report a pleasant and relaxing experience.

4 Keep a dream diary for several weeks. That means writing down as much of each night's dreams as you can remember. The suggestions in the box on page 43 should help. As you collect your dreams, analyze them according to the five-step procedure outlined on pages 42–44. By having a number of dreams to work with, you will probably discover some recurring symbols that will make analysis easier.

5 You probably have a pretty good idea of what law-enforcement agencies say about drug abuse. But what about other concerned professionals? With your teacher's help, arrange for a speaker to talk to your class about the drug situation in your own community. Sources of speakers include free clinics, drug abuse clinics, public health offices, psychologists in private practice, or organizations such as Alcoholics Anonymous and Nar-Anon.

FOR FURTHER READING

Bulkeley, Kelly. *Dreams of Healing: Transforming Nightmares into Visions of Hope*. Mahwah, NJ: Paulist Press, 2003. Rather than ignore your bad dreams, this useful guide shows you how to use dreams and nightmares to work through times of personal crisis. You'll find the collection of post-9/11 dreams of particular interest.

Cohen, David. *The Secret Language of the Mind*. San Francisco: Chronicle Books, 1996. Ready to explore the inner workings of the mind? This useful guide leads you through topics ranging from amnesia to Freudian slips to differences in male and female brain chemistry.

Faraday, Ann. *Dream Power*. New York: Berkley Pub., 1986. Faraday takes the mystery out of dream interpretation. Her book emphasizes the use of dreams in improving your ability to solve problems and to make decisions.

Marshall, Shelly. *Young, Sober and Free: Teen-to-Teen Stories of Hope and Recovery*. Center City, MN: Hazelden, 2003. Instead of preaching about the evils of alcohol and drug abuse, the author introduces you to teenagers who have been there. She backs up their personal stories with practical discussions of the Twelve Steps used to help addicts learn how to be "sober and free."

National Geographic Society. *You Won't Believe Your Eyes!* Washington, DC: National Geographic Society, 1994. This handsomely illustrated book explores the world of optical illusions. Chapter 1, "A World of Illusions," demonstrates and explains many standard "fool the eye" tricks. Of equal interest is the work of special-effect artists (Chapter 3) and illusions in nature (Chapter 4).

Romer, Daniel, ed. *Reducing Adolescent Risk: Toward an Integrated Approach*. Thousand Oaks, CA: Sage Publications, 2003. If you've ever wondered why your friends drive too fast, drink too much, or take crazy chances, you'll likely find the answers here. Although this book can be hard going at times, it brings together a useful collection of strategies that address the issue of teenage risk taking—and its prevention.

Sobel, Robert S. *Quit-for-Life*. Clearwater, FL: MDTA Press 1989. Sobel brings the enthusiasm and self-knowledge of an ex-smoker to this common-sense blend of psychology and self-management. The book helps smokers "kick the habit" by describing the deeply embedded behavior patterns they must overcome in order to end their chemical addiction.

Wallace, Benjamin, and Leslie E. Fisher. *Consciousness and Behavior*. Long Grove, IL: Waveland Press, 2003. This densely written book examines consciousness from many different angles. Wallace and Fisher explore the physiology of consciousness, the action of psychoactive drugs, hypnosis, sleep and dreams, and other important topics relating to the complex behavior of the human mind.

Chapter

3

The Brain and Behavior

Psychologists have long known that the mind and the body affect each other far more profoundly than most people think they do. Perhaps you've noticed how a flare-up of acne can send one of your friends into a depression. Or maybe you know a busy executive whose job has caused her to develop ulcers. In short, what happens to the body affects the mind. And—even more dramatically—what happens in the mind affects the body.

This relationship has been proven over and over in what doctors call the *placebo effect*. A placebo (the word comes from the Latin for "I shall please") usually takes the form of a harmless non-medicinal substance. Sugar pills and saline injections are typical placebos. In a double-blind test of a new AIDS drug, for example, half the patients receive the new drug, and a control group receives a placebo. Neither the patients nor the doctors know who is taking the drug and who is taking the placebo. If the new drug is effective, the experimental group should improve; the control group should remain unchanged.

It's not unusual for patients in the control group to show improvement. Although that makes it difficult to evaluate the experiment, it leads to an important conclusion: Since a placebo cannot affect an illness, it must be the patient's belief in the placebo that causes the body to fight off the disease.

Norman Cousins, a well-known journalist and editor, relied on a similar belief system to save his own life. In 1964, Cousins fell ill with a disease that caused his body's connective tissue to degenerate. His doctors did their best, but they were unable to halt the progress of the crippling disease. Faced with nearly certain death, Cousins realized that drugs weren't going to cure him. But, he rea-

FIGURE 3.1 ■ Norman Cousins devoted the last years of his life to promoting the role of healthy attitudes in medicine. He believed that patients are more likely to recover when they enlist the powers of the mind in their battle against illness and disease.

soned, placebos have been used to treat illnesses as varied as seasickness, headaches, arthritis, hay fever, high blood pressure, depression, and ulcers. If belief in a simple placebo can help those conditions, he asked himself, why can't I use a similar belief to beat my own illness?

First, Cousins cut out the painkilling drugs that were causing him to have a severe allergic reaction. But how could he cope with the pain? He decided that laughter was still the best medicine. Day after day he watched Marx Brothers movies and the television show *Candid Camera.* A nurse read his favorite humor books to him. In his book *Anatomy of an Illness,* Cousins wrote, "I made the joyous discovery that ten minutes of genuine belly laughter . . . would give me at least two hours of pain-free sleep."

To build up his immune system, Cousins also took large doses of Vitamin C. He moved out of the hospital and into a hotel room. Away from the busy, impersonal hospital routine, he felt more in control of his life. Slowly, to his doctor's amazement, his illness began to disappear. Within a few months he was able to return to work.

After he retired, Cousins devoted himself to spreading the word about his discovery. Some critics accused him of telling desperately ill people that they could "laugh their illnesses away." Cousins replied that he never counseled people to reject proper medical treatment. The point, he explained, is that pleasant emotions make us feel better. The more laughter, love, and friendship we have in our lives, the better we'll feel.

A number of studies inspired by Cousins's ideas seem to prove their value. In one study, two groups of cancer patients all received the same medical treatment. But one group also received information and counseling to promote their emotional well-being. This group reported less depression, and their bodies produced higher levels of cancer-killing cells. Similarly, patients with advanced breast can-

cers who received emotional support and counseling lived an average of 18 months longer than patients who did not receive the additional therapy.

Even when a good attitude doesn't cure the disease, it improves the life of the patient. "The important thing is what we do while we're alive," Cousins wrote. "The great tragedy of life is not death, but what dies inside us while we live." To doctors, he said, "If you treat just the disease without treating the emotional devastation caused by the disease, you're only treating half a patient."

Whatever the final decision on the usefulness of Cousins's ideas, doctors have learned not to ignore the mind when they treat the illnesses of the body. For their part, psychologists know that the mind itself is a product of the complex and fascinating organ called the brain. But before the brain can be put to work—whether the problem is curing cancer or tying a shoelace—it must receive data about the outside world through the eyes, ears, nose, skin, and other senses.

This chapter will provide you with a brief introduction to the study of physiological psychology. When you finish the sections that follow, you will have a better understanding of the body you inhabit—and the marvelous brain that controls it.

3.1 What roles do the brain and glands play in behavior?

3.2 What effect does vision have on behavior?

3.3 How does your sense of hearing affect behavior?

3.4 How do your senses of smell and taste work?

3.5 What effect do the skin senses have on behavior?

3.6 Do you have any senses beyond the basic five?

3.1 ▪ WHAT ROLES DO THE BRAIN AND GLANDS PLAY IN BEHAVIOR?

Just as a great airliner cannot fly without proper commands from its pilot, your body cannot function without its own command center, the brain. If you could look inside your skull, you'd see a mass of gray-colored tissue that is shaped somewhat like an over-sized walnut. Under a microscope you would see that the tissue is composed of individual nerve cells, called *neurons*. Don't try to count them—the human brain contains approximately 10 billion neurons.

If your brain is typical, it weighs about 3½ pounds. That may not sound like much, but in proportion to body weight, it's the largest of any living creature. By contrast, a dinosaur called the stegosaurus weighed two tons—but had to rely on a 2½ ounce brain to drive its huge bulk.

Brain size alone, however, does not correlate directly with intelligence. Some highly intelligent people have relatively small brains. Instead of size, a better measure of intelligence might be the individual brain's ability to store and retrieve data and to make connections between apparently unrelated events or objects. Thus, to most people a falling apple is something to eat. But, to a genius like the English scientist Sir Isaac Newton, a falling apple was the clue that led him to his discovery of the universal law of gravity.

Research shows that brain activity is both electrical and chemical in nature. This electrochemical activity is fueled by oxygen and sugar from the bloodstream. Twenty-five percent of the oxygen pumped by the heart is used by the brain. If that supply should be cut off for as little as four minutes, permanent damage results. Of all the body's nerve cells, only the olfactory neurons in the nose are capable of regenerating themselves. Medical researchers have worked on this problem for many years, but it wasn't until 1990 that sci-entists at Johns Hopkins School of Medicine learned how to keep a lab culture of cerebral cortex neurons alive and multiplying. Many years down the road, the researchers say, this breakthrough may lead to a procedure that will allow surgeons to replace brain tissue damaged by accident or an illness such as a stroke. For now, stroke victims must rely on physical therapy to help them regain control of muscles left paralyzed when blocked blood vessels cut off oxygen to the motor control centers in the brain. When successful, the therapy helps the patient transfer control of the affected muscles to networks of un-damaged brain cells.

Even as you read these words, a tornado of activity is taking place in your brain. One part, the forebrain, is actively engaged in translating letter symbols into ideas. This is the part of the brain that controls the process of conscious thought. Another part of the brain, the hindbrain, is also hard at work, taking care of essential body functions. Without it, you'd be dead within a few minutes. (A diagram that maps the basic parts of the brain can be seen in Figure 3.2.)

THE HINDBRAIN

Have you ever forgotten to tell your heart to beat? Of course not, you say—that vital function is taken care of automatically. But it's not fully automatic. The *hindbrain* regulates many of the body's basic activities, including heartbeat, breathing, balance, the physical appetites, and sleep. Three of the hindbrain's most important parts are the medulla, the cerebellum, and the reticular activating system (RAS).

MEDULLA. The *medulla* provides a connection between your brain and spinal cord. It

BASIC PARTS OF THE HUMAN BRAIN

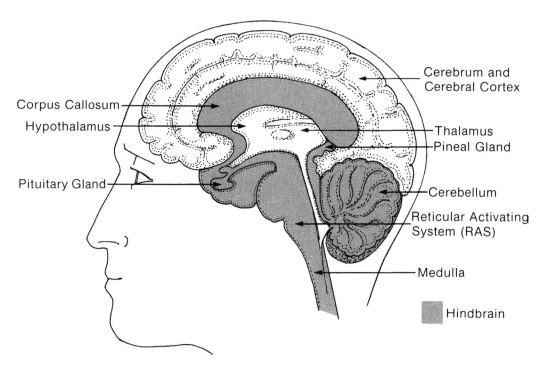

Corpus Callosum

Hypothalamus

Pituitary Gland

Cerebrum and
Cerebral Cortex

Thalamus
Pineal Gland

Cerebellum

Reticular Activating
System (RAS)

Medulla

Hindbrain

Interior of the Brain When Split on Midline

FIGURE 3.2 ▓ In this diagram, the brain has been split down the middle to show its basic internal parts. Hindbrain structures are shown in black; the forebrain appears in white. Both halves of the brain contain the same structures even though the left brain and the right brain control different behaviors.

helps regulate breathing, heartbeat, and blood pressure. Even if you deliberately stopped breathing, the medulla would take over within a very few minutes and would resume breathing for you. At the same time, your conscious mind would "black out" so that it could no longer interfere with this vital activity.

CEREBELLUM. The *cerebellum* helps maintain the body's balance and plays an important role in coordinating fine-muscle activity. When you thread a needle or repair a com-

puter, your cerebellum makes sure your fingers follow the orders of your conscious mind.

RETICULAR ACTIVATING SYSTEM (RAS). Are you sleepy right now or wide awake? Whichever state you find yourself in, the signals that control wakefulness and sleep, as well as arousal and alertness, originate in the *reticular activating system (the RAS)*. Chemicals created within the brain stimulate or depress the RAS, causing you to wake up or fall asleep. The RAS also helps sort out important messages from the constant flow of trivia reported by your sensory receptors. Thus, you can ignore normal traffic noises—until the screech of brakes alerts you to possible danger.

The hindbrain also connects directly to the *spinal cord*, a vital bundle of nerves that runs through the backbone. From the spinal cord, long cables of sensory and motor nerves connect the *central nervous system* (the brain and spinal cord) to the *peripheral nervous system* (the nerve pathways that stretch to all outlying parts of the body, including the muscles). But if you had to make do with only these structures, as wonderful as they are, you'd still be little more than a jellyfish. It is the forebrain that makes you a human being.

THE FOREBRAIN

Your highly developed *forebrain* makes it possible for you to experience the pleasures and pains of existence. Whether you're smelling a rose or solving a tricky math problem, the conscious thought that directs your activity takes place in the forebrain. Three of the most important parts of the forebrain are the thalamus, the hypothalamus, and the cerebrum.

THALAMUS. The *thalamus* connects the forebrain with the rest of the body. All incoming messages from the sense organs (except for smell) pass through the thalamus. Like a high-speed switchboard, the thalamus sorts out the signals and passes them on to the proper groups of neurons in the forebrain.

HYPOTHALAMUS. The *hypothalamus* plays an important role in controlling instinctive behavior, particularly when you are in danger. If you were threatened by a mugger, for example, your hypothalamus would order production of the hormones that prepare your body to protect itself. The hypothalamus also directs the body's responses to hunger and

thirst, sexual feelings, and stress. One way to cope with stress, research suggests, is to "take a few deep breaths—through your nose." Deep breathing through the nose cools the hypothalamus and stimulates it to release chemicals that have a calming effect on your mood.

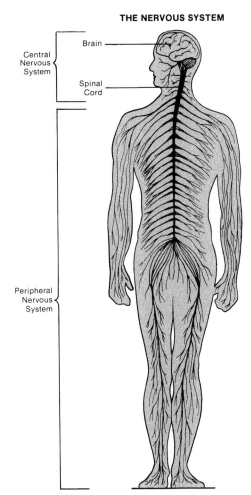

FIGURE 3.3 ▓ Your brain receives information and sends orders via two nerve networks. The central nervous system is made up of the brain and spinal cord. When this system is connected to the peripheral nervous system, it ties the body into a unified system under direct control of the brain.

65

THE FOREBRAIN: WHERE THOUGHTS BECOME ACTION

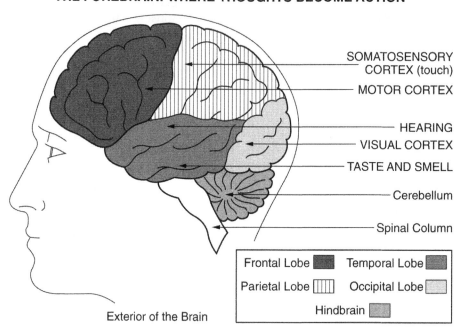

SOMATOSENSORY CORTEX (touch)
MOTOR CORTEX
HEARING
VISUAL CORTEX
TASTE AND SMELL
Cerebellum
Spinal Column

Frontal Lobe ▪ Temporal Lobe ▪
Parietal Lobe ▥ Occipital Lobe ▨
Hindbrain ▨

Exterior of the Brain

FIGURE 3.4 ▪ Exploration of the brain has enabled researchers to map the major parts of the forebrain. "Seeing," for example, takes place in the visual cortex at the back of the brain. Can you locate the control centers for the other senses?

The "pleasure center" described on pages 3–4 is also located in the hypothalamus. Imagine a future in which every member of society is "hooked up" at birth with a radio-controlled pleasure-center stimulator. Whoever controlled the transmitter would undoubtedly receive unquestioning obedience from everyone, so great would be the desire to receive regular jolts of pleasure!

CEREBRUM. The *cerebrum,* the great dome of tissue that lies atop the brain, allows you to experience consciousness. This area forms 60 percent of your brain's mass. By far the most important part of the cerebrum is the *cerebral cortex.* The cortex contains most of the specific areas that affect muscle coordination,

memory, concentration, problem solving, and decision making. This outermost layer represents a marvel of engineering, for the one-eighth-inch-thick cortex would cover an area of over six square feet if it were laid flat. In order to fit inside the skull, the cerebral cortex is folded many times. This folding gives the brain its wrinkled appearance.

The cortex is divided into four regions called *lobes* (see Figure 3.4). The *occipital lobe* is located at the back of the head. Here the brain interprets the signals transmitted by the eyes and creates the mental image that allows you to "see."

At the side of the head lies the *temporal lobe.* This lobe handles both your auditory sense and your sense of smell. When you hear popcorn popping and then inhale the aroma, it's the temporal lobe that's receiving and interpreting the stimuli furnished by your ears and nose.

The *parietal lobe* is found at the top of the head. This region governs your sense of touch and also keeps track of the different parts of the body. If the segment of the parietal lobe known as the somatosensory cortex were to be damaged, for example, you would lose awareness of your body's movements.

Finally, the *frontal lobe,* located just behind your forehead, adds its own roster of important functions. Some research suggests that the frontal lobe plays a key role in creativity, emotional control, and attention span. More certainly, the frontal lobe's motor cortex provides the coordination that keeps your feet, legs, arms, hands, and other body parts working together. A large portion of this area is devoted to the control of two small parts of your body, the hands and mouth. Because tool use and spoken language are the major developments separating humans from the lower animals, this unequal development makes biological sense. Even the simple act of saying "hello" to a friend requires the precise coordination of hundreds of muscles.

LEFT BRAIN VS. RIGHT BRAIN

The left and right sides of your brain look much alike, but their functions differ greatly. Research shows, for example, that your left brain controls movements on the right side of your body, and vice versa. Take a moment and scratch your nose with your right hand. It was the motor cortex on the left side of your

LEFT HEMISPHERE (Controls right side of body)	RIGHT HEMISPHERE (Controls left side of body)
Language Rational Mechanics, math Recognize objects Logic, analytic thought Perception of order Active	Music Creative Art, symbols Recognize faces Holistic, intuitive thought Perception of patterns Receptive

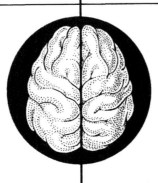

THE BRAIN DIVIDES UP THE WORK   Although the two halves of the brain work closely together, each hemisphere controls a different set of abilities. If you're a right-handed, left-brain-dominant person, writing a research paper calls for the left brain's verbal skills. But what if you want to draw a cartoon for the title page? Drawing requires a shift to the right brain's nonverbal, artistic skills. The chart above spells out the range of abilities that researchers have linked to each hemisphere.

brain that controlled your arm and finger movements.

One side of the brain always takes a dominant role. Left-brain dominance leads to right-handedness. Since more than 90 percent of the world's population are right-handed, you can conclude that most people are left-brain dominant. If you happen to be left-handed, you already know that you're in the minority. You may also have noticed that many left-handers use their right hands for everyday activities, such as throwing a ball or opening a jar. British scientist Oliver Zangwill believes that these left-handers are still left-brain dominant. He estimates that less than one half of all left-handed people are right-brain dominant.

Even more interesting to researchers has been the discovery that even though the two halves of the brain work closely together as a rule, they control different abilities. The dominant left brain takes charge of logical thought (solving mathematical problems, for example) and verbal abilities (talking to a friend or writing a poem). As a consequence, damage to the language areas of the left brain would leave you unable to speak or write. The right brain handles artistic, musical, athletic, and other nonverbal activities. When you dance a jig, paint a picture, or play a set of tennis, the right brain is exercising control.

A band of nerve fibers called the *corpus callosum* connects the two halves of the brain. This connection enables the brain to work as a single unit. But something interesting happens when the corpus callosum is cut or damaged. Since the two halves of the brain can no longer communicate freely, each side of the body loses some of its usual skills. Mary O., for example, had split-brain surgery to relieve the effect of severe epileptic seizures. Since she was left-brain dominant, she could still write with her right hand. Her right hand, however, could no longer draw pictures or work jigsaw puzzles—which are

right-brain, nonverbal activities! Observers reported that while Mary was struggling to work a jigsaw puzzle with her right hand, her left hand kept trying to take over. Under orders to use her right hand and annoyed by this "intruder," Mary finally sat on her left hand to keep it out of the way. When she was told to switch to her left hand she sighed with relief and quickly finished the puzzle.

TRANSMITTAL OF MESSAGES

One of the marvels of your body is the speed and efficiency with which messages move to and from the brain. Message impulses move along a network of nerve cells called a *neural pathway*. Each neuron (see Figure 3.5) is composed of three major parts: (1) a *cell body*, where the nucleus and other equipment vital to the work of the cell are located; (2) a number of branching fibers called *dendrites*, which carry the incoming signals to the cell body; and (3) the *axon*, a single arm that branches out at the end and carries impulses from the cell body to the dendrites of nearby neurons.

BASIC ACTION OF THE NEURONS. The basic nerve impulse is electrochemical in nature. When a dendrite belonging to one of your neurons receives a stimulus, a change takes place in the end of the dendrite. This change is like a signal that says "stop" or "go." If the signal is "go," the neuron fires. This means that a wave of electrochemical activity travels from the receiving dendrite to the cell body and onward through the axon to other neurons in the neural pathway. When the impulses reach the proper neurons in your brain, a thought, image, word, or emotion takes shape in your mind. Once a neuron has fired, it takes about a thousandth of a second to "recharge" and get ready for the next impulse to arrive.

Impulses can pass from one neuron to an-

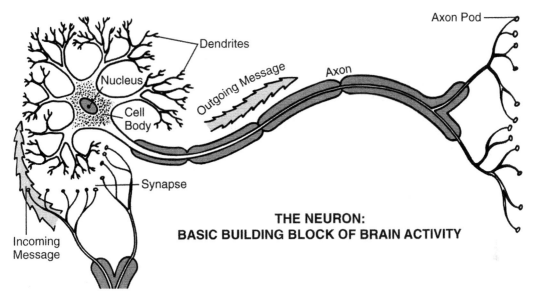

Dendrites

Nucleus

Cell Body

Outgoing Message

Axon

Axon Pod

Synapse

Incoming Message

**THE NEURON:
BASIC BUILDING BLOCK OF BRAIN ACTIVITY**

FIGURE 3.5 ■ The brain contains some ten billion nerve cells. Each neuron (shown here in simplified form) interconnects with hundreds of other similar cells. Impulses are carried across the synapse by chemical messengers called neurotransmitters. A hundred million of the brain's neurons would fit into a cubic inch.

other only by jumping a tiny space between the pods at the end of the axon and the neighboring dendrites. This space, only seven millionths (.000007) of an inch wide, is called the *synapse*. You can see the pods and the synapse in Figure 3.5. When an impulse reaches one of these pods, it releases a chemical called a *neurotransmitter*. The chemical crosses the synapse and triggers an impulse in the next cell. In this way, the impulse passes from one neuron to the next in the neural pathway until it reaches its destination. Impulses speed through the body as fast as 200 miles per hour.

BREAKDOWNS IN TRANSMISSION.   Any breakdown in the transmission of nerve impulses can cause serious problems. When multiple sclerosis attacks the insulation that covers the axons that carry messages to the muscles of the body, the result is paralysis and loss of

muscular control. Epileptic seizures take place when damaged neurons fire wildly. Mild epileptic seizures cause only a brief blackout, but more severe seizures can result in unconsciousness and convulsions. Although researchers are still searching for a cure for multiple sclerosis, drug or surgical treatments enable most epileptics to lead productive lives.

ROLE OF THE ENDOCRINE GLANDS

As important as the central nervous system is, your behavior is also affected by busy chemical factories called *glands*. Ducted glands pipe saliva, sweat, tears, and digestive juices to where they are needed. But some of your most important glands pump powerful chemicals called *hormones* directly into the bloodstream. These ductless glands, known as the *endocrine glands*, regulate everything from

▪ PRO & CON:

Is Psychosurgery a Proper Treatment For Mental Problems?

In 1891, a Swiss surgeon performed brain surgery designed to change the abnormal behavior of mental patients. Although these first experiments were not successful, a new method of dealing with the mentally ill had been created. Psychosurgery, as it is called today, involves the use of precise surgical techniques to destroy the brain tissue thought to be causing the abnormal behavior. Violently aggressive people, for example, can return to normal life, no longer dangerous to themselves or to others. The usefulness and ethics of such surgery, which is still being used on several hundred patients each year, have become a major issue in psychology. The main arguments on each side of the debate are summarized below.

PRO

1 Psychosurgery offers the only real hope for returning many severely disturbed mental patients to any type of normal life. Advanced techniques have made the procedures relatively foolproof.

2 The cost of keeping disturbed patients in jails or mental hospitals is immense. For a few thousand dollars and with little risk, many such people can be returned to society as productive citizens.

3 Although psychosurgery sometimes causes changes in the patient's personality, the price should be considered minor. Modern surgical techniques remove only the brain tissue responsible for the offending behavior.

4 Fears that psychosurgery will lead to loss of freedom are overstated. Every scientific advance carries with it the possibility for evil as well as good. Some people fear that psychosurgery might be used to control unruly citizens by linking them to mind-control computers. So far, this has happened only in science fiction.

CON

1 Psychosurgery's record is one of poor legal and scientific controls. Published studies often suffer from a lack of follow-up that makes it difficult to evaluate accurately the success of the surgery.

2 Psychosurgery is an unacceptable violation of individual rights. In most cases, psychosurgery is performed on those patients least able to object—the residents of mental hospitals and prisons.

3 Despite improved techniques, the surgeon cannot guarantee that severe personality changes won't occur. Drug treatments can be modified and hospital gates opened—but brain surgery cannot be reversed.

4 Reliance on psychosurgery could easily lead to even greater use of similar techniques for changing behavior. Today, the surgeon treats the mentally disturbed; tomorrow, psychosurgery might be performed on anyone who refuses to obey the rules of an all-powerful government.

Do you think psychosurgery should be allowed to continue? If so, what circumstances do you think should exist before a doctor is allowed to perform this type of surgery? Compare your answers with those of others who have read this Pro & Con.

physical growth to sexual functioning. The most important of the endocrine glands are the pituitary, the adrenal, the thyroid, and the sex glands (see Figure 3.6).

PITUITARY GLAND. The *pituitary gland* produces hormones that regulate a wide range of body activities. Most important, a properly working pituitary secretes a growth hormone that ensures normal growth. Too much or too little of this hormone can cause giantism or dwarfism.

Some pituitary hormones act as chemical messengers that turn other glands off and on. The sex glands, for example, would not turn a child into a sexually mature adult if they were not stimulated by the pituitary at the proper time. Female Russian gymnasts were once accused of trying to reverse this process by taking drugs to slow down sexual maturation. Slimmer, smaller bodies, it was thought, would give them a better chance of winning world titles.

Whether the charge was true or not, researchers can bring about seeming miracles with the use of pituitary hormones. One tiny six-year-old girl with an underactive pituitary grew over 20 inches in 18 months after doctors treated her with growth hormones. Like most drugs, the hormones have also been misused. Some sports-crazy parents have tried to give their sons and daughters a head start on athletic fame by treating them with illegally obtained growth hormones. Like the anabolic steroids some impatient athletes have used to build muscle mass, these powerful hormones have disastrous side effects that far outweigh any temporary advantage their use may give a young man or woman.

ADRENAL GLANDS. The *adrenal glands* produce their own family of hormones. Adrenaline, one of the most important products of the adrenals, prepares the body to cope with

ENDOCRINE GLANDS ALSO AFFECT BEHAVIOR

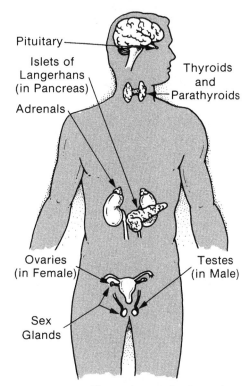

FIGURE 3.6 ▨ The *endocrine glands* regulate many important human behaviors. Too large or too small a quantity of the hormones secreted by these glands can lead to physical and emotional problems.

emergencies. Next time you find yourself in a stress-producing situation, check for these changes as the adrenaline begins to flow: You feel stronger and more energetic as extra sugar is released into the blood. Your blood pressure rises and your pulse rate increases. You breathe more easily as air passages in the lungs are enlarged. You see better as your pupils admit more light into the eyes. Your skin temperature rises, and your palms begin to sweat. In a few seconds, your body will be as ready as it can possibly be for the coming challenge.

José Delgado:
Prophet for a Brave New World of ESB

The fighting bull charged straight at the apparently helpless José Delgado. The speeding animal was only 20 feet away when Delgado pressed the button on a transmitter in his hand. The bull skidded to an abrupt stop. It looked blankly at Delgado, then wandered off.

What happened in that bullring? Before the demonstration, Delgado had implanted a tiny radio receiver called a *stimoceiver* in the bull's brain. When he activated his transmitter, the stimoceiver delivered tiny jolts of electricity to an area in the bull's brain that inhibits aggression. In effect, the stimoceiver "turned off" the bull's desire to attack.

Delgado's show-stopping research inspired further work on ways to harness the power of the brain. In one experiment, neuroscientists trained a brain-implanted monkey to send brain signals to a robot arm. Activated by the monkey's thoughts, the arm carried out reaching and grasping movements on a computer screen. The next step, the researchers believe, is to use similar "brain wiring" to enable disabled patients to control computers or robots "in real time, as fast as they can think."

The man who inspired these experiments was born in Spain in 1915 and trained in medicine at the University of Madrid. He came to Yale University in 1950 to carry on his research. Delgado states his goals by saying, "I would like to cure epilepsy, cure mental disorders, and construct a better world." What makes these goals seem possible to Delgado is his faith in research that uses the mind to influence its own behavior.

Delgado's special interests center on electronic stimulation of the brain (ESB). Through electrodes implanted in the brain, he believes, two-way radio communication between the brain and computers can be arranged. In this way, scientists could send information, instructions, and directions for planned behaviors to a subject's brain. Delgado claims that this method would allow an infant to be trained and educated to reach the highest possible levels of development. No longer will the accident of birth, which gives one child loving parents and another an abusive mother or father, cripple humankind.

To those critics who claim that the stimoceiver would lead to enslavement of people by ruthless dictators, Delgado replies that ESB cannot make robots of people. Behavior can be influenced, he says, but not controlled. From a practical standpoint, ESB has limits that can be overcome only in the pages of a novel. Used properly, it will help people develop their minds, train their thinking power, and control their emotions.

The stimoceiver has been used effectively to locate lesions in the brain that cause violent, uncontrolled rages. Why not go the next step, Delgado wonders, and apply this new technology to making the human personality more truly "human"?

Do you agree with Dr. Delgado that the United States should promote the exploration of "inner space"? Do you see any danger in allowing research on the use of ESB to continue?

The adrenals also work behind the scenes to regulate the chemical balance of the body. Most obviously, at puberty the adrenals cooperate with the sex glands to produce the physical changes that occur during early adolescence. Adult body hair sprouts, boys' voices lower, and girls' breasts develop. Adolescent acne, unfortunately, also seems to be related to the action of the adrenals and the sex glands during this period of rapid physical change.

THYROID GLAND.   The hormones produced by the *thyroid gland* help determine the body's energy level. If you have an overactive thyroid, you will lose weight, have trouble sleeping, and be full of nervous energy. Too little thyroid production leads to sluggish behavior and weight gain. Severe thyroid deficiency in early childhood can also affect intellectual development. This condition, known as *cretinism,* results in low intelligence and poor physical development. Early hormone therapy for children born with this condition can sometimes prevent mental retardation by restoring normal growth in the nervous system.

SEX GLANDS.   The *sex glands,* properly called the *gonads,* are the ovaries in women and the testes in men. These glands produce the hormones that regulate the development of the sex organs and prepare the body for reproduction. In most animals, the production of sex hormones leads to instinctive mating behavior. The sexual life of human beings, however, is so complex that the work of these potent glands should not be thought of only in biological terms. Human sexual behavior is also strongly influenced by psychological factors and social customs.

■ SECTION CHECKUP

1 What are the basic differences between the hindbrain and the forebrain?

2 Why is the cerebral cortex so important to your behavior as a human being?

3 How are nerve impulses transmitted from one neuron to another?

4 Why are the endocrine glands considered to be so important to an individual's growth and development?

3.2 ▪ WHAT EFFECT DOES VISION HAVE ON BEHAVIOR?

Close your eyes. Instantly, you lose much of your contact with the world around you. Even though you can still hear, smell, taste, and touch, you'll probably feel rather helpless. With care, you can still move around your house or find objects on your desk. But just try pouring a glass of milk! It won't take long to verify that about 75 percent of your information about the world comes to you through your eyes.

Technically, *vision* refers to your eye's ability to respond to light. But even the sharpest human eye is sensitive to only a limited part of the electromagnetic spectrum. You cannot see ultraviolet light, for example—but bees can. Similarly, you could be photographed in a dark room "lighted" only by infrared light. Since your eye cannot see infrared light, you wouldn't know the picture had been taken until someone showed you the print.

Vision provides you with a number of important abilities. These include (1) depth perception, which enables you to judge fast-moving traffic while you're driving. (2) Color discrimination, which allows you to pick out the ripe banana from the green ones. (3) Rapid focus (from short-range to long-range and back again), which lets you catch a hard-thrown baseball. (4) The ability to adjust quickly to differences in brightness, so that walking out of the shade into the sunlight doesn't leave you blinded.

MECHANISM OF THE HUMAN EYE

One way to understand the working of the eye is to think of it as a television camera. Like the camera, your eye continuously gathers reflected light from whatever scene lies in front of its lens. As the light varies, your eye adjusts automatically for changes in brightness. Then, just as the camera transmits pictures to a receiver, your eye converts the image focused by the lens into electrical impulses and sends them to the brain. As shown in Figure 3.7, the mechanism of the eye has six major parts.

MECHANISM OF THE HUMAN EYE

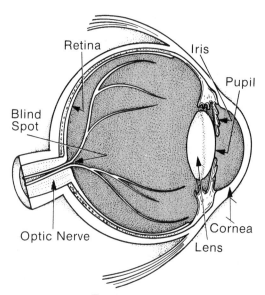

FIGURE 3.7 ※ The human eye is your personal "TV camera." It provides you with 75 percent of the sensory data you gather from the world around you. But the eye only collects and transmits visual data. "Seeing" actually takes place in the visual cortex of the brain.

1. The *cornea* is the transparent outer covering found at the front surface of the eye. The curved surface of the cornea enables it to gather light from a much wider field of vision than would be possible if it were flat.

2. The *iris* is a circular arrangement of muscles that regulates the amount of light admitted into the eye. When people tell you, "Oh, you have such beautiful eyes," they're talking about the color of the iris. The iris can be blue, green, or brown, with additional flecks of other colors. Brown is the most common color, however, probably because the darker shade gives the most protection from bright sunlight.

3. The *pupil* is the dark opening in the center of the iris through which light passes on its way to the retina. The size of the pupil is regulated by the contraction and relaxation of the iris. Pupil size normally varies with the amount of light reflected from the scene you're observing. Your pupil gets bigger in dim light and contracts to its smallest size in bright sunlight. You can test this size change for yourself with a mirror.

Researchers have found that pupil size is also affected by emotions. When you look at something you find exciting or interesting, your pupil size enlarges. When you look at something unpleasant, your pupils contract. This change in pupil size is entirely unconscious and cannot be controlled. In experiments to test this finding, groups of men and women were shown pictures of babies. All of the women—whether or not they had children—showed an increase in pupil size. Only those men who were fathers, however, had a similar reaction.

4. The *lens* is a focusing device. Its job is to deliver a sharp image to the retina. Special muscles adjust the shape of the lens so that you can see objects close up or far away with equal clarity.

5. The *retina*, the area at the back of the eye, is lined with about 125 million light-sensitive cells. These cells convert light into

YOUR REALITY HAS A HOLE IN IT

FIGURE 3.8 ⋙ You can prove the existence of this blind spot by holding the diagram at arm's length. Close your left eye and focus the right eye on the X. Now move the book slowly toward you. Somewhere along the way, the black spot will disappear. If you keep moving the book toward you, the spot will reappear.

electrical impulses for transmission to the brain. Ninety-five percent of the cells are *rods* (named because of their long, narrow shape). The rods are sensitive to low levels of light but "see" everything in shades of gray. The remaining cells in the retina, the *cones,* provide you with color vision. Cones are concentrated near the center of the retina, where your vision is sharpest. Since the cones do not respond to low light levels, your night vision tends to lack color perception.

6. The *optic nerve* is a bundle of nerve fibers that serves as a transmission line to the brain. The optic nerve is composed of over a million fibers, each of which carries impulses from many rods and cones at once. Because there are no rods or cones at the spot where the optic nerve leaves the retina, you have a "blind spot" in your vision (see Figure 3.8). You aren't normally aware of the blind spot, however. Psychologists believe that the brain "fills in" the "hole" by constructing a logical extension of the surrounding area.

COLOR BLINDNESS

Color perception depends on which type of cone receives the stimulation. Some cones are sensitive to red, others to yellow and green, and the rest to blue and violet. When

one type of cone or another is missing or does not work properly, color blindness results. About seven men out of a hundred have this condition, but only one woman in a thousand is color blind. Color blindness is thought to be a hereditary condition that is passed on to sons (and less frequently to daughters) by women who carry the defective gene.

Red-green is the most common color blindness, followed by blue-yellow. Because Ronnie L. is red-green color blind, he cannot tell a red apple from a green one. Ronnie can see that the apples are different, but both appear gray to him. Blue skies and yellow tulips look normal to Ronnie, but not to Sue N., who is blue-yellow color blind. Even so, Ronnie and Sue are better off than the one person in 40,000 who is totally color blind. With no working cones on their retinas, these people see only a black, white, and gray world.

VISION ADAPTATION

Remember the last time you walked into a darkened theater? At first you felt blinded, and you may have stumbled into someone standing in the aisle. But gradually your eyes adjusted to the darkness. Gray shapes emerged, and finally you spotted an empty seat. Full adjustment to near-total darkness would have taken almost an hour. By that time, your eyes would have become a hundred thousand times more sensitive to light than they are outside on a sunny day.

Vision also adjusts for extremes of size and distance. You can move easily from working on a tiny model train to watching a hawk as it alights upon a distant tree. If you have normal eyesight, you can probably see a ¼-inch-thick wire at a distance of 440 yards—almost the length of four football fields! Many people, however, cannot see clearly because of defects in the eye. If the lens does not focus an image clearly on the retina, for example, vision becomes fuzzy. Most problems of this kind can be corrected with eyeglasses, properly designed to compensate for the faults in the lens or cornea.

FOOLING THE EYE

Visual illusions work because the clues that you normally use to identify size or shape of objects have been changed. Look at the illusion in Figure 3.9, for example. Which line, A or B, is longer? Your perception will probably tell you that B is longer than A, but your ruler will show you that they're the same length. The illusion created by the converging "railroad tracks" tells your brain that B is farther away; in order to look as long as A, it must be

longer than A! Psychologists call this concept *size constancy.* To test the concept, hold one hand at arm's length, the other at half that distance. The two hands will look the same size, yet the image size of the far hand on your retina will be exactly one half that of the near hand. Only when you overlap the far hand with the near hand will the size difference become apparent.

An *afterimage* occurs when you stare steadily at an image for some time. As the retina's cells tire, the image becomes "fixed." Then, when you look away, an afterimage appears. You can test this illusion by using the target circle printed here (see Figure 3.10). After staring at the target for 60 seconds, look at a white wall. The target will now appear on the wall, but it will be many times larger than the original. That's size constancy at work again. In effect, the brain is saying, "If a retinal image that big is actually ten feet away, it *must* be quite large." A projected afterimage also reverses colors. You should see the target circle as white instead of black, a result of continued firing of the retina cells and optic nerve after they are stimulated.

The afterimage makes motion pictures possible. Film is actually a series of still pictures, each of which appears on the screen for about ¹⁄₂₄th of a second. Your own retina provides the illusion of motion by retaining an afterimage of each frame. This allows the next frame to blend smoothly into the last, creating the illusion of motion.

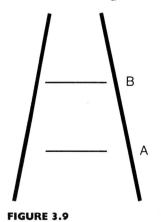

FIGURE 3.9

FIGURE 3.10

■ SECTION CHECKUP

1 How would your life be changed if you could not see?

2 Name the six major parts of the eye. What is the role of each part in providing you with vision?

3 Explain how size constancy and after-image work to create visual illusions.

3.3 ▨ HOW DOES YOUR SENSE OF HEARING AFFECT BEHAVIOR?

A door slams in a distant part of the house. You turn your head, waiting for footsteps. Automatically, a series of ear mechanisms have gone into action, converting the sound into impulses that speed to the brain. Was it the wind? Or an intruder? In the dark of night, your eyes won't help you find the answer. This time, you'll have to depend on your ears for help.

Physicists define *sound* as a form of energy consisting of air waves of changing pressure. These waves are measured in cycles per second (cps). *Frequency,* which is the number of vibrations per second, is expressed in cps. For example, middle C on the musical scale has a frequency of 256 cps. The human ear can detect sounds ranging from about 20 cps up to approximately 20,000 cps. At the low end of the scale, you hear the sound as deep, rumbling bass notes. High-frequency sounds are heard as high-pitched squeals. But technical terms hardly account for the wonderful world of sound that surrounds you. From the creepy noises outside your window at night to the soaring beauty of a great orchestra, your ears add an important dimension to your understanding of the world around you.

MECHANISM OF THE EAR

The working parts of your hearing mechanism are hidden from view. The *outer ear* merely collects sound waves and funnels them through the *auditory canal.* At that point, the ear really begins to go to work (see Figure 3.11).

1. The *eardrum* is a thin, flexible layer of tissue that stretches across the end of the auditory canal. Sound waves that strike the eardrum cause it to vibrate.

2. Three tiny bones, each hinged to the next, amplify the vibrations transmitted by the eardrum. As a result of the work done by this delicate mechanism, sound waves are 30 times stronger when they reach the cochlea.

MECHANISM OF THE HUMAN EAR

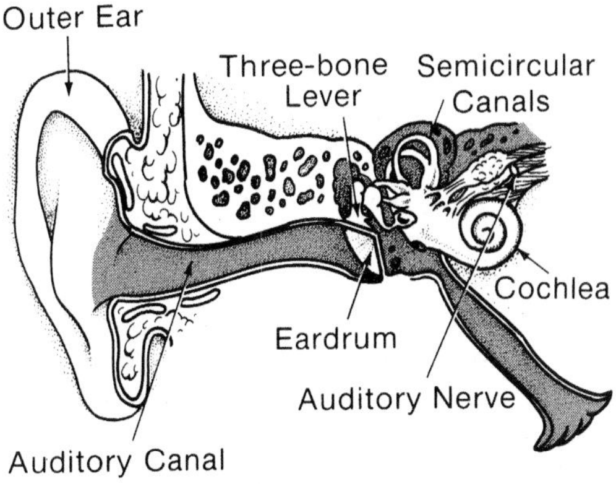

FIGURE 3.11 ▨ The human ear converts sound waves into electrical impulses for transmission to the brain. The semicircular canals control your balance and are not involved in hearing (see pages 86–87).

3. The *cochlea* converts sound energy into electrical impulses for transmission to the brain. The snail-shaped cochlea is filled with fluid and sensitive hair cells. When vibrations enter the cochlea, the fluid moves back and forth, stimulating the hair cells. In turn, the hair cells convert the movement into impulses that can be delivered to the auditory nerve.

4. The *auditory nerve* carries the impulses from the cochlea to the part of the brain responsible for hearing, the auditory cortex. Now your brain can get on with the job of making a decision about those noises you heard earlier. Listening intently, you hear another thump and a faint "meow." That's a relief. It's only the cat, jumping against the screen door and demanding to be let into the house.

THE ART OF HEARING

Each ear operates independently of the other. The fact that sound waves usually strike one of your ears a fraction of a second sooner than the other allows you to locate the source of a sound with good success. Confusion results when competing noises or echoes conceal the true source of a particular sound. Drivers on city streets, for example, often find it difficult to pinpoint the location of a siren because of traffic noise and the echo of the siren from nearby buildings.

In addition, the ear does not respond equally to all types of sound. Sound waves between 2,000 and 4,000 cps, for example, will give you few clues as to their source. Perhaps it is no coincidence that many smaller animals such as mice, birds, and insects give their warning cries in that frequency. That way, you and other larger animals will be less likely to find their location—and maybe they'll escape to live another day.

Some sounds are pleasant and other sounds are just "noise." Music creates a good feeling because the sound waves come in regular patterns, with each instrument adding

its own set of pleasing tones. When chalk screeches on a blackboard, however, it creates irregular waves with unrelated frequencies. That's why you cover up your ears and complain about such an irritating noise. The quality of a musical tone is also determined by the number of weaker vibrations (called overtones) that are added to the primary tone. Your ear can detect an amazing number of overtones. There's a world of difference, for instance, between a note played on the piano and the same note struck on a glass jar.

NOISE POLLUTION

Each year, American cities and towns become a little noisier. Is that really so bad? Some recent research suggests that too much noise can do more than keep you awake.

Scientists use a measure known as the *decibel scale* for measuring the range of sound to which the ear can respond (see Figure 3.12). Since the ratio (from the softest to the loudest noise you can hear) is something like 1 to 5 million, the scale has been simplified. It starts at zero (the point at which sound becomes audible) and moves upward to the 150 range (the incredible roar of a wind tunnel). Each 10-decibel (db) increase in noise actually means that the pressure on your eardrum increases 10 times. A typical residential street measures 50 db, but heavy rush-hour traffic might hit 90 db. The 40-decibel difference actually means a ten-thousand-times (10 × 10 × 10 × 10) increase in noise level!

But loud, sustained noise can do more than drown out your phone conversation or wake a baby. Prolonged exposure to sounds at 90 db or above can cause permanent hearing loss. At 130 db, most people find that the noise causes actual physical pain. This fact takes on particular importance when you realize that dance clubs often amplify their music to 110 db or more. Some hard-rock groups have been measured at 125 db.

Hearing experts warn that hearing damage

THE DECIBEL SCALE: HOW LOUD IS LOUD?

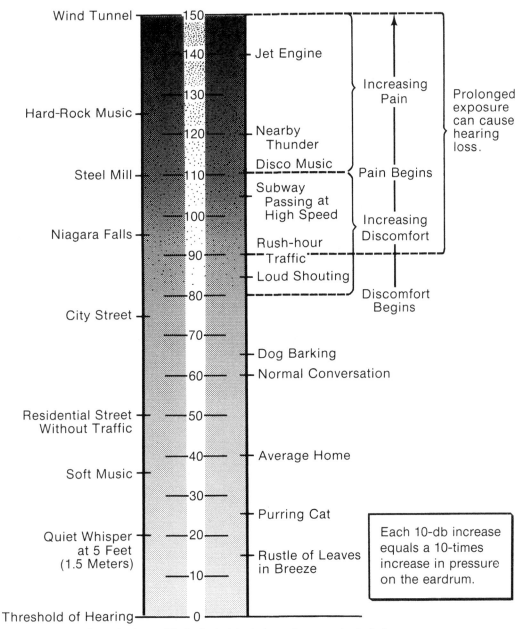

FIGURE 3.12 ■ Sounds above 80 decibels (shaded area) cause physical discomfort to the listener. Above 110 db, your ears will hurt from the additional pressure. Prolonged exposure to high decibel levels has been found to cause permanent hearing loss.

begins after 30 minutes' exposure to a decibel level of 110. At 125 db the damage begins within five minutes.

Tests show that people who listen regularly to high-decibel music at concerts or through headphones pay for their enjoyment with serious hearing losses, particularly in the high-frequency tones. One study at the University of Tennessee, for example, found that more than 60 percent of the incoming students had a "significant hearing loss." It's as if each of these young adults had traded in 20-year-old ears for those of a 65-year-old.

Living with loud noise day and night can cause even more serious problems. Dr. William Meecham of UCLA demonstrated this in a study of death rates near Los Angeles International Airport several years ago. Meecham discovered that death rates among residents living within three miles of the air-

port were 19 percent higher than among people living six miles away. In matched neighborhoods, the researchers found that 890 people died in the high-noise area, compared with 670 in the low-noise community.

Along with warnings about cigarettes, alcohol, and drugs, government may soon be telling you, "Too much noise is dangerous to your health."

■ SECTION CHECKUP

1 Trace the path of a sound from the time it enters the outer ear until it reaches the auditory cortex.

2 How do you locate the direction from which you hear a dog barking?

3 What are the dangers of excessive noise in the environment?

3.4 ▓ HOW DO YOUR SENSES OF SMELL AND TASTE WORK?

"The taste of your bread," an ancient Persian poet once said, "depends on whether you are hungry or not."

Perhaps more than any of your other senses, smell and taste are conditioned by your emotional state at any given moment. Imagine the delightful, mouth-watering smell of a bakery. Fresh bread, tangy tarts, and cinnamon rolls perfume the air. But what if you work there, and you don't like the job? Those same smells, so pleasant to your customers, will become distasteful reminders of your unhappy situation.

As the example also shows, the senses of smell and taste are closely related. Both smell and taste are "chemical senses." Sensory receptor cells in the nose and mouth react to chemical substances carried in the air or dissolved in liquids. Lower forms of life use smell and taste to help find food, select a

mate, and avoid danger. As a human being, these same senses enrich your life with some of the most delightful sensations known to our species.

THE SENSE OF SMELL

In comparison with dogs, bears, deer, and other animals, you do not have a highly developed sense of smell. Birds, on the other hand, apparently cannot detect odors at all. Insects may be the champion "smellers." Some male moths, for example, can detect the tiny amounts of sex-attracting chemicals released by females of the species at distances of up to 15 miles. One unhappy researcher proved this fact conclusively when he spilled a tiny amount of the chemical on his skin. For days afterward, he attracted love-struck male moths from miles around.

HOW THE SENSE OF SMELL WORKS. When an odor enters your nose, it excites two small areas at the roof of the nasal passage. These *olfactory patches,* one on each side of the nose, connect directly to the *olfactory bulbs* of the brain (see Figure 3.4). As with the other senses, you don't actually "smell" an odor until the brain analyzes and interprets the incoming messages. Your limited sense of smell grows out of two related factors. First, the olfactory patches are relatively small in human beings. Second, only 5 percent of the cerebral cortex processes data regarding odors, compared with 33 percent in dogs. A dog can be trained to sniff out heroin or cocaine no matter how carefully the drugs are sealed in their containers. One drug-sniffing dog, for example, found a packet of cocaine hidden in a truckload of onions! Thanks to these highly trained dogs, a number of drug smugglers are now serving long sentences in state and federal prisons.

CATEGORIES OF SMELLS. No exact scale has been worked out for putting smells into categories. One long-accepted system suggested that only six classes of smells exist—spicy, flowery, fruity, resinous, putrid, and burnt. Researcher James Evans of the University of California, Irvine disagrees. "[The nose has] about 150 types of odor receptors," he says, "which means that we can identify that many classes of smells." Your nose will tell you, in any event, that few smells fall into a single well-defined category. A woman's perfume will most likely combine a number of subtly different flowery scents. A freshly baked carrot cake, by contrast, will smell spicy and fruity—and burnt, if the baker left it in the oven too long.

THE SENSE OF TASTE

Take a bite of a juicy apple. What a lovely sensation! But imagine for a moment that you have a cold. That same apple will taste like a mouthful of straw, because you can't smell its fruity odor! Your sense of taste, then, begins in the mouth but also involves smell and touch. Scent, texture, and shape all combine to create this complex sense.

HOW THE SENSE OF TASTE WORKS. What happens when you bite into an apple? Taste begins with the sight of the apple; saliva flows as your mouth prepares for the first bite. Waiting inside your mouth are about 10,000 complex cell structures called taste papillae. Although the papillae are concentrated along the front of the tongue, they can be found in lesser numbers all over your tongue and throughout your mouth. Each of these tiny bumps contains a set of intertwined nerve fibers that act as sensory receptors. The key receptor is the taste bud. The other nerve fibers respond to temperature, pressure (touch), and pain.

Now let's get back to that bite of apple. Saliva dissolves bits of apple into a solution to which the nerve fibers within the papillae can react. The taste buds send a message to the brain that you experience as flavor. In a bite of ripe apple, the dominant flavor would be sweet. At the same time, the other nerve fibers add their own reports. Temperature receptors tell you that the apple is cold, not warm. Pressure receptors help you decide that it is firm, not mushy. The pain receptors would most likely send no reports at all. If you had bitten into a Jalapeño pepper, they would be ringing alarm bells.

While you're chewing, odors reach the nose and enable the olfactory sense to add its own judgment. How important is odor to your sense of taste? As a simple experiment, cut up identical chunks of raw potato and apple. Choose some subjects and ask them to close their eyes and hold their noses while they sample each in turn. Most people can't tell one from the other!

Your hardworking taste buds do not live very long. As they die out, new ones take

Yes, Chocolate Really Is Addictive

Food habits and cravings have always fascinated psychologists. One popular theory, for example, suggests that cravings are the body's way of satisfying nutritional deficiencies. If you're desperate for a cheeseburger, maybe it's because your body needs the extra fat that comes with a typical fast-food burger. Modern researchers add another corollary: Your emotional state also plays an important role in explaining food cravings. Chicken soup can be very comforting when you're sick, for example. Not only does it go down well on an upset stomach, it reminds you of the tender, loving care you received when Mom fed you soup as a child.

Here are some other common foods and the reasons we crave them:

Bread and pasta. A steak dinner without bread, potatoes, or pasta feels incomplete. That's probably because you want the mood-altering effect that carbohydrates provide. Eating a baked potato or a plate of spaghetti stimulates the brain to produce serotonin. This neurotransmitter has a calming effect on the body.

Chocolate. High-fat, high-sugar foods stimulate the production of the natural opiate-like brain chemicals called endorphins. Endorphins block pain and give you a mild "high" when they reach the brain's pleasure center. In addition, a chocolate bar contains tiny amounts of two mildly addictive stimulants, caffeine and theobromine. Finally, chocolate also provides a tiny trace of phenylethylamine (PEA), which is thought to heighten your sexual feelings. Now you know why so many people become chocoholics!

Carbonated beverages. Surprisingly, it's not the sugar or the caffeine that excites the nervous system when you drink soda pop. These can't be discounted, but it's the carbonation that really turns on the adrenaline. Expect almost the same rush when you switch to a caffeine-free diet soda.

Snack foods. The most popular snack foods, such as potato chips and pretzels, are both salty and crunchy. Researchers say there are two reasons for this preference. First, salty foods satisfy a genetically programmed need that all humans share. Second, eating crunchy foods is good for relieving boredom and frustration because they give us something interesting to bite and chew.

Does this research help you understand some of your food preferences? Are there any clues here that explain why it's so hard to stay on a strict weight-reduction diet?

their place. Year by year, fewer and fewer of the worn-out taste buds are replaced. That fact helps explains the complaints you often hear from older people. "My food has lost its flavor," Grandpa grumbles. Actually, it is his ability to taste his food that has decreased over time.

CATEGORIES OF TASTES. Research shows that taste buds respond to only four flavors:

sweet, sour, salty, and bitter. When you bite into a grilled steak, for example, your taste buds can report only its dominant flavor—a salty savor. The complexity of that delicious flavor derives from the interaction of your taste papillae with the reports from your olfactory sense. On the other hand, if you've doused the steak with hot sauce, be prepared to experience a brief, painful burst of flavor. For you, and for those who share your taste for hot, spicy foods, pain plays an unexpectedly important role in eating pleasure.

■ SECTION CHECKUP

1 Why are smell and taste considered to be chemical senses?

2 How does the sense of smell contribute to your sense of taste?

3 What are the basic odors? The basic flavors?

3.5 ■ WHAT EFFECT DO THE SKIN SENSES HAVE ON BEHAVIOR?

Popular usage refers to your fifth sense as the "sense of touch." In a psychological sense, that's a good name, because touching (hugs, handshakes, pats, and other direct contact between you and another person) is such an important means of communicating feelings. From a physiological viewpoint, however, a more accurate name would be the *skin senses*. What is commonly called touch actually involves three distinct types of sense receptors: pressure, pain, and temperature (heat and cold).

HOW THE SKIN SENSES WORK

Hidden beneath the surface of the skin lie countless specialized nerve endings and other types of receptors. When these receptors are stimulated, as by the touch of your finger on a jellyfish, they send signals to the brain. In turn, the brain interprets the signals (soft, squishy, cold) and decides on appropriate action (ugh! move away!). Most skin sensations, such as tickling, itching, burning, and the like, result from the mixing of several skin sensations at the same time.

Like the other senses, your skin senses are often fooled. You can prove this by lightly pressing a sharp pencil against the back of your hand. In certain spots, you'll feel a cold sensation rather than pressure or pain. This means that you've activated cold-sensitive receptors, and your brain perceives these impulses as the touch of something cold.

PRESSURE RECEPTORS

Sensitivity to pressure varies over different parts of the body. Your tool-using hands contain about 135 pressure receptors per square centimeter, but your upper arm has only one-tenth as many. Another area of your body that is richly supplied with pressure receptors is the lips. Perhaps that explains why a kiss on the lips is so much more exciting than a kiss on the shoulder. Both kisses send signals to the brain's pleasure center—but the kiss on the lips generates a far greater number of these pleasurable sensations.

Pressure receptors also demonstrate the principle of *sensory adaptation*. After the receptors have responded to a stimulus for a short time, they become adapted to the stimulus and no longer respond. The sensation disappears. Without sensory adaptation, your sense of touch would keep you constantly aware of anything in contact with your skin: clothes, air currents, the pack of gum in your pocket, and so on. After a few hours of such annoyance, you'd be ready to tell your brain, "Enough already!"

PAIN RECEPTORS

The next time you have a headache, think of those rare newborn babies who cannot feel pain. Without the early-warning system of danger that pain receptors provide, these children quickly run up high rates of bruises, scrapes, and bumps. Even eating a hot dog can be dangerous when there's nothing to tell you that you may be biting your own tongue.

The simple receptor cells that signal painful stimuli to the brain spread their dendrites out like the branches of a tree just beneath your skin. These *nociceptors*, as they're called, respond to a number of intense stimuli: cutting or pricking, twisting, heat or cold, damage to tissue, or pressure severe enough to cause injury. Pain receptors vary in number on different parts of the body. The bottom of your foot has only about 50 pain receptors per square centimeter, for example. But you have 230 in the same-sized area of your neck.

Pain signals travel to the brain along two types of neural pathways. One pathway is made up of fast-conducting fibers coated with myelin. The sharp, intense pain messages that reach the thalamus via fast-pathway fibers call for quick action to prevent further damage to the body. A second pathway is made up of slow-conducting, unmyelinated fibers. The slower, nagging pain messages that travel this pathway are routed to several brain areas, including the medulla, thalamus, and hypothalamus. These messages remind you that you've been injured and set up a persistent demand for further efforts to relieve the pain.

Your body also has different ways of responding to painful stimuli. For example, suppose that you're running water into the sink to wash the dishes. You dip your hand into the water and find that it's too cool. As you turn up the hot water, you keep your hand in the sink. That way, you'll know when the water's the right temperature. At the same time, the radio starts playing your favorite song. While you're listening, you suddenly realize the water's now too hot. You pull your hand out. In this case, the hand's pain receptors sent warning messages to the brain. Your brain then reacted to the danger by triggering a muscular reaction that moved your hand.

Now assume a second case. What happens if you accidentally put your hand on an iron that you think is cold but that is heated to 300° F (149° C)? If you left your hand on the iron until your brain took action, your skin could be badly burned. In this case, a special reflex action (called the "hot-stove reflex") will cause you to pull your hand away instantly. Only after your hand is safe will your brain scold you: "That was a hot iron, dummy!"

Not everyone feels pain in the same way. Even your state of mind can affect the intensity of the pain. Soldiers in wartime sometimes refuse morphine, for example, even though they have been severely wounded. Civilian patients, by comparison, demand painkillers for minor surgery far less painful than the soldiers' wounds. Psychologists who studied this contrast during World War II soon realized that the soldiers were *happy* to be wounded! Their injuries meant that they could escape the terrors of the battlefield, and the relief masked the pain. Researchers also found that the brain makes little distinction between physical and psychic pain. If your friends snub you, the social hurt activates the same brain regions as would a stubbed toe.

TEMPERATURE RECEPTORS

Skin receptors for heat and cold are called *thermoreceptors*. They measure temperature changes above or below normal skin temperature, about 90° F (32° C). Touch your heat receptors with a metal rod heated to 110° F

(43° C), and the receptors will send impulses that the brain will perceive as warmth. A cold rod that excites separate cold receptors will give you the opposite response. Cold receptors outnumber heat receptors by over three to one. This probably is related to your lack of insulating body hair. Unlike a furry bear or wolf, cold presents a greater threat to your survival than does heat.

Your body adapts quickly to temperatures within a range of 60° to 106° F. After spending a few minutes in 62° ocean water, for example, the initial shock of the cold water disappears, and you feel fairly comfortable. In fact, if you run into a current of 68° water, it will feel quite warm. If both heat and cold receptors are stimulated at the same time, however, a strange thing happens. Lay your arm on a row of tubes filled alternately with cold and warm water, for instance. Your first impression will be one of intense heat! Psychologists explain that reaction this way. When both heat and cold receptors are stimulated at the same time, the brain interprets

this as great heat. So far, no one understands exactly why.

IMPORTANCE OF TOUCHING

Can you remember what it was like to be a baby? Probably not. But the memory of those important months lies buried in your unconscious. Like most babies, you were probably held, carried, patted, rocked, kissed, tickled, stroked, and touched in a thousand tender ways. You felt loved and protected.

But now you're grown up. Do you still need the touching that made your early life so happy? Psychologists are unanimous in their answer: Yes, you do. Physical contact with other people seems to be a lifelong need. The problem is, of course, that social custom restricts the amount of touching that you're allowed to have. What was OK for a child becomes taboo for the adult (see Figure 3.13). As a result, many people in our society are "touch-starved."

FIGURE 3.13 ▪ It's no wonder a hug feels so good! For most people, the touching stops when they become adults. But the need continues, a reminder of the security and love they knew as babies.

A university library demonstrated this human need in a simple experiment. Librarians were instructed to casually touch the hand or arm of each person who checked out a book. These people were later interviewed about their attitude toward the library. Unlike library users who weren't touched, these subjects reported highly positive feelings about the library and its personnel. Apparently even a casual human contact is enough to change negative or neutral feelings into positive responses.

A popular bumper sticker asks, "Have you hugged your child lately?" Perhaps it should be revised to read, "Have you touched your friends today?"

■ SECTION CHECKUP

I What are the three types of receptors that make up the skin senses?

2 What does sensory adaptation refer to? Why do your pain receptors not show sensory adaptation?

3 Why do psychologists believe that touching is so important to emotional health and happiness?

3.6 ▓ DO YOU HAVE ANY SENSES BEYOND THE BASIC FIVE?

Quick, how many senses do you have? If you're like most people, you'll answer, "Five: vision, hearing, taste, smell, and touch (the skin senses)." Or perhaps you'll add a "sixth sense" of psychic powers. But most scientists do not accept telepathy, clairvoyance, or the other extrasensory (ESP) powers as proven fact (see Chapter 14).

Modern science, however, does accept the existence of three additional senses: (1) kinesthesis, the sense that reports the position and movement of your body; (2) the equilibratory sense, which provides your sense of balance; and (3) circadian rhythms, which give you your sense of the passage of time.

KINESTHESIS

Wiggle your fingers. Raise your arm. *Kinesthesis* is the muscle, tendon, and joint sense that enables you to make these seemingly simple movements. Because of sensory receptors located in the joints, you know the position of your arms and legs and can keep track of their movements. Additional receptors in the muscles and tendons enable you to know whether a muscle is relaxed or contracted.

This kinesthetic sense enables you to carry on all your physical activities, from walking and climbing to threading a needle or catching a frisbee. The importance of this sense will quickly be evident the next time your foot "goes to sleep." If circulation is cut off for a few moments, the normal flow of sensory data is severely reduced. Try to walk. Without the usual kinesthetic information, your brain is forced to the conclusion that your foot has turned into an awkward lump on the end of your leg.

EQUILIBRATORY SENSE

The orientation of your body in relation to the earth and the space around you is controlled by the *equilibratory sense*. Until you become dizzy, seasick, or disoriented after a whirl on a spinning carnival ride, you probably take this sense for granted. But with it, your body can respond and adjust automatically to changes from upright to not-so-upright. Bend over and touch your toes, for

FIGURE 3.14 ■ The equilibratory sense helps you stay oriented with respect to the earth. But take away gravity, as in space flight, and untrained astronauts would experience extreme dizziness. One Soviet cosmonaut, in fact, had to return to earth early because he could not overcome this problem.

example. Even with your eyes closed, you don't become confused about where you are. Similarly, you'll know when an elevator starts and stops, even though you cannot see any apparent motion.

The receptors of your equilibratory sense are located in the inner ear in organs called the *semicircular canals* (see Figure 3.11). As your body turns, a fluid inside the canal moves tiny hairlike filaments, which convert the movement into impulses to be relayed to the brain. Dizziness results when the brain receives an overload of messages from the

semicircular canals. To make it worse, these "motion detectors" are also connected directly to the parts of the brain that control your vomiting reflex. People who suffer from car or air sickness know all about this unpleasant reaction (see Figure 3.14).

CIRCADIAN RHYTHMS

Plants and animals feed and reproduce according to natural rhythms based on subtle changes in light, air pressure, and the pull of gravity. Human beings sometimes forget that they are also governed by internal body clocks. The pattern of your days seems so natural that you probably ignore the changes in body temperature, blood pressure, pulse, and mood that coincide with the passage from day to night. This natural cycle is called a *circadian rhythm* (from the Latin words *circa,* "around," and *dies,* "day").

Even when isolated from the outside world in a submarine or cavern, people keep their natural cycles of sleep and wakefulness. These human "body clocks" don't keep totally accurate time, however. Subjects in such experiments tend to gain one or two hours a day. Thus in ten days, a normal ten o'clock bedtime may have advanced to eight A.M.!

Jet airplane travel can also disrupt your body clock. After flying across several time zones, you will find your eating and sleeping patterns upset. For the first few days, you'll feel sleepy at the wrong time, and you'll wake up in the middle of the night. Sports teams and business executives know that this "jet lag" leaves people feeling sluggish and mildly depressed.

Evidence gathered in animal experiments points to the pineal gland, located near the center of the brain, as the source of your body's circadian rhythms. Although the main rhythm is 24 hours long, shorter subcycles have also been spotted. About every 90 minutes, for example, your brain relaxes its attentiveness. That's the time you're likely to get up from your desk to look for a snack. During the night, dreams appear in 90-minute cycles. Finally, life and death also seem tuned in on circadian rhythms. Alertness slips and accident rates rise soon after lunch, for example. Even more dramatically, more babies are born and more people die between the hours of midnight and six A.M. than at any other time.

■ SECTION CHECKUP

I Describe the roles of (a) kinesthesis, (b) the equilibratory sense, and (c) circadian rhythms.

2 Why would astronauts need artificial gravity to live normally on long space voyages?

3 Explain the problem of "jet lag" as it relates to circadian rhythms.

LOOKING BACK: A SUMMARY

I The human brain functions as the command center for all mental and physical activity. The hindbrain contains those brain structures primarily concerned with basic life functions: breathing, balance, digestion, heartbeat, and sleep. The forebrain handles most of those conscious activities associated with the pleasures and pains of existence. Of particular importance are the cerebrum and the cerebral cortex. These centers control the muscles, interpret sensory data, and regulate higher mental processes such as decision making, abstract thought, and language.

2 Each side of the brain takes charge of different abilities. Most people are left-brain dominant. In such people, the left brain takes responsibility for logical thought and verbal abilities. The right brain deals in artistic, musical, athletic, and other nonverbal activities.

3 Impulses travel quickly through the nervous system via neural pathways made up of individual nerve cells called *neurons.* Nerve impulses enter a neuron via the branching arms known as *dendrites.* The impulses then travel as a wave of electrochemical activity to the cell body before moving along the axon to the next neuron in the network. Since the axon does not actually touch the nearby dendrites, chemicals called *neurotransmitters* carry the message across the synapse.

4 The endocrine glands also play an important role in controlling growth and behavior. The pituitary gland regulates physical growth; too much or too little activity can cause giantism or dwarfism. The pituitary also acts to turn on other glands at the proper time. The adrenal glands produce adrenaline, which prepares the body to cope with emergencies. They also regulate the body's chemical balance and help produce hormones that are necessary for sexual maturation. The thyroid gland helps control the body's energy level and also plays a role in ensuring proper intellectual development. The sex glands, or gonads, regulate the development of the sex organs and prepare the body for the reproduction process.

5 Humans receive about 75 percent of their sensory data through their eyes. Like the other sensory receptors, the eye itself does not "see." Rather, it converts light waves into electrical impulses by means of specialized cells called *rods* and *cones* located in the retina. These impulses travel via the optic nerve to the brain, where "seeing" actually takes place. Color blindness results when the color-sensitive cone cells are missing or do not work properly. The eye is capable of adjusting to extreme ranges of light and dark, but it can also be tricked. Optical illusions are created when the brain misinterprets the image relayed from the retina.

6 Hearing begins when the ear picks up sound waves, which are converted into electrical impulses in the cochlea. The auditory nerve carries these impulses to the brain, where the sound is "heard." Whether a sound is pleasant or not depends on the pattern of sound waves it creates. Overexposure to noises over 80 db can cause hearing loss, deafness, and higher death rates.

7 The senses of smell and taste are called *chemical senses* because both react to chemicals carried in the air or dissolved in liquids. The sense of smell is located in receptors at the roof of the nasal passage. These receptors convert the stimulus into electrical impulses, which the brain analyzes and interprets. Taste depends on taste papillae located on the tongue and throughout the mouth. Each papilla contains sensory receptors for taste (the taste buds), temperature, pressure (touch), and pain. Taste buds respond to four basic flavors: sweet, sour, salty, and bitter. The sensations of taste and smell are strongly affected by a person's past experiences and current emotional state.

8 The skin senses respond to three distinct types of stimuli: pressure, pain, and temperature (heat and cold). Different parts of the body vary greatly in the number of receptors for collecting these stimuli. Within limits, pressure and temperature receptors adapt to the touch of clothing or the warmth of bath water, a process called *sensory adaptation*. Pain receptors do not provide the same type of adaptation. To do so would deprive the brain of the warning messages it needs to protect the body from further injury. As with the other senses, the brain can be "fooled" by vague or conflicting reports from the sensory receptors in the skin.

9 In addition to the familiar five senses, three other senses have been identified. Kinesthesis refers to the brain's ability to detect and control the position of the body and to monitor its movements. The equilibratory sense provides the sense of balance needed to keep the body properly oriented in relation to the earth. Circadian rhythms keep the body in sync with the environment by establishing a regular rhythm of sleeping and waking.

PUTTING YOUR KNOWLEDGE TO WORK

■ TERMS YOU SHOULD KNOW

adrenal glands	frequency	pituitary gland
afterimage	frontal lobe	placebo effect
auditory canal	glands	psychosurgery
auditory nerve	gonads	pupil
axon	hindbrain	reticular activating system
cell body	hormones	(RAS)
central nervous system	hypothalamus	retina
cerebellum	iris	rods
cerebral cortex	kinesthesis	semicircular canals
cerebrum	lens	sensory adaptation
circadian rhythms	medulla	sex glands
cochlea	neural pathway	size constancy
cones	neuron	skin senses
cornea	neurotransmitter	sound
corpus callosum	nociceptors	spinal cord
cretinism	occipital lobe	synapse
decibel scale	olfactory bulbs	taste buds
dendrite	olfactory patches	temporal lobe
eardrum	optic nerve	thalamus
endocrine glands	outer ear	thermoreceptors
equilibratory sense	parietal lobe	thyroid gland
forebrain	peripheral nervous system	vision

■ CHAPTER CHECKUP

I Which of these is a *true* statement about the human brain? (*a*) Nerve impulses travel from neuron to neuron at the speed of light. (*b*) Human beings no longer need the hindbrain, which is left over from an earlier stage of development. (*c*) Like all cells in the body, brain cells are replaced when they die. (*d*) The size of a person's brain does not correlate directly with his or her intelligence.

2 If Jerry is left-brain dominant, he'll use his right brain when he (*a*) translates English into Spanish (*b*) asks Karen for a date (*c*) picks a new color scheme for his room (*d*) counts his change at the auto-parts store.

3 When a mother hears her baby's cry and instantly wakes from a deep sleep, the part of the brain that controls waking and sleeping is the (*a*) cerebral cortex (*b*) RAS (*c*) pituitary glands (*d*) peripheral nervous system.

4 Conscious thought processes take place in the (*a*) hindbrain (*b*) medulla (*c*) thalamus (*d*) cerebrum.

5 Messages travel to and from the brain via a network of nerve cells that operate on the basis of (*a*) electrical impulses (*b*) chemical impulses (*c*) electrochemical impulses (*d*) mechanical impulses.

6 Three quarters of the sensory impulses received by the brain originate in the (*a*) eyes (*b*) ears (*c*) skin senses (*d*) kinesthetic sensory receptors.

7 Permanent damage to the ear may be caused by prolonged exposure to sounds starting at decibel levels of (*a*) 60 db (*b*) 90 db (*c*) 110 db (*d*) 130 db.

8 The senses that operate primarily through chemical stimuli are (*a*) the skin senses (*b*) circadian rhythms (*c*) smell and taste (*d*) kinesthetic and equilibratory senses.

9 Sensory adaptation is the process by which (*a*) sensory receptors in the skin no longer respond to a stimulus (*b*) you assume that the world is consistent—chairs have four legs, knives cut, and so on (*c*) you maintain your balance on a carnival ride or a skateboard (*d*) you set your body clock for the time zone you live in.

10 The endocrine gland that prepares the body to cope with emergency situations is the (*a*) adrenal gland (*b*) thyroid gland (*c*) pituitary gland (*d*) sexual glands.

■ EXPLORING CONCEPTS

1 Why is the brain called the "command center" of the body? What makes the human brain superior to that of the lower animals?

2 Imagine yourself in a Spanish bullring, facing the charge of a rampaging bull with only a bullfighter's cape in your hand. Describe what takes place in your mind and body from the moment you see the animal move toward you until you decide whether to face the bull or to run for your life.

3 List several activities that would be primarily controlled by the hindbrain. Now list several forebrain activities. What is the basic difference between the two lists?

4 Describe the activity of a single neuron from the moment a message is received from a neighboring nerve cell. What are some of the dangers that result when breakdowns occur in the transmission of impulses along the neural pathways?

5 Which of your eight senses would you be most willing to do without if you had to give up one of them? Explain why.

■ HANDS-ON ACTIVITIES

1 Prepare a poster collage to illustrate basic brain functions. For each major part of the brain, find a magazine picture that shows its function. For example, the sensory-motor cortex might be illustrated by a picture of a violinist, the medulla by a runner gasping for breath. Draw a line from your drawing of the brain to the picture and label the picture with the proper identification.

2 A number of books are available that explore the interesting topic of sensory illusions. Richard Held's compilation of readings from *Scientific American*, called *Image, Object, and Illusion*, is an excellent example. Obtain a book about illusions and copy a number of simple illusions to show to your family and friends. Keep a record of their reactions to each illusion. Do you find any consistency in the way people interpret such illusions?

3 Are you a supertaster? One in four people is extrasensitive to sweet, bitter, and sour tastes. To find out if you are one of them, dab a few drops of blue food coloring on your tongue and swish it around. The pink circles that show through the blue coating are fungiform papillae—the structures that house your taste buds. Next, lay a piece of notebook paper on your tongue. Count the number of papillae that show up in the binder hole. Nontasters will tally zero to 15, average tasters, 15 to 35—and supertasters, 35 or more papillae.

4 A simple experiment conducted with cold, lukewarm, and hot water will convince you of the confusing nature of temperature perception. Begin by filling pan *A* halfway with cold water from the tap. Then fill pan *B* halfway with lukewarm water (90° F or so) and pan *C* with hot water (but not too hot). Now ask your subject to place his or her left hand in pan *A* and report on the temperature. Do the same with pan *C* for the right hand. The subject will almost certainly report that *A* is cold and *C* is hot. Now tell the subject to place both hands at once into pan *B*. What report do you get this time? The reports from hand *A* ("warm") and from hand *C* ("cold") demonstrate that each hand had adapted to its first bath—and pan *B* now seems to contain both hot *and* cold water!

5 Past experience and long-ingrained habits greatly influence perception. If you need further proof, try the following experiment. Begin by counting the number of F's in the following sentence:

FINISHED FILES ARE THE RESULT OF
DECADES OF SCIENTIFIC STUDY
COMBINED WITH THE EXPERIENCE
OF MANY YEARS

Most people report that they find three F's. How many did you find? If you found fewer than six, try again. Right, there really are six F's! If you analyze the experience, you'll see that people typically skip over the F's in the three repetitions of the word "OF." Because you read by scanning several words at a time, you tend to ignore short connective words like a, the, on—and of. Only when you slow down and focus on each word in turn can you count all six F's. Try this test on your friends and family. It's a rare person who counts all the F's on the first trial.

FOR FURTHER READING

Ackerman, Diane. *A Natural History of the Senses.* New York: Random House, 1991. One reviewer called this beautiful book "a marvelous celebration of the senses." Ackerman writes with the feeling and insight of a poet about the physical and emotional dimensions of human sight, hearing, touch, taste, and smell.

Cousins, Norman. *Anatomy of an Illness.* New York: W. W. Norton, 1979. Cousins's book has become a landmark in the often controversial field of holistic medicine. First published as an article in a conservative medical journal, the book describes the unorthodox methods that enabled Cousins to defeat a crippling and usually fatal disease.

Crichton, Michael. *The Terminal Man.* New York: Knopf, 1972. Crichton uses his medical background to dramatize the issue of psychosurgery and mind control. This fast-paced novel convincingly argues that medical techniques are far ahead of society's ability to control their effects, particularly where the brain is concerned.

Edwards, Betty. *New Drawing on the Right Side of the Brain.* Los Angeles: J. P. Tarcher, 1999. Edwards promises to "teach you to draw even though you feel you have little talent and doubt you could ever learn." Her widely used methods are based on exercises calculated to release the creative abilities of the right half (or creative side) of the brain.

Keller, Hellen. *The Story of My Life.* Garden City, NY: Doubleday, 1902 (available in many modern editions). The inspiring story of Helen Keller's escape from the dark and soundless world of her childhood has lost none of its power. She also provides an honest and useful look at what it means to lose both sight and hearing.

Matthews, Paul M., et al. *Bard on the Brain: Understanding the Mind Through the Art of Shakespeare and the Science of Brain Imaging.* Washington, DC: Dana Press, 2003. Matthews and his co-writers use Shakespeare's timeless insights into the human condition as a springboard for exploring the beauty and mystery of our minds and brains. You're sure to be intrigued by the book's stunning images, products of the latest advances in brain imaging.

Ornstein, Robert, and David Sobel. *The Healing Brain.* New York: Simon and Schuster, 1999. This book explores the role of the brain in maintaining the stability and health of the human body. Ornstein and Sobel use research studies and anecdotal evidence to show how the brain exercises control over the immune system, regulates pain, and manages emotions to improve health.

Restak, Richard. *The New Brain: How the Modern Age Is Rewriting Your Mind.* Emmaus, PA: Rodale Press, 2003. This provocative book explores the subtle ways our brains are adjusting to life in a complex, data-filled world. Restak, a well-known neurosurgeon, focuses on new insights into brain physiology and digs into questions such as, "How does exposure to violent imagery affect our brains?"

Springer, Sally P., and Georg Deutsch. *Left Brain, Right Brain.* New York: W. H. Freeman, 1997. This book is sometimes hard going, but it does provide a thorough review of what scientists have learned about the contrasting roles of the two hemispheres of the brain. Of particular interest are the discussions of left-handedness, mental illness, sex differences, and learning disabilities.

HOW PEOPLE GROW

- THE CHILD GROWS UP
- THE ADOLESCENT SEARCHES FOR IDENTITY

Chapter

4 THE CHILD GROWS UP

Like most people, you're probably looking forward to life's great adventures. Maybe you plan to dive for sunken treasure, write a novel, compete in the Olympics, run for president. Or maybe you've thought about becoming a parent.

What's that! Is parenthood such a great adventure? Yes, say psychologists. Taking responsibility for the growth and development of a child will push your capacity for love and discipline close to the breaking point. In fact, when parents do not provide adequate love and care for their children, the results can be disastrous. Consider the case of Joey.

Psychologist Bruno Bettelheim called Joey "a mechanical boy" because Joey could exist only by imitating machines. Reality had become too painful for Joey. He was forced to escape into a world of illusion. So remarkable was Joey's "mechanical" behavior that his observers were almost convinced that they were watching a human machine at work.

When Joey arrived at Bettelheim's Orthogenic School in Chicago, he was nine years old. His behavior at mealtimes was typical. When he entered the dining room, he would string an imaginary wire from an imaginary electrical outlet. This provided him with his "energy source." When he sat down, Joey "insulated" himself with paper napkins, then "plugged" himself in. Only then could he eat, for Joey believed that his body could not ab-

sorb food without electrical energy. Joey's pantomime was so well done that hospital workers stepped carefully so as not to "trip" over the imaginary wires!

During the rest of the day, Joey led an equally unusual existence. Most of the time, he would sit quietly, his "machinery" at rest. Then he would suddenly "turn on." Like a wind-up toy, he would "run" faster and faster, yelling louder and louder, until he "exploded." Screaming "Crash, crash!" he would smash items from his collection of radio tubes, light bulbs, and other breakable objects. Afterward, he would slip once again into his speechless, motionless nonexistence.

What caused Joey's behavior? Bettelheim checked back into Joey's childhood for the answer. Some children become mentally ill because they are abused or because they are alternately loved and then rejected. Joey, however, had been completely ignored.

Joey's mother stated, "I never knew I was pregnant. I had no feeling of actual dislike—I simply didn't want to take care of him." She kept Joey on a rigid feeding schedule. She never cuddled the baby, nor did she play with him. Left alone most of the day, Joey was punished by his father if he cried at night.

When he began to talk, Joey spoke only to himself. He played with machines at an early age and quickly learned how to take an old fan apart and put it together again. When he

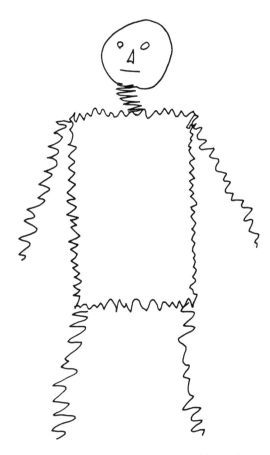

FIGURE 4.1 ■ Joey, the mechanical boy, drew this self-portrait soon after coming under the care of Dr. Bruno Bettelheim. Joey hid from human feelings by imitating the behavior of machines.

reached school age, Joey's withdrawn behavior made it impossible for him to stay in a regular classroom. Time after time, he found that human feelings led only to pain and to rejection.

By the time Joey came under Bettelheim's care, his skillful efforts to imitate his beloved machines almost totally dominated his life (see Figure 4.1). For weeks, his only answer

when someone spoke to him was "Bam!" His "explosions" served to keep people at a distance, for he feared contact with others. Machines, he told himself, were strong and tough. If he could be a machine, he reasoned, he couldn't be hurt.

Slowly, the loving care he received at the Orthogenic School began to break down Joey's defenses. Each day, gentle hands bathed and cared for him. Nurses, doctors, and teachers worked long and patiently to help him accept himself as a living, feeling person. Gradually, Joey's machinelike existence gave way to more childlike behavior. Instead of drawing robotlike trucks, he began to draw trucks and cars with human operators. In time, Joey even learned to make friends with other children.

By the time he was 12, Joey had rejoined the human race. The journey was a painful one, but Joey never wanted to retreat into his old prison. As he announced to Dr. Bettelheim, "Feelings are more important than anything under the sun."*

Most children never experience the neglect that robbed Joey of his humanity. More often than not, children move along predictable pathways of physical, emotional, and intellectual growth. In this chapter, you will learn about those first years of life, when many lifelong personality patterns begin to take shape. The questions discussed in this chapter include the following:

4.1 Why is the psychologist interested in child growth and development?

4.2 What effect does heredity have on human development?

4.3 What factors influence the physical development of the child?

---

* Bruno Bettelheim, "Joey: A 'Mechanical Boy,'" *Scientific American,* Vol. 200 (March 1959), pp. 116–127.

4.4 What are the stages of intellectual development?

4.5 How does a child develop emotionally?

4.6 What can parents do to ensure that their

children develop physically, intellectually, and emotionally?

4.7 What special problems do parents and children face today?

4.1 ■ WHY IS THE PSYCHOLOGIST INTERESTED IN CHILD GROWTH AND DEVELOPMENT?

Perhaps you've heard the old saying, "As the twig is bent, so grows the tree." Sigmund Freud translated that bit of folk wisdom into psychoanalytic terms by stating, "The child is father of the man."

However you say it, the earliest years of life play a major role in determining the emotional, intellectual, and physical qualities of

the mature adult. Locked within the mind and body of the infant, developmental psychologists believe, lie the basic blueprints for later growth and development (see Figure 4.2).

Strangely enough, human societies have not always recognized childhood as a distinct phase of the life cycle. In the 1700s, children as young as eight worked in mines and fac-

FIGURE 4.2 ■ At this stage of development, the infant chimpanzee is far ahead of the human baby in most physical and intellectual skills. But their heredity will take them on widely separate paths through life. The chimp's intellectual growth will soon end, while the baby may go on to become a poet, politician, or physicist.

tories. The modern child's years of play and education would have seemed wasteful, or perhaps even sinful, not too long ago. As society allows children more and more time for "growing up," the importance of childhood as a critical period of development has been increasingly recognized.

Human infants remain dependent on their parents longer than the young of any other species. Newborn turtles must fend for themselves immediately after hatching from their eggs. Even young chimpanzees receive only a few years of care from their mothers. And while a newborn chimp can grasp its mother's fur as she swings from tree to tree, humans have been forced to invent strollers and cradleboards to carry their helpless babies.

Can you imagine leaving two-year-old Perry to take care of himself in a wilderness? Birds don't need to be taught how to build nests, and a young lion is driven by instinct to stalk its first antelope. But Perry has none of these built-in survival instincts. Left alone, he would soon die. Human children need long-term care and training during all of their early growth stages.

STAGES OF GROWTH

The work of developmental psychology centers on two types of research. First, the psychologist studies the physical, intellectual, and emotional activities that take place during each stage of growth. Second, the psychologist tries to explain why children behave the way they do. Six stages of growth have been identified.

1. *Prenatal phase* (conception to birth). The Chinese long ago recognized the importance of the prenatal phase by saying that a baby's day of birth is also its first birthday. The importance of the nine months of life before birth is also accepted by medical doctors and psychologists. They know that the mother's physical and emotional health di-

rectly affect the baby. For example, the baby of a heroin or crack addict is born sharing her addiction. Even the birth process itself has been given renewed attention by doctors who believe that the baby's entry into this world should be as painless as possible.

2. *Newborn phase* (birth to one month). During this period, the baby makes its first contacts with the outside world. It must learn to breathe, cry, nurse from the breast or bottle, sleep in a cradle or bassinet, and begin learning to relate to its caregivers. It's a big job, but the newborn is more capable of adjusting to these demands than most people realize. Experiments show that a baby's ability to respond to adults is well advanced during these early days of life. In one study, one-month-old infants learned to control the spin of a colorful mobile by sucking on a special nipple. Previously, psychologists would not have believed that babies are capable of such learned behavior. (Figure 4.3 describes an experiment that is similar.)

3. *Infant phase* (one month to two years). The baby shows enormous growth in every aspect of life during this phase. At two months, the infant can respond to stimuli but is largely helpless. Each month that passes adds new interests and abilities to the baby's growing repertoire. Curiosity about the world outside the crib or playpen grows quickly. At six months, blocks are mostly good for putting in one's mouth. A year later, the same baby will find a dozen uses for the same blocks. One favorite game calls for throwing the blocks on the floor for the sheer pleasure of seeing someone pick them up. By their second birthday, most children can walk and have begun to develop language skills.

4. *Childhood phase* (age two to about 12). Childhood is often divided into preschool (two to five years) and the middle years (five to 12). During the childhood phase, the child learns to cope with the world outside the home. The most difficult challenge for most children comes when they're sent off to

Reducing the Trauma of Birth: Can—or Should—Anything Be Done?

As far back as 1923, Otto Rank, an Austrian psychoanalyst, described the theory of birth trauma. Rank claimed that after nine months of warm security in a protected womb (uterus), where all needs are met, the newborn experiences being born as a severe shock. Suddenly, without warning, the newborn is exposed to bright lights, cold air, and contact with hard, unyielding objects. Rank believed that this trauma of separation from the mother lasts throughout our lives.

Frederick Leboyer, a French baby doctor, has devoted his life to relieving this birth trauma. Leboyer likens birth to finding oneself suddenly transported to the moon:

> Out of the uterus, the body has a different weight and density. Its surroundings are vast and unfamiliar. The sounds it hears are tremendous and the air it breathes is different in substance. . . . I sought to make the transition from internal to external life a gradual development by prolonging some of the sensations felt in the uterus, and by slowly introducing the baby to the new ones.

Over the years, more and more doctors have adopted the concept of trauma-free birthing. In the delivery room, the Leboyer method requires that the following steps be followed.

1 *Light and sound.* The baby is delivered in dim, indirect light to protect the eyes after the near darkness of the womb. Silence is maintained in the delivery room to protect the baby's ears, for the world of the womb was hushed and quiet.

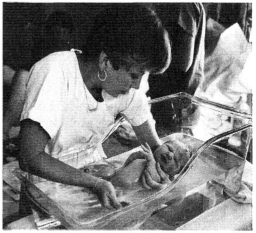

2 *Breathing and the spine.* Breathing air is a brand-new experience. The umbilical cord is not cut immediately, so that the baby has two ways of obtaining oxygen. To protect the spine, the baby is handled gently and massaged. The doctor never dangles the child upside down to promote breathing.

3 *Touch.* Because even the softest cloth will feel painfully harsh to the baby's skin, the infant is left naked. The doctor places it gently on the mother's abdomen. Nothing is hurried. The newborn is left to uncurl slowly from the fetal position, supported by the mother's hands.

4 *The bath.* The baby is bathed in water a little above body temperature. At this time, a real smile often appears on the baby's face. Leboyer believes that the infant is now at peace with the world.

Does Dr. Leboyer's method make sense to you? Some doctors feel that these methods complicate deliveries without providing any measurable advantage to the newborn infant. A growing body of research tells us otherwise. One study showed that Leboyer children are quicker to learn motor skills such as walking and feeding themselves. Parents also report that Leboyer children have less colic and are easier to toilet train.

school for the first time. Whether it's a play-school or a kindergarten, academic success requires the development of new social and cognitive skills. Perhaps you remember your own first days in elementary school. You had to obey new rules, make new friends, and probe the mysteries of reading, writing, and arithmetic. Every day seemed to bring an exciting—or painful—experience. There was the thrill of seeing your artwork displayed on the bulletin board for the first time. And there was the pain of being laughed at when you splattered paint on your new sweater.

5. *Adolescence* (age 12 to 18). The challenge of building a personal identity occupies the adolescent. You will learn more about this challenging and often confusing phase in Chapter 5.

6. *Adulthood*. No clear-cut age defines the passage from adolescence to adulthood. Most teenagers are accepted as adults when they take on adult economic and social roles. The community will probably consider you a full-fledged adult when you move out of your parents' home and begin to support yourself financially.

THEORIES OF BEHAVIOR DEVELOPMENT

Imagine a group of first graders at play. Watch them run, jump, and scream their way around the playground. You'll soon spot individual differences among the children. Lupe is large and strong for her age. She takes the lead in the dodge ball game. Jamaal is quicker at problem solving, so he's the one who steps forward to organize the teams. Then there are the Chang twins. They dominate their corner of the playground by sheer force of personality. Finally, look at those two lonely figures in the corner of the sandbox. Why are they left out of the games? Ask the other children. They'll tell you that Tim and Myra "just don't fit in."

How do these strongly individual behavior

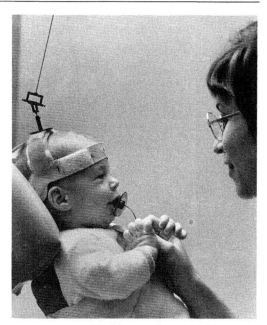

FIGURE 4.3 ■ In this experiment by Harvard Professor Jerome Bruner, a nipple is hooked up to a brightly colored light box. When the infant sucks hard enough on the nipple, the film in the box comes into focus. The baby's repeated efforts to make this happen seem to prove that even month-old infants will work to make their environment more interesting.

patterns develop? Despite all their research (see Figure 4.4), psychologists have not been able to agree on a single theory to explain why individual differences occur. Instead, they have developed three major concepts: the behavior-learning theory, the evolved-primate theory, and the psychodynamic theory.

BEHAVIOR-LEARNING THEORY. According to the *behavior-learning theory*, children learn new behaviors because they receive rewards for doing so. The development of language, social behavior, and other complex skills takes place because children cannot meet needs for security, love, approval, and shelter in any other way.

FIGURE 4.4 ▦ The psychologist can observe human children but cannot run experiments on them that might cause physical or emotional harm. Such studies, therefore, are done with monkeys, whose behavior is often similar to that of humans. Psychologist Harry Harlow first separated young monkeys from their mothers. He then found that the young monkeys preferred the warmth of a "cloth mother" to a "wire mother," even though they received their food from the "wire mother." What conclusion about the role of a mother's nurturing can you draw from this experiment?

Behaviors that bring rewards are continued. But behaviors that are punished or ignored tend to disappear. Newborn infants, for example, soon learn that they'll be fed if they turn their heads at the sound of a bell. Behaviorists such as B. F. Skinner (see Chapter 7) admit that certain skills (using a spoon, for example) cannot be learned before the child is physically ready to learn them. But behaviorists are quick to point out that a child who is never encouraged to use a spoon will probably not do so. They also believe that complex behaviors, such as truthfulness or a love of music, are learned through a similar conditioning process.

EVOLVED-PRIMATE THEORY. A second important way of explaining development is the *evolved-primate theory*. This theory is named for the belief that human behavior begins with the individual's biological inheritance. Sarah, for example, may be genetically programmed with the potential to be an Olympic volleyball player. But if she is raised in an environment that doesn't meet her growth needs, she may never achieve her full physical and emotional potential. Social forces, therefore, are the second crucial factor in Sarah's development. Unlike the behaviorists, psychologists who accept the evolved-primate theory believe that children take an active role in their own development.

Jean Piaget, a Swiss zoologist and child psychologist (see BioBox, pages 116–117), adds that children pass through critical stages during which behaviors must be learned. If Sarah does not learn to catch a ball at the critical time, Piaget says, she may never completely catch up with other children in that particular skill. There are also critical periods for the development of language skills. An American couple living in Mexico City, for instance, might find it difficult to learn Spanish. But their five-year-old child is capable of learning to speak and understand Spanish within a few months. In this case, the five-year-old is still within the critical period for developing language skills—while the parents have long since passed through that stage.

PSYCHODYNAMIC THEORY. Psychologists who believe in the *psychodynamic theory* of development emphasize the social aspects of a child's life. They do not overlook the realities of biological inheritance, but they believe that personality develops out of the interaction between one's inner needs and the demands of the environment. They see this as an active, dynamic process. Each child develops a "self" that tries to achieve identity and self-fulfillment within the framework of the culture. In this view, children grow and develop when their homes and communities meet their physical and emotional needs.

Every child, for example, is born with a capacity for violence. Left totally on their own, children might very well behave like savages (as British novelist William Golding predicted in *Lord of the Flies,* a novel about children stranded on an island after a plane crash). In the Yanömamo Indian culture of South America, for example, boys learn early that aggression pays off. The child who kicks his mother or pokes another child with a spear is applauded. But culture usually limits the ways children express their aggressions. In U.S. society, most children are taught to repress their aggressive tendencies. An argu-

ment over stolen food that would lead to bloodshed among the Yanömamo is usually resolved by verbal give and take in our culture.

⬛ SECTION CHECKUP

1 Describe the developmental phases that Pat will go through before graduating from high school. Why does Pat need a longer period of parental care than all the lower animals?

2 How would a psychologist who believes in the behavior-learning theory explain Pat's learning to talk? Contrast that view with the explanations given by those who believe in the evolved-primate theory and the psychodynamic theory.

3 Why would motherless monkeys prefer a cloth "mother" to a wire "mother"? Would you expect human babies to show the same behavior in a similar situation?

4.2 ⬛ WHAT EFFECT DOES HEREDITY HAVE ON HUMAN DEVELOPMENT?

One of the oldest debates in psychology centers on the question of *nature versus nurture.* In that debate, *nature* stands for the individual's biological inheritance, or *heredity.* Your parents contributed the genes that determine many of your physical, mental, and emotional characteristics. *Nurture* stands for the experiences and environment that have shaped your body, mind, and personality since you were born. Your height, for example, is determined largely by heredity. But whether you're happy or unhappy with your height is determined largely by your environment.

Today, psychologists realize that heredity and environment cannot be separated. In order to study child growth and development,

researchers must look at both influences. Scientists who study heredity, for example, know that a boy's height may be programmed by nature to end at 5′4″—and no amount of diet, exercise, or desire will give him the extra inches he needs to play center on his high school basketball team. Environmental factors, moreover, may prevent that same boy from reaching his growth potential. A poor diet during early childhood, for instance, could prevent him from growing to his full potential. Similarly, he may never develop the emotional "growth" needed to compete at any level of competitive athletics if his parents don't give him enough love, affection, and discipline.

ENVIRONMENTAL VARIABLES

The environmental factors that affect a child's development can be classified as either physical or social. Physical factors include a nutritious diet, pure air and water, and proper medical care. The child's physical environment also plays an important role. If Kitty grows up in a big city, her life experiences will be quite different from those of her cousin, Robyn, born on a Minnesota farm. Kitty may be quite good at finding her way around the city on buses and subways, while Robyn might be terrified by the traffic. But when it comes to saddling a horse, Robyn will be far ahead of her cousin. The only things Kitty knows about horses are what she's learned by watching television.

Social factors in the environment include children's families, the schools they attend, the television shows they watch, the books they read, and the friends with whom they play. A community that provides good schools and recreation for children makes an important contribution to proper development. Well-adjusted children can be found in any environment, rich or poor. But they are most often found in those towns and cities where families and communities work together to provide a supportive social, educational, and emotional environment.

One of the newer theories in child development is that of the "small moment." According to Dr. Daniel Stern, infant personalities are shaped by everyday interactions with adults. Although he doesn't entirely discard the theory that children pass from one critical phase to another, Stern believes that parents should not wait for children to reach these "milestones." Every day, he says, brings small moments in which the child seeks to confirm its sense of being connected to its caregivers. When little Sophie squeals, Mom should respond by matching the pitch of her voice. When Sophie shakes her rattle, Mom should gently shake her crib in the same rhythm. Babies who are ignored when they make these efforts to interact may become passive and withdrawn.

HEREDITY

Each new human being has a unique set of physical characteristics. When the male sperm combines with the female ovum (see following section), millions of years of human development ensure that the child will look and act like other members of the species *Homo sapiens*.

At the same time, the child's parents, grandparents, and great-grandparents have each contributed genes that will determine skin color, general body shape and size, hair and eye color, and a thousand other specifics. Experiments with laboratory animals, moreover, show that children can inherit other characteristics as well. Positive correlations have been established between a child's intelligence and that of the parents, for example.

Unfortunately, a connection also seems to exist between mental illness in parents and their children. Schizophrenia, for example, is a mental illness that causes severe distortions in the way people perceive reality. Although the condition occurs in less than 1 percent of the general public, psychologists have found that the figures rise to 16 percent for children with a schizophrenic parent. When both parents are schizophrenic, 68 percent of the children are affected. Despite these findings, researchers cannot say with any degree of certainty that schizophrenia can be inherited. It's equally possible that the emotional strain of growing up in a disturbed family might "teach" children to adopt schizophrenic behavior as a defense against a chaotic, unpredictable environment.

ROLE OF THE GENES IN HEREDITY

Nature locks in a child's heredity at the moment of conception. As the female ovum (egg) moves down the fallopian tube, a swarm of male sperm fight their way toward it. Each ovum and each sperm carries 23 threadlike bits of genetic material known as *chromosomes* (see Figure 4.5). Once the ovum has been fertilized by a single sperm, it contains a total of 46 chromosomes, 23 from each parent. Every chromosome contains at least 3,000 *genes*, which are the actual carriers of heredity. Both parents, therefore, share equally in the process of "drawing" their baby's genetic blueprint.

Even though they have the same parents, brothers and sisters seldom look exactly alike. The 23 chromosomes contributed by the first parent can occur in over eight million combinations. Add the second parent, with eight million different combinations, and the total possible number of combinations reaches an incredible 150 trillion. The combination inherited by any one child is the result of random selection. Only when a single fertilized ovum splits and creates identical twins do two human beings ever share the same genetic blueprint. Unless you're an identical twin, therefore, you are truly a unique person. No one exactly like you exists anywhere in the universe!

GENETIC COMPLICATIONS

Genes and chromosomes usually combine to produce healthy children. But not all genes and chromosomes are created equal. The random effect of dominant and recessive genes and the effect of chromosomal abnormalities can have enormous consequences for the newly conceived child.

DOMINANT AND RECESSIVE GENES. The genes that determine individual traits are either *dominant* or *recessive*. A dominant gene always prevails over a recessive gene when two sets of genes match up at the moment of conception. If the genes that determine eye color are isolated, for example, scientists

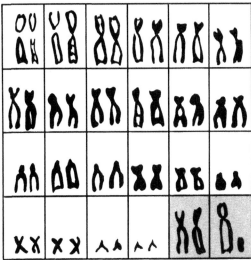
Female or Male

FIGURE 4.5 ▓ Under the electron microscope, human chromosomes look like this. Of the 23 pairs, only the last two are different (gray areas). XX is the female chromosome, XY the male.

know that the gene for brown eyes is dominant. The gene for blue eyes is recessive. Other typical dominant genes are those that determine curly hair and freckles.

Now let's see what color eyes baby Larry will have. Remember that he has two genes for eye color, one from each parent. If he receives a dominant gene for brown eyes from either parent, he'll have brown eyes. Only if he receives two recessive genes for blue eyes, one from each parent, will he have blue eyes. If Larry's parents each carry one dominant gene for brown eyes and one recessive gene for blue eyes, Larry's chances of having blue eyes are one in four (see Figure 4.6).

Eye color, of course, is actually of little importance in your life. But a number of serious illnesses and physical conditions are caused by recessive genes. When both parents carry a recessive gene, the odds are always one in four that each child they have will receive

THE ROLE OF DOMINANT AND RECESSIVE GENES

Pete and Millie have brown eyes. Genetically, however, each has one dominant gene for brown eyes (Br) and one recessive gene for blue eyes (bl).

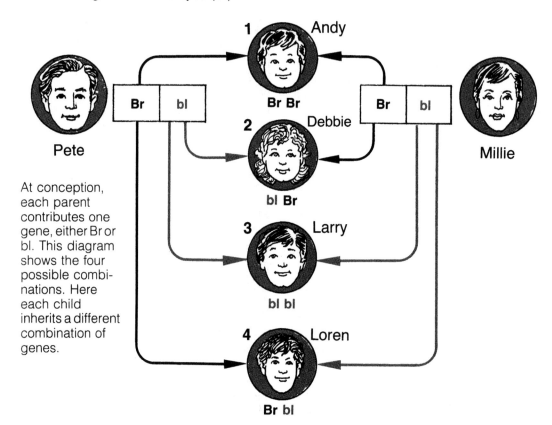

At conception, each parent contributes one gene, either Br or bl. This diagram shows the four possible combinations. Here each child inherits a different combination of genes.

When the Br gene appears, the child will always be brown-eyed. Only when two bl genes match up will the child have blue eyes. Which child has blue eyes in this family?

FIGURE 4.6 ▦ If the mathematical odds hold true, two brown-eyed parents who each carry the recessive gene for blue eyes can expect to have one blue-eyed child out of four. In actual practice, of course, they might have all brown-eyed children, all blue-eyed children, or some other combination.

two recessive genes and therefore will be affected by the disease. Hemophilia, Tay-Sachs disease, sickle-cell anemia, some forms of mental retardation, and dwarfism occur when a child inherits two recessive genes for these conditions. Fortunately, screening tests have been developed that warn would-be parents about possible genetic risks should they decide to have children (see Pro & Con, page 112).

HOW SEX IS DETERMINED

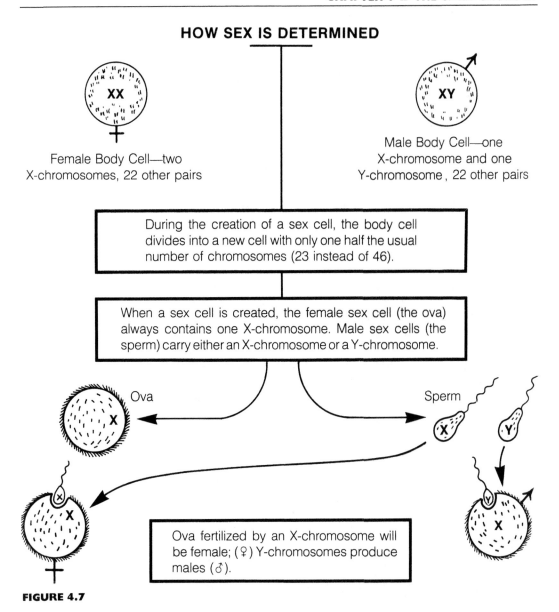

Female Body Cell—two
X-chromosomes, 22 other pairs

Male Body Cell—one
X-chromosome and one
Y-chromosome, 22 other pairs

During the creation of a sex cell, the body cell divides into a new cell with only one half the usual number of chromosomes (23 instead of 46).

When a sex cell is created, the female sex cell (the ova) always contains one X-chromosome. Male sex cells (the sperm) carry either an X-chromosome or a Y-chromosome.

Ova

Sperm

Ova fertilized by an X-chromosome will be female; (♀) Y-chromosomes produce males (♂).

FIGURE 4.7

CHROMOSOMAL ABNORMALITIES. Breakdowns in the transmission of chromosomal information can also cause serious physical or mental defects. Severely retarded children born with the condition known as *Down syndrome,* for example, carry an extra chromosome. Scientists believe that this extra bit of genetic information causes Down syndrome.

More controversial is the effect of the so-called XYY chromosome. Although most males are XY (females are XX—see Figure 4.7), some men carry an XYY abnormality. Evidence suggests that these men (about one in 2,000) may be inclined toward antisocial behavior. Like small children, XYY males tend to take what they want, when they want it. Most test below average in intelligence and are relatively law-abiding. However, hospitals for the criminally insane house a much larger percentage of XYY males than are found in the general population.

What should be done with XYY males? Psychologists know that if you expect a child to misbehave, it probably will. If parents are alerted to children who have the XYY abnormality, will the children receive proper training and love—or will they be seen as potential criminals with little to offer to the family or to society? As scientists learn more and more about behavior, these questions will become more common.

HELP IS ON THE WAY. Thanks to advances in medical science, there is hope for babies who suffer genetic defects. Screening techniques that analyze fetal cells early in a pregnancy can detect some 200 abnormalities. In hospitals, pioneering surgeons are using space-age instruments to repair some of these defects while babies are still in the uterus. Using a blood transfusion technique developed in France, doctors can now save 80 percent of the fetuses that would otherwise have died of Rh disease (a severe blood incompatibility).

A second line of research is helping women who hesitate to become pregnant because they are carriers of sex-linked diseases such as hemophilia. Doctors begin by fertilizing one of the woman's eggs in a test tube. When the egg develops to the ten-cell stage they test to see if it contains the Y (male) chromosome. If it does not (signifying that the child will be a girl who may be a carrier but who cannot inherit the disease), the egg is implanted in the woman's uterus. The pregnancy can then proceed normally.

Other groups of researchers predict that human genetic engineering lies just over the horizon. For now, geneticists are working mostly with plants and bacteria. In one experiment, researchers improved the flavor of commercially grown tomatoes by modifying a gene connected with the softening of the fruit. These new tomatoes ripen more fully without becoming too soft to pick by machine. These and other successes give doctors hope that they will one day be able to repair human genetic defects by "splicing" new genes into a developing fetus.

DISEASE AND DRUG USE DURING PREGNANCY

Infectious diseases that strike a woman just before or during pregnancy can seriously harm an unborn child. The greatest danger occurs during the first few months of the prenatal period. A pregnant woman who comes down with German measles (rubella) may give birth to a blind, deaf, or brain-damaged baby. The crippling effects of venereal diseases can also be passed on to the baby, as can anemia, jaundice, and AIDS. All of these diseases put the baby's life at risk, but doctors can treat most of them with some hope of success. Only AIDS, which destroys the body's ability to fight off infection, sentences the newborn to almost certain death.

Equally dangerous to the unborn child are the drugs the mother takes during pregnancy. The tranquilizer thalidomide, for example, caused an epidemic of severely deformed babies during the early 1960s. Even tranquilizers such as Valium and Librium can cause deformities. Drug use by pregnant women, particularly narcotics, has led to the birth of infants who are addicted to heroin or cocaine. These babies, innocent victims of their mothers' habits, suffer severe withdrawal symptoms at birth. Similarly, LSD and marijuana have been cited as causing chromosomal abnormalities and birth defects. Researchers who have studied the problem conclude that there are no totally harmless drugs when a pregnancy is involved.

Pregnant women are also being warned to give up cigarettes and liquor. Pregnant women who smoke generally give birth to

FIGURE 4.8 ▓ Cartoon by Jules Feiffer

smaller babies and have a higher rate of premature births than nonsmoking mothers. British doctors report that physical and mental retardation occur more frequently in children whose mothers smoke during pregnancy. A mother who drinks during pregnancy can also cause severe problems for the unborn. Alcohol builds up in the baby's body, retarding growth and causing subnormal development. Even two drinks a day may cause brain damage to the unborn child.

The hard facts lead to only one conclusion:

Mothers who drink or smoke during pregnancy are gambling with the health of their children.

■ SECTION CHECKUP

I What is meant by the debate over "nature versus nurture"? Which do you think is more important to the development of a healthy child? Explain your answer.

2 What role do chromosomes and genes play in determining a child's heredity? What is meant by a chromosomal abnormality?

3 What advice would you give to a pregnant woman who wants to do everything she can to give birth to a healthy baby?

4.3 ▓ WHAT FACTORS INFLUENCE THE PHYSICAL DEVELOPMENT OF THE CHILD?

During infancy and childhood, children grow and develop at a rapid pace. This development seems to follow a predetermined course. Premature infants, for example, even though born a month or two early, develop at approximately the same rate as infants who spend a full nine months in the womb. A poor diet can retard children's growth, and inadequate care can harm them emotionally —but neither care nor calories can speed up their development.

Many behaviors develop according to an orderly sequence that is not greatly influenced by the child's environment. Native American babies, for instance, are sometimes tied into a cradleboard that restricts their arm and leg movements. Despite this apparent handicap, studies showed that these children learn to walk at about the same age as children who grow up with full freedom of movement. Similar studies looked at infants in an orphanage who were left alone on their backs or stomachs for long hours at a time. These children developed simple hand-eye skills, such as putting their fingers in their mouths, on schedule. Although they did show a slight lag in other motor skills, such as standing and walking, researchers found that the delay wasn't permanent. The children eventually learned to run, jump, and climb as well as

children raised in more normal conditions. Lack of loving treatment during the first nine months of life, however, can leave deep emotional scars.

ROLE OF MATURATION

The process of growing to adulthood is called *maturation*. Psychologists find it useful to study maturation in infants because so many changes occur during the first years of life. Also, because babies cannot do much on their own, researchers can easily measure the effect of environmental factors on behavior. Studies show, for example, that babies tend to master most motor skills in sequence. About 95 percent of all children learn to walk according to a predictable schedule (see Figure 4.9).

Some infants will reach each stage ahead of others, and some infants will be slower than the average. Such differences fall into the range of normal behavior for babies. In fact, as generations of parents have learned, neither reward nor punishment can hurry the maturation process. One-year-old children cannot be toilet-trained, for example, because they have not gained control of the necessary muscles. During the second year of life, however, toilet training can proceed

THE CHILD'S DEVELOPMENTAL CALENDAR

at birth
fetal posture

1 month
chin up

2 months
chest up

3 months
reach and miss

4 months
sit with support

5 months
sit on lap
grasp object

6 months
sit on high chair
grasp dangling object

7 months
sit alone

8 months
stand with help

9 months
stand holding
furniture

10 months
creep

11 months
walk when led

12 months
pull to stand
by furniture

13 months
climb stair steps

14 months
stand alone

15 months
walk alone

FIGURE 4.9 ▨ Although babies do not develop at the same rate, they tend to develop their motor skills in the sequence described in the chart above.

efficiently. By that time, maturation has prepared the baby's body to do what its brain wants to do—please its parents by using the toilet.

Consider young Maria for a moment. As she grows, her ability to control her own body increases. When she was a few months old, she often jabbed herself in the eye when she tried to put a rattle in her mouth. By six months, however, she can easily stick almost anything into her mouth, much to her parents' dismay. Meanwhile, Maria has also been busy putting together individual movements into complex actions. Just to roll over requires that she coordinate arm, neck, stomach, and leg movements. No wonder she looks so pleased when she finally makes it!

EFFECT OF THE EMOTIONAL ENVIRONMENT

Frederick II, ruler of Sicily in the 1200s, believed that all babies came into this world with an inborn language. Curious to find out what this language was, he gathered a group of newborn infants for an "experiment." He turned the babies over to foster mothers with orders to raise the children in strict silence. Frederick never heard the children speak their "natural" language, however. Deprived of the love, encouragement, and stimulation normally given by parents to their children, all the babies died.

Indeed, as recently as the early years of this century, 90 percent of all newborn babies placed in Baltimore orphanages died within a year. They received adequate physical care, but no one had time to cuddle or hold them. When babies raised under these conditions don't die, they often suffer mental or emotional damage. Loving parents seem to have always known this, even though psychologists have only recently proved that babies cannot develop normally unless they receive proper emotional nurturing.

EFFECT OF PHYSICAL DEFECTS

Some children start life with a handicap. Faulty genetics, illness, or accident can leave a child with more than the usual difficulties in growing up. Unless such children receive proper care and counseling, they may feel themselves "different" from others, unworthy, and rejected. At the same time, if they are treated with pity rather than encouragement, they may not learn how to take responsibility for their own lives.

DISABILITY DOESN'T MEAN DISABLED. The hardest lesson to learn about the handicapped is that their disabilities do not automatically keep them from living productive lives. Given the opportunity, people with disabilities are capable of doing almost anything the nonhandicapped can do. In every corner of society, they are holding jobs, raising children, playing sports, and generally making valuable contributions in whatever fields they enter.

This lesson is driven home every time an athlete with disabilities competes in a sports event. Every year thousands of children with disabilities take part in the Special Olympics. Sponsored by the Joseph P. Kennedy Foundation, these games attract children with special needs for a day of competitive events. The smiles on the faces of the spirited young athletes reminds onlookers that win or lose, competing is good fun.

Winning is more important to the members of the Achilles Track Club. These challenged athletes, who range in age from 18 to 65, compete in wheelchairs, on crutches, with guide dogs, or on skates. They include paraplegics, the blind, the arthritic, and the mentally retarded. As 51-year-old Charlie Gale puts it, "Disabled people live in a kind of bubble—in society but not really a part of it—because of what society says you are—handicapped. [Competition] allows me to be seen only as an athlete. When I go flying past someone, they don't have time to stereotype me. It's equal respect out there [on the track]."

RELATING TO PEOPLE WITH DISABILITIES.
Psychologists believe that the most important gift you can give people with disabilities is to treat them with dignity and respect. Perhaps you know someone who is blind, deaf, or confined to a wheelchair. If so, you may have had the same experience 17-year-old Kathy C. had.

Over several months, Kathy developed a phone friendship with Nelson, a friend of her older brother. She knew that Nelson had been a victim of cerebral palsy since birth. Over the phone, his disability didn't show. She learned to relate to him as a warm, intelligent person. But when Kathy met Nelson for the first time, she realized that he was confined to a wheelchair and that he did not have full control of his facial muscles. Kathy broke down and cried. She couldn't face him. It took several meetings before she learned to see Nelson as a good friend who happened to have a physical disability.

Now, when they meet, Kathy sees only her good friend Nelson. It hasn't been easy, but she's learned not to feel sorry for him. She lets him take care of his own needs when he can, instead of jumping to help him every time he moves. She's also learned that he isn't perfect. Like everyone else, he can be annoying at times. But Kathy and Nelson agree that their friendship has enriched them both.

■ SECTION CHECKUP

1 What is meant by the term *maturation?* Describe the steps a typical child goes through before learning to walk.

2 What would you say to reassure a worried parent whose baby is slow to begin walking?

3 How important are love and affection to the proper growth of a child?

FIGURE 4.10 ■ Best-selling author Stephen Hawking (*A Brief History of Time*) is confined to a wheelchair by an incurable neuromuscular disease. Unable to speak, Hawking depends on a computer to communicate with his wife and children, friends, and coworkers. The disability has not dimmed his talent for thinking deeply and creatively about the physics of space and time. Like so many other people with physical limitations, he insists on living an active and productive life.

▓ PRO & CON:

Should Genetic Screening Be Made Compulsory for Couples Who Plan to Marry?

A number of serious illnesses and physical deformities can result from inherited genetic traits (see pages 105–106). In recent years, medical science has developed a *genetic screening* procedure that can identify the carriers of hereditary illnesses. Carriers are people who do not suffer from the illness themselves but who can pass the condition on to their children. A proposal has been made that would require genetic screening for everyone who applies for a marriage license. Would you agree to such a law? The following arguments might help you make up your mind.

PRO

I Most states already require that couples planning to marry take a blood test to screen for venereal disease. Since a simple procedure also exists that can predict who might give birth to a genetically defective child, society cannot morally refuse to use it.

2 The social costs of caring for defective children can be counted in dollars, time, and emotional harm to otherwise healthy families. Any measure that will prevent such births should be taken.

3 Genetic counseling can provide couples with the information they need to make good decisions about their future. Before they are married, couples who are carriers can think through the possibility that their children might be born crippled or retarded.

4 Once conceived, a genetically defective child must either be aborted or allowed to be born. Neither option presents a fair choice for the child or for the parents.

5 Society owes each child the best possible start in life. Modern existence is tough enough without adding the difficulty of a genetically linked handicap to that struggle.

CON

I Further limits on personal freedom of choice by government cannot be allowed. Genetic screening should be available for those who want it. But the decision should be a purely voluntary one.

2 Couples who truly desire to be parents will accept and care for their children, handicapped or not. Society should not interfere with the basic human right to have children.

3 Experience shows that many couples react badly to the knowledge that they are carriers of genetic defects. Instead of leading to positive decisions about the future, screening can lead to feelings of guilt, depression, and a sense of having lost control of their own lives.

4 Other options exist besides giving birth to defective children or having abortions. Couples who cannot face that possibility do have alternatives. They can adopt, use a sperm donor or surrogate mother, or even choose to remain childless.

5 Except for those genetically linked conditions that result in an early death, handicapped children can, and do, contribute a great deal to both their families and to society. They should not be denied that opportunity.

If you were about to be married and your doctor offered you a genetic screening test, would you take it? How would you react if the test showed that you and your spouse-to-be were carriers of a genetically linked disease?

4.4 ▓ WHAT ARE THE STAGES OF INTELLECTUAL DEVELOPMENT?

What goes on in the mind of a baby? No one knows for sure. Studies show, however, that even unborn infants respond to a variety of stimuli. The steady rhythm of the mother's heartbeat, for example, can be both heard and felt by the infant. Research psychologists have found, moreover, that newborn babies prefer nursery rhymes that their mothers read aloud to them *before* they were born. A month-old infant gives every indication of conscious thought as it reacts to its father's voice or the sight of a brightly colored ball. Undoubtedly, infants do not think in the same way you do, but their *cognitive processes* (thinking processes) begin very early. As psychologist Anthony DeCasper reminds us, "They're good learners, newborns are. They're exquisite learners."

Step by step, infants must learn to cope with the puzzling stimuli reported by their limited senses. "What happens to objects when they disappear from sight? Will Mommy come when I cry? What was that loud noise?" Gradually, infants develop cognitive skills that allow them to make sense out of questions such as these. But these processes do not develop in a vacuum. Motivation, emotional responses, and even birth order in the family (see box on page 114) play important roles in the maturation of a child's thinking skills.

PIAGET'S FOUR STAGES OF COGNITIVE DEVELOPMENT

The work of Jean Piaget has greatly influenced modern research on the cognitive development of children (see BioBox, pages 116–117). Piaget believes that the child's thinking processes move through four orderly stages. Progress from one stage to another depends upon maturation as well as favorable environmental factors. Even a bright three-year-old cannot grasp the same concepts that almost all seven-year-olds handle easily.

SENSORY-MOTOR STAGE. The sensory-motor stage begins at birth and generally lasts for two years. During this period, children learn to distinguish themselves from the objects around them. Curiosity develops, and the baby attempts to make interesting events last longer. Infants learn to coordinate sensory experiences with sucking, reaching, or grasping movements. Language use begins toward the end of this stage.

Another development during the sensory-motor stage is called *object constancy*. From the point of view of six-month-old Curt, for example, objects no longer exist when they disappear from sight. You can test this principle by letting Curt watch as you hide a favorite toy under a towel. Even though he can see the shape of the toy under the cloth, he will look confused and uncertain. If he does reach out to touch the hidden toy, it will be more by accident than design. No one should be surprised, therefore, that Curt cries when Mom leaves. He can't help but feel that she no longer exists and may never return! At two years, however, Curt will search for a concealed toy, certain that it is only hidden from view. He has developed the cognitive concept of object constancy.

PREOPERATIONAL STAGE. Piaget's second phase lasts from age two to age seven. During this stage, children focus on their own desires, pleasures, and pains, usually without thought for the needs of others. Children at this age are learning to use language as a tool for understanding and controlling the world around them. But their thought processes still do not conform to adult standards of realism or logic. Ask four-year-old Melissa to tell you

The Effect of Birth Order and Family Size on Intelligence

PEANUTS reprinted by permission of UFS, Inc.

A child's intelligence—its ability to solve problems and to learn new information—is determined by a number of related factors. These include heredity, family life, quality of education, even diet. But research also reveals that Linus (in the *Peanuts* cartoon) knew what he was talking about. Firstborn children, particularly in a family where the children are born close together, tend to score higher on intelligence tests than their younger brothers and sisters. Summed up, the evidence seems to show that (1) intelligence declines with family size; (2) the fewer children in your family, the smarter you are likely to be; and (3) the firstborn child will likely be the brightest.

These circumstances can probably be charged to environmental influences, not heredity. Psychologists Robert Zajonc and Greg Markus worked out the problem via a mathematical model. They believe that each new child lowers the intellectual environment of the family. Thus, if the mother and father together produce an intellectual environment rated at 100, each new child (whose adult intellect begins at zero) lowers the total intelligence level in the household proportionately. The first child reduces the rating to 67; the second child born two years later lowers the rating to 51. (These figures do not refer to IQ but to the total quantity of intellect—wisdom, skills, and experience—at the family's disposal.) With each new child the rating falls again because a child's cognitive growth is heavily influenced by the intellectual level of the other people in the household.

If you're a second, third, or fourth child, are you doomed to be a dumbbell? Not really. The differences created by birth order don't amount to much—about ten points on an IQ test. Even so, loving parents will want to make sure their younger children receive the extra nurturing they need to make up for their lower positions in the family's birth order.

Source: Robert B. Zajonc, "Dumber by the Dozen," *Psychology Today,* Vol. 8 (January 1975), pp. 37–43.

how flowers grow. She may tell you quite sincerely that ants are pushing them up from beneath the ground.

In the early years of this phase, from about two to four, children believe that if two objects share a feature in common, then all features must be shared in common. Thus two-year-old Celia believes that if her favorite ball is red, round, and bounces, then a round, red Christmas-tree ornament should also bounce. By the time she's four or five, however, Celia will understand that such logic doesn't work. She'll no longer expect all round, red objects to bounce.

| Three Years | Four Years | Five Years | Six Years |

FIGURE 4.11 ▩ Amold Gesell, one of the major figures in the study of child growth and development, collected these drawings from children of different ages. When told to "draw a man," the youngsters responded with their own unique ideas of what a "man" looks like. You can see how the children's cognitive development improved year by year in their ability to "see" and draw anatomically correct human figures.

Even with greater maturity, however, Celia won't be working with adult logic. Her thought processes will lead her to jump to conclusions, bypassing the usual rules of reason. During this period, children also learn to apply past experiences to new situations. They no longer are content simply to imitate what they see others doing. Figure 4.11 provides an example of how developing cognitive skills can be seen in children's drawings.

CONCRETE OPERATIONS STAGE. Between the ages of 7 and 11, children begin to think in more mature concepts. They understand and use a number of specific skills, including what Piaget describes as *grouping* and *conservation*. In grouping, children learn to form systems of classification that allow them to place similar objects into logical classes. For example, Patricia, who is eight, can now classify dogs, turtles, fish, and hamsters by their common identity. "They're all pets," she'll tell you.

When children learn the concept of conservation, they can no longer be fooled into thinking that two half-doughnuts are "bigger" than one whole doughnut. They understand that changing the shape or distribution of an object does not change its mass or volume. Before he understood this concept, young Tim insisted that milk poured from a shallow bowl into a tall pitcher had actually increased in volume.

FORMAL OPERATIONS STAGE. As early adolescence begins, so does Piaget's period of formal operations. Eleven- and 12-year-olds begin to understand abstract political, moral, religious, and scientific ideas. Children can now construct and test their own hypotheses. Within a few more years, Piaget believes, the average adolescent will have mastered all of the basic cognitive skills that he or she will ever need. What remains is learning to put those skills to use. Young people must finish school, begin careers, and develop adult relationships with family, friends, and lovers. Chapter 5 will explore these challenging problems in greater depth.

MASTERY OF LANGUAGE

Language specialists believe that an infant vocalizes every basic sound needed to speak any language. Out of a babble of squeals, coos, clicks, and grunts, growing children slowly put together the sounds that allow them to master their native language. While

Jean Piaget:
A Theory That Gives Meaning To the Timetable of Intellectual Development

For Jean Piaget (1896–1980) all human understanding grows out of the interaction between children and the people and objects with which they come in contact. When a baby grasps, throws, sucks, bangs, or strokes a teddy bear, a chain of learned behaviors is started that eventually will help the child take control of its environment. This seemingly simple concept has become one of the most influential in modern developmental psychology.

Born in Neuchâtel, Switzerland, Piaget became interested in both zoology and psychology at an early age. He published his first scientific paper at the age of ten! His revolutionary theories of intellectual development were drawn from his own observations. Many were based on experiments he and his wife conducted on their two daughters. During his lifetime, Piaget was often called "the greatest living psychologist."

Piaget's basic theory is that a child cannot master a new intellectual concept before he or she has reached the correct stage of maturation. Thus, Piaget said, knowledge cannot be separated from biology. His observations convinced him that children adapt to their environment only as fast as their biological development permits.

Piaget described how he first discovered what he calls the concept of *conservation*. Adults know that changing the shape of an object does not alter its volume. A ball of clay weighs the same, whether rolled into a ball or smashed into a pancake. But children under the age of seven or eight do not recognize this apparently basic fact.

putting thoughts into words may not seem very difficult to you, language remains one of humanity's greatest achievements.

When you began to talk, you had to cope with three problems common to everyone who learns a language. First, you had to learn the basic speech sounds used in the language. English vowels and consonants require the mastery of 45 different sounds. Second, you had to learn a vocabulary, the words that allow you to speak about concrete things (such as video games, fireworks, and swimming pools) and abstract things (fun, holidays, and the shock of diving into cold water). And third, you had to learn grammar, the way a language puts words together to convey meaning.

Social interaction with older people is crucial to the development of language. Children who spend their earliest years in total

Piaget had been trying to find some easy way of identifying children whose epilepsy hadn't been discovered. For a while he thought he'd found the method. He would place four coins and four beads in front of the subject (Figure 4.12A). Then he would hide one of the coins. If at the same time he stretched the remaining three coins out into a longer line, the epileptic child said there were more coins than beads (Figure 4.12B). Piaget thought that this simple test would separate epileptic children from other children. But when he tried the test on nonepileptics, he found that all children of this age lack the concept of conservation.

Now, Piaget wondered, do children lack this concept because the principle has never been taught to them? He had some children taught-the same language as that used by children who did understand the concept of conservation. These nonconservation children quite readily learned to use the words *long* and *short* and *wide* and *narrow* in a consistent way. But learning the language didn't teach the concept. When the instructor rolled a ball of clay into a snakelike shape, the children could describe it as "long" and "thin." But they also thought that the new shape contained a greater quantity of clay than the original ball.

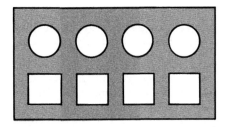

FIGURE 4.12A

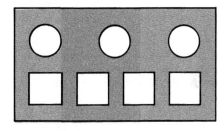

FIGURE 4.12B

Piaget believed that his principles hold true no matter how different children might be in intelligence, size, or emotional stability. Children, he said, can learn "tricks" to make their parents happy. But true understanding of the logic behind these concepts must wait until they reach the proper developmental stage.

You can test some of Piaget's insights. Perhaps you have a younger brother or sister, a young neighbor, or live near a nursery school. Test these children on their understanding of the concept of conservation, for example. Along with Jean Piaget, you'll very likely discover that "cognition follows biology."

isolation may remain permanently mute or mentally retarded (see the box on page 118). Psychologists also believe that the way you perceive reality changes according to the language you happen to speak as you grow up. That's why the authors of this book are careful not to use words such as *man, he,* and *his* when referring to both men and women. Many social psychologists believe that using male-oriented language promotes a belief in

male superiority. If women are to gain full equality, they add, our language must help by conditioning children to express themselves in ways that reflect a nonsexist society.

FORMATION OF CONCEPTS

Another major step in the cognitive process requires that children learn to form concepts. Simply stated, *concept formation* is the ability

The Wild Boy of Aveyron

Late in 1799, the Department of Aveyron in central France buzzed with gossip touched off by an unusual event. Hunters and farmers told of seeing a boy about 14 years old, who lived alone in the woods of the region. The reports described the boy as wild and uncivilized. They said he scavenged for food by digging roots and bulbs, drank from streams, and ran on all fours.

When he was finally captured, the Wild Boy came under the care of Jean-Marc Itard, a physician at the National Institute of Deaf-Mutes. Itard believed that he could civilize the child, but many people disagreed. The debate touched off by Itard's efforts centered on the question, "Was Victor (as the boy came to be called) abandoned because he was an idiot, or was he an idiot because he was abandoned?"

Itard stubbornly maintained that Victor could be helped. After all, he pointed out, the boy had managed to exist in the woods, living by his wits, for an unknown length of time. Victor, he believed, possessed a normal intelligence stunted by lack of contact with loving parents and the social interaction of everyday family life.

Despite Itard's five-year training program, Victor did not learn to speak more than a few words. He was never fully comfortable in clothing or sleeping in a bed, although he would do both to please the people who cared for him. Victor died in 1828, still "fearful, half-wild, and unable to learn to speak, despite all the efforts that were made."

Jean-Marc Itard, however, had opened new doors for the education of children, normal and retarded. His work with Victor, for example, inspired Maria Montessori, the famous Italian educator. Her approach to teaching children, revolutionary when she opened her first school in the early years of this century, emphasizes that children should be free to develop their own capacities for physical and intellectual development. Thanks to the Wild Boy of Aveyron, Montessori children learn carpentry, household tasks, and other how-to jobs in addition to art, music, and the traditional subjects.

to recognize the common features of situations or objects you encounter in the outside world. Children must learn to overlook unimportant features in order to determine which features are important. Cars and trucks are both motor vehicles, for example, even though they come in various sizes and shapes. But is an airplane a motor vehicle? Adult logic says, "Yes, it is." Like a car, an airplane carries passengers and cargo, is driven by an engine, and travels from place to place. But children who are just learning to form concepts might not agree. Airplanes fly, they'd argue, while cars and trucks travel only on roads and highways.

By the age of six, most children have also mastered the basic concept of categories. They can define almost any type of relationship in words. The two-year-old says, "A ball is to throw." But at six, the same child will categorize balls by size, features, or similarities to objects that are not balls. In this way, children learn to react to the constant bombardment of stimuli in a practical way. When faced with a new situation, they can reduce the complex to simple terms and make an appropriate response. Thus, at age four, young Adam may be frightened by a ride on a roller coaster. But three years later, he'll understand that amusement-park rides are meant to frighten in a "safe" way. He'll probably want to go on the roller coaster again and again.

■ SECTION CHECKUP

I Describe Piaget's four stages of cognitive development.

2 What is meant by object constancy? How can you test a baby to see if it has developed this concept?

3 Why is language development so important to the growth of a child's cognitive skills?

4 What is meant by concept formation? How does this cognitive skill help children make sense of the world around them?

4.5 ▓ HOW DOES A CHILD DEVELOP EMOTIONALLY?

Physical and intellectual growth represent only part of a child's development, for human beings also live in an emotional dimension. Your own catalog of emotions is a long one: you love, laugh, cry, and grieve; you feel joy, jealousy, anger, and disgust. Most people call themselves logical, thinking beings, but they are also creatures of emotion. And what a robot-like existence we'd all lead if that weren't so!

DEFINING EMOTIONS

Imagine two-year-old Mary playing in her backyard. Right now, she's the picture of sunny contentment. But watch what happens when her mother calls her to come inside. The joyous smile vanishes in an instant. Now she's sulking, her lower lip pushed out, her body sagging as she drags herself toward the door. Inside, Mary is told to take a nap. Mild displeasure turns into temper tantrums. She cries, holds her breath, and kicks at the rug as she's dragged off to bed.

What was going on in Mary's head? A psychologist would describe her behavior as the expression of *emotions,* the feelings that swept her along from joy to resentment to anger. Was Mary born with these feelings? Or did she learn them from other people? Researchers believe that emotions occur as a result of the body's reaction to events in the

outside world. But they also know that the mind receives and interprets a stimulus according to past experience. The mind, in turn, tells the body how to act.

To prove this relationship, try a simple experiment. Clench your fists, hunch your shoulders, and tighten your neck muscles. This is the body posture most people take when they're angry. And now, by deliberately copying the muscular tension associated with anger, chances are you'll actually begin to *feel* tense and angry.

Clearly the mind and body interact to determine your emotions and the way you deal with them. Think of how you'd feel if you were faced with the prospect of climbing down a cliff. The sight of the sheer drop to the rocks far below sends a cold shiver through your body. But if your best friend is trapped on the face of the cliff and needs help, your mind can probably overcome that fear. Slowly, adrenaline pumping, you make the descent. In doing so, you'll prove that emotions, no matter how primitive, can be controlled by the conscious mind.

EMOTIONAL BEHAVIOR IN INFANTS

Psychologists disagree over the number of basic emotions that infants feel. One viewpoint holds that there are only two basic emotions. One is delight, which results in

THE TREE OF FEELINGS: EMOTIONAL DEVELOPMENT FROM BIRTH TO TWO YEARS

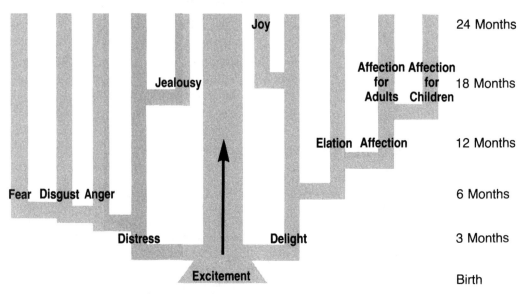

FIGURE 4.13 ≋ The complex nature of emotional development can be traced in this "tree of feelings." Note that by age two the child expresses almost all of the basic emotions normally associated with adulthood.

behavior designed to hold on to a stimulus. Its opposite is distress, which results in attempts to evade or lessen the stimulus. An approximate schedule for the appearance of specific emotions in babies through the second year can be seen in Figure 4.13.

Are emotions instinctive or learned? No one can give a final answer to that question, but research shows that learning does modify the way children display their feelings. Thus, at age three, Diane may express anger by kicking and screaming at her mother. A few years later, she'll be in better control. Instead of throwing a tantrum, Diane is now more likely to displace her anger by hitting her younger brother or by sulking in her room.

This process of taming children's self-centered behavior so that they can become productive members of society is known as *socialization*. Three basic forces work to help

children develop these emotional controls. First, children learn that certain behaviors bring them affection and acceptance. Children will do almost anything for rewards such as ice cream cones and affectionate hugs. Second, by adopting socially acceptable behavior, children avoid rejection and punishment. No child wants to be ignored or spanked. And finally, children naturally model their behavior on the people around them. If they have parents who behave in socially acceptable ways, they will learn to do likewise.

DEVELOPMENT OF MORALITY

One of the most important requirements of socialization is that children learn a system of morality. Society is changing rapidly, and social standards seem to turn upside down almost overnight. But each child must develop consistent standards of right and wrong, a sense of responsibility, and a basis for judging individual behavior.

The moral concepts of a child differ from those of adults. As a young adult, you understand that values can change. For example, most people agree that killing another human being is wrong. But if you were a police officer protecting school children from a sniper, *not* to kill might be equally wrong. Children, however, tend to see morality in absolute terms. Five-year-old Tommy, for example, has learned that it's dangerous to talk to strangers. Once he's absorbed that lesson, he'll probably turn and run when he's approached by any stranger.

As children grow up, their ability to deal with moral questions improves. At first, they simply memorize the moral principles their parents teach them. Later, their thinking process permits them to understand and evaluate the rules of behavior. Piaget thought that this process develops with maturity, just as other thinking skills develop when the child's mind is ready to handle them. Sigmund Freud, however, believed that moral behavior depends on the development of the conscience. He said that experience and training provide each of us with an inner "voice" that knows the difference between right and wrong. Without such inner controls, children would simply give in to their impulses. No one minds when a year-old baby does that. But such behavior in a six-year-old is difficult to tolerate—and unthinkable in an adult.

DEVELOPMENT OF SEX ROLES

Being male or female doesn't mean that a child will automatically learn masculine or feminine *sex roles*. By their third birthday, however, most children have adopted appropriate behavior based on the models provided by their parents and other key adults in their lives. If every adult presented a perfect model for such behavior, children would

have few problems. But many American parents and guardians carry on the stereotyped sex roles they learned from their own parents. These fathers tell their sons, "Don't cry, that's sissy stuff," and boys learn not to express their feelings. Some mothers teach their daughters to use "feminine" wiles when dealing with men. As a result, these girls may grow up to be manipulative and emotionally dishonest in their relationships.

Traditional sex-role modeling has created rather fixed ideas about men and women. Writing about his insights after taking a psychology course, Sam K. said:

> I learned that girls have the same feelings I do. I used to think they were some sort of different species, that they didn't think like us guys. I can talk to them a lot better now. I just treat them like people!

Changes of attitude such as Sam experienced are now more common in U.S. society. Even so, many men still say that women are more emotional than men—but also warmer, softer, and less aggressive. Women, on the other hand, tend to stereotype men as aggressive, domineering, and resistant to expressing emotion.

The feminist movement strongly challenges these stereotypes. Not only does such sex-role stereotyping limit the full development of the personality, the feminists point out, it doesn't reflect the reality of life in this country today. (Chapter 13 discusses sex roles and sexism at greater length.)

▪ SECTION CHECKUP

1 What two emotions does the newborn start life with, according to psychologists?

2 Why do children accept the process of *socialization,* even though it requires that they control their emotions?

3 How do children learn masculine and feminine sex roles?

Each Generation Raises Children in Its Own Way

Grandparents often watch with dismay as their adult children raise the grandchildren. "I think it's disgraceful that Debbie doesn't have two-year-old Chantal toilet trained," Grandma says with a shudder. What Grandma forgets is that her own mother often disagreed with the way she raised Debbie. Each generation adopts its own childraising practices, as this table illustrates.

Early 1900s	1920s–1930s	1940s–1950s	1960s–1970s	1980s to Present
		THUMB SUCKING		
Feelings varied, but was often discouraged.	Forbidden by most parents and doctors.	Allowed, along with pacifiers.	Encouraged, along with pacifiers.	Allowed, along with pacifiers, but not encouraged.
		TOILET TRAINING		
Enemas and bowel irrigation used to "clean" babies.	Begun as early as 2 months of age.	Delayed until 6 to 18 months.	Delayed until 6 to 18 months.	Child determines best time, often at age 2 or 3.
		DISCIPLINE		
Moral training began early.	Strict discipline used at an early age.	Common sense and nurturing behavior recommended.	Most discipline gave way to permissiveness.	Suit discipline to child's age. "Time-outs" replace spankings.

4.6 ▓ WHAT CAN PARENTS DO TO ENSURE THAT THEIR CHILDREN DEVELOP PHYSICALLY, INTELLECTUALLY, AND EMOTIONALLY?

When their needs for love, approval, security, food, and shelter are met, most children develop into vigorous, healthy adults. But the same new parents who take skiing lessons or who hire an expert mechanic to fix their car somehow assume that parenting comes naturally. Too late, they discover that caring for a baby demands nearly infinite amounts of patience, love, discipline, and endurance. All of a sudden they find themselves changing diapers, mixing formulas, caring for rashes and sniffles, and wondering what to do about toilet training. And even when they've mastered those skills, they still must face the moment when their six-year-old asks, "Where do babies come from?"

Fortunately, no one has to start from scratch when it comes to raising children.

If you touch me soft and
     gentle
If you look at me and
     smile at me

If you listen to me talk
     sometimes before you talk
I will grow, really grow.

BRADLEY (age 9)

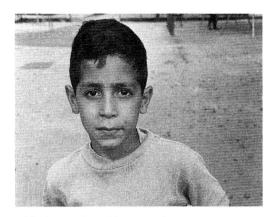

Muriel James and Dorothy Jongeward, *Born to Win* (pg. 44), © 1971, by Addison-Wesley
Publishing Company, Inc. Reprinted by permission of the publisher.

There is help available to parents from doctors, relatives, friends, and books on child raising. There's no way to guarantee that you won't make mistakes, but the following guidelines will help make success more likely.

LOVE AND AFFECTION

The need for *nurturing*—building warm, affectionate parent-child relationships—cannot be stressed too greatly. For the infant, this means cuddling, kissing, loving words, and frequent skin-to-skin contact. As the child grows, these needs for simple, physical displays of affection do not diminish. But older children also need verbal encouragement and approval. Watch 13-month-old Sharon take her first, hesitant steps. It's hard work, and the falls really do hurt. But her parents' cheers and inviting arms more than make up for temporary setbacks.

The child's entire world lies within the home. How can children develop a sense of self-worth unless the parents—those all-powerful and all-important givers of love and favors—provide ample supplies of love and emotional support? Urie Bronfenbrenner, a well-known child psychologist, summed up the need for love when he wrote, "The child should spend a substantial amount of time with somebody who's crazy about him."

ADEQUATE DIET

A child's nutritional needs begin at the time of conception. If the mother eats a diet rich in protein and essential vitamins and minerals, her unborn child will develop normally. Studies have demonstrated that IQ scores of poorly nourished children can be raised about ten points when they are fed a proper diet. Millions of children who grow up in poverty-stricken families will never reach their full physical and mental potential because their parents cannot afford to feed them properly. Sadly, growth losses suffered in the early childhood years cannot be fully reversed.

Adequate diet does not depend on expensive cuts of meat or rich desserts. In fact, many families suffer from "hidden hunger" because they rely too heavily on junk foods that are full of sugar and chemical additives.

123

As a result, 37 percent of U.S. children are obese, compared to 20 percent in Europe and 10 percent in China. Families that eat well understand the basic principles of food choice and preparation. Family doctors, health clinics, home-economics courses, and libraries can assist parents in planning well-balanced menus for growing children.

SENSORY STIMULATION

As a perceptive psychologist once noted, "Play is a child's work." Even babies need exciting, colorful objects to look at while they're lying in a crib or playpen. As the baby gains greater physical coordination, alert parents give it sturdy, safe toys that match its developmental level. Well-designed, inexpensive toys are good for banging, throwing, pushing, building, balancing, teething, and a hundred other useful activities. This type of rich, active environment, when coupled with proper nurturing, stimulates the development of the baby's cognitive and motor skills (see Figure 4.14).

The importance of sensory stimulation and proper nurturing was demonstrated in a study at Harvard University. Psychologists there became interested in why some children grow up better prepared to cope with life than other children. When they visited a kinder-

garten, for example, researchers quickly identified two kinds of children. They called them *A* and *C* children. Both groups were similar in motor and intellectual skills, but there the similarities ended. Group *A* children, as they were called, adjusted easily to change. *A* children were more outgoing, welcomed new experiences, and seldom seemed restless, bored, or upset. Group *C* children, on the contrary, cried easily and resisted change. School frightened them. Instead of welcoming the new experience, *C* children cried and clung to their parents' legs.

Since the parents were matched for economic and intellectual background, the researchers guessed that the difference in *A* and *C* behavior would be found in the children's home life. The study eventually showed that the contrasting childraising practices followed by *A* and *C* families between the ages of 10 and 18 months apparently made the difference. Before this age, the differences were not apparent; later, changes in parenting methods did not seem to change the children's behavior.

What happened during those critical months? *A* parents provided a rich variety of toys and allowed their children to roam freely around their living area. *C* parents, however, were overly protective and often left their children in playpens and highchairs for long periods. *A* parents often stopped to talk to their children. They challenged their curiosity, refused to help with problems until the children had made their own attempts, and reinforced the idea that adults can be used as a resource. *C* parents seldom encouraged their children to explore the world around them. Just as a *C* child started to look into the

FIGURE 4.14 ▦ Why are some children emotionally more mature and intellectually more vigorous than others? One study shows that such children received high-quality love, encouragement, and stimulation during the critical developmental period between 10 and 18 months.

mysteries of the vacuum cleaner or the dog's water dish, a *C* parent came running to hustle the child back to his playpen or crib. *A* children fell down and were encouraged to pick themselves up; *C* children were ignored or smothered with sympathy when they fell. In short, *C* parents failed to provide the stimulating environment that would have brought out the best in their children just when such stimulation was most important.

CONSISTENT DISCIPLINE

Have you ever met a spoiled child? If so, you probably agree that it wasn't a pretty picture. Children need discipline for their own protection. Proper discipline protects youngsters from obvious dangers, such as hot stoves and fast-moving traffic. But discipline also creates a balance between the child's desires and the desires of others. Children who expect everyone to give in to their wishes often feel compelled to fight with anyone who won't step aside.

The task for parents lies in finding a proper balance between permissiveness and repression. Too little discipline leaves children without proper guidelines for their conduct. Too much discipline keeps them from growing up free and independent. At its best, discipline comes from within. Self-disciplined children know how to act even when adults aren't around. But children also must learn to accept reasonable social controls. You may not agree with some school rules, for example, but you probably understand the chaos that would result if everyone ignored them.

Child psychologists suggest six basic rules of good discipline.

1. Fit the discipline to the child's maturity level. There's no sense in lecturing a two-year-old on philosophic concepts of right and wrong. If two-year-old Hank is "feeding" cookies to the goldfish, tell him to stop. Use a quiet, firm voice. If he doesn't respond, repeat the order and reinforce it by removing him from his perch by the fish tank. As you do so, divert his attention by offering him a favorite toy.

2. Discipline should be firm and consistent. Children feel much more secure when they know what the limits are. Throw out rules you're not willing to enforce. It's quite reasonable, for example, to establish a regular bedtime routine. Once you begin the routine, however, it will be effective only as long as the children know they can't talk you out of it.

3. Use physical punishment only when truly necessary and always in moderation. Punishments such as a "time-out" should be swift, reasonable, and related to the offense. Old-fashioned "whippings," often given in anger, do little to increase self-discipline and may build great resentment.

4. Help the child understand the reason for the discipline. The old line, "Do what I say and not what I do!" leaves the child more determined than ever to try the forbidden behavior.

5. Reward *good* behavior with your attention and praise. Too many parents ignore their children when they're playing quietly— but give them lots of attention when they're noisy or mischievous. This pattern just tells children that the way to get attention is to *be* noisy and mischievous.

6. Responsibility for discipline should be shared equally among all adults responsible for raising the child. The classic threat, "Just wait 'til your father gets home!" only sets Dad up as a fearful figure more to be avoided than loved. And most children are quick to learn how to manipulate parents who can't agree on how or when to discipline.

MOTIVATION

There's 15-year-old Luanne, changing the washer on the kitchen faucet. Dad's watching, quick to offer advice. But Luanne's fumbling with a stubborn screw. Pretty soon, Dad

FIGURE 4.15 ▓ When parents and teachers combine forces to provide an exciting, hands-on learning environment, children can—and do—succeed in school. Learning psychologists call the process "making programs fit the child instead of making the child fit the school." Instead of confining children to their desks and asking them to fill in worksheets, creative teachers allow their students to move, touch, and explore.

says, "Here, let me do that. You're too slow." A discouraged Luanne steps aside. The message is clear: girls don't have an aptitude for mechanical tasks.

Or join the dinner table conversation at the Simpsons'. Jimmy has just shown his report card to the family. "Well," says Mom, "that's pretty good. But in this family we expect all

A's. You'll just have to work harder from now on." You can see from Jimmy's pained expression that he feels doomed. How can he ever meet that nearly impossible standard?

Without knowing it, too many parents constantly tell children that they're dumb, slow, stupid, lazy, or bad. Eventually, those messages get through, and the children start acting dumb, slow, stupid, lazy, or bad. Psychologists call this condition a *self-fulfilling prophecy*.

Parents can also give their children positive self-fulfilling prophecies. In general, psychologists find that well-motivated children come from homes where parents provide four positive messages. First, they believe that learning is important, and they communicate that belief through their own actions. Second, they encourage their children to talk freely about their experiences and feelings. Third, they frequently express a warm interest in their children's accomplishments. When the childish voice cries, "Mom and Dad, look at me!" Mom and Dad take time to look and praise. Finally, they do not expect their children to achieve more than they are capable of achieving.

Adults tend to forget how important their responses can be to a child. Silence or inattention, for example, can devastate a child's sensitive feelings. Positive reinforcement, moreover, doesn't cost much. It means merely being present when needed, giving an extra smile or touch, and rewarding even small achievements with a hug, kiss, and extra attention. This simple principle can give every child the motivation he or she needs to succeed. And isn't that what parenting is all about?

■ SECTION CHECKUP

I Why should every child spend as much time as possible with "somebody who's crazy about him or her"?

2 What's wrong with parenting that protects a child from all danger and that prevents frustration by solving problems for the child?

3 Describe some of the rules for proper discipline.

4 What is meant by a *self-fulfilling prophecy*? How would you advise eight-year-old Patty's parents to act when she makes her first clumsy try at building a doghouse?

4.7 ▓ WHAT SPECIAL PROBLEMS DO PARENTS AND CHILDREN FACE TODAY?

Most people romanticize childhood. They see the child's world as secure, innocent, and loving. Sadly, the opposite is true for millions of babies and young children. A fetus that survives until birth may die in the first days or weeks of life. Some of the survivors are physically handicapped and many will be physically and emotionally abused by their parents. As they grow up, millions of children will never know the security of a close and loving family. Others must cope with the pressure of trying to meet unrealistic parental expectations.

INFANT MORTALITY

Doctors define a nation's infant mortality rate as the number of infants per thousand live births who die before their first birthday. Scientists often use this number as a yardstick for measuring the health and well-being of the population at large. At one time, the United States could boast of having one of the world's lowest infant mortality rates. Sadly, the U.S. infant mortality rate is now almost twice that of Sweden, and the nation's rating has slipped from sixth in the world to thirty-fourth.

The infant mortality rate does not apply equally to all Americans. African American babies, for example, are more than twice as likely to die in the first year as white babies. Some of this difference can be traced to eco-nomic factors. Many black babies are born into families who have incomes below the poverty level. Mothers in these circumstances have less access to health services and are more likely to give birth to babies weighing less than 5.5 pounds. Statistics show that low-birth-weight infants are 40 times more likely to die during the first month. They are also twice as likely to suffer disabling conditions such as blindness, deafness, and mental retardation.

The high cost of medical care also plays a role. Because of lack of funds, many counties in the United States have closed public health clinics that once offered prenatal care to the poor. In addition, three-quarters of the nation's family doctors no longer deliver babies. When asked why, they point to the high cost of medical malpractice insurance. As a result, hospital deliveries, which are safer should complications arise, have become less common.

THE TRAGEDY OF DRUG BABIES

Child abuse can begin soon after conception. Mothers who use cocaine, heroin, and other drugs share their habit with their unborn babies. Regular cocaine use during the first three months of pregnancy keeps the fetus from growing and developing normally. Continued drug use results in additional damage. Drug babies have low birth weights and are often born prematurely. Even if the birth goes normally, the babies are likely to suffer from mental and emotional problems.

Pediatricians and child psychologists are now trying to cope with the results of the nation's drug epidemic. Many babies born to crack cocaine users begin life suffering from withdrawal symptoms. Some are very excitable and jittery. Others are sluggish and depressed. Drug babies often withdraw from direct contact with their caregivers. They rarely smile or gurgle and seem most content when left to stare vacantly at a room's walls and ceiling.

Drug babies do not leave their physical and behavioral problems behind when they grow up. They are often hyperactive and lack the concentration needed for school tasks. Teachers report that they lag behind in language development and in their ability to organize information. Many are steered toward special education classes. Those who receive medical and psychological care at an early age can be helped to live normal or near-normal lives. Doctors worry, however, that many drug-affected children will not be helped until it is too late.

CHILDREN OF DIVORCE AND POVERTY

Until the 1960s, the typical American child was born into a two-parent family. Dad held a steady job, Mom worked at home as a housewife, and the child had 1.3 siblings.

Today, only 25 percent of American families fit that model. One in three first-time marriages ends in divorce. It's true that most people marry again—but many second marriages also end in divorce. Parents who are struggling to resolve their marital problems often involve their children in damaging emotional conflicts. The woulds children suffer during these stressful periods can make it difficult for them to achieve enduring relationships of their own when they become adults.

Changing social patterns and hard economic times also scar America's children. More women are working, and more children are being raised by single parents. Children in these families may spend as many as 10 or 12 hours a day in play schools or with babysitters. A majority of caregivers provide the security and affection children need, but far too many are ill equipped to serve as substitute parents. Poverty also scars children. Many children in low-income families grow up in neighborhoods shattered by gang warfare, drugs, and substandard housing. All too often, these children are born to unwed, teenage mothers. Finally, to make matters worse, governments, as they struggle to balance their budgets, have cut social and health care programs aimed at helping poor children.

CHILD NEGLECT AND ABUSE

Parents who are overwhelmed by their own economic and emotional problems sometimes neglect or abuse their children. A neglected child is one who does not receive adequate adult care and supervision. Government studies, for example, show that millions of children between 5 and 13 years of age come home to empty houses or apartments or to the care of older siblings. For many of these children, television has become the universal babysitter. The average child watches over 6,000 hours of television before starting first grade—and neglected children watch much more. Teachers report that excessive television watching can lead to low reading scores, shortened attention spans, and lower grades.

Even more alarming is the rapid increase in child abuse. Abuse can be emotional, physical, or sexual—and sometimes all three. Since 1975, reported cases of abuse have mushroomed from 60,000 to over 900,000 per year.

Abuse can be found at every level of society, but low-income parents are seven times more likely to abuse their children. There is no common factor in child abuse, but many abusive parents suffer from low self-esteem, have poor impulse control, and are likely to have been abused as children. Drugs, alcohol, marital problems, and mental illness also contribute to child abuse.

PARENTAL PRESSURE

Can a child receive too much attention? Child psychologists believe the answer is "yes." Some well-meaning parents fill their children's days with extra classes, organized sports, and other "enrichment" opportunities. These highly pressured children soon learn that failure will not be tolerated. They become "superkids," admired by adults but robbed of their childhood.

The superkid syndrome is part of a family commitment to success in school and athletics. Some parents overspend on name-brand clothing, dressing preteen children in sophisticated styles better suited to young adults. Free play and leisure give way to rigorous training and study sessions. As a result, doctors are now seeing more children at ages five to nine who are suffering from injuries once limited to college-age athletes. Growing children are thrown into weightlifting programs, and some junior high athletes are using steroids. As these highly stressed children grow up, they tend to be more anxious, less creative, and more likely to "turn off" to school.

FIGURE 4.16 ▦ In today's world, where most parents work, tens of thousands of young children spend time alone after school until an adult or an older brother or sister gets home. These "latchkey children" may learn a sense of responsibility and to be self-reliant, but they may also give in to dangerous temptations. Some people advocate keeping schools open later to provide safe places for children to stay until the workday ends.

▪ SECTION CHECKUP

1 Why does the United States have an alarmingly high infant mortality rate?

2 Summarize the ways in which a baby can be harmed by its mother's drug abuse during pregnancy.

3 What effects do (*a*) family breakup, (*b*) poverty, and (*c*) child neglect and abuse have on children?

4 Why is it risky for parents to pressure children to be overachievers in academics and sports?

LOOKING BACK: A SUMMARY

1 Psychologists emphasize that the experiences of early infancy and childhood play a critical role in determining future personality and behavior. The forces that shape the child's development include the biological limitations of heredity as well as the environmental conditions imposed by home, community, and the wider society. Behaviors not developed at the proper stage of life—prenatal, newborn, infant, childhood, or adolescence—may never be fully learned.

2 Individual differences in behavior develop as a child grows through the life stages. Psychologists have three major theories to explain these differences. (*a*) Behavior-learning theory states that children learn new behaviors because they are rewarded for doing so. (*b*) Evolved-primate theory holds that behavior results from the interaction between the biological development of the human species and the social environment into which the child is born. (*c*) Psychodynamic theory believes that personality develops as children search for ways to satisfy their basic needs within the confines of the culture.

3 Heredity and environmental influences cannot be separated when evaluating the forces that shape a child's life. Environmental influences include physical factors such as diet, medical care, and clean air; social factors include the family, schools, friends, and the community. Heredity is a gift of the child's parents, who pass on a random selection of traits through the 23 chromosomes and thousands of genes each contributes to the fertilized ovum. Some traits, such as physical features, height, and hair color, are clearly controlled by heredity. Other traits, such as intelligence, are influenced by both heredity and environment.

4 Genes are either dominant or recessive. Some physical defects can be traced to combinations of recessive genes or to chromosomal abnormalities. Disease or careless use of drugs during pregnancy can also damage the developing fetus.

5 Most children develop motor skills on a schedule set by the maturation of the nervous system. This schedule can be slowed down by injury, illness, or poor diet, but it cannot be speeded up. Most infants learn to roll over, sit up, and walk within a month or two of babies their own age. Handicapped children often need special care and counseling so that they can learn to take responsibility for their own lives.

6 Intellectual (cognitive) development also advances in stages. Jean Piaget described four such periods. (*a*) The sensory-motor stage, birth to age two, is when infants learn how to respond to sensory experiences in the environment. (*b*) The preoperational stage, ages two to seven, is when children focus on their own needs without thought for others. Language and more logical thought processes also develop during this period. (*c*) The concrete operations stage, ages seven to 11, is when children learn to use concrete cognitive skills such as grouping and conservation. (*d*) The formal operations stage, age 11 through adolescence, is when children learn to test their ideas against reality and to use advanced abstract reasoning.

7 Mastery of language is a major cognitive development. In order to communicate with others, the child must learn the complex mix of sounds, vocabulary, and grammar that makes up speech. Another essential cognitive skill involves the ability to form concepts. This process allows the child to solve more difficult problems by organizing data into logical patterns.

8 When the mind and body interact and respond to stimuli from the environment, the resulting sensation is called an emotion. Psychologists disagree over the number of emotions that infants can feel. At a minimum, the newborn shows clear evidence of delight and distress. Emotional responses become more complex as children develop and learn to adjust their basic needs to the demands of the world around them. This process is known as *socialization.*

9 Before age seven or eight, most children accept moral values (such as whether or not they should lie, steal, or obey orders) only when forced to do so. A more mature sense of morality develops when children learn to accept the needs and rights of others. Learning appropriate sex roles is an important part of a child's intellectual and emotional growth. Parents and other adults in the family help determine sex-role behavior because children tend to model themselves on adults of the same sex. Old, stereotyped sex roles have changed dramatically, but feminists believe that women still have work to do if they are to gain full equality in all areas of U.S. life.

10 The most important contribution parents can make to their young children is to provide an environment rich in nurturing and sensory stimulation. A balanced diet helps children grow strong and healthy. Firm, consistent discipline teaches children how to control their behavior. Praise and attention, as well as patience, help children develop the kind of motivation that can ensure later success in school, at work, and in building close personal relationships.

11 Parents and children today face a growing list of social, economic, and emotional problems. Infant mortality rates are rising because of drug use and cutbacks in health care for the poor. At the same time, more families are being broken up by divorce. The children who grow up in broken homes spend more time alone or in playschools. Some children are neglected and a growing number are physically, emotionally, and sexually abused. By contrast, some well-meaning parents rob their children of their childhood by burdening them with impossibly high expectations.

PUTTING YOUR KNOWLEDGE TO WORK

■ TERMS YOU SHOULD KNOW

adolescence	evolved-primate theory	nurturing
adulthood	formal operations stage	object constancy
behavior-learning theory	genes	prenatal phase
childhood phase	genetic screening	preoperational stage
chromosomes	grouping	psychodynamic theory
cognitive processes	heredity	recessive genes
concept formation	infant phase	self-fulfilling prophecy
concrete operations stage	maturation	sensory-motor stage
conservation	nature versus nurture	sex roles
dominant genes	newborn phase	socialization
emotions		

▪ CHAPTER CHECKUP

1 The childhood schizophrenia demonstrated so vividly by Joey the Mechanical Boy probably resulted from (*a*) a chromosomal abnormality (*b*) injuries suffered during the birth process (*c*) lack of nurturing on the part of the parents (*d*) inadequate diet during infancy.

2 Present-day psychologists agree that the most important factor in the development of personality is (*a*) heredity (*b*) the environment (*c*) the socialization process (*d*) the interaction of heredity and environment.

3 The first period of life during which the actions of the mother have any influence on the child is the (*a*) prenatal phase (*b*) newborn phase (*c*) infant phase (*d*) childhood phase.

4 Which of the following is a *true* statement about children whose parents are both mentally ill with schizophrenia? (*a*) The children have almost a 70 percent chance of also developing this serious mental illness. (*b*) The children of schizophrenics never develop this mental illness. (*c*) Only the younger children of schizophrenics develop this mental illness. (*d*) Children of schizophrenics show the same incidence of the illness as the general population—about 1 percent.

5 If each parent carries one dominant gene for black hair and one recessive gene for blond hair, the odds of their giving birth to a blond-haired baby are (*a*) zero (*b*) one in two (*c*) one in four (*d*) impossible to predict because the inheritance of physical features occurs at random.

6 Babies who are confined in a restricted environment during the first months of life (*a*) never catch up with other children (*b*) develop motor skills faster than other children (*c*) develop language skills faster than normal (*d*) follow much the same timetable for developing motor skills as other children.

7 According to Piaget, a child who understands the concept of conservation will be able to (*a*) recognize that changing the size or shape of a mass does not change its volume (*b*) solve a problem by using a new approach when the old one fails (*c*) make categories of objects with similar features (*d*) solve abstract problems involving social issues.

8 A child's cognitive processes first include the ability to understand fully abstract political or scientific concepts at about (*a*) age six (*b*) age eight (*c*) age 12 (*d*) any age from two to 20; all children develop at their own speed.

9 Children learn their most important lessons about masculine and feminine behavior (*a*) instinctively (*b*) from playmates (*c*) from watching television (*d*) from using parents as role models.

10 The most critical period for determining whether children will develop the intellectual and social competencies they need to succeed in our society occurs at (*a*) birth to two months (*b*) ten to 18 months (*c*) 18 to 36 months (*d*) four to six years.

▪ EXPLORING CONCEPTS

1 What does the psychologist mean by the statement, "The child is father of the man"? What does it tell us about the importance of early childhood?

2 Name some of the various hereditary and environmental forces that determine four-year-old Jamie's behavior. What would you say to Jamie's parents, who are worried that he's been slow to develop the same running and throwing skills as his friends?

3 Is there anyone else in the world exactly like you? Discuss the genetic and environmental reasons for your answer.

4 Name some physical and mental problems caused by (*a*) heredity and (*b*) environmental forces. Discuss ways in which each of these problems can be prevented.

5 Imagine identical twins (brothers or sisters who developed from a single divided ovum) who were separated at birth and raised apart—one in a large city in the United States and the other in a village in Kenya. What physical differences, if any, do you think they'd display at age 18? What cognitive and emotional differences would you expect?

▪ HANDS-ON ACTIVITIES

1 Do you know an infant or a child under three years of age? If so, arrange to spend some time in careful observation. Keep a record of the baby's play activities, television viewing, language skills, motor skills, and eating habits. Does the child seem to fit the developmental schedule for his or her age?

2 If your parents kept a baby book for you, read through it. How did your own developmental stages match up with the norms? Do you see patterns of behavior that still exist today? As a further insight, check your height at 18 months if you're a girl, 24 months if you're a boy. Studies show that at those ages most children are one half their adult height. Does it appear as though the prediction will work out for you?

3 Volunteer to spend some time helping out in a day-care center or play school. Pay particular attention to the teaching methods used and the amount of nurturing given to the children. Discuss your experience with your psychology class. What does the school do well? Are there any areas that need improvement?

4 Organize your class to survey a sampling of the television shows that children watch. Categorize the number and variety of violent acts committed during these programs. Can you draw any conclusions as to the possible effect this exposure will have on young children?

5 Write down a list of your basic values and beliefs concerning money, morality, sex, ways of expressing emotion, and the like. How many of your values are the same as those of your parents? How many are different? How do you account for the similarities and differences? When you look at the way you have been raised, would you change anything with your own children?

FOR FURTHER READING

Brazelton, T. Berry, and Stanley Greenspan. *The Irreducible Needs of Children*. Cambridge, MA: Da Capo Press, 2000. Two of the country's top baby doctors discuss the seven needs that make up the foundation of a healthy childhood. The authors spotlight the sad fact that society allows some children to grow up with their basic needs unmet.

Candland, Douglas. *Feral Children and Clever Animals*. New York: Oxford University Press, 1995. Candland retells stories of feral children such as the Wild Boy of Aveyron. Then he applies these insights to research with "clever animals." If a gorilla can learn to use sign language, maybe it's time to redefine what it means to be human.

Cattanach, Ann. *Introduction to Play Therapy*. New York: Taylor & Francis, 2003. Therapists who work with troubled children use play therapy to gain a child's trust and cooperation. Written by a leading expert in the field, this book uses dramatic case studies to show how play therapy works.

Dorris, Michael. *The Broken Cord*. New York: Harper & Row, 1990. The heartbreaking reality of fetal alcohol syndrome comes to life in this true story. The vivid prose allows the reader to share the struggles of a family whose adopted child was born to an alcoholic mother.

Serulnikov, Adriana. *Piaget for Beginners*. New York: Writers & Readers, 2000. Piaget can be hard going, but Serulnikov does a good job of making his work accessible. This reader-friendly book uses pictures and comic strips to amplify the text. A brief biography helps bring Piaget into focus, too.

White, Burton, *The New First Three Years of Life*. New York: Fireside, 1995. This classic work has been updated to include new research into the mental, physical, social, and emotional growth of infants and toddlers. White's advice on discipline, toilet training, and other parenting issues is invaluable.

White, Merry Isaacs. *Perfectly Japanese: Making Families in an Era of Upheaval*. Berkeley, CA: University of California Press, 2002. This study of Japanese culture will help you see family life in a new light. Japanese families, it turns out, are just as complex and conflicted as your own.

Your Growing Child. Alexandria, VA: Time-Life Books, 1987. This well-designed book provides a highly readable overview of the topic. The editors describe child growth and development in sections titled, "How Children Grow," "Developing Movement Skills," "Speech and Language," and "Learning Responsibility."

Chapter

5 THE ADOLESCENT SEARCHES FOR IDENTITY

Every adult has passed through adolescence. Despite their eight years of "on-the-job training," however, not every adult understands the emotional riptides that mark the transition from childhood to young adulthood.

Even when adults try to help, adolescents do not always respond in a predictable way. Perhaps you can sense some of the confusion Owen Harding is feeling as he talks to his homeroom teacher about his failing grades:

I wasn't even too worried about seeing Mr. Harris, but when I walked back to my home room at three-thirty I stood outside for a long time before I walked in. I wasn't too crazy about seeing Mr. Harris all of a sudden. . . .

Finally I just barged in, and Mr. Harris looked up from a whole bunch of papers he was leafing through.

"Be with you in a minute, Owen."

I just stood there like a dunce.

Then I asked him if he wanted the door closed and he said yes, so I closed it. I almost asked him if he wanted it locked too, but he didn't seem to be in a very happy mood.

"Have a seat," he said. . . . "I would like to help you, Owen," he said.

"What d'you mean, Mr. Harris?"

"You must realize that you're doing

very badly. For instance in Geometry and Biology"—he looked through some stupid records that must have been mine—"if you don't pass those examinations, you could be kept back a year." . . .

Mr. Harris drummed his fingers on the desk and looked at me in a funny way, like I was a stranger who'd just barged in on him. . . . He seemed very nervous the way he kept drumming his fingers. . . . He made me nervous doing that! . . .

He gave me the old X-ray eye treatment—one of those I-can-see-right-through-you looks. Sometimes he talked like he wasn't a teacher, when there was something wrong and he felt he had to know you. He did that sometimes, because he was a pretty good guy. But it always made me uncomfortable, because he really was a teacher and he didn't know very much about you at all. . . .

"All right. We'll get down to the facts." . . . He fiddled around with some yellow sheets that were probably my stupid records; it looked like he had a whole pile of them on his desk. . . .

"In junior high school you made the honor roll five times. Your total average

Thumbprint

In the heel of my thumb
are whorls, whirls, wheels
in a unique design:
mine alone.
What a treasure to own!
My own flesh, my own feelings.
No other, however grand or base,
can ever contain the same.
My signature,
thumbing the pages of my time.
My universe key,
my singularity.
Impress, implant,
I am myself,
of all my atom parts I am the sum.
And out of my blood and my brain
I make my own interior weather,
my own sun and rain.
Imprint my mark upon the world,
whatever I shall become.

Eve Merriam

through junior high school was eighty-nine percent. *Eighty-nine percent!"* he said. The way he looked at me I thought he was going to ask me if I'd paid off the teachers. He took out his handkerchief and blew his nose. . . . "I hate to tell you what your average is now. It's not good—I'll tell you that. You're doing very badly."

I stared at this half-rotten apple on his desk. I wondered if one of the hundred percenters had given it to him.

"I didn't do very well in the ninth grade, though," I said. "It's not only in high school I've done bad."

"Bad*ly*, Owen. Bad*ly*."

"*Bad*ly," I said. He was always correcting you instead of listening to what you said. "I did very badly in the ninth grade. Almost as badly as I'm doing now." . . .

"And since you've been in high school," he said, picking up one of the yellow sheets and squinting at it, "you've barely maintained a passing seventy-five." . . .

"The only reason is, I haven't studied."

"Yes, but why haven't you studied?" he asked me.

"I don't know. I don't like to study, I guess."

"Well, do you know why you don't like to study?"

"No," I said. "I don't know. The work doesn't seem to interest me." . . .

"What d'you suppose the answer is?" he asked me.

"Well," I said, "maybe I've gotten too smart for school." Boy, that was the biggest mistake going! He stuck the chewed-up pencil in his mouth again and almost bit it in two.

"Owen—I'm not going to become personal. . . . But if you'll permit me, I'd like to make a personal observation."

"I don't mind," I said. "Say anything you want."

"Well," he said, "after talking to some of your teachers, I've come to a conclusion. I think that you're unreasonable. You're very unreasonable."

Are adolescents unreasonable? Or does Owen have good cause to mistrust Mr. Harris? Whatever the answer, it's clear that for most young people, growing up involves a long and sometimes painful journey of self-discovery.

Psychologists have long been aware of the importance of adolescence. In this chapter, you'll learn about the changes that occur during these years. Some of these changes are physical; others are emotional. Mix them all together and you produce a sometimes explosive combination that challenges every adolescent. The questions to be discussed include:

5.1 What is adolescence?

5.2 What physical changes take place during adolescence?

5.3 What emotional challenges does the adolescent face?

5.4 What are the developmental tasks of adolescence that relate to the self?

5.5 What are the developmental tasks of adolescence that relate to others?

5.6 What special problems do adolescents face today?

5.1 ■ WHAT IS ADOLESCENCE?

Psychologists agree that adolescence is a state of mind as well as a physical reality. For some young people, it's a time of rapid and exciting growth. After all, the term adolescence comes from the Latin verb *adolescere*, "to grow up." That's how 16-year-old Maria K. sees it:

I can hardly wait to start each day. There's always something exciting to do, something new to learn. My parents give me a lot more freedom, and my boyfriend and I get along great. Also, since I decided to be a paramedic,

school makes a lot more sense. Sure, it bugs me that some adults still treat me like a little kid. But I'm not in any rush to grow up. I'm having a good time right now.

Other adolescents find it difficult to make sense out of their new physical maturity. Suddenly, the world seems to close in on them. As Hammond A. says,

I wasn't prepared for all the crazy feelings that go through my mind. Sometimes I feel OK, but other times I feel like dying. Girls scare me, and I

The Adolescent Challenge
Strange, Deep Yearnings for . . . Something
As interpreted by Thomas Wolfe

During these years, Eugene would go away from Pulpit Hill, by night and by day, when April was a young green blur, or when the spring was deep and ripe. . . .

He was devoured by a vast strange hunger for life. At night, he listened to the million-noted ululation [howling] of little night things, the great brooding symphony of dark, the ringing of remote churchbells across the country. And his vision widened out in circles over moon-drenched meadows, dreaming woods, mighty rivers going along in darkness, and ten thousand sleeping towns. He believed in the infi-

nite rich variety of all the towns and faces; behind any of a million shabby houses he believed there was strange buried life, subtle and shattered romance, something dark and unknown. At the moment of passing any house, he thought, some one therein might be at the gate of death, . . . murder might be doing.

He felt a desperate frustration, as if he were being shut out from the rich banquet of life. And against all caution, he determined to break the pattern of custom, and look within.

Thomas Wolfe, *Look Homeward, Angel* (New York: Scribner's, 1929), pp. 596–597.

can't seem to talk to my folks any more. It's like having a bomb inside me that might go off any minute. I wish people would get off my back and just leave me alone.

Why do some people seem to coast through adolescence, while others find it a constant struggle just to keep their heads above water? In truth, the years between 12 and 18 (as our society usually defines adolescence) are a period of tremendous physical, intellectual, and emotional growth. To make matters even more complicated, this is also the time when young people often come into direct conflict with their parents over the life-style choices they're making and the values they're adopting. But knowing something about the process of growing up may make it a little easier for you.

THE STAGES OF ADOLESCENCE

No one would suggest that the values and experiences of a 12-year-old seventh-grader are the same as those of an 18-year-old high-school senior. Social scientists, therefore, have divided adolescence into three stages: preadolescence, adolescence, and young adulthood.

PREADOLESCENCE. Childhood ends with a period of rapid physical growth, including the first signs of sexual maturation. *Preadolescence* can begin as early as eight or nine, but the typical ages are 10 to 14 for girls and 12 to 15 for boys. The behavioral changes typical of adolescence begin during these years. Parents may notice that once happy-go-lucky children now seem moody, withdrawn, and rebellious. These emotional

FIGURE 5.1 ▓ Formal ceremonies known as *rites of passage* mark the passage from childhood to adulthood in most cultures. Whether the ceremony involves special cultural rituals or the completion of a high-school course of study, such ceremonies tell everyone that the adolescent is now an adult. (At left, a young woman participates in her "sacred Sunrise Dance," a major celebration of Apache identity.)

changes are a normal part of growing up. They may even intensify after the adolescent has completed *puberty,* the physical development that signals the beginning of adult sexual maturity.

ADOLESCENCE. During the years between 15 and 18, teenagers must complete what psychologists call the developmental tasks of *adolescence* (described in detail later in this chapter). Adolescents need to work toward emotional and economic independence, for example. They must also come to terms with their own physical development. And they must find their own individual identity.

YOUNG ADULTHOOD. The passage from adolescence to adulthood begins at 18 or 19 and extends through the early twenties. By this time, the majority of teenagers have completed their adolescent development. As young adults, they are ready to accept their new responsibilities for career building, development of long-term love relationships, and making a life outside their family homes.

If you lived in a simpler, tribal society, you'd have become an adult shortly after puberty (see Figure 5.1). To mark the occasion, you'd have undergone certain ceremonies that social scientists call *rites of passage*. If you are male, you'd have been required to demonstrate your strength, endurance, and courage. Tribal elders would have taught you special chants and dances. You might have been sent to hunt dangerous game, such as an elephant or lion. If you are female, you'd have had your own rites of passage. As a woman, you would have learned special dances, and you might be tattooed to enhance your beauty. To complete the rites, older women would have introduced you to the mysteries of sex and motherhood in order to prepare you for marriage.

Adolescents in the United States, by contrast, attain adulthood in a confusing, hit-and-miss fashion. You may have reached puberty at 12, but in most states you can't drive a car until you're 15 or 16. You probably started paying adult prices at the movies when you were 13, but you're not allowed to see

X-rated films until you're 17. You can vote at 18, but insurance companies charge you "young-driver" premiums until you're 25. It's no wonder young people often feel confused as to what their status really is.

CONTRASTING VIEWS OF ADOLESCENTS

To a degree, adolescence is mostly a modern invention. Only in the 1800s did society begin to set aside a period between childhood and adulthood in which young people were given time to develop their adult personalities. As adolescence became a reality, social scientists began to look for theories to explain adolescent behavior. Out of those studies, two significant ideas emerged.

THE "STORM-AND-STRESS" THEORY.   In 1904, psychologist G. Stanley Hall described adolescence as a stormy passage from childhood to adult maturity. Hall saw this period of "storm and stress" as a natural expression of physical and emotional growth. Extremes of mood, in which the adolescent swings from joy to gloom, were seen as necessary to growth. Hall's theory claims that the teenager's rebellious behavior, idealism, and self-interest are normal. Many social scientists accept this concept as a useful explanation for adolescent behavior.

ADOLESCENCE AS A SELF-FULFILLING PROPHECY.   Other experts say that adolescence need not be a time of "storm and stress." Anthropologist Margaret Mead pointed out that adolescence in the traditional Samoan culture is a happy and peaceful time. She believed that advanced societies contribute to adolescent problems by cutting teenagers off from full participation in adult life. For example, well-meaning parents often try to "protect" their teenagers by excluding them from important family business. Adolescents are often the last to learn that their parents are experiencing health or financial problems.

Developmental psychologists who agree with Dr. Mead say their research shows that most adolescents pass through the teen years without great difficulty. These psychologists say that problems develop when society tells adolescents that they are expected to become rebellious, wild, or mixed-up. This expectation can become a self-fulfilling prophecy, they say, which creates the very behavior the adult society predicts—and dreads.

■ SECTION CHECKUP

1 How would you define adolescence? Why do psychologists believe that it is an important time of life?

2 What are rites of passage? Why are they important?

3 Contrast the "storm-and-stress" theory of adolescence with that of adolescence as a self-fulfilling prophecy.

5.2 ■ WHAT PHYSICAL CHANGES TAKE PLACE DURING ADOLESCENCE?

Have you noticed how small many of the ninth-grade boys are these days? What high-school senior has not stopped to marvel at the tiny people who appear on campus each September. "They're no bigger than third graders!" the fully grown seniors laugh, forgetting that two or three years ago many of their classmates were also that height.

The growth spurt that marks preadolescence is the most obvious signal that childhood has ended. But emotional development seldom keeps pace with physical development. Imagine that you have learned to ride a 50-cc moped. But suddenly you're given a giant 750-cc motorcycle. Learning to handle that powerful cycle is something like the job preadolescents face when their bodies suddenly take on adult dimensions and develop adult sexual drives.

EXTERNAL CHANGES

"What happened to my babies?" Mom says sadly. Her smooth-cheeked son has abruptly sprouted a mustache. He seems to have grown six inches taller overnight. His sister, meanwhile, has developed some distinctly feminine curves. And both of them are fighting troubling cases of acne.

This adolescent growth spurt, known as puberty, originates in the brain's hypothalamus. As the key control center for many body processes, the hypothalamus stimulates the pituitary gland. The pituitary, in turn, triggers the production of growth hormones in the thyroid, adrenal, and sex glands. This flurry of chemical activity brings almost immediate results. Typically, girls grow three to four inches and gain 22 pounds. Boys average increases of four to six inches and 40 pounds (see Figure 5.3).

During childhood, twins George and Patty looked much alike in their jeans and T-shirts. As they reach puberty, their body proportions and contours will begin to show significant differences. Patty will probably reach physical maturity first. Her slender, boyish figure will fill out as her breasts, hips, and legs develop rounded feminine contours. Patty's new figure will result from the buildup of underskin fat, along with changes in the bone structure, particularly in the pelvic area.

George, meanwhile, will develop a masculine body line, with broadened shoulders, slender hips, and straight legs. As he spurts past Patty in height and weight, his nose and jaw will become much more prominent. George's voice will take on deeper tones as his larynx (the "Adam's apple") enlarges. Patty's voice will also deepen, but not as much. George will probably suffer a period when his voice alternates treacherously between baritone and squeaky soprano. Finally, both George and Patty will grow additional body hair, nature's final signal that they have reached sexual maturity.

INTERNAL CHANGES

George's and Patty's rapid physical growth will also be matched by major internal changes. Neural tissue grows most rapidly between birth and age six. During adolescence, however, lymphoid tissue (intestines, lymph nodes, thymus, and tonsils) expand greatly, followed closely by the growth of genital tis-

LUANN By Greg Evans

FIGURE 5.2

ADOLESCENT GROWTH SPURTS

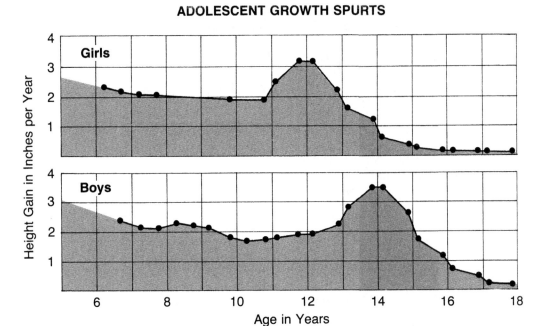

FIGURE 5.3 ▓ Girls reach their adolescent growth spurt approximately two years earlier than boys, but boys catch up quickly. The primary growth period for adolescent girls is 12 to 13; for boys it is 14 to 15.

sue. Neither George nor Patty will be much aware of these internal changes, but another profound signal awaits each of them. As puberty begins, Patty will experience her first menstrual cycle. For girls who have not been given clear, understandable information about the meaning of menstruation, this can be a frightening experience. A year or two later, George's body will begin producing sperm, giving him the physical capability of fathering a child.

Although George and Patty are now approaching physical maturity, they will need a number of years of further psychological maturation before they can adjust to their new bodies. Their sex drives, however, will not wait. The internal and external changes described above will lead them into a new world of sexual feelings, all of which carry

emotional consequences. These feelings are discussed at greater length in Section 5.3 (page 144–149).

COPING WITH PHYSICAL PROBLEMS

The physical growth that goes with adolescence doesn't always take place smoothly. As Harrison M. put it, "Here I am, trying to cope with all kinds of emotional changes—and my own body refuses to cooperate!" In Harrison's case, he's talking about an outbreak of acne. For other teenagers, the problems involve the effects of rapid growth or the consequences of early or late physical maturation.

ACNE. Few adolescents escape the torments of acne. The eruptions of pimples and black-

The Adolescent Challenge
Coping With the "Awkward Age"
As remembered by authors looking back

I feel self-conscious. I don't want to be handsome, but I hate my present appearance. Weak, pale, small ears, big nose, "peach fuzz," weak chin. Now my mouth is out of shape and I cannot smile, for Dr. Singer put my brace back yesterday.

DAVID S. KOGAN

My hands and feet grew farther and farther away from my body and set up on their own, reminding me of their distant connection by getting in the way and declining generally to do what they were told. I would have been glad to get rid of them and go handless and footless through life.

JOHN A. RICE

If there's one thing I desire in life, it's not to be as hungry as I am. I'm disgracefully hungry. I never had a day in my life when I didn't want to eat a lot.

HELENA MORLEY

When I was in about the tenth grade, I didn't consider myself to be especially popular. I was not particularly good-looking, I was ashamed of having acne, I wasn't a star athlete . . . and I didn't get especially good grades. . . . You can imagine how surprised I was, then, when I was elected president of my class.

JAMES L. COLLIER

heads on face, chest, and back cause new heartache every time they appear. Dermatologists (skin doctors) say that mild cases of acne are a normal part of growing up. They explain that acne results when certain hormone secretions that occur during adolescence cause a disturbance in the glandular functions of the skin. Frequent bathing with soap and water, mild medication, and a moderate exposure to sunlight generally produce marked improvement. Scarring can be kept to a minimum if the acne sufferer resists the temptation to squeeze the eruptions. More severe cases should be referred to a dermatologist for treatment and advice on how to smooth out the scars.

The psychological impact of acne is harder to treat. Just when they want most desperately to be physically attractive, some teenagers wake up one day to find their skin marked by red, blotchy pimples. Well-meaning friends and parents will tell these unhappy young people that "no one really notices," but kind words cannot erase the reality revealed by the mirror. Nor does the knowledge that most acne disappears with the end of adolescence help very much. Perhaps the best advice that psychologists can give to young people like Harrison is: Practice proper skin hygiene and see a doctor if the acne gets out of control. Meanwhile, work to develop such an outgoing, self-confident personality that no one will pay attention to a few short-lived blemishes.

RAPID GROWTH. Adolescence has often been called "the awkward age." During early adolescence, many young people do seem to spend a lot of time tripping on stairs or knocking over glasses at the dinner table. Psychologists explain that their sudden growth spurt outdistances the muscle coordination needed to handle longer arms and legs. Muscle strength also increases dramatically, almost doubling between preadolescence and late adolescence. The time lag between developing full body size and strength and achieving full neuromuscular control may last as long as 12 months. Boys usually run into greater problems with awkwardness, probably because their height and weight increases are almost double those of girls.

Like acne, awkwardness often arrives just when the adolescent wants to make the best possible impression on others. Even though no one laughs at acne, most people seem to find great amusement in watching a teenager spill the peas after misjudging the distance from serving dish to plate. The laughter and jokes may not be meant to hurt, but they do. Psychologists offer no cure for the problem except to recommend that adolescents develop a sense of humor—and patience. In this case, practice does make perfect.

EARLY OR LATE MATURATION. In the seventh grade, Greg was a well-adjusted, happy youngster. Although a few of his classmates had begun to show signs of physical maturation, he still fit in with most of his friends. But when he reached the tenth grade and still looked like a little kid, Greg began to feel desperate. Taller, stronger boys teased him, and the girls either ignored him or laughed at him. Like many other boys going through the same problem, Greg defended himself by becoming more aggressive. He became a discipline problem at school and at home. If there was trouble, he was usually at the center of it.

Sara, on the other hand, reached puberty earlier than the rest of her classmates. She began menstruating at ten, and the changes

" HI, FELLAS,... WANTA GO DOWN TO THE PARK AN' KNOCK THE OL' BALL AROUND ?"

FIGURE 5.4

in her body frightened her. To make matters worse, the other children were aware of her new figure. No matter what she wore, or how carefully she slouched to avoid standing out as the tallest person in her class, Sara couldn't escape their curious glances and cutting remarks.

Adolescents find it difficult to cope with being "different" from their friends. Yet nature's schedule of physical growth always leaves some people outside the "normal" age range for beginning puberty. Greg and Sara would find their out-of-sync growth patterns easier to bear if they could share their feelings with a parent or counselor. In turn, they would be assured that both early and late starters end up exactly where their own genetic blueprints specified they would. In the long run, the age of maturation matters far less than the individual adolescent's ability to handle the emotional challenges that go with growing up.

■ SECTION CHECKUP

1 Describe the basic physical changes that take place when Patty and George reach the age of puberty.

2 How can physical maturation during ado-lescence contribute to the emotional prob-lems of this time period?

3 What advice would you offer to a younger friend who is late in reaching his or her ado-lescent growth spurt?

5.3 ▓ WHAT EMOTIONAL CHALLENGES DOES THE ADOLESCENT FACE?

Perhaps you've heard adults say, "I wouldn't be 16 again for all the gold in the world." Actually, that's not really a put-down. What they mean is that they vividly remember their own adolescence, and they sympathize with those who are still coping with the emotional challenges of growing up. These challenges include learning to deal with sexual matura-tion, coping with restlessness and anxiety, and handling a profound shift in emotional ties.

RESPONDING TO SEXUAL MATURATION

Think for a moment about the last time you relaxed with a group of friends. You proba-bly talked about a dozen or more topics, from football to music and from religion to career plans. It's possible you didn't talk about sex. But you can be sure it was on just about everybody's mind.

Sexual maturation begins during preado-lescence and remains a powerful influence over behavior during the teenage years. All adolescents find that their developing self-image is tied closely to their success in deal-ing with sexual feelings. Because today's society permits people to express their sexu-ality more freely, more adolescents than ever before have become sexually active.

PARENTAL ATTITUDES. Adolescent sexual experimentation arouses resistance on the part of most parents, who prefer that their sons and daughters abstain from sex until they marry. Much of this resistance grows out of two beliefs. First, many adults were raised to believe that premarital sex violates main-stream standards of moral behavior. Second, experience shows that adolescent sex only seems carefree and romantic. All too often, the reality includes *sexually transmitted dis-eases* (STDs) such as AIDS and chlamydia, unwanted pregnancies, and hasty marriages.

Another group of parents communicates negative or mixed messages to their children. In the minds of these parents, sex and drugs seem to be linked. Thus, both are seen as evil. Or these parents may promote a double standard of behavior in which sex is okay for boys but taboo for girls. In the final analysis, almost all parents would prefer that their chil-dren bury their sexual feelings in school, sports, music, scouting, and other energy-consuming activities.

Despite parental hopes and fears, young people do seek out sexual experiences. Rec-ognizing this reality, many skillful and loving parents provide information and reassurance about the physical and emotional "facts of life." In addition, sex-education classes help teenagers learn about sex in a nonjudgmental atmosphere. Perhaps the most important out-come of such classes is that many young peo-ple begin to lose their doubts and fears of being "different." Teenagers who base their decisions about becoming sexually active on

Common Sexually Transmitted Diseases

One statistic is enough to tell the story: doctors treat over ten million Americans for sexually transmitted diseases (STDs) each year. Anyone who is sexually active runs the risk of infection. Because AIDS can also be transmitted by infected needles, drug users who share needles are also at risk. This chart lists only the most common STDs. (M-male; F-female)

STD	SYMPTOMS	TREATMENT	PROGNOSIS
AIDS	Fevers, infections, collapse of auto-immune system (M and F).	Experimental medications slow onset and relieve symptoms.	No known cure. Death results from secondary infections.
HERPES	Painful blisters on genitals and/or around the mouth (M and F).	Acyclovir controls recurrent outbreaks in most patients.	No permanent cure. Agonizing but not fatal.
SYPHILIS	Genital sore shows up in first stage. Later stages bring rashes, sores, hair loss, fever, brain damage. (M and F).	Diagnosed by blood test. Treated with penicillin.	Fatal if not treated. Early diagnosis and treatment offer full recovery.
GONORRHEA	Vaginal discharge (F). Discharge from penis (M). Burning urination (M and F).	Diagnosed by Gramstain test. Treated with penicillin or other antibiotics.	Proper treatment offers full recovery.
CHLAMYDIA	Burning urination (M and F). Discharge from penis (M).	Diagnosed by culture test. Treated with tetracycline and other antibiotics.	Full recovery if treated. Can cause infertility if left untreated.
GENITAL WARTS	Small clusters of warts on or near genitals (M and F). Warts are not visible in many infected persons.	Treated by freezing with liquid nitrogen or removed by laser surgery. Application of podophyllin or trichloracetic acid is an alternate treatment.	Full recovery if all warts are removed. The virus that causes the warts is linked to increased risk of cancer.

For information, contact your local helpline, the STD National Hotline (800-227-8922), or <www.ashastd.org/NSTD/>.

media hype and street wisdom run the risk of scarring themselves for life, both physically and emotionally.

PROBLEMS OF BEING SEXUALLY ACTIVE. Faced with rising divorce statistics, many young adults choose to live together before marriage. In this way, they hope to bypass the mistakes they see their elders making. The most mature of these young men and women see sex as a natural part of a larger love relationship. They believe that sex is not an end in itself but a means of deepening their feelings of affection and shared experience.

At the same time, the statistics show that

increased sexual activity has led to more pregnancies, the rapid spread of STDs, and increased emotional pressure on young people. Teenage pregnancies seldom work out well. All too often they place severe emotional and financial burdens on the young couple. Whether the young couple marries or not, life plans often collapse. If they do marry, the odds against success are dauntingly high.

Because they've heard that most STDs can be cured by antibiotics, some teenagers are tempted to look on infection as a short-term embarrassment. That attitude puts individuals and their sexual partners at great risk. Because guilt often accompanies the embarrassment, people tend to wait too long before asking for help. Only prompt medical care can cure the treatable STDs. Failure to begin the course of treatment in the early days of the disease can lead to more severe symptoms, sterility, and long-term emotional distress.

Medical science has not developed an inoculation to protect against STDs. Because the diseases are spread through sexual contact, the only sure protection against infection is to abstain from sex. For the sexually active, doctors advise (1) a careful choice of partners and (2) the use of condoms. Birth control devices such as diaphragms, jellies, and IUDs offer little or no protection. A healthy life-style keeps the body prepared to fight infection should one occur. Good health is no substitute for medical care, however. Syphilis, for example, is nearly always fatal if left untreated. In the case of AIDS and herpes, researchers have not yet found a cure.

Finally, greater sexual freedom puts pressure on adolescents who are not emotionally ready for intimate relationships. No one truly believes that the typical adolescent is mature enough to cope with the complexities of a sexual relationship. That doesn't keep the media from bombarding young people with an overload of sexually oriented messages. Caught up in this tangle of mixed messages, teenagers tend to follow their instincts—and

sex is a powerful drive. Psychologists can only shake their heads. Growing up, they say, is a full-time job. Becoming sexually active only makes the task more difficult.

RESTLESSNESS AND ANXIETY

Life sometimes seems full of contradictions. Consider Josie. At age 15, Josie's moods swing swiftly and unpredictably from sweet cooperation to angry aggression. She demands more responsibility, then ignores everyday chores and misses her deadlines for getting home at night. Fiercely independent in some things, she wouldn't dream of dressing differently from the other girls in her group. Josie worries a lot about her looks, her boyfriends, her relations with her parents. In short, she's caught up in typical adolescent feelings of restlessness and anxiety.

RESTLESSNESS. Adolescents often find it difficult to achieve inner peace. Boys and girls are driven by a general *restlessness*—a need to be in motion, to be doing several things at the same time. Nervous habits such as foot tapping, gum chewing, or fingernail biting may grow into long-term habits. Josie has lots of company when it comes to experiencing mood swings that send her spirits soaring one minute and plunging into depression the next.

Gradually, as Josie grows in maturity and self-awareness, her restlessness and mood changes will lessen. Ask her high-school teachers, who yearly see the difference between the noisy restlessness of the ninth graders and the more controlled behavior of the seniors. Like so much in adolescence, time usually eases the difficulties brought on by rapid physical and emotional growth.

ANXIETY. Psychologists define *anxieties* as vague fears that a person cannot pin down to a specific cause. Adolescents who fear failure in school, rejection, or loss of status may react to their anxieties by adopting hostile

Categorizing the Adolescent Personality

Despite the infinite variety of the human personality, researchers have discovered that people share certain well-defined personality traits. One study, for example, divides teenagers into four basic personality types. Read the descriptions below and see whether or not you agree. Remember, no one is a pure "type." Idealists sometimes abandon themselves to the Hedonist's quest for pleasure, and there's a touch of the Sociopath in all of us. On balance, where would you place yourself and your friends?

Conventionalists. Conventionalists feel most comfortable when they stay within the legal and moral guidelines established by their families and communities. If they do rebel, their rebellions are usually shortlived. They enjoy good times but look for them in approved athletic and social activities. This is the largest of the four categories.

Idealists. Most teenagers are aware of the injustices that afflict our society. Idealists carry that awareness a step further—they try to do something to help. Idealists march in demonstrations, help the homeless, join volunteer corps, and plan careers in the helping professions. Their passion and commitment often carry Conventionalists with them.

Hedonists. "Let's have some fun!" shout the Hedonists. Anything that stands in the way of pleasure—jobs, homework, family, their own health—takes second place. Consequences don't mean much to Hedonists. All too often, their search for new and more exciting kicks leads them to experiment with drugs and alcohol.

Sociopaths. Although they are often bright and charming, Sociopaths are totally self-centered. They devote themselves to achieving power and pleasure. Because they lack what society calls a conscience, taking advantage of friends or breaking the law troubles them not at all. Luckily, this group is the smallest of the four.

Which description best fits your own sense of who you are? When you slip out of that category, which personality type do you move toward? Self-examination gives you a chance to recognize your positive traits and to change those that feel negative.

The Adolescent Challenge
The Dilemma of Emotional Growth
As interpreted by Anne Frank

This passage is part of the final entry in the diary that Anne Frank kept while she and her family hid from the Nazis during World War II. Thanks to the heroic efforts of their non-Jewish friends, the Franks survived in their Amsterdam hide-away from 1942 until the Gestapo arrested them in 1944. The 15-year-old died a year later in the Bergen-Belsen concentration camp, only three weeks before the camp was liberated. If you want to read more of Anne's story, look for *Anne Frank: The Diary of a Young Girl* at your library. You can also see Anne's ordeal brought to life in a 1959 film, *The Diary of Anne Frank.*

Tuesday, 1 August, 1944

Dear Kitty,

"Little bundle of contradictions." That's how I ended my last letter and that's how I'm going to begin this one. . . .

I've already told you before that I have, as it were, a dual personality. One half embodies my exuberant cheerfulness, making fun of everything, my high-spiritedness, and above all, the way I take everything lightly. This includes not taking offense at a flirtation, a kiss, an embrace, a dirty joke. This side is usually lying in wait and pushes away the other, which is much better, deeper and purer. You must realize that no one knows Anne's better side and that's why most people find me so insufferable.

Certainly I'm a giddy clown for one afternoon, but then everyone's had enough of me for another month. Really, it's just the same as a love film is for deep-thinking people, simply a diversion, amusing just for once, something which is soon forgotten, . . . My lighter super-ficial side will always be too quick for the deeper side of me and that's why it will always win. You can't imagine how often I've already tried to push this Anne away, to cripple her, to hide her, because after all, she's only half of what's called Anne, but it doesn't work. . . .

behaviors. By directing their built-up feelings against parents, school, or other teenagers, they may find temporary relief from inner pressures. Anxious about her ability to attract a boyfriend, Josie may become a truant or turn to drug use. Other adolescents may take refuge in day dreaming, or they may put on a swaggering, tough-guy mask to hide their inner worries. A few may become physically ill, their symptoms caused by psychological stress rather than disease.

If Josie talked to a counselor, she might gain enough self-understanding to overcome her anxieties. With professional help, she would learn that most girls share her doubts. Her anxieties wouldn't disappear overnight, but if she is basically healthy, she will gradually work out a productive solution. To her surprise, Josie will discover that when she stops worrying about boys and turns to other interests, her heightened sense of inner peace will attract new friends—of both sexes!

SHIFTING EMOTIONAL TIES

"What's wrong with adults is that they knew us as children!" This statement by a teenage girl summarizes the dilemma of many young people. They see themselves as "new" people, unfairly tied by their families to a childhood long since outgrown. Because parents represent a constant reminder of those early years, some adolescents delight in challenging, shocking, or ignoring their parents. "With parents like mine," they seem to be saying, "this is the only way we'll ever be truly free to grow."

Carl, for example, knows that his parents are skeptical about the value of organized religion. By joining the Methodist Youth Fellowship, he distances himself from his family while also gaining a supportive new group of friends. Secure within this circle, Carl has time to reexamine his own values and beliefs. Ironically, even as he proclaims his independence, he continues to adjust his tastes in clothes, music, and hairstyles to match those of his school's "in" group. Parents, for their part, often feel that their teenage children embrace any new idea, from a dance craze to career plans, simply as a way of expressing contempt for adult values. This disagreement is often referred to as the *generation gap*—the difference of viewpoint that separates parents from their children (see Figure 5.5).

Adolescents also feel frustrated by another set of conflicting statements: "You're too young to do *this*," they're told. But the next minute someone says, "Grow up! You're too old for *that*." Young people rightfully resent such a muddled definition of their status. Wise parents give their teenage children gradually increasing amounts of trust and responsibility. Family councils meet to decide curfew hours, television viewing versus homework obligations, rules for the use of the family car, and other matters.

What can Carl do, for example, when his father vetoes his decision to take an after-school job? He can get angry, or he can beg. But that isn't very adult, is it? If Carl wants to be treated as an adult, his first job is to behave like one. Instead of giving way to anger or tears, he might try bargaining. "Let me try the job for a month," he could say quietly, using his adult voice. "You be the judge of whether I'm keeping up my responsibilities at school and here at home. If it doesn't work, I'll take responsibility for my failure."

Who knows? Carl might win with that sort of approach.

■ SECTION CHECKUP

1 Describe some of the emotional challenges faced by a typical adolescent.

2 Why is sexual maturation so difficult for most adolescents to handle?

3 What do you think parents can do to help their teenage children overcome the anxieties that go with adolescence?

CATHY   **by Cathy Guisewite**

FIGURE 5.5

5.4 ■ WHAT ARE THE DEVELOPMENTAL TASKS OF ADOLESCENCE THAT RELATE TO THE SELF?

Have you ever tried out for an athletic team or a part in a school play? If you were serious about your effort, you probably asked yourself a few questions: Am I physically ready to do this? Am I mentally prepared to cope with this challenge? Can I handle the emotional involvement? If you answered "yes" to all of those questions, you probably went ahead with the tryout. In a very real sense, you had developed in mind and body to the point where you were ready for a new challenge.

Before you can "try out" for adulthood, you must complete a number of what psychologists call *developmental tasks*. These tasks, completed successfully, are signs of your continuing maturation. Some developmental tasks involve the way you relate to yourself; others involve the way you relate to other people. In this section, you will find out about the developmental tasks that relate to the self.

TO ACCEPT THE REALITY OF YOUR PHYSICAL APPEARANCE

Adolescents often hear people say that "looks aren't all that important." But they look around them at the idealized body image promoted by the media, and they know that's not true. As children, they could still believe in the legend of the ugly duckling who turned into a beautiful swan. By middle adolescence, however, most young people realize that they will never be models or movie stars.

Some teenagers overcome their own negative feelings about their looks by achieving success in school, sports, or work. Others try too hard to compensate for their feelings of inadequacy. Quiet little Tracy startled her parents and friends by adopting the multicolored hairstyle of her favorite rap group. Desperate for attention, she put on a loud, swaggering manner quite at odds with her earlier self. A third group of adolescents may turn inward when they cannot come to terms with their body image. Shy and uncertain of their desirability, they often become withdrawn and depressed.

Plastic surgery may be helpful in remedying serious defects such as an unsightly scar, but most adolescents discover that heroic measures really aren't necessary. Sixteen-year-old Kim, for example, wasn't happy with her appearance. She hated her glasses, her chubby figure, and her straight black hair. She was a good student, but that didn't satisfy her desire for a more active social life. Finally, after talking to her parents about her feelings, she started a program of self-improvement. A new, shorter hairstyle accented her good bone structure. After exchanging her horn-rimmed glasses for contact lenses, she took up jogging and went on a diet suggested by her doctor. As the pounds dropped off, she bought a few stylish outfits. Then, buoyed by a renewed sense of self-confidence, Kim set out to make some new friends. As you might guess, her social life improved dramatically.

Was there any miracle in what Kim did? Of course not. If she hadn't been a basically likable person, the changes she made in her appearance wouldn't have accomplished very much. But by coming to terms with the reality of her looks, she was able to develop the self-confidence she needed to take chances in her relationships with others. In the long run, it was the attractive personality inside that really counted.

TO ACHIEVE IMPULSE CONTROL

Do you ignore the alarm clock when it rings? Do you make up excuses to escape those ever-present jobs around the house? If your answer is "yes," you've got plenty of company. No one—adult or adolescent—truly enjoys routine, repetitive work. The difference is that mature men and women have learned to forego pleasure when there's work to be done.

In U.S. society, adolescence is the time during which young people complete the task of socialization. As you approach adulthood, you are expected to develop what psychologists call *impulse control*. This means that you give up the childish insistence on having your needs and desires gratified instantly. You learn to defer the immediate pleasure of staying in bed for the longer-range pleasure of good marks in school or the paycheck that comes with your early-morning job.

Learning impulse control isn't easy. Many adolescents become impatient when the world does not respond to their wishes. They feel locked into an artificial world of school and family that seems far removed from "real" life. In time, however, most young people learn to exercise control over the impulse to strike out at what they don't like or to grab what pleases them. Those who don't learn this lesson as adolescents soon discover that the adult world has little patience with people who can't postpone their pleasures.

TO PREPARE FOR ECONOMIC INDEPENDENCE

Not too many generations ago, children usually followed in their parents' footsteps when they selected a vocation. Most boys went into business, industry, or the professions. Most girls settled down as wives and mothers. In the second half of this century, a number of factors have changed that limiting choice of careers.

1. Many parents no longer demand that their children follow in the family tradition. Today's young people tend to choose occupations that meet their own interests and needs, rather than those that fulfill family expectations.

2. Economists prophesy that at least half

BERRY'S WORLD By Jim Berry

BERRY'S WORLD reprinted by permission of NEA, Inc.

FIGURE 5.6

the jobs people will be working at ten years from now do not exist at the present time. Increased technology demands more specialized skills and decreases the number of low-skill, manual labor jobs. Employers are responding by providing on-the-job training courses. If new workers possess basic reading, writing, math, and computer skills, they say, the company will teach them the rest. Job applicants may be asked to take tests that measure aptitudes, skills, and personality. Managers know that honesty and the ability to work with others are just as important as highly developed technical skills.

3. With more time to grow up and study the world of work, many young people feel confused as to the vocation they want to pursue. On the one hand, they want jobs that pay well enough to support a comfortable way of life. On the other hand, they also demand jobs that give them a feeling of inner satisfaction. Unfortunately, jobs that meet both of these criteria are in short supply.

4. The old certainty that a degree from a

liberal arts college automatically opens the door to a well-paid, satisfying career no longer holds true. Magazines, newspapers, and television often report on Ph.D.'s who tend bar or work in heavy construction. As a result, parents and students are demanding that high schools and colleges teach skills that can be converted into jobs upon graduation. The civil rights and feminist movements have opened up new career opportunities to minorities and women. Equal opportunity and equal pay for equal work have been added to the legal and social foundations of U.S. society. Teenage girls, for example, can now aspire to be astronauts and engineers. Perhaps their grandmothers dreamed that Mr. Right would sweep them off their feet and carry them away to live in a vine-covered cottage. Today's young women often delay marriage and children to pursue well-paid, satisfying careers.

School and community agencies provide vocational counseling that can help young people connect the three corners of the career triangle: abilities, training, and job opportunities. You might have friends, however, who dropped out of school to take the first full-time job that came along. The lure of a quick paycheck that can be turned into a car, apartment, or expensive stereo often leads to boring, dead-end jobs. If you're willing to stay in school, you can use the insight provided by your counselors and the training provided by your teachers to begin preparing yourself for a satisfying, financially rewarding career.

TO DEVELOP A NEW CONCEPT OF SELF

Psychologist Erik Erikson believed that the single most important task any human being must face is that of achieving a clear sense of personal identity. He stressed that success in the tasks of adult life, such as building a career and achieving intimacy with friends, depends in large part upon completing the search for identity during adolescence.

To achieve *self-identity* means to adopt goals and values that will allow you to make good decisions about your life. You'll make some of these decisions consciously, others unconsciously. Your age, sex, ethnic background, religious training, school experiences, family goals, and personal values will all play a part in your choices. Developing a sense of pride and confidence in yourself is also part of self-identity. That feeling—what psychologists call self-worth—is a measure of your success in reaching the goals you set for yourself. People who lack self-worth tend to let others make their life decisions for them.

Another difficulty in achieving self-identity comes, surprisingly enough, from the "freedom to be" that most Americans enjoy. You can go practically anywhere and do practically anything. If you wish, you can join the Navy, learn karate, or apply to law school. Faced with so many choices, some young people become paralyzed. They fear that a single wrong decision will destroy their chances for future happiness. Psychologists are quick to point out, however, that life is made up of many choices. Some matter more than others. Life-shaping decisions should be made only after you've carefully evaluated all the factors involved. But if you do make a mistake, you can always correct it. The only person who can truly lock you into a bad choice . . . is *you.*

■ SECTION CHECKUP

I What does the psychologist mean by "developmental tasks"? Discuss the importance of the four developmental tasks that apply to the self.

2 Why would it be a mistake for a parent to tell a child, "Don't worry, dear. When you grow up you'll be even better looking than a movie star"?

3 Explain what Erikson meant by "achieving a clear sense of personal identity." Why is it so hard to do?

FIGURE 5.7 ▪ Cartoon by Jules Feiffer

5.5 ▪ WHAT ARE THE DEVELOPMENTAL TASKS OF ADOLESCENCE THAT RELATE TO OTHERS?

Most adolescents must grow and find their self-identity within the borders of their own communities. To do so requires that they add developmental tasks related to the people around them to those related to the self.

TO ACHIEVE EMOTIONAL INDEPENDENCE FROM THE FAMILY

True emotional independence comes only when adolescents and their families work to-

You Can't Make Anyone Love You

Psychologist-author Sheldon Kopp sat down one day to write a letter to a friend. What came out, he says, was "a visionary list of the truths that at my best shape my life." These are some of the things he wrote:

1 There is no way of getting all you want.

2 You can't have anything unless you let go of it.

3 You can't make anyone love you.

4 Everyone lies, cheats, pretends (yes, you too, and most certainly I myself).

5 Love is not enough, but it sure helps.

6 You are free to do whatever you like. You need only face the consequences.

7 We have only ourselves, and one another. That may not be much, but that's all there is.

Do any of Kopp's ideas match up with your own experiences? Can you use any of them to help shape your own sense of who you are and what you want out of life?

From *No Hidden Meanings,* by Sheldon Kopp. Palo Alto, California. Science & Behavior Books Inc., 1975.

---

gether to untie the bonds that have held them together. Because stressful parent-adolescent relationships sometimes cut off lines of communication, mutual cooperation may be difficult to achieve. Even if Neal R. packs his bags and runs a thousand miles away, the old emotional ties will still bind him. Growing up in his family left Neal with a heavy load of unfinished business. Before he can be truly free, he must take care of old debts and guilts, speak openly about his feelings, and listen to what his parents have to say. Some families make a ceremony of this, clearing the air by exchanging feelings in open, honest discussion. When the sons and daughters leave home, the parents give them a key to the house as a symbol of their right to return at any time, no questions asked.

Even in a stable, loving family, the adolescent's path to emotional independence is seldom smooth and untroubled. The transition is often complicated by the fact that young people and their parents approach the task with sharply contrasting points of view.

ADOLESCENT VIEWS. For most adolescents, the struggle with parents can be summed up in a single word: *independence*! Issues that are minor in themselves may lead to major battles when parental orders run counter to the young person's wishes. You've probably gone through debates over clothes, curfew hours, choice of friends, use of alcohol or drugs, tastes in music, or driving the family car. As adolescents mature, parents should give them progressively greater freedom and responsibility to make their own choices. A parent who exercises overly strict control in such matters runs the risk of touching off a rebellion. By the same token, permissive parents who set few limits run the risk of leaving their children with the conviction that Mom and Dad don't really care what happens to them.

More complex emotions also enter into parent-adolescent relations. Young people often experience vague guilt feelings about leaving the family circle. Rhonda may know, for example, that her parents want her to celebrate the Fourth of July at home in the traditional way. But she also knows that Shauna is planning a great party—and all of her friends will be there. To resolve the conflict, teenagers often attack the family's values, magnifying their faults as a means of justifying their own decisions. Thus, Rhonda will justify going to Shauna's party by saying to her parents, "These family picnics are really dull! You just want me to stay around home so I won't have fun with my friends."

In time, adolescents learn to see their parents in a more objective light. For many, this moment may not come until they reach adulthood. With maturity comes an appreciation of the positive contributions the family made to their growth. Even the parental faults that touched off an adolescent fury will be seen as forgivable. Mark Twain, creator of Tom Sawyer and Huckleberry Finn, summed it up when he wrote, "When I was fourteen, I wondered how a man like my father could be so dumb and still live. When I was twenty-one, I was amazed at how much the man had learned in seven years!"

PARENTS' VIEWS.   Many parents see adolescence as a long period of obnoxious behavior by the same children who only a few years earlier were sleeping contentedly in their arms. Even though they sincerely want to help their children achieve adult independence, they also want to protect them from pain and disappointment. Mr. Rose, for example, remembers the trouble he got into as a young driver when he smashed up the family car. So it's little wonder that he holds back on giving his son Bob permission to use the family car for a Saturday night date.

Many parents also experience unconscious emotions that keep them from giving independence to their children, even though the independence has been earned. Both Mom and Dad may unconsciously fear the "empty-nest syndrome," that sense of loss that follows when the last child has left home. Parents whose lives are filled with hard work

and worries may also unconsciously envy the apparently carefree existence of their adolescent children. Finally, watching their children move into adulthood tells the parents that they, too, are growing older. Middle-aged men and women can no longer pass for "almost 30" when a son or daughter is claiming adult privileges.

TO COPE WITH GROUP PRESSURES

"Everyone else is doing it, Sammy."

"Come on, Sue, don't be chicken!"

How many times have you heard similar statements from your friends? Or how do you feel if your *A* on the test draws a chorus of sarcastic comments from the rest of the class?

This type of peer pressure makes the search for self-identity even more difficult. Despite such conflicts, many courageous young people hold fast to the values they have gained from their family, their religion, and their own personal philosophy. In keeping with the teachings of her church, Nadia would never drink beer at a party. But Sophia, whose own religion has equally clear rules, may "go along" with the group in order to save face. Her feelings of guilt, however, will make it difficult for her to enjoy her hard-won popularity. That Sophia would continue to give in to peer pressure despite her discomfort demonstrates the powerful need adolescents have for approval from their peer group.

If you want to avoid being caught in this type of bind, take a careful look at the peer groups you join. Groups such as Explorer Scouts, church youth groups, community orchestras, and the like, generally are predictable. You know ahead of time exactly what you're getting into. But choosing a group of friends opens up other possibilities. Delinquency, for example, frequently grows out of peer-group associations. In a study of two matched groups from inner-city neighborhoods, researchers discovered that 98.4 percent of the delinquents ran around with other

FIGURE 5.8 ■ Like many teenagers, the members of this study group spend more time with their friends than with their families. Driven by their need for acceptance, teens with low self-esteem sometimes allow peer group values to override the values taught by their parents, schools, and churches. With added maturity, most will learn that true friends contribute to their social and emotional growth instead of hindering it.

delinquents. Only 7.4 percent of the nondelinquents who lived in the same neighborhood had friends among the trouble-prone youths.

Nevertheless, psychologists encourage you to spend time with your peers. Growing up, after all, requires that you spend more time with your friends and less with your family. The trick is to find those true friends with whom you can share your deepest thoughts and feelings. These are the people who accept you for the person you are. They don't try to change you, nor do they measure friendship in money or willingness to go along with the "gang." When you do find that

sort of friendship, it will lead to some of the most rewarding experiences of your life.

No matter how carefully you choose your friends, peer pressure is a fact of teenage life. The pressure is easier to resist if you have some strategies worked out ahead of time.

1. If your values are a little shaky, take some time to think them through. Peer pressure doesn't upset people who know who they are.

2. When faced with a choice that goes against your values, remember that you have the right to say, "No." You don't need to ex-

plain your reasons unless you feel comfortable in doing so.

3. Most young people worry that refusing to go along with their friends will cost them their place in the group. Be prepared for those fears. In the long run, your own self-approval is more important than the temporary approval of the group.

4. Form an alliance within your peer group of friends who share your values. By agreeing to support each other, you'll greatly reduce the effect of group pressure on each individual.

5. If your peer group persists in pressuring you, it may be time to make some new friends. True friends respect your individuality— your specialness.

■ SECTION CHECKUP

1 What are the developmental tasks of adolescence that relate to others?

2 Why do psychologists say that you can achieve emotional independence from your family only when you all cooperate to untie the bonds that hold you together?

3 What are some of the unconscious feelings that cause parents to hold on too tightly to their children?

4 Despite the possible dangers of giving in to peer pressures, why would it be unwise for 16-year-old Bill to refuse to join any peer group?

5.6 ▓ WHAT SPECIAL PROBLEMS DO ADOLESCENTS FACE TODAY?

Adolescence has never been an easy period for either parents or young people. A clay tablet from the ancient Fertile Crescent civilization of Sumer records the words of a father: "Why do you idle about? Perverse one with whom I am furious . . . Night and day am I tortured because of you. Night and day you waste in pleasures."

Today, 4,000 years later, the possibilities for mistakes and self-destructive behavior seem greater than ever before. Today's adolescent faces problems that make growing up both difficult and challenging. Some of the most critical of these problems are early marriage, unwanted pregnancy, use of drugs or alcohol, and delinquency.

EARLY MARRIAGE

With all the experiments in living together that have marked changing sexual patterns in the United States, you might wonder if anyone is getting married these days. In fact, large numbers of young people still fall in love and decide to marry. Even though studies show that teenage marriages often fail, very few couples would admit that the low odds apply to *their* marriages.

Even when a teenage marriage does not end in divorce, young couples face problems that include (1) interrupted or incomplete educations; (2) financial hardships caused by low salaries and soaring costs; (3) limited recreational opportunities (there never seems to be enough time or money for having fun); and (4) the likelihood that the husband and wife will grow apart as their adult personalities develop.

UNWANTED PREGNANCIES

Strangely enough, at a time when sex education and contraceptives are more available than ever before, more unmarried teenage

Do Many of the Problems of Adolescence Result From the Breakup of the Traditional Family?

Since the turn of the century, some psychologists have described adolescence as a natural time of "storm and stress." Others, however, believe that the problems of adolescence reflect changing social conditions. Many stresses of adolescence, they charge, lie in the breakup of the traditional U.S. family. The following arguments will give you a chance to make up your own mind about this debate.

PRO

1 Divorce, child abuse, drug addiction, and poverty are only four of the ills that menace the U.S. family. Each disrupts home life and threatens the emotional and physical health of children caught up in the resulting chaos.

2 Children raised in broken homes seldom receive sufficient nurturing. During adolescence, this neglect can lead to anti-social behavior. Indeed, self-destructive acts by teenagers can almost always be seen as demands for parental attention. Parents who really care spend time with their children.

3 Juvenile violence is increasing at an alarming rate. Some experts say that the current epidemic of gang-related violence is closely related to family breakup and to the loss of community values. A society that claims to love its children cannot afford to ignore this connection.

4 Teenagers who grow up in broken homes are often left without parental guidance. Left to find their own way, these young people are more likely to drop out of school, use drugs, join gangs, and commit crimes.

5 Even in intact families, busy schedules have turned many homes into dormitories where family members meet only to eat and sleep. Americans also give young people a negative message when they segregate themselves by age. Adolescents who seldom meet older people tend to adopt the values favored by the youth culture.

CON

1 Family life goes on, regardless of headlines. Most children grow up in healthy families. Even when both parents work and even though Mom or Dad is a stepparent, children survive. Social agencies intervene to protect the helpless.

2 Being raised by one's biological parents does not guarantee proper nurturing. Children can—and do—grow up healthy in many different family arrangements. Where family life has been disrupted, parents protect children by hiring competent caregivers. Quality of care, not quantity, determines adolescent stability.

3 The media spotlight juvenile crime but overlook the vast majority of law-abiding teenagers. Older adults tend to forget that yesterday's "pranks" are often defined as crimes today. Where teenage gangs are out of control, the police must protect the community. At the same time, social agencies must attack the root causes of violent behavior.

4 The fact that adolescents seek friends who share their values is a normal part of growing up. When society solves problems such as poverty and discrimination, teenagers will have a better chance to grow up to be productive adults.

5 Age segregation, if it does exist, is neither good nor bad. Social change happens; societies accept the change or reject it. The U.S. life-style that is emerging as the new century begins has many positive virtues. Social scientists are already finding a renewed emphasis on family togetherness and responsibility.

What evidence have you seen in your own family or neighborhood to confirm or deny these arguments? What advice would you offer to the parents of an 11-year-old about guiding their child through the adolescent years?

girls are becoming pregnant. Experts number such pregnancies at half a million each year—many to girls as young as 13 and 14. Those figures suggest that many adolescents have not been learning the "facts of life" as thoroughly as they should.

What are the facts of life that are being overlooked? One is the mistaken idea that sex is permissible and enjoyable only if it is done on the spur of the moment—which usually means without contraception. That wonderful "romantic" evening all too often leads to an unwanted pregnancy. Pregnancies also result from abuse of alcohol and drugs. With their inhibitions lowered, girls are more likely to agree to an unwise sexual encounter. Finally, some girls allow themselves to become

pregnant in the belief that a baby will provide the love that's missing from their lives. By the time they realize that babies take far more than they give, it is too late.

Psychologists urge adolescents to make mature decisions about their sexuality. Unwanted pregnancies create emotional consequences for all concerned. Abortion may be an option for some young women, but even successful abortions carry an emotional price tag. Many women report feelings of guilt and lowered self-esteem after having an abortion. Those young women who decide to give birth are usually ill-equipped emotionally and financially to take on the responsibility of raising a child. Teenage mothers often must choose between dropping out of school and

Erich Fromm on "The Art of Loving"

Erich Fromm (1900–1980), one of this century's most respected psychologists, believes that love is an art. Like all worthwhile achievements, people will experience true love relationships only when they learn how to love, Fromm tells us. First, one must master the theory; later, one can gain mastery through practice—much as an artist learns to paint or a woodworker to build beautiful furniture.

Why do so few people learn this art? Fromm suggests that we don't believe that love is important enough:

> In spite of the deep-scated craving for love, almost everything else is considered to be more important than love: success, prestige, money, power—almost all our energy is used for the learning of how to achieve these aims, and almost none to learn the art of loving.

How do we know when we are truly and rightly in love? Listen to these words:

Susan Lapides, Design Conceptions

If I truly love one person I love all persons, I love the world, I love life. If I can say to somebody else, "I love you," I must be able to say, "I love in you everybody, I love through you the world, I love in you also myself."

Erich Fromm, *The Art of Loving* (New York: Harper & Row, 1956).

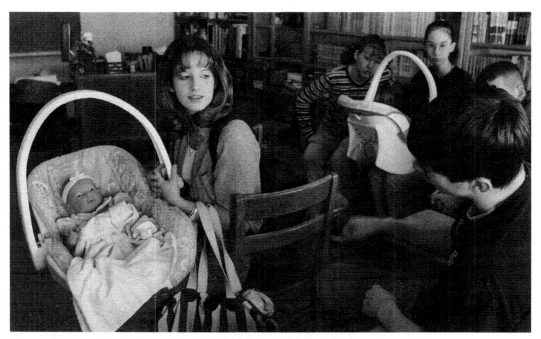

FIGURE 5.9 ■ The burden of full-time parenting is especially hard on teenagers, most of whom are still searching for their own identities. Students in this high school class are enrolled in a program called "Baby Think It Over," which uses battery-powered "babies" to drive home the hard fact that parenting calls for endless amounts of love and patience. Each "baby" is programmed to cry at random intervals, 24 hours a day. The "parental" response is monitored by electronic sensors that report instances of neglect or rough handling.

giving up their baby for adoption. Others are pressured into marriages that have little chance of success. Grandparents who thought their child raising days were over find themselves pressed into service as unpaid babysitters or as full-time foster parents.

DRUGS AND ALCOHOL

Americans are hooked on drugs. They live in what social scientists refer to as a *drug culture.*

You don't believe it? Remember that many drugs are substances that change behavior or create an altered state of consciousness. Then take a look around your own house. You'll probably find several of the following: diet pills, cold medications, tonics, pep pills, tranquilizers, sleeping pills, pain killers, liquor and beer, soft drinks and coffee (caffeine), and tobacco. Experts say the only surprise is that so many adolescents do *not* get hooked on drugs.

To be fair, most drugs are both helpful and benign. There's not much danger in starting the morning with a cup of coffee or in treating a headache with an aspirin. The danger comes when anyone—child, adolescent, or adult—deliberately uses reality-altering drugs to "get high." Thanks to a heavy-duty educational campaign, most people know that using narcotics and alcohol can lead to physical addiction. But many young people who would never experiment with hard drugs have developed psychological dependencies. A *psychological dependency* leaves users with an overwhelming sense of anxiety that can only be relieved by taking their drug of choice.

Long-term dependence on beer—or marijuana, or any other "soft" drug—can create a psychological addiction. The world may look better through a drug-induced high, but a temporary escape from reality only postpones life's problems. A few of the costs of such addiction are easy to spot: auto accidents, unwanted pregnancies, senseless crimes. Less easy to see, however, is the loss to society of people whose psychological dependence on drugs or alcohol leads them to "drop out" of school and careers. These people often drift into self-limiting nonproductive lives. A further negative attitude often develops among adolescents, for whom even the purchase of alcohol and tobacco is illegal. These young people may develop a disrespect for the law that can lead to more serious delinquency.

Psychologists look on the use of drugs and alcohol as psychological "crutches." They believe that dependence on any reality-altering substance denies the individual the chance to live fully and productively. Emotionally healthy people of any age, they insist, can live satisfying lives without hiding behind the blurred perceptions and relaxed inhibitions of stimulants, depressants, or hallucinogens.

DELINQUENCY

Headlines like these have become commonplace: JUVENILES VANDALIZE LOCAL SCHOOL. TWO TEENAGERS KILLED IN DRIVE-BY GANG SHOOTING. YOUNG THIEF MUGS PREGNANT MOTHER OF THREE. The youthful law-breakers featured in these reports are often called *delinquents*: those who violate laws, disobey authority, or behave in ways that endanger the safety or morals of the community. Juvenile delin-

quency is nothing new, however. Aristotle, writing over 2,000 years ago, complained that Greek youth "are in character prone to desire and ready to carry any desire they may have formed into action."

Psychologists believe that much delinquency grows out of the adolescent need to rebel against the restrictions of the adult world. Such rebellion in earlier times usually took the form of pranks, such as tipping over outhouses or hoisting a cow to the courthouse roof. Then, as now, some young people simply ran away from home. But the increase in more serious teenage crimes—muggings, burglaries, rape, car theft, vandalism, and assault with deadly weapons—is alarming. Many adults now feel that the courts should punish youthful criminals with the same sentences given adult offenders.

CAUSES OF DELINQUENCY. Delinquency is not restricted to the United States, nor is it to be found only in large cities. Studies of the problem have identified a number of possible causes for increased juvenile crime.

1. Parents no longer exercise the same supervision and control of their children that they once did. Working or divorced parents have less time to spend with their children, who sometimes turn delinquent as a way of saying, "Hey! Pay attention to me!"

2. For many inner-city youth, inadequate schools and high unemployment rates cause anger and despair. Without hope for the future, they turn to delinquency as a release for their frustrations.

3. Similarly, many communities provide few recreational facilities for youth. Left with nothing to do, teenagers may turn to delinquency just for "kicks."

4. Budget shortfalls and the press of drug-related crime have cut into the ability of the police, the courts, and the social service agencies to develop effective juvenile diversion programs. Moreover, delinquents are not treated equally throughout the country. In

FIGURE 5.10 ▪ One alternative to prison is a "boot camp" for young offenders who have not committed violent crimes. Usually run in a military-like fashion, boot camps teach self-discipline as well as work and education skills. Not everyone thinks that boot camps work. Critics charge that the real lesson taught at a boot camp is that "the loudest and meanest wins."

one state, a 14-year-old may be sent to prison for the same offense that leads to probation in a neighboring state. All too often, teenagers emerge from underfunded juvenile detention facilities better prepared for a life of crime than for a life as productive, law-abiding citizens.

5. The drug culture breeds its own delinquency. Hooked on expensive drugs, young people may turn to theft, prostitution, and other crimes to support their habits. On the other side of the equation, the lure of easy money has led youth gangs into drug trafficking.

6. World problems such as inflation, the threat of war, distrust of politicians, and worry about the environment cause many young people to drop out of the "straight" culture. Without hope for the future, they find it easy to distrust the adult world. Some of these alienated young people put their energy into changing the society, at times through radical or violent means. Others let their self-contempt, pessimism, and distrust of adult institutions lead them to drugs, vandalism, and crime.

TREATMENT FOR DELINQUENCY. Most treatments for delinquency have had only limited success. The law generally treats juveniles with greater leniency than it does adults. This "soft" approach has frequently returned young criminals to the streets without effectively changing their behavior. Fifteen-year-old Rod, for example, has been to court seven times for various juvenile offenses. Each time, he has received probation and has been returned to the custody of his parents. But the forces that make Rod a potentially dangerous criminal never change. Rod's father is still unemployed, and Rod still finds school totally alien to his needs.

Would a detention home, reform school, or an adult prison change Rod's behavior? These costly, harsher punishments do not seem to work much better than Rod's merry-go-round on probation. The only thing that had an effect on Rod was his visit to a local prison. There, he and some of his friends listened to the inmates tell about prison life. Their language was so tough and graphic that Rod has stayed out of trouble ever since.

Another hopeful experiment has taken place in Sweden. There, delinquents and their families gather on a remote island for a period of intensive counseling. The Swedish psychologists believe that delinquent behavior is a family responsibility. Until the entire family works together on the problem, they say, the delinquent's behavior will probably not change.

In the long run, adolescents will always have extra energy to invest. Perhaps one cure for delinquency will be programs that focus on positive uses for this energy and idealism. For convicted delinquents, state-run "boot camps" that combine remedial classes with strenuous outdoor work (building campgrounds, cutting fire trails, and the like) show some promise. Summer work and sports programs that "get kids off the streets" have been helpful in cooling off the inner cities. In the final analysis, only when parents, teachers, politicians, business leaders, and police officers combine to create positive outlets for adolescent energies will we find a cure for the costly ill called juvenile delinquency.

▩ SECTION CHECKUP

1 Why do psychologists believe that a teenage marriage has a poor chance for success?

2 Explain what is meant by a "psychological addiction."

3 How would you explain the high rate of juvenile crime in the United States today? What can be done to change this pattern?

LOOKING BACK: A SUMMARY

1 Adolescence is the period of growth and maturation that modern Western societies have defined as the years from about 12 to 18. During three stages—preadolescence (10–14 for girls and 12–15 for boys), adolescence (15–18), and young adulthood (18–25)—young people are expected to gain emotional maturity, achieve independence from parental control, choose and prepare for a career, and achieve self-identity.

2 Psychologists hold two contrasting views of adolescence. The "storm-and-stress" theory sees the mood swings and rebellion of adolescence as necessary to emotional growth. Others believe that adolescence is

stressful only when the adult society tells young people it will be so. Many teenagers, in fact, do live through the adolescent years without significant difficulty.

3 Physically, adolescents grow from children into adults within four to six years. Their height and weight change dramatically, and so do bodily proportions. Perhaps most notable of all, boys and girls develop the sexual characteristics of men and women. Physical appearance becomes critically important to adolescents, who must also cope with problems of acne, rapid growth, and the possibility of maturing earlier or later than their friends.

4 Emotionally, adolescents face the problem of coping with sexual maturation. Even though society permits young people to express their sexuality more freely than ever, unwanted pregnancies, STDs, and the difficulty of coping with powerful sex drives still make this adjustment difficult. Adolescents must also cope with feelings of restlessness and anxiety. So many changes take place so rapidly that teenagers feel overwhelmed by worries related to popularity, career choice, and relations with parents. Sometimes confused over their status, treated one day as children and the next as adults, adolescents must also begin the process of gaining greater independence from parental control. This process often intensifies what some have called "the generation gap."

5 Psychologists often speak of the developmental tasks of adolescence. These are physical and psychological steps teenagers must take before they can be called mature adults. Tasks that relate to the emotional and mental makeup of young people include (*a*) The need to accept the realities of physical appearance and to make the best of what nature has provided. (*b*) The need to build inner controls that allow the individual to postpone instant gratification of needs and to work for longer-range goals. (*c*) The need to make career choices that will provide economic independence as well as a satisfying way of life. (*d*) The need to achieve a clear sense of personal identity, with values and goals that will guide young people through the tough decisions of adult life.

6 Developmental tasks that relate to other people include (*a*) The need to achieve emotional independence from the family, a step that requires both adolescents and parents to respect each other's feelings. (*b*) The need to act maturely when peer pressures run counter to the individual's own values. These tasks become much more complex when each person's perception of the adolescent's needs comes from a different angle. Parents, for example, see questions of independence differently than do their children.

7 Life in today's rapidly changing society creates new opportunities for the adolescent and new problems as well. Relaxed sexual standards may bring the pressures of unwanted pregnancy and early marriages that too often fail. A drug-oriented culture tempts pleasure-seeking young people to experiment with drugs and alcohol as escapes from reality. Delinquency among adolescents may be seen as a sign of growing social unrest. Normal adolescent feelings of restlessness and rebellion may be compounded by lack of jobs or recreation and despair over social ills. The best cures for delinquency are close-knit families and community groups that direct youthful energy and idealism into positive channels.

PUTTING YOUR KNOWLEDGE TO WORK

■ TERMS YOU SHOULD KNOW

adolescence	generation gap	restlessness
anxiety	impulse control	rites of passage
delinquents	preadolescence	self-identity
developmental tasks	psychological dependency	sexually transmitted diseases (STDs)
drug culture	puberty	young adulthood

■ CHAPTER CHECKUP

1 Which of the following is a *true* statement about adolescence? (*a*) In every culture ever studied, adolescence is a time of rebellion and gradual development toward adulthood. (*b*) Since a 13-year-old and an 18-year-old are both adolescents, both are going through the same physical and emotional changes. (*c*) Because boys generally grow to be larger than girls, their adolescent growth spurt starts earlier. (*d*) The majority of young people pass through adolescence without becoming wildly rebellious or deeply disturbed.

2 Adolescents who have completed puberty generally (*a*) undergo rites of passage at home and in school (*b*) show little change from childish behavior (*c*) experience some emotional problems in learning to cope with their physical growth and development (*d*) take on full adult responsibilities.

3 Which statement is *true* about adolescents who mature later than their classmates? (*a*) Delayed growth can never be made up. (*b*) Professional counseling is always needed. (*c*) Some boys who mature later tend to work out their frustrations by being aggressive and rebellious. (*d*) Late maturation only affects boys.

4 The best way to treat acne is to (*a*) ignore it completely (*b*) look for a miracle cure at the drugstore (*c*) hide until it goes away (*d*) keep the skin clean, use a mild medication, and develop a positive outlook on life.

5 Adolescents often shock their parents with rebellious behavior as a way of (*a*) proving that all adolescents are delinquents (*b*) providing their own rites of passage (*c*) demonstrating that they're not children any longer (*d*) making up for the spankings and punishments of childhood.

6 An example of a decision that shows impulse control instead of instant gratification of desires is to (*a*) quit the tennis squad when you're not made captain (*b*) take a job to pay for car insurance instead of taking the science class you need for graduation (*c*) tell the boss where to get off when she doesn't accept your idea for changing the restaurant's menu (*d*) hold your tongue and get the job done when Granddad fusses at you for not raking the leaves.

7 The search for self-identity by typical adolescents (*a*) can be achieved only when they learn who they are and what they want to do with their lives (*b*) will take care of itself (*c*) requires many years of study (*d*) requires that they cut off contact with their families as soon as possible.

8 Ernest can achieve emotional independence from his parents by (*a*) leaving home (*b*) working toward a mutual acceptance of his growing ability to handle adult responsibilities (*c*) demanding his rights and forcing his parents to admit he's an adult (*d*) staying at home as long as his parents need him.

9 An adolescent with a good sense of personal worth will (*a*) never enjoy peer group activities (*b*) accept parental direction without question (*c*) engage in delinquent behavior, since it's part of growing up (*d*) not violate personal values in order to gain group approval.

10 Teenage marriages often fail because (*a*) the couple cannot cope with financial problems (*b*) one partner or the other feels tied down by the marriage and rebels (*c*) career opportunities are limited by the need to support the family (*d*) all of these reasons help explain the failure of many teenage marriages.

■ EXPLORING CONCEPTS

1 Imagine yourself as the parent of ten-year-old twins who are nearing puberty. What would you say to your son and daughter about the physical changes that lie ahead of them?

2 Why do some adolescents find it difficult to talk to their parents? Can you suggest any methods to make communication more open and more effective?

3 Your friend Newt is really worried about his looks. Why is his physical appearance so important to him at 16? Discuss some of the insights provided by psychology that can help young people like Newt who are worried about their lack of model-perfect looks.

4 One unexpected result of antidrug campaigns has been an increasing number of children and teenagers who report their parents' drug use to authorities. Why do psychologists advise caution when it comes to prosecuting these parents? How do you think such reports should be handled?

5 Explain some of the social and psychological forces that lie behind the nation's rising juvenile crime rate. Do you think this problem can be solved with stricter laws and harsher penalties? Why or why not?

■ HANDS-ON ACTIVITIES

1 Do you have an ongoing disagreement with your parents over an issue such as curfew, choice of friends, or use of the car? A useful technique for dealing with such problems is to hold an imaginary dialogue with the adult involved—mother, father, guardian, whomever. In this dialogue, you take both roles. First, state your case, using your best argument. Then switch roles and imagine how the other person would respond. What are his or her reasons? It will be difficult at first, but as you get into it, the dialogue will begin to flow. By speaking for the other person, you may gain some valuable insights into why he or she takes the position that is making you so angry.

2 As noted in the chapter, this culture does not provide rites of passage for every adolescent. We do have a few occasions to mark movement toward adulthood—the Jewish *bar mitzvah* and *bat mitzvah,* the granting of driving privileges, high-school graduation. Try designing a special ceremony that marks a person's becoming an adult in this society. You might want to include qualifications of age and achievement, testing of newly acquired adult skills, a formal ceremony, and a really great party. Share your ideas with your family and your psychology class.

3 Each generation invents its own version of adolescence, often without paying much attention to the wishes of the adult world. How do your customs, interests, and values compare with those of the significant adults in your life? The best way to find out is to talk with them about their teenage years. Ask them to reminisce about the clothes, hairstyles, foods, and music that were popular when they were teens. How did they feel about school, dating, work, and the like? You'll find that most people enjoy a chance to talk about their teenage experiences—and you may discover that the differences between *now* and *then* aren't as great as they often seem.

4 Psychologists like to challenge people to think about their values—what's important in their lives. Try this exercise yourself and share it with your friends. It's fun to do—and the insights you gain will be worth thinking about.

DESIGN YOUR OWN T-SHIRT

Cut a T-shirt shape out of poster board. Decorate it with any design of words and/or pictures that tells the world what you want to say about yourself *right this minute.*

5 Do you feel as though your life has been settling into a rut? Try a "new experience" experiment for a month. The procedure is simple. Every week, take time to try two new activities that you've never done before. What can you do? The list is endless, but here are some examples: fly a kite, go fishing, take up meditation, eat unfamiliar food (sushi, perhaps?), make a new friend, try a new hairstyle, go blindfolded for a day. Use your own ingenuity. After each experience, write a short description of how you felt about it. At the end of the month, you'll have eight new experiences to add to your list of things you like or don't like (after all, you may not like raw fish!). But more important, you'll have given yourself permission to take chances that can open up your life and give you renewed zest for living.

FOR FURTHER READING

Alpern, Michele, and Marvin Rosen. *Teen Pregnancy.* Broomall, PA: Chelsea House, 2002. This short, nonjudgmental book opens with the statement, "Bad things sometimes happen to good people." Each section features a real-life situation that dramatizes topics ranging from "Sexuality and Birth Control" to "Raising a Child." The authors' bottom-line advice to pregnant teens: Find a reliable support person to turn to for help.

Freed, Alvyn M. *TA for Teens (and Other Important People).* Sacramento, CA: Jalmar Press, 1976. Don't be misled by the age of this book. It is as up-to-date today as it was when it was first published. TA (Transactional Analysis) teaches you how to use this powerful concept as a way of coping with the daily dilemmas of living. Freed's book gives it to you in straightforward, no-nonsense terms, with lots of exercises and activities to make TA both useful and practical.

Hershorn, Dr. Michael. *Cool It! Teen Tips to Keep Hot Tempers from Boiling Over.* Far Hills, NJ: New Horizon Press, 2003. Does your temper keep you from fully enjoying school, sports, or social activities? If so, Dr. Hershorn suggests, you need to cool it! This useful and nonjudgmental book teaches teenagers that anger is a normal, human emotion that can be managed as surely as you manage your diet or your homework. Each section tackles a different aspect of anger in direct, down-to-earth language, and provides exercises that help you practice your newly learned anger management skills.

McCoy, Kathy, and Charles Wibbelsman. *The Teenage Body Book.* New York: Perigee Trade, 1999. This useful "owner's manual" answers questions from teenagers about the physical and emotional changes of adolescence. The authors give sound, nonjudgmental advice on topics as varied as dieting, depression, and dating.

Parks, Gordon. *The Learning Tree.* Greenwich, CT: Fawcett, 1963. The famous black photographer writes about growing up in a small Kansas town. A beautifully written book that speaks to all people, everywhere.

Patnaik, Gayatri, and Michelle Shinseki, eds. *The Secret Life of Teens: Young People Speak Out About Their Lives.* Minneapolis: Sagebrush Education, 2000. The editors, both former teachers, invited teenagers to write to www.bolt.com to tell them about their lives, thoughts, and hopes. Out of the 5,000 submissions that flooded in, Patnaik and Shinseki picked 200 letters that cover such universal topics as friendship, parental divorce, love, religion, substance abuse, and teen sexuality. You'll have to decide whether or not these well-written letters speak for you and your friends.

Shepherd, Jean. *Wanda Hickey's Night of Golden Memories and Other Disasters.* Garden City, NY: Doubleday, 1971. Shepherd's antic imagination recreates his disaster-prone adolescence with perception and comic style.

UNIT III
PERSONALITY DEVELOPMENT

- FREUD'S THEORY OF PERSONALITY
- PERSONALITY THEORY SINCE FREUD

Chapter

6 FREUD'S THEORY OF PERSONALITY

The mysteries of the human personality have fascinated philosophers and scientists since men and women first walked the face of the planet. A lonely girl, for instance, starts out for the supermarket. But without being aware of what she's doing, she drives a mile out of her way and is startled to discover that she has parked in front of her best friend's house. Then there's Rob, who really meant it last night when he said he'd never cut psych class again. . . . Today's he's already left campus, unable to hold to his promise.

Why do people act in ways that don't seem to make sense? Why do they keep on doing things that harm themselves and others? Until Sigmund Freud made his landmark discoveries in the 1890s, no one had a satisfactory answer to these questions. The workings of the personality seemed as mysterious as the far side of the moon.

Freud was a Viennese doctor who specialized in illnesses of the nervous system. As he worked with his patients, he gradually realized that some emotional force they weren't aware of and couldn't control was influencing their behavior. A woman named Anna O., whom Freud never met, helped him find that hidden force.

Freud learned about Anna O. (whose real name was Bertha Pappenheim) from his friend, Dr. Joseph Breuer. Anna's mother had called Dr. Breuer to treat the 21-year-old woman, who was ill and refused to leave her bed. Before her breakdown, Anna had spent six months nursing her dying father. Her symptoms, Breuer discovered, included partial paralysis of her arms and legs, poor vision, some loss of speech and hearing, and a painful cough. Anna also suffered hallucinations in which her father's face appeared to her as a death's head. Over and over, Anna insisted that something was tormenting her.

Breuer was interested in the case of this beautiful, intelligent woman. As was his custom, he tried hypnosis as a means of treating her. Under hypnosis, Anna talked about her passionate fondness for her father. When she spoke of the difficult months of nursing him, she bust into tears, laughed wildly, and flew into terrible rages.

To Breuer's surprise, these emotional sessions led to a remarkable change. Afterward, Anna's mind would be perfectly clear. She would leave her bed and spend hours writing letters to her friends. As Breuer wrote, "It was truly a remarkable contrast: in the daytime

170

the irresponsible patient, pursued by hallucinations, and at night, the girl with her mind completely clear." At the same time, he found that her physical symptoms were also disappearing. Breuer concluded that by revealing her feelings, she was "talking away" the emotions that she had been unable to face during the long nights of caring for her father.

One by one, Anna's symptoms faded as their cause became clear. For example, her vision improved after she described a night when she had been sitting by her father's bed. As she thought about his dying, her eyes had filled with tears. Just at that moment, he asked her to tell him what time it was. Not wanting him to know that she was crying, she ignored her tears. But in order to see her watch, she had to bring it close to her face, squinting as she did so. From that moment on, the squint had become permanent—and it was the squint that caused her poor vision.

Her hearing loss had begun when her brother caught her listening outside her father's bedroom. Angry, he grabbed and shook her. Anna wanted to hit him back, but she was afraid of making a scene. Her partial deafness started that night. Similarly, her cough had begun the night she heard dance music while on duty beside her father's bed. The music reminded her of the fun she was missing. Briefly, she daydreamed about going to a party. Then, just as quickly, she was swept by waves of guilt and remorse, for her daydream made her feel as though part of her wanted to desert her father. The cough came as a welcome relief, for she could then say to herself, "No one with a cough like mine could possibly go out to a party."

Unfortunately, Anna also transferred her affection for her father to Dr. Breuer. This forced him to break off her treatment, for his wife was jealous of the time he spent with Anna. His abrupt withdrawal from the case led to a relapse, and Anna had to be put into a sanitarium. She later recovered and went to live in Germany. There she became a pio-

FIGURE 6.1 ▓ Bertha Pappenheim, better known in the literature as "Anna O.," was one of the most famous patients in the history of psychotherapy. Sigmund Freud's friend Joseph Breuer treated Anna's disabling physical symptoms by encouraging her to "talk out" her repressed feelings. After studying the case, Freud became convinced that the roots of her problems were psychological, not physical.

neering feminist and a champion of progressive political and social causes.

Freud remembered the case of Anna O. when he began treating his emotionally disturbed patients. He found that long-forgotten events usually lay at the root of their problems. In time, he traced these buried memories to a part of the mind he called the *unconscious*. The unconscious serves as a storehouse for powerful feelings, Freud decided. He also realized that the unconscious has the power to affect behavior. Anna O.'s physical symptoms, Freud concluded, grew out of her conflict over her father's illness.

One part of her wanted to love and care for him, but another part of her yearned to be free of the sickroom and the fear that he would die.

Freud turned his theories into a system of therapy called *psychoanalysis*. Freed of their unconscious conflicts, many of his patients recovered and returned to normal life. In time, he also developed a consistent theory of personality and behavior based on psychoanalysis. Today, psychologists and psychiatrists trained in Freudian techniques still follow in the footsteps of this man who "shook the sleep of the world." Even though modern psychology does not accept all of Freud's ideas, any study of personality must consider his insights.

Your study of personality will take you through Chapters 6 and 7. This chapter will begin the investigation by looking at the following questions:

6.1 How do psychologists define personality?

6.2 How have philosophers and scientists tried to explain personality?

6.3 What contributions did Sigmund Freud make to the understanding of personality?

6.4 How does Freud explain the defense mechanisms that the ego uses to protect the personality?

6.5 Why did Freud's theory of psychosexual development arouse so much controversy?

6.6 What happens during psychoanalysis?

6.1 ▓ HOW DO PSYCHOLOGISTS DEFINE PERSONALITY?

Everyone uses the word "personality." Pressed for a definition, however, only one person in ten will be able to come up with one. Don, for instance, talks of personality as if it were something that can be measured. "Debbie has a lot of personality," he says. At other times, Don uses the word as if it stands for something good or bad. "Mark's personality will make him a successful police officer," Don tells his friends.

Psychologists can't let such an important idea be defined so vaguely. They believe that a good definition of personality must apply to all people and all behavior.

DEFINING PERSONALITY

Can any general truths about human personality be found? In a field notable for its disagreements, most psychologists would agree on three basic observations about a normal personality.

1. Each person generally behaves in a consistent way from one situation to another. Thus, if Anne is usually aggressive in her relationships, you can count on her to come on strong in most social situations.

2. This consistent pattern of behavior grows out of a complex system of conscious thought, unconscious drives, and life experiences. This system also creates the personal values and goals that help you set priorities from day to day. Thus, Anne may decide, "I'm tired of always being behind in my biology class. From now on I'll tape my soap operas and watch them *after* I've finished my assignments."

3. Every person possesses a unique personality. No two will behave in exactly the same way, even when faced with similar circumstances. Both Don and Anne might have aggressive personalities, for example. When they're stopped for speeding, however, their reactions differ greatly. Don becomes fright-

ened and passive, while Anne flares up, ready to do battle. A careful study of their childhood experiences with authority figures would help explain the differences.

By putting these observations together, psychologists can arrive at the following definition: *Personality is the unique pattern of thought, feeling, and behavior by which each person reacts to the external world.* How can anyone understand something as complex as a human personality? Psychologists rely on observation, tests, and people's limited ability to express their inner thoughts and feelings. With all of these variables at work, it is not surprising that theories about personality development vary widely.

CONTRIBUTIONS OF HEREDITY AND ENVIRONMENT

Many individual differences begin with a person's genetic inheritance. To some extent, genes determine such factors as your physical strength and coordination, your ability to resist sickness, and your physical appearance. Such physical traits obviously influence behavior. Most psychologists, nevertheless,

conclude that a person's environment has a greater effect on personality than heredity does.

The environmental factors that influence your physical and mental growth include such basics as a good diet, adequate health care, and freedom from worry. The most important environmental factors, however, are your interpersonal relationships. The feelings you share with family and friends, it turns out, have more to do with shaping your personality than anything else (see Figure 6.2). In experimental situations, for example, monkeys have been isolated from the rest of the troop. Although they received proper food and health care, these lonely monkeys developed into neurotic (disturbed) adults. Under stress, they became withdrawn and depressed. In test situations, they solved problems poorly. Meanwhile, their brothers and sisters, raised in a normal social environment, developed into well-adjusted adults.

What do such experiments prove? For one thing, they show the importance of proper nurturing during childhood. For another, they reinforce the idea that no child is born either "good" or "bad." Both good citizens and mass murderers are made, not born.

FIGURE 6.2 ▓ The importance of affectionate nurturing during childhood has been demonstrated by raising monkeys in isolation. What if these children were treated the same way? Would they grow up as withdrawn and unhappy as the young monkey shown here?

IMPORTANCE OF PERSONALITY THEORY

Psychologists continue to search for a systematic theory of personality to help them explain the behavior of healthy and unhealthy individuals everywhere. Such a theory would explain why Eskimos react one way to change and Swedes another. It would help scientists predict how Americans in general will react to an energy crisis—and how individuals like Emilio and Juanita will feel when faced with a mile-long gas line. A valid personality theory will help explain human values, motivations, emotions, and abilities.

Finally, once a solid theory of personality has been established, it can be used as the basis for inquiry into specific problems. Such conditions as mental illness, depression, ad-olescent suicide, and antisocial behavior can all be attacked more successfully. In time, an answer might even be found for the question voiced by people of every age: "What must I do to make my life happier and more productive?"

■ SECTION CHECKUP

1 Define personality in terms that your nine-year-old neighbor would understand.

2 Which is more important to the development of personality, genetic inheritance or environmental influence? Why?

3 Why do psychologists believe that developing a workable theory of personality is so important?

6.2 ▓ HOW HAVE PHILOSOPHERS AND SCIENTISTS TRIED TO EXPLAIN PERSONALITY?

The search for a universal theory of personality isn't new. For thousands of years, philosophers and scientists have tried to find a consistent system that can be applied to all people and all cultures. Albert Einstein was able to sum up the energy potential of the atom in a single equation: $E = mc^2$. No such breakthrough formula seems likely for personality. In this section you will learn about five of the theories that have been used to explain personality. Some are ancient; others were created during this century.

SUPERNATURAL FORCES AND PERSONALITY

Until relatively recent times, most cultures believed that personality was under the direct influence of the supernatural. Surrounded by gods, demons, and spirits, humans were forced to balance their own needs against the demands of these unseen forces. The Incas of Peru went so far as to treat mental illness by opening the patient's skull to allow the demons trapped inside to escape. The ancient Greeks, on the other hand, sometimes challenged the gods and dared their wrath. Homer's *Odyssey,* for example, tells how the hero Odysseus angered Poseidon, god of the sea. The vengeful god then sent a great storm that wrecked Odysseus's ship. A lesser man would have died, but Odysseus called on the pride and determination that were the bedrocks of his own personality—and survived the storm.

Few Americans today believe in demons, spirits, or sea gods. But about one out of five people still thinks that the position of the sun, stars, and planets can influence the human personality. This ancient pseudoscience, known as astrology, assigns personality traits according to the position of the sun and planets at the time of birth. People born under the sign of Aquarius (January 20–February 18), for example, are said to be spiritual, loving, and life-giving. Pisces people, born a month later (February 19–March 20), are thought to be compassionate, tolerant, and long-suffering. Experience indicates that these predictions sometimes seem to come true. Careful study shows, however, that astrological forecasts have about the same ratio of success to failure as would any random predictions. After all, don't most people possess the traits astrology assigns so arbitrarily to Aquarians and Pisceans? It might make as much sense to predict your personality by the birthdate of the doctor who delivered you.

PHYSICAL ATTRIBUTES AND PERSONALITY

As scientific viewpoints began to compete with supernatural beliefs, early peoples began looking for the sources of personality in the body itself. Ancient Hebrews, Egyptians, and Greeks often described organs other than the brain as the center of behavior. Some writers pointed to the liver or stomach as the key to understanding personality. In the fourth century B.C., the Greek philosopher Aristotle described the heart as the organ of understanding. Aristotle thought that the brain was an inert organ whose main function was to absorb the heart's excessive heat.

PHRENOLOGY. In the Middle Ages, Albertus Magnus, a German writer and teacher, revived the idea that the brain was the supreme organ. Albertus Magnus went so far as to locate various aspects of personality in different parts of the brain. In the early 1800s, another German, a doctor named Franz Joseph Gall, picked up the concept and founded a short-lived science he called *phrenology*. Gall claimed that he could read a per-

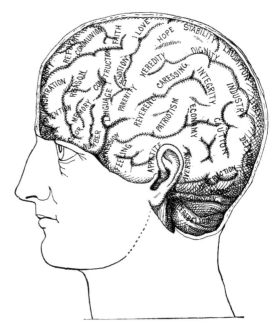

FIGURE 6.3 ▓ Phrenologists claimed to have scientifically charted the location of individual character traits, as shown in the diagram. In the 19th century, people used this fake science as a way of choosing careers or hiring people for jobs.

son's character and abilities by studying the shape of the skull, along with its bumps and depressions. Taken over by con artists and frauds, phrenology quickly became a popular fad. Speaking abilities, for example, were said to be located behind the eyes, while parental love could be measured at the back of the skull (see Figure 6.3). Research soon disproved the claims of the phrenologists. The part of the brain that controls speech turned out to be in another part of the brain entirely. Today, scientists know that the shape of your skull has no more to do with personality than do the bumps in the sidewalk outside your home.

SOCIOBIOLOGY. A new theory to explain behavior, based on genetic attributes, appeared in 1975. In that year, Harvard zoologist Edward O. Wilson launched a controversial concept called *sociobiology*. According to this theory, behavior and personality are genetically based, the result of evolutionary processes dating back two to four million years. Genes, the sociobiologist claims, program the behavior of all organisms, whether housefly or human being, in order to protect their continued existence. Studies of 44 sets of identical twins separated at birth seem to support this theory. Even though the twins were raised in different American families and communities, they developed similar likes and dislikes and even chose similar ways of making a living.

Sociobiologists believe that this basic drive to survive explains the most complex social behaviors. Ethnic pride, for example, is explained as the human preference for a mate who will produce children with facial features, hair, and skin color similar to one's own. Also, maternal love may be seen as an attempt by the mother to ensure that her genes will be carried on in the children of the next generation.

Sociobiology's severest critics point to the lack of evidence that specific genes account for aggression, altruism, or other social behaviors. They also fear that belief in the all-powerful gene could lead to an attempt to genetically engineer the next generation. Does any society truly know which personality traits are "best"? In the 1980s, officials in Singapore thought they knew. Until the policy ended in 1985, Singapore urged college graduates to have large families—and paid poorly educated women to be sterilized after giving birth to one or two children.

Wilson responds to his critics by agreeing that cultural and environmental forces do shape the personality—but that genetic influences should not be ignored. "Admitting that we are all influenced in different ways by our genetic coding doesn't reduce our freedom to do what we want to do," he says.

TYPOLOGIES AS A WAY TO EXPLAIN PERSONALITY

THE HUMORS. As early as 400 B.C., the Greek physician Hippocrates took a step toward placing the study of personality on a scientific basis. In his writings, he created a *typology* (a system in which people are classified into a limited number of categories) based on the "humors" of the body. Hippocrates thought that one of four humors, or body fluids, is dominant in every person. This dominant humor, he believed, determines both physical health and individual character. Hippocrates identified the four humors and the character traits each controlled as follows:

BODY HUMOR	CHARACTER TRAITS
Phlegm	Passive, careful, slow-moving
Black bile	Melancholic, anxious
Yellow bile	Irritable, angry
Blood	Easygoing, optimistic

Fourteen centuries later, the people of the Middle Ages still accepted the ideas of bodily humors. And even today, you may have heard someone described as "melancolic" or "phlegmatic." Hans Eysenck's updating of the four humors into their related character traits is illustrated in Figure 6.4.

SHELDON'S SOMATOTYPES. In the 1940s, psychologist William Sheldon developed a typology based on careful measurement and observation. After studying photographs of more than 4,000 male college students, Sheldon decided that he could divide his subjects into three basic body types. The *endomorph,* he said, has a soft, round body with highly developed digestive organs. The *mesomorph,* in contrast, has an athletic, well-muscled body. And finally, the *ectomorph* can be recognized by a tall, thin, fragile body (see Figure 6.5).

Since few people can be classified as pure endomorphs, mesomorphs, or ectomorphs,

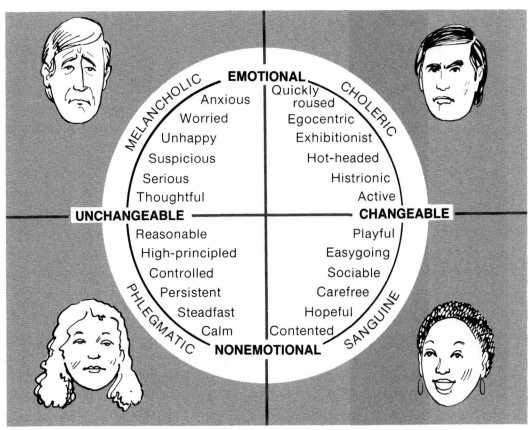

FIGURE 6.4 ▓ British psychologist H. J. Eysenck drew upon both ancient and modern theories of personality to design this representation of the structure of personality. Can you locate yourself in this chart of character traits? (From H. J. Eysenck, *The Biological Basis of Personality,* copyright © 1967 Charles C. Thomas, Publisher. Courtesy of Charles C. Thomas, Publisher, Springfield, Illinois.)

Sheldon assigned a score of 1 to 7 for the degree to which the individual possesses each body type. He called this three-part score the *somatotype.* According to this system, a typical athletic build would be rated 3-6-2: average in endomorphy, high in mesomorphy, and low in ectomorphy. A halfback for a professional football team, however, might rate a highly mesomorphic 1-7-1.

Sheldon's research convinced him that a high correlation exists between character traits and somatotypes. An endomorph, he believed, is comfort-loving, social, gluttonous, slow to react, and even-tempered. Mesomorphs, he went on, are aggressive, courageous, love vigorous activities, and tend to dominate others. Ectomorphs, Sheldon concluded, seem to be introverted, self-conscious, poorly coordinated, and interested in intellectual activities.

Psychologists admit that Sheldon's typology holds up fairly well when tested against actual personalities. They are not certain, however, that body type actually influences

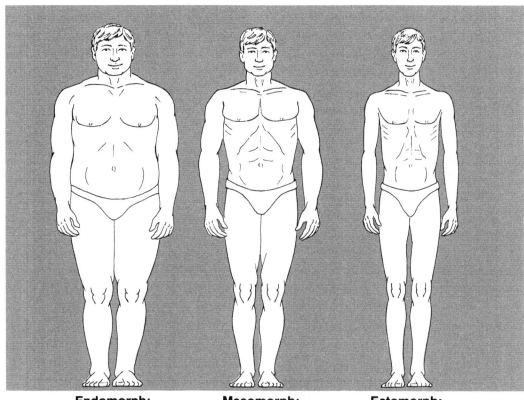

Endomorph:
Sociable,
Comfort Loving,
Fond of Eating

Mesomorph:
Aggressive, Athletic,
Courageous

Ectomorph:
Introverted,
Intellectual,
Poorly Coordinated

FIGURE 6.5 ■ Psychologist William Sheldon developed a typology that linked personality with an individual's physical characteristics. The three somatotypes he identified appear above. The typology can be used for females as well as males. Can you find your own somatotype here? Are your interests similar to those Sheldon assigned to that particular somatotype?

behavior. One pro-Sheldon theory suggests that a particular body type pushes its owner toward certain kinds of activities. Thus, endomorphs feel best when they are eating and relaxing—so that's what they do. But Sheldon's correlation might also grow out of a self-fulfilling prophecy. If society demands that fat, muscular, or skinny people behave in certain ways, they probably will behave as expected. In any event, you need not feel that you're captive to your own somatotype. Your body shape may influence your interests, but it probably won't determine them. Only you can do that.

PERSONALITY DEFINED BY TRAITS

Psychologists define *traits* as the tendency to respond to most situations or people in a particular way. If you usually make your decisions regardless of what others think, you possess the trait of independence. Psychologist Raymond Cattell, a pioneer in mental testing, used a trait-rating scale to divide people into specific personality types. On his scale, 12 pairs of traits are tested to provide a measure of how an individual relates to his or her environment.

In the rating scale on page 179, each pair of traits represents the end points of a range of behavior. Where would you place yourself on Cattell's scale for each pair of traits? Does your trait profile give you any insights about strengths or weaknesses in your personality?

PSYCHOSOCIAL THEORY OF PERSONALITY

What would happen if identical twins were separated at birth and raised in two different cultures? Imagine that one twin grew up in Puerto Rico, her sister in Cuba. The girls would still look alike, except for their haircuts and clothing. They may even find that they have similar sleeping and eating habits. The experience of growing up in societies that em-

brace such contrasting ways of life, however, would inevitably stamp them with different political, social, and economic values.

The example illustrates what psychologists call the *psychosocial theory* of personality. The theory states that heredity and environment interact to shape each person's unique pattern of behavior. As children grow, their family, friends, and community all join to reward some behaviors and punish others. In this way, the girl in Cuba would be punished for the same spirit of independence for which her sister in Puerto Rico would be rewarded. This socializing process teaches children how to function as members of their particular culture. The psychosocial theory, therefore, does a better job than other theories in explaining the differences in behavior found in varying cultures.

Sigmund Freud devised the first major psychosocial theory of personality, but he did not stop there. Freud's work also marked the beginning of psychology's efforts to explain the influence of the unconscious on behavior. Before Freud, psychologists had been content to explain personality on the basis of

CATTELL'S RATING SCALE FOR PERSONALITY TRAITS

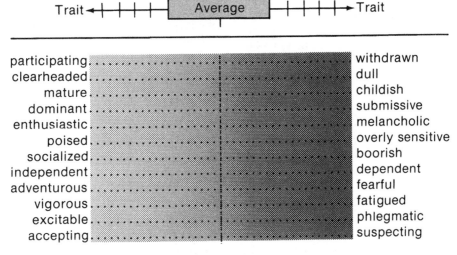

FIGURE 6.6

Sigmund Freud:
Pioneer Explorer of the Unconscious

Sigmund Freud (1856–1939) was born in Freiberg, Moravia (now part of the Czech Republic), but his family moved to Vienna when he was four. A bright, ambitious student, Freud studied at the University of Vienna. In 1886 he set up practice as a neurologist, a specialist in diseases of the nervous system. That same year, Freud married Martha Bernays, and the marriage produced six children. The youngest, Anna Freud, later became a world-renowned psychoanalyst in her own right.

The Freuds lived and worked at Berggasse 19, an address that has become famous as the birthplace of psychoanalytic theory. In 1938 the Nazi takeover of Austria forced the family, which was Jewish, to leave its home and take refuge in England. Freud was already suffering from the cancer of the jaw that eventually killed him, but he was determined to "die in freedom."

Freud's theories grew out of the discoveries he made while treating his emotionally disturbed patients. At first, he tried the traditional treatments: hot baths, electrotherapy, and rest cures. But as he became aware of the powerful influence of the unconscious, he turned to his new "talking out" therapy. Psychoanalysis seemed the only way of uncovering the forgotten events that were causing his patients' emotional problems.

But Freud's work did not go smoothly. In order to help his patients, he felt that he must first overcome his own neurotic fears. It was during this period, in 1897, that he wrote about his self-analysis:

> Business is hopelessly bad, it is so in general, right up to the very top of the tree, so I am living only for "inner" work. . . . Some sad secrets of life are being traced back to their first roots, the humble origins of much pride and precedence are being laid bare. I am now experiencing myself all the things that as a third party I have witnessed going on in my patients—days when I slink about depressed because I have understood nothing of the day's dreams . . . and other days when a flash of lightning brings coherence into the picture, and what has gone before is revealed as preparation for the present.

At one time, Freud was so full of anxiety and fear that he couldn't bring himself to leave his house. But by gradually—and painfully—working through his own analysis, he opened long-closed doors to the proper treatment of the mentally ill. Before Freud, emotionally disturbed people were shunned like lepers or locked up like criminals.

Essentially a modest man, Freud at times refused to take full credit for his accomplishments. In his autobiography, he wrote:

> Looking back, then, over the patchwork of my life's labors, I can say that I have made many beginnings and thrown out many suggestions. Something will come of them in the future, though I cannot myself tell whether it will be much or little. I can, however, express a hope that I have opened up a pathway for an important advance in our knowledge.

Did Freud "open up a pathway" for new advances in psychology? The following sections will help you make up your mind.

observable conscious behavior. After Freud, psychologists never again believed that human actions derive totally from the exercise of conscious will.

■ SECTION CHECKUP

I Why have astrology and phrenology been rejected by psychologists as explanations for human behavior?

2 How does William Sheldon's theory of somatotypes explain human personality? Contrast the three somatotypes Sheldon describes—endomorph, mesomorph, and ectomorph.

3 Why is the psychosocial theory thought to be a better way of explaining personality than typologies or trait theory?

6.3 ▮ WHAT CONTRIBUTIONS DID SIGMUND FREUD MAKE TO THE UNDERSTANDING OF PERSONALITY?

Imagine for a moment that an earthquake has struck your community. As the earth rumbles and sways beneath your feet, you'll probably feel a surge of unreasoning terror. If you can't trust the stability of the ground beneath your feet, what can you trust?

In the late 1800s, the writings of an unknown Viennese doctor created a similarly unnerving reaction. The existence of childhood sexual feelings, the influence of the unconscious, the enormous power of the mind—all of Sigmund Freud's ideas seemed to challenge the stability of 19th-century culture. Disturbed and angry, psychologists joined the public in accusing Freud of trying to undermine the foundations of society. Many objected particularly to Freud's theory that the adult personality is almost totally shaped by childhood experiences. Even today, this apparent denial of free will bothers people who otherwise would accept Freudian ideas more readily. As Freud wrote in *An Autobiographical Study,* ". . . I had no followers. I was completely isolated. In Vienna I was shunned; abroad no notice was taken of me. My *Interpretation of Dreams,* published in 1900, was scarcely reviewed in the technical journals." Recognition of the importance of Freud's work came slowly. Finally, by the 1920s, his theories gained widespread acceptance.

What are the basic principles of Freud's theory? In this and the following sections, you will have a chance to examine the key concepts of psychoanalysis.

POWER OF THE UNCONSCIOUS

Sigmund Freud described the human mind as an iceberg with the great bulk of its mass hidden beneath the dark surface of the sea. The tip of the iceberg represents the *conscious mind,* where everyday thought processes take place. At the water line, Freud identified a crossover zone called the *preconscious.* Here you store memories that can be called back to consciousness when you need them. You're reaching into the preconscious when you hesitate, then say, "Just a minute. I've got that name on the tip of my tongue."

Submerged and closed off from direct contact with the conscious mind lies the unconscious (see Figure 6.7). This great storehouse contains all your life experiences, particularly the harsher, more savage emotions—your fierce hates, secret loves, uncivilized passions. These memories, feelings, and desires are buried (*repressed,* the psychologist would say) because they are too powerful to be handled easily by the conscious mind. But out of sight doesn't mean out of mind. These hidden memories and emotions influence almost

WHAT'S GOING ON INSIDE YOUR HEAD:
THE THREE LEVELS OF CONSCIOUSNESS

Conscious mind
Everyday thought processes take place here: decision making, problem solving, daydreaming, reactions to events in the environment.

Preconscious
A crossover zone between the conscious and unconscious. Material not being used at the moment but not repressed can be found here.

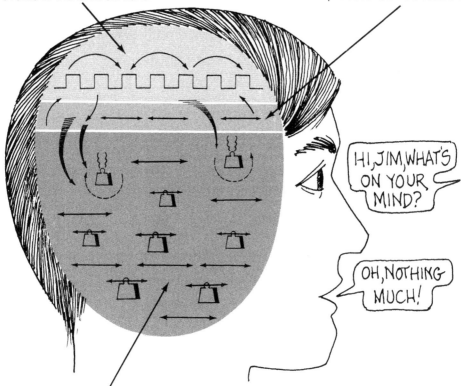

UNCONSCIOUS
The great storehouse of our basic drives, sexual desires, more savage emotions, and most painful memories. Even while repressed, these "forgotten" feelings can greatly influence our everyday conscious thought and behavior.

LEGEND

⊓⊔⊓⊔ Organized thought

⌒ Random, nonfocused thought

⟷ Stored material

⊤ Repressed material

Repressed material released during dreams and free association

Material moving from one level of consciousness to another

Experience so painful it is repressed immediately

FIGURE 6.7

182

FIGURE 6.8 ■ Is photographer Arthur Tress in touch with the hidden realms of the unconscious mind? This dream-like image seems to confirm Freud's belief in the existence of a subterranean storage vault of memories and emotions that lie deep within every human being. What does this eerie study of a young woman and her mother suggest to you?

everything you think, feel, and do (see Figure 6.8).

If you aren't convinced that you really do have an unconscious, Freud would ask you to keep careful track of your speech and everyday actions. If you're like most people, every once in a while you "slip" and say or do something you didn't mean to say or do. Perhaps you have reluctantly agreed to go with your family to visit Aunt Edna at the nursing home. Is it any surprise that you're late getting ready and everyone has to wait for you? Or have you ever been making polite conversation and had something embarrassing slip out? After class one morning, Patrick tried to impress his teacher by telling

her how "really interesting" her lectures were. "All of them," Patrick assured her, "are rarely interesting." Freud would have smiled at this "Freudian slip" and said, "Yes, young man, we know what you really think of Ms. Barker's lectures."

Psychoanalysis, Freud's method of treating mentally ill patients, grew out of his research into the unconscious. As his friend Dr. Breuer had discovered with Anna O., repressed memories seemed to lose their awesome power once patients begin talking freely about "forgotten" experiences. The unconscious does not give up its treasures easily, however. The psychoanalytic method requires a long-term commitment to therapy between the patient and the analyst (see Section 6.6, pages 194–196).

LIFE AND DEATH FORCES

According to Freud, all behavior ultimately can be reduced to two fundamental drives: eros and thanatos. *Eros* (derived from the name of the Greek god of love) stands for the life drive—the satisfaction of hunger, thirst, sex, and the need for self-preservation. Freud said that a reservoir of energy was needed to fuel the life drive. He found this psychic energy in the *libido*. The libido includes all of the different kinds of love experienced by human begins. Along with energizing your sexual drives, the libido provides the energy for love of self, parents, friends, country, even works of art.

Thanatos (derived from the Greek word for death), stands for the death drive. Freud believed that all people carry this death wish inside them. When the drive becomes overwhelming, it can lead to suicide. More often, thanatos leads a disturbed individual into a pattern of aggressive behavior that can result in brutal crimes against the larger society. Psychoanalysts believe that war and genocide are the ultimate expressions of the death wish.

ROLE OF THE ID, EGO, AND SUPEREGO

As Freud studied human behavior, he came to believe that the raw energy of the libido derives from and is modified by other powerful forces in the mind. Human beings, he said, are caught between their own needs and those of society. Three forces within the mind help people resolve this conflict. He called these forces the id, ego, and superego (see Figure 6.9).

THE ID.   Buried within the unconscious is the *id*, a storehouse for all your instincts and passions and the source of many of your habits.

Like a great savage infant, the id constantly demands satisfaction of your needs. If your body needs food, the id says, "Eat! Now!" If you're angry, the id says, "Hit back! Now!"

The goal of the id is to maximize pleasure and to avoid pain. Freud coined the term *pleasure principle* to describe this desire of the id to reduce tension and to gain immediate satisfaction without counting the cost. Although the id's untamed appetites can cause you trouble, you cannot do without it. From the id comes the energy that allows you to find joy in sharing a good meal with friends, playing a video game, fixing a broken toy, or writing songs.

THE EGO.   Computerlike, almost always in control, the *ego* acts as a moderating force between the demands of the id and the reality of the world around you. Without the ego to exercise control, the id would send you bolting for the cafeteria at your first hunger pangs. Instead, the ego measures the risk of leaving class early. If the cost is too great, the ego tells the id, "Wait 20 minutes till lunchtime, and we'll get a hamburger." This process of analyzing the consequences of future actions, in order to provide pleasure with the least amount of pain, Freud named the *reality principle*.

The ego also helps you repress desires that conflict too strongly with reality. You may have a powerful urge to take a joy ride in your neighbor's expensive new car, but the ego helps you deal with the impulsive voice of the id. The id whispers, "Look, the key's in the ignition! Let's boogie!" The ego responds, "Slow down! We're sure to be caught. It's not worth the risk." Note, however, that the ego's primary task is to satisfy the id, not to frustrate it. The ego doesn't know right from wrong; that role is filled by the superego.

THE SUPEREGO.   Freud believed that the *superego* absorbs the social and moral values taught by your parents, teachers, and other

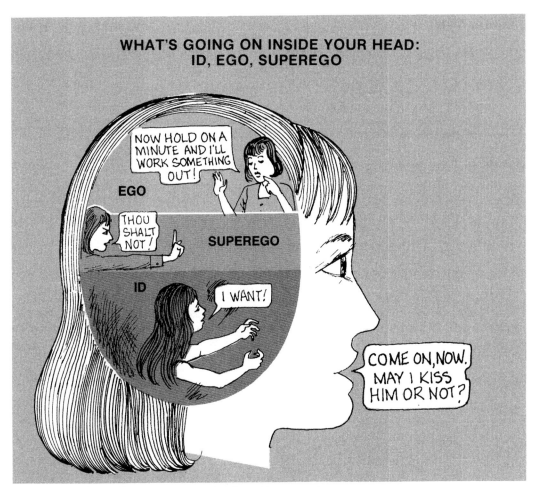

WHAT'S GOING ON INSIDE YOUR HEAD:
ID, EGO, SUPEREGO

FIGURE 6.9 ▩ The conflicting demands of the id, ego, and superego are represented here. The id demands immediate satisfaction but must work through the ego to achieve it. The superego upholds standards of morality taught during childhood. The ego's job is to reconcile these conflicting demands with the reality of the external world.

adults. During your childhood, these "rules for living" were enforced by rewards, punishments, and restrictions. The superego demands that you practice a perfect morality, a goal that often brings it into conflict with the id's desire for pleasure.

Imagine that you're walking through a department store. You see an expensive watch.

Your id says, "I want!"—even though you don't have any money. The ego, aware of the state of your finances, quickly evaluates your chances of stealing it. When the clerk's back is turned, it signals "Go!" But the superego quickly overrides the ego with its own "Stop!" command. Fearing punishment and unwilling to face the guilt feelings the superego is

▦ **PRO & CON:**

How Would Today's Women Debate Sigmund Freud?

For all his genius, Sigmund Freud was a man of his time and culture. In the late 1800s, Victorian society expected women to take a passive, submissive role in relation to men. Women who spoke out for equality or who did not repress their sexuality were put down as traitors to their sex. Given this repressive condition, it is no wonder that Freud saw many female patients. Most suffered from hysteria, a mental illness caused by repression of natural feelings.

If Freud were alive today, many women would want to argue with him about his attitudes toward their sex. With that in mind, a "debate" has been arranged between Dr. Freud and a modern feminist. After you "listen" to both sides, you can make up your own mind as to whether times have changed or not. Freud's words, by the way, are taken directly from his writings.

DR. FREUD

1 A comparison with what happens in the case of the boy shows us that the development of the little girl into a normal woman is more difficult and more complicated.

2 The little girl is as a rule less aggressive, less defiant, and less self-sufficient; she seems to have a greater need for affection to be shown her and therefore to be more dependent and docile.

3 ... for women to be loved is a stronger need than to love. Their vanity is partly a further effect of penis envy, for they are driven to rate their physical charms more highly as a belated compensation for their original sexual inferiority.

4 The great question that has never been answered, and which I have not been able to answer despite my 30 years of research into the feminine soul, is: What does a woman want?

FEMINIST

1 No such difficulty exists. Girls and boys are simply people, with all the problems and potentials that go with being human. If any greater difficulty in growing up exists, society creates it.

2 Does this mean that boys don't need affection? The fact is that girls are taught to need attention, while boys are encouraged to develop greater independence. Why can't both sexes be treated alike?

3 Freud projected his own male feelings of superiority upon women. Men have been exaggerating the importance of genital differences ever since. Of course, little girls notice the differences between themselves and their brother or father. But do they also have beard envy or muscle envy? The answer is obvious: Freud was flat-out wrong.

4 Women want to share equally with men in building a decent, peaceful society. They want equal opportunity and equal pay when they work outside the home. They want men to join them in raising their children. In brief, they want to see a world in which people are judged by who they are rather than by sex, race, or religion.

Times have changed, haven't they? Some psychologists believe that, if Freud were alive today, his attitudes toward women would be quite different. What do you think?

so good at giving you, you walk away from the temptation. These feelings of guilt derive from the *conscience,* a part of the superego. The superego also contains the *ego ideal,* which rewards you with approval when you act according to the superego's moral code. In this way, the superego not only makes you feel guilty and unhappy when you violate a rule, but it also rewards you with a pleasurable feeling of satisfaction when you do the right thing.

■ SECTION CHECKUP

1 Describe the roles of the conscious, the preconscious, and the unconscious.

2 Describe some human activities that would derive from eros, the life drive; from thanatos, the death drive.

3 Imagine that you're standing by the teacher's desk and that the test answers are in plain sight. What messages will the id, ego, and superego give you at this point?

6.4 ■ HOW DOES FREUD EXPLAIN THE DEFENSE MECHANISMS THAT THE EGO USES TO PROTECT THE PERSONALITY?

Sometimes the competing demands of the id and superego trap the hardworking ego into a no-win position. Imagine that you've just backed Dad's car into a neighbor's expensive new car. The id screams, "No one saw us! Get out of here fast before we get caught!" But superego jumps in, mercilessly moralistic: "It would be wrong to run away. You caused the accident with your careless driving. Stay and accept the consequences."

Both drives are too strong to be ignored. Caught in such a bind, the ego often chooses a response that disguises or compromises the id's socially unacceptable desires. In this case, the ego might choose to stay with the damaged car, thus obeying the law. To reduce the anxiety level, the ego may also choose to distort reality by rationalizing (alibiing) the accident: "It was either hit your car, Mr. Krukow, or run over the little kid who ran in back of me."

Freud made one of his most enduring contributions to psychology when he identified a number of these ego-protecting behaviors. Known as *defense mechanisms,* their use is thought to be largely unconscious. Even though you may in time become expert at spotting their use by others, you're unlikely to be aware of the degree to which you depend on one or more of the following defense mechanisms.

REPRESSION

When she was seven years old, Rachel was attacked by a large watchdog. She was bitten on the legs but escaped without serious injuries. Today she does not remember that incident, but she is terrified of dogs. Whether the dog that runs toward her is a German shepherd or a toy poodle, Rachel feels almost suffocated by fear.

Repression protects you from disturbing memories, forbidden desires, or painful feelings by burying such material in the unconscious. Repressed feelings remain "alive," however, capable of influencing behavior without the person's awareness. Part of Rachel wants to like dogs, but whenever she gets close to one, the old repressed fear takes over. Similarly, repressed material can affect normal physical drives such as hunger or sex. Doctors also know that repression can lead to physical ailments. Anna O. (see pages 170–172) was an extreme example of someone who experienced a *psychosomatic illness.* Even today, some medical experts estimate that up to 40 percent of the patients a physician sees each day may be suffering from illnesses with origins that are psychological, not physical.

Since you cannot "remember" what you have repressed, it sometimes takes a lengthy period of therapy before the hidden material can be uncovered. Even when unearthed, you must still accept and deal with what you've repressed. In Rachel's case, that would not be too difficult; her fear of dogs gives an obvious clue as to where to look. But repression also acts to conceal drives and feelings that people cannot admit having—even to themselves. In such cases, the patient often vigorously resists any attempt to open up the repressed material.

DISPLACEMENT

Harry's day had gone from bad to worse. He forgot his math homework, his girlfriend broke a date, and he missed the bus after school. Seething with the injustice of it all, he walked into the house just in time to hear his mother say, "Harry, did you get a haircut as I asked you?" Just then his baby brother ran up to be hugged. Harry released all his built-up aggressions by pushing Huey away with a violent shove.

When you can't focus your feelings on the person or thing that caused them, you often strike out at a less threatening person or object. Freud called this *displacement.* Harry couldn't strike out at his girlfriend or his mother, so baby Huey became the substitute. If Huey hadn't come by just then, Harry would likely have displaced the built-up en-ergy created by his anger to his dog or bedroom door.

Anger isn't the only emotion that can be displaced, but it is the most common. People sometimes displace nervousness or fear by chewing gum or picking at their fingernails. Some psychologists have described prejudice as displaced aggression, as when an unemployed worker blames all of his troubles on a minority group. If you learn to recognize your displacement behavior you can channel it into useful, less harmful ways of releasing tension. If Harry had put in some time running, chopping wood, or punching a bag, he would have felt better. And baby Huey wouldn't be crying.

SUBLIMATION

Susan thought her world was going to end when her parents told her they couldn't afford to send her to college. After a period of depression, she took a job at a local law office. The work proved interesting, and she was soon putting in extra hours. At night she took extra training at the local community college. Within a year, her boss promoted her to the level of executive secretary and gave her increased responsibility as well as a raise.

Without knowing it, Susan was practicing *sublimation,* the defense mechanism that detours powerful, frustrated drives into socially useful behavior. Freud believed that civilization could not exist without sublimation, for it allows people to contribute to society while also achieving their own inner peace (see Figure 6.10). In this way, a rock-throwing youngster in trouble with the law might find release from his inner tension on the baseball field. Or a woman who has just ended a love affair might feel better if she puts all her energies into creating beautiful ceramic figures. A childless couple who befriends stray cats and dogs may also be sublimating the desire

FIGURE 6.10 ※ Sublimation provides a release from inner stress and frustration by directing energy into socially useful activities. Can any of your own interests in sports, art, music, or volunteer work be considered sublimation?

to have children of their own. Sublimation does not always absorb all the energy created by frustration, however. The aggressive youngster described above did find success in baseball—but he often lost his temper when an umpire's decision went against him.

PROJECTION

Jimmy secretly wishes he had as much money to spend on clothes as some of the other kids in school. On campus, however, he goes out of his way to put down classmates who wear expensive outfits. "Look, there comes Vernon," he yells, "and he's wearing that ugly suede jacket again. What's the matter, Vernie, can't you afford anything better?"

Your ego can cope more easily with tension if it originates in the external world. Stress that actually comes out of the conflict between the id and the superego, therefore, is often projected by the ego upon an outside

target. Jimmy is using *projection* to cope with his own feelings of inadequacy. If he had more self-insight, he'd admit that he would like to have a suede jacket, too. Similarly, a husband who frequently accuses his wife of not loving him may really be saying, "I don't love you (but I can't admit it to myself)." You might suspect projection almost anytime someone, in Shakespeare's phrase, "doth protest too much." Thus, adults who loudly criticize young people and their music may secretly wish they could be young again.

REGRESSION

Overheard in the teachers' lounge: "I don't know what to make of my ninth graders this year. Usually they're great—alert, interested, cooperative. But just mention extra work or toss them a tough problem, and they come unglued! They pout, stamp their feet, practically throw temper tantrums. I can't figure them out."

189

A psychologist would instantly identify the students' antics as *regression,* a return to an infantile stage of behavior. When faced with frustration or stress, some people fall back on anxiety-releasing techniques that worked when they were young. Regression is not limited to young people. Under stress, adults often revert to childlike behavior—chewing their fingers, eating or drinking to excess, or throwing temper tantrums. Caught in the pressures of an unhappy marriage, husbands and wives have been known to stomp out of the house, perhaps to "go home to momma." Finding refuge from reality in alcohol or drugs is also considered regressive behavior.

Since regression usually means a refusal to face reality, overuse of this defense mechanism can lock a person into a pattern of non-productive behavior. As for those unruly ninth graders, give them a few years. Most of them will leave that regressive behavior behind as they mature.

REACTION FORMATION

> The neighbors marvel over John's devotion to his aging mother. After all, he's 38 years old and gave up his marriage plans to take care of her. Despite Mrs. R.'s cranky disposition, he plays the role of dutiful son with a smile and a cheery willingness to do whatever's necessary. "And what's so marvelous about it all," says old Mrs. Richmond next door, "is that she never gave him much love or attention when he was little."

Maybe John really enjoys his limited role in life, but the odds are good that he's using *reaction formation* to deal with unconscious feelings of bitterness and rage. In reaction formation, the unconscious converts a forbidden feeling into its opposite. John has good reason to dislike his mother, but he's also been taught to honor and respect her. Unable to deal with his anger, he has converted it into love and devotion, feelings that relieve his underlying anxieties. In much the same way, kidnapping victims sometimes become willing partisans of the people who are holding them captive. To do otherwise would expose a hostage to both physical and psychological injury.

You may have run into reaction formation around school without being aware of it. Think of someone like Margaret, for example. No one works harder or is more serious about her studies, right? But if you could see inside her head, you'd find out that Margaret bitterly resents the demands placed on her by her ambitious parents. But to rebel would be unthinkable. Instead, she turns the urge to give up on school into an obsession with all-*A* report cards.

RATIONALIZATION

> "Anne, did you call your editor? He'll want to know about the problem you ran into when you tried to research that story."
>
> "No, his line is always tied up. And besides, I was really busy this morning. I practiced piano for an hour and worked on my new dress, and then Tom called . . ."

No one likes to be criticized. All people have an ideal image of themselves built up in their minds. When they don't live up to that ideal, they feel guilty about it. *Rationalization* is the process of finding reasons or excuses for thoughts, feelings, or actions that don't measure up to your expectations of yourself. In this way, you "get off the hook," as when you look Dad in the eye and say, "I know it's late, but Ivan's car ran out of gas. We couldn't help it."

Anne didn't want to admit her difficulty, so she postponed her confrontation with her editor by inventing reasonable excuses for her inaction. Similarly, a salesclerk who takes merchandise from the store might say, "Sure I took a few things, but so does everybody else. The company can afford it." Rationalization makes living easier (who hasn't used it?), but a psychologist would be concerned about someone like Ben, who rationalizes his every action. Ben's behavior is unhealthy, the psychologist would conclude, because he never takes responsibility for anything he does.

PROCRASTINATION

"Louise! Have you started your ten-page book report yet?" Dad called. Louise looked up from her jigsaw puzzle. "Well, not yet," she said. Then she smiled and added, "But how long does it take to read a ten-page book?" Dad laughed at the joke and remembered his own high school days. His mom had often called him "Last-Minute Mike." Still, he worried about Louise. It didn't seem healthy to always be behind in one's work.

Like Louise's dad, society has never made up its mind about promptness. Proverbs tell us, "He who hesitates is lost," then add a conflicting message: "Look before you leap." Many people, it turns out, overdo the looking. They try to escape unpleasantness by postponing a task or action. This common defense mechanism is known as *procrastination*. At one level, we can all agree that watching television is more pleasurable than mowing the grass. But some people procrastinate for less obvious reasons. Postponing a task also postpones the possibility of experiencing failure. Unfortunately, procrastination all too often guarantees failure. If you don't leave enough time to complete a task, you're unlikely to do it well.

In *Gone With the Wind,* Scarlett O'Hara spoke for all procrastinators when she said, "After all, tomorrow is another day." In choosing the temporary solution, however, procrastinators create stress for themselves. Putting off an unpleasant task does not end your awareness that it must be done. You'll likely find yourself complaining about how little time you have to do the many tasks and services your teachers, family, employer, and friends ask of you. It's not unusual for procrastinators to waste as much time complaining about their burdens as it would have taken to actually do the jobs.

At what point does procrastination become unhealthy? To be sure, everyone procrastinates occasionally. Psychologists become concerned when an individual lives in a constant state of trying to catch up with yesterday. These are the people who should ask themselves, "What am I afraid of? Why do I find it so hard to get on with tasks I know must be completed?" Giving yourself an honest answer to these questions is the first and most important step toward ending habitual procrastination.

■ SECTION CHECKUP

▌ What purpose do defense mechanisms serve in human behavior?

2 Define and give an example of each of the following defense mechanisms: repression, displacement, sublimation, projection, regression, reaction formation, rationalization, and procrastination.

6.5 ▓ WHY DID FREUD'S THEORY OF PSYCHOSEXUAL DEVELOPMENT AROUSE SO MUCH CONTROVERSY?

To your great-great-grandparents, children represented one of life's puzzles. The popular literature of the Victorian period described

boys and girls as "pure, innocent, and unspoiled"—terms usually reserved for angels. In fact, then as now, children seldom lived up

The Influence of Sexual Drives: A Thumbnail Summary of Freudian Theory

1 Sex, in the broad Freudian interpretation, is the single most powerful force in determining our feelings, thoughts, and actions.

2 Sexual feelings (again in the broad meaning of that term) can be traced as far back as infancy. Anyone who has watched a baby at play has noticed the enjoyment it receives from its own body.

3 Emotional problems are caused by the repressive influence of individual and group taboos on our sexual feelings. These taboos begin in childhood, when our parents first scold us for doing or saying what to the child is a natural expression of sexuality.

4 All people carry within themselves a hidden reservoir of sexual desires, memories, and tendencies. Because society labels some of these tendencies "abnormal," the individual represses them.

5 Repressed sexual feelings fight their way to the surface of our lives in disguised but socially acceptable forms. They do so in many ways—through dreams, myths, art, literature, slips of the tongue, clothing styles, and even jokes and wisecracks.

---

to that unrealistic image. Even so, few people stopped to wonder about the gulf that separated the ideal child from the flesh-and-blood one.

In 1900, Sigmund Freud's statement that all children lived an unconscious but passionate sex life shocked people everywhere. The reaction to Freud's idea of *childhood sexuality* was as great as the shock that had greeted Darwin's theory of evolution just 50 years earlier. As one critic noted, "Freud has murdered childhood." Today, even though many of Freud's theories have gained wide acceptance, the controversy over childhood sexuality has not fully abated. Many people still reject the concept on religious or philosophical grounds. In addition, modern psychologists believe that Freud overemphasized the importance of sexual forces in shaping the personality. (The feature on this page summarizes Freud's views on this subject.)

Basically, Freud believed that personality is formed when children are forced to learn new methods of reducing tensions. Each stage of life, he said, brings new physical and emotional challenges for which old solutions no longer work. Of the five stages Freud described, three occur during the first six years of life. To followers of psychoanalytic theory, this fact seems proof enough that the ages from birth to six are the most decisive period in shaping personality.

ORAL STAGE

For the first year of life, the infant's pleasures and frustrations center on the mouth. In this *oral stage*, pleasure grows mostly out of stimulation of the lips and mouth, either through sucking, eating, drinking, or licking. Babies reject unpleasant sensations by literally spitting them out, as anyone who has ever tried to feed a baby strained liver can testify.

Freud thought that many adult character traits have their origins in this stage of life. A baby who isn't given enough food during the oral stage may become a possessive adult who can never get enough of anything. Likewise, a baby who is allowed to bite people without being disciplined may mature into a destructive grown-up. Freud guessed that many adult behavior patterns such as gum chewing or pipe smoking may be substitutes for the simple pleasures enjoyed during the oral stage.

Psychoanalysts also believe that because of unresolved conflicts during this or later stages, people may become *fixated* (locked into infantile behavior patterns). Physically, they continue to grow, of course. But emotionally, they remain dependent on behaviors that worked for them during that crucial stage. Compulsive eaters, who use food as a compensation for a lack of love in their lives, may be acting out a fixation from the oral stage of development.

ANAL STAGE

Freud placed great emphasis on the behaviors learned during the second and third years of life. He called this the *anal stage,* for the child finds pleasure during these years in the daily bowel movement. Toilet training, which usually begins in the second year, gives the child a first experience with the need to regulate an instinctive, impulsive behavior.

Freud believed that harsh, overly strict toilet training may cause development of one of two extreme personalities. Some children may develop a retentive personality, becoming stingy and stubborn. Other children may grow into expulsive personalities—rebellious, destructive, and disorderly. Freud also said that adults who find all their security in making money may be resolving the sense of loss they experienced during the anal stage. Parents can help their children through this stage by making toilet training a low-pressure, natural development that takes place only when the child is ready for it.

PHALLIC STAGE

Between ages four and six, children go through the *phallic stage*. The search for plea-sure now centers on the genitals, and boys and girls often engage in sex play during this time. Freud observed that the most important challenge of this period is the working out of the *Oedipus complex.** Boys and girls in the phallic stage feel an unconscious sexual attraction to the parent of the opposite sex. A boy wants to "marry" his mother, so that he can have all her affection. Similarly, a girl fantasizes about having her father all to herself. These unconscious drives bring the child into competition with the parent of the same sex. It's not unusual, for example, to see a boy of four or five deliberately place himself between his parents, as if trying to keep his father away from his mother. Girls and boys may have vivid dreams involving the death of their "rival."

Freud explains that these Oedipal feelings must be resolved if the child is to grow into a sexually normal adult. Children have little power to control their lives, however. Complications arise when the boy begins to fear that his father will punish him for his feelings by cutting off his penis. Freud called this fear the *castration complex*. He claimed that girls develop penis envy, which he defined as a jealousy of males, who own something important that they lack. Torn by guilt over their secret desires and fearful of punishment, children eventually repress their Oedipal feelings in favor of identifying with the same-sex parent. The rapid development of the superego during the phallic stage helps resolve the Oedipus conflict by building social and moral values related to sex roles into the child's personality.

---

* The name derives from the classic tragedy by the Greek playwright Sophocles. The play tells the story of Oedipus, doomed by the fates to kill his father and marry his own mother. Oedipus unknowingly fulfills his destiny. When he's confronted with the terrible knowledge of his incestuous marriage, he gouges out his own eyes.

LATENCY PERIOD

After the stormy years of the phallic stage, the child enters the relative calm of the *latency period*. Between the age of six and the onset of puberty, most sexual feelings are repressed. Children prefer the company of their own sex and invest enormous amounts of energy in school, sports, hobbies, and play activities. You may remember your own involvment in Scouting, Y groups, Little League, model building, street games, music lessons, and similar activities during those years.

GENITAL STAGE

Following puberty, adolescents enter the *genital stage,* the period of adult sexual growth. Previously, children were mostly interested in their own bodies. Now, as young adults, teenagers begin to explore the pleasures and pain of genuine love relationships. Individuals develop interests in career plans, join peer groups, and debate the desirability of marriage and having their own children.

Normal development during the early years now provides a firm foundation for achieving productive, satisfying personal relationships. For people who were fixated at an earlier stage, or who didn't work out an Oedipus complex, the genital stage may represent a difficult ordeal. Driven by unconscious forces they can only vaguely sense, these people often need a counselor or therapist to help them unravel the tangled threads of their personality problems.

■ SECTION CHECKUP

I Why did the theory of childhood sexuality alarm the Victorian world?

2 Name the five life stages that Freud described. What is the key growth pattern of each stage?

3 Why does psychoanalysis put so much emphasis on the Oedipus complex? What exactly did Freud mean by it?

6.6 ▓ WHAT HAPPENS DURING PSYCHOANALYSIS?

None of Sigmund Freud's 24 volumes of writings would be of more than theoretical value if his insights could not be applied to real people with real problems. Whatever else psychoanalysis teaches about personality, it is essentially a system of therapy.

How does psychoanalysis work? You may remember that almost all psychoanalysts are psychiatrists who have taken special advanced work in Freudian analytic methods. Psychoanalysts, therefore, use Freud's own techniques to help their patients unscramble long-forgotten experiences that still have the power to influence today's behavior. Armed with insights about their past, patients can then overcome the barriers that prevent them

from living happy, productive lives. Psychoanalysis works best with patients whose emotional problems, however painful and limiting, are relatively mild. Because the therapy involves a lengthy period of talking about the patient's past life, those who cannot (or will not) communicate freely will probably not benefit from analysis.

Each analysis is individual, of course, but the procedures that Freud used still dominate each therapy session. Because you may never talk directly to an analyst (short for psychoanalyst) yourself, here are some of the questions and answers you might hear if you could eavesdrop on a patient who is beginning therapy.

PATIENT: What do you mean by the psycho-analytic contract?

ANALYST: Before you start therapy, you and I must agree upon certain basic principles. You will promise to visit my office two or more times a week. You will agree to speak freely about anything that comes into your mind, without feelings of shame, guilt, or embarrassment. This is a Freudian technique known as *free association*.

For my part, I will listen carefully to everything you say. I won't give advice, criticize, or make decisions for you. My job is to interpret, not to take control. I'll also refuse to make snap judgments about your illness, for each new insight that emerges from your free association will probably modify my diagnosis.

PATIENT: Why do patients lie on a couch during analysis?

ANALYST: Actually, many analysts no longer use a couch. It has become a rather unfortunate stereotype. But a couch does have its purposes. First, you must be relaxed in order to free-associate. Second, you can't see my face while you're lying on the couch. That way, you can't try to guess from my expressions what I think of your remarks. If you could, you might try to impress me, or you might turn away from embarrassing material. Finally, I can see you, and often your face will give away what your words try to hide.

PATIENT: Why will I do so much of the talking? Will you always remain silent?

ANALYST: I'll speak when it's time. But Freud taught that the analyst's silence is an important part of therapy. I want to maintain a tension in our relationship. If we talk freely back and forth, that's a conversation. But if I remain silent, you will be forced to fill the spaces with your own words. And eventually those words will lead to repressed material that lies at the heart of your problem.

PATIENT: What do analysts mean by transference?

DENNIS the MENACE

"THE BEST THING YOU CAN DO IS TO GET VERY GOOD AT BEING YOU."

FIGURE 6.11

ANALYST: Freud considered *transference* the key discovery in the analytic process. He believed that it shows you are beginning to make real progress. You see, as our relationship develops, you will begin to transfer your feelings about important people in your life to me. What you feel about your father, mother, brother, or whomever will become part of our relationship. You will rely on me more and more, but you'll also hate me at times. These feelings will be powerful and upsetting. But transference means that you're asking yourself what you want from me—and from your life. When you love me, I will understand. And when you hate me, I will understand that emotion, too. You cannot upset me. You cannot make me think less of you. At the same time, I will be guarding against something called *countertransference*—the analyst's tendency to develop strong personal feelings for the patient. Also, your privacy is guaranteed. Nothing you say to me will ever leave this office.

PATIENT: Do you mean that I will feel free to tell you everything?

ANALYST: By no means! Your unconscious won't give up its secrets without a struggle. As we approach more painful episodes in your life, you will set up *resistances*. You will "forget" your appointments. You will tell me you can't remember your dreams. Days will go by in which you will lie silent for our entire hour, unable to find a single word to speak. You may even talk about ending the analysis. But your resistance means that we are approaching the most important stage of the analysis! That is the time to redouble our efforts, for it means a breakthrough is possible.

PATIENT: When do you do your job? Will you ever give me an interpretation of what's been happening?

ANALYST: That's a fair question. Remember, it isn't always easy for the analyst to remain silent. But the time does come when all the elements of your problems have been opened up. Then it's my job to point out the connections and meanings that you might otherwise miss. I will confront you with omissions, contradictions, and inconsistencies. Perhaps your relations with older people trouble you. I'll help you clarify those feelings and lead you back through the childhood experiences that caused them. If my insights are correct, you will begin to adopt new and more mature behavior patterns. Your old, self-defeating hang-ups will be left behind.

PATIENT: I've heard that analysis sometimes goes on for years. Won't the time come when I can end my therapy?

ANALYST: No analysis is ever complete. The childhood experiences that lie at the root of your problem won't go away; they're part of you. We'll both know, however, when you're ready to end your treatment. You'll be satisfied with the progress you've made and impatient at the lack of further insights. You'll feel much better about yourself, and you'll be able to handle your relationships with other people. Your life will never be all smooth sailing—but you'll be able to handle any storms that blow your way.

PATIENT: Ummm, as you know, analysis is terribly expensive. Why is that?

ANALYST: I could make a joke out of that, as when the yacht salesperson says, "If you have to ask how much it costs, you can't afford it." But you've asked a fair question. First, it took me 12 years of university study to learn my profession. While I was in training at the Psychoanalytic Institute, I went through an analysis myself. Second, I can see only a handful of patients each week. I need time to write up my notes, do my study and research, and run my office. I'm sorry, but the fee we agreed to is what my services are worth. And if analysis helps you put your life in order, I think you'll agree that it was worth every penny.

PATIENT: I read a report that said, "Freud has been proved wrong in nearly all of his notions." How do you respond?

ANALYST: It's true, the debate over Freudian theories still rages. Critics charge that psychoanalysis is based more on belief than on science—but no one disputes the influence of Freud's ideas. You hear references to defense mechanisms, the unconscious, dreams, and other Freudian constructs all the time. Concepts such as the Oedipus complex haven't fared well. But even psychoactive drugs can't compete with Freud's insights when it comes to helping my troubled patients.

■ SECTION CHECKUP

1 Define the psychoanalytic terms *free association, transference,* and *resistance.*

2 What is the purpose of the analyst's silence? At what point does the analyst begin to add interpretations and commentary?

3 Why does psychoanalysis take so long?

LOOKING BACK: A SUMMARY

1 *Personality* can be defined as the unique pattern of thought and behavior by which each person reacts to the outside world. Both heredity and environment play key roles in shaping personality, but environment is the more important factor. Psychologists are interested in personality theory as a way of explaining human behavior for all people, everywhere.

2 For centuries philosophers and scientists have searched for a workable theory of personality. The earliest theories said that behavior resulted from the action of supernatural forces. Various parts of the body, such as body fluids, have also been described as controlling the emotions. Later research tried to define personality through systems of categories, or typologies. One such typology is Sheldon's somatotypes, which use three basic body types to predict individual behavior. Other efforts centered on the measurement of individual traits, such as dependent-independent or dominant-submissive. Finally, modern psychosocial theory sets forth the idea that behavior results from the interaction of genetic inheritance and the socialization process. Of all the theories, the psychosocial approach does the best job of explaining cultural differences in behavior.

3 When Sigmund Freud announced that personality derives from psychological forces rather than hereditary influences, few people accepted his revolutionary theories. Starting with the concept of the unconscious, Freud showed that every human being is driven by two basic forces: eros (the life force) and thanatos (the urge to self-destruction). The life force is energized by the libido, which includes love in all its forms: sexual love, friendship, love of family, patriotism, and love of beauty.

4 Freud divided the mind into three parts. The conscious mind carries on everyday thought processes. The preconscious stores material not currently in use. The unconscious serves as the storehouse of all repressed feelings and memories: loves and hates, painful experiences, and primitive passions. Freud believed that neurotic fears and irrational behavior can usually be traced to events hidden in the unconscious.

5 Three powerful forces modify and use the raw energy of the libido: the id, the ego, and the superego. The id represents instincts, passions, and habits. It seeks tirelessly to gratify its needs, a process Freud called the *pleasure principle*. The ego acts as a moderating force between the id and the external world. Like a computer, the ego processes the id's demands and attempts to satisfy them within the limitations of reality. Freud thought of this process as the *reality principle*. Moral behavior derives from the superego, which contains the conscience and the ego ideal. When people violate the values they have learned from their parents and other adults, the conscience makes them feel guilty. When they act according to the superego's moral code, the ego ideal allows them to feel pride in their "good" behavior.

6 The ego sometimes denies or distorts reality when caught between the demands of the id and the superego. This process is known as a defense mechanism. Freud identified at least eight such mechanisms: (a) Repression—"forgetting" painful experiences by burying the memory in the unconscious. (b) Displacement—the transfer of a strong emotion from the person or situation that caused it to another, generally less threatening person or object. (c) Sublimation—the conversion of powerful, frustrated drives into socially useful behavior. (d) Projection—the concealing of one's inner fears and needs by "finding" them in the behavior of others. (e)

Regression—a return to childish behavior when under stress. (f) Reaction formation—the unconscious conversion of a stress-causing impulse or drive into its opposite emotion. (g) Rationalization—the tendency people have to use excuses as a means of protecting the idealized image they have of themselves. (h) Procrastination—the habitual postponing of actions or tasks that seem unpleasant or that carry the risk of failure.

7 Freud alarmed Victorian parents when he asserted that children pass through five sexually oriented stages of development. During the first year, an infant is in the oral stage, when all pleasure and displeasure center on the mouth. The anal stage, ages two to three, shifts the child's attention to the daily bowel movement. Improper methods of toilet training can fixate a child at this stage, creating a number of undesirable adult personality traits. During the third stage, ages four to six, the child enters the phallic period. At this time the Oedipus complex (the child's attachment to the parent of the opposite sex) must be worked out if the child is to achieve a normal adult sex life. Following a period of latency in which sexual feelings are repressed, puberty marks the beginning of the genital stage. As they become sexually mature, adolescents end the self-involvement of childhood and begin to develop more mature love relationships.

8 During Freudian therapy, usually known as *psychoanalysis,* the patient slowly works through the layers of the unconscious to the underlying causes of disturbed behavior. The analyst remains mostly silent, allowing the patient to talk about whatever comes to mind. This "talking out" process is called *free association.* In time, the patient experiences transference, the shifting of strong feelings about parents and other significant people to the analyst. Points of resistance appear, signaling the presence of important feelings that must be opened up. Finally, the analyst helps interpret the accumulated insights gathered over the preceding weeks and months. Analysis ends when patients understand the causes of their self-defeating behavior and learn new techniques for coping with difficult problems and relationships.

PUTTING YOUR KNOWLEDGE TO WORK

■ TERMS YOU SHOULD KNOW

anal stage	id	rationalization
castration complex	latency period	reaction formation
childhood sexuality	libido	reality principle
conscience	mesomorph	regression
conscious mind	Oedipus complex	repressed feelings
countertransference	oral stage	repression
defense mechanism	personality	resistance
displacement	phallic stage	sociobiology
ectomorph	phrenology	somatotype
ego	pleasure principle	sublimation
ego ideal	preconscious	superego
endomorph	procrastination	thanatos
eros	projection	traits
fixated	psychoanalysis	transference
free association	psychosocial theory	typology
genital stage	psychosomatic illness	unconscious

■ CHAPTER CHECKUP

1 Which of the following is *not* a true statement about Freud's psychoanalytic theory? (*a*) Children go through a period during which they love and desire the parent of the opposite sex. (*b*) Once sexual feelings have been repressed, they have no further power to influence people's lives. (*c*) The repressed memories contained in the unconscious can dramatically influence the thinking of the conscious mind. (*d*) Disturbed or unhealthy behavior can be resolved only when the patient understands the underlying causes of the problem.

2 The attempt to develop a universal theory of personality (*a*) is useful because such a theory would provide a way to understand all aspects of human behavior (*b*) will fail because the influence of supernatural forces on personality makes it impossible to understand what shapes human behavior (*c*) is useless because human behavior is so unpredictable it can never be summed up in a workable personality theory (*d*) ended with the Greeks, whose personality theory is still the basis for modern psychology.

3 A personality theory that is based on a typology is (*a*) phrenology (*b*) Freud's psychoanalytic theory (*c*) Cattell's trait theory (*d*) Sheldon's somatotypes.

4 Philosophers tend to be tall, thin, self-conscious, and mostly interested in intellectual pursuits. According to somatotype theory, they should be classified as (*a*) endomorphs (*b*) mesomorphs (*c*) ectomorphs (*d*) fixated personalities.

5 During a baseball game, Steve has been "brushed back" by a pitch that almost hits him. He rushes toward the mound, ready to swing his bat at the pitcher. The part of Steve's personality that seems to be in control at that moment is the (*a*) id (*b*) ego (*c*) superego (*d*) libido.

6 Which of the following statements about the id is *true?* (*a*) Human beings would be much happier if the id could be removed at birth. (*b*) The id is the source of the energy that drives the personality. Without it, there would be no creativity, love, or strong emotion. (*c*) The id is the only element in the personality that keeps people from behaving like wild beasts. (*d*) The id provides the energy and intellect needed to solve complex problems.

7 Depressed because her SAT scores were too low to get her into a well-known university, Sally

goes to a party and drinks too much. She is using the defense mechanism of (*a*) repression (*b*) reaction formation (*c*) regression (*d*) sublimation.

8 Recovered from her hangover, Sally tells her friends that she didn't really want to go away to college anyway. "Besides, my lousy high school didn't prepare me properly for the SAT," she says. Now Sally's using (*a*) repression (*b*) rationalization (*c*) regression (*d*) projection.

9 Probably the most critical of the psychosexual stages, because it is the time when the Oedipus complex must be resolved, is the (*a*) oral stage (*b*) anal stage (*c*) phallic stage (*d*) genital stage.

10 During his psychoanalysis, Stanley began to forget his appointments even though he had been seeing Dr. Murdock on Monday afternoons for nine months. Dr. Murdock suspects that Stanley has reached a point of (*a*) transference (*b*) resistance (*c*) free association (*d*) regression.

■ EXPLORING CONCEPTS

1 How would you define personality? Why are psychologists so interested in developing a workable personality theory?

2 Can you spot examples of Sheldon's somatotypes among the people around you? Do their personality characteristics seem to match their physical attributes?

3 Describe the roles of the id, the ego, and the superego. What kind of behavior would result if the superego failed to develop properly? Cite some examples from your own recent experience of the influence of these forces.

4 Some critics charge Freud with saying that the adult personality is shaped during childhood, and that it can never be changed. How would a Freudian answer that charge?

5 Name the psychosexual stages of development. What behaviors would you expect from a child as he or she passes through each of these stages?

6 Give a real-life example of someone using each of the eight defense mechanisms. Which ones seem potentially most harmful? Which ones seem least harmful (when not used to excess)?

■ HANDS-ON ACTIVITIES

1 Does astrology give any real insights into personality? You can run an interesting test that may give you at least a partial answer to this question. First, consult an astrology book and list the personality traits associated with each sign of the zodiac. Next, draw up a list of ten notable figures from history, such as Madame Curie, John Kennedy, Julius Caesar, Susan B. Anthony, Martin Luther King, Jr., Mohandas Gandhi, Benito Juárez, and the like. Look up these people in encyclopedias, biographies, and other sources. List their actual personality traits along with their birthdays. Do they correlate with the astrological predictions? Adolf Hitler, for example, was a Taurus. Did he have the predicted Taurus qualities of generosity and caring for others?

2 Do the psychosexual stages actually exist? After carefully defining the behaviors that would be expected at each stage, observe children and infants of differing ages to see if you can spot oral, anal, phallic, and latent activities. It might help to consult with the child's mother or father, since they see the youngster on an intimate, daily basis. Present your findings in a paper or make an oral report to your class.

3 Free association is one of the key techniques of Freudian psychoanalysis. You can experiment with a similar method for getting in touch with your own unconscious. First, choose a time and place where your privacy is assured. Equip yourself with paper and a pen. Begin by jotting down anything that seems important or interesting—your feelings, recent experiences, personal problems. Don't make a conscious effort to direct the writing in any way. Forget about grammar and style. Just keep on writing. After a while, your thoughts should begin to flow. Let them go, one idea picking up from another. You may come up with some useful insights into repressed emotions, or you may come across solutions to what seemed like unsolvable problems.

4 Try making a poster or collage representing the roles the id, the ego, and the superego play in your behavior. The id, for example, might be represented by pictures that show basic drives, creativity, open expressions of love, satisfaction of hunger, and the like. The ego can be shown as people *doing* things, such as driving, playing, working, and studying. The superego represents morality and authority. Show it with pictures of a house of worship, parents scolding a child, a police officer or judge, and so on. A few old magazines will probably provide all the material you need for making an artistic poster.

5 Keep a "defense mechanism" diary for a few days. This diary will serve two purposes. First, it will help you get in touch with your own behavior patterns, a useful goal under any circumstances. Second, you will gain a greater appreciation of the role defense mechanisms play in protecting the ego. You may not find yourself using all of the defense mechanisms described on pages 187–191, but almost everybody resorts to rationalization, displacement, and regression on a fairly regular basis.

6 To find out more about the best-known name in psychology, use the Internet's magic carpet to explore the Freud Museum in London < *www.freud.org.uk/* >. The home page provides links to wherever you choose to go in the museum—but be sure to save some time for poking around in the Dream Exhibition. Click on any dream title and you'll be taken to Freud's interpretation of its meaning. Share your favorite dream analysis with your classmates.

FOR FURTHER READING

Appignanesi, Richard. *Freud for Beginners*. New York: Phantheon Books, 2003. This seriously lighthearted look at psychoanlytic theory is billed as a "documentary comic book." Appignanesi's text, ably illuminated by Oscar Zarate's drawings, provides a refreshingly down-to-earth introduction to Freud, his work, and his times.

Freud, Sigmund. *The Interpretation of Dreams*. New York: Oxford University Press, 2000. For readers who want to explore Freud's writings, this seminal 1900 book contains his first comprehensive description of the role of the unconscious. Although this new edition remains faithful to Freud's style and beliefs, Professor Joyce Crick's modern insights add greatly to the value of her translation.

Janda, Louis. *The Psychologist's Book of Personality Tests*. New York: John Wiley & Sons, 2000. This book puts 24 psychological tests in your hands, each designed to identify the barriers that stand between you and a more productive life. The tests zero in on personal barriers, interpersonal barriers, and your capacity for change.

After you score each test, Dr. Janda provides expert advice on how to make use of the results.

Meyers, Ted. *Shrink Yourself.* New York: St. Martin's Press, 2001. This humorous look at psychoanalysis allows you to "consult" with Dr. Freud himself. Your fifty-minute therapy session will introduce you to ink blots, the Oedipus complex, repression, dream analysis, Freudian slips, and much more.

Reef, Catherine. *Sigmund Freud, Pioneer of the Mind.* New York: Clarion Books, 2001. This very readable book starts by walking you through the life experiences that helped mold the creator of psychoanalysis. Freud emerges as a dedicated doctor who was forced to endure public ridicule as he struggled to give voice to the insights that would help his patients conquer their personal demons.

Stone, Irving. *The Passions of the Mind.* New York: Penguin Books, 1987. As an alternative to works of straight biography, this fictionalized account of Freud's life and work provides a humanized approach to the great pioneer of the psychoanalytic theory.

Storr, Anthony. *Churchill's Black Dog, Kafka's Mice, and Other Phenomena of the Human Mind.* New York: Grove Press, 1990. This collection of essays explores the role of the personality and the "divine discontent" that motivates both artistic and scientific creativity. The title essay, an analysis of Winston Churchill's depressive personality and its effect on his leadership of Great Britain during World War II, is particularly interesting.

Chapter

7 PERSONALITY THEORY SINCE FREUD

The revolution inspired by Sigmund Freud at the turn of the century opened a debate that still echoes through modern psychology. Many young psychologists became firm supporters of Freud and his psychoanalytic theories. Others followed Freud for a time but then broke away to establish their own schools of thought. And a sizable group never accepted Freud's interpretation of personality at all.

As a result, psychology today seems a little like the automobile market. You can "shop around" for a system that matches your own insights about human behavior. If you want to find out which system is "best," however, that's a little like trying to choose between a Ford and a Chevrolet. Each school of psychology insists that its own theories best explain the complexities of human personality.

Behavioral psychologists, for example, have little use for Freudian ideas about the unconscious or the Oedipus complex. They believe that almost all behavior is a reaction to stimuli from the world around you. Control the stimuli, they say, and you can control behavior.

During a long and productive career, the famous behaviorist B. F. Skinner never hesitated, when given the opportunity, to apply

his theories to real life. Dr. Skinner startled the country in the mid-1940s when he raised his baby daughter in an enclosed crib. Skinner called the crib a "baby tender," but critics labeled Deborah Skinner "the baby in the box."

Skinner designed the baby tender because he wanted Deborah to have the best possible environment. The baby tender was actually a glassed-in, temperature-controlled crib (see Figure 7.1). Skinner thought that if his invention worked for Deborah, it would change the way all babies were raised. As a behaviorist, he was certain that baby tenders would produce healthy, happy children.

Skinner had observed that babies raised in tropical climates need little clothing. In colder climates, parents must bundle their babies in several layers of clothing and blankets. The clothing restricts movement and can cause rashes. When they're freed of confining clothing, babies seem more content. Skinner also noted that someone has to change and wash all those diapers, shirts, and sheets.

Skinner designed the baby tender so that the only clothing Deborah needed was a diaper. Temperature and humidity controls kept her warm and comfortable. She never developed a rash or caught a cold. "She has

FIGURE 7.1 ▓ Behaviorist B. F. Skinner raised his daughter in this baby tender. The experiment was part of his effort to design an environment that develops healthy, stable adult personalities. Why didn't the baby tender become popular? Would you raise your child in one?

never shown any sign of not wanting to be put back and simply does not cry," Skinner wrote in his autobiography. "The only times she has cried in the past four months . . . have been when she had diphtheria shots . . . , when I nipped the tip of her finger while trimming her nails, and once or twice when we have taken her bottle away to adjust the nipple!"

As a bonus, the baby tender was so efficient that the Skinners had to bathe Deborah only twice a week. Skinner installed a single 10-yard-long sheet so that a clean section could easily be cranked into place. The glass

sides of the air crib also kept out noise, and a shade protected Deborah from light when she was sleeping.

Eve Skinner enthusiastically supported her husband's attempts to simplify child care. She reported that the baby tender reduced her own work load and kept Deborah free from the colds and sniffles that often afflict babies. Not everyone admired the invention, however. After the baby tender was pictured in a national magazine, many people called it a "human goldfish bowl" that cut Deborah off from normal human contacts. Rumors started in later years that Deborah became psychotic because of her stay in the baby tender. In fact, she graduated from college, married happily, and earned an international reputation as an artist.

Skinner defended his invention. He told his critics, "The baby is not at all isolated socially. She is taken up for feeding, of course, and at six months spends about one and one-half hours per day in a play pen or teeter-chair. . . . She . . . greets us with a big smile when we look at her though the window."* As Skinner noted years later, many hundreds of babies have been reared in similar devices.

OK, you're probably saying at this point, "Hold on a minute. Would Freud agree with Skinner that raising a baby 'in a box' is a good thing?" Probably not. So how can anyone have faith in psychologists if they're always so far apart?

Most of psychology's critics forget that modern psychology barely predates the airplane. Wilhelm Wundt opened the first psychology lab in 1879. And no matter how hard Wundt and later researchers tried to put their field on a strictly scientific basis, human nature refuses to fit neatly into a test tube. As a result, psychologists have seldom agreed

upon the meaning of the data they gather. Given this basic handicap, perhaps a young science like psychology should be applauded for its successes rather than blamed for its lack of consistency.

In this chapter, you'll learn about five major schools of psychology to go with your understanding of Freud: the behaviorists, the neo-Freudians, the Jungians, the humanists, and the existentialists. And if you're still wondering what Skinner was trying to prove when he put Deborah in her "box," it seems only fair to begin with the behaviorists.

7.1 How do the behaviorists describe the development of human personality?

7.2 What have the neo-Freudians contributed to personality theory?

7.3 What contributions did Carl Jung make to personality theory?

7.4 How do the humanist psychologists approach personality theory?

7.5 What have the existentialists and other creative thinkers added to personality theory?

7.1 ▓ HOW DO THE BEHAVIORISTS DESCRIBE THE DEVELOPMENT OF HUMAN PERSONALITY?

Throughout the history of psychology, researchers have been faced with a curious paradox: They must study the workings of the mind without ever knowing exactly what goes on inside the brain. John B. Watson (1878–1958) tried to cut through that problem in 1913 by announcing that psychology should no longer deal with the mind. Only

* From B.F. Skinner, *The Shaping of a Behaviorist* (Knopf, 1979), pp. 275–305.

behavior is observable and verifiable, he said. Therefore, behavior is the only proper subject for the psychologist.

Watson's theories were greatly influenced by Ivan Pavlov's historic work on classical conditioning (see pages 7–8). Pavlov, a Russian physiologist, proved that he could condition (that is, train) dogs to salivate when they heard a musical tone. Pavlov sounded the tone whenever he fed a meat powder to the dogs. After six to eight trials, sounding the tone caused the dogs to salivate whether food was present or not. What particularly interested Watson was the fact that salivation in dogs is a reflex action. Pavlov had trained his dogs to do something over which they had no conscious control.

Watson went on to describe behavior as a system of *stimulus-response* units. In behaviorist terms, any behavior can be represented as S→R (stimulus causes response). When an infant sees its mother, for example, the sight of the mother is the stimulus, S. The stimulus activates certain circuits in the nervous system (signified by the arrow) that are conditioned to interpret that particular stimulus as signifying food, warmth, and love. The baby's response, R, is determined by the strength of the stimulus. When mom's face comes into focus, the baby smiles, coos, and waves its arms. Clearly, it's expecting to be picked up and cuddled.

B. F. Skinner (1904–1990), Watson's successor as the leading American behaviorist, also dismissed the psychoanalytic approach. Freud, Skinner lectured, "loves the superego, the ego, and the id, and the various geographies of the mind and all that stuff. I say we can get along without that. In fact, we can get along better without it."

Skinner also believed that the development of the personality is too important to leave to parents and the random learning experiences that are part of growing up. In his novel *Walden Two,* Skinner invented a self-sufficient community run on behaviorist principles. Professional nurses raise the children, shaping their personalities to the type of behavior needed to maintain a stable and productive society. When Skinner applied these same principles to all of American society in *Beyond Freedom and Dignity,* the reaction was loud and angry. Critics accused him of trying to solve social problems by sacrificing free choice and individual responsibility. (The Pro & Con on page 208 debates this issue at greater length.)

BEHAVIORIST THEORY: HOW RESPONSES ARE LEARNED

Behaviorists believe that infants are born with only three instinctive responses: fear, rage, and love. All other behaviors, they reason, develop through learning. Skinner classifies all behavior as either respondent or operant.

RESPONDENT BEHAVIOR. When a stimulus causes a reflexive, automatic, or involuntary response, it is termed *respondent behavior.* For example, if someone directs a puff of air at your eye, you will blink. The air puff is the stimulus: the reflexive blink is the response (puff → blink). But that same eye blink can be conditioned, just like the salivation of Pavlov's dogs. Suppose that the experimenter sounds a clicker at the same instant the air puff hits your eye. Now the S→R is $\left.{puff \atop click}\right|$→blink. If that stimulus is repeated a number of times, you will eventually be conditioned to blink when you hear the click, even when no air puff is used. Now the S→R can be read as click → blink.

OPERANT BEHAVIOR. Behaviors that act on the environment in order to gain a reward are called *operant behaviors.* Most human activities, from eating a grape to flying a 747, fall into this category. Behaviorists believe that operant behaviors can be conditioned by *reinforcement* (any event that increases or decreases the probability that the behaviors take place). For example, when her parents praise nine-year-old Rosa for taking good care of her pets, they're using *positive reinforcement.* Rewards, such as praise, money, promotions, and other desirable things, make people feel better. Positive reinforcement, therefore, tends to increase desired behaviors.

Rosa's parents also have other choices. For example, they might choose *negative reinforcement* instead of positive reinforcement. In this case, Mrs. Tarrant begins yelling at Rosa to feed Snoopy and Garfield every af-

FIGURE 7.2 ▪ Skinner's Ping-Pong-playing pigeons learned their "sport" through operant conditioning. Do you see any similar conditioning in the behavior of these human "pigeons" working at their slot machines?

ternoon at 4:30. She goes on yelling and scolding until her daughter completes her tasks. In time, Rosa will learn the desired behavior (feeding her dogs) as a way of avoiding something she doesn't like (her mother's yelling).

Finally, Rosa's parents might try *punishment* as a way of forcing Rosa to do her work. Punishment means to penalize a person after an undesirable behavior takes place. To punish Rosa, her parents might take away a privilege, such as watching TV, every time she forgets to fill the dogs' supper dishes. To avoid the punishment, Rosa will probably start caring for her pets on time.

As a way of dramatizing his theories, Skinner used positive reinforcement to teach pigeons a number of remarkable behaviors. Pigeons make good subjects because they seem to enjoy their work! They will put in long hours doing a task over and over for a small number of food pellets. By using the shaping process described in the next paragraph, it took Skinner only a few hours to teach his pigeons to bowl, play Ping-Pong, and peck out a tune on a piano (see Figure 7.2). During World War II, in fact, Skinner proved he could train pigeons to guide self-propelled bombs to their targets. In lab exercises, the pigeons "flew" the bombs by pecking at a control panel each time the target image drifted off center in a viewscreen. Even though his pigeon bombardiers showed promise of being more accurate than the electronic gear then in use, military planners refused to give Skinner's pigeons a chance to demonstrate their skills in combat.

SHAPING BEHAVIOR. You may not want to train pigeons to blow up battleships, but you can train both people and animals to perform complex operant behaviors through a process known as *shaping*. The desired behavior must first be broken down into small steps. As the subject performs each step, you provide reinforcement. Your dog might respond to a biscuit, your little brother to a smile and praise. Step by step, you build up the more complex behavior by reinforcing each link in the chain. If your subject shows undesirable behaviors, you ignore them.

If you're teaching little Mark to swim, for example, you'd start by breaking swimming into individual movements. If Mark is shy of the water, you'd start by coaxing him to sit on the step with his feet in the shallow water.

After he learns to stand waist deep in the pool, he'll be ready to put his face in the water. Each bit of progress earns him your praise and encouragement. Gradually, as you add the arm and leg movements, a delighted Mark will one day find that he's actually swimming. You don't have to be a psychologist to see that this approach is much more effective than the old "sink-or-swim" method of throwing Mark off the dock to learn on his own. (Activity 3 on page 234, gives you an opportunity to experiment with shaping behavior.)

BEHAVIORISM APPLIED TO THE PERSONALITY

Behaviorists believe that they can also explain the underlying causes of neurotic behavior. Even though they reject concepts such as the unconscious, they recognize that early life experiences can condition adult behavior.

In an experiment carried out in 1920, Watson introduced 11-month-old Albert to a tame white rat. At first, Albert played happily with his new pet. But one day, just as the baby reached for the rat, Watson sounded a sharp, startling noise just behind Albert's head. Albert withdrew his hand and began to cry. After several repetitions, Albert cried whenever the rat was brought in, even after the noise was stopped. In behaviorist terms, Albert had been *conditioned* to fear the rat because he connected it with the fear-producing noise ($\left.{\text{rat} \atop \text{noise}}\right| \rightarrow \text{fear}$). Albert also generalized his fear to other furry animals and even to inanimate objects such as a fur coat and a Santa Claus mask.

Behaviorists, therefore, classify neurotic behaviors as poorly chosen responses to stimuli. Underlying these responses (an unreasoning fear of high places, for example) is a general anxiety that makes it impossible for the individual to cope with the symptoms. In therapy, a behavioral psychologist might learn that Eunice's fear of heights began when she was trapped in a tree overnight by playmates who took away the ladder. The behaviorist would largely ignore this childhood event and concentrate on helping Eunice overcome her specific disability.

One common technique is called *systematic desensitization*. Over several meetings, Eunice will first be taught to relax. Then she will gradually be led to think about being in high places. When she can think about heights without disabling fear, she might be taken to a second-story window. With that conquered, she can then go up to the third story. Eventually, she'll "graduate" by walking freely to the edge of the observation deck of the tallest building in town.

In brief, behaviorists believe that if people behave "normally" they probably are healthy human beings. Unlike Freud, the behaviorists have no desire to backtrack through the dark maze of the mind to discover some distant childhood trauma. By concentrating on relieving the symptoms of disturbed behavior, they feel that they can benefit the greatest number of people. Time is too short and the pressures of modern living too great, they believe, to do anything else.

▪ SECTION CHECKUP

1 How does the behaviorist use stimulus-response theory to explain human behavior and personality?

2 Contrast respondent and operant behaviors. Give an example of each.

3 Explain the concept of conditioning. How could you use positive reinforcement to train a dog to jump through a hoop?

4 Use the Little Albert experiment to explain the behaviorist's concept of neurotic behavior. How could you use systematic desensitization to end Albert's fear of furry objects and animals?

▓ PRO & CON:

Is Behavior Modification the Answer to Social Problems?

Most psychologists prefer to treat individual patients. But one group of behaviorists, influenced by B. F. Skinner, has more ambitious ideas. In *Beyond Freedom and Dignity,* Skinner said that social problems, such as crime, violence, racism, and other antisocial behaviors, can be eliminated if society adopts behaviorist conditioning techniques. But the debate over the behaviorist approach arouses considerable controversy. Listen to the two sides argue their case; then decide how you would vote on this issue.

PRO

1 Since all behavior is learned, society can guarantee that people act in socially desirable ways only if it uses behaviorist conditioning techniques to shape the behaviors it wants.

2 What actually goes on inside the human mind cannot be studied scientifically. Psychologists, therefore, must limit their work to behavior that can be observed and verified.

3 The belief that behaviorist techniques will inevitably lead to a "Big Brother" brand of dictatorship is groundless. The fact that conditioning techniques have been misused in the past, such as in the brainwashing of war prisoners, should not count against their use in a free society.

4 Traditional methods of dealing with social problems have been tried for centuries—with incredibly bad results. Isn't it time society tried a scientifically proven method of curing social problems? Why wait until humanity destroys itself?

5 Behaviorism offers the only experimentally validated method of coping with emotionally disturbed people in today's mixed-up society. Other schools of psychology depend on "insights" and observations that cannot be proved or disproved experimentally.

CON

1 Behaviorism ignores almost everything that psychology has learned about personality since Freud opened the doors to the unconscious. Conditioning can alter behavior, but it cannot erase the powerful influence of the unconscious.

2 Behaviorists seem to believe that humans are little more than "complicated" animals. But treating people as animals that can be easily and safely conditioned ignores the immense complexity and potential of the human mind.

3 Who will design the behaviorist "blueprint" for people's future behavior? History provides little assurance that any form of government can be trusted with that much power. In fact, many people are already alarmed by the growing tendency of big government to invade the private lives of its citizens.

4 Today's political, economic, and social systems are not perfect, but neither are they total failures. Most people enjoy freedom of choice and freedom to grow and become what they will. Social peace bought at the cost of turning everyone into a programmed robot is too expensive.

5 Behaviorist techniques can be useful for modifying simple habits such as smoking or overeating. But the behaviorist flounders when called on to treat patients who suffer from deeply rooted emotional problems such as schizophrenia.

Do you think the opponents of behaviorist techniques win the debate? Or do you believe that the problems facing humanity today are so pressing that behaviorist techniques must be adopted in order to preserve civilization?

7.2 ▨ WHAT HAVE THE NEO-FREUDIANS CONTRIBUTED TO PERSONALITY THEORY?

Although Sigmund Freud's theories generated widespread interest and support, they were opened up to question by the research of 20th-century sociologists and anthropologists. These new studies described human beings as highly adaptable to changes in the environment. In keeping with these newer insights, a number of psychoanalysts began to modify Freud's ideas. Among these *neo-Freudians,* as they are often called, are such important names as Alfred Adler, Karen Horney, and Erik Erikson. (The work of another great neo-Freudian, Erich Fromm, is discussed in Chapter 5, page 159.) The neo-Freudians believe that social influences play a greater role in shaping personality than do heredity and early childhood experiences (see the box on page 212).

ALFRED ADLER

Alfred Adler (1870–1937), a Viennese psychiatrist, broke with Freud in 1911 to form a new school he called "individual psychology." Adler believed that Freud put too much emphasis on the role of sexuality in personality development. Instead, Adler placed social needs on an equal basis with Freud's sex drives. He claimed that personality develops through expression of inborn *social urges.* Each society modifies these social urges according to its own values.

THE CREATIVE SELF. The *creative self* was Adler's name for the inner system that guides the individual toward a fulfilling style of life. In a sense, the creative self *is* the person, for it makes you the unique person you are. Each person chooses a particular role because society seems to reward that choice. Your creative self may emerge as happy-go-lucky, intellectual, romantic, or melancholy. If choosing a melancholy role seems strange, remember that the melancholy person receives rewards of sympathy, attention, and the "right" to blame others for misfortune.

All of your drives to be a superior person grow out of this creative self. Unlike Freud, Adler believed that the individual consciously chooses the kind of person he or she will become. By awarding that role to the unconscious, Freud seemed to deny freedom of choice to the individual.

OTHER KEY CONCEPTS. Although Adler is not as important a personality theorist as Freud and Carl Jung (see the following section), a number of his ideas have gained widespread acceptance.

1. *Feelings of inferiority.* Adler believed that *feelings of inferiority* (the belief that other people are better than you are) greatly

FIGURE 7.3 ▨ Nobody knows better than Charlie Brown what it means to struggle with feelings of inferiority. How could Charlie compensate for his lack of social standing?

PEANUTS reprinted by permission of UFS, Inc.

Positive Reinforcement Can Train A Boss, a Beagle, or a Backhand

Thanks to the pioneering work of behaviorists like B. F. Skinner and the practical lessons taught by animal trainers like biologist Karen Pryor, the world is a better place for both humans and animals. Pryor says you can train almost any animal if you have a generous supply of food and a bottomless supply of affection and patience. "People don't realize how easy it is to train even difficult, dangerous animals without knocking them around," she points out. "All dolphin shows are based entirely on positive reinforcement, not aversive control. You cannot use a whip or a bridle, or even your fist, on an animal that just swims away."

Positive reinforcement works on humans just as surely as it works on animals. Here are some real-life examples that show this powerful mechanism at work:

■ Back in colonial times, wise old Ben Franklin used behavior modification to help an army chaplain increase church attendance. When the chaplain complained that the soldiers were not coming to services, Franklin reminded him that as chaplain, he was also the unit's rum steward. Hand out the rum ration just after prayers, Franklin advised, and you'll soon have soldiers flocking to your services. The chaplain followed the advice, Franklin wrote in his autobiography, and "never were prayers more generally and . . . more punctually attended."

■ Most students suffer in silence when a teacher scolds the class because some students haven't done their homework. A clever senior named Evangeline, tired of hearing the daily tongue-lashing, decided to teach her English teacher about positive reinforcement. "Instead of berating the class," she advised Dr. Marshall, "praise the students who do the homework." Marshall saw the value in Evangeline's suggestion and decided to try the experiment. Over the next several weeks, he started each class by reinforcing his students with public praise

influence behavior. Basic inferiority begins during childhood, when adults have almost total control of your life. To the child, everyone else seems bigger, stronger, and more powerful. Most people gradually overcome these feelings as they grow up. But mental disabilities, lack of social skills, poverty, and discrimination can also cause painful feelings of inferiority in both children and adults (see Figure 7.3).

Healthy people try to overcome their feelings of inferiority. Nonreaders will work hard to master basic reading skills. The classic "90-pound-weakling" will take up weight lifting. Adler called this *compensation,* the attempt to deal with the specific causes of inferiority. History records many examples of such compensation. Napoleon, for example, overcame his self-consciousness about his height and Corsican background to become a great French military and political leader. President Theodore Roosevelt refused to let his weak body and poor eyesight keep him from achieving success as a boxer, horseman, soldier, writer, and politician.

Adler also warned that compensation can

for the assignments they completed. By the third week, the class was happier, grades were improving, and three-fourths of the class was turning in the assigned work.

■ Andrew liked to let his beagle off the leash during their walks in the country, but the excited dog often refused to return when called. Tongue-lashings did not change Shadrack's behavior. At last, armed with some good advice from an animal trainer, the boy decided to try positive reinforcement. On the next walk, he made a huge fuss over the dog the first time Shadrack returned without being called. Each time the dog came back, he greeted it with enthusiastic praise, pats, and hugs. At the end of the walk, Shadrack came running as soon as Andrew called. The boy repeated the reinforcement each time he took Shadrack for a walk, and the dog was never again a problem.

■ B. F. Skinner loved to demonstrate the effectiveness of his theories. As a guest of honor at a convention, he was given a golden opportunity when one of the speakers, psychoanalyst Erich Fromm, attacked his behaviorist theories. Noting that Fromm was chopping the air with one hand for emphasis, Skinner began to nod and smile each time the speaker made his chopping motion. Sure enough, Fromm (who could see the grand old man of behaviorism smiling and nodding in the front row) began to chop more and more vigorously. At one point his wristwatch slipped over his hand, propelled by his nearly constant chopping motions.

■ Sheri was a fine young tennis player, but she could not control her backhand. Each time she pounded a ball into the net, she grew more tense and angry. Finally, Coach Berry took Sheri aside. "Forget the bad shots," Berry said, "and concentrate on the good ones. If you miss, ignore it and focus on the next point. Every time you hit a good backhand, give yourself a pat on the back. Tell yourself, 'Way to go, Sheri!' " Because Sheri's strokes were basically sound, the positive reinforcement worked. Instead of dreading the times when she was forced to use her backhand, she was soon hitting solid winners from both sides of the court.

Can you think of a behavior that you'd like to change—either in yourself or in a friend, relative, or coworker? Do you have a pet that has a bad habit or two? Positive reinforcement, properly and consistently applied, should do the trick.

turn into overcompensation. People may become so determined to compensate that they go too far. Caught up in his own sense of destiny, for example, Napoleon plunged Europe into a long and bloody war. Overweight adolescents sometimes go on diets so severe that they endanger their health.

2. *Fictional finalism.* Adler thought that people are sometimes driven by ideals that may be pure fiction but are ones they pursue with great determination. Common examples of what he called *fictional finalism* include "Honesty is the best policy," and "If I'm good, everyone will love me." Healthy people can see beyond these overly simple rules, but neurotic personalities often let such slogans rule their lives. Honesty *is* a good policy. But can you imagine the strain of being totally honest, in word and deed, at all times?

3. *Social interest.* Most people want to make their communities better places in which to live. Adler believed that this feeling is an inborn characteristic. He showed that *social interest* explains why people will risk their lives to rescue a stranger or will give generously to a charity. In more and more

Freud Versus the Neo-Freudians: Major Areas of Agreement and Disagreement

FREUD AND THE NEO-FREUDIANS AGREE:

1 Unconscious motivation is a powerful force in human behavior.

2 Repression is an important method for coping with anxiety.

3 The defense mechanisms play a key role in protecting the ego.

4 Early childhood is the time when the basic personality is formed.

FREUD AND THE NEO-FREUDIANS DISAGREE:

FREUD SAYS:

1 Sex is the basic human drive and the greatest single influence on behavior.

2 Childhood sexuality must be understood for its critical effect on development of the personality. This process often requires psychoanalysis.

3 Resolution of the conflicts caused by the Oedipus complex is essential to proper emotional growth. This process is common to all peoples, everywhere.

4 Women are an inferior sex.

5 The id, the ego, and the superego actually exist and play an important role in the working of the human mind.

THE NEO-FREUDIAN SAYS:

1 Social and cultural forces, not sex, are the most important influences on behavior.

2 The personality can fully develop if people are given the skills and insights they need to handle personal relationships successfully.

3 Resolution of conflicts that grow out of the clash between individual needs and the demands of the environment is basic to proper emotional growth.

4 Neither sex can be considered superior to the other.

5 Concepts such as the id, the ego, and the superego should not be thought to have an actual existence.

---

communities, however, fears for personal safety now override social interest.

KAREN HORNEY

Karen Horney, a German psychiatrist (see BioBox on page 214), has been called "the gentle rebel of psychoanalysis." Although trained in Freudian methods, she came to believe that instinctive urges and childhood sexuality were not enough to explain all neurotic behavior. In addition, Horney also objected strenuously to Freud's labeling of women as the inferior sex. In *The Neurotic Personality of Our Time*, she described the importance of social forces in shaping personality. She believed that the development of the ability to cope with life is directly related to how well the child copes with threats to his or her security. The adult personality, Horney explained, grows out of the child's success or failure in coping with this basic anxiety.

BASIC ANXIETY. Unable to control its environment, the infant feels helpless and insecure. This *basic anxiety* is often increased by negative parental behaviors, such as indifference, harsh criticism, lack of guidance, overprotection, and erratic discipline. Unless children overcome this basic anxiety during childhood, they will often choose neurotic behaviors during adolescence and adulthood. Horney defines neurotic behaviors as poorly chosen strategies for solving problems. For example, Jason, a basically healthy person, feels angry when he's denied a raise for which he's worked hard. But he understands the real world. He resolves his anger by asking the boss for an explanation. If the interview goes badly, he begins looking for another job. But Roger, who has never resolved his basic anxiety, cannot control his anger in the same situation. He curses the boss and quits his job on the spot.

NEUROTIC NEEDS. Karen Horney made a major contribution to personality theory by identifying the basic neurotic needs. These needs, she believed, grow out of the strategies people use to combat anxiety. She considered them neurotic because they often force people to make unrealistic demands on themselves or on others.

1. *Neurotic needs that move an individual toward people.* (a) The neurotic need for affection and approval: The individual must please others and live up to their expectations. (b) The neurotic need for a "partner" who will take over one's life: Afraid to be alone, the individual gives all control of his or her life to someone else. (c) The neurotic need for prestige: Self-confidence and personal identity rest totally on the expectation of receiving recognition from others. (d) The neurotic need for personal admiration: The individual expects to be admired on the basis of a false self-image.

2. *Neurotic needs that move an individual away from people.* (a) The neurotic need to restrict one's life within narrow borders: To be noticed is frightening or painful, so the individual withdraws into as narrow a corner

of life as possible. (b) The neurotic need for self-sufficiency and independence: The individual has been hurt when attempting to build relationships with others, so refuses to accept love or friendship. (c) The neurotic need for perfection: To make a mistake is to admit weakness, so the individual tries to be infallible at all times.

3. *Neurotic needs that move an individual against people.* (a) The neurotic need for power: Power and control are so important that the individual will do anything to attain them. (b) The neurotic need to exploit others: Taking advantage of other people serves as a way of relieving feelings of helplessness and insecurity. (c) The neurotic need for personal achievement: The individual tries desperately to achieve ever more splendid successes, even though the triumphs come at the expense of others.

Can these neurotic tendencies be eliminated from people's lives? Horney believed that the best solution would be to raise all children in an atmosphere of warmth, security, love, and respect. Adults who find their lives controlled by these self-defeating needs often require the assistance of a therapist. In therapy, Karen Horney's insights can help a troubled person become happier and more productive.

ERIK H. ERIKSON

Erik Erikson (1902–1994) is one of the key names in modern psychology. He began his career while teaching art in Vienna at a school founded by Anna Freud. With her encouragement, he turned to the study of psychoanalysis. In 1933, he moved to the United States, where he became an eminent therapist and teacher. Erikson first came to public attention in 1958, when he published a biography called *Young Man Luther.* In this book, he interpreted Martin Luther's religious career in psychoanalytic terms. This new approach to interpreting history, called *psychohistory,* has

Karen Horney:
The Gentle Rebel of Psychoanalysis

If a team of neurobiologists set out to clone the perfect psychologist, they might well use Karen Horney (1885–1952) as their model. The German-born psychoanalyst brought a warmth, dedication and joy of living to her work that touched all who knew her.

Karen Horney was born into a world that did not accept women as the equals of men. In order to become a psychiatrist, she had to overcome centuries of built-up prejudice. But she was strong-minded and intelligent. By the time she finished medical school and was ready to take the state exams, her professors had learned to respect her abilities. As a result, they let her schedule her tests so that she would have time to nurse her infant daughter.

That same determination served her well when she began to rebel against Freudian teachings. The more she worked with neurotic patients, the more she came to believe that psychosexual drives could not explain all disturbed behavior. Even though her new ideas cost her a teaching position, she refused to back down. Today, Horney's insistence on the role of cultural factors in causing basic anxiety has been largely accepted by most psychologists.

One of Horney's useful insights relates to what she called "the tyranny of the *should*." She described how people contribute to their own emotional distress in these words:

> Let us consider another demand: I should always be understanding, sympathetic, and helpful. . . . I had a patient [who felt as though she should be as forgiving as a priest]. But she did not . . . have any of the attitudes or qualities which enabled the priest to act as he did toward the criminal. She could act charitably at times because she felt

that she *should* be charitable, but she did not feel charitable. As a matter of fact, she did not feel much of anything for anybody. . . . Without being aware of it, her neurosis had made her egocentric and bent on her own advantage—all of which was covered up by a layer of compulsive humility and goodness.

Where do such conflicts come from? Horney believed that the problem begins in childhood with "a lack of genuine warmth and affection. A child can stand a great deal of what is often regarded as traumatic—such as sudden weaning, occasional beating, sex experiences—as long as inwardly the child feels wanted and loved. Needless to say, a child feels keenly whether love is genuine and cannot be fooled by any faked demonstrations."

Along with such insights, Horney also believed that human beings can change, grow, and escape their neuroses. She herself remained a growing, vibrant person all her life. A therapist, writer, and teacher, she also liked to sing, eat good food, and drink good wine.

As her friend Paul Tillich, the great theologian and philosopher, said of her, "Few people were so strong in the affirmation of their being, so full of the joy of living. . . . She wrote books but loved human beings."

Can you see why Karen Horney was so highly regarded by all who knew her? How would you summarize her insights into the causes of the troubled personality?

since become an accepted—but controversial—tool of historical research.

THE THEORY OF PSYCHOSOCIAL DEVELOPMENT.

Erikson's theory of psychosocial development ranks as a landmark contribution to our understanding of personality development. The theory is based on three concepts:

1. At the same time that people pass through the Freudian stages of psychosexual development, they also move through a series of *psychosocial stages* of ego development. At each stage, people must achieve a new way of seeing themselves in relation to society and to other people. In other words, 18-year-old Jeanne must face life on different terms than she did when she was eight years old.

2. Personality development continues throughout each person's life cycle. In popular terms, Erikson is saying that no one "has it made" at any age.

3. During each stage of life, a conflict develops between positive and negative ego qualities. These conflicts are present at every age, but each life stage requires that you focus on a particular crisis. Failure to resolve that particular crisis will result in damage to the ego. This damage makes the next stage that much harder to overcome.

STAGES OF PSYCHOSOCIAL DEVELOPMENT.

In Erikson's concept, each of us moves through eight stages of personality development during the life cycle. Each stage brings its own crisis that must be resolved.

1. *Trust vs. Mistrust* (infancy, birth to one year). Babies learn to trust or fear the world depending on their experiences with other people, particularly their parents. They need to feel that the world is orderly and predictable. Without the ability to trust, the infant will face the second stage handicapped by anxiety and personal fears.

2. *Autonomy vs. Doubt* (early childhood, ages two and three). During this stage, chil-

dren must develop confidence and independence. Typically, this means that they learn to feed and dress themselves and become toilet trained. Children who are not given the opportunity to explore new skills and develop self-confidence will be left full of shame and doubt about their abilities.

3. *Initiative vs. Guilt* (play age, ages four and five). Active and curious, children of the play age should be encouraged to develop their intellectual resources and their individual interests. They should be free to run, play, fantasize, and question everything. Guilt feelings result when parents clamp down too hard on the vigorous, self-motivated activities of this age. Instead of saying, "Look at me!" the child may be forced to whisper, "I hope they don't see me doing this."

4. *Industry vs. Inferiority* (school age, ages six to 11). Most children enter school eager to learn and to demonstrate their growing intellectual skills. They want to learn about new things and love trying to make things with their hands. Group games give them a chance to explore their relationships with others. Teachers and parents who push too hard, however, can cut off their children's feelings of industry. Too much pressure may cause feelings of inferiority, for children cannot help but *feel* inferior when asked to complete tasks beyond their abilities.

5. *Identity vs. Role Confusion* (adolescence, ages 12 to 18). This critical period requires that adolescents find their own identity. This crisis is made more difficult by the other challenges of adolescence: dealing with sexual maturity, choosing a career, and working out relationships with parents. Erikson himself spent two years, from ages 18 to 20, wandering aimlessly through Germany and Italy, trying to resolve his own identity crisis. In time, he achieved a sense of identity, as his later career reveals. Young people who do not achieve their own identities enter adulthood confused about their goals, values, and vocational possibilities.

(Text continues on page 219.)

How Many Ages Are There, Anyway?

Are there three, five, seven, or eight "ages" along the way to our biblical "three score and ten"? The question has challenged philosophers and psychologists from ancient times to the present.

THE RIDDLE OF THE SPHINX (AN ANCIENT GREEK MYTH)

One day, while Oedipus was on his way to the city of Thebes, a terrible Sphinx stopped him. This winged monster, which had the body of a lion and the head of a woman, asked all who passed a riddle. The penalty for not guessing the answer was to be killed and eaten. The terrified Thebans had offered the throne and the hand of their widowed queen to whomever should answer the riddle and overcome the monster.

"What animal," the Sphinx asked Oedipus, "walks on four legs in the morning, two at noon, and on three at night?"

Oedipus quickly replied, "Man, for in the morning, the infancy of his life, he creeps on all fours. At noon, in his prime, he walks on two feet. And when the darkness of old age comes over him, the stick he uses for support becomes a third foot."

Thereupon the Sphinx threw herself over the rocky precipice and perished. Oedipus became King of Thebes and married (unknowingly) his mother, Jocasta, thus sealing the fate that had been prophesied for him at his birth.

FREUD'S PSYCHOSEXUAL STAGES

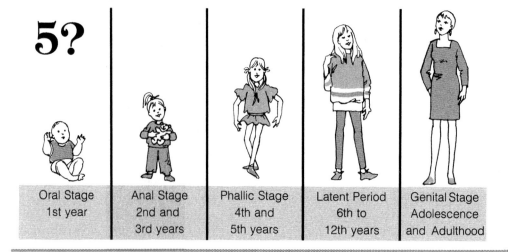

| Oral Stage 1st year | Anal Stage 2nd and 3rd years | Phallic Stage 4th and 5th years | Latent Period 6th to 12th years | Genital Stage Adolescence and Adulthood |

SHAKESPEARE'S SEVEN AGES OF MAN

All the world's a stage,
And all the men and women merely players.
They have their exits and their entrances,
And one man in his time plays many parts,
His acts being seven ages. At first the infant,
Mewling and puking in the nurse's arms.
Then the whining schoolboy, with his satchel
And shining morning face, creeping like snail
Unwillingly to school. And then the lover,
Sighing like a furnace, with a woeful ballad
Made to his mistress' eyebrow. Then a soldier,
Full of strange oaths, and bearded like
                    the pard,
Jealous in honor, sudden and quick in quarrel,
Seeking the bubble reputation
Even in the cannon's mouth. And then,
                    the justice,
In fair round belly with good capon lined,
With eyes severe, and beard of formal cut,
Full of wise saws and modern instances,
And so he plays his part. The sixth age shifts

Into the lean and slippered pantaloon,
With spectacles on nose, and pouch on side,
His youthful hose, well saved, a world too wide
For his shrunk shank, and his big manly voice,
Turning again toward childish treble pipes
And whistles in his sound. Last scene of all,
That ends this strange eventful history,
Is second childishness and mere oblivion,
Sans teeth, sans eyes, sans taste,
                    sans everything.

As You Like It, by William Shakespeare,
Act II, Scene vii

ERIKSON'S EIGHT STAGES OF DEVELOPMENT

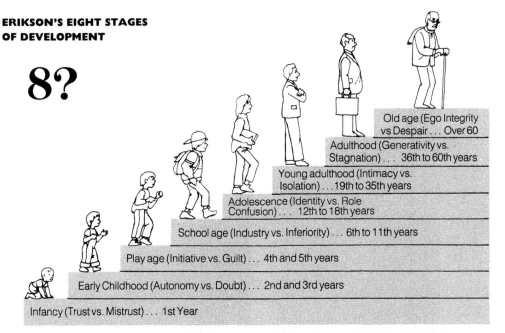

Old age (Ego Integrity vs Despair . . . Over 60

Adulthood (Generativity vs. Stagnation) . . . 36th to 60th years

Young adulthood (Intimacy vs. Isolation) . . . 19th to 35th years

Adolescence (Identity vs. Role Confusion) . . . 12th to 18th years

School age (Industry vs. Inferiority) . . . 6th to 11th years

Play age (Initiative vs. Guilt) . . . 4th and 5th years

Early Childhood (Autonomy vs. Doubt) . . . 2nd and 3rd years

Infancy (Trust vs. Mistrust) . . . 1st Year

Which interpretation makes the most sense to you? Why did you make that choice?

FIGURE 7.4 ■ From infancy to old age, each stage of the life cycle brings its own crisis and requires its own solution. Can you identify the five life stages illustrated here? What crisis does each of these persons face?

6. *Intimacy vs. Isolation* (young adult-hood, ages 19 to 35). Young adulthood usually finds people looking for a partner with whom they can share their lives. Erikson warned, however, that young adults will also find their values and identity challenged by both friends and lovers. This stage of life requires that young adults develop the strength to stick to commitments, even when they call for sacrifice or deferred gratification.

7. *Generativity vs. Stagnation* (adulthood, ages 36 to 60). Mature adults begin to plan for future generations, either through their children or by contributing their time and talents to their community. Such "generativity" adds greatly to the quality of life in any society. Examples of such activities include volunteer work in hospitals and at city hall, coaching youth athletic teams, going without a new car to pay for a child's college tuition, or joining a crusade to clean up the local water system. Erikson labeled "stagnant" those adults who are concerned only with themselves. They try to deny the aging process by concentrating solely on material pleasures.

8. *Ego Integrity vs. Despair* (old age, 60 and over). You probably know some well-integrated elderly people. These are men and women who cherish their successes, learn from their failures, and accept the inevitability of their own deaths. They remain active and involved right to the end, like the 80-year-old man who returns to college to "find out what's going on in the world." Elderly people who fill their conversations with, "I wish I'd had a chance to . . ." and, "It's not fair!" have not achieved ego integrity. Such

people often fear death and wake up each morning with a sense of despair that robs them of any joy during the years that remain.

IMPORTANCE OF ERIKSON'S WORK. Erikson's life-cycle theory allows psychologists to treat adult emotional crises as genuinely adult. By contrast, the Freudian analyst must always search for infantile traumas. Erikson's teachings, moreover, provide hope that early failures can be offset by later successes. A child who does not resolve the crisis of industry vs. inferiority at age seven, for example, can still overcome feelings of doubt and inadequacy later on. Often, added maturity enables people to develop on their own. In other cases, the help of a therapist may be needed. With Erikson's insights to draw on, you have a better idea of what lies ahead in your next life stage. Recognizing the crisis may be halfway to resolving it.

▓ SECTION CHECKUP

1 What is meant by the term *neo-Freudian?* What basic differences separate Freud and the neo-Freudians?

2 What did Adler mean by the creative self? What have feelings of inferiority to do with mental health?

3 How would Karen Horney define *basic anxiety?* How did she relate anxiety to neurotic behavior?

4 What does Erik Erikson mean when he says that each life stage carries with it a crisis that must be overcome? What is the crisis of your particular life stage?

7.3 ▓ WHAT CONTRIBUTIONS DID CARL JUNG MAKE TO PERSONALITY THEORY?

For seven years, from 1906 to 1913, it appeared that Carl Jung (1875–1961), a Swiss psychiatrist, would inherit Sigmund Freud's

role as leader of the psychoanalytic movement. The friendship that had grown between the two men ended, however, when

Jung refused to accept Freud's emphasis on sex as a primary force in personality development. Where Freud thought primarily of primitive drives, Jung placed equal emphasis on the spiritual and moral aspects of life. Jung's ideas were so original and his influence so great that he cannot be classified as a neo-Freudian. His concept of the personality, known as *analytic psychology,* stands on its own.

A jovial, vigorous man, Jung possessed a keen, active intellect. His investigations carried him far beyond the boundaries of psychology. During his busy life, he studied such varied fields as the occult, extrasensory perception, yoga, religion, mythology, and art. For a time, he even conducted a study of flying saucers! But Jung's passion remained the study of the *psyche,* his name for the human personality. Although he accepted many Freudian concepts, Jung enlarged the concept of the unconscious by adding several new ideas of his own.

THE JUNGIAN UNCONSCIOUS

Jung divided the unconscious into two parts, the personal unconscious and the collective unconscious.

THE PERSONAL UNCONSCIOUS. The *personal unconscious,* Jung believed, contains experiences that were once conscious but have since been forgotten, ignored, or repressed. Like Freud, Jung thought that these memories could influence an individual's conscious behavior. In this way, Jung's personal unconscious is quite similar to the Freudian unconscious.

Jung went on, however, to describe a number of organized groups of feelings, thoughts, and perceptions within the personal unconscious. He called each of these a *complex.* Jungian analysts often speak of a "mother complex" or a "power complex." Since a strong complex usually dominates the per-

sonality, it can be harmful if it prevents the person from establishing a realistic, freely chosen identity. A "money complex," for example, may lead Neal to sacrifice family and friends in his quest for financial gain. He may not be aware of this central theme in his behavior; he knows only that he must have money in order to feel at peace with himself.

THE COLLECTIVE UNCONSCIOUS. During his studies of art and literature, Jung found evidence of what he identified as universal instincts, drives, and memories. This *collective unconscious,* as he named it, forms a "racial memory" shared by all members of the human race. Jung believed that these collective memories cross all boundaries of time, skin color, and geography.

If you're wondering why you can't remember back to the Stone Age, Jung would say that no one can recall such ancient memories. They do exist, however, as unseen forces that influence your thoughts, feelings, and perceptions. The fact that many people love to hunt and fish wouldn't surprise Jung. He would say that the age-old urge to hunt and fish is an example of how the collective unconscious translates its influence into conscious behaviors.

Despite Jung's persuasive arguments, many psychologists refuse to accept the idea of the collective unconscious. Jung, however, insisted that two million years of evolutionary experience must have left their mark on the human brain. He pointed to the work of anthropologists, who have described apparently universal behaviors among widely separated peoples. What is a smile, a blush, a handshake, Jung asked, but an automatic physical response to the common pool of behaviors found in the collective unconscious?

ARCHETYPES. Jung was fascinated by the reappearance of common themes and symbols in dreams, literature, mythology, and art. Throughout history and in widely varied cul-

FIGURE 7.5 ▪ Carl Jung believed that art and literature provide clues to the existence of universal symbols that derive from our collective unconscious. Whether it's St. George dispatching a dragon or a silent movie hero risking his life above the wheels of a speeding locomotive, the hero archetype appears in all ages and all cultures. Can you think of other hero archetypes (male and female) that you've seen in recent films or television programs? (*St. George and the Dragon;* Raphael; © 1993 National Gallery of Art, *Washington; Andrew W. Mellon Collection.*)

tures, he found images of birth and rebirth, death, magic, God, the devil, the hero, the wise old man, and the earth mother. He called these universal thought patterns *archetypes*. These ideas come out of the collective unconscious, he believed.

Unlike complexes, which can dominate the personality, individual archetypes create images on which you base your understanding of the world around you. From them comes your sense of wholeness and completeness. Thus, your hero archetype gives you a sense of what it means to protect those you love and to fight for what is right. (See Figure 7.5.) Your earth-mother archetype, meanwhile, helps you understand the miracle of life and the nurturing of children.

Four of Jung's archetypes have evolved to

the point where they are treated as separate systems within the personality. These are the persona, the anima and animus, the shadow, and the self.

1. *Persona.* All people wear masks in public, Jung believed, behind which they hide their true natures. He called this mask the *persona.* Each individual forms his or her persona in response to social pressures, traditions, and the need to be accepted by others. Heidi's persona, for example, is that of the "good girl." She judges the "rightness" of everything she does according to her rigid concept of behavior. At times, Heidi would like to "break loose" from her self-created restrictions, but her persona is so important to her that she cannot admit to having such "bad"

feelings. That's not to say that it's unhealthy for Heidi to cling to her "good girl" persona. A Jungian analyst would become alarmed only if she allows the persona to dominate her life.

2. *Anima and animus.* Jung believed that all people carry elements of the opposite sex within their personalities. The *anima* is the feminine side of men, and the *animus* is the male side of women. These archetypes provide shading and balance to the personality. They enable each sex to understand and respond to the other. Some people have so idealized these archetypes, however, that no one can live up to their expectations. Joe's anima, for example, was shaped by his remarkably close relationship with his mother. Because his "ideal woman" archetype grew out of that idealized relationship, he "knows" that the woman he marries must not have a single blemish. Thus, it's little wonder that Joe is still looking for someone perfect enough for him to love.

3. *Shadow.* The *shadow* represents the primitive side of the personality. Perhaps you can see some elements of the Freudian id in the shadow, but the parallel is not exact. Socially unacceptable thoughts and desires that come from the shadow are usually repressed into the personal unconscious. Most people hide the shadow behind their persona. You could never love me, they seem to be saying, if you caught a glimpse of the terrible passions and selfish needs contained in my shadow.

4. *Self.* Analytic psychology places great emphasis on the concept of the *self.* Jung regarded the self as a life goal, a striving for unity and completeness. Few people reach this point, however, for all other elements of the personality must be fully developed first. Perhaps only a few great religious leaders and philosophers have attained the joining of the conscious and unconscious minds that is necessary for emergence of the completed self.

JUNG'S OTHER CONTRIBUTIONS

The popular terms that refer to shy and outgoing personalities, *introversion* and *extroversion*, were introduced in Jung's work. Introverts look inward and find pleasure in pursuing their own thoughts and feelings. They are happiest when they're alone or in small groups. Too many people tend to make them nervous. Extroverts, on the other hand, invest their psychic energy outside of themselves. They need company, excitement, and activity. Successful salespeople are usually extroverts. You've probably already discovered that you have both elements within your own personality. Jung said that one or the other usually dominates and that most people are aware of which one it is.

The word association test (see the box on page 223) also derives from Jung's analytic techniques. The test is widely used as a tool for revealing repressed or concealed personal data.

Carl Jung also brought a new compassion and openness to psychoanalysis. Despite the complexity of his ideas, people could relate to his outgoing personality. Jungian analysts sit facing the patient and take an active role in the therapy. As a consequence, Jung's approach to therapy has been described as warmer and less mechanical than Freud's.

■ SECTION CHECKUP

1 What are some of the basic differences between Jung's analytic psychology and Freud's psychoanalytic theory?

2 Distinguish between the personal unconscious and the collective unconscious.

3 What did Jung mean by a complex?

4 What is an archetype? How do archetypes affect behavior?

Using Free Association to Trap A Suspected "Criminal"

The Jungian free-association test is based on a simple principle: As the subject responds to a list of prepared words, repressed or concealed material will slip past the mind's censors and enter into speech. This experiment makes use of Jung's technique to expose a criminal suspect, much as the polygraph (lie detector) does, but without the elaborate equipment.

Step 1 On a slip of paper, write a description of a fictional crime. Include details of time, place, the identity of the victim, the amount of money stolen, the colors of the suspect's clothing, and the like.

Begin the description, "You have committed a serious crime. Last night, you. . . ." Make up several other slips of paper that simply state, "You are a subject in a psychological experiment. Thank you for your help."

Step 2 Extract from the scenario of the crime a list of ten key words. For the stickup of an armored car, these words might include *diamond, note, guard, shotgun, car,* and the like. Don't use too-obvious words such as *stickup, robbery,* or *getaway*. Now add to the list 15 general words that have no connection to the crime: *flower, breakfast, football,* and the like. Complete this step by adding the ten key words at random to the second list of 15.

Step 3 Select three or four suspects. Appoint a jury to judge the guilt or innocence of the suspects.

Step 4 The suspects should be kept isolated from one another and from the jury. Give each suspect a slip of paper. One person will receive the description of the crime, while the others will receive the meaningless second statement. Distribute the slips at random—it's best if the experimenter doesn't know the identity of the criminal. Give each jury member a copy of the word list.

Step 5 Bring the suspects one at a time before the jury. Instruct them to remain silent until asked to respond to the list of words you are going to read to them. Tell them to reply to each word with whatever second word comes to mind. Do not give any further explanation. Now read the list of words to each suspect, pausing after each word for the suspect's response. The jury should write down the suspect's replies, as well as any physical reactions—long pauses, laughter, nervous mannerisms, and the like.

Step 6 After all suspects have been "questioned," ask the jury to identify the criminal. If your word list has been properly keyed to the crime, the guilty person's responses to the key words will usually give him or her away.

7.4 ■ HOW DO THE HUMANIST PSYCHOLOGISTS APPROACH PERSONALITY THEORY?

Humanist psychology is based on the research and influence of Abraham Maslow (1908–1970). An American psychologist, Maslow told his fellow psychologists to stop the practice of defining personality in terms of their disturbed patients. Instead, he said, psychology should study healthy people.

Along with Carl Rogers, the other guiding

223

spirit of the humanist movement, Maslow believed that all members of society should be given the chance to realize their full potential as human beings. This goal is achievable, he thought, because people are basically good. His beliefs contrast with those of Freud, who seemed to define human beings as victims of their biological and psychological past. Not so, Maslow claimed. If their basic needs are met, most men and women build happy, productive lives for themselves.

MASLOW'S DEFINITION OF HUMAN NATURE

Maslow criticized the older schools of psychology for what he saw as their negative attitudes toward human nature. He attempted to paint a brighter, more optimistic picture of emotional life. In doing so, Maslow defined five basic concepts that relate to the human personality.

1. Humanity's essential nature is made up of needs, capacities, and tendencies that are good (or natural) rather than harmful.

2. Full, healthy personality development comes when people develop their basic natures and fulfill their potential. People must grow from within rather than be shaped from without. Unless they do, they can never reach true maturity.

3. Mental illness results when people's basic needs are not satisfied, thereby frustrating

or twisting their inner nature. The role of the therapist is to restore the patient to the path of growth and self-knowledge along the lines dictated by the patient's own inner nature.

4. Each person's inner nature is weak, delicate, and subtle, unlike the overpowering instincts of animals. Although a person's inner nature can grow tall and strong, it begins as a tiny seed. As it grows, it can easily be stunted by cultural pressures, the failure to satisfy basic needs, or unhealthy habits. No one's basic goodness ever disappears, even though it may be submerged for a while under self-defeating behaviors.

5. As people mature, their potential goodness shows itself even more clearly. The *self-actualizing* person, as humanist psychologists describe the fully mature personality, stands out in any environment (see Figure 7.6). Perhaps only a few people reach full self-actualization. But even those who are making progress toward that level of maturity are recognized and sought after by others.

BASIC NEEDS AND METANEEDS

Maslow believed that people must satisfy their *basic needs* for health, safety, and love before they are free to fulfill their higher growth needs. He defined the basic needs as:

1. Physiological needs: satisfaction of the body's requirements for food, drink, air, sex, sleep, and relaxation.

FIGURE 7.6 ▨ Abraham Maslow wouldn't agree with Lucy's opinion. According to Maslow, how could Charlie Brown achieve self-actualization?

PEANUTS reprinted by permission of UFS, Inc.

How Do You Recognize a Self-Actualizing Person?

Abraham Maslow described the healthiest of all personalities as belonging to the self-actualizing person. Based on his research, he identified a list of characteristics that describe the self-actualizing personality. Do you know anyone who rates high on eight or more of these qualities?

SELF-ACTUALIZING PEOPLE:

- Perceive reality better than most individuals.
- Accept themselves, others, and the natural world without worrying about what they cannot control.
- Are spontaneous in their thoughts and behavior but seldom engage in bizarre or unusual behaviors.
- Focus on problems outside themselves, rather than being self-centered.
- Refuse to bend to the social pressures that rule most people's lives.
- Find fresh enjoyment in activities that they have experienced many times before.
- Are open to profound spiritual or mystic experiences, although they are not necessarily religious.
- Identify with the rest of humanity in a positive way.
- Maintain deep emotional relationships with a limited number of people.
- Are democratic in their values and attitudes and free of prejudice.
- Enjoy the process of reaching a goal as much as the achievement itself.
- Enjoy a funny situation without turning the humor into hostility.
- Are capable of great creativity, often in a number of different fields.
- Are part of their culture but do not blindly conform to its standards.

2. Safety needs: feeling secure and safe from danger in an orderly, predictable world.

3. Love needs: satisfaction of the need to belong to groups, to receive and give affection, and to maintain friendships.

4. Esteem needs: attainment of acceptable levels of recognition, achievement, and competence.

Maslow called these basic needs *deficiency needs* because they must be met before people can bring beauty, goodness, and justice into their lives. Striving to attain the higher growth needs (Maslow called them *metaneeds*) is just as much a part of human nature

as is working to satisfy basic needs. Maslow defined the metaneeds as:

1. Cognitive needs: satisfaction of the mind's need to know, understand, and explore.

2. Aesthetic needs: the desire to bring beauty and order into one's life.

3. Self-actualization needs: the desire for self-fulfillment; the realization of individual potential.

You can see how deficiency needs and metaneeds work by looking at the career of Gilda G. When Gilda was a young, aspiring actress, she was forced to take any job she could get. With rent to pay and food to buy, satisfying her deficiency needs took all her time and energy. She did commercials, worked at trade shows, and took roles that did little more than pay the bills. In time, she was given better parts and finally landed a leading role in a Broadway hit. Today, wealthy and sought after, Gilda chooses roles that allow her to express her creativity and dramatic abilities. She takes time off from her career to raise her child. Happy and self-fulfilled, her deficiency needs satisfied, she now concentrates on satisfying her metaneeds.

SELF-ACTUALIZATION

As part of his research for his influential book *Toward a Psychology of Being,* Maslow studied the lives of a number of successful people. If he could find the common qualities that made these men and women successful, he reasoned, he would have defined the concept of *self-actualization.* Among the figures that Maslow counted as self-actualizing were Thomas Jefferson, Albert Einstein, Eleanor Roosevelt, George Washington Carver, and Jane Addams. He also included personal friends, people he thought demonstrated the qualities of health and creativity that characterize self-actualization.

Self-actualizing people, Maslow discovered, can satisfy both their basic needs and their metaneeds. They tend to be outgoing, creative, self-reliant, nonconforming, and democratic. You probably know several people who fit this description (see the box on page 225). Look for people who live their lives to the fullest, yet always seem to have time to help others. They have problems as everyone else does, but somehow they never let those problems dominate their lives.

Perhaps most interesting of all, self-actualizing people enjoy frequent *peak experiences.* Humanist psychologists define peak experiences as those moments of intense awareness when you feel totally alive. You're in tune with the universe and fully aware of the beauty, naturalness, and rightness of the moment. For some people, that moment may come as part of a religious experience, during prayer or a solemn ceremony. For others, it develops out of their passionate commitment to the activity of the moment. A former professional football quarterback, for example, described a peak experience that came during a game. He said that as he faded back to pass, he suddenly felt totally alive, with every sense heightened. Time seemed to stand still. He could "see" every player and knew exactly what he would do next. The football fitted his hand perfectly, and he knew with total certainty that when he threw the pass it would go for a touchdown. When his split end took the long spiral in for a score, the moment passed. But no one who experiences such high points forgets them.

Sadly enough, some people try to find shortcuts to peak experiences. They use drugs or alcohol to create an artificial environment that they hope will give them the insights and sense of well-being that self-actualizing people create for themselves. But true peak experiences cannot be ordered up or created with drugs. Maslow believed that anything that subtracts from the "will of health" moves people away from the path toward self-actualization.

■ SECTION CHECKUP

1 Why did Abraham Maslow suggest that psychologists study healthy people instead of disturbed people?

2 What are basic needs? What are metaneeds? Why must the basic needs be satisfied before the metaneeds can be met?

3 Define the concept of self-actualization. How would you recognize a self-actualizing person?

▓ BIOBOX

Rollo May:
Life Is More Than a Sentence Imposed by the Past

As a young man, Rollo May (1909–1994) fell ill with tuberculosis. Already interested in the study of human behavior, he "lived in a state of constant anxiety, like a horse running wild. I accepted it and recovered through the sheer exertion of my will. . . . I learned along the way to tune in on my being, my existence in the *now*, because that was all there was—that and my tubercular body. It was a valuable experience to face death, for in the experience I learned to face life."

The American Psychological Association awarded existentialist psychologist Rollo May its prestigious Gold Medal in 1987. The public knows him better, however, as the best-selling author of such books as *The Meaning of Anxiety, Man's Search for Himself,* and *The Cry for Myth.*

In his first book, *Love and Will,* May declared that awareness is not opposed to but essential to life. He also disagrees with the Freudians by suggesting that people need not be held prisoner by their past. He believes that people are prisoners only if they choose to be. As an existentialist, May encourages people to take responsibility for their own lives. He believes that teenage suicide and gang violence are the result of society's tendency to "take away from them something to love, the ideals, the

centers around which one is integrated. There's nothing that touches their souls."

When he was asked the value of psychotherapy, May replied:

> Before you begin psychotherapy, you might feel completely alienated, without anyone who believes in you. But when you establish a relationship with a therapist, you have found someone who is listening. The therapist might be the first person who has ever really listened, the first person who believes in you. . . . You feel like you are worth something, and you can venture forth into the world, because a strong person has confidence in you.

May refuses to work with anyone who is "looking for kicks" or who thinks it's fashionable to be in analysis. The patient he does want is like the woman who gave up a job in the Midwest and moved to the San Francisco area just because she wanted to talk regularly with May. Because she committed herself completely to the therapy, he took her on.

What do you think May means by "taking responsibility for your own life"? As an existentialist, why is commitment in his patients so important to May?

Key Personality Theories: How Do They Compare?

SCHOOL	IMPORTANT FIGURES	BASIC PERSONALITY THEORY	ORIGIN OF NEUROTIC BEHAVIOR
Psychoanalytic	Sigmund Freud	Human personality is formed by working out the conflict between the desire of the individual to seek pleasure and the demands of the outside world. Much behavior results from the influence of the unconscious, where the repressed experiences of childhood are stored.	Neurotic behavior develops when the ego cannot cope with the conflicting demands of the id and the superego. Unresolved traumas from the past can also cause the individual to act neurotically.
The Neo-Freudians	Alfred Adler Karen Horney Erik Erikson	Social and cultural forces combine to shape the personality. The healthy person has learned to cope with the conflict caused by individual needs and the demands of the environment.	Anxiety growing out of an inability to develop good personal relationships causes neurotic behavior. An inability to resolve the periodic crises of life also contributes to neurotic behavior.
Analytic Psychology	Carl Jung	The human personality, or psyche, develops out of the interrelationship of the personal unconscious with its complexes, the collective unconscious with its archetypes, and the conscious mind, or ego.	Failure to cope with a complex that forces unrealistic behavior can cause neurotic behavior. Forces from the collective unconscious can also overwhelm the ego and cause neurotic behavior.
Behaviorism	John Watson B. F. Skinner	All behavior grows out of the individual's response to stimuli from the environment. Any desired behavior can be developed by using proper conditioning techniques.	Neurotic behaviors are poorly chosen responses to stimuli. Many such behaviors were learned in the past and later became generalized to an entire series of responses.
Humanist Psychology	Abraham Maslow Carl Rogers	Human beings are essentially good and have a will to health. They grow by meeting basic needs and metaneeds, thus building a self-actualizing personality.	Neurotic behavior results when an individual's basic needs are not met. Cultural pressures or unhealthy habits can also submerge a person's basic goodness.

SCHOOL	IMPORTANT FIGURES	BASIC PERSONALITY THEORY	ORIGIN OF NEUROTIC BEHAVIOR
Existential Psychology	Rollo May Viktor Frankl	Every human being is free to make choices. People are free to grow and change, or they can choose not to develop their full potential. Happiness comes from commitment and acceptance of responsibility.	Anxiety and despair result from the sense of aloneness and risk that go with being responsible for making choices about life. Faced with that sense of hopelessness, people may make poor choices or decide to make none at all.

7.5 ▓ WHAT HAVE THE EXISTENTIALISTS AND OTHER CREATIVE THINKERS ADDED TO PERSONALITY THEORY?

A patient once asked psychologist Viktor Frankl (1905–1997) to tell him the true meaning of life. Frankl answered the question with another question: "What is the best move in a game of chess?"

Frankl wasn't trying to be difficult. As an existentialist, he was reminding his patient that there is no universal *best* move. You always have a choice, depending on the circumstances of a particular game. In a sense, that defines *existential psychology:* Human beings are free agents; they determine their behavior by choice. They are not controlled by unconscious forces over which they have no control. According to existential psychologists such as Rollo May (see BioBox, page 227), no one is bound to the past.

THE EXISTENTIAL APPROACH TO PERSONALITY

Existentialism grew out of the chaos that engulfed Europe during World War II. The cruelties of war, magnified by the Nazi concentration camps, convinced many people that life was empty of meaning. To help fill that vacuum, existential psychology was born. Even today, it does not offer a unified body of personality theory. But it does provide a set of attitudes that help explain such personal qualities as love, appreciation of beauty, and the urge to develop fully the human potential. For many people, existential psychology's belief in the nobility of the human spirit helps to give meaning and purpose to their lives.

KEY EXISTENTIAL BELIEFS

1. The central concept of life is *being*. Human beings live in a world made up of the physical environment, other people, and one's own consciousness. All you can know is what you perceive of that world. The existentialist explains, "You are part of the world, and the world is part of you."

2. *Being* also means *becoming*. Unlike a rock or a mathematical formula, you have potential. You can grow, change, commit yourself to projects—or you can give in to frustration and a sense of futility. To realize your potential requires that you explore your own being.

3. Each person must take responsibility for his or her own life. This means that you must make choices, even though that action can

involve taking a risk. If you make a poor choice, you are still free to make a better choice in the future. No one has the right to say, "That's the way I am. My parents hit me when I was little, and I can't change." You *can* change—and you have an obligation to do so.

4. Happiness is a by-product of committing yourself to the choices you have made. In a sense, you should make each choice in your life as if you were making it for all of humanity. Anxiety and existential despair result when you refuse to take responsibility for making decisions about your own life or give in to the knowledge that you are alone.

Perhaps you've been tempted at times to say, "That isn't fair!" when you didn't get the job, the grade, or the love you wanted. The existentialist would nod and say, "You're right. Life *isn't* fair. The world is full of unfairness. Look at the senseless death, disease, and other disasters that afflict humanity. But once you know that life is unfair, you are free! You no longer need to wait for good things to happen. Instead, you can begin living your life as fully and as richly as is humanly possible."

THE EXISTENTIAL VIEW OF NEUROTIC BEHAVIOR

The existentialist believes that anxiety and despair are inescapable parts of the human condition. Making choices means taking chances. If you decide to ask someone for a date, you may be turned down. You can apply for a job, but the employer may not like your looks. And so it goes. Each new choice brings a new anxiety. If you cave in under the pressure of anxiety, you will probably begin to behave in a neurotic way. Some people react by withdrawing from contact with other people. Others throw themselves into a desperate search for pleasure, using whatever means are available. Far too many become conformists, allowing others to determine what they will say, do, and think.

Existential despair results when people's inborn "will to meaning" is frustrated. Frankl called this the "existential vacuum." Here's how 18-year-old Gary B. described his own existential vacuum:

> All at once I knew that life didn't have any meaning. Like, you know, everyone else was faking it. I just felt hollow, all emptied out inside. Everything I tried to do fell apart. My job, my girlfriend, my family, nothing seemed worthwhile.

Most people experience this feeling at one time or another. Frankl saw it often in the World War II concentration camp to which he was sent. He found that those who survived were the men and women who had a task in life to complete. When someone else or some cause is dependent on you, you can rise above human limitations and overcome despair. Frankl summed up his own commitment by saying, "I have seen the meaning of my life in helping others to see in their lives a meaning."

Rollo May adds that anxiety, in small doses, can be constructive. He believes that it sharpens your sensitivity and sparks your creativity. Both Frankl and May would also agree that living up to your responsibilities will strengthen you. You can take risks when you're a healthy person because you have your own resources to fall back on. In freedom and commitment, the existentialists believe, you will find the happiness that seems to elude so many people today.

WILL THE MILLENNIUM YIELD A MAJOR ADVANCE IN PERSONALITY THEORY?

As humanity moves into a new century, psychologists haven't given up hope of developing an all-encompassing theory of personality. Each new theory, from Freud onward, has attracted followers who believed that it answered their questions about individual and group dynamics. In time, however, new generations stepped forward to chip away at the old system's blind spots.

Several promising systems have emerged from this ferment. *Family systems theory* instructs therapists to focus on the family, not the individual. Personality, the theory teaches, is largely shaped by family interactions. If José is anxious and depressed, a family systems therapist will assume that his family is dysfunctional. In their sessions, the therapist with urge José to talk about breakdowns in his personal relationships.

Other trends in personality theory emphasize the role played by increasing ethnic diversity and the role of gender at home, school, and in the workplace. No longer, we're told, can we assume that all Americans share the same cultural values. In their work, these therapists help their clients explore the ethnic and cultural forces that helped shape their personalities.

The fresh interest in gender takes note of the behaviors common to each sex. As gender theory reminds us, for example, the fact that boys tend to be more aggressive than girls has consequences when it comes to understanding behavior (see Chapter 13).

For a truly up-to-the-minute look at personality theory, point your browser to < *http://personality-project.org/personality.html* >.

■ SECTION CHECKUP

I Why would the existentialist say that "there's no best choice in life"?

2 What brings happiness to the individual, according to existential theory?

3 Describe the existential concepts of anxiety and despair. How can they be overcome?

LOOKING BACK: A SUMMARY

I Psychologists have not found—and may never find—a single, all-purpose theory to explain how the personality develops. Different theories place different values on biological, psychological, and environmental influences. Six major schools that provide a wide range of contrasting opinions about personality theory are the psychoanalytic (Freudian), the behaviorist, the neo-Freudian, the analytic (Jungian), the humanist, and the existentialist.

2 Behavioral psychologists John Watson and B. F. Skinner dismiss the study of mental processes that cannot be seen or measured. They believe that psychologists must study behavior, which can be observed, measured, and identified. Behaviorists explain that behavior is a system of stimulus-response units (S→R). When the stimulus is modified, the

response will change. Responses that are reflexive or involuntary are called *respondent behaviors*. Responses that act on the environment are called *operant behaviors*. Desirable operant behaviors can be strengthened by positive reinforcement. Undesirable behaviors can be eliminated by applying either negative reinforcement or punishment.

3 Behaviorists view neurotic behavior as inappropriate responses to stimuli. Therapy, therefore, consists of helping patients "unlearn" the unhealthy behavior through conditioning techniques. Society can also be improved by applying the same conditioning principles to shape "desirable" behaviors. This view has been hotly contested by humanist psychologists.

4 The neo-Freudian school of psychology rejects Freud's emphasis on sexual drives and his mechanistic view of adult life. Instead, neo-Freudians give greater emphasis to the influence of social forces. Alfred Adler stressed people's needs to find positive expression for their inborn social urges. He also explained the process of overcoming natural feelings of inferiority through compensation. Karen Horney described the neurotic personality, which she thought developed out of basic anxieties unresolved in childhood. She also listed the neurotic needs that grow out of people's attempts to combat anxiety. Erik Erikson identified eight psychosocial stages of development that all people must pass through during their lifetimes. Each stage brings a new crisis, which must be mastered if a person is to move on freely to the next stage. The crisis of adolescence, for example, is that of identity vs. role confusion.

5 Carl Jung made important contributions to personality theory. Of particular interest is his concept of the collective unconscious, which he said contains the ancient memories and experiences of the human race. Within the collective unconscious, Jung identified universal thought patterns he called *archetypes*. Some archetypes, which help people understand the world around them, include the earth mother, the hero, the wise old man, and death and rebirth. Four archetypes have become separate systems within the personality. These are (a) the persona (the public mask people wear to conceal the secret person underneath); (b) the anima and animus (elements of the opposite sex found in every person); (c) the shadow (the repressed, primitive side of the personality that is kept hidden from others); and (d) the self (the goal of wholeness and fulfillment sought by healthy personalities). Another part of the mind, the personal unconscious, contains organized groups of feelings, thoughts, and perceptions called *complexes*. Complexes have the power to dominate a personality if the individual is not able to deal with the influence of a "mother complex" or a "power complex."

6 The humanist psychologist believes that people are essentially good. Given the opportunity, they can become self-actualizing, a state in which they reach their full potential within the social environment. Abraham Maslow, the outstanding humanist psychologist, described a series of human needs he termed *basic needs* and *metaneeds*. The metaneeds (the desire for knowledge, beauty, and self-actualization) cannot be satisfied until the basic needs (physical, safety, love, and esteem needs) are met. Maslow described the self-actualizing person as one who is outgoing, creative, democratic, and independent. Self-actualizing people have more peak experiences (emotional high points) in their lives than do other people.

7 Existential psychologists believe that human beings are free agents; that is, all men and women must determine their own behavior by making choices. They are not controlled by unconscious forces. Existentialism teaches that the central concept of life is being. People can grow, change, and commit themselves, or they can give in to anxiety and despair. People must take responsibility for their own lives. Happiness results when they make a commitment to goals in which they believe. Making choices involves risk, however, and the anxiety that arises from fear of making poor choices can cause neurotic behavior. With existentialism and the other personality theories as a foundation, psychologists are hoping to build an all-embracing theory of personality. Some theorists have shifted focus from the individual to the family, to gender roles, and to the larger culture's role in shaping behavior.

PUTTING YOUR KNOWLEDGE TO WORK

■ TERMS YOU SHOULD KNOW

analytic psychology	family systems theory	psychosocial stages of
anima	fictional finalism	development
animus	humanist psychology	punishment
archetypes	inferiority (feelings of)	reinforcement
basic anxiety	introversion	repondent behavior
basic needs	metaneeds	self (Jungian)
behavioral psychology	negative reinforcement	self-actualization
behaviorist	neo-Freudians	shadow
collective unconscious	neurotic needs	shaping
compensation	operant behavior	social interest
complex	peak experience	social urges
conditioning	persona	stimulus-response
creative self	personal unconscious	(S→R)
deficiency needs	positive reinforcement	systematic
existential psychology	psyche	desensitization
extroversion		

■ CHAPTER CHECKUP

1 The experiment in which B. F. Skinner raised his daughter in an enclosed, temperature-controlled crib demonstrates the behaviorist belief that (*a*) infants should be isolated from human contact (*b*) infants have no defense against infection at birth and must be protected from the outside environment (*c*) society can create a race of strong, mentally healthy children only if their environment is carefully controlled (*d*) infants must be protected from traumatic childhood experiences until they have control of their unconscious minds.

2 The personality theory *furthest* removed from Freudian psychoanalysis is (*a*) neo-Freudian (*b*) Jungian (*c*) humanist (*d*) behaviorist.

3 Which of the following is a *true* statement about Jung's theory of the collective unconscious? (*a*) The collective unconscious is of almost no interest, since Jung believed that it has little influence on behavior. (*b*) Jung believed that the archetypes located in the collective unconscious represent some of the most powerful forces in the human mind. (*c*) Jung borrowed the idea of the collective

unconscious from Freud. (*d*) Jung said that the collective unconscious determines the degree of introversion or extroversion in personality.

4 The feelings of inferiority that Alfred Adler believed all people are born with can be overcome through (*a*) compensation (*b*) positive reinforcement (*c*) self-actualization (*d*) systematic desensitization.

5 Karen Horney believed that the basic anxiety felt by infant Carole may later be expressed as (*a*) neurotic needs that move her away from or against other people (*b*) an unresolved Electra complex (*c*) a feeling of emptiness and despair known as the existential vacuum (*d*) an inability to solve the crises that accompany each of the eight stages of psychosocial development.

6 According to Erikson, the crisis that must be overcome during adolescence is that of (*a*) Trust vs. Mistrust (*b*) Industry vs. Inferiority (*c*) Identity vs. Role Confusion (*d*) Intimacy vs. Isolation.

7 The basic concept of existential psychology can be summarized as the belief that all people must (*a*) overcome feelings of inferiority (*b*) maintain

233

ego integrity (c) have numerous peak experiences (d) take responsibility for the choices that affect their lives.

8 A school of psychology that focuses its attention on the healthy, "normal" personality is the (a) neo-Freudian (b) existential (c) behaviorist (d) humanist.

9 Saul isn't a self-actualizing person. Which description best describes him? (a) He is content with satisfying basic needs. (b) He maintains deep emotional relationships with a small number of other people. (c) He enjoys many peak experiences. (d) He stays in touch with reality better than most people.

10 A parent who wanted to improve the table manners of little Tony would probably have the most success with (a) punishment (b) psychoanalytic techniques (c) hypnotism (to get in touch with Tony's "food complex") (d) positive reinforcement.

■ EXPLORING CONCEPTS

1 Why do psychologists find it so difficult to agree on a single personality theory?

2 Imagine that Sigmund Freud and B. F. Skinner have just met for a debate. What would Freud criticize about Skinner's behaviorist ideas? How would Skinner, in turn, criticize Freud's psychoanalytic theory?

3 Do Erikson's psychosocial stages of development accurately describe the people you know? How well do you think they are coping with the crises Erikson assigns to each life stage?

4 Define the concept of self-actualization as used by Maslow. What do you think keeps many people from achieving this level of development?

5 Would you like living in a society in which everyone is self-actualizing? Why or why not?

6 Discuss how behaviorist theories could be applied to training a chimpanzee to eat with a fork instead of its fingers.

7 Imagine that everyone could be hooked up to a computer-controlled mind probe at birth. Socially desirable behaviors could be rewarded with a jolt of pure pleasure, while harmful behaviors could be punished by inflicting pain. Would you be for or against such a plan? Why?

■ HANDS-ON ACTIVITIES

1 After reading about the various personality theories in the last two chapters, you may have found one that appeals most strongly to you. Others in your class may have picked a different theory. This difference of opinion could be the basis for an interesting roundtable discussion with your class as the audience. Select the panel members and allow them time to prepare statements that explain why they think the theory they have chosen is the most successful in describing the roots of human behavior. On the day of the roundtable, allow each speaker five minutes for a formal presentation. Then allow time for other class members to question the panel on the theories and goals of the schools they represent.

2 How well do you know your own personality? You can gain some useful insights by making a "self-box" to represent your values, goals, and past experiences. Begin by finding an empty box. Decorate it with pictures from magazines or with your own photographs and artwork. Each picture should represent an aspect of your persona—the self you show the outside world. Now, rummage through your past—baby book, closets, junk drawers, everywhere you keep mementos. Place in the box only those items that have meaning to you. Your future can be represented by symbols—a college catalog, a doll dressed for a wedding or hoped-for job, a map of Europe. Some people organize their boxes quite carefully; others drop things in helter-skelter. However you organize it, your self-box will end up being important to you—because in a way, it will *be* you.

3 Ask a group of friends to join you in this experiment in shaping behavior. Choose a subject. Send the subject out of hearing while the rest of your group selects a specific action to which you will shape your subject's behavior. For example, you may choose to have your subject sit backward on a certain chair or open and close a window. Don't make the behavior too complicated. Select one person to be the controller. When the subject returns, no one is permitted to speak. The subject is told only that some form of behavior is expected and that when the subject performs any movement that is part of the desired activity or moves to the proper location, the controller will "reward" the action by clapping three times. The controller ignores actions that are not part of the desired behavior. Because most human subjects are smarter than laboratory rats, they usually can be shaped to the desired behavior in ten minutes or less.

4 Do you know someone who you think is self-actualizing? Write a short paper about that person in which you identify those specific personality traits that make him or her a self-actualizing person. Later, tell that person how important he or she is to you. That may be hard to do, but both of you will feel rewarded by this honest sharing of feelings.

5 One of the symbols that Jung identified as growing out of the collective unconscious is the *mandala*—a circular symbol of wholeness, completion, and renewal. Examples of mandalas can be seen in the Oriental yin-yang symbol, the sun-disk symbol, the ruins of Stone Age forts, etc. Make up a collection of mandalas to display on a poster along with an explanation of the significance of this eternal symbol. See Jung's *Man and His Symbols* for background reading on the mandala and other archetypes.

6 As a class project, assign a different culture to each group of three students. Ask them to research the myths, legends, and folk tales of the culture to find archetypal figures (wise old man, hero or heroine, earth mother, trickster, witch, and the like). Then compare the archetypes and the plots to see if Jung's prediction of similarities is true or not. One group might examine modern movies and television programs to see if the archetypes still appear. If you're inspired to dig deeper into Jung's ideas, you'll find a Website devoted to his work at < *www.cgjungpage.org* >.

FOR FURTHER READING

Burgess, Anthony. *A Clockwork Orange*. Cutchogue, NY: Buccaneer Books, 1996. Burgess looks into the future and finds it filled with teenage violence. Desperate to end the senseless bloodshed, behavioral scientists decide to use behavior-modification techniques to end the protagonist's violent tendencies. Horrifying, and yet thought-provoking, the novel vividly examines both sides of the issue regarding behaviorist theories of social control.

Jung, Carl G. *Man and His Symbols*. Garden City, N.Y.: Doubleday, 1975. In this book, completed just before his death, Jung tried to convey his ideas to the general public. The book offers a fascinating exploration of symbols, the unconscious, and Jungian dream interpretation.

Kunkel, John H. *Encounters with Great Psychologists; Twelve Dramatic Portraits*. Toronto: Wall & Thompson, 1989. Kunkel's subjects represent the major schools of modern psychology. Each "encounter" begins with a biographical sketch. Then comes the truly interesting part—an imagined "conversation" between the psychologist and some friends (both real and fictional). The reader meets Abraham Maslow, for example, at an informal get-together with several college students. Other psychologists "encountered" include Wundt, Freud, Adler, Jung, Skinner, and Piaget.

Pryor, Karen. *Don't Shoot the Dog!* New York: Bantam Books, 1999. Are you tired of Rover's midnight howling? Is your boss making unreasonable demands? This useful guide shows you how to use behaviorist principles to change behavior—your own as well as that of your pets, relatives, friends, and coworkers. Pryor, a pioneer in the training of dolphins, writes about positive reinforcement and shaping techniques in a down-to-earth, nontechnical style.

Reiss, Steven. *Who Am I? The 16 Basic Desires That Motivate Our Actions and Define Our Personalities*. New York: Berkley Trade, 2002. Drawing on the best research available, Dr. Reiss describes the 16 desires and values that shape your behavior. From that point, it's possible to analyze those desires and values in terms of how they helped shape your personality. After coming to terms with these valuable insights, you'll be ready to build better relationships with your family, friends, teammates, and workmates—each of whom has chosen a different mix of motivations.

Rogers, Carl R. *On Becoming a Person*. Boston: Houghton Mifflin, 1995. This comprehensive description of humanist psychology was written by one of the movement's founders.

Skinner, B. F. *Walden Two*. Upper Saddle River, NJ: Pearson Education, 1991. Behaviorism takes on a more human dimension in Skinner's novel about a commune in which behavior is scientifically "engineered."

235

UNIT IV

WHEN PERSONALITY IS DISTURBED

- UNDERSTANDING THE TROUBLED PERSONALITY
- HELPING THE TROUBLED PERSONALITY

Chapter

8 UNDERSTANDING THE TROUBLED PERSONALITY

You're not the only one whose life doesn't always go smoothly. History tells you that. The newspaper tells you that. And life itself tells you that.

What happens when people lose the ability to cope with the pressures of everyday living? Psychologists say these individuals are likely to substitute confused, irrational behaviors for the behaviors that no longer protect their egos. Unfortunately, the new defenses are almost always worse than the old ones. That's how the American poet Sylvia Plath described the dilemma in her autobiographical novel *The Bell Jar:*

> I was still wearing Betsy's white blouse and dirndl skirt. They drooped a bit now, as I hadn't washed them in my three weeks at home. The sweaty cotton gave off a sour but friendly smell.
>
> I hadn't washed my hair for three weeks, either.
>
> I hadn't slept for seven nights.
>
> My mother told me I must have slept, it was impossible not to sleep in all that time, but if I slept, it was with my eyes wide open, for I had followed the green, luminous course of the second hand and the minute hand and the hour hand of the bedside clock through their circles and semi-circles, every night for

seven nights, without missing a second, or a minute or an hour.

> The reason I hadn't washed my clothes or my hair was because it seemed so silly.
>
> I saw the days of the year stretching ahead like a series of bright, white boxes, and separating one box from another was sleep, like a black shade. Only for me, the long perspective of shades that set off one box from the next had suddenly snapped up, and I could see day after day after day glaring ahead of me like a white, broad, infinitely desolate avenue.
>
> It seemed silly to wash one day when I would only have to wash again the next.
>
> It made me tired just to think of it.
>
> I wanted to do everything once and for all and be through with it.

As you can see, Esther, the narrator of *The Bell Jar,* retains some insight into her problems. But the troubled teenagers in Theodore Isaac Rubin's *Jordi, Lisa and David* have crossed over the boundary. In the following excerpt, Rubin, a well-known psychologist, introduces Lisa. We meet her in the dayroom of a private hospital, talking to John, one of her therapists.

"John, John, begone begone—enough, enough of this stuffy stuff."

"Are you angry with me, Lisa?"

"Angry, angry—bangry, wangry,—be gone, John; John, be gone."

"I guess you are angry. What is it that makes you so angry?"

"You foo, you foo—it's you, it's you—it's you, you foo; foo you, foo you." . . .

She looked up at the big man and grinned—an inane, foolish kind of grin. Her mood changed suddenly. . . . She faced the wall and talked to herself in a barely audible whisper.

"He won't give me anything. He's big and fat and mean and why won't he give Lisa the crayons? He would give them to Muriel [Lisa's other personality]. He likes the Muriel me—but today I'm Lisa me, Lisa me."

In his coldly superior way, Lisa's friend David, who is also a patient, diagnoses Lisa's behavior. He explains that her "rhyming serves as a decoy or camouflage for what she actually feels." Then, as David turns to leave, John reaches out and pats the teenager on the shoulder. The innocent touch causes a violent break in David's icy control.

The boy lurched away and screamed, "You touched me, you boor, you unmitigated fool—you touched me! Do you want to kill me? A touch can kill. . . ." His face was contorted with rage. He turned and left them, muttering to himself, "The touch that kills, the touch that kills."

The power of the mind to alter the logic that most people live under can also be seen in *Mania,* L. M. Jayson's account of his own encounters with a voice that started talking to him from nowhere.

The sounds were so clear and so loud, I knew that pretty soon the people next to me would hear them. So I got up, and started walking slowly away, down the stairs of the boardwalk to the stretch

FIGURE 8.1 ▦ When people feel overwhelmed by the problems in their lives, they may adopt behavior that itself becomes a problem. How well do these inmates of a mental institution appear to be dealing with the pressures in their lives?

of sand below. . . . I waited until the voice came back, the words pounding in this time, not the way you hear any words, but deeper, as though all parts of me had become ears, with my fingers hearing the words, and my legs, and my head, too.

"You're no good," the voice said slowly, in the same deep tones. "You've never been any good or use on earth. There is the ocean. You might just as well drown yourself. Just walk in, and keep walking." As soon as the voice was through, I knew, by its cold command, I had to obey it.

Jayson listened so well to his "voice" that it took the combined efforts of lifeguards and police officers to keep him from committing suicide that day.

Esther, Lisa, David, L. M. Jayson—all are troubled, unhappy people whose lives have slipped out of control. What causes mental illness and other disturbances that change behavior? Psychology and medical science have come a long way since the days when people blamed devils and demons for all emotional distress. In this chapter, you will explore the problems of troubled personalities by examining the answers to the following questions:

8.1 What is a troubled personality?

8.2 What are the causes of mental illness?

8.3 What specific abnormal behaviors does the psychologist label as neurotic?

8.4 How does the psychologist classify different types of psychotic behavior?

8.5 What abnormal behaviors have been identified as personality disorders?

8.6 What personality problems can be traced to brain damage or dysfunction?

8.1 ■ WHAT IS A TROUBLED PERSONALITY?

Look carefully at the next ten people you pass on the street. They're almost certain to look perfectly normal. But appearances can be deceptive. Mental health experts estimate that at least three of the people you walked past will need help for an emotional problem at some time in their lives.

Does having a troubled personality mean that these people are "crazy"? Should they be locked up, drugged with tranquilizers, given shock treatments, forced to undergo psychotherapy?

The answer isn't a clearcut "yes" or "no." Most troubled people manage to cope. They hold down jobs, raise families, go to concerts, attend school, jog, garden, and do just about everything that other people do. But somewhere along the way, something pops up that interferes with their ability to manage their lives in a healthy and productive way.

Sometimes a troubled personality results from emotional stress. Mrs. S., for example, can't handle the day-to-day demands of raising three active children. She loses her temper over petty mischief and most afternoons she takes several drinks too many. Carey A., a neighbor, has spells of depression brought on by a biochemical imbalance in his body. It's not unusual, moreover, for the two factors—stress and physical disorders—to occur together, one triggering the other.

DEFINING NORMAL BEHAVIOR

Where would you draw the line between normal and abnormal behavior? Most cultures have different definitions. Horsemeat is a delicacy in Spain, and monkey brains were once a prized dish in China. But don't suggest either food for Sunday dinner. Your family would instantly conclude that you've taken leave of your senses. Some things that are normal in other cultures are definitely abnormal in the United States.

Psychologists, therefore, define *normal behavior* as the range of actions that are socially acceptable in a given culture. People who usually exhibit normal behavior are considered *well adjusted*. Those who consistently act in a socially unacceptable way are labeled *maladjusted* or *troubled personalities*. Psychologists assume that well-adjusted people will enjoy stable, productive, and relatively happy lives. Troubled people often suffer feelings of depression, guilt, rage, and general unhappiness. The contrast between the two is described in the box on page 241.

DEGREES OF ABNORMAL BEHAVIOR

In Figure 8.3A, the black circle *A* represents society's definition of normal behavior. The white circle *B* represents behaviors judged to

The Contrast Between Well-Adjusted And Troubled Personalities

WELL-ADJUSTED PEOPLE:

■ Can see others as they really are.

■ Accept others as they are and do not try to change them.

■ Can express warm, intense feelings.

■ Have the ability to respond to life's pleasures and challenges.

■ Maintain a serenity and calmness in most situations.

■ Treat other people fairly and show good impulse control.

TROUBLED PEOPLE:

■ See others as they wish them to be.

■ Demand that others meet their standards, no matter how unrealistic.

■ Have difficulty coping with feelings and emotions.

■ Are defeated by the realities of life.

■ Exhibit inappropriate extremes of emotion.

■ Adopt a self-centered and demanding life position.

be abnormal; that is, they lie outside the range of normal behavior. Punishing a child by giving a "time out" for painting the cat would fall into *A*. But breaking the child's arm for the same prank would fall into *B*. In theory, a normal person remains safely within the boundaries of *A*, never straying into *B*. In reality, most people cross that boundary at times, as shown in the second figure, 8.3B. Here the individual stays mostly inside the center area *A* but occasionally strays into *B*. By definition, *abnormal behavior* (the time spent in *B*) is a psychologically unhealthy choice of responses to life situations.

FIGURE 8.2 ▓ Mental health experts estimate that about three out of every ten Americans will need help in dealing with emotional problems at some time during their lives. Unfortunately, many of them will never visit a psychologist or a mental-health clinic. Why do you think so many people hesitate to ask for help?

FIGURE 8.3A

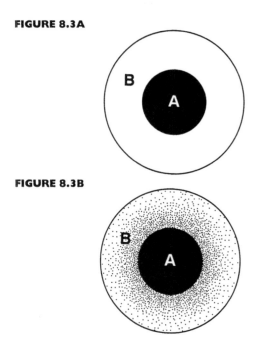

FIGURE 8.3B

Most people who show some abnormal behavior can still function at an acceptable level of efficiency. But as more and more behaviors fall into *B,* these people find that the everyday problems of living become increasingly harder to handle. The resulting behaviors are often labelled neurotic or psychotic, depending on their seriousness.

MENTAL HEALTH PROBLEMS IN AMERICAN SOCIETY

In an old story, one farmer says to another, "Everyone's crazy but you and me—and sometimes I worry about you."

The farmer's estimate that 99.9 percent of the population has emotional problems turns out to be much too high. A 1992 study by the National Institute of Mental Health (NIMH) estimates that over 20 percent of all Americans—some 62 million people—suffer from a mental disorder in any given year. In economic terms, the direct and indirect costs of caring for the mentally ill are estimated

at $160 billion. Sadly, children are not exempt. A 1988 study of 17,000 children found that one in five had a developmental, learning, or emotional problem. The NIMH study defined mental health problems as conditions that prevent the individual from living a happy, productive life. Along with psychotic conditions such as schizophrenia and clinical depression, the definition includes personality disorders and neurotic behaviors; alcohol and drug abuse; social isolation of the chronically disabled and the elderly; and the anxiety, depression, and anger triggered by poverty and discrimination.

This broad-scale definition of mental health problems has angered some psychologists. They fear that the public will begin to reject everyone who has a mental health problem, no matter what the cause. It is true that a few seriously disturbed people have committed terrible crimes. But to see all troubled people as potential murderers or sex offenders is both unfair and inaccurate.

Perhaps the best approach would be to apply the same judgment to emotional problems as you do to medical problems. If you break your leg or catch pneumonia, you go to a doctor. Why shouldn't emotional problems receive the same immediate, unquestioning treatment? One useful step would be to better educate the public to the causes, symptoms, and treatment of troubled personalities. After all, most emotional problems are short-lived. When the episode ends, people return to their normal, productive activities. Another step forward would be to make treatment available to all without counting the cost. Given the realities of cutbacks in federal and state mental health budgets, that goal currently seems beyond reach.

You can help at a more personal level. Hold out a supporting hand to anyone you know who suffers from an emotional problem. In many cases, the knowledge that you care may help that person begin the journey back to mental health.

▓ **BIOBOX**

Karl A. Menninger:
Everyone Is Subject to the Pressures That Lead to Mental Illness

The name of Menninger has been linked with mental health care in the United States ever since 1919. In that year, Karl Menninger (1893–1990) and his father, Charles Menninger, opened the Menninger Clinic in Topeka, Kansas. Along with their pioneering work in helping the mentally ill, the Menningers used their growing fame to educate the public to the need for humane treatment of mental illness.

Karl Menninger has been called the father of American psychiatry. He viewed mental health and disease as opposite ends of a continuous line. At one end lie health and happiness; at the other wait depression, anxiety, and delusion. Menninger believed that mental health varies according to people's stage of life and the stresses they encounter. When individuals cannot obtain satisfaction with a simple defense technique, they resort to more extreme measures. They may burst into tears or take a few drinks. But if the problem continues, they may move on to more desperate behaviors—fainting, use of drugs, or violence against others. Much criminal behavior, Menninger added, is a pathological reaction to severe punishment suffered early in life. Further punishment, he concluded, will only worsen criminal tendencies.

Dr. Menninger's deep concern for his patients and his understanding of their needs comes through in these words:

What we cannot prevent we must deal with, especially the extreme and disabling attacks of mental illness which are so costly to the individual and those around him. For these we should provide first of all accurate diagnosis . . . of the factors which have combined to produce it, the internal factors and the external factors. . . .

Being realistic, we know that in spite of the best diagnosis and the best treatment some patients will not recover. This is a minority, but of all people we psychiatrists should be the last to ignore a minority. And there are some who in spite of everything will continue to need our sympathy, our patience, and our help in the hope that some vestige of inner strength will sustain them. . . .

In one of his later books, Menninger took a compassionate look at the world he had devoted his life to helping. "Life is too precious to waste or to be wasted. Our country is too beautiful to be selfishly ravished. Our world, . . . is still too wonderful . . . to be destroyed by our . . . failure to use our intelligence."

Dr. Menninger doesn't promise any miracles. But the helping hand he and other therapists hold out to troubled people can be the difference between emotional health and mental illness.

■ SECTION CHECKUP

1 How would you distinguish between normal and abnormal behavior? Why is it unfair to label people's behavior abnormal just because you disagree with it?

2 Contrast the behavior of well-adjusted and troubled people.

3 What percentage of the population has a serious mental-health problem? Why do these people often fail to seek the help they need?

8.2 ▪ WHAT ARE THE CAUSES OF MENTAL ILLNESS?

At what point does abnormal behavior cross into the region where the medical term *illness* becomes appropriate? No hard lines divide a "life scale" that ranges from self-actualization to Menninger's fifth level of mental illness. But a graphic indication of that scale would look like Figure 8.4, with each level of adjustment, from self-actualization to total mental breakdown, fading gradually into the next.

Why do people move from one area to another on the scale? If you pressed mental health experts for an answer, they would say that it's seldom possible to locate a single cause. Instead, they believe that a combination of environmental and physical conditions usually causes mental illness.

ENVIRONMENTAL CAUSES OF MENTAL ILLNESS

Everyone experiences difficulty in adjusting to the demands of the outside world. You've probably felt some of that frustration when your wants and needs run headlong into the realities of parental rules, limited cash, and the desires of your friends. Well-adjusted people learn to cope with such problems. If they can't have their own way, they work out an acceptable compromise. By contrast, the poorly adjusted person often can't find a way to resolve everyday problems.

Research and common sense have combined to point out the specific forces in the environment that cause the greatest problems. These areas include (1) dealing with stress, (2) handling frustrations, (3) coping with anxieties, (4) functioning within the family, (5) functioning on the job, and (6) functioning in society.

DEALING WITH STRESS. In a psychological sense, *stress* results when pressures upset the body's emotional balance. Stress may grow out of unmet personal needs, work pressures, poor personal relationships, or inner drives that push people past their capabilities. When stress becomes unbearable, the poorly adjusted person unconsciously chooses a behavior that seems to promise an escape from tension. For example, Mary feels greatly pressured by her guardian's demand that she excel in school. Faced with that kind of stress, Mary often "forgets" test dates and "misplaces" her notes and essays.

HANDLING FRUSTRATION. *Frustration* results when people cannot satisfy a personal need or desire. Everyone suffers frustrations, such as the traffic signals that slow your ride home or the summer job that falls through. A common symptom of the mentally ill, however, is their inability to put off gratification of their needs. When frustrated, they often behave in illogical or bizarre ways. Some become excessively angry, while others withdraw from contact with the frustrating situation. Pete, for example, was frustrated because the payments on his new van ate up every dollar he made. When an older man accidentally scraped the side of the costly

MENTAL HEALTH-ILLNESS SCALE: FROM SELF-ACTUALIZATION TO TOTAL MENTAL BREAKDOWN

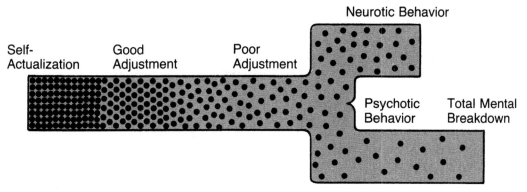

FIGURE 8.4

van, Pete took one look at the torn metal and punched the man in the jaw. Fortunately, the judge who heard the case recognized Pete's problem and arranged for him to enter therapy. A less sympathetic judge might have slapped Pete with a six-month jail sentence.

COPING WITH ANXIETIES. Psychologists define *anxiety* as vague worries about something that might happen in the future. Some people worry more than others and experience greater anxiety. Mentally healthy people know how to put such anxiety in proper perspective. But one in 50 Americans is thought to suffer from an extreme form of anxiety known as a panic disorder. If the radio reports that a hurricane is coming, everyone in its path will rightly worry about the danger. Most people will take reasonable precautions and then wait out the high winds. Anxiety-prone individuals will continue to worry, their panic mounting with each passing hour. When the real danger does strike, they may be so depressed and fatigued that they cannot cope with the emergency.

Anxiety can also lead troubled people to fasten onto a single thought pattern or behavior. They recite nonsense rhymes or give in to

an overwhelming urge to step on all the cracks in the sidewalk. When their attention is focused on such trivial concerns, they don't have to face the things they truly fear.

FUNCTIONING WITHIN THE FAMILY. Troubled people have a hard time maintaining the close relationships demanded by family life. Some have grown up in families in which emotional stress is a daily fact of life. Trying to cope with a chaotic home life can lay the groundwork for future mental health problems. Under the stress of day-to-day living with another person or with their own children, troubled adults sometimes take refuge in neurotic or psychotic behaviors.

When Don and Joy were married, for example, everything seemed perfect. They loved each other, and their families encouraged them. But Don soon developed a taste for going out frequently "with the guys." Left alone with no close friends nearby, Joy began behaving strangely. Sometimes she felt on top of the world with energy to spare. But more often she sank into periods of depression. Her moods upset Don, who reacted by staying out more often.

The day Joy discovered that she was preg-

245

The Double Bind: You're Caught No Matter Which Way You Turn

Most of us can empathize with Garry Larson's hapless goldfish. We've all been caught in no-win situations like this one. Psychologists call it the *double bind*. Here's a classic example:

JERRY: Bye, Mom, I've got to run. I'm late for the game as it is.

MOM: Oh, are you going out again tonight? I was hoping you'd stay home for once and keep me company. I thought we could make some popcorn and play a few games of cribbage.

JERRY: Aww, Mom, I told you I was going out with the guys. I'll stay with you some other night. This is the biggest game of the season!

MOM: Well, dear, you just go ahead. I'll be lonely sitting here all by myself, but that's okay. There's certain to be something good on television that will take my mind off my troubles.

JERRY: Yeah, right, Mom. Well, goodnight. See ya later.

THE FAR SIDE By Gary Larson

"Well, thank God we all made it out in time. . . . 'Course, now we're equally in trouble."

Can you spot the double bind in this dialogue? If Jerry goes to the game, he'll spend most of the evening feeling guilty. If he stays home, he'll feel angry and resentful at being manipulated. Either way, he's caught.

Children who grow up in households where parents consistently use double-bind messages learn that the world is a confusing, contradictory place. No matter what they do, it feels wrong. Psychologists say that the disordered thinking characteristic of much neurotic and psychotic behavior may begin with the impossible-to-resolve conflicts created by the double bind.

nant was not a happy one. She couldn't handle the thought of taking care of a child. That night Don came home to find Joy had locked herself in the bathroom. Over and over she screamed that she wanted to die. It took a call to the paramedics and several months of therapy before Joy could again cope with her life.

What could Don have done? First, marriage requires a mutual sharing of experiences. It's okay for him to see his friends, but not to the exclusion of his wife. Second, when he saw her wild mood swings, he should have gone with her to a counselor. Even if the thought of talking to a psychologist was too scary, they could have talked to their family doctor, a counselor at a free clinic, or a member of the clergy. Finally, Don should have been aware of his own withdrawal from Joy at a time when she needed him most. A liberal dose of TLC (tender loving care) might have prevented Joy's later explosion.

In fairness, Joy also shares the responsibility. Instead of confronting the issue of Don's nights out, she remained quiet. She could have made an effort to make friends on her own or to get involved in school or charity work. Unfortunately, Joy entered marriage with the expectation that Don would take care of her every need, and he had neither the will nor the inclination to play that role.

FUNCTIONING ON THE JOB. U.S. society looks on success at work as a sign of personal achievement. Many people, therefore, see their jobs as more than a way of making a living. Their salaries, promotions, titles, and other measures of progress up the ladder give these men and women their basic identity. But even though work can provide personal satisfaction, it also puts people in competition with each other. Many poorly adjusted people already feel insecure and unworthy. When their jobs force them into stress-causing situations, their anxieties and fears increase greatly.

The complicated nature of individual reactions to job stress can be seen in the cases of Jill and Andrew. Jill drifts from job to job. She can't seem to hold a position for very long, even though she has excellent clerical skills. Responsibility makes her feel anxious, and as soon as the boss begins to depend on her, she starts calling in sick. Before long, she resigns or gets fired. Andrew, meanwhile, *wants* to work. But every time he takes a job he breaks out in a rash. Even though he knows the rash is probably psychosomatic, he can't work when his body is covered by red, itchy welts.

Based on the evidence, you might hazard a guess that Jill and Andrew are psychologically "allergic" to work. A psychologist, how-

FIGURE 8.5 ▪ The social pressures to conform to peer-group standards of behavior can be particularly high during adolescence. Why would such pressures sometimes lead an individual into abnormal behavior?

ever, would first have them checked to make sure their problems aren't rooted in a medical condition. If the tests turn out negative, the psychologist might then conclude that their problems begin with personality troubles. The stress of the workplace triggers the mechanisms that protect them. Both would profit from counseling. If they don't receive help, the odds are good that their poor adjustment will grow worse, not better.

FUNCTIONING IN SOCIETY. In any society, freedom of action is always limited by the rights of others. Perhaps you'd dearly love to race the family car on the nearby highway. What stops you is the knowledge that "putting the pedal to the metal" endangers other drivers and risks a costly speeding ticket. Reluctantly, you stick to the 55-mile-per-hour limit. Emotionally disturbed people find it hard to accept limits when their own desires and needs seem so overwhelming. Society's pressures to conform often cause them to behave in ever more abnormal ways (see Figure 8.5).

Society seems to tell young men, for example, that their masculinity is measured by their success with girls. At 17, Ray's shyness made it difficult for him to talk to girls, much less to ask them for dates. To make matters worse, his friends teased him about his problem. His insecurity increased, and he withdrew even further into himself. Driven by anxiety and unconscious sexual needs, Ray started prowling the neighborhood at night, peeking into bedroom windows. Fortunately, he was caught by a neighbor and his parents were alerted. With the help of a counselor, Ray will probably be able to overcome his poor adjustment. Otherwise, his inner drives will continue to create even greater anxieties.

PHYSICAL FACTORS THAT CAUSE MENTAL ILLNESS

If you've ever had a high fever, you know that changes in your body's internal chemistry can affect your mental state. A rise in body temperature of only a few degrees can cause you to feel depressed and listless. You may experience mild hallucinations. It shouldn't come as a surprise, therefore, that psychologists have identified a number of physical factors that can cause abnormal behavior: accidents of heredity, biochemical imbalances, disease, accident trauma, and posttraumatic stress.

ACCIDENTS OF HEREDITY. Scientific "detectives" are making good progress in their search for genes that predispose the individuals who carry them toward some forms of mental illness. Schizophrenia, which is characterized by severe thought disorders, affects about 1 percent of the population. But, the DNA detectives point out, anyone who has a schizophrenic grandparent carries a 4 percent risk factor, and someone who has a schizophrenic parent has a 16 percent chance of also becoming schizophrenic. In identical twins, if one develops schizophrenia, the second has a 50 percent chance of developing the illness.

On the other hand, many psychologists argue that environment, not heredity, is the crucial factor. Children who grow up in a household torn by the emotional chaos of schizophrenia tend to learn faulty ways of coping with the world. Given this environmental handicap, perhaps it's no wonder that schizophrenic parents are more likely to produce schizophrenic children.

BIOCHEMICAL IMBALANCES. Scientists have long known that an excess or deficiency of otherwise useful chemicals can upset the nervous system. Some people create this *biochemical imbalance* through drug or alcohol abuse. Percy O., an alcoholic, has built up enough toxic substances in his body to cause memory loss, feelings of persecution, and visions of nonexistent snakes. Some schizophrenics show excessive blood levels of a protein called leu-endorphin. Scientists who are researching this discovery suggest that the protein excites the brain into behaving erratically. Long-term depression has also been treated with a trace element called lithium. When the lithium brings the body's sodium level into balance, depression generally disappears.

Athletes who use anabolic steroids to increase their weight and strength run a similar risk of creating biochemical imbalances. One study of steroid users showed that one-third displayed psychiatric symptoms severe enough to affect their daily lives, while another one-third had milder symptoms. The symptoms ranged from feelings of rage, recklessness, and hyperactivity to paranoid delusions and hearing voices. In addition, doctors report that 'roid users will be more likely to suffer heart disease and strokes later in life. Fortunately, the personality problems usually disappear when users stop taking the drugs. Withdrawal symptoms are generally mild, although some athletes become depressed at the thought of losing the strength and bulk they have gained.

Researchers caution that correcting biochemical imbalances may not provide the simple solution to mental illness that some people hope for. Schizophrenics have been helped by the drug Clozapine, although this powerful medication also carries the risk of serious side effects. But a critical question remains. Does the chemical imbalance cause the schizophrenia? Or does the schizophrenia cause the imbalance? Perhaps the best that can be said is that a hopeful avenue of research has been opened up.

DISEASE.   Diseases, particularly those that affect the nervous system, can lead to abnormal behavior. Memory loss, disruption of speech, hearing "voices," and outbursts of violent behavior may result from inflammation of the brain or tumors that put pressure on certain parts of the brain. Strokes that interrupt blood flow to the brain often result in loss of memory and speech. Sexually transmitted diseases and other infections may cause the breakdown of brain tissue.

ACCIDENT TRAUMA.   In medical terms, a trauma is an injury or shock to the body. Any blow to the head that causes damage to the brain can also lead to personality changes. Trauma can also occur during birth, when brain tissues may be destroyed by lack of oxygen or by severe pressure on the skull. Symptoms resulting from such accidents include memory loss, speech impairment, inappropriate emotional responses, and partial paralysis. When damage occurs in only a small area, proper therapy can often restore all or partial function to mental and physical processes. Severe brain damage cannot be

reversed, however, because brain tissue does not grow back once it has been destroyed.

POST-TRAUMATIC STRESS DISORDER (PTSD).   Overwhelmingly stressful events such as a natural disaster, military combat, or a physical assault can cause *post-traumatic stress disorder*. As much as possible, victims avoid situations and activities that recall memories of the traumatic event. They often dread bedtime, for their sleep is troubled by terrifying nightmares. Other symptoms include emotional numbness, depression, sudden rages, jumpiness, and an inability to concentrate. This recently recognized disorder is relatively rare, even among the Vietnam combat soldiers who first brought it to public attention. One survey found that 15 percent of the veterans interviewed displayed some PTSD symptoms, but fewer than 1 percent suffered from the full disorder.

DEPRESSION—A CAUSE AND A SYMPTOM

You probably recognize the symptoms. Something unpleasant has happened and you feel "down." You don't have much energy, food tastes like straw, and no idea seems worth pursuing. People try to cheer you up, but you push them away. You'd rather be left alone to brood and feel miserable. Those feelings of sadness and hopelessness are part of what psychologists call *depression*. Everyone has depressions, but a good night's sleep or a heart-to-heart talk with a friend is usually enough to snap most people out of them.

Psychologists do worry, however, when otherwise healthy people remain depressed for weeks or months. This type of clinical depression often begins when people feel they cannot control their own lives. Personal problems, such as divorce, a death in the family, or loneliness, can bring on depression. Social ills such as poverty, discrimination, and unemployment also can trigger a depressed

FIGURE 8.6 ■ Everyone feels depressed now and then. After a few hours or a few days, the mood lifts and life seems worth living once again. Long-term clinical depression, which leaves the victim unable to cope with normal life routines, is another matter. Why is it so important to obtain professional help for someone who is experiencing the despair and hopelessness of clinical depression?

state. Whatever the cause, if depression is left untreated, it can lead to a suicide attempt. Each year, 7 percent of the adult population suffers from clinical depression—a group that numbers twice as many women as men. Nor does youth offer protection. At any given moment, 3 to 5 percent of all teenagers are experiencing the feelings of despair and hopelessness that mark this disorder.

As one woman said, "I felt desolate and abandoned. My brain was telling me that I was not abandoned, but the feeling was that I was bereft even by God. It was as if the earth had opened at my feet, and I was standing at the edge." In these severe cases, doctors sometimes recommend antidepressant drugs or electroconvulsive therapy (ECT) as well as talk therapy. ECT has many critics (see Pro & Con, page 264), for it works by using an electric current to produce a convulsion in the patient. But seriously depressed patients agree that any treatment that gives them hope is better than their illness.

■ SECTION CHECKUP

1 List some of the environmental forces that can cause abnormal behavior or mental illness. Why are stress, frustration, and anxiety considered so important in evaluating the causes of poor adjustment?

2 Describe some of the physical factors that can bring about abnormal behavior or mental illness.

3 Why are psychologists reluctant to point to any single factor as a cause of mental illness?

8.3 ■ WHAT SPECIFIC ABNORMAL BEHAVIORS DOES THE PSYCHOLOGIST LABEL AS NEUROTIC?

You'd enjoy meeting Nick S. He's a pleasant, middle-aged man, soft of speech and an expert on trivia questions. Nick is shy, but generous and anxious to please. There's just one thing. If you want to meet Nick, you'll have to visit him at his house. You see, Nick lives in a single windowless room that he almost never leaves. He'd like to go shopping at the nearby Mega Mall, but he can't. He suffers

from agoraphobia, an unreasoning fear of open spaces, crowds, traffic, and the other hallmarks of city life.

In psychological terms, Nick suffers from a *neurosis*—a repeated, inappropriate, and involuntary response to stress or a fear-provoking situation. Like most neurotic behaviors, Nick's fear of going outdoors started with some unpleasant experiences.

He was mugged twice within ten days, and soon afterward, he lost his way in a strange part of town. He began to stay closer to home, and gradually the area he felt safe in became smaller and smaller. His inability to meet his basic needs for personal safety led to his current neurotic behavior.

All fears and feelings of nervousness shouldn't be labeled as neuroses. Many of the worries that afflict modern society are based on realistic concerns. Where does neurotic behavior begin? The signs include (1) excessive tension or nervousness; (2) an inability to work at a level in keeping with one's abilities; (3) an overwhelming need for love and approval; (4) an inability to relate to other people; (5) rigid, repetitive behaviors; (6) overreacting to what others say or do; and (7) an inability to make decisions. The following sections describe five of the most common neuroses.

OBSESSIONS AND COMPULSIONS

A TV detective named Adrian Monk works overtime to bring order to his often chaotic life. Monk washes his hands many times a day, and he spends a lot of time making sure that everything in his apartment is neat and tidy.

When Monk washes his hands over and over, he is demonstrating what psychologists call obsessive-compulsive behavior. People with such a neurosis can be recognized by their endless attention to detail and the performance of ritual (repetitive) acts. *Obsessions* are thoughts, impulses, or feelings that are repeated continuously and that the individual cannot control. When the person translates these thoughts or impulses into repeated, involuntary actions, the resulting behavior pattern is called a *compulsion*. People sometimes joke about "shopaholics" and "pack rats," but when the behavior is truly compulsive, it causes the victim far more pain than pleasure.

You've probably endured a day when a song or jingle filled your head with nonsense rhymes. Even when you make a conscious effort to erase that particular tape, it hangs on, endlessly repeating. Luckily, after a few hours or a day, it goes away. Troubled people, however, discover that unwanted thoughts or actions threaten to take over their lives. Most psychologists believe that obsessive-compulsive behaviors develop because the individual fears that "unacceptable" impulses originating in the unconscious may "break loose." In order to control these impulses, the neurotic works out a behavior that will suppress those urges. Monk's obsession with cleanliness may be intended to keep him from giving in to an unconscious impulse to surrender to the disorder he sees all around him. Freud, in fact, described obsessive-compulsive behavior as a personal religion that acts to ward off evil.

PHOBIAS

When Carole was four years old, she hid in a closet during a game of hide-and-seek. The door snapped shut, trapping her in the dark, almost airless closet for several hours. Today, Carole cannot bear to stay in any small, enclosed space. Once she had to cancel a cruise to the Bahamas because she discovered that just stepping into the small stateroom made her feel panicky.

When fears become irrational, intense, and uncontrollable, they are called *phobias*. Everyone experiences such fears, but most people learn to handle them. You may have a slight fear of heights, for instance, but it doesn't keep you from flying to Nebraska or enjoying the view from the top of a skyscraper. Occasionally, however, a phobia becomes strong enough to dominate a person's life. These phobic fears (see Figure 8.7) include almost every life situation you can imagine.

Psychologists explain phobias as the result of frightening experiences that condition a

FIGURE 8.7

PHOBIAS: SOMEONE FEARS JUST ABOUT ANYTHING

Claustrophobia
(fear of enclosed places)

Nyctophobia
(fear of dark or night)

Hydrophobia
(fear of water)

Ophidiophobia
(fear of snakes)

Acrophobia
(fear of heights)

Gamophobia
(fear of marriage)

Entomophobia
(fear of insects)

Haphephobia
(fear of being touched)

Thanatophobia
(fear of death)

bet, once she decides to face up to her phobia, would be to undergo a program of systematic desensitization with the help of a therapist skilled in behaviorist techniques.

CONVERSION HYSTERIA

On the morning of an important concert, guitarist Rudy S. woke to find that his left hand was paralyzed. Instead of raging at his sudden misfortune, the up-and-coming musician remained calm. When his nearly hysterical manager reached the hotel room, Rudy simply shrugged and said, "Well, I guess the concert will have to be canceled."

If Rudy had been totally honest, he would have admitted to feeling extremely fearful about that concert. His paralysis developed when those inner fears became so great that his ego couldn't cope with them any longer.

person to fear a particular situation. The original fear may later become generalized to related situations. Carole's claustrophobia began with her terrifying experience in the closet, but now it extends to any small, enclosed space. For Carole, that list includes elevators, tents, and tunnels, as well as a cruise ship stateroom. Telling her to ignore her fears won't solve the problem. Her best

His condition is known as *conversion hysteria,* a neurotic behavior in which repressed emotions are turned into physical disabilities. Symptoms vary from patient to patient but range from partial paralysis to deafness, blindness, or fainting spells.

In many cases, the physical symptoms relate in some way to the fears that underlie them. A dancer, for example, would be more likely to experience paralysis of her legs than of any other part of her body. One new father, overwhelmed by the sense of responsibility he foresaw in raising a child, promptly "lost" his eyesight.

Victims of conversion hysteria usually seek medical attention. The condition causes doctors great difficulty, for the physical symptoms are all too real. Once physical causes have been eliminated and the proper diagnosis has been made, the patient must be helped to recognize the underlying fear that caused the symptoms. At that point, the paralysis or other problem often disappears as quickly as it appeared (see the box on page 254). In cases in which the hysterical disability has lasted for months or years, prolonged therapy may be necessary.

DISSOCIATIVE REACTIONS

Most of his neighbors would agree that Jack W. is a gentle man. He takes good care of his family, supports every charity that knocks on his door, and feeds the neighborhood songbirds. But several nights a year, Jack slips out of his house and creeps silently through the nearby streets. Whenever he sees a cat, he offers it a tidbit of poisoned fish. When morning comes and the news of the dead animals spreads, Jack is as amazed as anyone else about the crime. If he were to take a lie-detector test, he'd swear to his innocence and pass with flying colors.

Neurotic responses to fear or stress in which parts of the personality or memory dissociate (split off) are known as *dissociative*

reactions. Like most of us, you probably integrate several different "people" within your personality. You may be a fierce competitor at school or at work, but then you turn into an easygoing charmer when you're safe within the family circle. Some people, however, reach a point at which their egos can no longer cope with the stress caused by the different needs of the "people" who live inside them. In Jack's W.'s case, he has long been enraged by the cats that hunt and kill his beloved birds. His own personality would never let him harm a cat. But his unconscious desire to revenge the dead birds breaks out in a separate personality who calls himself Rocky. Rocky can—and does—punish the cats for killing his birds. Under a similar strain, someone else might develop amnesia instead of a multiple personality.

AMNESIA. *Amnesia* is a state in which people literally "forget" all or part of their identity and past life. Amnesia may result from a blow on the head or other brain injury. Patients almost always recover from this type of amnesia. Memory loss may also occur when the mind "blacks out" a painful life situation. To treat this type of amnesia, therapists try to find the particular conflict that caused the loss of memory.

Evelyn I., for example, lost her memory when a chain of events put her under unendurable stress. A widow, she had to give up her apartment because of a rent increase. She traveled to California to stay with a friend, only to find that the friend had become ill and had moved to New York. At that point, Evelyn blanked out, leaving her purse and her identity behind. The police later found her wandering aimlessly around town, unsure of who she was and where she was. Rest and therapy eventually helped her recover her memory.

MULTIPLE PERSONALITIES. This most dramatic form of dissociative reaction was made

Small Miracle in the Emergency Room: Coping With Conversion Hysteria

In *The Making of a Psychiatrist,* David Viscott takes us inside the emergency room of a large New York City hospital. There he finds a young woman named Charlotte waiting for him. Charlotte's legs are paralyzed. The man who's with her tells Viscott that they've just come to New York from North Carolina. Charlotte, he says, was fine when she left home. After talking to her mother on the phone, however, she became upset. By the time they reached New York, she couldn't walk.

A report shows that another doctor wasn't able to find a physical cause for the paralysis. After mentally diagnosing acute conversion hysteria, Viscott says:

"Charlotte, what's wrong?"

"It's my feet, doc. I can't move my feet." Charlotte looked very calm. She stared at the ceiling. "I have to be at work tomorrow. . . ."

"You don't seem very worried about your feet," I said.

"Why should I, doc? You're the doctor. It's your problem. I don't know nothing about no feet. You know about feet." This detached attitude of a hysteric toward her symptoms is typical . . .

"What did your mother have to say about your coming north?"

"That's my business," said Charlotte, moving one leg.

"It's important."

"It may be important, but it ain't none of your business."

"Mothers sometimes see situations very differently from their daughters." . . .

"We sure do." Charlotte looked angry. "She thinks just because I'm going north with a man means I'm a tramp. She says I should marry Warren first, but I say I don't have to. I'm gonna live with him . . ."

"If you could say what you wanted, what would you have said? Go on, pretend I'm your mother. What would you say to me? Go ahead, let me have it. . . ."

Charlotte . . . got right into it. "You have no right telling me what to do with my life. I went to high school. I didn't get pregnant like half my girlfriends did. You can't tell me I got to spend my life in this place."

"But, Charlotte, your father and I have plans for you—"

"You're always talking about you and your plans," she yelled at me. "You keep telling me I gotta do this and I gotta do that because Jesus is watching me. Well, I'm watching me too and I don't like what I see. I'm sick and tired of North Carolina and I got plans of my own."

"You're going to stay right here if I have anything to say about it," I said, . . .

"You shut your big fat . . . mouth," she said, and stood up. "I'm old enough to do what I want and go where I want, and I don't need to ask your permission."

Charlotte was standing in front of me, glaring and making a fist.

"You sure sound like you've got a lot of reasons to be angry," I said.

"Yes, I do," she snapped.

"I think maybe you were afraid of getting angry and weren't as sure of yourself as you sounded. Your mother obviously made you angry and you seem to have felt guilty about something."

With that seemingly miraculous cure, Charlotte is ready to pick up her life again. After making an appointment for a further checkup, she turns to Viscott.

"Too bad [I won't see you at the clinic]," she said as she left. "You sure know how to fix a girl's legs."

What does Charlotte's spontaneous recovery tell you about the nature of conversion hysteria? Is it possible that many of the "miracle cures" claimed by faith healers, witchdoctors, and psychics are actually based on the successful treatment of this neurotic condition?

famous by Robert Louis Stevenson's fictional account of *The Strange Case of Dr. Jekyll and Mr. Hyde.* In the story, the kindly and upright Dr. Jekyll swallows a mysterious liquid that changes him into the evil Mr. Hyde. In true-life cases of *multiple personality,* the individual develops one or more separate identities in addition to the original personality. These new personalities are usually born out of childhood abuse and neglect.

In Flora Schreiber's case history, *Sybil,* young Sybil's strict religious training required that she love and honor her mother. Sybil's mother, however, was a severely disturbed woman who alternately loved and tortured her child. In self-defense, Sybil's personality dissociated into 16 separate personalities. Each personality represented a different aspect of Sybil's character. Vickie, for example, was calm and worldly, dressed well, and liked to speak with a French accent. By contrast, Martha was depressed and suicidal.

Can you imagine the shattering impact of such dissociation on the personality? Imagine waking up to find your room painted a different color and your closet filled with new clothes. Or imagine meeting someone who seems to know you quite well—but whom you don't remember at all! Like most multiple personalities, Sybil didn't suspect the existence of her other selves. It took years of therapy and great patience on the part of Sybil's therapist to bring all of her personalities together again. Fortunately, such multiple personalities are rare. Only 5 percent of the neurotics who seek help from a therapist are found to be suffering from either hysterical conversion or a dissociative reaction.

ANXIETY DISORDERS

When the alarm goes off, Perry stays in bed for a while, thinking, "I've got to get moving." But as his mind focuses on the school day that lies ahead, he feels the first signs of panic. His head hurts, his hands sweat, and

his stomach churns. When questioned, Perry admits that his new school really isn't too bad. His teachers treat him well and he's made a few friends. Most days, in fact, he manages to get himself off to class. But when he's facing an especially stressful day, he stays in bed, a victim of his neurotic feelings of anxiety.

Researchers estimate that as many as 11 million Americans like Perry are in need of treatment for *anxiety disorders* in any given year. These heightened states of anxiety often leave the victim hovering on the edge of panic. Physical symptoms can include a general feeling of ill health, stomach disturbances, fatigue, and diarrhea. Certain periods of life (early childhood, adolescence, and the onset of middle age) seem to trigger more anxiety attacks. Most doctors, once they rule out medical causes for the symptoms, prescribe tranquilizers for anxiety. But if the underlying causes go untreated, the anxiety may return later, perhaps in a more disabling form.

If a patient describes feelings of general nervousness, fatigue, and insomnia, psychologists refer to the condition as *neurasthenia* (literally, "nervous weakness"). Most neurasthenics complain of chronic fatigue, the feeling of being worn-out and unable to carry on regular activities. Many of their anxieties are "free floating." That is, the individual has no specific idea as to what is causing the worn-out, nervous condition. Typically, such anxiety reactions grow out of repressed conflicts that arise from the individual's inability to satisfy basic needs: sex, security, achievement, and self-esteem.

■ SECTION CHECKUP

I What is the difference between being afraid to pet a tiger and being afraid to pet a house cat? At what point does a behavior stop being normal and become neurotic?

2 Describe the behavior you would expect from someone suffering from each of these neurotic reactions: obsessive-compulsive behavior; a phobic fear; conversion hysteria; a dissociative reaction; an anxiety disorder.

3 Why do psychologists say that the underlying cause of a neurotic reaction must be uncovered before the condition can be fully overcome?

8.4 ■ HOW DOES THE PSYCHOLOGIST CLASSIFY DIFFERENT TYPES OF PSYCHOTIC BEHAVIOR?

Somewhere in the United States there's probably a man who compulsively buries chicken and beef bones in his backyard. His mild neurosis doesn't harm anyone, and his neighbors probably kid him about his unusual behavior. But what if that same man began kidnapping and burying the neighborhood children "to save them from the devil"? The diagnosis would undoubtedly then shift from neurosis to *psychosis*.

An old joke has also been used to describe the difference between a neurosis and a psychosis. One psychologist asks, "What is the difference between a psychotic and a neurotic?" The second psychologist replies, "Psychotics know that 2 + 2 = 5. Neurotics know that 2 + 2 = 4 . . . but it makes them angry."

Even though the public tends to apply terms like "crazy," "mad," "daft," or "cracked" to all neurotics and psychotics, psychologists avoid the use of slang terms. Sticking labels on troubled people, they explain, is a way of distancing ourselves from those who need help and understanding. Most neurotics carry on their daily lives with some success, but psychotics are sometimes a danger to themselves and to others. In legal terms, they may be judged insane and committed to a mental hospital. Mental health experts also remind us that psychoses are not more extreme forms of neurotic behaviors. The neurotic personality rarely becomes psychotic, even in the face of increased frustration or failure.

Psychoses may be divided into two major types, organic and functional. Organic psychoses begin with disease, accident trauma, a breakdown of nervous tissue, or a biochemical imbalance that affects thought processes. Functional psychoses originate primarily in painful emotional experiences.

MAJOR SYMPTOMS OF PSYCHOTIC BEHAVIOR

Psychotic behavior usually develops rather suddenly, even though the underlying causes of the psychosis have existed for a long time. Almost overnight, the psychotic person loses contact with reality, becomes highly defensive and withdrawn, or begins to exhibit bizarre behaviors. In many cases, psychotics lose the ability to express themselves. Unable to explain their feelings, they may become highly agitated, or they may give up trying to speak. Two other major symptoms of a psychotic condition are the experiencing of hallucinations and delusions.

HALLUCINATIONS. Psychotics who see rats crawling out of the walls or who describe visits from long-dead relatives are suffering from false perceptions known as *hallucinations*. Hallucinations can involve tasting, smelling, hearing, touching, and seeing things that do not exist. It is not unusual for psychotics to claim that phantom figures are threatening them (see Figure 8.8). Other psychotics assert that they feel weird vibrations, experience atomic radiation, or see the walls closing in on them.

DELUSIONS. A patient who "sees" Batman chasing the Joker is hallucinating. But if he says he *is* Batman, he's experiencing a *delusion,* a false belief. Delusions often lead psychotics to announce that they are the living Buddha, Queen Elizabeth I, the President, or some other powerful authority figure. Other delusions involve persecution, the feeling that outside forces are threatening the individual's safety.

If your friend Woody begins hallucinating, your natural reaction would be to assure him that his ceiling isn't dripping with tarantulas. But logic and physical evidence cannot convince psychotics that their hallucinations or delusions are false. To Woody, those creepy crawlers do exist. He can see them, feel them, sense them. People who treat psychotics must first look for physical conditions that could cause their illness. Once medical causes have been eliminated, therapists look for unconscious needs that the patients generally cannot describe or understand. Faced with some overwhelming fear or need, their minds take refuge in the illogic of psychotic thinking and behavior.

ORGANIC PSYCHOSES

Any psychosis that can be traced to damage to the central nervous system is known as an *organic psychosis.* The organic psychoses result from disease, accident trauma, damage to the nervous system, or a biochemical imbalance that affects behavior. Symptoms of organic psychoses may include any or all of the typical psychotic behaviors, including bizarre actions, loss of memory, hallucinations, and the like. Three typical organic psychoses are described in this section.

PARESIS. If left untreated, the spirochetes that cause syphilis make their way through

FIGURE 8.8 ■ The schizophrenic girl who drew this hallucination saw herself "threatened on all sides by hideously grimacing heads of monsters" who wanted to tear her to bits. Can you sense some of the terror she must have experienced?

the bloodstream and into the brain. Years may go by before the deadly results of this invasion become evident. Patients suffering from the advanced stages of syphilis show a breakdown of intellectual and behavioral functions known as *paresis.* Symptoms include delusions, episodes of extreme excitement, and deep depression. Even though early diagnosis and modern antibiotics should have made paresis a relatively rare disorder, syphilis has made a comeback in recent years. The causes are easy to spot and difficult to fix. People in the at-risk population have become complacent about the need to protect themselves from this silent killer at the same time that the funding for public health programs is being slashed.

DELIRIUM TREMENS (D.T.'S). Mental health authorities consider alcoholism a serious illness. Not only does long-term alcohol abuse cause alcoholics and their families emotional and financial harm, but the psychotic reactions that appear after prolonged alcoholic

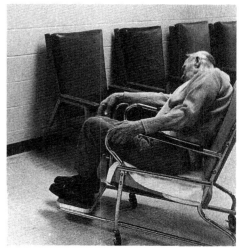

FIGURE 8.9 ▓ Jessica Tandy and Hume Cronyn were still actively performing in the theater and in motion pictures in their eighties. Many older people end their days "warehoused" in rest homes. What can be done to keep the elderly healthy and active?

binges are severe and frightening. This condition, known as *delirium tremens,* or the *D.T.'s,* occurs when the chronic alcoholic's blood-alcohol level drops suddenly. The psychotic reactions include hallucinations, delusions, trembling, sweating, and confusion. The vitamin deficiencies associated with alcoholism may also cause memory lapse. The D.T.'s often last for several days, during which alcoholics may think they are being attacked by swarms of terrifying creatures. Therapists who work with alcoholics must treat their physical condition as well as the emotional problems that led them to become alcoholics.

SENILITY.   One of life's saddest experiences is to visit a much-loved grandfather, only to discover that *senility* has robbed him of his capacity to relate to you. Senility is the psychosis of old age. Its symptoms include disorientation (inability to recognize time or place), memory lapses, and delusions. With people living longer than ever, senility has become an increasing problem. Studies of se-

nile patients reveal that their brains have deteriorated, a condition often accompanied by a restricted blood flow to the brain.

Far from being an inevitable part of the aging process, the onset of senility can often be avoided or slowed. The best prescription comes from the example set by numerous elderly people: Stay healthy and active, and you'll have a good chance of remaining vigorous and alert right to the end. Your own community probably has many senior citizens who jog, play golf, do volunteer work, attend adult classes, and live independently in their own homes and apartments (see Figure 8.9). Even some apparently hopelessly senile patients have recovered at least part of their vitality when therapists put them on good diets and give them the affection and attention so often missing in the lives of America's elderly.

No discussion of senility would be complete without mention of *Alzheimer's disease (AD).* Many of the symptoms of Alzheimer's mimic those of senility. Victims suffer from memory lapses, learning disabilities, personality changes, and a general inability to cope with everyday routines. The symptoms and physical deterioration grow worse over time. Researchers estimate that about 5 percent of the 65-and-over age group may have AD. For those 80 and over, the rate climbs as high as one-third of the population. When autopsies are done, the brains of AD victims show characteristic masses of tangled neurons.

Despite heroic research efforts, the causes of AD are still unknown. Heredity may play a role, for the disease is more common in people whose relatives have been diagnosed as having AD. Other possible causes include viral infections, substandard diet, excessive amounts of aluminum in the system, and a falloff in the production of key neurotransmitters. A brain protein known as amyloid B has been found to cause the nearly complete collapse of cell function when present in high concentrations.

Although AD cannot be cured, proper treatment can slow its progress. One promising approach uses drugs such as Exelon and Aricept that prevent the breakdown of acetylcholine, a brain chemical essential to the proper functioning of memory. Until researchers find a cure, therapy will continue to focus on improving the individual's diet, general fitness, and access to social and recreational activities. Despite their increasing disability, it's not unusual for AD patients to live for many years. Their need for long-term care places an increasing burden on both families and the health care community.

FUNCTIONAL PSYCHOSES

Unlike organic psychoses, *functional psychoses* are believed to originate in painful emotional experiences. The influence of heredity and biochemical imbalances cannot be ignored in diagnosing and treating such illnesses, however. One popular school of thought sums up the debate this way: Heredity, biochemical imbalances, and other physiological factors may very well predispose an

individual to a psychotic breakdown. But it is stress, poor interpersonal relationships, substance abuse, being abused as a child, a dysfunctional family life, and other environmental factors that tip the balance toward mental illness.

So varied are the symptoms of the common functional psychoses that psychologists often disagree on how to categorize them. One relatively simple system uses three main headings: (1) schizophrenia (psychoses marked by thought disorders), (2) affective reactions (psychoses marked by mood disorders), and (3) paranoid reactions (psychoses marked by systematic delusions involving feelings of persecution). To make matters more complicated, individual patients often display symptoms that fit more than one of these categories.

SCHIZOPHRENIA. About one half of all patients in mental hospitals are diagnosed as schizophrenics. In fact, schizophrenia has become so common that some psychotherapists accuse other therapists of lumping all difficult psychotic cases under this catchall label. However diagnosed, schizophrenics display five general disturbances of their thought processes: bizarre, erratic personal behavior; delusions and/or hallucinations; loss of contact with reality; breakdowns in communication; and the display of inappropriate emotions. If you were to follow a staff member through the wards of a mental hospital, you'd probably see the four most common forms of schizophrenia.

1. *Simple schizophrenia*. That's Barbara, sitting so quietly over there. She's lost interest in the outside world, and she probably won't talk to you. If she does, her speech will very likely break down into a "word salad," with nouns and verbs and adjectives thrown in at random. She looks terrible, since she seldom combs her hair or worries about her clothing.

2. *Catatonic schizophrenia*. Paul has been sitting in that contorted position with arms outspread since early this morning. It's as if

The Psychotic Experience: Firsthand Accounts

Many former mental patients have described their experiences while locked in the grip of their psychoses. These short excerpts express the painful reality of mental illness from a very personal point of view.

DELIRIUM TREMENS

I . . . sprang in among the hissing serpents. They leaped at me and entwined themselves around my legs and arms. They . . . tore and lacerated my flesh. . . . Seizing a large heavy one, I pulled off its head and used its body for a weapon. . . . I had only one more monster between me and safety. . . . "Too late! Too late!" said the boatman, and as I flung the serpent behind me the boat moved off [to safety].

DELUSION OF PERSONAL POWER

My radar beam was a source of delight to me. . . . I could repel attendants or patients at will. All that was necessary was to recognize the central source of heat in my solar plexus and move it into my eyes, stare angrily at my enemy and he would become pale, frightened and usually leave. Since the source of the power was definitely located inside me, in my chest, it must obviously come from the sun. Solar power, solar plexus. For this reason . . . I gazed at the sun, absorbing its light and warmth.

PARANOID SCHIZOPHRENIA

During the paranoid period I thought I was being persecuted for my beliefs, that my enemies were actively trying to interfere with my activities, were trying to harm me, and at times even to kill me. . . . In order to carry through the task which had been imposed upon me, and to defend myself . . . I was endowed in my imagination with truly cosmic powers. . . . I felt that I had power to determine the weather which responded to my inner moods, and even to control the movement of the sun in relation to other astronomical bodies.

---

he's been frozen in place. Occasionally he'll break into wildly aggressive behaviors; that's why he's locked in that padded room. Doctor Thorn says it's as if Paul has withdrawn into the deepest reaches of his mind and slammed the door shut. When he does talk, he reveals deeply paranoid delusions. Last week he screamed over and over that the ward orderlies were poisoning his food.

3. *Paranoid schizophrenia.* Watch out, Mrs. L. knows you're new here. She'll want to show you the scars of her martyrdom and plead with you to carry an urgent message to the bishop. She's certain that she's being held because of her religious beliefs and that she's being denied sainthood. Some days she changes roles and tells everyone that she's God. It's hard to keep up with her shifts in attitude and behavior, but they mostly involve persecution of one type or another.

OBSESSIONS AND COMPULSIONS

I am forced to remember everything; I hear something on the radio and then I have to know all about the words of that song; when I look at the window I have to keep counting all the windows and try to remember them; when I go to bed at night I have to keep repeating the names of the patient on my left and the one on my right for fear I won't remember them in the morning and this keeps me from sleeping; I know I am incurable; this drives me mad.

DEPRESSION

That night, the creeping tide of depression washed away the sand of self-esteem. I was a fool to think I could win. There was no victory for such as me. I was a crippled puppy running by the road, dust on a cathedral floor, a blind lion, for me there was no hope. Was there anyone at all? There was no one at all. My wife had betrayed me to my enemies. I was separated from my family, afraid for my children. . . . All was depression.

SCHIZOPHRENIA

I felt so light that I was certain I should have risen off the ground if I had not had hold of his [the attendant's] arm. . . . and as I got lighter and lighter, I got quite frightened, and clutched hold of him, saying I had not the slightest idea where I was going to if I "went up." Instantly I felt as heavy as lead, and could hardly lift my feet off the ground. . . . I had a strong suspicion that he was "willing" me to feel these sensations; indeed, I felt somewhat afraid, and went off by myself . . .

PLEAS FOR HELP

Being crazy is like one of those nightmares where you try to call for help and no sound comes out. Or if you can call, no one hears or understands. You can't wake up from the nightmare unless someone does hear you and helps you to wake up.
All this other raving and howling going on around me—will not someone come and awaken me—so that I may go free?

Excerpts from VARIETIES OF PSYCHOPATHOLOGICAL EXPERIENCE by Carney Landis and Fred A. Metter, Jr., copyright © 1964 by Holt, Rinehart and Winston, Inc., and renewed 1992 by Fred A. Metter, Jr., reprinted by permission of the publisher.

4. *Hebephrenic schizophrenia.* According to cartoonists, every mental hospital has Napoleons and Florence Nightingales, right? This is Quintin—who will demand that you use his proper name—Julius Caesar. Quintin usually acts the role of the great Caesar, but he also regresses to childish behavior at times. That's when he giggles and cries, falls into rhyming speech, and forgets his toilet training. In a way, he combines many of the behaviors associated with the other forms of schizophrenia. Listen, he's trying to tell you something.

I'm Julius Caesar, old geezer just squeez'er, why don't you? The noblest Roman of them all, a dandy randy fandy sandy silence on the wing on the sling on the cling. Thank you, fank you, I Caesar rank you.

Schizophrenics tend to stay in the hospital a long time. The severity of their symptoms often defies the best efforts of the hospital therapists to reach them. Traditional talk therapies have had only limited success. Better results have been achieved with other treatments, including antipsychotic drugs, strict diet, and massive doses of vitamins. Therapies vary because researchers are still conducting studies to find the exact cause (or causes) of schizophrenia.

AFFECTIVE REACTIONS.   Psychoses that cause extreme variations in mood are known as *affective reactions.* A *manic-depressive psychosis,* for example, causes cyclical mood swings that carry the individual from the heights of elation (the manic phase) to the depths of despair (the depressive phase). The illness sometimes locks its victims into continuing cycles of either manic or depressive behavior.

Annette M. flew into a large Midwestern city just after two deaths in her family and the breakup of her marriage. She was taken to a hospital after a series of outbursts that totally disrupted the hotel where she was staying. She broke windows, argued profanely over her bill, flirted with every man she saw, and capped her performance by taking off her clothes in the hotel restaurant. At the hospital, her manic phase continued. She played practical jokes, sang bawdy songs in the hallways, and broke more windows. Then, without warning, she withdrew into a severe depression. She announced that her soul was damned to hell and that her only solution was suicide. As the depression deepened, Annette became totally inactive and refused to eat. Her behavior was described in the hospital records as that of a classic manic-depressive.

Long-term depressive psychosis has become an increasingly common problem. The simple depression most people experience is as unlike Annette M.'s depressive phase as a cold is to double pneumonia. Fortunately, therapists have begun to zero in on the biochemical causes of some long-term depression. Carefully controlled dosages of lithium and norepinephrine have worked well with some patients, while others respond well to electroconvulsive therapy (ECT). Thanks to treatment that combined talk therapy, an antipsychotic drug, and proper diet, Annette was able to leave the hospital after four months. She says her life is now under control, and she doesn't expect to return.

PARANOID REACTIONS.   People who suffer from *paranoid reactions* have delusions that center on feelings of persecution and overblown feelings of self-importance. For many paranoids, the delusions take the form of imaginary plots directed against them by powerful groups such as the FBI, foreign drug lords, or aliens from Mars. Unlike the confused and contradictory delusions reported by paranoid schizophrenics, true paranoids often have good contact with reality—except for their convincing tales of persecution.

Just listen to Roland N.'s story of his persecution by the big oil companies. Roland is

FIGURE 8.10

well dressed, his handshake is firm, and his manner is sincere. He projects an air of utter conviction when he tells his listeners about the tap on his phone, the interception of his mail, and the mysterious agents who follow him everywhere. When asked why the oil companies are after him, Roland talks vaguely about having perfected a secret, cheaply made fuel. But if you ask too many questions, he'll quickly become suspicious of your motives. When you leave him, you won't be positive that he *doesn't* have an invention. Roland can be quite convincing.

Like Roland, paranoids often believe themselves gifted with superpowers. They sometimes assume the identity of a famous person, complete with elaborate details that seem to confirm their delusion. These delusions often involve religious figures, such as the Virgin Mary, or celebrities, such as Elvis. Paranoid patients show up more often in fiction than in fact, however. Only one percent of the patients who enter therapy are diagnosed as having a true paranoid reaction.

▓ SECTION CHECKUP

1 How would you define the difference between a neurosis and a psychosis?

2 Contrast the specific symptoms commonly found in schizophrenia, affective reactions, and paranoia.

3 Distinguish between an organic psychosis and a functional psychosis. Why do psychiatrists hesitate when asked to identify schizophrenia as either a functional or organic psychosis?

8.5 ▓ WHAT ABNORMAL BEHAVIORS HAVE BEEN IDENTIFIED AS PERSONALITY DISORDERS?

What can society do about people who show none of the common symptoms of neurotic or psychotic behavior but who consistently ignore accepted standards of normal behavior? Psychologists find it difficult to help such people because they seldom recognize their need for therapy. They rarely lose contact with reality, and they often appear to be charming and intelligent. But people with personality disorders cannot be called well adjusted for they often cause great distress to themselves and to those around them. Their behavior problems usually begin in childhood or adolescence and tend to be both inflexible and self-defeating.

Some personality disorders, such as schizotypal personality disorder and paranoid personality disorder, create symptoms that are milder and less disabling than the psychotic conditions whose names they borrow. Of greater interest for this discussion are four personality disorders that are not linked to psychoses: antisocial personality disorder, histrionic personality disorder, passive-aggressive personality disorder, and narcissistic personality disorder.

ANTISOCIAL PERSONALITY DISORDER

Brett V. laughs when told he's been diagnosed as having an *antisocial personality disorder.* "Those shrinks don't bother me," he snickers. "The way I see it, the world is made up of dopes and smart guys. Me, I'm one of the smart guys. I take what I want when I want it. If someone gets hurt, that's too bad. The dopes have to watch out for themselves."

Fans of mystery novels and suspense films will recognize Brett by an older label, that of the sociopath or psychopath. By whatever name, the men and women who warrant the diagnosis of antisocial personality disorder

Should Depressed Patients Be Given Electroconvulsive Therapy?

Electroconvulsive therapy (ECT) was first introduced for the treatment of mental illness in 1938. The therapist begins the procedure by administering muscle relaxants and a general anesthetic. After attaching electrodes to the comatose patient's skull, the therapist shocks the patient's brain. Although the body stays relaxed, the shock triggers a severe brain convulsion. Many patients are given double-barreled therapies that combine antidepressant drugs with ECT treatments every three to six months.

Despite its widespread use, ECT remains something of a mystery. No one knows exactly why it helps some severely depressed patients who have not responded to other forms of therapy. A heated debate has arisen over the use of ECT, as the following arguments demonstrate.

PRO

1 ECT benefits patients who would otherwise remain mentally ill. Sixty to 70 percent of depressed patients who receive ECT show marked improvement in their ability to cope with life.

2 Despite numerous scare stories, ECT is "safer than aspirin," particularly for pregnant women, the elderly, and the infirm. If memory loss does occur, it is almost always temporary. Therapists now minimize the problem by confining the treatment to one hemisphere of the brain.

3 Following ECT therapy, many potential suicides discard their plans for self-destruction and respond to therapy. Unfortunately, some patients have reaped publicity by blaming ECT for their own failure to come to grips with their mental problems.

4 State and federal agencies have approved ECT as a proven and successful treatment when administered by qualified psychotherapists under proper conditions.

5 Therapists have learned to restrict ECT to those patients who are most likely to benefit from it. Its success makes it a reasonable choice when nothing else seems to work.

CON

1 Depressed patients often show improvement even when no therapy is given. ECT has not been successful with schizophrenic patients, but it is still being used to treat them.

2 ECT results in the death of one patient in every thousand. Memory losses caused by ECT often last for four weeks or more, and some patients have a permanent memory loss. Ward orderlies sometimes use the threat of ECT as a means of controlling patients.

3 No statistics exist to prove or disprove the argument that ECT prevents suicides. Many depressed patients talk about suicide but never attempt it. Ernest Hemingway, in fact, blamed ECT for destroying his ability to write. He committed suicide one month after his second ECT session.

4 Studies of ECT effectiveness suffer from lack of adequate controls. Government agencies have approved many procedures that later proved useless or even dangerous.

5 Up to 100,000 Americans receive ECT treatments every year, at $2,500 per session. This high volume proves that some therapists turn to ECT when they don't know what else to do.

Critics of ECT describe its continued use as little better than burning incense over the patient. Its supporters say that it works, so why quarrel with success? If you were suffering from a serious depression, with no hope of quick improvement, would you accept a series of ECTs? Why or why not?

can be expected to wreak havoc in the lives of those around them. Unlike schizophrenics or manic-depressives, antisocial personalities do not display obviously neurotic or psychotic symptoms. Many climb to positions of power and influence because they are often gifted with quick minds and creative abilities. If blocked in their ambitions, however, they lie, cheat, steal, and exploit others to reach their goals. Success in business or politics does not guarantee personal happiness for people with antisocial personalities. Their lack of empathy and their aggressive, exploitive behavior prevent them from developing close social, sexual, and work relationships.

The case history of Gwen T. illustrates the point. As a tenth grader, Gwen did not receive the grades she thought she deserved. Untroubled by a sense of right and wrong, she used a laser copier to print herself a report card full of *A*s and *B*s. Too lazy to learn the routines, she talked her way into the Pep Club by charming the sponsor. When she was thrown off the squad for missing too many games, she retaliated by pouring sugar into the gas tank of the sponsor's car. Gwen left school early and altered her sister's diploma so that she could get a job. Her looks and ready smile couldn't make up for her poor work habits, however. She was fired three times in a month. Jobless, she started hanging out in bars and soon married an older man with two children. The marriage ended when Gwen disappeared one day, "tired" of taking care of the house and children. She then served time in a state prison after the police picked her up for writing bad checks. Although Gwen is full of promises about changing her life, her probation officer doesn't have much hope. She was fired from her last job for drinking while on duty.

Antisocial personalities can be graded by degree. Gwen might well be termed an *inadequate antisocial personality,* for she cannot cope with the demands of a normal life-style. Like Gwen, "inadequates" often respond to stress by lying, swindling, resorting to petty crimes, or deserting their families.

FIGURE 8.11 ■ The aggressive psychopath often turns to crime or other antisocial activities as an "easy" way of satisfying basic needs.

Even more troubling is the *aggressive antisocial personality,* whose outbursts of violent behavior occur suddenly and with no apparent cause. "Aggressives" frequently choose a life of crime as the easiest way of meeting their perverse, irrational needs. Because they see others as objects to be exploited, many aggressives commit violent crimes if hurting others seems likely to provide a thrill or a payoff. What society calls random, senseless violence makes perfect sense to the aggressive antisocial personality. Abuse of alcohol or drugs often contributes to this pattern of violence.

Studies of brain-wave activity in aggressives reveal a pattern more typical of children than of adults. Other research adds the possibility of linking antisocial behavior with abnormal sex chromosomes (see Chapter 4, pages 105–106). Most psychologists, however, still believe that the antisocial personality grows out of an unhealthy environment during childhood and adolescence (see Figure 8.11). The childhood of antisocial personalities often includes desertion by one or both parents, life in a foster home, a poor school record, delinquency, an unstable work record, and dependence on drugs or alcohol. Because antisocial personalities do not learn from experience, fear of punishment does not deter them from committing the same offenses over and over. If forced into therapy, they tend to tell their doctors what they want to hear—and then go back to their old antisocial ways.

HISTRIONIC PERSONALITY DISORDER

Have you ever met someone like Roger? Any happening, large or small, sends Roger into a highly emotional state. He dramatizes every injury and expects his friends to take care of his needs. Whatever he doesn't like, he represses. Most of his friends think he's terribly immature.

A psychologist would diagnose Roger as suffering from *histrionic personality disorder*. His tendency to repress information about the

FIGURE 8.12 ▪ Jules Feiffer must have known some passive-aggressive personalities, for he captures their technique perfectly in this cartoon. Do you know anyone who uses similar tactics to control friends and family?

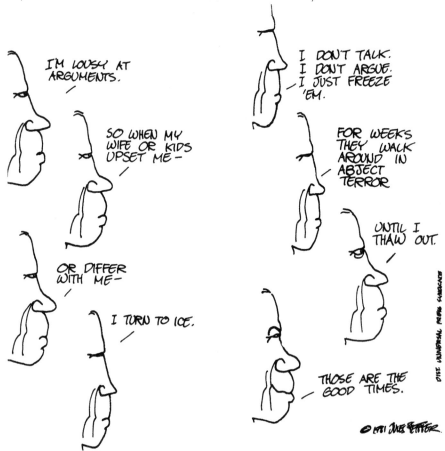

world, his overly emotional reactions, and his dependence on others mark this type of personality disorder. Like most histrionic personalities, Roger can change abruptly from wild laughter to childlike tears. His emotional outbursts are aimed at attracting attention and sympathy.

THE PASSIVE-AGGRESSIVE PERSONALITY DISORDER

It's late afternoon, and Mrs. Yates asks, "What would you like for dinner?" Mr. Yates replies, "Oh, I don't know. Just fix something simple." Taking him at his word, Mrs. Yates cooks a noodle casserole and calls the family to the table. Mr. Yates takes one look at his plate and starts to pout. He makes sure his wife sees that he's eating only a few bites of the casserole. When she asks him what's wrong, he sighs loudly and says in a whiny voice, "I'm just not very hungry. You know I don't like casseroles. I need steak and potatoes if I'm going to go out and break my back on the job every day."

Can you see Mr. Yates's technique for getting his way? He never speaks up for what he wants. It's up to others to guess, and when they guess wrong, he lets them know about it. That's the tip-off to the *passive-aggressive personality disorder*. These people cannot show normal aggression in a healthy, open way. Instead, they arrange situations in which the other person cannot possibly succeed. At work, Mr. Yates reacts to conflict by quickly agreeing with his coworkers—but then he finds underhanded ways to sabotage the compromise.

Beneath the "nice guy" face that passive-aggressives show the world lies a deep pool of hostility. Because they cannot admit to their anger and resentment, they can only express it in ways that do not attack the other person directly. If they do throw a tantrum, they're likely to focus their anger on a pet or an inanimate object. That's why no one should be surprised that Mr. Yates blew up at work last week and smashed the soft-drink machine.

NARCISSISTIC PERSONALITY DISORDER

Barbara O. was dressing for the homecoming dance when her date called to say he'd hurt his ankle playing tennis. Instead of sympathizing, Barbara flew into a rage. "Billy, how could you be so careless?" she shouted into the phone. "Everyone expects to see me wearing my new dress at the dance, and now I won't be able to go."

Barbara's disregard for Billy's injury suggests that she might be afflicted with *narcissistic personality disorder*. Psychologists have been diagnosing this disorder with greater frequency in recent years. In brief, narcissistic personalities display an overblown sense of self-importance. The specific symptoms include feelings of superiority and uniqueness, exaggeration of talents, boastfulness, and an overwhelming need for attention and admiration. Deep feelings of inferiority often lie hidden beneath their superior attitudes.

Billy might well be better off without Barbara. Narcissists tend to exploit others, picking their friends for what they can take from them. They fake feelings in order to impress people with their sincerity and depth. Looks are more important than talent. If you know any narcissists, do not expect them to accept criticism or to pay back favors. To these self-centered individuals, arrogance seems to come naturally.

■ SECTION CHECKUP

1 What is meant by *personality disorders?*

2 Why is the aggressive antisocial personality considered to be a possible danger to society?

3 Contrast the behavior patterns of the histrionic, passive-aggressive, and narcissistic personalities.

8.6 ▧ WHAT PERSONALITY PROBLEMS CAN BE TRACED TO BRAIN DAMAGE OR DYSFUNCTION?

Four-year-old Hillary A.'s mother was a crack cocaine addict. To a casual observer, Hillary's learning disabilities, hyperactivity, and frequent tantrums might suggest some form of neurotic or psychotic behavior. But is it fair to label a child as mentally ill when the causes are largely physiological? Psychologists don't think so. They do believe, however, that people whose behavior problems or troubled personalities result from brain damage or dysfunction need special attention. In many cases, these children and adults can be helped to develop far healthier personalities than once was thought possible.

IMPERFECT BRAIN DEVELOPMENT

When the brain does not develop properly, infants are born profoundly retarded. In aplasia, for example, the child's cerebral cortex

FIGURE 8.13 ▧ With proper early education and training, many people with Down syndrome can hold jobs and care for themselves.

never develops, leaving the brain's capacity for high-level thought and problem solving badly crippled. In microcephaly, the bone of the upper skull does not grow to full size. Caught within a constricted space, the brain cannot develop to its full potential. Children born with these conditions can often perform some self-care activities and can learn to perform simple tasks. Their abilities will not increase with age, however. Those who live to adulthood must stay in a protected environment. In most cases, that means custodial care in a state or county institution.

Down syndrome is a less severe form of mental retardation. The condition is caused by a genetic defect. Down syndrome children carry an extra chromosome that apparently prevents their brains from generally developing past a mental age of three to seven years. About one in every 900 births produces a Down syndrome child, but the odds increase as a woman ages. At age 29 or under, a woman's chances of having a Down syndrome child are about 1 in 1,500; by age 45 the chances are 1 in 30. When the risk factors are great, a pregnant woman can elect amniocentesis. This procedure can detect the presence of chromosomal abnormalities in the developing fetus well before the end of the first trimester.

At one time, because they often develop serious heart or lung problems, Down syndrome children rarely lived past childhood. Today, with better medical care, many live into adulthood. When properly trained and supervised, teenagers and adults work successfully in sheltered workshops. A few have found regular work in restaurants, stockrooms, and other workplaces that need dependable employees who welcome hard, repetitive tasks. Instead of being warehoused in institutions, many Down syndrome adults now live with their families or in board-and-care facilities.

BRAIN TRAUMA

Any injury to brain tissue is termed a *trauma*. In difficult births, the infant's head may be compressed so severely that brain damage results. Fortunately, such birth traumas have become quite rare. Later in life, any severe blow to the head that causes swelling and bleeding can damage brain tissue. This condition is sometimes seen in "punch drunk" boxers who have taken too many blows to the face and head. Accident trauma, in which a bone fragment or a foreign object damages the brain, can cause the growth of scar tissue or the death of brain cells. In all three cases, the trauma can interfere with normal physical and mental behavior. Accident trauma may also lead to unexpected personality changes (see Figure 8.14).

Trauma sometimes results from conditions inside the body itself. The slow growth of brain tumors will eventually interfere with normal brain functioning. Strokes are cerebral "accidents" in which a segment of the brain loses its blood supply. Strokes often cause paralysis, speech difficulties, and personality changes.

ENDOCRINE AND METABOLIC DISORDERS

Changes in the internal chemistry of the brain can also affect the personality. The most common disorders involve the thyroid and adrenal glands. An overactive thyroid, for example, can cause symptoms often associated with extreme anxiety states. These symptoms include hyperactivity, hallucinations, and feelings of great apprehension. A deficient thyroid, by contrast, leaves the individual feeling depressed and lacking in energy.

An underactive adrenal gland can lead to

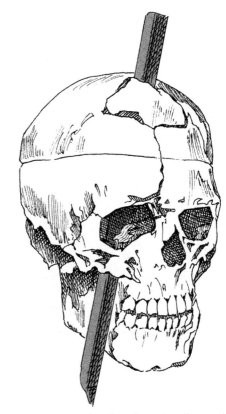

FIGURE 8.14 ■ A railroad construction accident in the 1880s left Phineas Gage alive—but with a tamping iron driven completely through his skull. Incredibly enough, Gage lived through the ordeal. Doctors repaired the damage to his skull, but the trauma to the frontal lobe of his brain changed his personality. Once a popular, easygoing man, he became moody, stubborn, and profane. This sketch, based on a drawing made by Gage's doctor, shows the path taken by the tamping iron.

depression, anxiety, and withdrawal symptoms. A rare condition caused by an overactive adrenal gland leads to obesity and extreme shifts in mood, ranging from total withdrawal to outbursts of violence. Fortunately, all of these conditions can be controlled by medical therapy. President John F. Kennedy, for example, had Addison's dis-

FIGURE 8.15 ■ The haunting gaze of Vincent van Gogh conveys the same power and anguish we find in his paintings. In 1889, when these works were painted, van Gogh was depressed over his recurring mental illness. He committed suicide in 1890.

ease. Regular medication restored his under-active adrenal gland to normal functioning and made it possible for him to carry on his political career.

Other related disorders are caused by inflammation of brain tissue and higher-than-normal body temperatures. A group of illnesses known as encephalitis (sleeping sickness), for example, can lead to prolonged periods of lethargy and sleep, convulsions, disorientation, and hallucinations. Some children exhibit personality changes following their recovery from such illnesses. They may develop aggressive, cruel antisocial personalities. High fevers also interfere with normal brain activity and can lead to a state of delirium. In a delirium, the patient experiences delusions, anxiety, confusion, and periods of unconsciousness.

BRAIN DYSFUNCTION

Some people must live with conditions that originate in a disorder of the nervous system itself. These dysfunctions can result in abnormal behavior, both physical and emotional. Three relatively common examples of brain dysfunction include epilepsy, hyperactivity, and autism.

EPILEPSY. *Epilepsy* (also known as *convulsive disorder*) has been recognized for centuries. Julius Caesar and Vincent van Gogh were both epileptics (see Figure 8.15). The condition may be caused by a variety of factors, including heredity, brain injury, tumors, or infection. Just as frequently, no known organic cause can be isolated.

The typical epileptic seizure involves a second or two of unconsciousness and an almost invisible convulsion. This is a petit-mal seizure, and it generally causes little interruption in normal activities. Grand-mal seizures, which occur in a small percentage of epileptics, cause general convulsions and a longer loss of consciousness.

Oscar D.'s parents suspected his epilepsy early, and their doctor confirmed it with an EEG. With medication, Oscar's seizures are well controlled, and he carries on a normal, productive life. One of his friends had a more serious condition that required surgery before the seizures could be brought under control. But like many other epileptics, Oscar finds that the idea of epilepsy upsets people who don't know much about it. He laughs about that, a little grimly:

> You won't believe how many people expect me to fall down in a roaring fit at any moment. And the parents of the girls I date! All they can imagine is a family of epileptic grandchildren. Don't they know that heredity is only one of the possible causes of epilepsy? My condition started with a case of measles when I was a baby. As long as I'm taking my medicine, I can even drive a car safely. After all the campaigns against prejudice we've had in this country, it's about time people stopped being prejudiced against people like me. Almost all epileptics have normal intelligence, and we can do just about everything anyone else can do. It would make as much sense to discriminate against diabetics or people who wear glasses.

HYPERACTIVITY. "Bobby, can't you sit still? And stop wiggling!" The chances are good that Bobby can't sit still if he's one of the 10 percent of the elementary-school population that suffers from *attention deficit disorder* with *hyperactivity*. Bobby's symptoms include restlessness, constant movement, a short attention span, and aggressive outbursts of temper. Even if his parents have learned to cope with his demanding, explosive behavior, it's unlikely that the school will be that patient. Hyperactive children frequently become discipline problems because of their inability to concentrate, work quietly in their seats, finish tasks, and share materials and equipment. Although the ceaseless, haphazard motor activity tends to end during adolescence, the behavioral problems do not always disappear.

Hyperactive behavior has been described as a group of symptoms rather than as a disease. Its causes have not been pinpointed, but may include brain injury, biochemical imbalance, or allergies to something in the child's diet. Most doctors prescribe a drug therapy that relies on an amphetamine such as Ritalin. Usually a stimulant, Ritalin helps hyperactive youngsters focus on the task at hand. Under proper dosage, they begin to function more normally at home and in school. Many psychologists fear, however, that too many difficult, nonhyperactive children are being put on drugs simply as a shortcut to controlling them. Such therapy may cover up their real problems and may also create a long-term drug dependency. Fortunately, there is a better way to help hyperactive children. Several studies have shown that about half of the hyperactive children who are put on diets high in protein and free of chemical additives soon became symptom free.

AUTISM. To look at Avis, you wouldn't guess that she has a serious neurological problem known as *autism*. She looks as normal as any other attractive, healthy four-year-old. But don't expect a response when you talk to her, even though she isn't deaf or mute. Avis lives in her own inner world most of the time. Today she's playing with her favorite toy, a wooden hammer. Over and over, hour after

FIGURE 8.16 ▓ The forces that lock autistic children into their own private worlds make therapy difficult and time consuming. Would you have the love and patience needed to work with autistic children?

hour, Avis bangs a special spot on the floor with the hammer. If you take the hammer away, she's likely to bang her head on the floor—over and over.

The parents of autistic children say it's as though their sons and daughters live in another dimension. Last month, for example, Avis came down with a sore throat. Unable to explain the problem to her parents, she turned into a screeching, scratching wild thing. Her father still carries the scars left by the scratches Avis inflicted on him when he tried to calm her down.

Avis is the one child in 150 who suffers from autism (or its milder, more common variant, Asperger syndrome). Unlike childhood schizophrenia, autism's symptoms appear during infancy. Autistic children tend to respond mainly to inner drives and needs.

Self-stimulating behaviors such as rocking, arm flapping, and head banging are common. Unable to communicate with their caregivers, autistics veer between silent withdrawal and sudden, violent tantrums. Tests have found abnormally high levels of the neurotransmitters serotonin and dopamine in the brains of these children. Researchers tend to blame a combination of genetic and environmental factors, including exposure to toxic chemicals such as mercury and lead.

The efforts of psychologists and educators to break through to self-isolated children such as Avis have been only partially successful (see Figure 8.16). Drugs that inhibit the production of dopamine seem to relieve some of the symptoms, particularly self-mutilation and repetitive movements. When it comes to teaching autistic children, patient, repetitive "shaping" techniques, combined with love and affection, seem to work best. Teachers break each task into tiny steps and ask the child to repeat each step over and over. Rewards of small treats or hugs and praise are given when the child responds to the training. A variation on the reward technique uses mild electric shocks, spankings, or other aversive therapy to eliminate destructive behaviors. As might be expected, the use of punishment in any form arouses controversy. Defenders of aversive therapy say they give 15 rewards for every punishment handed out.

Whatever training methods are used, only a disappointingly small percentage of autistic children escape from their isolated worlds. Many are sent to institutions when their families can no longer cope with their uncontrollable behavior.

■ SECTION CHECKUP

1 Define what is meant by the term *brain dysfunction*.

2 Contrast the behavior patterns of a hyperactive child and an autistic child who have been placed in a first-grade classroom.

3 How would you explain to your friends that they shouldn't be fearful of, or prejudiced against, someone who has epilepsy?

LOOKING BACK: A SUMMARY

1 Every culture defines normal and abnormal behavior according to its own standards. When people consistently behave abnormally, they are termed *maladjusted*. As the abnormal behavior increases in severity, the individual is often spoken of as being neurotic or psychotic. People with troubled personalities tend to have difficulty coping with the realities of life and often exhibit inappropriate behaviors and emotions.

2 Psychologists see mental illness as a temporary breakdown in the individual's ability to handle the problems of work and personal relationships. Mental health experts believe that over 30 percent of the population will need help with an emotional problem some time during their lifetimes. Improved mental health care and changing attitudes have made it possible for many people to seek help for emotional problems that formerly would have been kept hidden.

3 No single factor can be pointed out as the cause of all mental illness. Instead, environmental and physical factors frequently combine to cause neurotic or psychotic behavior. Environmental factors that affect behavior include dealing with stress, handling frustration, coping with anxieties, functioning within the family, adjusting to job pressures, and finding a place in society. Physical factors at the root of some troubled personalities include heredity, chemical imbalances, disease, and accident trauma. People who have been exposed to an overwhelming shock, such as wartime combat or a vicious mugging, sometimes develop the symptoms of post-traumatic stress disorder (PTSD) in the months following the event. The most common symptom of emotional distress today is depression, a feeling of hopelessness and sadness that affects almost everyone at some time or another. Troubled personalities, however, often become trapped in long-term clinical depression.

4 Almost everyone occasionally shows mildly neurotic behaviors. Neurotic personalities respond to stress or fear-causing situations with repeated, involuntary, and inappropriate behaviors. Common neuroses include obsessions and compulsions, which are continuously repeated, involuntary thoughts or actions. Phobias are irrational, uncontrollable fears, and anxiety disorders are feelings of general nervousness, fatigue, and physical upset. Less common types of neuroses include conversion hysteria, in which inner conflicts surface in the form of paralysis or some other physical disability, and dissociative reactions, which cause parts of the personality to "split off," as in amnesia or multiple personalities.

5 Psychotic behavior, popularly and legally termed *insanity,* involves a loss of contact with reality. Because psychotics live in an unreal world, they can be dangerous to themselves or to others. Hallucinations (false perceptions) and delusions (false beliefs) are common symptoms of psychotic behavior. Organic psychoses begin with damage to the central nervous system. Three types of organic psychoses are paresis, an advanced stage of syphilitic infection; delirium tremens, the hallucinations and confusion that accompany advanced stages of alcoholism; and senility, the disorientation and memory loss caused by old age. The symptoms of Alzheimer's disease, which include progressive memory impairment and a loss of physical function, are often mistaken for those of senility.

6 Functional psychoses originate primarily in painful emotional experiences but may have organic causes as well. The symptoms of schizophrenia include breakdowns in communication, disorientation, delusions, and bizarre behaviors. Affective reactions, another type of functional psychosis, put the individual through wild mood swings that range from mania to deep depression. Paranoid reactions involve delusions of persecution and self-importance.

7 Some personality disorders do not involve loss of contact with reality. Antisocial personality disorder creates individuals who exploit other people in order to satisfy their needs and to achieve material success. Inadequate antisocial personalities cannot cope with life's demands and often react by turning to petty crime, lying, or running away from responsibilities. Aggressive antisocial personalities often use violence to achieve their goals. The histrionic personality represses information that sounds unpleasant and reacts emotionally to almost any situation. The passive-aggressive personality expresses his or her anger indirectly, often by arranging situations in which the other person cannot succeed. The most commonly diagnosed personality disorder is that of narcissistic personality disorder. Narcissists, because of their grandiose sense of their own importance, cannot accept criticism or give of themselves to others.

8 Abnormal behavior can also result from brain damage or dysfunction, which are primarily medical problems. Incomplete brain development can cause profound retardation, as in aplasia and microcephaly. Down syndrome results from a genetic defect. Brain trauma that damages brain tissue can be caused by difficult births, blows to the head, tumors, or a loss of blood supply to a part of the brain. Severe trauma may cause paralysis, loss of speech, or personality changes. Symptoms of endocrine disorders, which are caused by malfunction of the thyroid or adrenal glands, include hallucinations, depression, and mood changes. Memory loss, personality changes, and delirium may follow a high fever or an attack of encephalitis.

9 Brain dysfunction, a breakdown of normal brain activity, can cause abnormal physical and emotional behavior. People with brain dysfunction should not be considered mentally ill. They need medical treatment and often psychotherapy to help them handle their problems. Three disorders associated with brain dysfunction are epilepsy, attention deficit disorder with hyperactivity, and autism. Epileptics and hyperactive children who receive prompt treatment can live normal lives, but autistic children are often trapped within their self-isolation despite every effort to free them.

PUTTING YOUR KNOWLEDGE TO WORK

■ TERMS YOU SHOULD KNOW

abnormal behavior	dissociative reaction	normal behavior
affective reactions	Down syndrome	obsessions
aggressive antisocial personality	electroconvulsive therapy (ECT)	organic psychoses
Alzheimer's disease	epilepsy	paranoid reaction
amnesia	frustration	paranoid schizophrenia
antisocial personality disorder	functional psychoses	paresis
anxiety	hallucinations	passive-aggressive personality
anxiety disorder	hebephrenic schizophrenia	phobias
attention deficit disorder	histrionic personality disorder	post-traumatic stress disorder
autism	hyperactivity	psychosis
biochemical imbalance	inadequate antisocial personality	schizophrenia
catatonic schizophrenia	maladjusted personality	senility
compulsion	manic-depressive psychosis	simple schizophrenia
conversion hysteria	multiple personalities	stress
delirium tremens (D.T.'s)	narcissistic personality disorder	trauma
delusions	neurasthenia	troubled personality
depression	neurosis	well-adjusted

■ CHAPTER CHECKUP

1 Lisa's compulsive, rhyming speech (see page 239) is a symptom of (*a*) conversion hysteria (*b*) paranoia (*c*) manic-depressive reaction (*d*) schizophrenia.

2 A mentally healthy person will (*a*) never show signs of maladjustment or abnormal behavior (*b*) occasionally behave in self-defeating or unhealthy ways (*c*) eliminate all stress from his or her life (*d*) experience some sort of brain dysfunction several times during a lifetime.

3 Imagine a typical classroom of 36 students. The number that will need psychological help for a severe emotional problem sometime during their lifetime is approximately (*a*) 6 (*b*) 12 (*c*) 16 (*d*) 18.

4 Percy has a tendency to worry about future events, whether he can control them or not. This causes an emotional state known as (*a*) anxiety (*b*) frustration (*c*) stress (*d*) autism.

5 Sam T. feels panicky and faint whenever he drives through a tunnel or rides in an elevator. His condition would best be called (*a*) a phobia (*b*) a manic-depressive reaction (*c*) a dissociative reaction (*d*) a hysteric conversion.

6 Tammy K. has periods in which a separate personality emerges who is different from Tammy in many ways. This neurotic behavior is properly described as (*a*) a dissociative reaction (*b*) schizophrenia (*c*) conversion hysteria (*d*) free-floating anxiety.

7 Wilson B. believes that the FBI has tapped his phone and has been opening his mail in an attempt to steal his plans for an antigravity machine. This psychotic behavior is properly described as (*a*) an affective reaction (*b*) a manic-depressive reaction (*c*) psychopathic (*d*) a paranoid reaction.

8 Toni O. exhibits symptoms that include disorientation, hallucinations, and bizarre behavior. This psychotic condition is properly described as (*a*) an affective reaction (*b*) schizophrenia (*c*) a paranoid reaction (*d*) narcissistic personality disorder.

9 During a bank robbery, a man kills a guard without apparent reason. When questioned, he shows no guilt over his action. In all other respects, he has perfect contact with reality. His disorder can be described as that of (*a*) a schizophrenic (*b*) an antisocial personality (*c*) a manic-depressive (*d*) a neurasthenic.

10 Damage to the brain, whether caused by trauma, lack of oxygen, or a chemical imbalance, is of great concern because (*a*) it always causes insanity (*b*) it leads to paresis (*c*) it causes genetic damage (*d*) it can result in personality changes, hallucinations, memory loss, and disorientation.

■ EXPLORING CONCEPTS

1 List five behaviors you would consider normal in this culture and five behaviors you would label as abnormal. Would everybody in your culture agree with your choices? Why or why not?

2 Whitney E. is presently being treated for schizophrenia in a mental hospital. His three brothers show no sign of mental illness, nor do his parents. List a number of possible causes of Whitney's psychosis, both environmental and physiological. Why do you think that he became mentally ill while the rest of his family remains healthy?

3 Explain the difference between neurotic and psychotic behavior in regard to (*a*) contact with reality (*b*) orientation in time and place and (*c*) chances for recovery.

4 Describe briefly the behaviors you would expect from a person who has been diagnosed as (*a*) schizophrenic (*b*) manic-depressive (*c*) paranoid and (*d*) an aggressive antisocial personality.

5 How does the average person react when faced with the unpredictable behavior of the mentally ill? What do you think can be done to overcome this reaction, so that people can learn to treat a person suffering from mental illness as compassionately as they treat someone with a physical illness?

6 List some of the ways American society might be changed to reduce the incidence of mental illness. Why would such changes be a good investment for the future?

■ HANDS-ON ACTIVITIES

1 Prepare a collage that demonstrates the contrast between mental health and mental illness. Use cut-out pictures, your own original artwork, and copies of the artwork produced by the mentally ill. (You'll find samples of such artwork in most books on abnormal psychology.) Discuss the meaning of the images you chose for your collage with your class.

2 If you're like most people, you probably follow a regular routine as you get up in the morning and get ready for the day. Just for one day, vary the routine. Get up on the opposite side of the bed (if possible), eat breakfast before combing your hair, put your shoes on in the opposite order, take a different route to work or school, and so on. Do you find it difficult or easy to change the way you do things? This experience may give you some insight into compulsive behaviors. A truly compulsive person, however, wouldn't be able to change his or her routine at all.

3 If there is a school for exceptional children in your area, try to arrange a visit. Such a school may teach autistic, retarded, and cerebral-palsied children. Observe the procedures that have been developed to help these children. If your career plans include the possibility of working with exceptional children, you might want to volunteer to work at the school.

4 All people have fears that they seldom notice until the fear-causing situation arises. Make an inventory of your own fears. Then survey your friends to find out what fears are most common. Can you figure out how your own fears became part of your personality? For a full listing of known phobias, check out <*www.phobialist.com*>.

5 Ask the members of your class to join in examining the theme of mental illness in current literature, films, and television. Each person can report on one such work or program. Is mental illness being fairly treated in the media, or is it being exploited? After the general discussion, try to pull together an evaluation of current attitudes toward people who have troubled personalities.

FOR FURTHER READING

Berger, Diane and Lisa. *We Heard the Angels of Madness*. New York: William Morrow, 1991. In compiling their deeply personal account of Mark Berger's struggle with manic depression, his mother and aunt have also provided a survival handbook for anyone who is called on to help a family member cope with mental illness. The book is full of useful information about symptoms, diagnosis, therapies, and the community resources available to the mentally ill.

Davison, Gerald, et al. *Abnormal Psychology*. New York: John Wiley & Sons, 2003. If you want to check out current trends in the field of mental health, this well-illustrated text is the place to go. In addition to its coverage of current research, the new edition spotlights the role of gender and ethnicity in the treatment of mental illness.

Green, Hannah. *I Never Promised You a Rose Garden*. New York: Henry Holt & Co., 1995. This engrossing novel focuses on a 16-year-old girl and her long struggle with schizophrenia. Green takes you into the chaotic inner world of mental illness and describes the long, often painful process of therapy that enabled Deborah to return to a normal life outside hospital walls. (You might also enjoy the film that was made from this book.)

Greenfeld, Josh. *A Client Called Noah*. New York: H. Holt, 1986. Greenfeld, in this third volume of his ongoing "family journey," writes honestly and lovingly about life with his autistic son. Whether you begin with this book or with one of the earlier books (*A Child Called Noah* [1972] and *A Place for Noah* [1978]), you will share the family's struggle to help Noah break out of his silent, self-involved world.

Hermelin, Beate, and Michael Rutter. *Bright Splinters of the Mind*. London: Jessica Kingsley Pub., 2001. "John" is an autistic boy who has trouble feeding and dressing himself—but hum any tune that comes to mind, and he can play it on the piano. This well-researched book focuses on autistic children and adults who demonstrate remarkable gifts in such fields as music, language, art, and math. Known as autistics savant, they have much to teach us about the nature of special talents and their relationship to intelligence.

Porter, Ray. *Madness: A Brief History*. New York: Oxford University Press, 2003. The author, a medical historian, traces the history of mental illness from ancient times to the present. Madness, it turns out, is a fascinating subject, and Porter leads you through a survey of topics that range from witchcraft and dunking stools to psychoanalysis, ECT, and Prozac.

Whitaker, Robert. *Mad in America: Bad Science, Bad Medicine, and the Enduring Mistreatment of the Mentally Ill*. Cambridge, MA: Perseus Publishing, 2001. Whitaker, a medical journalist, takes a poleax to the psychiatric profession for its treatment of the mentally ill—both in the past and in this new millennium. This social and medical history of madness in America may upset you at times, but it will also give you a fresh perspective on how best to meet our obligations to those who have been judged to be insane.

Chapter

9 HELPING THE TROUBLED PERSONALITY

Dr. David Viscott makes his living helping people. That's not unusual for a doctor, but the patients Dr. Viscott works with suffer from anxiety reactions, phobias, depression, and other emotional problems. Like most modern psychotherapists, Dr. Viscott doesn't pretend that he can furnish "miracle" cures. Instead, he uses his skills and insights to help his patients help themselves.

In the following excerpt from *The Making of a Psychiatrist,* Dr. Viscott is working with Roberta Goldman. Roberta has made a great deal of progress since she began her therapy. But today, something has gone wrong . . .

Roberta was in the OPD [Outpatient Department] waiting room. She was twenty minutes early and looked uncomfortable, restless. There was no sense making her wait since I had free time.

We walked down the hall toward my office. What could have happened to upset her? . . . the divorce had been an anxious struggle for her. Many times she'd thought she'd made a mistake and wanted to go back to Gary. . . . Law school, though, had been a breeze for her and she had received an offer with an excellent law firm in town. She had even learned to cope with her mother by being firm and saying no when her

mother infringed on her rights. She had also been dating, but . . . why did Roberta look so terrible?

"I think I'm going crazy," Roberta said, near tears, collapsing in her chair. "Yesterday was the worst day of my life. Everything seemed unreal. Floors seemed to be rising and falling, and the perspective of rooms kept changing. I felt I was losing my mind. . . . I couldn't stand being with people, and yet I wanted someone to help me." . . .

"When did all this start, Roberta?"

"I'm not sure. I think I woke up with it."

"Did you have a dream that night?" I asked, playing a hunch.

"Oh, God, yes, a horrible dream."
. . . "I dreamt I went back to Gary. Oh, yes, there was a bizarre religious ceremony! . . . I . . . had to crawl down the aisle on my hands and knees, begging forgiveness from all the relatives for leaving him. I wanted to turn around and run, but I couldn't. I just went on crawling. . . . Please, tell me what's *happening!*"

"I think, Roberta, that you reacted to your dream as if it were real, even though you couldn't remember it. The feelings you had during the day were mostly fear. The feeling in the dream was the fear of being caught again in

278

FIGURE 9.1 ▩ Psychotherapists work at helping people whenever and wherever they're needed. No matter what type of therapy they use, their goal is to help their patients regain control of their lives.

the trap of your marriage. I think they were both the same fear but you didn't know it."

Roberta suddenly seemed more relaxed. "That feels very true," she said.

"I had a similar thing happen to me once," I said. "I had a dream I couldn't remember. I had a horrible day. The way I felt was the way I would have felt if the events in my dream had actually happened."

"You had the same thing happen to you and you didn't crack up?"

"And neither did you. The feelings you had were real, but the event that caused them, your dream, was only a dream."

"It's really strange," said Roberta, "the things that happened in the dream were like losing everything I've worked so hard for in here. I mean my independence, my ability to stand on my own two feet."

"Sometimes," I said "a dream reveals a part of yourself that you find very hard to face." . . .

Finally she said, "I guess I'm still afraid of being alone, and I guess I'm afraid of being better. If I'm better, it means I don't have you anymore and I'm *really* on my own. I know I can

make it but I guess there always are some doubts." . . .

It suddenly struck me how many of my patients, like Roberta, spent their lives reacting to a feeling from a forgotten event, a feeling whose source was obscure but would be felt whether they wanted to feel it or not. And unless they found out where the disconnected feeling came from and measured it, it would make them distort the world around and inside themselves and they would begin to lose their sense of what was real.

Roberta Goldman's story demonstrates that psychotherapy *can* help people regain control of their lives. This chapter will help you focus on some of the different techniques therapists use to treat the troubled personality. The four sections that follow answer these questions:

9.1 What is psychotherapy?

9.2 What types of individual psychotherapy are available?

9.3 How do different group therapies work?

9.4 Where can troubled people go for help?

9.1 ▓ WHAT IS PSYCHOTHERAPY?

Although some people might argue the point, psychologists do have a sense of humor. For instance, they enjoy a variation on the old neurotic/psychotic joke (see page 256) that goes like this:

> What is the difference between a neurotic, a psychotic, and a psychologist?
> The neurotic builds castles in the air, . . . the psychotic lives in them, . . . and the psychologist collects the rent.

The psychologist who treats troubled people earns that "rent" fairly. In the same way that your family doctor might set a broken arm or heal an infection, specially trained *psychotherapists* help their patients regain their mental health.

HISTORICAL APPROACHES TO PSYCHOTHERAPY

The term "mental illness" reminds you that people can be mentally as well as physically ill. At different times in human history, however, there were less enlightened ways of thinking about those who suffered from emotional problems.

SUPERNATURAL EXPLANATIONS. Humanity's oldest explanation for disturbed behavior is known as the *demonological model*. When a primitive cave dweller alarmed the tribe with episodes of violent, manic behavior, the elders stepped forward with a ready explanation. "Demons have invaded our friend's body," they said. Perhaps the elders prescribed rest, herbal drinks, and fasting. Or they may have called in the tribal shaman (healer) to perform ritual dances and chants. The ancient Incas of Peru sometimes "released" the demons by drilling a hole in the disturbed person's skull. Although the methods were crude, the treatments sometimes worked. Rest and quiet are almost always helpful, and drilling the skull may have relieved pressure caused by a tumor or head injury. Most primitive peoples still believe that the demonological model fully explains the mysteries of abnormal behavior.

In a society organized by priests and based on more sophisticated religious values, mental illnesses were diagnosed differently. According to the *religious model*, mental illness resulted when someone violated God's will. As a result, people who suffered from emotional illnesses were thought to have sinned so terribly that they merited their punishment. Only the priests could help them. First, the individual had to confess his or her sins and pray for forgiveness. Next came an assigned penance in the form of fasting, making gifts to the church, or punishing one's own body. In cases in which the devil was thought to have taken possession of the person's body, the individual was put through an exorcism. In this ceremony, the priest performed special prayers and chants to drive out the evil spirit. Some religions still perform exorcisms when supernatural forces are thought to be causing the disturbed behavior.

MEDICAL EXPLANATIONS. Over 2,500 years ago, the Greek physician Hippocrates refused to treat abnormal behavior as an invasion by demons. Instead, he thought of it as an illness to be treated like other illnesses. When dealing with a mentally ill person, Hippocrates prescribed rest, avoidance of stress, special exercises, and a vegetarian diet. Troubled people often regained their emotional health after being treated in this simple, humane way.

Despite the insights provided by the ancient Greeks, the demonological model revived during the Middle Ages. Anyone who acted "strangely" ran the risk of being accused of practicing witchcraft. The "treat-

FIGURE 9.2 ■ Traditional and modern cultures treat troubled personalities in their own ways. How do methods of psychotherapy differ in these two societies? In what ways are they the same?

ment" for witches was to burn them at the stake. It was not until the 1800s that a more scientific approach to mental health problems appeared. Doctors of that time came to believe that disturbed behavior was caused by a breakdown in brain function. This *neuropathological model* relied on surgery, massage, and other physical therapies to relieve symptoms. If the patients' behavioral problems originated in organic dysfunctions such as brain tumors, infections, or other medical conditions, the treatment had a good chance of helping them. Functional illnesses with roots in emotional stress did not respond well to such treatment.

Other doctors, meanwhile, decided that mental illnesses such as depression were caused by poisonous substances in the body. This *toxin model* sometimes led them to remove the spleen, which was thought to be the source of the behavior-altering toxins. Changes in diet and doses of various drugs were also tried. Surprisingly enough, today's researchers have revived interest in this theory. Evidence has been gathered that shows a connection between biochemical imbalances in the body and some forms of mental illness.

PSYCHOSOCIAL EXPLANATIONS. The medical approach to treating mental illness

achieved some success in treating organically caused problems. But not all emotional problems can be blamed on infections or biochemical imbalances. Beginning with the theories of Sigmund Freud (see Chapter 6), a *psychosocial model* for abnormal behavior began to take shape. According to this model, abnormal behavior is the end result of harmful environmental (social) forces acting on the personality of the individual. As a result of those pressures, some people adopt abnormal behaviors as a way of coping with unendurable problems.

According to Freud's *psychoanalytical model,* for example, mental illness is the result of painful childhood sexual feelings. The powerful influences of the child's family and community, he said, affect the adult's ability to cope with personal relationships. Thanks to Freud, mental illness came to be seen as a condition based on past experiences rather than as a battle with demons or a breakdown in brain function. When patients lay down on Freud's couch, they were encouraged to come to terms with repressed memories. In time, they gradually uncovered long-forgotten experiences that lay at the heart of their troubled personalities.

Freud's insights and those of the great therapists who came after him created a large

The Causes of Mental Illness: Changing Viewpoints Suggest a Complex Interaction of Physical and Social Factors

	MODEL	CAUSE	TREAMENT	THERAPIST	CURRENT STATUS
SUPERNATURAL EXPLANATIONS	Demonological	Demons invade the body.	Rituals, prayer, herbal medicines, and fasting.	Shaman or priest.	Belief abandoned by all but primitive peoples.
	Religious	Mortal sin. Devil takes possession of the soul.	Confession and penance; exorcism.	Priest or minister.	Exorcism still practiced by some religions.
MEDICAL EXPLANATIONS	Neuropathological	Breakdown in brain function.	Surgery, psychotropic drugs, massage, hydrotherapy.	Surgeon, physical therapist, psychiatrist.	Certain organic mental illnesses still treated in this way.
	Toxin	Poisonous toxins prevent brain from working properly.	Surgery to remove organ causing the problem, changes in diet, treatment with specific drugs.	Surgeon or other medical practitioner.	New research confirms connection between biochemical imbalances in the body and certain mental illnesses.
PSYCHOSOCIAL EXPLANATIONS	Psychoanalytic	Painful emotional experiences in childhood, mostly sexual in nature.	Help patient come to terms with repressed memories.	Therapist trained in Freudian techniques.	Psychoanalysis has given rise to a number of "talk" therapies that place less emphasis on sexual causes.
	Behaviorist	Learned behaviors interfere with normal life adjustment.	Behavior modification (reward "good" behaviors and punish or ignore "bad" behaviors).	Psychologist trained in behaviorist techniques.	Popular because of emphasis on changing behavior; most useful with neurotics.
	Radical	A sick society generates sick behavior.	Uses existential concept that patient must take responsibility for behavior.	Radical or existential psychiatrist.	Emphasis on patient responsibility has influenced other forms of therapy.

FIGURE 9.3 ▨ London's St. Mary of Bethlehem hospital clearly deserved its name of "Bedlam." In this scene, one man is being chained to prevent him from committing suicide, while others act out their sad states of delusion and melancholy. What effect do you think the visit of the two curious society ladies had on the inmates?

"family" of related talk therapies. As the years passed, two therapy systems arose that refused to buy into the psychoanalytic model. In the *behaviorist model,* therapists believe that mental illness results from learned responses to stimuli. By following a program of behavior modification, patients learn to change harmful and self-defeating habits. Step by tiny step they move closer to regaining control of their lives.

By contrast, the *radical model* blames mental illness on the stress placed on the individual by a severely disturbed society. If society is sick, the *radical psychiatrist* tells us, it's not surprising that so many people lose their ability to cope. In therapy, patients discard guilt feelings and learn to take responsibility for their own behavior. Thera-

pists remind them that living in a sick society is no excuse for being sick yourself.

TREATMENT OF THE MENTALLY ILL

Until recent times, the mentally ill were often subjected to cruel and inhumane treatment. In the 1600s, mental hospitals were grim prisons in which patients were isolated from the rest of society. London's St. Mary of Bethlehem asylum stands out as a terrifying example. Londoners soon shortened the hospital's name to "Bedlam," a term that has come to mean any place of wild confusion (see Figure 9.3). For a penny, visitors could watch the inmates "perform." Bedlam's patients mostly took care of one another, for medical care was sadly lacking. Therapy consisted of chains, whips, straitjackets, and other restraints. Improvements in patient treatment came slowly. In one early hospital, the patients were doused with buckets of ice water as part of their therapy.

In the late 1700s, a French physician took a new and revolutionary position. Philippe Pinel believed that the mentally ill were no different from anyone else, except for their severe personal problems. Pinel walked into his asylum one day and ordered that the inmates be freed from their chains and dungeons. He moved them to sunny, well-furnished rooms, where they ate well and were no longer mistreated. Pinel sat down with each patient, listened to individual problems, and began to compile case histories. Thanks to this enlightened treatment, many patients recovered and were able to resume their normal lives.

In the United States, similar reforms began. Dr. Benjamin Rush, a signer of the Declaration of Independence, took the first steps toward providing humane treatment of the mentally ill in the late 1700s. But much remained to be done. In 1842, Dorothea Dix, a Boston school teacher, campaigned for proper hospital facilities for the mentally ill. Dix discovered that most emotionally disturbed people were being held in prisons and poorhouses. They were often whipped and confined in cages, closets, cellars, and pens. Thanks to Dix's effective publicity, the public voted to pay for properly equipped mental hospitals. Despite these advances, the struggle to maintain good hospitals has not yet ended, as you will learn in Section 9.4.

CHOOSING A TYPE OF THERAPY

Imagine that for some time you have been feeling increasingly anxious. You wake up each morning with a strong feeling of dread, yet you know there's no real reason for your anxiety. Finally, you decide to seek help.

But how do you choose the right therapy?

Should you try a psychoanalyst? A behaviorist? Should it be individual or group therapy? The choices seem endless.

Everyone going into psychotherapy faces these decisions. Fortunately, the dilemma isn't as daunting as it may seem. Almost any recognized therapy can be helpful as long as two factors are present. First, the individual must admit to having a problem and must ask for help. Therapists can't force their insights on unwilling patients. Second, the therapist must inspire trust. As it develops, trust stimulates the open and free dialogue that is essential to any therapy relationship.

Even when all systems are go, therapists can't give guarantees. Many troubled people recover, but others stay the same or slip backwards. Win or lose, however, all good therapists subscribe to the following four practices:

A GOOD THERAPIST PROVIDES SUPPORT IN TIME OF CRISIS. Therapy provides an emotional safety net for troubled people. Good therapists furnish this support without reservations. They believe that every person has a right to unconditional support, no matter what he or she may have done in the past. In turn, patients know that the therapist will be available whenever they feel themselves losing control.

A GOOD THERAPIST SCREENS PATIENTS FOR MEDICAL PROBLEMS. Just as some physical ailments are psychological in origin, some abnormal behavior is caused by organic conditions. A careful psychotherapist will always have patients checked for possible chemical imbalances, infections, brain tumors, and other medical problems that can cause disturbed behavior.

A GOOD THERAPIST DEVELOPS CATHARSIS. *Catharsis* (from the Greek for "to purge or clean out") is the release of tension through talking or otherwise working out painful memories and repressed feelings. When patients talk about long-buried emotions, they often feel a release from anxiety. At the same time, both the patient and the therapist gain valuable insights into the causes of the behavior that led to the therapy sessions.

A GOOD THERAPIST HELPS PEOPLE CHANGE.
Once the emotional problems have been identified, the therapist helps patients discard nonproductive behaviors. The next step is to use the insights gained in therapy to learn healthy, productive ways of satisfying needs. Comedian Bob Newhart went into therapy because he wasn't satisfied with the way his life was going. He summed up his feelings about the experience in these words: "I think the whole experience of therapy was painful at first but, . . . I like where I am now and I didn't like where I was before. The shrink helped me get to the point where I am today. It's made my life better: I've gotten to know myself better, and I like myself a little more."

■ SECTION CHECKUP

1 Contrast the causes of mental illness as described by the three major theories—the supernatural, medical, and psychosocial.

2 Why was Philippe Pinel's approach to therapy for the patients of his asylum so revolutionary?

3 List several of the services that good psychotherapists provide for their patients.

Strengths and Weaknesses Of Individual Therapy

STRENGTHS

1 Therapist and patient develop the mutual trust and closeness that are a prerequisite to successful treatment.

2 Individual therapists are free to choose the approach they think will best help patients.

3 Many patients prefer the privacy and one-to-one attention they receive in individual therapy. Because they feel more comfortable, they make better progress than they would in group therapy.

4 Strict licensing requirements for individual therapists generally ensure that patients receive competent care.

WEAKNESSES

1 Individual therapy is expensive. Public health agencies and free clinics do provide low-cost or free one-to-one therapy, but their resources do not stretch to reach all who could benefit from the service.

2 Because of the expense, many patients drop out of therapy before the benefits become evident. A typical course of therapy may take six months to a year; psychoanalysis lasts even longer.

3 Because patients develop a close relationship with their therapists, they are often reluctant to end the sessions. This rule holds true even when it becomes clear that the therapy has failed.

9.2 ▓ WHAT TYPES OF INDIVIDUAL PSYCHOTHERAPY ARE AVAILABLE?

Take one therapist. Add one troubled patient. Encourage the patient to start talking. The therapist listens, counsels, and occasionally guides the discussion. The patient gradually gains in self-understanding and recovers control of his or her life. Stripped to its essence, that's *individual therapy.*

Ever since Freud, this one-to-one relationship has been the heart of psychotherapy. Even today, despite the growing popularity of group therapies, individual therapy remains the first choice of most troubled people when they seek help. Choosing from among the many different therapies available, however, presents a further challenge. Since no single psychotherapy can be rated as "most effective" or "least effective," a sampling of the more commonly available therapies might help you understand what goes on in the therapist's office.

PSYCHOANALYSIS

Although Chapter 6 describes a typical Freudian analysis (pages 194–196), a brief review may be useful. After all, most modern systems of therapy depend to one degree or another on the insights and techniques developed by Sigmund Freud.

BASIC CONCEPTS. Psychoanalysts believe that emotional disorders have their origins in childhood. That is when the demands of the id first come into conflict with the superego. Caught between the "I want" drives of the id and the "Thou shalt not" commands of the superego, the ego must work overtime to moderate childhood's powerful sexual drives. When this struggle leads to painful conflicts, feelings and experiences are repressed into the unconscious. Freud believed, for example, that Oedipal conflicts are always repressed.

Repressed experiences can lead to feelings of depression and other emotional problems later in life. Most people manage to live normal lives despite the certainty that they are repressing many of childhood's terrifying conflicts. Psychoanalysts would agree with that point. But they'd also say that everyone's life could be even more productive if he or she had the chance to go through analysis.

What is it like to lie on an analyst's couch? Martin Shepard, himself a psychiatrist, describes his own experience.

> It was not the lying on a couch four times a week that "cured" me. Nor was it my analyst's interpretative skills that made me realize the absurdity of my self-contemptuous, vicious cycle. That that was a blind-alley way of thinking emerged gradually as I listened to all of the claptrap I was free associating. . . .
>
> Another thing that helped was my daring to go beyond my fears and old ways of dealing with myself and others. . . . Last, and perhaps most significant, was the fact that I felt fully accepted by this woman analyst of mine.
>
> I could tell her about my "worst self"—both historically (stealing money from my mother and lying about it) and in the present (passing by an auto accident at a roadside and not stopping to see if I could help)—and I felt she still was interested in me. I dared to ask her if she liked me, and she said that she did. I dared to insult her by sneering at her "superkindness," and yet she remained kindly disposed. . . .
>
> It was this acceptance by her of all these parts of me that I felt also led to my accepting myself.

THREE STAGES OF ANALYSIS. An analysis such as the one that Shepard went through takes place in three stages. Because each patient brings different problems to the therapy sessions, no one can predict how long each stage will take.

First, in order to uncover the roots of their troubled behavior, patients learn to *free-associate*. They lie on the analyst's couch or sit in a comfortable armchair and say anything that comes to mind, particularly as it relates to their past. During this stage, the patient meets *resistances,* those locked compartments of the unconscious where the most troubling memories lie waiting. Patients also begin to experience *transference* during this period. All the love/hate emotions they feel about parents, lovers, and the other significant people in their lives become part of their feelings toward the therapist.

In stage two, *catharsis* begins. Tensions disappear as patients talk more freely about experiences dating back to early childhood. After months of near silence, the analyst begins to offer evaluation and interpretation.

Finally, in stage three, the patients are ready to *work through* the final resistances. They must replace the last self-defeating attitudes and feelings with increased control, insight, and acceptance. Therapy ends when the patients achieve greater independence and healthier ways of coping with the reality of everyday existence.

THE NEO-FREUDIAN APPROACH

Even during Freud's lifetime, a number of psychoanalysts disagreed with his insistence that the personality is largely shaped by sexual drives. The neo-Freudians shifted their emphasis to the psychosocial forces, both cultural and environmental, that influence behavior. They also insisted on a more active dialogue between the therapist and patient.

Among the important analytical therapies that emphasize psychosocial causes of disturbed behavior are those developed by Alfred Adler (1870–1937) and Harry Stack Sullivan (1892–1942).

ALFRED ADLER: INDIVIDUAL PSYCHOLOGY. Adlerian analysts see themselves in a role similar to that of a parent. As a parent interprets social customs and rules to a child, so the analysts help their patients understand the nature of their neurotic behaviors. Adler particularly looked for behaviors linked to his patients' feelings of inferiority, which he believed all people experience in one degree or another.

According to Adler, abnormal behavior results from misguided attempts to compensate for feelings of inferiority. Seventeen-year-old Oliver, for example, tries to compensate for his poor performance in the classroom by playing the role of class clown. His jokes and pranks gain him some of the recognition he needs. But clowning around doesn't resolve the basic problem, as a sympathetic analyst would point out. In therapy, Oliver would learn how to develop the social and academic skills that will help him increase his feelings of self-worth. Once he masters these new skills he will be free to discard his clownish behavior as an overcompensation he no longer needs.

HARRY STACK SULLIVAN: INTERPERSONAL THERAPY. The American psychiatrist Harry Stack Sullivan emphasized the role of culture in causing disturbed behavior. The individual can be defined only in the light of his or her relationships with other people, Sullivan insisted. Children learn love, responsibility, and generosity from their parents and other adults. But they also learn loneliness, despair, guilt, and anxiety.

Sullivan believed that it was a waste of time for the therapist to try to free patients from the causes of their unhealthy behavior. For example, if a young woman named Betty has learned to see her parents as cold and unapproachable, she will tend to transfer that image to all the authority figures in her life. In this way, her relationships with teachers, bosses, and even her husband will be colored by her early experiences. The analyst's job, as Sullivan saw it, is to help Betty "see" others as they really are. She can then discard the false images as she relates more openly and honestly with friends, family, and co-workers.

THE EXISTENTIAL APPROACH TO THERAPY

The unconscious, childhood sexuality, and other psychoanalytic concepts have little meaning for existential therapists. In their view, only the present moment matters. Each person stands alone. You cannot blame other people for what you feel, nor does it pay to explore repressed desires as a means of freeing yourself from unhealthy behaviors.

Anxiety arises, the existentialist will tell you, from being unable to face what you already are. The only route out of that terrible feeling of existential despair, out of the emptiness of life, is to face the fact that you must take responsibility for your own choices. In taking that responsibility, you can tap your potential for growth toward the highest human qualities—love, commitment to a cause, appreciation of beauty.

No two existential therapists follow the same rules. But therapists Viktor Frankl and R. D. Laing have developed some interesting approaches to helping the troubled personality overcome unhealthy behaviors.

VIKTOR FRANKL: LOGOTHERAPY. In his therapy, Viktor Frankl (1905–1997) emphasized the search for meaning (logos). He believed that all humans are motivated to find meaning in their lives. The troubled personality is created when this "will to meaning" is frustrated. To a teenage obsessive-compulsive named Maura, the logotherapist says, "You may not be able to control the circumstances of your life. But you can control your attitudes toward those circumstances. You have the freedom to take a stand."

In therapy sessions with Maura, the logo-therapist helps her explore the underlying causes of her obsessive-compulsive behavior. In time she will realize that the compulsion that requires her to keep her desk, locker, and room perfectly neat at all times stems from an underlying fear of disorder. Maura now remembers a chaotic period in her life when her parents were divorcing and the house, as well as her life, seemed to be in constant turmoil. The logotherapist becomes her partner in exploring these feelings.

Gradually, Maura accepts the fact that in order to overcome her obsessive-compulsive behavior, she must do exactly what she most fears. First, she learns to be disorderly in her personal habits. In small, "baby steps," she leaves clothes lying around her room and jumbles the books in her locker. As she discovers that she *can* endure this amount of disorder, she then leaves her bed unmade, the dishes unwashed, and so on.

As she takes her first steps toward overcoming her compulsive behavior, Maura is asked to redirect her energies. Her therapist encourages her to join the swim team and to do volunteer work at a nursing home. As Frankl would tell her, "The cue to your cure is not self-concern, but self-commitment." Maura will always be rather tidy in her personal habits, but she will now do so through choice, not compulsion.

R. D. LAING: RADICAL PSYCHIATRY. British psychiatrist R. D. Laing (1927–1989) wrote that the insane are perhaps the only truly sane people in a world gone crazy. As an illustration of this antipsychiatric view, he asks you to imagine two people. One is a girl who believes that an atom bomb is ticking away inside her, ready to explode. The other is a submarine captain ready at any moment to launch a salvo of nuclear missiles. Most psychologists would label the girl as psychotic, says Laing, perhaps schizophrenic. These same therapists would call the captain normal. So, who's truly crazy, asks Laing: a girl

Radio Psychologists Offer a Phone Line Instead of a Couch

The phone lines are jammed even before the show goes on the air. In a small studio at radio station KFI (Los Angeles) a woman screens the calls. "See if you can stop crying, Marie, long enough to tell me that," she says soothingly.

In a nearby studio, outspoken and often controversial therapist Laura Schlessinger prepares for another evening of radio psychology. In the hours that she's on the air, people will call from as far away as Canada. The stories they tell will be full of pain, loneliness, frustration, anger, and despair. In the few minutes she spends with each caller, Schlessinger must clarify the problem and suggest a possible solution. Drawing on her many years of radio experience, she is able to send most callers on their way with some useful advice and the sense that someone cares about them.

Traditional psychotherapy requires weeks or months of interaction between the client and the therapist. Can anyone, no matter how gifted, reduce that process to a quick three to five minutes? Schlessinger, Dr. Phil McGraw, and their counterparts across the country do not claim to be doing psychotherapy. When they detect serious emotional problems in their callers, they advise them to seek counsel-

ing. Their job, they say, is to help basically healthy people solve everyday problems.

What kind of calls light up the switchboard? Young Stuart calls to ask for help in coping with a teacher "who hates me." Betty asks for advice on how to discipline a rebellious teenager. Charley says he despairs of finding a job where he can use his artistic talent. Pat doesn't know how to deal with her traumatic memories of being abused as a child.

Michael is one of the evening's last callers. He feels drained after months of caring for a friend dying of AIDS. He's also worrying about a long-delayed job search. Schlessinger talks to him about self-renewal, about being unable to give if you're empty. Then she gives Michael a deadline for mailing two job applications.

"That's it?" Michael asks. Clearly, he's expecting a bit of advice that will magically fix his problems.

"What did you think I was going to do? Come over and make you spaghetti?" Schlessinger responds.

"You do make me laugh," Michael chuckles. He sounds happier as he hangs up.

who admits that her world may blow up at any moment or a naval officer who stands ready to kill millions of people?

Laing uses this argument to reinforce his belief that society uses mental illness as a way of coping with people who make the rest of us uncomfortable. Once patients are labeled schizophrenic, for example, they can be confined to a hospital, drugged into tranquility, shocked into forgetfulness, and even have

odd bits of their brains removed. After a while, they'll stop saying, seeing, hearing, feeling, and doing whatever it is that's so strange. Laing and other radical psychiatrists think that this "psychiatric assault" is often used to quiet the rebellious, nonconformist personalities.

Given this philosophy, how would a radical psychiatrist treat a schizophrenic? First, Laing says that schizophrenics need a life-

The Double Bind of the Troubled Personality

Radical psychiatrist R. D. Laing believed that mental illness grows out of the impossible demands society places on the individual. In the short poems he called "Knots," he tried to put that concept into terms that can speak to the heart as well as the mind.

In this "Knot," Laing asks you to think about the double bind that affects so many disturbed people.

There must be something the matter with him
   because he would not be acting as he does
      unless there was
   therefore he is acting as he is
   because there is something the matter
      with him
He does not think there is anything the matter
      with him
   because one of the things that is
   the matter with him
   is that he does not think that there is anything
   the matter with him
therefore
   we have to help him realize that,
   the fact that he does not think there is
      anything
   the matter with him
   is one of the things that is
   the matter with him

support system that will nurture them while they find their way through the maze of their madness. At Kingsley Hall, a residential center Laing established for psychotic patients, people were given the chance to work with and through their crises in living. Those who were "up" took care of those who were "down." The doctors dressed like everyone else and served as "guides" rather than therapists. In this atmosphere of acceptance,

love, and support, psychotic patients showed remarkable improvement. For example, 41 of the Kingsley Hall residents had previously been hospitalized. After their stay, only 12 were so out of touch with reality that they needed further hospitalization.

In describing her experience at Kingsley Hall, Mary Barnes writes:

> My fear of love was even greater than my fear of anger. All twisted up and matted together in my mess state, I didn't know much what was happening.
> Joe [Dr. Joseph Berke, Mary's doctor] assured me it was all right to paint. . . .
> Paint I did. Gradually, it seemed to *me,* perfectly right again, to paint. Painting, when I wasn't too "bad" to do it, got me together, my body and soul. All my insides came out, through my hands and my eyes and all the colour. It was free and moving, loving and creative.

CLIENT-CENTERED THERAPY

Unlike psychoanalysis and existential therapies, with their European background, *client-centered therapy* carries a made-in-America label. Psychologist Carl Rogers (1902–1987) developed this humanistic form of therapy. Rogers defined neurotic behavior as the result of life experiences that make people defensive, prevent them from communicating freely and openly with others, and keep them from becoming fully self-actualizing.

As the name suggests, client-centered therapy spotlights the client as a person capable of directing his or her own therapy. Rogers believes that the word *patient* automatically puts the person seeking help in an inferior position. *Client,* in contrast, implies that therapist and client share equal interests and responsibility. In this relationship, the therapist's job is to provide understanding, warmth, and acceptance.

Client-centered therapists do not attempt

to find out what is "wrong" with their clients. Rogers described his task as creating a sympathetic setting in which clients can find their own path to self-awareness. In the following excerpt, Rogers describes his discovery of what he came to call *nondirective therapy:*

An intelligent mother brought her very seriously misbehaving boy to the clinic. . . . We decided in conference that the central problem was the mother's rejection of her son. . . . In interview after interview I tried . . . to help the mother see the pattern of her rejection and its results in the boy. To no avail. After about a dozen interviews I told her I thought we both had tried but were getting nowhere, and we should probably call it quits. She agreed. Then as she was leaving the room, she turned and asked, "Do you ever take adults for counseling here?" Puzzled, I replied that sometimes we did. Whereupon she returned to the chair she had just left and began to pour out a story of the deep difficulties between herself and her husband and her great desire for some kind of help. I was bowled over. What she was telling me bore no resemblance to the neat history I had drawn from her. I scarcely knew what to do, but mostly I listened. Eventually, after many more interviews, not only did her marital relationship improve, but her son's problem behavior dropped away as she became a more real and free person. . . . This was a vital learning for me. I had followed *her* lead rather than mine. I had just *listened* instead of trying to nudge her toward a diagnostic understanding I had already reached. It was a far more personal relationship, and not nearly so "professional." Yet the results spoke for themselves.*

* Carl R. Rogers, "My Philosophy of Interpersonal Relationships and How It Grew," address at Association for Humanistic Psychology, Honolulu, Hawaii, September 1972.

Today's client-centered therapist follows Rogers's three basic principles.

1. All clients receive the therapist's *unconditional positive regard.* By demonstrating empathy and personal involvement, the therapist assures clients that they are valued as people, no matter what they have done in the past. This security frees clients to express their feelings without risking the loss of the therapist's respect.

2. Client-centered therapists do not hide behind professional masks. They reveal themselves to their clients as genuine, warm, well-adjusted, and caring human beings.

3. Client-centered therapists do not judge their clients, nor do they prescribe solutions to their problems. The therapist's job is to reflect back the client's feelings for evaluation and exploration.

Thus, if 12-year-old Gordon says, "I hate my father!" Dr. Gonzales doesn't look shocked, nor does she begin probing for an unresolved Oedipal complex. Instead, Dr. Gonzales replies, "Oh, you do have strong feelings about your father, don't you?" That gives Gordon a chance to reflect on what he's said. Now he continues, "Well, he does make me terribly angry. Just last week I wanted to buy a new camera, and he wouldn't let me, even though I worked for the money!" To which Dr. Gonzales replies, "You must want that camera quite badly to become so angry about not getting it."

As the dialogue continues, Gordon begins to understand the causes of his emotional problems. Once he realizes what is missing from his life, Dr. Gonzales will help him choose new behaviors to replace the old, self-defeating ones.

Client-centered therapy works best with mildly troubled people who have enough contact with reality to respond to the challenge of self-discovery. The nondirective techniques pioneered by Carl Rogers have found widespread use among counselors, social workers, ministers, and other people in the helping professions.

COGNITIVE THERAPY

Psychologists are constantly searching for new insights into human behavior. One of the newest and most influential therapy systems to emerge from this search is known as *cognitive therapy*. According to this theory, the best way to solve emotional problems is to change the client's way of thinking. Once faulty thinking processes and belief systems have been exposed, client and therapist can work together to modify them. Cognitive therapy seems best suited for treating depression and anxiety disorders. Some therapists have also found it useful in the treatment of marital conflicts, hyperactive behavior, and eating disorders.

Albert Ellis (1913–) has emerged as a leader in the field with a system he calls *Rational Emotive Therapy* (RET). Ellis sees disturbed behavior as growing out of a three-step process. First, there is an activating experience (Ivan G. takes advantage of his girlfriend). Afterward, the individual experiences consequences (Ivan's guilt feelings lead to depression). The incident and the emotions it causes reinforce a faulty belief (one of Ivan's life assumptions is that "certain acts are so wicked and cruel that they merit severe punishment"). Ellis takes the position that the incident does not create the disturbing emotion. Ivan's depression, he believes, grows out of his irrational belief system.

RET therapists do not look for past life experiences as the cause of disturbed behavior. Instead, they work with their clients to correct false and self-defeating ways of thinking. In Ivan's case, the therapist's job would be to help him understand that making mistakes does not make someone a bad person. During therapy, Ivan might be asked to play different roles as a way of gaining greater insight

into his relationships with others. The therapist might also ask him to build new models for thinking and behaving in social situations. Other techniques include the use of humor to expose the absurdity of some beliefs and simple persuasion. The breakthrough comes when clients realize that changing faulty beliefs can lead to the resolution of their emotional problems.

BEHAVIOR THERAPY

Behaviorists believe that all human behavior is the result of learned responses to the environment. Psychologists who practice *behavior therapy* (often referred to as *behavior modification*) reject most of the techniques favored by psychoanalytic and client-centered therapists. They pay little attention to the causes of abnormal behavior or to increased self-awareness. Instead, they try to change the behavior itself, using techniques that replace unproductive behaviors with healthier ones.

Most behavior therapists today use the *operant conditioning theories* of B. F. Skinner (see Chapter 7, pages 205–206, and Chapter 10, pages 322–325). Skinner believed that children learn at an early age to "operate" on the environment in particular ways. These learned behaviors are either rewarded or punished by parents and other adults. Typically, a child learns to use the behaviors that pay off. For example, if saying she's ill earns Monica extra sympathy and a day off from school, she'll probably continue to use illness as a way of coping with stress when she's older. In time, Monica's "colds" or "fainting spells" will become automatic responses to any situation in which she feels threatened.

In the following case study, behavior therapy was used to treat a case of school phobia. At age 14, Lance literally could not stay in school. After 15 minutes in the classroom, he would become dizzy and nauseated. Then, palms sweating and pulse rate rising, he would run out of the room. No amount of

■ PRO & CON:

Does Psychotherapy Work?

At first glance, you might think that's a silly question. Of course psychotherapy works! If it doesn't, why are so many people paying so much money for therapy sessions, drug treatments, ECT's, and other ways of resolving their emotional problems? Surprisingly enough, a number of serious doubts have been raised about the value of most psychotherapy.

PRO

1 Psychotherapy produces positive changes in the behavior of troubled people. If someone starts therapy with a particular problem and completes the therapy no longer locked into that unhealthy behavior, the improvement must be credited to the course of therapy.

2 Qualified therapists bring two essential ingredients to therapy. One ingredient is professional training and experience. The other is the warmth, intelligence, and insight of a caring human being. Without them, their patients would remain locked into their self-destructive behaviors.

3 Therapists have the training and experience needed to make accurate diagnoses of their patients' problems. Otherwise, useful therapy cannot take place.

4 Without psychotherapy, countless people would be sentenced to lives of misery and despair. Although it's not perfect, psychotherapy is still the best solution anyone has found for helping emotionally troubled people.

CON

1 Positive changes in patients' lives can take place whether they go into therapy or not. One major study showed that one third of the people in therapy improve, one third stay the same, and one third get worse. Troubled people who don't go into therapy get better or worse in about the same ratio.

2 Almost any sympathetic person who is willing to listen can provide as much help as most trained therapists. The key factor in therapy is a motivated patient who wants to get better. If that ingredient is there and if the patient believes in the therapy being used, improvement is almost certain.

3 Therapists seldom agree on a diagnosis. The definitions of the various mental illnesses are woefully inexact. A patient who talks to three different therapists may receive three different diagnoses.

4 Statistics show that more severe mental illnesses are the least likely to respond to treatment. This means that the benefits of psychotherapy are granted primarily to those who need them the least.

Do you think that psychotherapy is a giant con game? Or do you think that therapists provide an invaluable service to troubled people? You might want to talk to some people who have been in therapy before you decide on your answer.

punishment could force him to stay. Lance's despairing parents finally took him to a hospital for therapy.

At the hospital, a friendly psychologist put the teenager on a behavior-modification program. Lance agreed that he could handle five minutes a day in the special classroom run by the hospital. When the five minutes were up, Lance was free to leave the room and carry his completed assignment to the psychologist's office. Then he could do anything he wanted for the rest of the day.

293

When Lance brought his work to the office, the psychologist entered his progress on a large chart. After praising Lance for his accomplishment that day, the psychologist would ask him to set his target for the next class period. Challenged by the chart and pleased by the praise, Lance steadily increased his time in the classroom. By the fifth day, he had reached 30 minutes, and on the sixth day, he stayed for 40 minutes. At the end of the month, Lance was attending class full-time. Soon afterward he was discharged from the hospital.

A follow-up showed that Lance kept up his good attendance and improved his grades. What made this turnaround possible? The positive reinforcement Lance received from the psychologist for each day's improvement kept him motivated to overcome his phobia. Behavior-modification therapy thus accomplished in a few weeks what traditional psychotherapy might have taken months to achieve. You will note that the behaviorist focused on changing Lance's behavior. A therapist trained in a cognitive-behaviorist approach would have spent more time talking with Lance about the thoughts and beliefs that lay beneath his phobic behavior.

Once the patient has "unlearned" the inappropriate behavior, the behaviorist feels that the therapy is complete. Non-behaviorists claim that eliminating one neurotic behavior in this way often leads the patient to substitute another, equally unhealthy behavior. They point to former smokers who give up cigarettes only to start overeating. Behaviorists respond by saying that *symptom substitution* doesn't happen often enough to be a cause for concern. The former smoker who is overeating, they add, should now receive therapy for that new symptom.

Behavior therapy works quite well for phobias, bedwetting, compulsive behaviors, and other specific personality problems. Its critics point out that it has less success with more complex disorders. Schizophrenia, alcoholism, anxiety reactions, and feelings of existential despair do not respond well to behavior modification.

■ SECTION CHECKUP

1 Contrast the Freudian psychoanalytic approach to therapy with the psychosocial theories of Adler and Sullivan.

2 Why would the various types of therapists described in this section (psychoanalytic, existential, client-centered, cognitive, and behaviorist) all have difficulty treating a schizophrenic?

3 Ed is now 23, and he still can't cope with his fear of airplanes. He's about to lose a good job if he can't fly to sales meetings. What type of therapy would you recommend for Ed? Why?

9.3 ■ HOW DO DIFFERENT GROUP THERAPIES WORK?

Have you ever taken part in a *group therapy* session? No? But surely you've attended a football game, gone to a movie, or joined your friends for a picnic. These group experiences, while not technically a form of therapy, did give you something, didn't they? Afterward, you probably felt different. Happy, perhaps, or excited. The interaction of people in social situations creates these feelings. And that's what group therapy is all about.

Group therapy brings 8 to 10 people to-

5·28

© 1972 WASHINGTON POST WRITERS GROUP

AFTER A COUPLE OF
HOURS, DR. RAZZE
BEGAN TO QUESTION
HIS THEORY OF
CURING FEAR OF
PUBLIC APPEARANCE
THROUGH GROUP
THERAPY

WILEY

FIGURE 9.4

gether to meet with a therapist. During the time they're interacting, the participants form a miniature society. The interpersonal relationships that develop within the group become an important part of the treatment. Group members are encouraged to share their personal problems, feelings, and insights. Within the safe and supportive environment of the group the therapist helps the members discard unhealthy behaviors. A recent survey showed that about 16 percent of all Americans have taken part in group therapy sessions.

The number of types of group therapy available would fill a good-sized directory. A few of the most common group therapies will be discussed here: conventional group therapy, psychodrama, encounter groups, Gestalt therapy, family therapy, and mutual aid groups.

CONVENTIONAL GROUP THERAPIES

Most psychotherapists also conduct group therapy sessions, using their own "conventional" approach to therapy. In some cases, therapists recommend group therapy because they believe that the social interaction generated by the group will contribute to the patient's recovery. In other cases, group therapy permits patients to remain in treatment when they cannot afford individual therapy.

One common rule applies to all of the conventional group therapies: enforced participation. Group members must talk about their feelings, hang-ups, and life experiences. If the therapist doesn't draw a member out, the other group members will. The group also joins the therapist in discussing, judging, attacking, and supporting each other's statements. When the process "clicks," group members begin to see themselves as others see them. This self-knowledge often serves as the first step toward achieving more positive attitudes and behaviors.

PSYCHODRAMA

Since the 1940s, *psychodrama* has ranked as one of the most popular and effective of group therapies. Psychiatrist J. L. Moreno developed psychodrama as a means of exploring and analyzing the real-life roles that cause neurotic behavior. In a typical psychodrama session, group members take turns acting out scenes related to their problems. The therapist acts as "director," with other members joining the "protagonist" in dramatizing the relationships that are causing the person's emotional difficulties.

Thirty-year-old Bobby M., for example, is still neurotically dependent upon his mother. He has never learned to separate himself from her control, even though he says he yearns to

295

Strengths and Weaknesses of Group Therapy

STRENGTHS

1 Psychotherapists can reach a greater number of people by using group techniques.

2 Costs of therapy are reduced as each patient pays a smaller share of the therapist's fee.

3 Patients learn that other people suffer from the same (or similar) painful feelings and problems.

4 The support, advice, and criticism of other group members play an important role in advancing the course of therapy.

5 Group members learn to help one another and in doing so are often helped themselves.

WEAKNESSES

1 Each group member receives only a small fraction of the therapist's time and attention.

2 The success of the group depends almost entirely on the skill of the therapist, who must provide each member with proper insights and direction.

3 Many group therapists are not properly trained. In some states, anyone with a gift of gab can open a "clinic" and start group sessions.

4 New group therapies appear regularly. Only a few are backed up by solid research.

5 A percentage of group members cannot handle the give-and-take of the typical group session. Some people leave their groups in worse condition than when they started.

---

be free. In his psychodrama, Bobby will play himself. Alice, another group member, will play Bobby's mother, and Smitty will take the role of Bobby's *alter ego*—the angry person inside Bobby. The alter ego wants independence and despises Bobby for not being able to achieve it. The director will control the action, keeping it on track and intervening when the actors become too emotionally involved in their roles.

Psychodrama sometimes uses trained actors to get the scene started. The therapist-director usually limits the patients to roles they have experienced personally or to those they would normally fear or avoid. Patients often start a scene playing themselves only to be asked to "reverse" roles and play the other person in the same scene. In the following psychodrama, Suzy is the protagonist. She is free, for once, to talk openly to her husband, played by another group member.

SUZY [*speaking to her husband about their children*]: I've been having difficulty with John again. I wish you would talk to him about picking on Marie. He will not leave her alone. I find it is all becoming too much to handle by myself.

HUSBAND: They will work it out themselves. I'll talk to them tomorrow [*yawning*].

DIRECTOR: Is that the way it was?

SUZY: No, not exactly.

DIRECTOR [*to Suzy and "husband"*]: Reverse roles.

SUZY [*as husband: Looks up impatiently from newspaper "he" has been reading*]: You make too much out of it. They are just like all kids. You are as capable as I am in dealing with these little arguments. [*"He" continues reading.*]

DIRECTOR: Reverse roles.

SUZY [*as herself*]: You seem more concerned

Psychopoetry: Finding Yourself Through Verse

Psychologist Gilbert Schloss of Manhattan College, one of the pioneers in the field of psychopoetry, believes that poetry can serve as a bridge between a person's past experiences and present feelings. In psychopoetry groups, members read their own poetry or the poems of others that have special meaning to them. Through the poetry they come to know one another and themselves. Schloss cautions, however, that poetry therapy is a technique, not a magical cure for emotional problems.

M.B. is a 20-year-old teacher whose first poems touched upon the hurt and anger she was feeling:

My World

My world's a world of
darkness
Groping
I do not see
That's how I want
it—In my w   orld
is nothing
only brain gray
grinding out the circles
that enclose
me.

After many sessions with her psychopoetry group, M.B. was able to express her new sense of awareness and confidence:

At the Beauty Parlor

Inside there is something stilled
I am quiet
after many sleepless
days.
I've bought a gown of blood red.
I know what jewels I want to wear.
I am performing in one single line of
black.
What is this quiet?
Is it all right to stop?
To grasp this piece of me?
May I parade it for a night?
My hair dries quietly.
Soon I shall be
crowned.

Why not try putting your own feelings into a poem? You don't have to worry about rhyme or meter. Just write what you feel inside.

---

about your paper and the TV than about me. I'm left on my own to deal with all the dirty work. . . . [*Her emotions rise to the surface.*] I guess I'm trying to say I feel lonely. Somehow we don't communicate. I feel I'm losing you, and I can't handle the children without your support. . . .

DIRECTOR: How do you feel?

SUZY: All right—not nearly as tense.

DIRECTOR [*to "husband"*]: Could you share with Suzy as her husband?

HUSBAND [*to Suzy*]: You made me feel guilty. I could feel your anger. Then later I suddenly felt very warm toward you.

SUZY: That makes me feel better because I really love you.*

* Jacob L. Moreno and Dean G. Elefthery, "An Introduction to Group Psychodrama," in George M. Gazda, ed., *Basic Approaches to Group Psychotherapy and Group Counseling,* pp. 82–86. Courtesy of Charles C Thomas, Publisher, Springfield, Illinois.

After the role playing is over, the therapist leads the group in a discussion of the day's session. This gives the members a chance to relate their new insights to the real world outside the group.

When psychodrama works well, the patient-actors gain the same kinds of insight into the causes of their behavior as they would have gained in longer-term psycho-therapy. Because the other group members tend to identify with the protagonist, they often gain insight into their own feelings.

ENCOUNTER GROUPS

Encounter groups come in all shapes and sizes. At different times they have been called *confrontation groups, sensitivity groups, human-relations groups, personal-growth groups, human-potential groups,* and so on.

Unlike more traditional therapies, encounter groups appeal mostly to people who want more joy, warmth, and growth in their lives. Other encounter members join because they sense that they have lost contact with themselves and the world around them. For these people, the group experience promises honest interpersonal relations, self-discovery, and an escape from isolation. This aspect of the encounter movement grew out of humanist psychology's emphasis on self-awareness

and growth. Although encounter-type groups can be found in most communities in the country, the original groups began at Esalen in Big Sur, California. Psychologists such as Abraham Maslow, Fritz Perls, and Carl Rogers pioneered the movement.

Most encounter groups range in size from 8 to 20 members, plus a therapist or leader. Many groups meet for a limited number of hours or days, then disband. During the sessions, the groups generally focus on the "here and now." They discard politeness in favor of stripping away the masks that people hide behind. The leader's job is to zero in on the "unfinished business" in each person's life. If you join a group, you are expected to accept responsibility for your feelings. Everything you say must be open and honest.

Encounter groups depend heavily on *sensory-awareness games* as a way of pushing people toward self-awareness. These "games for grown-ups" require group members to "be" or do any number of exercises or activities (see Figure 9.5). Some games are fun, others are challenging, and a few are likely to embarrass the shy members of the group. In *Own Your Own Life,* Richard Abell describes his experiences during a sensory-awareness exercise at an encounter workshop:

> "Each of you take a sheet," Gloria said. "You are to be born under the sheet; feel what it's like just to be born; begin to move around and explore the environment and gradually grow up." . . .
>   I got under my sheet. "Now imagine that you are being born." I curled up in the fetal position and made little

FIGURE 9.5 ▓ Encounter groups provide activities designed to help people develop a richer, more satisfying outlook on life. What do you think these workshop members are learning about themselves in this awareness exercise?

whimpering noises and felt completely helpless. It was a good feeling, feeling helpless and not feeling afraid.

"Now begin to move around with your sheet over you, just a little at a time, and explore the environment." I began to move my body, my hands, my feet, still lying down. Then I began slowly crawling around. . . . I tried to take the point of view of a baby toward the end of the first year, for whom the world is new, unexplored.

"Now move more, until you bump into something or someone. Then explore that," Gloria said. . . . I bumped into a big irregular object, very muscular and solid. A man. . . . I kept on bumping for about fifteen minutes until I was beginning to feel pretty grownup. Just before the exercise ended, I had the impulse to grab the last girl I bumped into and roll over and over again in the deep grass, down the slight hill that we were on. I did, and we laughed. I was still under my sheet and couldn't see her.

Later, as group members discuss their feelings, insights emerge. People begin to express their emotions more openly. If a man says, "My wife left me and I feel lonely," several women may reach out and hug him. A woman who believes she's homely will be reassured that she has many attractive qualities. Encounter language often becomes vivid and unrestrained, but as long as the leader thinks it's honest, nothing is censored. After several sessions in which they have openly expressed their true feelings, many participants say that for the first time in their lives they understand the inner conflicts that keep them from being truly happy.

DOES ENCOUNTER WORK? Not all psychologists applaud the encounter movement. One complaint centers on the old question that applies to all therapies: Is it useful? A study at Stanford University yielded mixed results. Of 170 students who joined one or another of 18 encounter groups headed by

well-trained leaders, almost 60 percent of the participants judged themselves as having changed. But 52 percent of the control group reported the same thing, even though they did not take part in an encounter activity.

Since no therapy helps everyone, those uneven results might be rated as consistent with other therapies. But the same study showed that 10 percent of the participants had been hurt by the encounter process. The casualties suffered injuries that ranged from damaged self-esteem to mental breakdowns. Most of the casualties resulted from verbal "attacks" on the individuals by group leaders. One student reported, "The leader dismissed me and my whole life." Another said sadly, "The leader said I was on the verge of schizophrenia." Other surveys have uncovered instances where group members have been physically abused during encounter sessions. In short, encounter is no magic road to mental health. (See the box on page 300 for some rules to follow when you're thinking about joining a group.)

TYPICAL ENCOUNTER GROUPS. Among the hundreds of encounter groups, three represent the range and vitality of this approach to psychotherapy: T-groups, Gestalt groups, and marathon groups.

1. *T-groups*. The *T* in *T-groups* stands for *training*. Psychologist Kurt Lewin designed T-groups as a way of training people to do a better job of coping with their job or life situation. A group of new college students, for example, might join a T-group as a way of preparing for the demands of academic and dormitory life. The T-group leader provides useful information and leads a series of exercises designed to build human relations skills. The group members share their personal feelings, fears, and insights. This shared experience has the potential of providing each member with the tools and confidence needed to face the challenges ahead.

How to Choose a Group Experience: Look Before You Leap

A successful group experience can change your life—or it can leave you more unhappy than when you started. No one can guarantee you a rewarding experience, but the following rules will help you avoid a bad one.

1 Never respond to a newspaper ad. The best groups, run by trained professionals, do not advertise in newspapers.

2 Never take part in a group of less than six members nor in one of more than 16. Small groups do not develop the necessary group interactions, and large groups cannot be properly controlled.

3 Never join an encounter group on impulse. Important decisions deserve careful thought. If you sense that your life is spinning out of control, seek regular psychotherapy instead.

4 Except for T-groups, never join a group made up of close friends, schoolmates, or co-workers. Keeping group discussions and revelations confidential is a tricky business even when the group members are strangers.

5 Never stay with a group that insists that everyone *be* something—whether that identity is political, artistic, or intellectual. Self-actualizing people set their own goals and seek their own self-expression.

6 Never join a group whose leader does not possess proper credentials or training. The encounter movement has attracted far too many well-meaning but poorly prepared amateurs.

---

2. *Gestalt therapy groups*. Frederick "Fritz" Perls (see BioBox, page 301) almost single-handedly made Gestalt therapy one of the most popular of all group therapies. Perls borrowed the idea that any unsatisfied need creates tension from traditional Gestalt psychology. Just as you instinctively want to complete the circle shown here, you normally feel compelled to complete a task or satisfy a need.

In a healthy person, needs emerge, are satisfied, and disappear. This process, Gestalt psychologists say, is continuous. Each need is met in turn. For example, young Derrick is totally absorbed in a television program. But his gestalt (sense of completeness) does not last. His back starts itching. At first he ignores it, but the itching continues. An incomplete gestalt—the need to remove the discomfort—now becomes the center of his attention. Once he finds a stick and scratches the itch, he can go back to his program—until another need emerges that must be taken care of, such as hunger pangs or a drippy nose.

Gestalt therapists define neurotic behavior as confusion over how to respond to each new need. They say that this confusion takes three forms. Some people literally cannot "see" what troubles them. Others are unable to express their needs openly. Lillian may need love but not know how to ask for it.

▧ BIOBOX

Fritz Perls:
"I Am Not in This World to Live Up to Other People's Expectations"

When Frederick S. Perls (1893–1970) arrived in the United States from Europe in 1946, he looked very much like what he was—a psychoanalyst well trained in Freudian theory. He sported a carefully tended mustache, white spats, and cane. Twenty years later, Perls wore a full beard, love beads, and a jump suit. He had become the "guru" of a new and influential nonanalytic therapy called Gestalt. Tens of thousands of people flocked to his group sessions at Esalen in California to undergo an intense emotional experience.

Fritz Perls demanded openness, honesty, and cooperation from his group members, and he applied the same standards to himself. Perls was not a simple person. He could be wise and earthy, loving and spiteful, wildly outgoing and intensely personal. His wife, after their separation, referred to him as "half prophet and half bum." Perls rather liked the description, and perhaps it helps explain the enormous appeal of his therapy.

Perls wrote colorfully and well about his theories. For example, he saw the parent-child relationship differently from the way most psychologists did.

> Possibly the most difficult mental feat for any patient is to forgive his parents. Parents are never right. They are either too stern or too soft, too strong or too weak. There is always something wrong with parents. And the balance between guilt feelings (that he owes them something) and resentment (that they owe him something) is achieved by a very

peculiar phenomenon—gratefulness. Gratefulness leads to closure. Neither party owes the other anything. . . .

Responsibility also plays a major role in Perls's thinking. He described the need to take responsibility for yourself in these words:

> Full identification with yourself can take place if you are willing to take full responsibility—*response-ability*—for yourself, for your actions, feelings, thoughts; and if you stop mixing up responsibility with obligation. . . . You are responsible only for yourself. *I* am responsible only for *myself*. This is what I tell a patient right away. If he wants to commit suicide, that's his business. If he wants to go crazy, that's his business. . . . But I am not in this world to live up to other people's expectations, nor do I feel that the world must live up to mine.

Fritz Perls loved a good argument. If you disagree with his ideas, do you think he'd be upset? What would you say to him if he were standing beside you right now?

From Joen Fagan & Irma Lee Shepherd's *Gestalt Therapy Now* (Science and Behavior Books Inc. Palo Alto, CA, 1970).

The Gestalt Prayer

I do my thing, and you do your thing.
I am not in this world to live up to your expectations
And you are not in this world to live up to mine.
You are you and I am I,
And if by chance we find each other, it's beautiful.
If not, it can't be helped.

Source: Frederick S. Perls, *Gestalt Therapy Verbatim* (© Real People Press, 1969. All rights reserved).

Another group represses feelings through muscular tension. These people often contract their facial muscles and tense their hands, arms, and shoulders as a way of bottling up their anger.

Perls designed his therapy to put people in touch with these blocked emotions. He combined elements of psychoanalysis, Gestalt concepts of treating the "whole person," and existential ideas of "here-and-now" reality. Perls strongly believed that too many people live in the past ("Oh, I wish I'd done that") or in the future ("Someday I'll be able to do that"). In his therapy sessions, he insisted that his clients adopt a realistic attitude toward their needs. The Gestalt prayer (on this page) includes the essence of a major tenet of Perls's philosophy.

The Gestalt therapist pays close attention to posture, movement, gestures, and involuntary sounds. The "whys" of behaviors are of little concern. Exercises in awareness help the group members regain contact with their blocked feelings. The therapist might ask a woman to complete the sentence, "At this time I'm aware that . . ." Or a man might be told to conduct a dialogue between the opposing sides of his personality. Perls said that everyone has these warring voices—the *topdog* and the *underdog*. Topdog is the stern voice of conscience and duty. By contrast, the tricky, submissive underdog tries to explain away the failures that are part of everyone's life.

In a typical Gestalt session, someone like June takes center stage. The therapist suggests a subject for a dialogue. Then June sits on a stool and starts by having her topdog say, "Get to work, dummy." After topdog has spoken, she shifts stools and responds to topdog's complaints. "I can't, I've been sick," her underdog might reply. The therapist guides her dialogue, alternately babying her, threatening her, and scolding her. The aim is to push June through the blocks that keep her from expressing honest feelings. If she fights back, the therapist may ask her to play the role of therapist in order to better voice the criticism she feels.

3. *Marathon groups.* Beginning in the 1960s, some encounter-group leaders decided that faster breakthroughs to self-awareness could be made if the encounter experiences were lengthened. As a result, *marathon groups* meet for prolonged sessions of up to 48 hours. Participants remain together for the entire marathon, except for a sleep period after the first long session. (In the early marathons, no one was allowed to sleep.) Meals are taken as part of the group's ongoing program. Under the pressures generated by constant group interaction, participants begin to speak freely and

honestly. Old barriers are swept away as people weep, laugh, fight, scream, and hug each other.

At the end of the marathon, many participants report feelings of catharsis, as if they had finally been able to release years of built-up emotions. Follow-up studies, however, show that the insights gained during marathons tend to disappear when people return to their regular lives. Critics also caution against the intensity of the marathon experience. People who seem to be in control of their lives may be tipped over into neurotic or psychotic behavior by emotional experiences too strong to handle.

FAMILY THERAPY

Many people who show gains during therapy fall back into old habits when they return home. Hard-won insights and new behaviors soon fade within the harsh environment of a disturbed family setting. Patients are often thrown back into contact with family members whose dysfunctional behavior may have been the original cause of their emotional problems. Clearly, it isn't enough for patients to change. Their families must change, too.

Although family therapists bring many different techniques to their sessions, all begin with a single concept: one family member's disturbed behavior is often a symptom of deeper family disturbances. A "family" is defined as any group of people living together as a family unit. Thus, childless couples, parents and children, or extended families that include grandparents are all candidates for family therapy.

The family therapist works with a six-step program:

1. Make contact with family members. Obtain agreement (however grudging) that each will participate in the group sessions.

2. Establish a nonjudgmental atmosphere in which family members are free to express their feelings.

3. Help the family define its problems in concrete behavioral terms. Give each person a chance to explain what he or she is doing to resolve the problem or problems.

4. Help the family members set realistic goals by which they can measure their progress.

5. As counseling proceeds, periodically review the progress made, decisions taken, and new behaviors adopted.

6. Bring the therapy to a close when the family has built strong conflict resolution skills of its own.

Many family members go into therapy reluctantly. Therapists know that parents, in particular, find it difficult to admit they may be the cause of their children's emotional problems. Zandy N.'s eating disorder, for example, is linked to her father. Mr. N. had unconsciously withdrawn his love from Zandy as she matured into womanhood. In therapy, he will be helped to confront his own fears about losing his "baby." Polly S., who showers her son with affection, will see for the first time how smothered Carlos feels by her constant attentions.

Family therapists know that the group experience can turn a dysfunctional family into a healthy one. Their biggest problem, they say, is making sure that everyone attends the sessions.

MUTUAL AID GROUPS

Therapy, whether group or individual, can work wonders. When the last session ends, however, the individual must go back to living in a world full of problems, stress, hardship, and pain. For millions of others, their descent into addiction leaves them unable to climb back into the daylight. For all of those troubled people, *mutual aid groups* provide much-needed help. The members understand each other because they share a common experience.

No individual- or group-therapy system has

FIGURE 9.6 ■ Joining a group session at a rehabilitation center is a big step for a recovering drug addict. Members join with the therapist in tough-talking sessions that force addicts to shed their defenses and take responsibility for poor choices. Why do encounter methods work with addicts when conventional therapies so often fail?

had much success with the treatment of addicts. Whether the individual is addicted to drugs, alcohol, or food, something more than psychoanalysis or encounters is needed. To fill this need, several mutual aid groups that focus on addictive behavior have been developed. Two of the best known are Daytop Village and Alcoholics Anonymous.

DAYTOP VILLAGE. Conventional methods of treating drug addicts seldom achieve their goals. Over 90 percent of the patients released from U.S. Public Health Service hospitals fall back into their habits within two or three years. At Daytop Village, a live-in treatment facility on New York's Staten Island, 75 percent of the addicts who stay more than three months never return to drugs. The Daytop philosophy works because it was developed by ex-addicts. Everyone on the staff is a former junkie, so new residents can't get

away with the well-polished lies that they have always used to excuse their addiction.

Daytop Village was founded in 1963 and set up its first center on Staten Island, N.Y. It now operates facilities in 26 states, and its treatment methods have taken root in 66 countries. Most of Daytop's early residents were male felons and heroin addicts. Today there are more women, multi-drug abusers, and teenagers. Residents must agree to abstain from all drug use, including alcohol, while they are living at Daytop.

Therapy at Daytop emphasizes participation in encounter groups. Daytoppers call it "the game," "attack therapy," or the "pressure cooker." Three times a week, residents take a turn on the "hot seat." Let's say it's Alan's turn today. As a new resident, Alan might begin by explaining why he turned to drugs. He describes his abusive parents, the poor neighborhood he grew up in, and—but Sylvia breaks in. "Alan, we know why you're a junkie! It's because you're *stupid!*" she shouts at him. Others join in. Alan has no choice but to submit to these attacks. He withers under criticism of his former life, his personal habits, his excuses. But Alan will soon learn that the violent criticism is offered out of love, in the hope that his life can be saved. He also knows that no one escapes the "hot seat," not even the manager of the facility.

Daytop estimates that it takes a year and a half to two years to transform a drug addict into a responsible human being. For many former junkies, Daytop represents the first time in their lives that they have accepted responsibility for their own actions. Surrounded by caring people, working at useful tasks within the house, addicts begin to grow out of their immature, empty ways.

ALCOHOLICS ANONYMOUS. Every member of Alcoholics Anonymous is a reformed alcoholic, including the leaders. The million-member group was founded in 1935 by Bill and Dr. Bob (to preserve privacy, the group uses only first names). Like Daytop Village, AA does not seek out its members. Instead, alcoholics must want help badly enough to attend their first meeting. At all AA meetings, alcoholics tell about the misery that liquor has caused them and their families. With tears in their eyes, they tell how they found a fresh life through AA. This testimony gives hope to new members, who are encouraged to concentrate on remaining sober one day at a time.

The American singer Lillian Roth overcame her alcoholism with the help of AA. Here she describes her first testimony at an AA meeting and the reaction to it.

I stood up. I had faced many audiences without qualms. This was the toughest appearance I had to make. I couldn't act. . . . This was the real me on display for the first time in my life.

Stammeringly I tried to tell about myself. These are all my blood brothers in the audience, I thought. We all suffer from the same illness, and these talks we give are our blood transfusions to one another. We all have an incurable disease—alcoholism.

"I can't get up here and tell you I'm a happy person," I said. "But I am sober. I am trying to contact God as I understand Him. I don't yet have the peace of mind I know many of you have, but I'm told that if I hold on, it will come. . . ."

I was limp when I sat down. "What a beautiful talk," one woman said. A girl approached me. "This is my first meeting," she confided. "You don't know how you've encouraged me. I have such a terrible alcoholic problem. I looked at you and I thought, 'If she can do it, after what she's gone through, I can do it, too.' "

Her words left me with a warm glow. Was this what they meant when they said I would be happy again? Because I had helped someone?

Alcoholics in AA must admit that they are powerless over alcohol and that their only hope lies in giving themselves up to a power greater than themselves. These admissions are two of the Twelve Steps, a recovery program that alcoholics are encouraged to follow. Experience shows that a member who fails to understand and practice the Steps usually remains an addict. Father Joseph Martin, cofounder of the Maryland treatment center, explains it this way: "I believe the founders of AA suggested that we use the Twelve Steps in the same way that a parachute instructor suggests that we use a parachute when we jump out of an airplane. We don't have to take the suggestion, but there are definite consequences if we don't." Because the Twelve Steps have been so successful, many other groups who work with addicts have adapted the Steps to fit their own self-help programs.

AA also promotes the "buddy system." Members can pick up a phone and ask for help at any time of day or night. Several AAers will soon arrive to provide support. This mutual aid system has helped create an international network of AA chapters. Nor have the families of alcoholics been forgotten. Al-Anon provides support for the wives and husbands of alcoholics. Alateen gives special attention to the needs of adolescents who live with alcoholic parents or guardians. Each chapter maintains a library of books and pamphlets written with teenagers in mind. The needs of younger children are met by Pre-Alateen and Alatot groups. Even though Al-Anon and Alateen are not part of AA, the groups work closely with local AA chapters.

Not every alcoholic who joins AA remains with the program. Some find the emphasis on religious faith difficult to accept. Others are not ready to face the problems that alcohol helps them hide from. But of every hundred alcoholics who attend at least seven AA meetings, 75 will never take another drink.

■ SECTION CHECKUP

❚ Summarize some of the strengths and weaknesses of group therapies.

2 Describe what happens at a psychodrama session. Why would psychodrama probably not work for a drug addict or an alcoholic?

3 Who would be better suited for an encounter group: a man with a phobia about snakes or a woman who is having difficulty relating to her family?

4 What do Gestalt therapists mean when they say, "I am not in this world to live up to your expectations"?

9.4 ▦ WHERE CAN TROUBLED PEOPLE GO FOR HELP?

Let's say it's four in the morning and your phone rings. Your friend Ginny is on the line. She sounds upset, frightened about something. You know she's been having trouble with her personal life. Out of her confused complaints of anxiety, sleeplessness, and depression, you finally piece the story together. Ginny feels as though she can't cope with her problems any more, that she may be having a "nervous breakdown." Her parents are out of town, and she's turned to you for advice on where to go for help.

What can you tell her? You're fairly certain that your community has resources for people with emotional problems. But where? Is there anyone Ginny can turn to at four o'clock in the morning?

Take a deep breath and sort out your options. Your first task is to help Ginny regain control. You might be able to do this on the phone, or you may have to go and stay with her for a while. Just knowing that someone cares will probably help her make it through the night.

Next, you can help Ginny and her parents find professional help. The following section describes the typical mental health services found in most communities.

COMMUNITY RESOURCES

Most mental health problems can be resolved without hospitalization or lengthy therapy. Publicly funded agencies provide their services without charge. Private doctors and clinics charge the "going rate," although some may offer their services on an ability-to-pay basis. With a few phone calls you should be able to find a helping agency that will fit Ginny's needs and pocketbook. If you're not sure how to begin, check the emergency numbers listed in your phone directory. You can also contact your local Mental Health Association, a community hot line, a school counselor, a hospital emergency room, a member of the clergy, or a doctor.

CRISIS INTERVENTION. If Ginny is threatening suicide or if her condition seems desperate, she needs immediate help. Most towns and cities today have one or more *hot lines,* some of which operate around the clock. These telephone services are staffed by volunteers who are trained to give advice and a sympathetic ear to anyone who calls. Most hot lines also direct the caller to an appropriate agency for more in-depth counseling. Some hot lines specialize in particular problems, such as preventing suicides or helping rape victims.

A few hospitals provide emergency mental health services along with their regular medical care. If the hospital doesn't have a mental health unit, however, it may not have qualified doctors on duty. Call ahead, and make sure the staff can handle Ginny's needs. In addition, *community mental health centers* often offer emergency services. Most are connected with a general hospital and serve a specific geographic area. Because they are funded by state and federal money, their services are usually free or low cost. Like most public agencies, they tend to be busy and underfunded. Ginny may have to wait several hours before a doctor or psychologist is available to see her.

Most doctors and members of the clergy are trained in crisis intervention. Even if they don't know Ginny personally, their ability to access mental health resources can be invaluable to you as you try to help her.

COUNSELING SERVICES. If Ginny is still in school, encourage her to make an appointment to talk to someone on the counseling staff. Remind her that school counselors specialize in educational counseling and may not be trained to handle complex emotional problems. In the larger community, you might help her find a clinic where she can talk to a trained mental health worker. Counseling services have become more common as the need for them has grown. Free clinics often offer personal counseling in addition to their medical services. Finally, don't overlook Ginny's religious group and her family doctor. Even if they don't provide counseling, they can help her contact an appropriate counseling center.

If Ginny looks or sounds suicidal, contact a suicide prevention center. The counselors there can help her through the critical hours when she is most likely to try to take her own life. Later, they will help her rebuild her self-esteem and coping skills. Similarly, rape crisis centers work with rape victims to support them through the emotional shock and legal complications that accompany this crime of violence.

No exact line can be drawn between the point at which counseling stops and therapy begins. In general, counseling is geared to short-term emotional problems and emergencies. Skilled counselors recognize the point at which their clients need referral to a psychotherapist. By the same token, counseling ser-

FIGURE 9.7 ▓ Ginny has decided that she can no longer cope with her feelings of anxiety and depression. If she asked you for help, what would you tell her?

vices tend to be less expensive and more available than individual or group therapies. Vocational, marriage, and family counseling are also available in most communities.

PRIVATE PSYCHOTHERAPISTS AND CLINICS. If Ginny elects to try a more intensive therapy, she will have to choose between a private psychotherapist and a clinic. Private therapists work alone or in groups. They are in business for themselves and usually do not accept patients who cannot afford their fees. Clinics, on the other hand, are organizations that employ therapists, social workers, and counselors for the purpose of providing mental health care. Some do operate on a private basis with a regular schedule of fees. Other clinics receive support from public funds or charities and can offer their services based on ability to pay. Ginny and her parents will have to choose a therapist on the basis of cost, availability of treatment, and the type of therapy with which she, in particular, feels most comfortable.

MENTAL HOSPITALS

Ginny may not need to enter a mental hospital, but one American in ten will spend time in a mental hospital during his or her lifetime. What will these troubled people find when they reach the hospital? Some will find pleasant, well-managed facilities. Professional staffs of doctors, nurses, and orderlies will provide individual and group therapy sessions, medical care, occupational therapy, recreation and social events, home visits, and frequent contact with the outside world. The best hospitals clearly project a sense of belonging to a healing community.

Not all hospitals match that bright picture. For every quality facility, another stands as a living monument to society's age-old practice of ignoring the needs of the mentally ill. Kenneth Donaldson found that out when he was sent to a state hospital for "observation." After doctors diagnosed him as a paranoid schizophrenic, Donaldson spent the next 15 years in the hospital. He was kept in a locked ward, denied the right to go outside, and refused occupational therapy. Donaldson's doctors apparently believed that his attempts to obtain a release marked him as mentally ill! Donaldson later sued the state, and his $38,500 award was upheld by the U.S. Supreme Court (*Connor* v. *Donaldson*, 1975). In what legal experts call the single most important decision in mental health law, the Court ruled that no one may be locked up unless it is for treatment. Only when patients are hazards to themselves or others, or cannot care for themselves, may they be confined.

The Donaldson case has not ended neglect in many state and private hospitals. As one state mental health director puts it, "If you have to choose between children and the mentally ill or senior citizens and the mentally ill, the mentally ill will lose every time." Overworked doctors and nurses are tempted to overprescribe tranquilizing drugs in order to keep patients quiet. Hospital workers, particularly the orderlies who clean the wards and care for the patients on a daily basis, are often poorly paid and undertrained. As a consequence, those who do remain to work under these conditions may be careless at best and sadistic at worst. Newspapers sometimes publicize such scandals, but efforts at reform too often die for want of adequate funding.

HOSPITAL TREATMENT. Once admitted, patients receive treatment that ranges from wonderful to abysmal. At the bottom of the scale, they may receive little more than the basics of food, clothing, and a bed. In these hospitals, described so vividly in Ken Kesey's novel *One Flew Over the Cuckoo's Nest,* people are treated as objects. The nurses and orderlies have little time to spend in personal contact with patients beyond handing out medication and maintaining order. Visits from the staff psychologist are brief and infrequent. A television set dominates the dayroom. Organized sports, games, outings, and occupational therapy are conspicuous by their absence. All too often, moderately disturbed patients become worse under these conditions. Boredom, loneliness, anxiety, and adverse reactions to medications all contribute to the decay of people warehoused in such hospitals.

At better hospitals, pleasant physical surroundings, a dedicated staff, and individually prescribed therapy all play a role in shortening the time patients spend there. A good hospital may be public or private, large or small. What seems to count most is an enlightened attitude toward patient care and a budget large enough to provide the following treatment techniques.

1. *Psychotherapy.* Staff psychologists and psychiatrists provide individual and group therapy sessions for the patients. The type of therapy used ranges from analytic techniques to behavior modification, depending on the needs of the patients and the philosophy of the hospital administration. Typically, patients see their therapists two or three times a week. They also attend group therapy sessions. Many hospitals emphasize *milieu therapy,* which means that the hospital environment itself becomes part of the therapy. Milieu therapy involves the patients in organizing and administering the social activities within the hospital. This approach keeps patients active who might otherwise become withdrawn and depressed when subjected to an impersonal hospital routine.

2. *ECT and psychosurgery.* Electroconvulsive therapy (ECT) and psychosurgery (brain surgery) are both used in the hospital setting. Electric shock remains a popular treatment for severely depressed patients despite its possible side effects (see Pro & Con, page 264).

Although ECT has numerous defenders as well as critics, psychosurgery is a far different matter. Surgical removal of brain tissue was once a common treatment for conditions of abnormal excitement or uncontrollable outbursts of violence. The use of surgery to change these behaviors was drastically reduced after a 1977 study alerted the public to its dangers. Psychosurgery almost always affects the patient's personality, particularly in the areas of creativity and other high-level thinking skills. Surgery that is used to control or change behavior should not be confused with necessary procedures for the removal of diseased or injured brain tissue, as in the case of tumors or head injuries.

3. *Drug therapy.* The introduction of tranquilizers and other *psychotropic* (behavior-changing) *drugs* in the 1950s changed the course of modern psychotherapy. Between 1969 and 1974, for example, the number of patients in U.S. mental hospitals dropped by 50 percent—from 500,000 to 250,000. With the help of properly prescribed drugs, many chronically ill patients were able to respond positively to psychotherapy.

Today, drug therapy has become a standard therapy tool in and out of hospitals. Most therapists use drugs in combination with more traditional therapies. Unfortunately, these powerful drugs can also be abused. Budget-starved hospitals sometimes overdose their patients to keep them quiet. Zonked-out patients don't make much trouble for the staff, but neither do they get well.

The most commonly used psychotropic drugs fall into three categories: antipsychotic drugs, minor tranquilizing drugs, and antidepressant drugs.

Agitated or violent patients who once would have been restrained in padded cells can now be treated with antipsychotic drugs. Typical drugs in this group include chlorpromazine (Thorazine), haloperidol (Haldol), and fluphenazine (Prolixin). These powerful drugs relieve panic, delusions, and other behavior disturbances. Therapists restrict their use to the most severe psychotic conditions, such as schizophrenia. Side effects include drowsiness, dizziness, weight gain, loss of motor control, and restlessness. Proper dosage usually controls these problems.

Minor tranquilizers are the most widely prescribed of all psychotropic drugs. Tranquilizers provide a calming effect that relieves anxiety without reducing mental alertness. Among the best-known members of this group are chlordiazepoxide (Librium) and diazepam (Valium). Side effects are rare, with one troubling exception—many people develop a drug dependency habit after prolonged usage. These "Valium addicts" suffer withdrawal symptoms when they try to end their dependency. Buspirone (BuSpar), one of the newer tranquilizing drugs, relieves anxiety without exposing patients to the danger of addiction.

Antidepressant drugs have mushroomed in number and popularity. Originally, the amphetamines were used to treat depression, but their potential for abuse made them a poor choice. Today, the preferred antidepressants include such drugs as fluoxetine (Prozac), sertraline (Zoloft), and venlafaxine (Effexor). Although these drugs are usually prescribed for depression, they are also helpful in relieving panic attacks, obsessive-compulsive disorders, eating disorders, and severe insomnia. Side effects are mild, and the drugs are not normally addictive. Lithium carbonate (Eskalith) has brought new life and hope to many manic-depressives and long-term depressives. Carbamazepine (Tegretol) sometimes works for patients who do not respond to lithium therapy.

4. *Occupational and recreational activities.* Well-run hospitals provide a number of additional activities for patients as part of milieu therapy. Workshops and training programs in fine arts, homemaking, and crafts encourage self-expression and build self-esteem. Dances, field trips, sports activities, and frequent contact with the outside world keep patients alert and encourage social interaction. Some hospitals also offer educational programs that allow patients to earn high school or college credits. The staff encourages family members to visit often and arranges home visits for qualified patients. These trips often mark the first step toward a return to life outside the hospital.

THE HALFWAY HOUSE. In 1955, only one in four mental patients could be treated on an outpatient basis. By the late 1990s, three out of four were able to live at home while undergoing therapy. Halfway houses were established to help patients make the transition from the hospital to life at home. Like mental hospitals, not all halfway houses receive proper funding. Many are little better than skid-row hotels. The best, however, provide a much-needed service.

Twenty-eight-year-old Chester W.'s experiences illustrate how a well-run facility can help. When Chester realized that he could no longer cope with his overwhelming feelings of anxiety, he voluntarily signed himself into a state mental hospital. After two months of rest and therapy, he felt much more in control. The tranquilizer he was taking controlled his anxiety, and his weekly therapy sessions put him in better touch with his feelings.

Anxious to return to work but still not ready to live on his own, Chester moved to a halfway house run by the county mental health agency. He lived in a private room but received therapy and support from a well-trained staff. In the evenings, he made new friends in the lounge and crafts shop. Returning to work was frightening at first, but without the pressure of taking complete care of himself, Chester was able to meet the challenge. Gradually, his doctor decreased the dosage of his tranquilizer.

Six months after his initial breakdown, Chester was ready to return to his own home. For the first time in years, he was free of his crippling anxieties.

Despite their proven effectiveness, many halfway houses have fallen victim to funding cuts. Others have been converted to shelters that lack essential resources. Without trained staff to guide and counsel them, the mentally ill forget to take their medications. Before long they wander away to join the ranks of the homeless mentally ill who now roam the nation's streets.

THE HOMELESS MENTALLY ILL

Not since the 1820s have so many mentally ill Americans gone untreated. Half a million of the nation's most seriously disturbed people now live on the streets, in public shelters, or in jail. Fewer than 60,000 are housed in mental hospitals.

Thanks to a 1970s-era Supreme Court

decision that allowed the states to greatly reduce the number of hospital beds for the mentally ill, much of the burden of care was shifted to the police. After Los Angeles County closed some of its mental health clinics, the number of 911 calls asking for help in dealing with disturbed individuals soared to 30,000 a year.

When the police pick up mentally ill people, they have little choice but to put them in jail. Often the only charge is "disturbing the peace" or a petty crime such as shoplifting. Jail time means long, monotonous days in crowded cells. With no time or budget for providing therapy, the jail's medical staff tends to use psychotropic drugs as a shortcut way of controlling behavior. After completing their sentences, the mentally ill are returned to the streets to begin the cycle all over again. A visitor from the 1700s could be excused for complaining that our "enlightened" era seems intent on creating its own version of Bedlam.

■ SECTION CHECKUP

1 If a friend asked you for help in finding a source of mental health care in your community, where would you send that person?

2 Contrast the treatment given in a good mental hospital with that found in a poor one.

3 Why have drug therapies become such an important part of modern psychotherapy? Why do mental health experts worry about the widespread use of minor tranquilizers to treat "everyday" anxiety?

LOOKING BACK: A SUMMARY

1 Throughout history, many different ideas have been advanced to explain disturbed behavior. According to the demonological model, mental illness was caused by evil spirits that invaded the body. In the religious model, emotional problems were viewed as punishment for sins against God. Later, more scientific explanations centered on the medical and the toxin models, which taught that mental illnesses start with organic brain dysfunctions or with poisonous substances in the body. Finally, believers in the psychosocial model point to environmental forces that cause conflicts between individuals and their surroundings as the primary cause of most mental illness.

2 Only in modern times have the emotionally disturbed been treated with sympathy and understanding. Early treatments were painful and largely useless. In the late 1700s, Philippe Pinel began the movement to free mental patients from the chains and dungeons that had formerly been their lot. Dorothea Dix did the same for America's emotionally disturbed in the 1840s, with the founding of this country's first modern mental hospital.

3 Psychotherapy is the process of helping patients replace neurotic behaviors with more healthy responses to stress, anxiety, depression, and other symptoms. All established psychotherapists have certain qualities in common. Each provides support in time of crisis, screens patients for medical problems, develops catharsis (the release of tension), and attempts to change disturbed behavior.

4 Freudian psychoanalysis began the tradition of individual therapy, with its one-to-one relationship between therapists and patients. According to Freud, adult neurotic behavior begins when the sexual drives of the id come into conflict with the superego during childhood. Psychoanalysis tries to resolve this conflict through free association, transference, catharsis, and overcoming resistances. During the lengthy period of analysis, patient and analyst work together to penetrate the patient's deepest and most painful memories.

5 Later psychoanalysts placed less emphasis on sexual conflicts and more on cultural influences as the causes of disturbed behavior. Alfred Adler believed that therapy must help the patient recover lost feelings of self-worth as a way of overcoming feelings of inferiority. Harry Stack Sullivan pointed to interpersonal relationships as the cause of mental problems and tried to help his patients "see" people as they really are. Existential therapist Viktor Frankl says that human beings develop neurotic behavior out of the frustration of being unable to find meaning in their lives. Only when people take responsibility for their decisions and make a commitment to something outside themselves can they return to mental health.

6 Another existential therapist, R. D. Laing, believes that only the insane are truly sane in what he sees as a crazy world. Laing believes that society uses mental illness as an excuse for locking up people who make the "normal" population uncomfortable. His therapy involves giving schizophrenics and other seriously disturbed people a life-support system that enables them to find their way down into madness and back again.

7 Client-centered therapy, as developed by Carl Rogers, concentrates on helping clients find their own path to self-awareness. Therapists use unconditional positive regard to assure their clients that they are valued human beings no matter what they have done in the past. Rogers also believes in a nondirective relationship between clients and therapists. Clients are given the primary responsibility for changing their own self-defeating behaviors. Cognitive therapy, a closely related system, teaches that the best way to help clients solve emotional problems is by identifying and changing faulty thought processes.

8 Behavior therapy is based on the theory that all behaviors, healthy and unhealthy, are learned responses to the environment. Behaviorist therapists pay little attention to unconscious motivation. They rely on operant conditioning techniques to cure specific phobias, compulsive behaviors, and the like.

9 Group therapies have grown in popularity in recent years. Each group acts as a miniature society, in which the interaction of therapist and patients brings about the needed changes in behavior. Most individual therapies also run group sessions using the basic techniques of that therapy system. All group therapies require that each member participate. This leads to self-knowledge that can become the first step toward more positive behaviors and attitudes.

10 A psychodrama group casts its members in roles and scenes taken directly from their own lives. The therapist directs the action and assigns the roles to be played. By acting out the scenes, participants gain insight into their feelings. This insight can lead to meaningful change under the guidance of the psychodrama leader.

11 Encounter groups challenge their members to grow and change through direct confrontation. They emphasize the here-and-now aspects of life and often use tough-minded techniques to force people to discard their defenses. T-groups are a type of encounter group designed to train people to deal with the challenges of new or changed life situations. Gestalt groups, developed by Frederick Perls, emphasize "how" over "why" and put group members in touch with their blocked-off feelings. Marathon groups are speeded-up encounters of twenty-four to forty-eight hours, during which group members work through their current life problems under the stress of enforced participation and fatigue. When a patient's emotional problems are caused by a troubled home life, family therapy brings the entire family together for group therapy sessions. With the help of the therapist, all family members learn healthier ways of relating to one another.

12 Mutual aid groups provide an effective way of dealing with drug and alcohol addiction. Daytop Village uses the stress of confrontation with other ex-addicts to force drug addicts to take responsibility for their own lives. This process of mutual caring also works at Alcoholics Anonymous, where ex-alcoholics testify about their past lives and provide one another with the support an alcoholic needs to stop drinking.

13 Most communities provide a number of places where troubled people can go for help. Crisis-intervention services are provided by hot lines, suicide-prevention centers, emergency facilities in hospitals and community mental health centers, family doctors, and members of the clergy. Counseling for less immediate problems can be found in schools, clinics, and the like. Psychotherapy can be obtained from either private or public therapists and clinics, depending on need and the ability to pay.

14 Modern mental hospitals have come a long way from the grim asylums of the past. Physical conditions have been improved, patients stay for shorter times, and release rates are higher. Not all hospitals meet these standards, however. Low budgets and public apathy leave some state hospitals with overcrowded wards and overworked staffs. Patient care in the better hospitals includes traditional individual and group therapies, along with occupational and recreational activities. ECT and psychosurgery are still found in mental hospitals, although little psychosurgery is being done today. Drug therapy with tranquilizers and other psychotropic drugs has enabled many patients to return home with their behavior problems under control. Many drugs have side effects, however, and unruly patients are sometimes overdosed to keep them quiet.

15 The halfway house has helped many former mental patients by giving them support and therapy during the critical period when they first leave the mental hospital. Unfortunately, cutbacks in mental health budgets have cut deeply into halfway house programs and other community-based services. As a result, thousands of homeless mentally ill people are now wandering the streets. Many end up in jails, which are ill-equipped to provide the therapy these people need.

PUTTING YOUR KNOWLEDGE TO WORK

■ TERMS YOU SHOULD KNOW

alter ego	halfway house	psychotherapy
behaviorist model	hot lines	psychotropic drugs
behavior-modification therapy	individual therapy	radical model
catharsis	marathon groups	radical psychiatrist
client-centered therapy	milieu therapy	Rational Emotive Therapy (RET)
cognitive therapy	mutual aid groups	religious model
demonological model	neuropathological model	sensory-awareness games
drug therapy	operant conditioning theory	symptom substitution
encounter groups	psychoanalytic model	T-groups
family therapy	psychodrama	toxin model
Gestalt therapy groups	psychosocial model	unconditional positive regard
group therapy	psychotherapist	

▪ CHAPTER CHECKUP

1 The first modern psychotherapist was (*a*) Ivan Pavlov (*b*) Sigmund Freud (*c*) Carl Rogers (*d*) B. F. Skinner.

2 Catharsis plays an important role in therapy because it allows the patient to (*a*) release tension (*b*) overcome paranoid schizophrenia (*c*) get through therapy without the help of a therapist (*d*) overcome neurotic behaviors related to brain dysfunction.

3 A good therapist will (*a*) refuse to treat any patient who has committed a crime (*b*) help patients learn to solve their own emotional problems (*c*) never use psychoactive drugs (*d*) know that medical problems have nothing to do with disturbed behavior.

4 Which therapy system teaches that patients can find meaning in their lives only if they take responsibility for their life choices? (*a*) Freudian psychoanalysis (*b*) behavior therapy (*c*) Frankl's existential therapy (*d*) Rogerian client-centered therapy.

5 A key requirement for client-centered therapists is that they give their clients (*a*) group encounter experiences (*b*) unconditional positive regard (*c*) time for free association (*d*) treatment with the latest psychotropic drugs.

6 The most rapid treatment for overcoming Nick's phobia about snakes would probably be (*a*) psychoanalysis (*b*) client-centered therapy (*c*) behavior modification (*d*) an encounter group.

7 A group therapy that would ask Lydia to act out a role based on her actual life problems is (*a*) a marathon encounter group (*b*) a psychodrama group (*c*) an Alcoholics Anonymous group (*d*) a T-group for young actors.

8 The type of therapy *least* concerned with an adult patient's childhood experiences would be (*a*) existential therapy (*b*) psychoanalysis (*c*) client-centered therapy (*d*) behavior modification.

9 Overcrowded, poorly staffed mental hospitals (*a*) never existed except in novels and films (*b*) no longer exist because mental patients are now cared for in halfway houses (*c*) exist only in underdeveloped countries where money is scarce (*d*) exist wherever the public turns its back on the mentally ill and refuses to provide adequate budgets for therapy.

10 The major danger Chet faces from prolonged use of a minor tranquilizer such as Valium is that he will (*a*) become dependent on the drug (*b*) suffer serious side effects (*c*) never be allowed to leave the hospital (*d*) soon develop psychotic behaviors.

▪ EXPLORING CONCEPTS

1 Contrast the different approaches to psychotherapy based on the theories of Sigmund Freud and Carl Rogers. Which would you prefer if you were to undergo therapy? Why?

2 List the different explanations people have offered as to the cause of mental illness over the centuries. What type of therapy was developed for each of these models?

3 How does the idea of encounter groups fit the attitudes of today's society? What are some of the advantages and disadvantages to such groups?

4 Why do the Daytop Village and Alcoholics Anonymous approaches to addiction group therapy work where other therapies frequently do not?

5 Suppose you were on a state board investigating mental hospitals. What would you look for when you visited a hospital? What questions would you ask the hospital administrator? The staff? The patients?

6 Which of the therapies discussed in this chapter would be most effective in dealing with schizophrenia? Which would be least effective? Give reasons for your answers.

7 Many people have said that the Gestalt prayer (page 302) helps them by stating that they are not responsible for changing other people. But some critics point out that the last three lines seem to say that no one is responsible to anyone else. How do you feel about the Gestalt prayer? Does it lead to mental health or to greater selfishness?

▪ HANDS-ON ACTIVITIES

1 If possible, arrange for a class visit to a mental health facility in your area. Most hospitals provide guided tours of the wards, recreation rooms, and offices. Ask for a chance to talk to some of the patients. In many hospitals you will be encouraged to join in their games, read to them, or simply visit. Observe the care provided by the staff. Perhaps you can arrange in advance to talk with one of the staff psychologists about the therapy programs provided. Write a report describing your experience. If you discover seriously deficient conditions, you should communicate your findings to your state mental health commission and to your state legislator.

2 Alcoholics Anonymous meetings are held in almost every city of any size in the United States. Visitors are usually welcome, though you might want to check ahead of time. Try to discover what makes AA so effective. Listen to the testimonials, and talk to the members. What impressions do you come away with? A similar visit to a meeting of Overeaters Anonymous can also be interesting and instructive. Note the similarities and differences between the two organizations.

3 Find a friend or relative who is both a good listener and someone you respect. Tell that person that you want to talk about a personal problem. Pick a situation that is honestly bothering you. Share your feelings as openly as you can. Afterward, analyze the experience. Were you able to express your emotions clearly and honestly? How well did your partner listen? Were his or her remarks directive or nondirective? How could the situation have been improved?

4 Work with your psychology teacher to invite a local psychiatrist or clinical psychologist to speak to your class. If the therapists in private practice are too busy, ask the school psychologist to come in. Suggest to your guest that he or she answer the following questions: "What type of training have you had? What kind of psychotherapy do you specialize in? Tell us about some typical patients you've worked with. What would you recommend as good mental health advice?"

5 As an alternative to Activity 4, ask your psychology teacher to contact Recovery, Inc. (312-337-5661 or <*www.recovery-inc.com/*>) to arrange for a demonstration panel to speak to the class. Recovery's panels are made up of former mental patients. They discuss their own therapy experiences and the help they received from Recovery's mutual aid programs. Before they leave, ask the panel members to discuss their present lives. Do they feel discriminated against in social or work situations? Why are they willing to speak in public about their emotional problems?

6 Do some research on the expanding use of psychotropic drugs, such as Prozine, in psychotherapy. Compare the advantages of such treatment with its possible dangers. Report to the class on your findings.

7 With the help of your psychology teacher, organize your class to survey the mental health facilities available in your community. Resources might include hospitals, mental health clinics, community service organizations, hot lines, and special counseling programs provided by schools and religious groups. If your community does not have such a list, use a word processor to turn your research into a booklet that lists the name, address, telephone number, services offered, hours, and costs of each helping agency. Make the list available for distribution through schools, religious groups, city hall, and libraries. You'll probably be amazed at just how many resources are available to those who need help.

8 Do you know a COA—a Child of an Alcoholic? If you'd like to help your friend, your local Al-Anon or Alateen chapters can be of immense help. If you can't make that connection, contact the National Association for Children of Alcoholics (888-554-2627 or <*www.nacoa.net/*>). This organization is dedicated to helping COAs. Ask for literature (such as the pamphlet "Guidelines for Helping a COA Child") that you can read and pass on to concerned adults at school or in the home.

FOR FURTHER READING

Burns, David. *The Feeling Good Handbook*. New York: Plume Books, 1999. Dr. Burns believes that changing the way you think can change the way you feel and behave. His book presents a step-by-step method that he promises will free you from fears, phobias, and panic attacks. Readers are taught how to uncover self-defeating attitudes, build self-esteem, and improve relationships. Perhaps no book can deliver on all of these promises, but Burns does provide a number of useful insights.

Kaysen, Susanna. *Girl, Interrupted*. New York: Random House, 1996. In this vivid memoir, the author describes the terrifying reality of the two years she spent on a psychiatric ward in the late 1960s. After reading Kaysen's book (or watching the film that it inspired), you will be left with a far greater awareness of what it means to be diagnosed and treated for a mental illness.

Kesey, Ken. *One Flew Over the Cuckoo's Nest*. New York: Viking Press, 1962. This explosive novel hinges on the conflict between one man and a mental hospital that would rather keep patients sick than make them well. Tough-minded and profane, the novel's insights into hospital life are unforgettable, as is the Academy-award-winning film based on the novel.

Sacks, Oliver. *The Man Who Mistook His Wife for a Hat*. New York: Simon & Schuster, 1998. Case histories tend to be a bit on the dry side—but not when your guide is "one of the great clinical writers" of our time. Sacks introduces you to patients who suffer from bizarre disorders that affect perception, memory, and muscle control. The title case stars a man who literally could not be sure he was looking at his wife—or at a hat.

Seligman, Martin. *Authentic Happiness*. New York: Free Press, 2004. Professor Seligman says it all in the subtitle to this user-friendly book— *Using the New Positive Psychology to Realize Your Potential for Lasting Fulfillment*. To reach that goal, he provides guidelines and self-tests designed to help people identify and develop their personal "signature strengths." Incorporate these attributes into everyday living, he says, and you, too, can experience "the good life."

Szasz, Thomas. *Lexicon of Lunacy: Metaphoric Malady, Moral Responsibility, and Psychiatry*. Somerset, NJ: Transaction Publishers, 2003. Dr. Szasz relishes his role as a leading critic of the psychiatric establishment. In this book he sets out to prove that the way we diagnose mental illness is subject to shifting social values. Is Szasz correct when he writes that the misuse of psychiatric language has led to a medicalized approach to therapy that denies free will and personal responsibility? You'll have to decide for yourself.

Vitkus, John. *Casebook in Abnormal Psychology*. Columbus, OH: McGraw-Hill, 2003. This casebook describes 18 detailed case histories that represent a broad spectrum of mental disorders and the therapies chosen to treat them. Vitkus takes the reader through each stage, from presenting symptoms to choice of therapy to prognosis for future progress. The cases are drawn from actual material provided by practicing psychotherapists.

UNIT V

HOW PEOPLE LEARN

- LEARNING, THINKING, AND DEVELOPING CREATIVITY

- PSYCHOLOGICAL TESTING

10 LEARNING, THINKING, AND DEVELOPING CREATIVITY

At age two, Mandy and Glenn spoke only a handful of words. They couldn't tie their shoes, write their names, or count past four.

Today, the twins are all grown up. Along the way, they have mastered language, shoe tying, arithmetic, and a thousand other complex skills. What happened in those in-between years isn't much of a mystery. With the help of their parents, teachers, and friends, they learned the skills and information needed to cope with the world around them.

Psychologists have long been interested in the learning process. Much of their research is done with animals. Rats find their way through mazes, dolphins retrieve objects on command, cats escape from puzzle boxes, and dogs stand patiently while technicians scan their brain waves. The psychologists' favorite subjects for learning experiments, however, are the animals closest in intelligence and physical abilities to Mandy and Glenn—the great apes.

One line of research pursues the goal of teaching gorillas and chimpanzees to "talk." If primates can learn to communicate with us, learning psychologists will have accomplished two valuable tasks. First, science will gain new insights into how language develops in human children. Second, the age-old

barrier to communication between humans and animals will finally be overcome. Early experiments, however, quickly proved that gorillas and chimps cannot duplicate human speech. Only when trainers turned to the sign language used by the hearing impaired were these intelligent animals able to live up to expectations.

Is "ape talk" conducted in sign language the equivalent of human speech? Some scientists point out that dogs can be taught to "count" on command and that parrots can mimic dozens of words and phrases. These skeptics want proof that the messages that flash between apes and their teachers represent more than rote learning or mimicry.

One fascinating study of primate speech started in 1972. That was the year Penny Patterson, a graduate student in psychology at Stanford University, caught her first glimpse of a tiny, undernourished baby gorilla at the San Francisco Zoo. Patterson had no way of knowing then that the sickly little ape would become her constant companion in the longest continuous experiment ever undertaken to teach language to another species. Within a year, Project Koko was up and running.

Koko tried to bite as Patterson shaped her

FIGURE 10.1 ⬛ Koko's teacher Penny Patterson holds up a kitten for Koko's inspection. Koko loved her kitten playmates.

hands into the signs for *food, drink,* and *more*. Despite her initial resistance, Koko caught on quickly. As the months passed, her vocabulary increased to over 1,000 words. By then the experiment had outgrown its quarters at Stanford. Patterson, delighted with Koko's progress, formed the Gorilla Foundation and moved to a new headquarters in Woodside, California. There a male gorilla named Michael joined the experiment.

Patterson and Koko's other teachers learned long ago not to discount their prize student's intelligence. Although Koko scores a below-average 75 on IQ tests, Patterson is quick to point out that the tests were designed for human children, not gorillas. One test, for example, asked Koko to pick two good things to eat from a series of five pictures. Koko picked the apple and the flower.

The test unfairly counted flower as a wrong answer. After all, gorillas *do* eat flowers.

Koko captured the nation's heart when *Life* magazine printed a picture of her holding a pet kitten. When Koko first asked for a pet, Patterson had tried to give her a toy cat. Koko refused the toy, insisting that she wanted a live kitten. When the tailless Manx kitten arrived, Koko named it All Ball and cuddled it as if it were an infant gorilla. Six months later, All Ball was run over by a car. When she was told that her pet was dead, Koko cried. Patterson and Barbara Hiller later had several talks with her (in sign language) about the incident.

P: Do you want to talk about your kitty?

K: *Cry.*

P: What happened to your kitty?

K: *Sleep cat.*

P: Yes, he's sleeping.

K: *Koko good.*

H: What are you going to get for Christmas?

K: *Frown bad.*

H: Why bad?

K: *Gorilla love visit.*

H: What do you mean? [Koko does not respond.] What would you like to get for Christmas?

K: *Cat cat tiger cat.*

H: Well, pretty soon you'll have another cat, maybe not for Christmas. Can you think of anything else you'd like?

K: *Trouble trouble. Koko good.*

H: You are good.

K: *Koko gorilla love good.* [A few minutes later she cried again.]

Koko, the "loving gorilla," was given a second kitten a few months later. She named him Lipstick, a tribute to his reddish fur. As she cradled Lipstick in her arms, she called him *Baby.* When the lively kitten scampered away, she signed, *Obnoxious.*

Koko's language skills have grown over the years. She tells lies to escape punishment and often teases her human friends. A teacher once asked her to name the color of a white towel. Koko signed, *Red.* When the teacher repeated the question, Koko signed, *Red, red, red!* Then, grinning like a mischievous child, she picked a small red thread off the towel. Koko is also learning to communicate via a computer keyboard. When she presses the A key, a computerized voice says, "Apple." The keyboard "voice" allows her to reply to questions without using signs.

Patterson's long-range plans for Koko and Michael failed when the two gorillas refused to mate. In December 1991, Patterson arranged for Ndume, a ten-year-old male, to join the Gorilla Foundation. Because Ndume was younger and slightly smaller than Michael, Patterson hoped that Koko would be attracted to him. Koko, however, has shown little interest in mating. Her reluctance keeps a key piece of the research on hold. If she does give birth, will she teach her offspring to sign? So far, only Koko knows the answer to that question.

Along with the fun and excitement of watching the great apes learn to "talk," psychologists are finding out about human learning as well. Most of the classic learning experiments, such as Pavlov's work with conditioned reflexes, started with animals. Over the years, new data about the process of thinking, memory, problem solving, and creativity have found their way into psychology's ever-widening knowledge of human behavior. This chapter will introduce you to some of the important concepts in learning psychology:

10.1 How do people learn?

10.2 How does memory work?

10.3 How do people think?

10.4 How can you improve your learning and problem-solving abilities?

10.5 How can you improve your creativity?

10.1 ■ HOW DO PEOPLE LEARN?

Every summer, organizations such as the American Field Service and Youth for Understanding send high school students to live with families in other countries. Would you accept this once-in-a-lifetime opportunity to explore a different culture? A little hesitation would be understandable.

What if you were sent to Japan, for example? You'd want to learn at least a few words of the language. And you'd want to prepare yourself to cope with new social customs, unusual foods, and different ways of bathing and sleeping. That's a lot of learning to cram into a few weeks, but it's not an impossible task. *Homo sapiens* learn quickly.

DEFINING LEARNING

Learning, by definition, is the lasting change in a person's behavior brought about by study, training, or experience. Temporary changes in behavior due to fatigue, drug use, or instinctive reactions don't count as learning. Nor is learning restricted to gaining new knowledge and skills. You also learn to grow as a person. This type of learning includes new ways of relating to other people; new insights into your goals and values; and new attitudes toward people, issues, and problems. On your trip to Japan, for example, your learning would divide into three basic types.

1. You would learn new *information*. Before you flew home again, you'd have crammed thousands of facts related to language, geography, weather conditions, transportation, schooling, and many other aspects of Japanese life and customs into your head.

2. You would learn new *skills*. After some awkward fumbling, you'd learn how to use chopsticks. You might learn how to write your name in Japanese characters and how to wear the kimono. After a while, thanks to your new skills, you'd begin to feel more comfortable in your Japanese surroundings.

3. Finally, you'd learn new *social behaviors*. Some of these would involve politeness and respect for tradition. You'd learn how to greet your Japanese family and how to behave during the tea ceremony. But you'd also gain insights into your own ability to cope with change. You'd learn to adjust to the different dating customs in Japan, for example, and you'd discover what it's like to live far from home.

You don't have to travel overseas to encounter new learning opportunities. Every day brings chances to grow as a person, to adjust to changes in your environment, to gather new information, to modify old skills and learn new ones. Not everyone learns at the same speed, however. Elliot may be a whiz at learning to play the drums, but he barely scrapes through in biology. Nettie picks up math quickly, but she's all thumbs around the kitchen.

Psychologists also know that children cannot learn certain skills or concepts before they are intellectually ready. Try as you might, you won't be able to teach five-year-old Bertie the concept of historical time. To Bertie, last month is about as long ago as 1066.

Even though psychologists have gathered a mountain of information about *what* people learn and *when* they learn it, they haven't reached agreement on *how* learning takes place. Opposing camps divide the field into two basic learning theories. One approach is called stimulus-response theory; the other is known as cognitive theory. Neither theory totally excludes the other, but each emphasizes different factors in a learning situation.

STIMULUS-RESPONSE THEORY

American learning psychologist Edward L. Thorndike published his first descriptions of the *stimulus-response (S→R) theory* of learning in 1898. Thorndike described learning as the relationship between a *stimulus* (any event or impulse) and a *response* (the resulting behavior). He called the connection between stimulus and response a *bond*. When bonds are strengthened by repetition, they become habits or behavior patterns.

Thus, as a child you may have watched everyone else eating with forks while you had to make do with a spoon. In that case, the stimulus was the desire to mimic your parents. The response was to eat with a fork. At first you probably had trouble picking up the food and guiding each forkful safely to your mouth. But you kept at it, and soon you

FIGURE 10.2 ■ The challenge of learning to putt with the accuracy demonstrated by his teacher will call on all the learning ability this young golfer can bring to his new sport. What other skills, information, and social behaviors will he need to learn as he struggles to improve his game?

could stab peas and carrots with the best. Through repetition, you established a habit.

Remember, Thorndike adds, only successful responses become habits. Unsuccessful responses will be extinguished (fade out). Think of the S → R learning that many children go through when they first pull a dog's tail. The wagging tail is the stimulus; grabbing and pulling it is the response. But tail pulling doesn't become a habit because parents scold and dogs bite. After a few unsuccessful tries, the response is extinguished, even though the stimulus remains.

TRIAL-AND-ERROR LEARNING. Thorndike believed that most learning takes place through *trial and error*. When faced with a problem, he explained, people try different solutions until they find one that works. If a response works often enough, they add that response to their arsenal of behaviors that become permanent.

Thorndike ran a series of experiments to test this theory. He collected stray cats and put them inside puzzle boxes, which could be opened only when the cat pulled on a latchstring. Tempted by food placed outside the box, the cats mewed, scratched, and poked about until they accidentally released the latch. One cat, for example, took 230 seconds on the first trial. By the sixth trial, its time had improved, but only to 170 seconds. Then, on the seventh trial, it apparently learned the routine, for it escaped in 30 seconds. Thorndike concluded that the cat had learned from its earlier trial-and-error efforts. Later experiments with both animals and humans seemed to verify these results, at least for simple tasks.

OPERANT CONDITIONING. E. L. Thorndike's theories dominated learning psychology until the 1930s, when B. F. Skinner's ideas about operant conditioning added an important new concept. (See also Chapter 7, pages 205–206.) Skinner identified two types of behavior: respondent and operant. *Respondent behavior* takes place, he said, when a specific stimulus causes an involuntary response in the subject. Respondent behavior is also known as *classical conditioning* and can be related back to Pavlov's landmark experiments (see Chapter 1, pages 7–8).

Pavlov's dogs salivated at the smell of the meat powder. Their conditioned response to the sound of the bell was an automatic one; that is, they salivated when the bell rang whether they wanted to or not. In the same way, the pupil of your eye contracts in bright light. If someone hit C# on the piano every time a bright light was flashed in front of you, six to ten repetitions could establish a respondent behavior. For some days afterward, your pupils would contract whenever you heard a

C#. Respondent behavior, therefore, is passive and mechanical. The appropriate stimulus will always cause the related response.

Skinner was much more interested in *operant behaviors*. Operant behaviors, he noted, are active rather than passive. The individual must decide which behavior will gain the desired reward. A rat, for example, will learn to press a lever to gain a reward of food. Let's say that the rat must choose from five levers, each a different color. Only the red lever will produce a food pellet. The rat can press none of the levers, it can press them all, or it can press only the food-producing lever. As you might guess, the rat chooses the red lever and enjoys the reward. Skinner would say that it has voluntarily learned an operant behavior.

Most human behavior is operant, Skinner said, whether it is reading a book, playing a piano, or running for president. The important point, he continued, is that human operant behaviors can be conditioned, just as the rat's choice of levers was conditioned by the lure of a reward. To understand just how that conditioning works, several additional principles related to operant behaviors must be considered.

1. *Reinforcement.* According to behaviorist theory, operant behaviors depend on rewards and punishments. *Rewards,* or *positive reinforcement,* tend to increase the chances that a particular behavior will be repeated. You can see the principle at work in everyday life. Teaching a dog to do a trick can be as simple as rewarding the desired behavior. Out of the thousands of movements a dog can make, it will learn to select those specific moves that you are rewarding. In this way, step by step, you can teach Prince to sit up, beg, roll over—or jump through a fiery hoop. The same principle works with people. Reward six-year-old Sophia for straightening up her room, and she'll be more likely to do it again. In time, if the rewards continue, keeping her room neat will become a habit.

Punishment tends to extinguish operant behaviors. If you hit Prince very time he sits up, he'll soon stop sitting up. Training Prince with punishment instead of reward, however, is likely to backfire. If he learns at all, the price will be steep. Prince is likely to develop some undesirable behaviors, such as barking, biting, or slinking around with his tail between his legs. Similarly, if Sophia's parents ridicule her for keeping her room "like a pigsty," they're likely to make the problem worse. Discouraged and unsure of herself, Sophia may give up entirely on her ineffectual efforts to keep the room neat.

Even when rewards stop, operant behaviors seldom extinguish immediately. Prince will still sit up every now and again, hoping for one more dog biscuit. That's one reason people hold on to nonproductive behaviors longer than they should. Unconsciously, they keep hoping that the rewards they once enjoyed will return.

FIGURE 10.3 ■ This rat is learning how to get food by pressing a lever in a special research cage known as a Skinner box. If the rat learns to press the lever whenever a light flashes, would you call that a respondent or an operant behavior? Why?

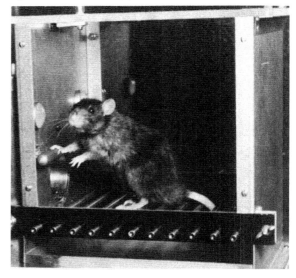

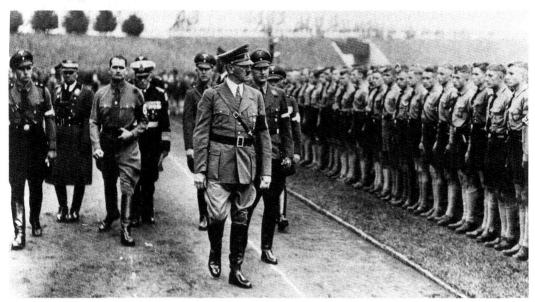

FIGURE 10.4 ■ Different societies have always produced different kinds of people. What rewards and punishments do you think were used to train a generation of German youth to absolute obedience to Adolf Hitler? Could mass conditioning ever happen in the United States?

2. *Signals.* Have you ever crossed a street against the red light? Even if you have, you probably hesitated for a moment, because the red light acted as a stimulus for a particular operant behavior—waiting until it's safe to cross. Your daily life is full of stimuli that serve as signals for particular behaviors. Your alarm going off in the morning signals that it's time to start the day. A bit of theme music signals that your favorite television program is about to start. In each case, the signal tells you that reinforcement is likely to follow.

Signals can also become generalized. You learned about red lights, perhaps, when you first began crossing streets. But now you interpret all red signal lights as "Stop, avoid danger." Green lights give you the go-ahead to proceed, whether on the street or while you're operating a computer.

3. *Schedules of reinforcement.* Surprisingly enough, you can build a more stable set of

operant responses if you don't reward the behavior every time. Let's say that, after training Prince, you now reward him every fifth time he sits up. He'll soon learn that schedule and will work happily for reinforcement that comes only one time in five. Now, try an experiment. Stop the rewards completely. Prince will sit up, certain that the reward will follow. The behavior will extinguish in time, but Prince will keep on working at it for quite a while. If he's used to being rewarded every time, the behavior will extinguish much more quickly when the rewards stop.

The most effective schedule of reinforcement seems to be a *variable-interval reinforcement,* meaning that the rewards come at unpredictable times. If you've ever watched people feeding money into a slot machine, you've seen an excellent demonstration of variable-interval reinforcement. Think about it. Would you play the slot machine if you knew that it paid off only on each 21st pull of the handle? The casino operators know the answer: "No, of course not." They set their machines to make small payoffs at irregular intervals, thus conditioning gamblers to go on hoping that the really big jackpot is just a few plays away.

COGNITIVE THEORY

Many modern psychologists do not believe that stimulus-response theory gives proper weight to the mind's higher mental processes. Human beings, they observe, carry on a number of high-level mental activities called *cognition*. Reasoning, abstract thinking, and problem solving, they believe, amount to more than S → R behavior. According to *cognitive theory,* learning is the process of putting bits of experience and information together to create a new understanding. It is an active process that involves the "whole" person.

A psychologist at the University of California at Berkeley, E. C. Tolman, described this process as building up experiences based on what you already know about the environment. Tolman's experiments seemed to show that rats were capable of insights that shortcut laborious trial-and-error learning. In a typical experiment, rats were turned loose in mazes containing a network of alleys and dead ends. Many paths led through the maze to a reward of food, but one path was always shortest. The rats clearly preferred the shortest path. When it was blocked, they immediately shifted to the next shortest route. Apparently, Tolman concluded, they had built up a mental map of the entire maze and could quickly move from one path to another without resorting to trial and error. In this way, the cognitive theory makes the rats—and people—active participants in the learning process.

You can see cognitive learning at work if you watch Libby learning to ride her first two-wheel bicycle. First, you might notice that some S → R learning is taking place. Libby quickly discovers what happens if she runs into a curb or loses her balance. She also responds positively to the praise of her parents. These responses could all be explained as operant behaviors. But watch closely. You'll see Libby pause as she plans each new step, using past experiences as a guide. This set of responses is cognitive learning at work. If she can't straddle the seat easily, she'll figure out how to use the curb to get started. If her dress-up shoes slip off the pedals, she'll change them for sneakers that won't slip. Libby will also watch older children riding their bikes, and she'll apply those observations as a way of speeding up her own learning.

To see Libby learning to ride her bike is to see her totally focused on learning something that's important to her. Simple conditioning theory doesn't fully explain that type of learning. Libby will certainly enjoy the rewards of learning to ride. But the inner satisfaction that comes from using all her mental and physical resources to master a difficult skill will be her most important reward.

FACTORS THAT INFLUENCE LEARNING

How well a person learns skills, attitudes, and values is influenced by a number of factors. Here are some of the most important.

1. *The self.* Learning takes place more readily when what you learn matches your self-concept. If you think of yourself as athletic, for example, you'll learn a new sport faster than someone who doubts his or her athletic ability. Personality traits, such as laziness or stubbornness, can also interfere with learning.

2. *Past experience.* You tend to relate what you see and hear and feel to past experiences. If the new material doesn't match

up to past learning, you'll be more likely to reject it. That's why it's often so hard to talk someone into trying an unusual food or a new hairstyle.

3. *Intelligence.* Intelligence is the ability to solve problems and to absorb new information quickly. Scores on intelligence tests tend to give the impression that intelligence is a single quantity, something like the amount of money you have available in a bank account. But intelligence is really the sum of a number of specific abilities. Mechanical skills, verbal skills, artistic skills, athletic skills, and dozens of other skills all make up individual intelligence. Your ability to learn depends to some degree on your ability to apply one or more of these skills to the learning task.

4. *Motivation.* Anything that makes you want to learn is called *motivation.* When you *want* to learn a new skill, such as typing, you'll make more rapid progress than you will if you're taking the course only to satisfy a graduation requirement. That's probably why you do better in some classes than in others. If you are motivated to learn a body of material, you'll do the work more willingly and receive greater satisfaction from it.

5. *Emotions.* Your emotions can either help or hinder learning. Enthusiasm is a positive factor, while anxiety generally gets in the way of learning. For example, you may have had the experience of tackling a textbook assignment, only to realize later that you hadn't absorbed anything you read. As you think about it, you realize you weren't able to set aside the day's burden of worries. Anxiety clearly interfered with your ability to concentrate and remember what you were studying.

6. *Rewards and punishments.* Rewards are important stimuli to learning. They are often given in the form of money, recognition, or grades, but praise and affection create an even greater incentive to learn. Punishment, as noted earlier, is generally less effective as a learning tool. When it is used, punishment should be administered immediately. This makes it possible for the learner to connect the punishment with the incorrect behavior. On an adult level, punishment works only if it is coupled with rewards. If your employer criticizes you for poor work but never rewards you for a good performance, you'll lose interest in learning how to improve.

7. *Feedback.* You'll learn more rapidly if you know right away whether your response was correct or not. When you're learning to shoot pool, the feedback is immediate: the ball either falls into the pocket or it doesn't. By delaying feedback (witness the teachers who don't return student papers until weeks later), schools lose much of the learning value tests and assignments should have provided. Computer-assisted instruction (CAI) attempts to overcome that problem by providing instant feedback (see the box on page 327).

8. *Guidance.* When you receive guidance from a more experienced person, you can often shortcut errors and move quickly to the correct solution. Think of trying to teach yourself how to perform heart surgery by reading a textbook! Teachers who provide positive feedback can make learning both efficient and enjoyable.

9. *Novelty.* Dull routine interferes with learning. You'll learn better when new and unexpected factors are added to the learning situation. Skilled teachers provide this novelty by varying classroom routine with films, guest speakers, debates, and other techniques. Overuse of novelty, however, can detract from learning. A teacher who tells too many jokes may disrupt the class's concentration. Students may enjoy the jokes, but they won't learn as much as they would with a more businesslike approach to teaching.

10. *Cumulative learning.* Do you want to learn a subject—and hold on to what you've learned? The secret, says psychologist Harry Bahrick, is twofold. First, learn the material

Computer-Assisted Instruction: Putting the PC to Work in the Classroom

A typical classroom operates on a time-honored ratio. One teacher organizes the instructional program for 20 or more students. Because students do not all learn at the same rate, some run ahead and others fall behind. A ratio of one teacher to each student would increase learning efficiency, but the costs would be astronomical. Thanks to computer technology, however, the solution lies close at hand. Infinitely patient and surprisingly resourceful, the personal computer (PC) has been drafted into the struggle to improve the nation's educational system. With one human teacher and 20 PCs, the classroom *can* provide individualized instruction.

Computer-assisted instruction (CAI) builds on the operant learning theories of B. F. Skinner. Programmers break the subject matter into individual frames that allow the learner to focus on one concept or fact at a time. A typical frame presents the information and asks for a response. The learner responds via a mouse or the computer keyboard—and receives instant feedback. If the response was correct, the learner is allowed to go on to the next frame. If the response missed the mark, the computer explains why the answer was wrong and asks the student to try again. Instructional games use stories, competition, and game-like graphics to prove that learning can be fun. Educational simulations create "microworlds" that allow students to test the effects of their choices on people, communities, and the natural world.

CAI works well with both slow and quick learners. Slow learners work at their own pace, reviewing difficult concepts over and over until they master them. Quick learners need not suffer boredom while waiting for the rest of the class to catch up. As soon as they complete one level of instruction, they can move on to a more advanced level.

Students in well-equipped classrooms use computers to do research, complete CAI assignments, and design their own Web pages.

The proponents of CAI acknowledge that start-up costs are high but believe that improved learning efficiency makes the investment worthwhile. They further remind the critics who charge that CAI takes the human interaction out of learning that computers are not meant to replace a trained and caring teacher. Like a chalkboard, textbook, or VCR, the computer is just one more tool for helping students learn.

over a long period of time (months instead of weeks). Second, spend at least 40 percent as much time reviewing (or using) what you've learned as you did learning it in the first place. Bahrick found that people who went on to take college math remembered 80 percent of their high school algebra as long as 50 years later. Another group earned equally good grades in high school but did not go on to take high-level math in college. This group scored only slightly higher than a control group that had never taken algebra.

WHAT'S YOUR LEARNING STYLE?

Learning styles are as different as hairstyles or clothing styles. That fact shouldn't surprise anyone because each person brings different abilities, preferences, and habits to the learning experience. Learning psychologists know that you can improve your own learning style, but becoming a peak learner begins with self-examination.

First, figure out your learning physiology. Some people are visual learners who learn best by watching and reading. Others depend more on their ears; listening to a lecture works well for them. A third group learns most efficiently with a "hands-on" (tactile) approach. Your body clock also plays a role in learning efficiency. At what time of day are you mentally most alert? If you're a "morning person," for example, it pays to get up early to study or to tackle a creative project. "Night people" are advised to put off important learning tasks until after supper. Either way, seize your peak moments—then shut down before you run out of gas.

Next, ask yourself, "Am I a *grouper* or a *stringer*?" Groupers take a broad view of a subject, searching out general principles and drawing parallels. The best way for a grouper to learn is to jump in and "go with the flow." Stringers, by contrast, like to master specific details before moving on to general concepts.

They learn best when they can point toward a series of clearly defined goals. Stringers often earn higher grades than groupers because most academic work is organized to suit their strengths.

Finally, think about your general attitude toward learning. Ned Hermann of the Whole Brain Corporation says that most people fall into one of four categories. Style A learners like to tackle a subject by building up a hard core of solid data. These logical, rational learners are most comfortable when dealing with verifiable facts. Style B learners want everything laid out in neat, orderly stacks. They don't want to blaze new trails if someone else has already been over the route. Style C learners love to talk about what they're learning. They believe in free and open discussion, whether it's in the classroom or around the dinner table. Style D learners aren't interested in facts as much as they are in grasping the underlying spirit of a subject. They relish the challenge of looking at data in new and creative ways.

No one fits neatly into a single prefabricated style, of course. That shouldn't keep you from constructing your own learning profile. Learning how to learn at peak efficiency can pay big dividends now and throughout your life.

■ SECTION CHECKUP

1 Define learning. List some of the things you've learned in the past months: new information, new social behaviors, and new skills.

2 Your friend Nathan wants to teach his pet cockatoo to pull a toy wagon with its beak. How can Nathan use stimulus-response theory to train his bird?

3 Why wouldn't cognitive theory be of any

value to Nathan in training his bird? Describe a situation in which you've seen cognitive learning taking place.

4 Think of two types of learning, one that is easy for you and one that is difficult. What factors influence your learning in each case? How could you improve your performance in the types of learning that give you trouble?

10.2 ▓ HOW DOES MEMORY WORK?

How old are you? What's your telephone number? Who's the President of the United States? Which team won the last World Series? What did you eat for lunch yesterday?

Simple questions? Yes, if your memory works properly. A psychologist would define *memory* as the process of using the brain to store and retrieve information. Thanks to the brain's immense capacity, you carry an astounding amount of data around with you. The answers to tens of thousands of questions pop up instantly, seemingly without effort. But not if you're Henry M.

Henry M. doesn't have a memory. He lost it in 1953, when a surgeon cut too deeply into a part of his brain called the *hippocampus.* The psychosurgery was done in an effort to cure Henry's massive epileptic seizures, but today he lives in a world without a past. Henry retains only those memories that predate the operation. His motor skills and intelligence weren't affected. By day he earns a living doing light assembly work. At home, he finds contentment in performing such activities as raking leaves and shoveling snow.

If you were to meet Henry, you'd find him pleasant to talk to but vague about details. Experience slips through his mind like water from a leaky pail. Henry does recognize John F. Kennedy's picture and connects it with the assassination of the former president in 1963. Apparently, the emotional impact of that event impressed itself on Henry's faulty memory, just as it did for millions of other people. But for the most part, Henry is truly a "child of the moment," unable to retrieve recent memories. Talk to him one day and he won't remember meeting you the next. He can read the same magazine every day, and it's new to him each time. No one can restore Henry's memory, but researchers have put together a fairly complete picture of how a normal memory functions.

THE PHYSICAL BASIS FOR MEMORY

Researchers have concentrated on two questions regarding the physical basis of memory. Where is memory located in the brain? How does the brain process and store incoming data to create memory?

THE SEARCH FOR A "MEMORY CENTER." Researchers now believe that a true "memory center" may never be found. The hindbrain, which regulates automatic body functions, contains structures that are necessary to memory, but memory itself doesn't seem to be located there. Karl Lashley (1890–1958), an outstanding physiological psychologist, turned to the forebrain when he tried to locate the elusive memory center in rats. First, he trained the animals to run a maze. Then, little by little, Lashley cut out ever larger pieces of their cerebral cortex. Although he removed 90 percent of the visual cortex, the rats were still able to limp, hop, or stagger through the mazes they'd learned to run before the surgery.

Related studies on human patients, in which large amounts of brain tissue have been removed for medical reasons, yield similar results. Even though the surgery produces changes in personality and some loss of learning ability, most memory functions of the brain are not affected. As Henry M. demonstrates so tragically, the hippocampus plays a key role in laying down or retrieving new memories. Lashley and other researchers have concluded, however, that memory storage itself seems to be spread throughout the cerebral cortex.

MEMORY AS AN ELECTROCHEMICAL PROCESS. A simplified approach to explaining memory begins this way: Look at the capital *A* that opens this paragraph. As that image is picked up on the retina of your eye, electrochemical impulses carry a message about its size, shape, and color to the brain. This sets off a burst of activity in the visual cortex. Circuits of neurons fire or don't fire according to the impulses delivered by their neighbors.

If you had never seen an *A* before, a new pattern of neurons would be activated. The information-carrying RNA molecules in that chain of neurons would be coded, or rearranged, to store the new memory. You can think of it as similar to the programming of a computer. New data is coded into the memory bank and kept for future use.

In order to recall that capital *A*, the coded neurons must be stimulated by a "search" signal. When the search scores a "hit," the response is returned to the processing center of the brain, where you "remember" the letter. When you think of 10 billion neurons handling over 100 million electrical impulses each second, you can begin to appreciate the enormous computing power the brain brings to this task.

The role of RNA becomes clearer when you look at the research of University of Michigan psychologist James McConnell. McConnell's work apparently demonstrates that RNA-stored memory can be transferred from one animal to another. Experiments have been carried out using flatworms, goldfish, and rats.

Let's say that McConnell has taught a flatworm named Moe to turn right each time he is placed in a simple T-maze. The scientist then cuts Moe into tiny bits and feeds him to Curly, who has never run the maze. After Curly digests his meal, McConnell puts him in the maze. Behold, Curly runs the maze beautifully! Other experimenters have extracted brain matter from trained rats and injected it into untrained animals. Once again, the untrained rats "learned" skills that the donor rats had previously mastered.

Although these studies show considerable statistical validity, no one can yet explain how the transfer of training takes place. Some scientists, including McConnell, believe that RNA molecules carry the message. If the research holds up under further study, we'll know that memory exists as a physical change in the brain's electrochemical makeup.

THREE TYPES OF MEMORY

Have you ever gone through this frustrating experience? You look up a phone number, close the phone book, and start to dial. Then you stop, scold yourself for being so scatterbrained, and look up the number again. Between closing the book and picking up the phone, that seven-number sequence has either vanished or become hopelessly jumbled.

Memory researchers tell us that looking at or listening to a "packet" of information doesn't move the data into permanent memory. Before that happens, you have to work at retaining the phone number or whatever else you want to remember. Psychologists recognize three types of memory, each serving a different purpose.

SENSORY MEMORY. As you read, your body and brain are monitoring temperature, drafts, the comfort of your chair, the intensity of the

THE PROCESS OF MEMORY: INPUT TO OUTPUT

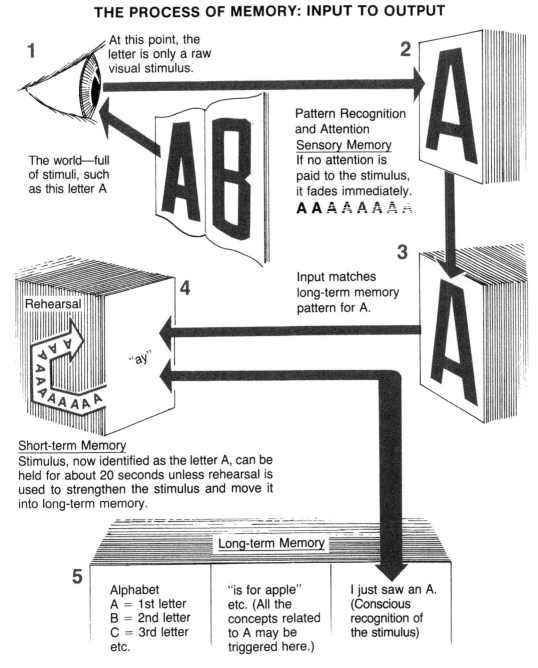

1 At this point, the letter is only a raw visual stimulus.

The world—full of stimuli, such as this letter A

2 Pattern Recognition and Attention
Sensory Memory
If no attention is paid to the stimulus, it fades immediately.
A A A A A A A A

3 Input matches long-term memory pattern for A.

4 Rehearsal
"ay"

Short-term Memory
Stimulus, now identified as the letter A, can be held for about 20 seconds unless rehearsal is used to strengthen the stimulus and move it into long-term memory.

Long-term Memory

5

Alphabet	"is for apple"	I just saw an A.
A = 1st letter	etc. (All the	(Conscious
B = 2nd letter	concepts related	recognition of
C = 3rd letter	to A may be	the stimulus)
etc.	triggered here.)	

All memory relating to the world, our own experiences, and our inner feelings is stored here. Data relating to the alphabet and the various uses of the letter A take up only a tiny corner of this immense storehouse.

FIGURE 10.5

light, and a thousand other sensory impressions. This continuous stream of data registers on the *sensory memory*. Sensory memory fades almost as quickly as it registers. Otherwise, no one's brain could cope with that flood of mostly useless data. But when something important happens, as when the room suddenly goes dark, the information is immediately called to your attention. Think of sensory memory as an early-alert system. Although it constantly monitors your body's state of well-being as well as the surrounding environment, it only sounds the alarm when a change merits your attention.

SHORT-TERM MEMORY. Psychologists describe *short-term memory* as a "holding tank." Experiments show that it holds five to nine items (words, sounds, faces, and so on) for about 20 seconds. After that, unimportant items are discarded. Thus, short-term memory is perfect for remembering a phone number—but only if you rehearse the number while you dial. *Rehearsal* is the process of concentrating on the item you want to remember, perhaps by repeating it several times. Since you're often distracted while you're picking up the phone and dialing, you tend to lose the number unless you do something to hold it. Short-term memory also explains the common experience that begins when someone asks you a question. You weren't paying attention, so you ask, "What did you say?" Even as you speak, however, you realize you *do* know what the original question was. It was held in short-term memory, waiting to be noticed.

LONG-TERM MEMORY. Everything you know is stored in *long-term memory*. This huge data bank includes more than just names, dates, and spelling words. Landscapes, plots of old movies, the scent of a rose, childhood friendships—all are kept in long-term memory. Moving data from short-term to long-term memory requires effort on your part. One experiment on remembering words, for example, found that people can move only about 12 unrelated words into long-term memory in a two-minute period. If you're highly motivated or if the material arouses strong emotions, greater chunks can be transferred. Watch your level of concentration soar when a teacher says that the next block of information will appear on tomorrow's test!

REMEMBERING AND FORGETTING

Wilder Penfield's experiments (described more fully in Chapter 2, page 33) confirmed the existence of long-term memory. Penfield triggered specific recollections of long-ago events with an electric probe during brain surgery. Except for the loss of brain cells during the aging process or through accidental injury, long-term memories are never completely lost. With new data arriving every day, your mind works constantly to organize its memories. Like an inefficient office worker, it sometimes misfiles important data. As you know from experience, it's relatively easy to store a file in long-term memory. Retrieving it, however, is often far more difficult.

REMEMBERING. To *remember* is to respond to a stimulus by retrieving one or more of the memories you've stored away. Psychologists speak of *recollection* or *recall* when they refer to the process of using word cues, stimuli, or "reminders" to remember something you've learned. If someone asked you, "Who invented the telephone?" you probably wouldn't have to search your memory for a long list of inventors' names. The cue word *telephone* would quickly recall the proper name: Alexander Graham Bell. Similarly, the brain stores details about the environment in which learning takes place alongside the new material. Suppose, for example, that you were eating chocolates the day you memorized the batting averages of the 1936 Yankees. Today, the taste or smell of chocolate

MNEMONIC DEVICES: SHORTCUTS TO IMPROVING YOUR MEMORY

Memory experts promise that you can improve your memory through the use of techniques they call *mnemonic* (pronounced ne-MON-ik) *devices*. The following techniques are typical; using them will improve your memory almost overnight if you're willing to practice them and use them consistently.

MNEMONIC DEVICE	TECHNIQUE	EXAMPLE
First-letter code (list of related items)	Make a sentence out of the first letter from each word in the list.	Memorize the notes on the lines of the musical staff: E-G-B-D-F. Mnemonic sentence: Every Good Boy Does Fine.
Association (names and faces)	When meeting people, first concentrate on the name. Then form a visual image from the name. Couple this with an impression of the person—a strong facial feature of some type. Rehearse this coupled image several times, and you'll have it.	Mr. Page Mrs. Robinson
Pegwords (shopping lists, errands, dates of historical events—anything that can be visualized as an object)	Begin by memorizing a simple list of rhymes for one to ten. A typical list: one/gun; two/shoe; three/tree; four/door; five/hive; six/sticks; seven/heaven; eight/gate; nine/twine; ten/hen. When you have a list to remember, hook each word to the rhyme word with a vivid mental picture—the more bizarre, the better. For example, when you need the items, say "one/gun..." and a mental picture will pop immediately to mind.	Try this shopping list: bread, milk, apples, butter, steak. 1/gun = 2/shoe = 3/tree = 4/door = 5/hive =

will help you recall those names and numbers even though you haven't thought about them for years.

RECOGNITION. By contrast, *recognition* depends on visual stimuli to retrieve a particular memory. Familiar shapes, patterns, or combinations of letters trigger a memory of what similar images meant at an earlier time. Bird-watchers who can identify a meadowlark in the brief instant before the bird flies away are demonstrating this type of remembering.

A few people have been gifted with almost total recall, an ability known as *eidetic recall* (or, as it is more popularly known, a photographic memory). Most adults, for example, can recite the alphabet without stopping to think about the proper sequence. In their memory, process *A* triggers *B, B* triggers *C,* and so on. These same people are stumped, however, when asked to recite the alphabet backwards. People with eidetic recall, by contrast, can call up a visual image of whatever they've seen. Reciting the alphabet backwards is no great challenge. They simply call off the letters as they flash on their mental viewing screen.

One study showed that about four percent of elementary school children have eidetic recall, but most lose the ability during puberty. Adult thought processes apparently interfere with the visual images needed for eidetic recall.

FORGETTING. If little is ever lost from long-term memory, why can't people remember whatever they want to remember? This inability to retrieve material when you want it is called *forgetting*. No single theory accounts for everything you forget. Most likely, each of the following explanations plays a part.

1. *Interference* occurs when newly learned material blocks retrieval of data you learned earlier. Learn your new phone number, for example, and you'll very likely lose your old one. Another kind of interference occurs when an old memory, such as a strong prejudice, blocks retention of new learning. An older man who dislikes children, for instance, may soon forget how hard the neighborhood kids worked to raise money for the local free clinic.

2. *Distortion of memory patterns* is a polite way of saying that people's memories change and distort reality. Ask five different eyewitnesses to describe the same robbery, and you'll probably get five different reports. The most common type of distortion is *leveling*. The eyewitnesses see what happens but remember only the general events. They may remember that the holdup men came into the store and emptied the cash register, but may not agree on what threats were made, the type of weapons used, or the make of the getaway car. *Sharpening* also distorts memory by focusing on a few unusual details. The witnesses may remember the money that was scattered on the floor but forget more important details, such as the physical description of the criminals. Finally, *assimilation* distorts memory by altering events to fit people's expectations or stereotypes. If the eyewitnesses were prejudiced against a particular ethnic group, they might very well report that the masked crooks were "obviously" members of that group.

3. *Repressed material* is forgotten because to remember it would be too painful. If Nelda witnesses a violent crime, for example, her mind may quickly repress that memory as too disturbing for her to handle. The unconscious stands guard over such memories and permits disclosure only under special conditions—during dreams, hypnosis, or free association. In some cases, repressed memories of childhood abuse surface abruptly much later in life. Resolving the lacerating emotions aroused by such memories often requires the help of a psychotherapist.

4. *Decay through disuse* suggests that memories fade when you don't rehearse them. But walk through your childhood

FIGURE 10.6 ✳ How good an eyewitness would you make? Study this scene for 60 seconds. Then cover the picture and write down all the details you can remember. Afterward, check your notes against the actual scene. What did you leave out? Did you add any new details? How do you explain any errors you made?

neighborhood some day, and apparently forgotten memories will spring back to vivid life. Learning psychologists tend to downplay decay as a factor in forgetting. Interference, they believe, plays a much larger role.

CAN CHEMISTRY IMPROVE LEARNING AND MEMORY?

"Hello, is this the Future Pharmacy? I've got a big math test tomorrow. Do you have anything that will help?"

"Did you say math? That means you don't want the new creativity pills. You better pick up a box of Cortex-A. Those babies will increase your attention span and improve your visual memory."

"Sounds great. I'll be right over."

No one has made that phone call—yet. So far, only one drug has weathered centuries of laws, taxation, and health scares. Taken as a pick-me-up in coffee, tea, or soft drinks, caffeine still rates as the world's most popular drug.

The chances are good that more powerful drugs will soon be available. Experiments with drugs that aid learning and memory have excited the imaginations of scientists everywhere. Researchers are working on cognition enhancers that provide positive results without unpleasant side effects. Donepezil, a cholinesterase inhibitor often prescribed for Alzheimer's patients, is being tested on healthy people who need to improve their performance on tasks that demand high levels of concentration. In one double-blind study using flight simulators, a group of pilots who took donepezil for 30 days outperformed the placebo group.

The armed forces are doing their own work with cognition enhancement drugs. As one researcher put it, the goal is to improve training and performance so that "our guys are a whole lot better than their guys." Enhancement drugs, for example, could be used to help soldiers stay sharp on missions that force them to go without sleep for several days.

What Are You Most Likely to Remember...
and Forget?

In *Techniques for Efficient Remembering,* Eleanor and Donald Laird summarize a number of interesting findings relating to the way memories work. Based on their research, they can predict what you're most likely to remember and what you'll probably forget.

YOU'LL PROBABLY REMEMBER:

- Pleasant experiences

- Whatever you review before you go to bed

- Things you feel are worth remembering

- Whatever you let sink in before going on to new material

- Things you talk about often

- Difficult material you have worked hard to learn

- Material you think about often or rehearse frequently

- Your successes

- Things that make sense to you

- Memories tied in with motor skills

- What you use frequently

YOU'LL PROBABLY FORGET:

- Names of things and people

- Numbers and dates

- Unpleasant things

- Facts that don't fit with your beliefs and prejudices

- Anything you learn by cramming

- Your failures

- Whatever you pick up casually without trying to remember

- Things you think of only once or twice after remembering them

- Material you don't understand

- Anything you try to remember when embarrassed, frustrated, in poor health, or fatigued

Drug companies are keeping their eyes on the market for memory enhancement drugs. Along with the millions who suffer from Alzheimer's disease, tens of millions of Americans are coping with problems that range from mild forgetfulness to the type of cognitive impairment that leads to AD. While they wait for a breakthrough drug treatment, worried people are spending more than $1 billion a year on gingko biloba and other herbs—even though proof that these remedies actually improve memory is hard to find.

The quest for a quick-and-easy shortcut to improved cognitive abilities also has a darker side—the under-the-counter sale of "smart drinks" and "smart drugs." The "smart drinks" are usually a witch's brew of vitamins, minerals, and other nutrients that supposedly stimulate the brain. The "smart drugs," which include vasopressin, Hydergine, and Piracetam, are actually prescription medications. Anyone who wanders into a disco-like nightclub called a Smart Lounge, however, will find "smart drugs" being sold in the same way street pushers sell cocaine. Drinking a vitamin-and-mineral cocktail probably won't do any harm; swallowing a handful of "smart pills" threatens the user's mental health and physical well-being.

■ SECTION CHECKUP

1 Describe the general process by which a memory is stored in the brain. Why have re-searchers never been able to discover a "memory center"?

2 Explain the different roles assigned to sensory memory, short-term memory, and long-term memory.

3 What are some of the reasons you forget things you really thought you would always remember?

4 What role will memory-aiding drugs one day play in helping ease memory disabilities?

10.3 ▓ HOW DO PEOPLE THINK?

Have you noticed the process people go through when something interesting or important happens? Whether they've stepped on an earthworm or survived an earthquake, they seem driven to study the event, label it, and file it for future reference. Later, if someone asks, "What happened?" they retrieve the data from storage and find words to describe it.

This complicated behavior is *thinking:* the active, conscious process that enables people to reorganize their memories so that they can develop ideas, establish relationships, and ask questions. The thinking process depends on images, symbols, concepts, and rules.

1. An *image* is the pictorial recall of a specific object or event. Most images lack specific detail, as if only the highlights remained in your memory. When you visualize your grandmother's house, the ice cream you made last summer, or the chaos in your closet, you're using images.

2. *Symbols* allow people to label objects, events, and feelings. The words you're reading right now are the most common symbols of all. With words, you don't need to bring an elephant into the room to think or talk about elephants. Words also enable you to deal with abstract ideas. How could you discuss love, freedom, and justice without words?

Commonly accepted graphic images also serve as useful symbols. People the world over recognize the symbolic meaning of the Red Cross and of their national flags.

3. *Concepts* allow you to put things into categories and to establish relationships. *Dog* is a word, but the concept of "dog" stands for a class of four-footed animals that bark, chase sticks, wag their tails, and shed hair on the sofa. When someone says *sports,* an entire family of relationships comes immediately to mind. Young Harry's ability to form and express ideas will take a quantum leap forward when he begins to grasp conceptual thinking.

4. *Rules* describe the relationship commonly believed to exist between different concepts. "Honor your father and mother" is a rule, as is the statement "Broccoli is good for you." In mathematics and science, you learn useful rules that establish accepted facts, such as "7 times 7 is 49" and "Matter can be neither created nor destroyed." You take another set of rules for granted because they are part of your cultural heritage. "The Constitution and Bill of Rights safeguard our individual freedoms" is an example of such a rule. A final class of rules affects your sense of who you are ("You're just like your father!"). Rules that help shape your life should

Pitfalls in the Pathway of Logical Thinking

The wonderful mechanism called the human mind is capable of towering achievements . . . and of monumentally foolish mistakes. Have you ever stumbled into any of these common pitfalls in logical thinking?

PITFALL 1: THE GAMBLER'S MISTAKE

If a coin turns up heads six times in a row, what are the odds that it will land tails on the next toss? Despite the temptation to assume that chance is not on the side of tails, the odds remain exactly what they were before: 50–50. Over thousands of tosses, the heads and tails will always even out. The coin never "learns" from experience. People *can* learn, however. Using the lessons taught by study and experience will improve your success rate well above 50–50.

PITFALL 2: FAITH IN SMALL NUMBERS

If you reached into a bag of apples and pulled out a rotten apple, would you assume that every apple was bad? Probably not, but people often assume that a small sampling is representative of a larger group. Television newscasters do this when they interview three people on the street and then announce, "The public believes Senator Foghorn will win re-election easily."

PITFALL 3: THE AWARENESS TRAP

Most people believe that a particular event is more likely to happen if they're conscious of similar happenings in the past. For example, suppose the newspapers play up a series of muggings in a high-crime area. Everyone living nearby will begin to worry about being attacked. People will stay home at night, buy new locks for their doors, and demand better police protection. In reality, the danger always existed. It was only the residents' increased awareness of the danger that changed their behavior.

PITFALL 4: ILLUSIONS OF CORRELATION

People find it easy to discover correlations (positive relationships) when their biases point in a particular direction. Thus, someone who disapproves of divorce may notice that many juvenile delinquents come from single-parent families and jump to the conclusion that divorces *cause* delinquency. These same people will conveniently overlook statistics about stable single-parent families, along with data on delinquents who live in traditional two-parent families.

PITFALL 5: THE P. T. BARNUM EFFECT

It was P. T. Barnum who said, "There's a sucker born every minute." The canny showman made his fortune by gambling on the human tendency to believe almost any claim that sounds factual or that carries the weight of authority. Barnum's spirit lives on in the rumors that sometimes sweep through a community or in the celebrity endorsements that pitch everything from automobiles to sports shoes.

always be tested for both accuracy and usefulness.

THE THINKING PROCESS

What a wonderful world you carry around in your head! Without ever stirring from your chair, you can fly in space, climb Mt. Everest, or figure out a way to finance the new CD you've been wanting. Using images, symbols, concepts, and rules, you can think about issues, decide on a course of action, or enjoy a daydream. Whatever thinking you do, some of it will be directed and some of it is certain to be nondirected.

DIRECTED THINKING.   Rhea is walking down the street, nothing much on her mind. Then she spots Ivy coming toward her. Rhea owes Ivy some money, and she's not ready to pay it back. In the few seconds she has left before Ivy sees her, Rhea thinks through several possible solutions to her problem. Systematically, she weighs each option, checking it against recollections of her past transactions with Ivy. Finally, she has her story ready and puts on her best smile. "Oh, hi," Rhea says, "I was just thinking about you . . ."

Rhea's quick juggling of alternatives represents *directed thinking*. Some experts on thought processes also call it straight-line or left-brain thinking. You start at point A, and proceed in logical fashion to points B, C, and so on, until you reach your goal. In a way, it's like working through a problem in geometry. Each step builds on the ones before. Without directed thinking, you'd soon sink under the weight of the unending series of problems that make up daily existence.

NONDIRECTED THINKING.   The process of *nondirected thinking* relies mainly on images and feelings. Lean back and daydream for a moment. Enjoy a fantasy about finding a 100-dollar bill in a letter from rich Uncle Amos. Relax and enjoy the prospect of spending the unexpected treasure. One image will lead to another and another. Such daydreams, fanta-

sies, and drifting thoughts are known as nondirected thinking. This type of right-brain thinking taps into the rich resources of the unconscious to provide relief from tension and boredom. More important, nondirected thinking often rewards you with your most creative ideas.

No great work of art ever grows entirely out of directed thinking. In order to paint, for example, you need to plan logically to the extent of obtaining the necessary materials. But decisions regarding what to paint are often produced by nondirected thinking. As you think about possible subjects, a series of images drift through your consciousness. Then, almost without knowing why, one scene emerges that "feels right." Some people call this "playing a hunch," or intuition. Creative thinkers don't question such feelings. They've learned to trust the right brain's intuitive talents.

THE ROLE OF LANGUAGE IN THE THINKING PROCESS

At one time, scientists believed that language erected an impassable barrier between humans and animals. Experiments in recent years have partially demolished that theory. Rats can learn to find their food under a triangle, for example, ignoring squares and circles. While a triangle isn't a word, it is a symbol that the rat learns to associate with food, just as you might associate a red-and-white striped bucket with fried chicken. At a higher level, Koko and other trained apes have learned to use their limited sign-language vocabularies quite effectively. But higher levels of thinking are tied to a more complex level of language than any gorilla or chimpanzee can reach. Without language, human culture might never have left the hunting and gathering stage. With it, our species has reached toward the stars.

LANGUAGE DEVELOPMENT.   Thinking in infants apparently begins with simple language concepts. For example, babies learn to match the word *bottle* to the actual object. Later, they acquire the ability to recognize broader relationships. Older children recognize both milk and marshmallows as foods because they have learned the concept of food. As language skills increase, abstract concepts appear, along with grammar and word order. The child says, "I miss you," and understands the feelings that these three words convey.

Language expert Noam Chomsky says that only human beings are born with this inborn capacity for language. He bases his belief on the evidence that despite all the inaccurate language children hear, they still learn to express themselves clearly and forcefully. Chomsky points out that children learn to speak at about the same age in every culture. Moreover, despite the apparent differences among languages, all languages are built from similar concepts about sentences, subjects, and predicates. These structures provide workable rules for grammar and word usage.

Children can be counted on to make errors while learning to talk. Watching his mother trip over the dog, little Stan might laugh and say, "Mom fell down." No matter. Stan has followed grammatical rules for forming the past tense. As he grows older, he'll learn to use irregular verbs. What Stan won't do is tangle up his word order. He'll never say, "Down fell Mom." Koko also learned to construct simple sentences with the words in proper order but only after extensive training.

LANGUAGE INTERACTS WITH CULTURE. Limitations of language may also influence behavior. The traditional Hopi Indian language, for example, has no past or future tenses. Where English says, "He ran," the Hopi would use the present tense, "*Wari* (Running occurs)." For the future tense ("He will run" in English), the Hopi would say, "*Warikne* (Running occurs I daresay)." Because they did not think in future terms, schedules and future plans meant little to the people of the old Hopi culture. The Eskimos of North America, by contrast, have a number of different words to identify various types of snow. These variations make sense in a culture in which snow is an overwhelming fact of life. Perhaps, if air pollution continues to worsen in this country, Americans will someday invent new words to describe the different types of smog they must endure.

■ SECTION CHECKUP

1 Define thinking. Why would a dream not be considered thinking?

2 What are the differences among images, symbols, concepts, and rules? Give an example of each.

3 Describe a situation that requires directed thinking. Now add a second situation in which nondirected thinking would be useful.

4 Why is language so important to the thinking process?

10.4 ▓ HOW CAN YOU IMPROVE YOUR LEARNING AND PROBLEM-SOLVING ABILITIES?

A farmer once sent his children to the well to bring back some water. "Take these two pails," he told them, "and don't come back until you have exactly five gallons." Then he handed them a two-gallon pail and a nine-gallon pail. How did the children solve the problem?

Here's what the clever children did. First, they filled the nine-gallon pail. Then they filled the small pail by pouring two gallons from the large pail. Next, they dumped out the two gallons from the small pail and filled it again. That left exactly five gallons in the large pail (nine gallons minus two minus two). After dumping out the contents of the small pail once more, they carried the large one home, their problem solved.

That's only a puzzle of course, an exercise for the fun of it. But the type of logical thinking that solves puzzles and riddles can also be applied to real-life problems. For many people, the first step toward better problem solving is the application of more efficient learning techniques.

IMPROVING YOUR ABILITY TO LEARN

In Section 10.1, pages 320–329, you learned something about how people learn. Here are some ways to make learning easier.

1. *Overlearning* is the process of repeating a skill over and over even after you've mastered it. Major-league baseball players, for example, practice every day, as do professional musicians. You can also apply overlearning techniques to other types of learning. Anyone studying a foreign language, for example, can profit from daily practice. Useful activities include listening to records, making up conversations, and reading simple stories (in addition to the constant chore of memorizing vocabulary).

2. *Removing negative conditions* that prevent efficient learning might be as simple as finding a quiet place to study. For many, it means turning off the radio—and especially the television. Because emotional problems disrupt concentration, they must also be thought of as negatives. If possible, take time off to resolve the emotional difficulty, then return to the learning session.

3. *Adjust the type of practice,* depending on the material to be learned. There are two basic types of practice: distributed practice and massed practice. Distributed practice, which divides the task into small segments, generally works best. Learning the names of

THE CASE OF THE SUDDEN SPENDTHRIFT

FIGURE 10.7 ▓ When confronted with a puzzle, good problem solvers begin by scanning the entire range of possible solutions. How good are you at finding multiple possibilities? Test yourself on "The Case of the Sudden Spendthrift." Harry Parker has always been a thrifty person. Suddenly, however, he has begun to spend money quite freely. How many reasons can you list to explain the sudden change in Harry's spending habits? (See page 354 for a discussion of your list of reasons.)

the major skeletal bones for physiology should be tackled in several short study sessions. It might be easier, however, to memorize your lines for a difficult scene in a play with massed practice. This means working without interruption until the script has been memorized. Since each speech within the scene links to the one before, you profit from the associations that build up as you rehearse the entire scene over and over.

4. *Verbalization* means to talk out the steps of a procedure, either to yourself or to others. Verbalization helps learning even when you're working on skills such as dancing or finishing a bookcase. Go ahead and talk to yourself. You'll get better results than with nonverbal methods. In fact, the more senses you involve whenever you're trying to learn something, the better. That's why taking notes when you read helps you learn more efficiently and why schools use audiovisual materials. Studies on learning efficiency show that people remember only about 10 percent of what they read and 30 percent of what they see happening around them. But they remember 90 percent of the self-instruction they give themselves while carrying out a particular activity.

5. *Improve your listening skills.* Dr. Robert McMillan, an expert in communications skills, estimates that 70 percent of your waking day is spent in verbal communication. Of that time, almost half is given over to listening to others. It makes sense, he concludes, to improve listening skills, since most people operate at only a 25 percent level of efficiency. Even though most of his suggestions for improving listening skills make good sense, few people take the time to apply them. For example, Dr. McMillan advises that when you're listening to someone, concentrate as if you're determined to learn something useful. Keep your emotions under control, for once you're emotionally aroused you'll probably stop listening. Try to pick out the speaker's main ideas and focus on them rather than try to memorize a lot of facts. Finally, Dr. McMillan notes that people speak at about 100 words per minute, but you think at about 400 wpm. Since you can literally "think circles" around any speaker, it's easy to drift off into some nondirected thinking of your own.

COMMON TYPES OF PROBLEM SOLVING

Ready for another puzzle? This one would have challenged Edison or Einstein. Look at the matchsticks in Figure 10.8. They've been arranged to form the Roman numerals VI = II. Obviously, six doesn't equal two in any numbering system, so your job is to move one of the matchsticks into a new position to create a correct equation. (The answer can be found on page 354.) Here are the ways people go about solving problems.

TRIAL AND ERROR.   Before Thomas Edison found the carbonized thread that served as the filament in his first light bulb, he tested hundreds of materials. Animals use *trial-and-error methods* randomly, as Thorndike proved with his cats in the puzzle boxes (see page 322). Skilled problem solvers, however, use this technique in a methodical fashion. They start by ignoring possibilities that obviously won't work. Edison, for example, didn't waste time trying to use cooked spaghetti as a filament. As problem solvers eliminate each of the more likely possibilities, they are left with fewer places to look for the correct answer. Mechanics call this troubleshooting. That's a shorthand way of saying, "I've got a mental list of all the reasons why this machine usually breaks down. Now I'm going to check out each of them until I find out what went wrong."

You can try trial and error when you tackle the matchstick puzzle. That means moving each matchstick to every possible position and evaluating the results. If you have enough patience this type of brute force approach will yield a solution—but only if you're alert to unexpected possibilities.

INDUCTIVE AND DEDUCTIVE REASONING. To reason is to reach a conclusion by systematically collecting data and thinking through a problem or situation. *Inductive reasoning* uses specific cases as the basis for establishing a principle or generalization. Suppose, for example, that every time you see a horror movie you have trouble sleeping for the next few nights. Since you normally sleep like a log, you can reason inductively that watching horror movies interferes with your sleep. Similarly, a research psychologist might use inductive reasoning while testing the effects of overcrowding on rats. If the rats respond to overcrowding by developing signs of neurotic behavior, such as fighting and not caring for their young, the researcher can induce a principle: Overcrowding causes disturbed behavior in rats.

Deductive reasoning, by contrast, uses general principles to provide a prediction or insight into specific cases. You might deduce, for example, that going to see a Marx Brothers comedy won't interfere with your sleep because you've seen many of their films and none ever has. In the same way, a scientist who has taught numerous pigeons to play table tennis can deduce that Pigeon K-4 will learn to play table tennis if given the same training.

Will either type of reasoning work with the matchstick puzzle? You can deduce that obvious solutions won't work, or it wouldn't be much of a puzzle. For that reason, you can stop trying to make the VI into $\frac{\text{II}}{\text{I}}$. Remember, you're only allowed to move *one* matchstick.

INSIGHT. Have you ever experienced an "Aha" reaction? Perhaps it happened the last time you were stumped by a problem. You tried one approach and then another, but nothing budged. Then, suddenly, a great idea popped into your head. You said "Aha!"— and happily put your solution to work.

That's *insight,* the sudden perception of key relationships that leads directly to a solution. Wolfgang Köhler's chimpanzee, Sultan, figured in one of the important early demonstrations of insight over 60 years ago. Köhler, a Gestalt psychologist, thought that animals were capable of more than trial-and-

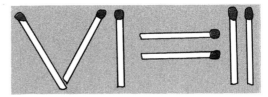

FIGURE 10.8

error learning. He gave Sultan a stick, then dropped a banana outside the cage. Sultan soon learned to use the stick to rake in the banana. But then Köhler changed the problem by giving the chimp two shorter bamboo sticks. Only if Sultan fitted the sticks together would he be able to reach another banana. Sultan tried one stick and then the other. No luck. Frustrated, he took the sticks and sat in a corner. After a period of apparent thought, he slipped the smaller stick into the hollow end of the longer one. Then, clutching the new, longer tool, he raced to the side of the cage and raked in his prize.

As Sultan discovered, insight usually comes only after some hard thinking. Perhaps insight is a right-brain activity, not reachable through directed thinking. Insights often come when you're relaxed, when you've "turned off" your directed thinking for a while. One good rule for applying insight is to "sleep on it." Review every aspect of the problem just before you drift off, thus programming your unconscious to work while you sleep. In many cases, the solution will appear in a dream or will be waiting in your conscious mind when you wake up.

Now, have you solved that matchstick puzzle? The people who do solve it report that the solution usually comes through insight. What if the answer required the use of mathematical signs as well as numbers? Check your solution against the answer on page 354.

MIND SET

When a certain way of thinking becomes habitual, that mental position is called a *mind set.* If Evan is convinced that the hometown

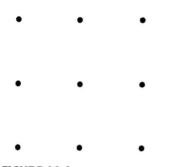

FIGURE 10.9

FIGURE 10.11 ▦ Problem: How can you use the one saucer to keep both cups of coffee warm? (See page 355 for the solution.)

team is the best baseball team in the league, it's doubtful that he'll listen to a reasoned argument as to why they won't win the pennant. When it comes to problem solving, mind set can either help or hinder you. For example, if you believe that speed is important in solving math problems, you'll probably accept a higher error rate than someone who thinks that accuracy is more important than speed.

FIGURE 10.10 ▦ The problem here is to tie the two strings together. They're far enough apart so that you can't hold on to one and reach the other. Once you overcome functional fixedness regarding the screwdriver, the solution becomes obvious. (See page 355 for the answer.)

344

Mind set can also lead people to assume limitations that don't really exist. As an example, try the problem in Figure 10.9. Copy the nine dots on a separate sheet of paper. The challenge is to draw four straight, connected lines that touch all nine dots. You may not lift your pencil off the paper.

Any luck? Before you look at page 355, ask yourself, "Am I placing any restrictions on my search for a solution that aren't really there?"

Mind set can hinder problem solving in two ways. *Rigidity* leads people to cling to a behavior because it once worked, even though circumstances have changed.

Functional fixedness is the inability to imagine new uses for familiar objects. As an example of functional fixedness, look at the problem in Figure 10.10.

The woman who replaces a lost hinge pin on a pair of sunglasses with a paper clip has overcome functional fixedness. And so has the man who figured out a way to keep his coffee warm. How did he solve his problem? (See Figure 10.11.)

IMPROVING YOUR ABILITY TO SOLVE PROBLEMS

Problem solving, it turns out, depends more on knowing how to define a problem and search for solutions than on an IQ score. In this section, you'll learn two strategies for attacking problems. One method uses a type of directed thinking called vertical thinking; the second uses a type of nondirected thinking called lateral thinking.

VERTICAL THINKING. A logical, straight-line approach often works quite well. Let's say you are determined to improve your grade in psychology. The determination to change old behaviors is the first step. Without sufficient motivation you probably won't be able to see the process through to completion.

1. The first step is to gather every scrap of information that applies to the problem. Consider your feelings about the class. Take an objective look at your study habits. Zero in on the specific factors that contribute to your lack of success. An old misunderstanding with the teacher may be distracting you, or you may not be setting aside enough time for reading outside of class. Some of this data may turn out to be useless, but you can't take the next step until you've fully defined the problem.

2. Make a list of all the ways you can improve your performance. A typical list will include extra study time, working with a tutor, resolving to take an active role in class discussions, talking to the teacher about your work, and so on. Write down every possibility that comes to mind. You can discard the less useful ideas later.

3. Commit yourself to a plan of action. You'll probably choose the approach that seems most logical, but it's okay to play a hunch. Discuss your decision with someone you trust, such as the teacher or a counselor. Above all, stay flexible. Be ready to throw out what doesn't work and try something else.

4. Dig in and implement your plan. After a week or two, evaluate your progress. Is your plan working? You can use your grades as a yardstick, but your own sense of progress also counts. If you don't see any change in a reasonable period of time, go back to step one. Use your experience of the past few weeks as a guide in drawing up a revised action plan. Then try again.

LATERAL THINKING. Edward de Bono (see BioBox, page 346) identified a nondirective type of thinking that's useful for problems that don't lend themselves to straight-line, vertical thinking. He calls it *lateral thinking* and defines it as a way of freeing the mind to use its creative potential. Remember Sultan and his two sticks? Dr. de Bono wants you to use insight to solve problems when other approaches don't work.

Look at the following puzzle. The driver must maneuver his truck through the underpass and deliver a load of emergency medicines. The underpass is inches too low, the truck can't be unloaded, and to back up and find another route will take hours. What can the driver do?

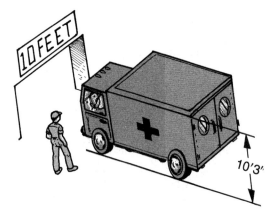

FIGURE 10.12

Conventional problem solving won't work here. Breaking loose from rigid patterns of thinking, however, will lead you to a quick, neat solution. While you're mulling over the problem, take a look at some of de Bono's suggestions for improving your lateral thinking.

1. *Open yourself up to alternatives.* If obvious solutions don't work, look for other possibilities. Forget for the moment about a *best* way and look at all ways. An old saying sums up the way of the lateral thinker: "If you can't raise the bridge, lower the river."

Edward de Bono:
The Case for Lateral Thinking

Dr. Edward de Bono (1933–   ), a man who thinks about thinking, reasons that the brain is an information processing system that does more than store data like a computer. Instead, it picks and chooses and alters the information it receives.

A native of Malta, de Bono came to his study of thinking and brain function as both a medical doctor and a student of philosophy. He is best known for his concept of lateral thinking, a way of solving problems when neither trial and error nor directed thinking (De Bono calls it vertical thinking) will work. De Bono tells a story about himself that illustrates how easily people can allow mind set to make their lives more complicated:

While he was a student at Oxford, de Bono came back late from a party. Finding the gates locked, he climbed one fence and then another. At that point he discovered that he was outside again; he had climbed in and out across a corner. On his second try, he found the proper second wall. The wall's iron gate, he noticed, offered better footholds than the stone wall itself. A few minutes later, as he was sitting astride the gate, it swung open. Feeling foolish for having climbed an unlocked gate, de Bono jumped down and went on to his room.

How would lateral thinking have helped de Bono avoid his futile climb? If he'd started by checking out the alternatives, he would have tried the gate *before* he started climbing.

When he processes information, de Bono expects to be wrong part of the time. Lateral thinking, he says, restructures incorrect data by reducing the gap between the current arrangement you hold in your mind and the best possible arrangement. His concepts have been put to use by some of the world's largest companies, including IBM, Shell, and General Foods. His 1992 book, *Serious Creativity: Using the Power of Lateral Thinking to Create New Ideas,* updated and expanded his ideas. De Bono's students—whether they're grade schoolers or corporate executives—find that they soon begin to think more clearly and creatively. Lateral thinking, they say, also leads to improved communication and decision making.

De Bono likes to remind his listeners that "thinking is the ultimate human resource. Yet we can never be satisfied with our most important skill. No matter how good we become, we should always want to be better."

Can you think of a problem you've faced recently that could be solved more efficiently by lateral thinking? Why not give it a try? There's no law that says life's problems can be solved only by vertical thinking.

2. *Undo your selection process*. Avoid the logical, step-by-step approach that works so well for most problems. The goal is to make sure that no useful solution is ignored. In short, avoid mind set. You don't need to justify each step according to "rightness" or logic. The only test is "Does it work?"

3. *Shift your attention*. If you can't find a solution to the problem, perhaps you can change the problem. This is called *transfer*. You can see the technique illustrated in the case of the carpenter who decided to steal wheelbarrows from the factory where he worked. Each day at quitting time the carpenter showed up at the factory gate, pushing a wheelbarrow filled with trash. The guards at the gate couldn't find anything hidden in the trash, so they waved the man through. If they'd transferred their attention from the trash to the wheelbarrows, they'd have caught their thief.

Still working on getting that truck through the underpass? Since you can't raise the underpass, can you lower the road? (Sorry, it's reinforced concrete. Try again.)

4. *Try brainstorming*. When several people get together and start throwing out ideas, each new idea tends to spark several others. Out of the blizzard of useless or bizarre proposals generated by a typical *brainstorming* session, a few ideas of genuine merit often emerge. The primary rule of brainstorming is that no one is allowed to poke fun at anyone's ideas. A few "That's stupid!" comments will quickly short circuit the nondirective thinking necessary to good brainstorming.

Okay, how are you going to get that truck through the underpass? You couldn't raise the underpass or lower the road. So why not lower the truck! Perhaps you could hacksaw a few inches off the top, but there's an easier way. Start by letting some air out of each tire. When the truck settles low enough, the driver can maneuver it through the underpass. Then, after pumping up the tires again, he'll be on his way. That's lateral thinking!

FIGURE 10.13

Want to try another one? While changing a flat tire far from any garage, a driver lost the lug nuts that fasten the wheel to the car (Figure 10.13). How would you solve the problem? Once again, lateral thinking will save the day. (See page 355 for the solution.)

■ SECTION CHECKUP

1 What advice would you give to friends who want to improve their learning skills?

2 What is the difference between trial-and-error problem solving and using insight to solve problems? Give an example of a problem that would be solved best by trial and error and one in which you should depend on insight.

3 Why does mind set get in the way of problem solving?

4 What is lateral thinking? Name some of the rules that would help you use this type of nondirected thinking.

10.5 ▨ HOW CAN YOU IMPROVE YOUR CREATIVITY?

Have you ever made something original, useful, or beautiful? Did you ever solve a problem in an unexpected way? Perhaps you made decorations for a friend's party, scored a touchdown on a clever new play, or raised money for your club by organizing a monster-movie festival. If so, that reorganization of old ideas and processes into something novel and useful demonstrated your *creativity*.

Being creative makes people feel good. Creative thought gives you the sensation of being original, of doing something no one else has done. Psychologists estimate that only about 1 percent of the population is capable of highly creative thought. But almost all people can develop a greater degree of creativity. You may never discover antigravity or write a great novel, but you can probably do more original thinking than you give yourself credit for.

A CREATIVITY TEST

The following exercises will help you measure your creativity. Allow two minutes for each item.

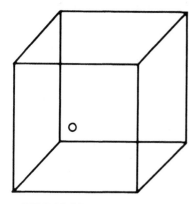

FIGURE 10.14

1. Look steadily at the drawing in Figure 10.14. How many times does the small circle move from back to front (or vice versa) in two minutes?

2. Name as many objects as you can that are white, soft, and edible.

3. How many uses can you think of for a piece of brown paper?

Finished? Don't look at the analysis until you've done the tests.

Test 1. Count 1 for each change in perspective. The more often the cube flips back and forth, the more flexible you are. Score: 1–3 changes, low creativity; 4–5, average; over 5, high creativity.

Test 2. Count 1 point for each answer. Score: 0–5, low creativity; 6–10, average; over 10, high. Typical answers include marshmallows, mushrooms, white bread, noodles, and yogurt. But did you think of bean curd, divinity fudge, shredded coconut, vanilla frosting, or (shudder) grubs?

Test 3. Count 1 for each answer. Count 2 for truly original uses. Typical answers include wrapping a package, writing a letter, starting a fire, and making a paper airplane. More creative uses include drawing a treasure map, plugging up a sink, mending a torn kite, or making a mask. Score: 0–5, low creativity; 6–10, average; over 10, high.

What does your score mean? Not a great deal, except for giving you a little insight into how the creative mind works. Neither creative nor noncreative people have a monopoly on happiness or intelligence. Some jobs reward creativity more than others, but there are just as many careers for hardworking, low-creative people as for brilliant innovators—probably more, in fact. The key point is that you had a potential for creativity when

▓ PRO & CON:

Should Schools Teach Creative Thought?

No one seems satisfied with what U.S. schools teach or with how they teach it. Along with the old "Johnny can't read" criticism, schools are also being attacked for not developing creative thought in their students. Typically, the "Pro" argument for teaching creative thought says that children start out brimming over with creative ideas, but that rigid and subject-centered teaching soon discourages them. In a debate, the argument would sound like this.

PRO

1 Most schools teach traditional methods of problem solving. They apparently believe that creative thinking interferes with such teaching.

2 Children who show signs of creative thought are often singled out as "different," and pressures are placed on them to conform.

3 Creative thinkers do not always score well on IQ tests, which reward straight-line thinking. As a result, creative children are often put in classes that do not challenge or reward their special skills.

4 Too many teachers treat creative children as discipline problems. Teachers of this type often turn creative thinkers into either sheep or rebels.

5 Because few teachers think creatively themselves, most do not understand the needs of the creative minority. Left unchallenged and unrewarded, creativity soon dies.

CON

1 Society has a right to insist that children be taught to think logically. Creative thought cannot be taught. Either children have it or they don't.

2 Critics often mistake lack of discipline for creative thought. Even highly creative people need to learn basic skills and study traditional subjects.

3 IQ scores are only one of several criteria used for placing children in a class suited to their abilities. Whatever the placement, if creative children outperform their classmates, most teachers quickly recommend a transfer to higher-level classes.

4 Schools must handle many children at a time. The so-called creative youngsters often interfere with the right of other children to learn.

5 The schools offer all students many opportunities for developing creative thought and expression. Most teachers cherish creative thinkers and give them as much attention as they can.

Can you remember any school experiences that would support either side of this argument? If you were a parent, would you want traditional subjects and strict discipline in the classroom? Or would you prefer a more open classroom, where children can learn and create according to their own needs and abilities?

you were a child. You can still fulfill that potential if you're willing to work at it.

ELEMENTS OF CREATIVITY

Creative thinking requires that you actively seek new answers to old questions. The elements necessary for that type of thinking include flexibility, persistence, and insight.

FLEXIBILITY.   Rigid thinking defeats creativity. *Flexibility,* which is a willingness to adopt new ideas, is the opposite of functional fixedness. Flexible thinking leads to nonrigid, creative solutions. When asked what can be done with a brick, the rigid person thinks mainly of doorstops or bookends. A flexible thinker, however, comes up with more original uses: a step for watching parades, a marker for drawing on the sidewalk, a tombstone for a pet animal's grave, and so on.

PERSISTENCE. Creative solutions don't always come to mind quickly. You must keep working at the problem, even after you've tried dozens of ideas that didn't pay off. Almost all great inventions have been the products of *persistence* by highly creative people. If Edison hadn't persisted in his research, the electric light might not have been developed until years later.

INSIGHT. Flexibility and persistence often combine to produce the breakthrough idea, or *insight* (see also page 343). The insight itself may come as a blinding flash of inspiration or in a dream, but it doesn't happen if the necessary preparation has been ignored. People had been growing and eating peanuts and sweet potatoes for centuries, but it remained for George Washington Carver to see the possibilities in these simple crops. Out of the peanut, for example, he developed some 300 synthetic products, including milk, butter, cheese, coffee, flour, breakfast food, ink, dyes, soap, wood stains, and insulating board. Such insights are payoffs for years of patient preparation. When a creative thinker invests that type of effort, the rewards can be great, both for the individual and for society.

IMPROVING CREATIVITY

Creativity comes in various forms. Mozart literally "heard" symphonies in his head and wrote them down. The words to "The Battle Hymn of the Republic" came to Julia Ward Howe in a dream. Faced with "instant" creativity of this sort, many people assume that creative thought is beyond their reach. This assumption might be termed the ultimate mind set, at least as far as creativity is concerned: "I know I can't do it, so I won't embarrass myself by trying." But techniques do exist for improving the creative abilities of any person.

PRESCHOOL CHILDREN. With preschool children, play provides an important opportunity for creative expression. Infants in their cribs and playpens profit from an abundance of simple, colorful toys and mobiles. If you want to develop creativity in three-year-old Jocelyn, for example, you could start by giving her a "supertoy"—a sturdy child-sized table equipped with levers, buzzers, bells, and counting devices. Each time Jocelyn moves a lever, buzzers sound, bells ring, colored disks move up and down, and so on. Jocelyn will spend a lot of time with her supertoy, because it has so many interesting things to see, hear, push, pull, touch, and investigate. If you test Jocelyn for creativity four years later, you'll probably find that she'll score higher than children who didn't have the same opportunities.

Child psychologists urge parents to allow their children to express their own views of the world. When children color the sky purple and the grass orange, adults are advised to admire their originality. Freehand drawing, no matter how simple, is better than the traditional coloring book with its preset limits on where to color. Children's fantasies should also be encouraged. Authority figures who insist on blue sky, green grass, and a world without imaginary animals soon convince youngsters that creativity doesn't pay off—and that conformity does.

OLDER CHILDREN AND ADULTS. You don't have to be a child to enjoy your own "supertoy." Games and puzzles that reward insight and ingenuity are both fun and mindstretching. Scrabble, Pictionary, charades, handicrafts, cooking, painting, ceramics, creative writing, chess, and other challenging activities fit into this category. Personal computers loaded with challenging software can tap into unexpected reservoirs of creativity. Sports and games, when played for the sheer joy of competing, can fill the same need. Continuing education classes, whether taken on a college campus or at a nearby adult school, provide unlimited opportuni-tiets for exploring new ideas and learning new skills.

Too many people give up because they listen to the voice inside their heads that says, "Don't take the risk. You'll surely fail." Per-haps it's true that you'll never be a David Hockney, a Jonas Salk, a Michael Jordan, or a John Lennon. So? Who's to say that growing a beautiful rose or surfing a perfect wave isn't just as creative? You can tap into that well-spring of creativity that exists in all of us—but only if you're willing to try. The decision is up to you.

■ SECTION CHECKUP

1 How would you define creativity? Give an example of noncreative uses for a paper clip. Now give some creative uses for the same paper clip.

2 How do flexibility, persistence, and insight relate to creativity?

3 What can parents do to encourage creativity in their children?

FIGURE 10.15 ■ Creative thought at its best led to the design of this solar-powered vehicle, which won a solar car rally in Japan. If the sup-porters of solar power have their way, it won't be long before descendants of such vehicles replace their smog-producing cousins on the nation's highways.

LOOKING BACK: A SUMMARY

1 Learning is a lasting change in your be-havior or performance brought about by study, training, or experience. Psychologists have two major theories about how learning occurs. Stimulus-response $(S \rightarrow R)$ theory puts emphasis on the relationship between a stimulus (any event or impulse) and the re-sponse (the resulting behavior). Successful responses are learned and become part of behavior; unsuccessful responses fade away. Edward Thorndike thought that learning is basically trial and error. B. F. Skinner added the concept of operant behaviors: those com-plex reactions to stimuli that the subject

chooses in order to gain a reward or avoid a punishment. Operant behaviors can be in-creased by reward (positive reinforcement) and extinguished by punishment. Signals trig-ger operant behaviors by alerting the subject to the reward or punishment to follow. More stable operant behaviors can be obtained by a schedule of reinforcement that rewards the behavior only part of the time.

2 Cognitive-learning theorists believe that stimulus-response theory ignores the higher mental processes. Human learning, they say, results from new understandings built up of individual experiences. Cognitive-learning theorists accept the influence of S → R learning, but they also believe that humans recognize the joy of learning for its own sake and can choose a mode of behavior without going through a conditioning process.

3 A number of factors influence the learning process. These include one's self-concept, past experiences, intelligence, motivations, and emotions. Rewards and punishments, feedback, guidance, and novelty also play a role. Learning can—and does—take place under almost any circumstance. Peak learning takes place when learners work within their own learning profiles and when they receive encouragement and assistance from family, friends, teachers, employers, and coworkers.

4 The electrochemical process called *memory* seems to be located generally in the cerebral cortex. New information is stored in networks of neurons by specially coded RNA molecules. When a new stimulus triggers these neurons, you "remember" the original data. Experiments show that learned behaviors can apparently be transferred by feeding or injecting untrained animals with material from the brains of trained animals.

5 Three types of memory serve your body's different needs. (a) Sensory memory receives data from the senses and almost immediately discards what you don't need. Important information is called to your attention. (b) Short-term memory provides a 20-second "holding tank" for processing words, numbers, sounds, and other stimuli. Any data that's not rehearsed is discarded. (c) Long-term memory stores the permanent data and experiences of a lifetime. Remembering is based on what you retain in long-term memory. Most memories are triggered by cues and stimuli from the environment, a process known as *recall* or *recollection*. Recognition is a visual form of memory retrieval, while forgetting is an inability to retrieve information from long-term memory. People forget because stored data is blocked, distorted, repressed, or fades through disuse.

6 Research is well advanced on a family of drugs that promise to improve memory, concentration, and alertness. Donepezil is one of several drugs being used to treat the memory and learning disabilities that mark the progress of Alzheimer's disease. Another group of drugs that improve overall brain function may one day help the average person improve his or her learning ability. The researchers who are developing these powerful drugs warn that they should not be used carelessly, but people seeking enhanced mental abilities are experimenting with herbal remedies, "smart drinks," and "smart drugs."

7 Cognition includes thinking, remembering, problem solving, and creativity. Thinking is the process of gathering, classifying, and using the data stored in long-term memory. Images, symbols, concepts, and rules are used in the thinking process, which can be either directed or nondirected. Directed thinking moves in a straight line from point A to point B, and so on. Nondirected thinking relies on images and feelings, as in fantasies and daydreams. Images are pictorial recalls of specific objects or events. Symbols, particularly words, allow you to label objects and events and to deal with abstractions. Concepts enable you to put things into categories and to establish relationships. Rules define the relationships that exist between concepts, establish standards for behavior, and explain how things work.

8 Language plays a vital role in thinking. Babies develop language skills in predictable steps, for they are apparently born with a capacity for learning the complex structure of spoken language. Language interacts with culture, one influencing the other.

9 A problem-solving situation occurs whenever needs are blocked or a question needs answering. Good problem solvers are also good learners. They know how to use learning techniques such as overlearning, removal of negative conditions, use of different types of practice, verbalization, and improvement of listening skills. Typical methods of problem solving include trial and error (using all possible solutions until the right one is found), inductive reasoning (using particular facts to reach general conclusions), deductive reasoning (using general principles to solve specific cases), and insight (the sudden perception of key relationships).

10 Mind set is a person's consistent way of thinking about a particular situation or problem. Rigidity means that someone will continue using a certain behavior even when it doesn't work any longer. Functional fixedness keeps people from finding new uses for familiar objects. Vertical (directive) thinking provides a logical, step-by-step approach to problem solving. Lateral (nondirective)

thinking teaches you how to break rigid patterns of thinking by freely considering new and unexpected alternatives.

11 Creativity is the reorganization of old ideas and processes into something novel or useful. Only a few people are highly creative, but others can improve their creativity by learning how to free their minds from self-imposed restrictions. Creative thinking requires flexibility (the willingness to give up nonproductive ways of thinking), persistence (the willingness to keep working when the first attempts don't pay off), and insight (the breakthrough that allows for recombination of existing materials or ideas). Creativity can be nurtured or improved by encouraging creative thought in young children. Stimulating toys and games and other ways of rewarding imagination seem to help. Older children and adults can profit from activities such as games, handicrafts, and artistic pursuits that encourage creativity.

PUTTING YOUR KNOWLEDGE TO WORK

■ TERMS YOU SHOULD KNOW

bond	insight	rehearsal
brainstorming	lateral thinking	respondent behavior
classical conditioning	learning	rigidity
cognition	long-term memory	rules
cognitive theory	memory	sensory memory
concepts	mind set	short-term memory
creativity	mnemonic devices	signals
deductive reasoning	nondirected thinking	stimulus-response theory
directed thinking	operant behavior	stringer
eidetic recall	overlearning	symbols
flexibility	persistence	thinking
functional fixedness	positive reinforcement	trial and error
grouper	punishment	variable-interval reinforcement
image	recall	verbalization
inductive reasoning	recognition	vertical thinking

Solution to Figure 10.7 (page 341)

Since Harry isn't talking, there may be many different reasons to explain his change in spending habits. Here are some sample explanations. How many more did you write down?

1. Harry just learned that he has an incurable illness and wants to enjoy his money before he dies.

2. Harry just won a lottery and is celebrating his good fortune.

3. Harry has inherited a fortune from a rich aunt and is determined to enjoy his new wealth.

4. Harry's wife has filed for divorce. He's spending as much money as he can so he won't have the cash to pay her demands for alimony.

5. Harry has had a nervous breakdown and isn't aware of what he's doing.

And so on. Try this problem with a group of friends. It's not only fun, it's also a good exercise for developing your thinking abilities. Brains improve with exercise, just as muscles do.

Solution to Figure 10.8 (page 343)

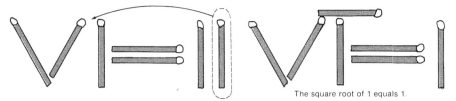

The square root of 1 equals 1.

You should also give yourself credit for either of these alternative answers:

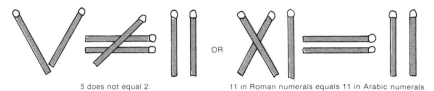

5 does not equal 2.   OR   11 in Roman numerals equals 11 in Arabic numerals.

■ CHAPTER CHECKUP

1 Which statement best summarizes the importance of Koko the gorilla's use of sign language? (*a*) Koko's thinking skills are probably equal to those of human beings. (*b*) Gorillas should be reclassified as members of the species *Homo sapiens*. (*c*) Koko's language skills demonstrate an ability to think and reason at a level higher than any other animal has yet shown. (*d*) Koko's "speech" is nothing more than copycat behavior, similar to the speech of a parrot.

2 Which of the following would *not* be considered an example of learning? (*a*) You touch a hot kettle and instantly pull your hand away. (*b*) You master the art of baiting a fishing hook. (*c*) You travel in Mexico and become comfortable with the different customs. (*d*) You complete a backpacking trip over a mountain trail you've never seen before.

3 A dictator who wanted to train a generation of children to obey any order without question would be most likely to use (*a*) classical respondent conditioning techniques (*b*) operant condi-

Solution to Figure 10.9 (page 344)

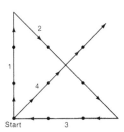

Many people make the assumption that they must stay *within* the square formed by the nine dots. Once you break free of this unnecessary mind set, a solution becomes possible.

Solution to Figure 10.10 (page 344)

As soon as you realize that the screwdriver can be used as a weight instead of a tool, the problem is solved.

Solution to Figure 10.11 (page 344)

Use one of the cups to cover the other. Then put the saucer on top.

Solution to Figure 10.13 (page 347)

Borrow one nut from each of the other wheels. Then drive slowly to the nearest repair shop.

tioning techniques (*c*) the cognitive theory of learning (*d*) none of these. People cannot be conditioned to behave in ways that violate basic human values.

4 If you were writing a story in which mad scientists set out to destroy people's ability to form new long-term memories, you would have them destroy (*a*) the hippocampus (*b*) the visual cortex (*c*) the memory center (*d*) any part of the old brain.

5 The process that allows you to move data from short-term memory into long-term memory is (*a*)

retrieval (*b*) recall (*c*) reinforcement (*d*) rehearsal.

6 Sheila says, "I don't remember anything the nuclear power company president said. I'm against building nuclear generating plants anyway." Her statement suggests that she's demonstrating a type of forgetting known as (*a*) interference effect (*b*) distortion (*c*) repression (*d*) decay through disuse.

7 Which of the following is an example of nondirected thinking? (*a*) Susan plans a hiking trip through the High Sierras. (*b*) Tom lies in a hammock, watching the clouds form patterns in the sky. (*c*) Pete works through a series of geometry problems. (*d*) Mrs. Thorne tries to figure out how to make the food budget stretch to the end of the month.

8 When someone solves a problem unexpectedly after working on it for a long time, the solution is said to come through (*a*) positive reinforcement (*b*) rigidity (*c*) assimilation (*d*) insight.

9 All of the following are techniques of lateral thinking *except* (*a*) brainstorming (*b*) opening up to alternatives (*c*) shifting attention (*d*) inductive reasoning.

10 Which of the following is a *true* statement regarding creativity? (*a*) All people have the same potential for creativity. (*b*) Mind set is a useful aid to creativity. (*c*) Creative people stick to straight-line thinking when solving problems. (*d*) Even noncreative people can improve their ability to think creatively.

▪ EXPLORING CONCEPTS

1 Imagine that someone has just given you a six-week-old puppy. It's your job to train the dog to be a well-behaved member of the family. How could learning theory help you? Why would stimulus-response learning theory work better in training the puppy than cognitive theory?

2 What are the three types of memory? Why do you think humans need all three? If everything people learn is stored in long-term memory, why do they still forget things?

3 How does straight-line, vertical thinking differ from lateral thinking? Which would be better for solving a problem in mathematics? Which would be better for figuring out a way to increase attendance at school dances? Why?

4 How can teachers and parents encourage creativity in a young child?

5 How does mind set interfere with problem solving? Why would brainstorming be a useful method of overcoming rigid thinking and functional fixedness?

▪ HANDS-ON ACTIVITIES

1 Compile a number of puzzles, some easy, some difficult. (James Fixx's two books, *Games for the*

Superintelligent and *More Games for the Superintelligent* are good sources.) Give the puzzles to several friends and relatives. Pay special attention to their problem-solving techniques. Note the types of reasoning they use, how long they persist, what role insight plays in their thinking. You may find a few people who immediately say, "I can't do puzzles" and refuse to try. What does that tell you about their mind set?

2 Would your relatives or friends make reliable witnesses? Set up a test for them, following this general procedure: At a time when you have a group of people together (a family get-together would be perfect), arrange for several "actors" to put on a dramatic scene. It can involve a fight or an accident. The entire scene should not take longer than a minute. As soon as it's over, ask each witness to write an account of what he or she saw happen. Do not let the witnesses talk to one another. Collect the reports and compare them. You'll probably find a wide diversity of opinion as to what actually happened. Why?

3 Research the current developments in the use of drugs that enhance learning by altering brain chemistry. Try an Internet search engine such as <*www.google.com*>, or use the library's *Readers' Guide to Periodical Literature* to search for articles in current news and science magazines. How close are learning-enhancing drugs to wide-spread use? What restrictions should be placed on their use? Report on your findings to your psychology class.

4 A simple, interesting exercise in creativity can take place either in a classroom or with a group of friends. Start the exercise by inventing a main character and a situation. Take your hero to a cliff-hanging moment, and then pass the story on to the next person to continue. Each person adds his or her own creative touches and sets up wilder adventures for the next storyteller. The experience will undoubtedly have its humorous moments. But it also has the potential to inspire unsuspected creativity in just about everyone.

5 You can set up your own learning experiment by first making a simple maze for your subjects to "run." On an 8″ × 18″ piece of wood, Celotex, or wallboard, stick thumbtacks as shown in the dia-

gram at the top of this page. Each tack should just touch the next. Do not show the maze to your subjects (Ss). Blindfold each S and ask him or her to find a path through the maze by tracing it with a finger. As the experimenter (E), your job is to time each trial and keep a record of the number of errors each S makes during each trial. Allow ten trials for each S. Anyone who solves the maze twice in succession without an error can stop. Afterward, use your data to draw conclusions about the performance of your Ss. For example, did age or sex make any difference in their performance? Did the Ss use strictly trial-and-error learning, or did they show some cognitive learning? Did any of the Ss show more persistence than others?

FOR FURTHER READING

Gross, Ronald. *Peak Learning*. Los Angeles: Jeremy Tarcher, Inc., 1999. This well-designed paperback uses the latest research in neuroscience, cognitive studies, and developmental psychology to help you become what Gross describes as a "peak learner." His insights include ways of using the computer to help you develop a clear, systematic set of learning techniques.

Higbee, Kenneth. *Your Memory: How It Works and How to Improve It*. Englewood Cliffs, NJ: Marlowe & Co., 2001. If you want to do a better job of remembering the important stuff, from shopping lists to Aunt Ida's birthday, this is the book for you. Higbee provides easy-to-follow memory techniques that will help you expand your natural abilities well beyond what you thought possible. The bottom line: a well-honed memory is a big step toward better grades.

Keyes, Daniel. *Flowers for Algernon*. New York: Harcourt Brace Jovanovich, 1984. Charly Gordon is retarded—until doctors perform an operation that turns him into a genius. You'll never think of the retarded in the same way again after reading this book, which also became a successful movie called *Charly*.

Myers, Tona Pearce, ed. *The Soul of Creativity: Insights into the Creative Process*. Novato, CA: New World Library, 1999. What is creativity? Instead of offering a definition, this fine collection lets you discover the answer for yourself. Each aspect of creativity is discussed and illustrated in a thoughtful essay contributed by a renowned teacher, artist, or spiritual leader. Their stories focus on the role creativity has played in their lives.

Turkington, Carol, and Joseph Harris. *Understanding Memory: The Sourcebook of Memory and Memory Disorders*. New York: Checkmark Books, 2001. Do you have an elderly relative who is suffering from memory loss? You'll find an up-to-date explanation for that all-too-common dilemma in this detailed look at memory and memory dysfunction. Along the way, the authors explore a broad range of memory-related topics, including absentmindedness, childhood memories, posthypnotic suggestion, and how to improve long-term memory.

von Oech, Roger. *A Whack on the Side of the Head*. New York: Time Warner, 1998. Far too many authors who tackle the subject of creativity undercut their message by taking themselves too seriously. Roger von Oech doesn't make that mistake. When von Oech counsels the use of humor in problem solving, for example, he writes, "Go ahead and be whacky. Get into a crazy frame of mind and ask what's funny about what you're doing." His book helps set the proper mood with its generous use of cartoons, puzzles, and anecdotes.

357

Chapter

11 PSYCHOLOGICAL TESTING

FIGURE 11.1

Did you look at the picture above this paragraph before you started reading? If you're like most people, you probably glanced at it and then went on. In a moment, though, you'll be asked to take a longer look.

Is this some sort of memory test? No, it's not even one of those tricky questions psychologists sometimes spring on unwary subjects. No hidden figures lurk in the shadows. You won't be asked to remember whether or not the woman is wearing an apron. The picture *is* part of a test, however.

Ready? Look carefully at the picture for a full minute. Think about the tiny slice of life that's been captured by the camera. When you're ready, make up a story based on what you see happening in that doorway. Describe

the events that took place just before the picture was taken, as well as the scene in front of you. You can write your story on a piece of paper or you can compose it in your head. When you've finished, go on to the explanation below.

You've just completed a test item similar to those found in a number of personality tests. When interpreted by a *psychometrist* (a specialist in psychological testing), these tests provide useful clues about the test taker's emotions, interests, values, and thought processes. Interpretation can be difficult, for no two people respond exactly alike to test items such as this one. For example, 18-year-old Marian made up this story:

> It's one o'clock, and the cop is bringing Frank home for breaking curfew again. Mrs. Smith is worried, but she feels helpless. She's just been divorced, and without a father around, Frank won't listen to her. The cop doesn't understand the problem. He's warning her that Frank is on the way to becoming a gangbanger. What is Frank thinking? I don't know. He's pretty mixed up. Maybe Mrs. Smith should whack him a few times.

Marian obviously saw elements in the picture that reflected some of her own feelings and experiences. Perhaps in your story you identified with one of the people in the picture. If you took the boy's point of view, for example, it might mean that you're relating to a similar incident in your own life. In the same way, your description of the woman and the man wearing the helmet might reveal your general attitude toward authority figures. Did you agree with Marian that the man is a police officer? Most people do, but the man is actually a messenger for a motorcycle delivery service.

The psychometrists who evaluate test responses look for recurring themes, such as hostilities, fears, and anxieties. Although they tend to focus on negative traits, they'll also be alert to interpretations that point to positive outlooks on life.

In contrast with Marian's story, this one was written by 16-year-old Zoë:

> Tonight will be a happy time at the Foster house! Young Sid was kidnapped four days ago, but he escaped and was rescued by the police. Officer O'Neal has just brought him home, and his mother is just about to give him a hug. Sid did more than escape; he told the police exactly where to find the kidnappers, down to the license number of their car. As soon as Sid's dad comes home, they'll have a big celebration, with all kinds of good things to eat.

Zoë's colorful story demonstrates her strong sense of family unity. A psychological evaluation would also point out the lack of anxiety in Zoë's writing. If she thinks she can cope with a kidnapping, the challenges of everyday life probably won't be able to frustrate her.

Personality tests represent only one type of psychological test. Even though you may never be asked to take a personality test of this type, your school career has exposed you to other types of testing: measures of intelligence, achievement, aptitude, and interests. This chapter will discuss each of these different types of tests, as well as some of the controversy that surrounds their use.

11.1 What do psychologists mean by intelligence and IQ?

11.2 How do psychologists measure a person's intelligence?

11.3 Do intelligence tests really measure what they claim to measure?

11.4 What do achievement and aptitude tests reveal?

11.5 What can you learn from personality tests?

11.1 ■ WHAT DO PSYCHOLOGISTS MEAN BY INTELLIGENCE AND IQ?

Try this experiment. Ask three people to define intelligence. Everyone understands, more or less, what the word means, but it's still difficult to define. Most of your subjects will probably fall back on the use of synonyms. "Intelligence? Well, you know, smart, uh . . . clever." Keep track of the definitions people give you, and compare your findings

with those collected by your classmates. Which definition do you think is best?

Psychologists have long wrestled with the same problem. Before they could measure intelligence, they had to define it. In 1923, Professor Edwin Boring, of Harvard University, stated flatly that "intelligence is what the tests test." The writers of intelligence tests,

Almost Everyone Has Tried to Define Intelligence

In 1905 Alfred Binet and Theodore Simon defined intelligence in these words: "To judge well, to comprehend well, to reason well, these are the essential activities of intelligence." A half century later David Wechsler, a famous name in intelligence testing, expanded that definition: "Intelligence is the . . . global capacity of the individual to act purposefully, to think rationally, and to deal effectively with [the] environment." Those sterling efforts have not kept others from adding their own interpretations. Here are a few of the more interesting efforts.

Intelligence consists of recognizing opportunity.
CHINESE PROVERB

Much learning does not teach a man to have intelligence.
HERACLITUS

The difference between genius and stupidity is that genius has its limits.
UNKNOWN

Intellect annuls fate. So far as man thinks he is free.
RALPH WALDO EMERSON

The test of a first-rate intelligence is the ability to hold two opposed ideas in the mind at the same time, and still retain the ability to function.
F. SCOTT FITZGERALD

The intellect is the tool to find the truth. It's a matter of sharpening it.
SYLVIA ASHTON-WARNER

An intelligent person is one who has learned . . . that good is better than evil, that confidence should supersede fear, that love is superior to hate, that gentleness is better than cruelty, forbearance than intolerance, compassion than arrogance, and that truth has more virtue than ignorance.
J. MARTIN KLOTSCHE

The true test of intelligence is not how much we know how to do, but how we behave when we don't know what to do.
JOHN HOLT

Which definition do you like best? Try writing your own. The game is open to everyone.

Boring argued, were defining intelligence by how well people scored on their tests. Although a long time has passed since Boring issued his criticism, psychologists still haven't agreed on a definition of intelligence that is universally accepted.

INTELLIGENCE DEFINED

Albert Einstein stands out as a perfect example of the problems involved in defining intelligence. The Nobel Prize winner in physics, the man who unlocked the power of the atom, was once asked to leave school because his grades were so poor. Einstein failed his en-

trance examination for technical school, and the University of Zurich in Switzerland later turned down his doctoral dissertation. Even after he graduated, he had a hard time finding a job. Despite these apparent failures, can you find anyone who would say Albert Einstein wasn't intelligent?

Clearly, the same person can be a brilliant executive—and a failure when confronted by the task of building close personal relationships. It follows, therefore, that intelligence is not a single mental quality. Instead, *intelligence is the totality of all the mental abilities that give people the ability to solve whatever problems they think are worth working on. In* his early years, Einstein did not find routine schoolwork worthy of his time and attention. Thus, despite his immense intelligence, he earned poor grades.

Not all psychologists have been satisfied with this general approach to defining intelligence. L. L. Thurstone, a pioneer in the field of mental testing, said that intelligence is built from seven basic mental abilities. After testing yourself on the seven questions that follow, look for the answers on page 391.

1. *Word fluency:* a measure of your ability to think of words rapidly in response to a cue consisting of initial letters or rhymes.

> Write as many words as you can that begin with the letter *d* and end with *r*. The length of the words doesn't matter. You may use proper nouns or foreign words.

2. *Reasoning ability:* a measure of your ability to use the process of deductive or inductive reasoning.

> Look at the row of letters *abacada* ___ . The next letter should be *e*. Now use the same procedure to complete these series: *azbycxd* ___ . *mmmlllkkk* ___ . *acegik* ___ .

3. *Memory:* a measure of your ability to learn word lists or other material rapidly.

> Study the following code: a = 2, e = 4, l = 6, m = 8. Now, without looking at the code, translate the following words: 8264, 264, 468.

4. *Spatial perception:* a measure of your ability to think in visual terms, such as interpreting drawings or recognizing a geometric figure.

> The following figure is shown from a bird's-eye view, looking directly down on it. Which of the other figures represents a proper side view of the same object?

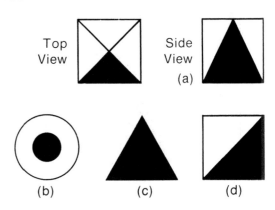

5. *Perceptual ability:* a measure of your ability to see and understand what's happening around you.

> In each row of faces, one face is different from the others. Which one is it? If you guessed the first face in row (a), you're correct. Now do the same with rows (b) and (c).

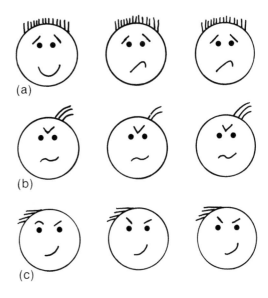

6. *Numerical skills:* a measure of your ability to use simple arithmetic.

> Select the proper answer to the following problems. Don't work out the entire problem, as the correct answer is always given. Use any shortcuts you can.

(a) 5.8681×8.1197 = ____ (a) 47.647211
(b) 40.824419
(c) 19.723092
(d) 54.098340

(b) $\sqrt{105.3468}$ = ____ (a) 8.4398295
(b) 10.263858
(c) 15.7836212
(d) 32.982712

7. *Verbal relationships:* a measure of your ability to read and understand written material.

Read the following proverb: Too many cooks spoil the soup. Now, which two of the following statements have nearly the same meaning as the proverb? (a) Many hands make light work. (b) If you want a job done right, do it yourself. (c) Big oaks from little acorns grow. (d) Necessity is the mother of invention. (e) If you want to make sure a job doesn't get done, give it to a committee.

Developmental psychologist Howard Gardner won the prestigious Grawemeyer Award in 1990 for "extending the notion of intelligence beyond the narrow cognitive domain." Gardner believes that all of us possess seven different kinds of intelligence: linguistic, musical, logical-mathematical, spatial, bodily kinesthetic, interpersonal (the ability to understand others), and intrapersonal (the ability to understand oneself). Most intelligence tests, he charged, measure only linguistic and logical-mathematical intelligences. Other psychologists have tried to resolve the argument by breaking mental abilities into smaller and smaller components. One researcher drew up a list of 238 different types of intelligence.

Less ambitious, but potentially more useful, is psychologist J. P. Guilford's concept. He sees intelligence as made up of 120 distinct "blocks," each identified by (1) the kind of material acted on, (2) what actions were carried out with the material, and (3) what products resulted. Sample intelligence factors

in Guilford's model include the ability to identify classes of words; the ability to remember a system of numerals, symbols, or letters; the ability to state the correct deduction from given facts; and the ability to produce novel responses.

Guilford believes that everyone has all 120 of these abilities, but in varying degrees. If Elton Y. takes one of Guilford's diagnostic tests, for example, he might find that he's strong in the ability to evaluate but weak in dealing with word meanings. Elton's counselor could then prescribe exercises that would build up his vocabulary and word-usage skills. Elton will also be encouraged to plan for a career in which his ability to evaluate alternate choices would be useful, such as in business administration.

THE CONCEPT OF IQ

Most people recognize the widely used term *intelligence quotient (IQ)*. Unfortunately, many people confuse the *quality* (intelligence) with the *measure* (IQ). As defined earlier, intelligence is the basic human ability to solve problems, slowly or quickly. IQ, on the other hand, is a convenient yardstick for comparing an individual's mental abilities with those of the rest of the population.

Psychometrists remind their clients that IQ is nothing more than a numerical score derived from a specific test. They know, however, that the concept of a single, easily understood number called IQ is deeply embedded in the national consciousness. As a replacement, they suggest the use of "standard deviations from the mean" or the "standard age scores" generated by the revised Stanford-Binet Intelligence Scale. Whatever form the score takes, its usefulness depends on the accuracy and fairness of the test, the conditions under which the test is given, and the way people interpret the score.

As an example, look at how 15-year-old Dwight's traditional IQ score is figured.

WE CAN'T DO THE INTELLIGENCE EXPERIMENT — THE LADDER WON'T FIT INTO THE LAB.

FIGURE 11.2

Dwight begins the process by taking an intelligence test. The examiner then translates his raw score into a *mental age* (MA) score. This number tells Dwight how he scored in relation to other 15-year-olds who have taken the test. To calculate his IQ, Dwight must also factor in his *chronological age* (CA). The formula looks like this:

$$IQ = \frac{\text{Mental Age (MA)}}{\text{Chronological Age (CA)}} \times 100$$

Thus, if Dwight tested at an MA of 16 years, two months, the equation works out to an IQ of 108 $(\frac{16.17}{15} \times 100 = 108)$.

The basic assumption behind the IQ score is that the average person's CA and MA will be the same. By this system, therefore, the typical six-year-old would be expected to score $(6 \div 6) \times 100$, which yields an IQ of 100. In actual test situations, about half the population ranks above 100 and the other half falls below 100.

Extensive testing has established the percentage of people who will fall into any specific segment of the IQ scale. This prediction is based on a mathematical model known as the *normal curve of distribution*. If you set up a scale and weighed every student in your school, the graph of their weights would fol-

low a bell-shaped curve, or normal curve of distribution. A few of your classmates would fall at the extreme ends, but most people would bunch up toward the middle, or average, weight (see Figure 11.3 on page 364).

A study of the distribution of IQ scores from a sample of 2,904 subjects yielded a nearly perfect bell-shaped curve. (See Figure 11.4. The original Stanford-Binet was standardized with the use of this group.) Over the years, psychologists have quantified the percentage of the population that can be expected to fall into each segment of the curve.

According to this curve, Dwight's 108 IQ score places him near the top end of the middle (average) segment. Does that mean that he's a better person than someone with an IQ of 98 and inferior to someone else who scored 130? Psychologists are quick to point out that IQ scores don't measure real-life achievements. Qualities such as motivation, persistence, and stability count just as heavily as intelligence. At this point in his life, Dwight wants to be a mechanic. Because he's gifted with good mechanical abilities and is highly motivated, he'll probably make a crackerjack mechanic. Bryan, with an IQ of 128, also would like to be a mechanic, but he prefers to "hang out" with his buddies. He learns quickly, and he's good at bluffing his way through. (Of course, bright people are

CURVE OF NORMAL DISTRIBUTION: STUDENT WEIGHTS
IN A TYPICAL HIGH SCHOOL POPULATION

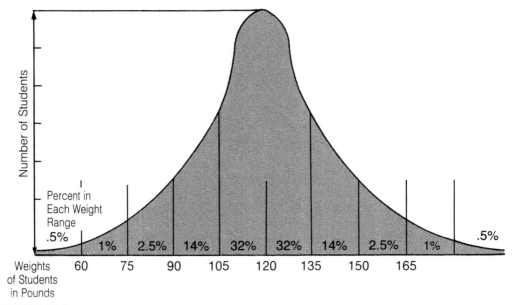

Number of Students

Percent in
Each Weight
Range

.5%   1%   2.5%   14%   32%   32%   14%   2.5%   1%   .5%

Weights   60   75   90   105   120   135   150   165
of Students
in Pounds

FIGURE 11.3

THE NORMAL DISTRIBUTION OF IQ SCORES

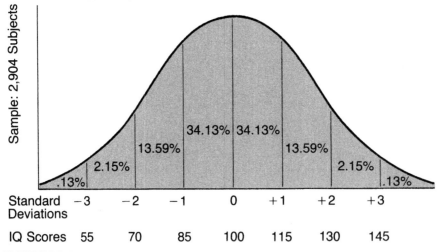

Sample: 2,904 Subjects

34.13% 34.13%

13.59%   13.59%

2.15%   2.15%

.13%   .13%

Standard   −3   −2   −1   0   +1   +2   +3
Deviations

IQ Scores   55   70   85   100   115   130   145

FIGURE 11.4

no more lazy than others. Bryan is just one particular person who is both bright and lazy.) In practical terms, many people would wonder if Bryan is really more intelligent than Dwight.

■ SECTION CHECKUP

1 Give a working definition of intelligence.

2 List some of the individual abilities that

364

make up the general quality people consider to be intelligence.

3 Ursula has a mental age of 12 years, 6 months, and a chronological age of 10 years. Use the traditional formula to calculate her

IQ. Would you put her in the average, high average, or superior category?

4 Is Ursula's high score on an intelligence test a guarantee of success in life? Why or why not?

11.2 ▓ HOW DO PSYCHOLOGISTS MEASURE A PERSON'S INTELLIGENCE?

Imagine for a moment that it's 1524 and you're an adviser to King Henry VIII of England. War clouds are gathering, and the army must be built up quickly. Henry orders you to select the bravest, most skillful, and most intelligent archers to support his royal knights. You swallow hard, because you know that Henry will throw you into the dungeon if you make a mistake. How would you choose the best archers?

Throughout history, people have been challenged by similar dilemmas. At various times they have chosen their candidates by simple guesswork, by careful observation, or by controlled testing. As a clever adviser, you'd probably think up some tests for your candidates. Let the archers prove their skill by shooting for distance and accuracy. Send them through an obstacle course under fire to test their bravery. And as the centerpiece of your program, set up a series of problems that will test the archers' "battlefield IQ"— their coolness, initiative, and resourcefulness during battle.

Although such testing and evaluation are far from new, formal testing of intelligence only began in the early 1900s. The breakthrough came with the work of two French psychologists, Alfred Binet (see BioBox, page 367) and Theodore Simon. In 1905, Binet published a series of intelligence tests intended for use with schoolchildren. Binet grouped his tests by chronological age and coined the term "mental age" to represent an

individual child's score. Suzanne, for example, might do well in those tests usually passed by nine-year-olds but fail those passed by ten-year-olds. Whatever Suzanne's birth age, Binet believed that his test had established her mental age at nine. Under the traditional IQ formula, Suzanne was given an IQ score of 113 if she was eight but only 75 if she was 12.

Although intelligence testing has become more complex since Binet, the basic approach has changed very little. The test maker constructs questions and problems that seem appropriate for testing general intelligence. After a number of people have taken the test, the results are evaluated. Poor questions are discarded and new ones written. Once enough data has been gathered on how typical seven-year-olds score, for example, the raw scores can be converted into mental age equivalents or standard age scores for all seven-year-olds who take the test.

That's basically what Dr. L. M. Terman did at Stanford University in 1916, when he revised the original Binet test for use in the United States. Terman's version of the test, known as the Stanford-Binet, gave credit for each level passed. If Lola, age six, passed all tests rated for six-year-olds, she received credit for a MA of six. If she also passed four of six tests at the seven-year level, eight months were added to her MA. If she then failed to pass any tests at the eight-year level, her MA remained fixed at six years, eight

The Search for Artificial Intelligence

Remember Dr. Frankenstein and the monster he built from recycled body parts? If Dr. Frankenstein were alive today, he might well be channeling his energies in a different direction—the search for artificial intelligence. In his new lab, computer chips and software programs would take the place of scalpels and formaldehyde.

Computer scientists define *artificial intelligence* as the computerized simulation of human thought and reasoning. While a true "thinking machine" is still only a theoretical dream, institutions as diverse as the U.S. Air Force and Mrs. Fields' Cookies are finding numerous applications for a form of artificial intelligence known as *expert systems*. An expert system applies the know-how of real-life experts to everyday problems. Jake Hamblin ran into an expert system when he bought a ring for his wife.

Jake, a prosperous film producer, began a cross-country trip in Seattle. He used his American Express card to pay an $800 hotel bill before catching a cab to the airport. In New York, he whipped out his card again when he decided to purchase the $1,400 ring. As a matter of routine, the clerk contacted Amex to ask for approval. The computer that handled the contact knew at once that the two purchases were too large for routine processing. The computer kicked the problem on to an expert system called Authorizer's Assistant (AA).

Within milliseconds AA had checked Jake's travel history, spending patterns, and general credit worthiness. Should it ask the clerk to confirm Jake's identity by asking for his Social Security number? No, the system decided, the purchase fit within its guidelines. AA then called on a human supervisor to finalize the decision. Ms. Sloan glanced at the data displayed on her own screen. After reading a summary of AA's reasoning, she nodded and punched a key. An instant later, the store clerk's computer flashed an electronic okay. Jake never knew that it had taken both human and artificial intelligences to decide that he was a good risk.

Artificial intelligence is already changing the way we live. Thanks to expert systems, small businesses can "hire" the kind of troubleshooting expertise that once was available only to giant corporations. The near future, the programmers say, will bring driverless trucks, fully automated assembly lines, and word processors that interact with writers to help them clarify ideas. As for the more distant future, look for *artificial life* programs that recreate many of life's processes. The first A-life programs are already "teaching" robots to cope with simple problems they were not specifically programmed to solve. Wherever he is now, Dr. Frankenstein must surely be applauding.

---

months. Under the traditional method of calculating IQ, the examiner then translated her MA into a Stanford-Binet IQ score of 111.

CRITERIA FOR CONSTRUCTING TESTS

Measuring intelligence with a carelessly constructed test would be like using a rubber ruler to lay out a new house. None of the measurements would make any sense. Before any IQ test can be used for measuring intelligence, therefore, it must meet four criteria.

OBJECTIVITY. A test achieves *objectivity* when it can be taken and evaluated without allowing the examiner's personal feelings to affect the scores. Multiple-choice questions,

■ BIOBOX

Alfred Binet:
Creator of the Intelligence Test

Intelligence testing on a scientific basis began with the French psychologist Alfred Binet (1857–1911). Binet had a background in medicine and law when he entered the relatively new field of psychology in 1886. Paris school officials soon asked him to find a way to classify retarded children so that they could be given the best possible education. Binet began by trying every measure of intelligence available at the time. He compared head sizes, looked into palmistry, and made careful measurements of reaction time. None of those techniques seemed to correlate with a child's mental abilities.

In the early 1900s, Binet collaborated with psychologist Theodore Simon in an attempt to establish exact standards for the measurement of intelligence. The two men agreed to develop a series of tests, each test to be of increasing difficulty. The tests, they said, should start from the lowest intellectual level that could be observed and end with that of normal intelligence. When given to children, the tests were expected to provide ratings of the intelligence level of each individual child within his or her group.

Binet wrote about his work:

Our principal conclusion is that we actually possess an instrument which will allow us to measure the intellectual development of young children. . . . Of what use is a measure of intelligence? Without doubt one could conceive . . . of a future where the social sphere would be better organized than ours; where everyone would work according to his known aptitudes in such a way that no particle of

psychic force should be lost for society. That would be the ideal city. It is indeed far from us.

Binet also looked forward to a time when parents and teachers could make use of intelligence tests as a way of better understanding their children.

A father and mother who raise a child themselves, . . . would have great satisfaction in knowing that the intelligence of a child can be measured and would willingly make the necessary effort to find out if their own child is intelligent. We think especially of teachers who love their profession, who interest themselves in their pupils, and who understand that the first condition of instructing them well is to know them.

What would Binet say if he heard a counselor tell a student, "I'm sorry, but with IQ scores like yours, you shouldn't plan on going to college"? Why would he agree or disagree with this use of IQ scores? What would a modern psychometrist say?

for example, meet this criterion because the scorer's biases cannot influence the results. Tests that give the examiner the responsibility of interpreting answers or that award weighted scores for partially correct answers diminish a test's objectivity. If all other variables are held constant, a test with good objectivity will yield consistent results, no matter who does the scoring.

STANDARDIZATION. By *standardization,* psychometrists mean first that a test must be administered consistently. Time allowances, instructions, and other details of the testing situation must be handled the same way each time the test is given. Standardization also refers to the establishing of *norms*—tables that specify how well average or "normal" people performed on the test. What if you scored 84 on a test? That sounds like a good score, but is it? Before you can decide, you'll need to know how other people did on the same test. If the average score was 67, your 84 would be an excellent mark. But if most people score 95 or better, your 84 would rank below average. That's why norms must be set up for standardized tests. Only after the test maker gives the test to a carefully chosen cross section of the population can raw scores be translated into meaningful results.

To make scores easier to interpret, results are often given in *percentile rankings.* Perhaps your raw score of 84 puts you in the 67th percentile. That means that you scored better than 66 percent of the people who have taken the test in the past. In the same way, a score at the 34th percentile would mean that you outscored only 33 percent of the norm group.

RELIABILITY. A test that gives consistent scores whenever a subject is retested is said to have *reliability.* To achieve reliability, test makers first try to eliminate test items that can be answered correctly by sheer guesswork. They also stay away from items that refer to a narrow field of knowledge. A question based on chess moves, for example, would be easy for chess players but quite unfair for most other people. Most important, test questions should be culturally neutral. No questions should appear on the test that bias results in favor of any race, ethnic group, or social class.

Test makers also pursue reliability by making the test long enough to cancel out the effect of a few lucky guesses. Further, a reliable test must be written clearly and simply. Technical words, slang terms, ambiguous questions, and references to changing fads can soon make the test obsolete. Even the most reliable test, however, cannot compensate for test takers who don't care about the results or who are fatigued, sick, or emotionally upset. In order to retain reliability, those people should be excused to take the test at another time.

VALIDITY. A test has *validity* if it measures what it claims to measure. Intelligence tests have been found that actually measure reading comprehension rather than intelligence. Using a flawed test is like trying to measure a pound of apples with a yardstick. Test validity can be judged best by comparing the later performance of test takers with their scores. Remember that test you were asked to set up for King Henry's archers? To check its validity, select men whose scores range from low to high. Then send them into battle and rate their performance. If high-scoring archers do well in combat and low-scoring men do poorly, you can consider your test valid. If your high scorers lose the battle, common sense suggests that emigration may be preferable to facing King Henry's wrath. (The feature on page 370 tells you how to make your own contemporary intelligence test, using only the dictionary as a resource.)

INDIVIDUAL INTELLIGENCE TESTS

The most valid and reliable intelligence tests are administered by trained examiners on a

The Tests Aren't Always Perfect: Ambiguous Test Items

No matter how hard test makers work to make their tests perfect, some ambiguous items still slip through. The following items appeared in an intelligence test that was once sold to the general public. Answer the two questions before reading further.

1. Which one of the five shapes is least like the other four?

A Z F N M

2. Which one of the five designs is least like the other four?

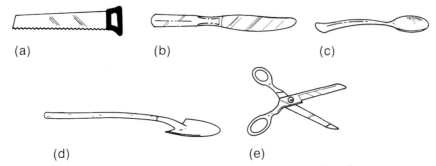

(a)　　　　　　(b)　　　　　　(c)

(d)　　　　　　(e)

The answers and explanations given by the test makers can be found on page 391. Can you think of any answers other than those given? If so, and if your logic is valid, then the questions must be classed as unfair. In a properly standardized test, items like these two would be thrown out and replaced with better ones.

one-to-one basis. For this reason, individual intelligence tests are also the most expensive to administer. The two best-known tests of this type are the Stanford-Binet and the Wechsler.

STANFORD-BINET. If you take the Stanford-Binet Intelligence Scale, the examiner often begins by chatting for a few minutes as a way of helping you relax. Then, as the test begins, you will be asked to respond to a series of questions. You can answer some of the ques-

tions with a word or definition, while others require the use of more complex problem-solving skills.

The 1986 revision of the Stanford-Binet divides the test into 15 subtests. Each asks questions that are graded in difficulty from simple to intensely challenging. With two items allotted to each level, a few subtests have as many as 21 levels. The examiner begins by asking you questions geared to your chronological age. If the questions stump you, the examiner moves to easier items. If you an-

How to Write Your Own Intelligence Test

Dr. L. M. Terman of Stanford University, who published the U.S. version of Binet's original intelligence test, wrote in 1918, "The vocabulary test has a far higher value than any other single test of the scale." He claimed that in most cases the vocabulary test alone would give an IQ score 90 percent as accurate as the complete Stanford-Binet. Terman compiled his vocabulary list by selecting words at random from a dictionary.

You can compile your own intelligence test based on the Terman model. Open a college-level dictionary at random to the middle of the *A*'s and write down the last word on the right-hand page. From that point, select the last word in every sixth column. When you've collected 100 words, test yourself on your ability to define the words chosen in this random fashion. If you think you've looked at the definitions as you went along, exchange your list with a classmate.

Score yourself as follows:

WORDS CORRECT	MENTAL AGE
20	Eight years
30	Ten years
40	Twelve years
50	Fourteen years
65	Average adult
75	Superior adult

Do you agree with Terman that a vocabulary test provides a valid test of intelligence? Why or why not?

---

swer them correctly, you graduate to more difficult items. Every subject eventually reaches a ceiling, known as the basal level. The scores for each of the four sections of the test, as well as a total score, are expressed as standard age scores (SAS). As with traditional IQ scores, the mean SAS score is 100.

In the *Verbal Reasoning* section, a child of six or eight would be asked questions similar to these:

1. *Vocabulary:* Define *dollar* and *envelope.*
2. *Comprehension:* Why do people comb their hair?
3. *Absurdities:* What is wrong with this picture? (The drawing shows a girl riding a bicycle on a lake.)

4. *Verbal Relations:* In the list *scarf, tie, muffler,* and *shirt,* what do the first three items have in common? How is the fourth item different?

In the *Abstract/Visual Reasoning* section, the child must duplicate a design made with blocks and copy a simple geometric figure. The *Quantitative Reasoning* section calls for simple arithmetic skills, such as picking the die that represents the sum of a two-spot die and a four-spot die. In another subtest, the child is asked to name the next two numbers in the sequence 4 6 5 8 6 10. Finally, a series of *Short-Term Memory* tests challenge the child with tasks such as repeating a sentence heard only once or duplicating a string of colored beads.

FIGURE 11.5 ▪ Individual intelligence tests often seem more like a game than an examination. What do you think the examiner is looking for in this exercise?

The examiner grades answers for correctness, originality, and maturity of thought. Any obvious signs of nervousness, anxiety, or lack of interest are also recorded and included in the evaluation. Lower-level tests tend to be concrete and often use pictures and objects to focus the child's attention. At the upper levels, the tests emphasize abstract reasoning and verbal skills. At all levels, subjects are expected to display good recall of past experience, judgment, interpretation, a long attention span, immediate memory, and other cognitive processes.

WECHSLER SCALES. In 1939 David Wechsler developed an intelligence test that attempted to balance the Stanford-Binet's reliance on vocabulary and word usage with greater emphasis on performance tests. Today, the revised Wechsler scales consist of three separate age-group tests: the Wechsler Preschool and Primary Scale of Intelligence, Revised (WPPSI-R), the Wechsler Intelligence Scale for Children, Revised (WISC-R), and the Wechsler Adult Intelligence Scale, Revised (WAIS-R).

If you took the WAIS-R you would be asked questions similar to the following:

1. General information: When is Labor Day celebrated?

2. Arithmetic reasoning: If the sales tax is 6 percent, what is the total price of a 60-cent ballpoint pen?

3. Digit span: Listen carefully, and then repeat the numbers—9 4 7 2 8 3.

4. Picture completion: What important part of the picture shown here is missing?

J U L Y						
S	M	T	W	T	F	S
1	2	3	4	5	6	7
8	9	10	11	12	13	14
15	16	17	18	19	20	21
22	23	24	25	26	27	28
29	30	31				

5. Block design: Use the four blocks shown here to make a design like the completed figure. (Actual blocks are provided on the Wechsler.)

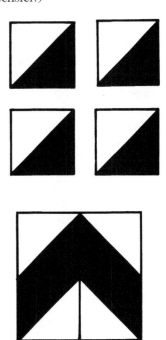

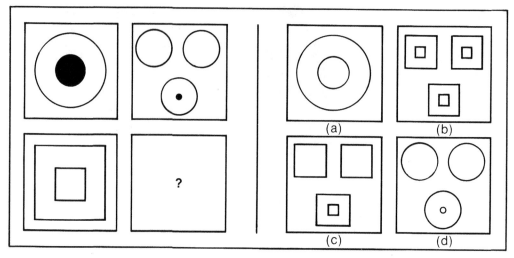

FIGURE 11.6

The Wechsler provides three separate IQ scores: a verbal IQ, a performance IQ, and a total IQ. Psychologists find this breakdown useful when dealing with subjects who are handicapped by language, educational, or cultural differences.

SPECIALIZED INTELLIGENCE TESTS.   The Stanford-Binet and Wechsler tests do not have the field of individual intelligence testing all to themselves. Other tests have been developed for testing special subjects. Tests of infants, for example, are based on observation of the child's behavior at a particular age. Does Suzy sit up? Walk? Does she turn to look at a new sound? Can she pick up a block? How does she react to strangers? Studies of large numbers of infants have established norms for scoring Suzy's developmental progress.

Similarly, a nonverbal test has been designed for use when language and cultural variables invalidate other tests. Testing a Russian-speaking immigrant with an English-language test, for example, would be an exercise in futility. The Progressive Matrices Test attempts to solve this problem by using sets of two-dimensional figures to test the subject's ability to perceive relationships. The figures range from relatively simple forms to complex patterns. A sample of items similar to those used in the Progressive Matrices Test can be seen in Figure 11.6. Your job is to choose the proper figure to complete the relationship.

GROUP INTELLIGENCE TESTS

For most people, taking an intelligence test means sitting down in a large room with a number of other people, all of whom are taking the same test at the same time. Although the process seems to deny individual differences, it does have a number of advantages. First, testing large groups greatly lowers the costs of testing. Also, the examiners can do their jobs without undergoing extensive training. The scoring is quick and objective. Another advantage of group testing lies in the well-developed norms that have been gathered over the years. The Army General Classification Test (AGCT), for example, has been given to literally millions of men and women. This 40-minute test has been extensively standardized and possesses a high validity.

The disadvantages of group tests, however, cancel out some of these strengths. One problem lies in the fact that the examiner cannot make allowances for the emotional or physical health of the test takers. If you are fighting a cold or if you were up all night caring for a sick parent, you're probably not going to be at your best. A strong performance on a group test also depends heavily upon your ability to read quickly and follow directions exactly. These factors may not have much to do with native intelligence, but failure to follow test-taking rules can lower your score. Another disadvantage is that you might be "turned off" by the length and impersonal nature of the test. After a while, some people get bored and fill in their answers at random. Finally, simple errors in using the answer sheet can completely invalidate the test. Psychometrists generally believe that IQ scores based on group tests tend to underestimate a subject's actual intelligence.

Despite these problems, group intelligence tests are among the most widely used of all psychological tests. Like individual intelligence tests, the Cognitive Abilities Test has sections on verbal, numerical, and nonverbal skills. The examiner adjusts the difficulty of the items for the age and ability range of the group being tested. Students taking the test receive a test booklet and an answer sheet. Each section of the test is timed. The Cognitive Abilities Test asks such questions as these:

1. Vocabulary: *impolite* (a) unhappy, (b) angry, (c) rude, (d) faithless, (e) talkative.
2. Verbal classification: *vulture, hawk, falcon, owl,* ____ . (a) robin, (b) bat, (c) eagle, (d) parrot, (e) woodpecker.

3. Verbal analogy: *Swim* is to *pool* as *run* is to ____ (a) street, (b) meadow, (c) sand, (d) floor, (e) track.
4. Number series: 7   10   14   19   ____ (a) 22 (b) 23 (c) 24 (d) 25 (e) 26.
5. Figure analogy:

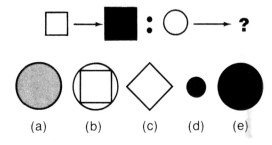

(a)   (b)   (c)   (d)   (e)

(Answers can be found on page 392.)

The CogAT, as it is often called, also provides a two-level primary test for kindergarten to grade three. Examiners read the directions for each item aloud when working with nonreaders. The primary CogAT includes two verbal, two quantitative, and two nonverbal subtests. A typical verbal item pictures a refrigerator, a sofa, a drinking fountain, and a store window. The child is asked to "fill in the oval under the *refrigerator*." A quantitative item pictures four slices of pie of various sizes. The examiner asks the child to "mark the oval under the *biggest* piece of pie."

■ SECTION CHECKUP

1 What reasons can you think of for using intelligence tests?

2 If you wrote an IQ test to help select the next group of astronauts, how would you make sure it was reliable? Objective? Valid? Standardized?

3 Contrast the advantages and disadvantages of individual and group intelligence tests.

11.3 ▓ DO INTELLIGENCE TESTS REALLY MEASURE WHAT THEY CLAIM TO MEASURE?

Many well-meaning people once believed that intelligence tests truly measured basic human intelligence. From that point, it wasn't a terribly big step to the belief that a person's value to society was directly related to IQ. No one was really against low-IQ people, but it did seem as though high-IQ's were more useful and should be given preferred treatment. Jobs, benefits, opportunities—all could be allocated on the basis of IQ.

But a strange thing happened on the way to that particular brave new world. Thoughtful people began to question the validity of pigeonholing men and women on the basis of intelligence tests. After all, the critics said, there's no guarantee that the tests truly measure anyone's actual abilities. And even more important, they went on, it's wrong to judge a person's worth by an IQ score. "It's bad enough that we give enormous financial awards to star athletes and entertainers simply because they possess a highly specialized talent," they argued. "Let's not carry that process to absurd lengths by creating an IQ elite as well."

By the mid-1960s, these debates had begun to have an effect. In March 1964, the New York City Board of Education banned the use of group intelligence tests in New York schools, and other large cities followed. Alarmed by what it felt was a continuing misuse of IQ data, the state of California followed suit in 1971. A new philosophy evolved that called on society to judge children and adolescents by their performance, rather than by IQ scores that too often proved to be poor predictors of future success. This position was reinforced at the convention of the National Association of School Psychologists in 1971. There a group of psychologists charged that intelligence tests were being used to place minority students in special education

classes. The effect of this, they said, was to segregate these students from the rest of the school population.

In 1979 a federal court ordered California schools to end the practice of using IQ tests to evaluate children thought to have learning disabilities. Judge Robert Peckham's ruling was based on findings that accused the schools of using racially biased tests to shunt African American children into dead-end programs for the retarded. The ruling held firm until 1992, when Peckham reversed himself. In his new ruling, the judge said that the ban was unfair to African American families who wanted their children to take the tests, which some school districts use to qualify students for admission to special programs for the mentally gifted. While waiting for the courts to issue a definitive ruling, the state department of education adopted a policy that discouraged the use of IQ tests for the placement of children of any race or ethnic group.

On another front in 1971, the United States Supreme Court ruled unanimously that the intelligence tests given to prospective employees by an electric-power company were unlawful. If employers want to give tests, the Court said, the tests must be related directly to the skills required for that particular job. The decision was followed in 1984 by what is now called the Golden Rule case. The Golden Rule Insurance Company had charged in a suit against the Educational Testing Service (ETS) that the differences in passing rates for blacks (52 percent) and for whites (77 percent) on the Illinois Insurance Licensing Examination proved that the test was racially biased. Without admitting guilt, ETS finally agreed to purge the test of items that yielded a difference greater than 15 percent. This case quickly became a national model for similar test situations.

Despite these setbacks, defenders of intelligence tests insist that test results are valid when used with appropriate safeguards. First, tests should be administered under proper conditions. Lighting, seating arrangements, phrasing of directions, and other elements must be set up so as to give test takers the best possible chance to do well. Second, test results should be used only to measure certain carefully defined abilities. A test can point out a weakness in reading comprehension, for example, but should not be used to make a final judgment about overall intelligence. Third, only specially trained people should be allowed to interpret test results. Finally, examiners must choose tests properly standardized for the group being tested. Thus, tests standardized for white, middle-class children should not be used to test children recently arrived from Southeast Asia, and so on.

Whatever the merits of this debate, two interesting questions concerning the use of intelligence tests have developed. Can intelligence be taught? Has the problem of cultural bias in intelligence testing been fully explored? These are two of the most controversial issues in modern psychological testing.

"TEACHING" INTELLIGENCE

For many years, most psychologists believed that intelligence was an inborn trait. An individual has a certain amount of intelligence at birth, the theory states, and no one can increase that amount. Supporters of this concept saw little need to give special attention to children of low-IQ parents or to children who come from low-income communities. In effect, they said to parents, "It's too bad, Mr. Bradford, but your Terry tests out at 85 IQ. You'll just have to accept the fact that he'll always be limited in what he can do."

Parents like Mr. Bradford can draw fresh hope from an experiment that started at Milwaukee's Infant Education Center in 1966.

Researchers selected 20 infants whose mothers had IQ scores of 75 or less. Earlier studies had shown that children raised by low-IQ parents tend to test below average. But these children were given a wide variety of stimulating play and educational experiences, starting soon after birth. Doctors, nurses, and social workers worked with the children and trained the mothers in better methods of child care. At age five, the children achieved an average IQ of 124, compared with a 95 average for a carefully matched control group. Although the Milwaukee experiment was limited in size, its conclusion has been backed up by other studies: IQ scores rise when a child's early environment is enriched.

Psychologist H. M. Skeels obtained similar results in the 1930s when he took retarded babies from an orphanage and placed them in a home for the mentally retarded. Surrounded by loving "foster parents" and given extra attention by nurses and attendants, the apparently retarded babies blossomed into children with normal and above-normal IQ's. The children were then placed with adoptive parents. The average IQ of a control group left in the cold, uncaring atmosphere of the orphanage actually decreased. A follow-up study revealed that almost all of the adopted children went on to complete high school. They all married—and produced 28 children with an average IQ of 104.

These findings suggest that intelligence tests measure learned skills, not inborn abilities and talents. Intelligence, rather than being seen as an inherited characteristic, is now generally accepted as a variable that is highly responsive to the environmental forces that a child encounters during infancy and childhood (see Figure 11.7). While no child's IQ score is likely to climb from 75 to 180, proper stimulation and nurturing can add IQ points. The children in the Skeels experiment showed an average increase of 28 points. One child gained a remarkable 58 points. Developmen-

FIGURE 11.7 ▓ Educational television programs can give extra stimulation to preschool children. Here Kermit the Frog is teaching number concepts. Can such programs also affect IQ levels?

tal psychologists believe proper nurturing from day one of our children's lives will go a long way toward ensuring that they reach their full intellectual potential. This fact became particularly pertinent in the 1990s, with its epidemic of drug-addicted babies and an increasing number of children who were growing up in inner-city neighborhoods racked by crime and poverty.

RACE AND INTELLIGENCE

One of the great controversies in modern American social science involves the extent to which intelligence is determined by heredity. If intelligence is largely a product of genes rather than environment, as some have claimed, then special programs such as Head Start classes for low-income preschoolers cannot change a child's intelligence to any great extent.

Others have claimed that there are genetic differences between races that affect intelligence. Any scientific issues raised by such theories tend to be clouded over by people who use the theories to support their own prejudiced notions of racial superiority.

The majority of scientists have refused to allow these ideas to go unchallenged. They insist that no proof of genetically based differences in intelligence can be found among the races.

CULTURAL BIAS IN INTELLIGENCE TESTS. Until recent years, the people who write intelligence tests assumed that every child of a certain age had received equal exposure to the basic elements of U.S. culture. In simple fact, that assumption was not valid. Many Americans, particularly those from low-income minority groups, do not grow up with the same educational and cultural backgrounds as do white, middle-class children. Thus, when asked to take an intelligence test, minority children often face a built-in *cultural bias*. Their vocabulary, grammar, knowledge of tools, utensils, music, literature, and the like may differ greatly from the norms established by the test makers.

As a step toward overcoming this problem, *culture-free tests* that do not depend on cultural or language skills available only to the white middle class are replacing the older tests. Test makers now understand that inner-city children cannot be expected to answer questions that describe a world that lies outside their experience. Similarly, the assumption that Standard English is superior to Black English or other dialects has been discarded. The 1986 revision of the Stanford-Binet, for example, relied on representatives from minority groups to screen test items for content they thought was gender-biased or race-biased. The publisher later ran a statistical analysis that was based on the responses different ethnic and racial groups gave to each item. The analysis helped the editors weed out additional items before the test went into general distribution.

Typically, a culture-free test modifies the traditional intelligence test in three ways: (a) language is simplified, (b) more nonverbal items are used, and (c) references are made to experiences that minority children recognize and to which they relate. The box on

How Bright Are You? Take the CBIT* and Find Out

1 *¿Cuantos huevos hay en una docena?* (a) 2, (b) 6, (c) 12, (d) 18.

2 A *six-penny nail* is (a) one inch long, (b) one and a half inches long, (c) two inches long, (d) three inches long.

3 On a musical score, the *fermata* (⌢) sign means (a) play faster, (b) play softer, (c) hold the note for extra time, (d) repeat the phrase.

4 If someone says your conversation is *fatuous,* you've been (a) complimented, (b) ignored, (c) insulted, (d) misunderstood.

5 If Harry tells you that the umpire called his favorite batsman out "leg before wicket," you can conclude that he has been watching a game of (a) rugby, (b) badminton, (c) cricket, (d) croquet.

6 Your host has just put a big bowl of *cous-cous* on the table. You know the meal is going to be (a) Japanese, (b) Swedish, (c) Algerian, (d) Brazilian.

How did you do? Most people complain that this isn't a fair intelligence test. After all, not everyone speaks Spanish or does carpentry work. And who knows that much about music or exotic foods? Not everyone, obviously. But without meaning to, some IQ tests use culturally biased items not remarkably different from these. When such tests are used to evaluate the IQ of people who have not had similar cultural experiences, the results are predictable.

* Green-Sanford *Culturally Biased Intelligence Test*

Answers: (c) is the correct answer to all items.

this page gives you a chance to try out a "counterbalance" intelligence test.

SUBTLE EFFECTS OF DISCRIMINATION. Centuries of discrimination have left their mark on African Americans. When asked in one study to estimate their own IQ's, African American students generally guessed lower in comparison with their actual scores than did white students. In another study, African American students averaged 6 IQ points higher when tested by African American examiners, as opposed to their scores when tested by a white examiner. In addition, many African American children approach test situations with the feeling that they'll do poorly. In the way of most self-fulfilling prophecies, they often do.

From 1981 to 1991, the U.S. Labor Department practiced a controversial policy known as "race norming" in an effort to reverse centuries of racism. Before reporting an applicant's percentile ranking to prospective employers, the department would "norm" the raw scores according to the applicant's race or ethnic background. Whites were ranked according to a "white" scale, African Americans according to a "black" scale. As a result, a white worker who scored 327 on a vocational aptitude test was ranked at the same 70th percentile as an African American worker who scored 283. Sociologists and psychologists alike generally agree that race norming is a dubious practice at best. They argue that the cause of social justice would be better served by equipping every American with the

Should You Be Given Your Scores on Psychological Tests?

All through your school career, you've taken psychological tests of one type or another. In some schools, teachers and counselors pass on test scores to students, but in others this information is kept in a confidential file. In such cases, students receive interpretations of the scores but not the actual test data. Would it hurt you to know your own IQ or your scores on achievement and personality tests? Many psychologists and counselors believe that the potential for damage does exist. The arguments go like this:

PRO

1 The schools claim that tests are given for the benefit of the students. The scores, therefore, rightfully belong to the people taking the tests.

2 In order to make rational decisions about school, career, marriage, and the like, students need to know all there is to know about their abilities.

3 People are hardly ever affected in a negative way by learning that they aren't geniuses or that their abilities don't suit particular careers. Everyone faces the challenge of learning to live with limitations.

4 Historically, schools have shared test data with teachers, parents, administrators, and law enforcement officials. Why don't they also share them with the people who take the tests?

CON

1 A psychological test isn't comparable to a quiz in math or history. The scores must remain under the control of the school because only trained counselors know how to interpret them.

2 Only when interpreted in the light of all available data about an individual do test results serve a useful purpose. Raw test scores are useless by themselves.

3 Handing out raw test data tends to create a self-fulfilling prophecy. Those who score poorly on an IQ test may begin to live down to that "prophecy." Children are most at risk of accepting adult pronouncements as facts not to be questioned.

4 The individuals mentioned in the Pro argument have a legal right to look at test data. Schools in many states also recognize the right of 18-year-olds to have access to their records.

What is the policy in your school about giving test scores to students, parents, and other people? What changes would you make in that policy, if any?

skills and experiences they need to reach their full potential.

IQ SCORES CAN BE IMPROVED. As discussed earlier in this section, IQ scores can be improved when caring adults reverse the environmental factors that contribute to low scores. Deficiencies can be fully remedied only if the improved health care and nurtur-

ing begin during infancy. A well-rounded program provides better nutrition and medical care, enrichment activities, and improved school services aimed at overcoming specific weaknesses. Hispanic and Asian children often need special help with language skills, for example. Along with hot lunches, dental checkups, and after-school enrichment programs, every community should be working overtime to provide its children with a greater feeling of value and self-worth.

■ SECTION CHECKUP

1 Why have many cities and states banned the use of group IQ tests for school children?

2 If Mrs. Hammond asked you for advice on

how to ensure that her new baby would grow up as intelligent as possible, what would you tell her?

3 If you heard someone argue that African Americans score lower than whites on IQ tests because of racial differences in intelligence, what arguments could you use to counter this prejudiced assumption?

11.4 ■ WHAT DO ACHIEVEMENT AND APTITUDE TESTS REVEAL?

Becky K. is about to finish her senior year of high school. With hopes of a career in dentistry to spur her on, she carried a heavy course load of mathematics and science. Along the way, she took dozens of quizzes and examinations. But when she took the SAT, she felt rather confused.

"Look," Becky told her counselor, "I know what an *achievement test* is. That's a test that measures how much I learned in a particular course. But as I understand it, the 'A' in SAT used to stand for 'Aptitude.' How can that be? The test I took mainly focused on how much I knew about English and math."

Mr. Topping smiled. "That's understandable. Even psychologists sometimes have difficulty telling where an achievement test ends and an aptitude test begins. Achievement tests look backward to see where you've been. *Aptitude tests* look ahead to measure your chances of success in learning a new body of knowledge or a new skill."

"So if I did well on the SAT, I'll do well in college?" Becky asked. "Can't the admissions officers figure that out from my grades?"

"The colleges don't really trust your high school grades, Becky. They don't know exactly what they mean, since every school tends to grade differently. That doesn't mean that the SAT is a perfect instrument. Students and educators alike have charged that it is biased against women and minorities, that

many questions are poorly written, and that coaching clinics are teaching students how to use the mechanics of the test to their advantage. The College Board, faced with the fact that a growing number of colleges no longer require applicants to take the SAT, is rewriting the test. The new version will replace the math and verbal sections with multiple-choice grammar questions, an essay question, and a math section that includes problems from Algebra II. The test-makers' goal is to rebuild confidence that SAT scores can predict how well a student will do in college."

Becky relaxed. "Well, I guess that makes sense. The colleges use the SAT to make sure that I've mastered the basic high school subjects. Then, if I don't lose my motivation or run out of money, they predict that I'll make it through to a degree."

Mr. Topping nodded and pulled out Becky's records. "This is a good time to look over your test scores. See, it's just as I expected. Your SAT scores correlate nicely with your overall achievement test results."

ACHIEVEMENT TESTS

Like Becky, you will take a number of different types of achievement tests during your school career. Your individual teachers will write tests to check up on your progress in their classes. Your school district will probably give you standardized achievement tests to check up on your general progress. Before you graduate, you may be asked to take a competency test to make sure you've reached a minimum level of achievement in basic skills such as reading, writing, and arithmetic. Even with school behind you, your chances of landing a job may depend on passing an achievement test. The Civil Service merit examinations, for example, test for the specific skills you'll need if you want to work for the government.

STANDARDIZED ACHIEVEMENT TESTS. When high schools want an overall picture of student progress, they turn to tests such as the Iowa Tests of Educational Development (ITED). This well-known battery was written to test the educational experiences gained by veterans while in the armed forces during World War II. Today, the ITED is composed of nine subtests, which also yield a composite score and an overall reading score:

- Vocabulary
- Reading Comprehension
- Language: Revising Written Materials
- Spelling
- Math: Concepts and Problem Solving
- Computation
- Analysis of Social Studies Materials
- Analysis of Science Materials
- Sources of Information

Results from tests like the ITED allow a school to compare its students with students across the country. If the school's reading scores come in lower than the average, administrators and teachers can take steps to improve the teaching of reading. Individual student scores can also be used to diagnose faulty skills so that remedial work can be assigned. A study by John Cannell in the late 1980s, however, set alarm bells ringing in the nation's schools. Cannell found that 70 percent of the country's students and 90 percent of its 15,000 school districts were testing

above the national norms on standardized achievement tests. American kids, he concluded with tongue in cheek, are "all above average." The root of this clearly faulty conclusion, Cannell said in a later report, is easy to find. First, the norms are based on obsolete data. Test publishers, he suggested, should compile annual national norms. Second, many schools are "teaching the tests" in order to make themselves look good. We can fix that problem, Cannell said, by making sure that teachers do not see the tests in advance.

Seniors who plan to continue their education often begin their assault on college admissions offices by taking either the SAT or the American College Testing Program (ACT). A smaller number sign up to take subject area achievement tests. Whatever challenge awaits you, prudence suggests that you can profit from extra work on the following skill areas:

1. *Vocabulary.* Success on most achievement test batteries relates closely to mastery of the language. Since vocabulary and word usage skills are so essential to scoring well on achievement tests, it pays to begin preparation early. Start by reading a variety of books, newspapers, and magazines on a regular basis. When you run across an unfamiliar word, look it up, rehearse it, and move it into long-term memory. When tackling a writing assignment, use a thesaurus (a dictionary of synonyms and antonyms) as a means of enriching your vocabulary. Word games such as anagrams, Password, and Scrabble also build up vocabulary. As the test date nears, spend some time with study guides that give directed practice in the kinds of questions that will appear on the actual test. If one is available, sign up for an evening or weekend "cram" course. Focused, well-organized review sessions can give you the confidence you need to do your best on the test.

If you were taking the vocabulary section of an achievement test today, you'd be answering questions such as these:

1. Choose the word that means the same as the word in capitals. CHRONIC (a) mild, (b) temporary, (c) healthy, (d) long-lasting, (e) regular.

2. Supply the word that best completes the sentence. No animal, with the exception of human beings, has had its ____ probed more thoroughly than the chimpanzee. (a) mental health, (b) genetic inheritance, (c) intelligence, (d) natural language, (e) sense of smell.

3. Select the pair of words that expresses a similar relationship to that expressed by the word in capital letters. PICADOR : BULL (a) heckler : speaker, (b) mote : eye, (c) executioner : victim, (d) singer : song, (e) matador : cow.

2. *Reading ability.* Both reading speed and reading comprehension count heavily in achievement tests. Typically, the test asks you to read a paragraph and answer questions about the content. Some readings are taken from literary works, others from nonfiction books. The usual reading comprehension question looks like this:

> The psychoanalyst attempts a measurement with an overhead that runs into years and thousands of dollars. The brain watcher, or personality tester, as we shall see, claims to be able to measure this same elusive human imponderable as easily and as accurately as counting compact cars off an auto assembly line. He can, he says, measure the psyche for anyone who wants to know, in as little time as five minutes, and as cheaply as $20 a head, less normal business discounts.
>
> In his attitude toward "brain watchers," the author expresses (a) uncertainty, (b) approval, (c) confidence, (d) sarcastic criticism, (e) optimism.

College admissions offices emphasize reading ability because most college students find their reading load increased by a factor of three (or more) over what they were assigned in high school. Fortunately, poor reading habits can be cured. Counselors recommend that students who read at 200 words per minute or less should enroll in a reading-improvement course.

3. *Mastery of numbers.* Achievement tests also emphasize mastery of basic numerical operations. Except for those that test specific mathematics skills, achievement tests seldom ask for computations and problem solving beyond algebra and geometry. They often include problems involving number series, ratios and proportion, and practical problems in area, volume, and percentages. Are you prepared to answer questions like these?

1. What comes next in the series 1 3 7 15? (a) 17 (b) 21 (c) 25 (d) 31 (e) 36

2. How many digits are there to the left of the decimal point in the square root of 863722.40815? (a) 3 (b) 4 (c) 5 (d) 6 (e) none of these

3. Pilots in a cross-country race know they must cover 225 miles in exactly 45 minutes to meet a checkpoint. At what speed should they fly to do this? (a) 169 mph (b) 225 mph (c) 275 mph (d) 300 mph (e) 450 mph

Achievement tests are also written to examine competency in a specific field. Depending on the college and your future field of study, you might be asked to take an achievement test in English composition or literature, American history, a foreign language, biology, chemistry, or physics. At this level, generalized reading and mathematics skills won't be enough. Subject-area tests demand that you demonstrate mastery of a particular body of knowledge.

Along with standardized, computer-scored achievement tests, you may be asked to take a *performance test.* If you have a driver's license, it's probable that you've already experienced your first performance test—a test that proved to an examiner that you can drive a car safely. Similarly, a secretary may be asked to take a performance test in word processing, and a mechanic may be given a malfunctioning engine to repair. Performance testing is also showing up in standardized achievement testing. Instead of relying solely on multiple-choice questions, test makers are adding open-ended word problems to math tests and asking for "real world" essays to demonstrate writing skills.

APTITUDE TESTS

If Becky K. goes on to a successful college career as a predentistry major, grades alone won't open the doors to dental school. As part of her application, she'll be expected to take the dental-school aptitude test. This test, like the SAT, will focus on Becky's reading skills, reasoning ability, mathematics skills, and her knowledge of science. She may also be asked to demonstrate a satisfactory level of hand-eye coordination. If the test is properly administered and interpreted, school officials will have a sound basis on which to judge Becky's potential as a dental student.

AREAS TESTED. Aptitude tests have been standardized to measure your talents in such areas as language, mathematics, art, music, mechanics, clerical skills, and manual dexterity. Most people, unless they are aiming at a specific field, take *multiple aptitude batteries.* These tests provide a complete profile of aptitudes in as many as nine different areas. The General Aptitude Test Battery (GATB), developed by the U.S. Employment Service, uses both written and performance tests to make sure the test taker meets minimum standards for typical occupations.

Another popular multiple aptitude battery is called the Differential Aptitude Tests (DAT). When used for vocational counseling, the DAT provides the kind of information students need to make career plans. The complete test takes about four hours over two separate testing sessions. You can get an idea of the DAT's eight sections by trying these sample questions:

1. *Verbal Reasoning:* ____ is to night as breakfast is to ____ (a) supper—corner (b) gentle—morning (c) door—corner (d) flow—enjoy (e) supper—morning.

2. *Numerical Ability:* 8 = ____% of 24. (a) 20 (b) 25 (c) 30 (d) 33⅓ (e) none of these.

3. *Abstract Reasoning:* Select the figure that completes the series.

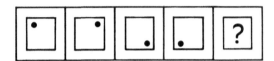

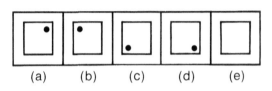

   (a)   (b)   (c)   (d)   (e)

4. *Clerical Speed and Accuracy:* Each item is made up of five combinations of symbols, one of which is underlined. Mark the same combination on the answer sheet.

		K	bB	BC	c̲B̲	bC	Cf
		L.	4B	4̲4̲	B4	BB	4C
Answer	K.	bC	BC	bB	Cf	cB
sheet	L.	B4	4C	44	4B	BB

5. *Mechanical Reasoning:* Which man has the heavier load? (If equal, mark C.)

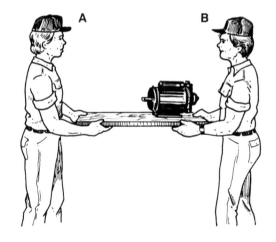

6. *Space Relations:* Which three-dimensional figure can be formed by folding the flat figure on top?

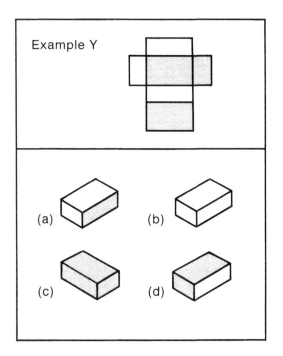

Example Y

(a)

(b)

(c)

(d)

7. *Language Usage (Spelling):* Tell whether each word is spelled right or wrong by marking R for right and W for wrong. A. alot B. friend C. summary D. nervous.

8. *Language Usage (Sentences):* Which section of the sentence contains an error?

Everyone are / invited to / the party / next Friday.
   (a)   (b)   (c)
   (d)

Figure 11.8 shows a typical profile of DAT scores. By matching this profile to the student's career plans, a counselor can help the student judge the suitability of his or her vocational choices. The DAT also provides a Career Planning Program. This program gives each test taker a computer printout that summarizes the information from the DAT profile. Jesse, for example, scored low in Mechanical Reasoning. In polite but firm language, the Career Planning Program will tell Jesse that his plan to become a machinist probably isn't the best choice for him. At the same time, the printout will point Jesse toward careers that match his higher scores.

Keith, by contrast, scored in the 90th percentile in Mechanical Reasoning. Because he's never done well in school, Keith has not made any career plans. His DAT results, however, have alerted him to an aptitude that has the potential of leading him into a better-paying, more satisfying job. An aptitude, however, is not the same as a developed talent. Aptitude tests can point Keith in the right direction, but they cannot supply him with motivation, training, or a strong work ethic.

■ SECTION CHECKUP

1 What is the difference between aptitude tests and achievement tests?

2 Why do colleges put so much emphasis on tests such as the SAT? How could you prepare yourself to do the best possible job on tests of this type?

3 The counseling office is offering you a chance to take the DAT. You've already decided on a business career. Would it make any sense for you to take the test? Why or why not?

11.5 ▓ WHAT CAN YOU LEARN FROM PERSONALITY TESTS?

Psychologists have long accepted the truism that each person is unique. In order to explore the cognitive dimensions of that uniqueness, they developed intelligence tests, achievement tests, and aptitude tests. A greater challenge arose when they tried to develop a standardized method of exploring emotions. Personality testing grew out of that

The Differential Aptitude Tests

The Psychological Corporation

Report for Anna Sample
09-Jan-01

DAT For Schools: Aptitude Profile
Reference Group: M + F Year 10 students
Educ. Plans: Voc./Tech. School

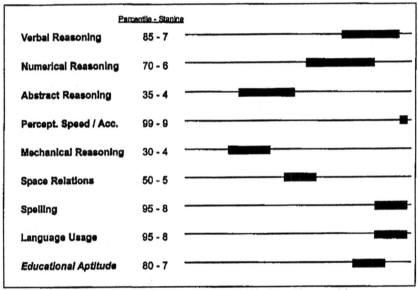

Differential Aptitude Test - Fifth Edition. Copyright © 1990 by Harcourt Assessment, Inc.
Reproduced by permission. All rights reserved.

FIGURE 11.8 ■ Anna just received this printout from her DAT. If you were helping her interpret it, what would you say are her strongest skills? Which are her weakest areas? What would you say about her desire to be a technical writer for an aerospace company?

quest. These tests are designed to measure emotions, motivations, attitudes, and the ability to relate to others. Properly used, they can help people bridge the gap that often exists between their self-image and the image they project to others.

Despite their widespread use, personality tests have a major weakness. To obtain valid results, the people who take the tests must report their innermost feelings openly and honestly. Some people cannot take that risk, so they answer the way they think they should answer. In fact, the test takers who most need help are the ones most likely to give dishonest or evasive answers. Moreover, the scoring of many personality tests is quite subjective. Even the most skillful examiners may find it difficult to evaluate vague and inconsistent data.

Despite their inherent flaws, personality tests play an important role in both counseling and in psychotherapy. This large family of tests can be divided into two general categories: interest inventories and clinical tests. *Interest inventories* help people learn more about their preferences in life-style, occupations, leisure-time activities, and friends. *Clinical personality tests,* by contrast, are designed to uncover emotional problems and tendencies toward neurotic or psychotic behavior.

THE INTEREST INVENTORY

Most students meet their first personality test when they take an interest inventory. These tests have been developed because of two related factors. First, ability does not guarantee success. Success comes when you possess a deep and abiding interest in a particular job or activity. Just as important, an interest inventory can put you in touch with interests that had previously gone unrecognized.

A TYPICAL INTEREST INVENTORY. The Strong-Campbell Interest Inventory (SCII) is the latest version of an older test called the Strong Vocational Interest Blank. The test begins by asking you to respond to 325 items. Under occupations, for example, you'll find architect, auctioneer, auto racer, and airplane pilot. For each item, you mark *like, dislike,* or *indifferent.* Later in the test, you'll be asked to respond in the same way to lists of activities and types of people. Once you've marked all the items, the test can be scored by hand or by computer. Separate scoring scales are provided for men and women.

Perhaps you have been thinking about a career in farming. With the SCII, you can compare your interest profile to that of suc-cessful farmers. If the two profiles match, you'll probably be happy and successful in that career. The SCII can presently be scored for more than 80 occupations, from actor to zoologist. People who enter occupations that match their SCII scores have shown a definite tendency to stay in those jobs.

INTERESTS AND JOB SUCCESS. Interest tests cannot take abilities and motivation into account. Low-energy city dwellers who lack manual dexterity may show a high interest in animal husbandry, but their chances of becoming successful ranchers would be nil. Similarly, people who couple high abilities with a total disinterest in a specific career are almost certainly doomed to failure. One investigation in the insurance field, for example, divided employees into three groups: *A* group, whose interests and abilities were geared to selling insurance; *B* group, whose interests were high but whose abilities were low; and *C* group, whose abilities were high but whose interests were low. The *A* group outsold the *C* group three to one, with the *B* group somewhere in between. Psychologists conclude, therefore, that interest inventories only point you in the right direction. You'll have to take it from there.

CLINICAL PERSONALITY TESTS

Clinical personality tests measure actual or predicted behaviors. If Reggie S. makes an appointment to begin psychotherapy, Dr. Olcina might ask him to take one or more personality tests as a shortcut way of gaining additional insight into Reggie's emotional makeup. Each test provides therapist and client with rating scales that describe a wide variety of behavior patterns. These scores, combined with a case history and Reggie's own talks with the therapist, will build a fairly complete picture of Reggie's attitudes, anxieties, fears, and reactions to stress.

A Prescription for Doing Your Best on a Test

Do you approach a test situation with a nervous, sinking feeling? A lot of people do, whether it is a psych quiz, a driving test, a tryout for the school orchestra, or a college entrance exam.

The secret to coping with test anxiety is to go into the test with the feeling that you're well prepared. Remind yourself that the test is *not* the enemy. Look on it as an ally in achieving something you want. Next, learning to be "test smart" will help you build the confidence you need to do your best work. The following guidelines apply primarily to tests taken in large groups and assume that you are familiar with the material covered by the test.

PREPARE YOURSELF FOR THE TEST

1 Follow a "business-as-usual" routine the day before the test. You won't build up an overload of nervous energy if you continue with your regular activities.

2 Try to get a full night's sleep. Spend an hour or two in a final review if you wish, but no amount of cramming will compensate for not feeling rested and relaxed on the day of the test.

3 For a morning test, set your alarm for two hours ahead of the scheduled starting time. To keep your energy level high, eat a breakfast high in protein and carbohydrates. Avoid fatty foods that tend to leave you feeling sluggish. You want your mind and body working at top efficiency when you open the test booklet.

4 Do not drink too many liquids. Some tests do not allow for restroom breaks.

5 Double-check to make sure you have the necessary equipment. Bring pens and pencils, a watch for keeping track of the time, a snack for energy, and a handkerchief or package of tissues. (Have you ever heard 50 people sniffling at once?) If you need a pass or receipt to enter the exam room, keep it readily available.

BEFORE THE TEST STARTS

1 Arrive early. You'll want time to become accustomed to the test environment.

2 Pick a seat that appeals to you. Look for good lighting, sufficient elbow room, and a clear view of the examiner.

Depending on Reggie's needs, Dr. Olcina has two basic types of clinical tests from which to choose. She might prefer an *objective personality test,* or what is also known as a self-report inventory. Objective tests require forced-choice responses, usually *yes, no,* or *cannot state*. Reggie's scores will be "graded" against a norm group established by the test makers. If she isn't convinced that Reggie will benefit from an objective test, Dr. Olcina can also use a *projective personality test*. On this type of test, Reggie will respond to the test items in a free, unstructured way.

OBJECTIVE PERSONALITY TESTS.   One of the best-known objective personality tests is the Minnesota Multiphasic Personality Inventory (MMPI) and its newborn sibling, MMPI-2. Although the MMPI-2 was written to correct some of the problems that had become apparent in a test originally developed and standardized during World War II, many clinical

3 Take some deep breaths and try to relax. Think of the test as a challenging game. It's not a matter of life or death, but you want to be slightly keyed up to do your best.

4 Listen carefully to the directions given by the examiner. If you don't understand something, ask to have it explained.

5 Survey the entire test before you begin—or as much of it as the directions allow. Check to see how much time you have for each section, so that you can budget your time.

WHILE TAKING THE TEST

1 Complete the answer sheet according to directions. The computer that scores it can't read your mind. Fill in the answer boxes fully, and erase old marks completely if you change an answer.

2 Check frequently to make sure that the number on the answer sheet corresponds to the number of the item you are working on.

3 Read the questions carefully. If you read directions too quickly, you may miss important words or phrases. Watch for qualifiers—words like *always* or *never*. Such words can affect the meaning of a statement or question. If you run into questions that you think could be answered several ways, make a reasonable choice and move on.

4 Most tests give equal credit to every question. If you're working against the clock, skip the difficult items and go on to the easier ones. Return to the puzzlers if you have time left over.

5 Work at top speed during the entire test. If your muscles start to feel cramped, take a 60-second break to stretch and take a few deep breaths. Relax your eyes by staring out the window or at the ceiling.

6 Don't assume that questions will become more difficult as you near the end of a section. More often than not, hard and easy items recur in cycles. Keep going, even though you feel discouraged.

7 Don't be afraid to trust your "educated" guesses. If the test doesn't penalize wrong answers (most count only the number of correct responses), eliminate the obvious distractors and go with the best of what's left.

WHEN YOU'VE FINISHED

1 Use the full time provided for the test. Even if you feel completely drained, try to save a few minutes to double-check everything.

2 Worrying about the test after you've walked out of the examining room won't change the results. Tell yourself you did your best and go on with your life.

---

psychologists and psychiatrists still favor the older test. Whichever version their therapist favors, test takers are asked to respond to over 550 statements as *true, false,* or *cannot say.* The items probe a variety of personal feelings and attitudes, including health, psychosomatic symptoms, marital and sexual attitudes, and occupational problems. If the subjects answer honestly, the test items are capable of revealing evidence of phobias, depression, conversion hysteria, paranoia, and other emotional disturbances. MMPI-2 adds scales that reveal tendencies toward eating disorders, substance abuse, and family dysfunction. The MMPIs also contain a built-in validity scale. Scattered through the test are key items such as "I never get angry." Too many "true" answers to these statements tell the examiner that the subject is lying to create a good impression or to cover up actual feelings. Sample items from the MMPI read like the following:

	T	CS	F
1. I have a good appetite	☐	☐	☐
2. I wake up fresh and rested most mornings	☐	☐	☐
3. I am easily awakened by noise	☐	☐	☐
4. These days I find it hard not to give up hope of amounting to something.........................	☐	☐	☐
5. At times I have very much wanted to leave home........................	☐	☐	☐
6. I usually have to stop and think before I act even in trifling matters	☐	☐	☐
7. Someone has been trying to poison me........	☐	☐	☐
8. I think I would like the work of a librarian	☐	☐	☐

Because it's easy to use and has well-established norms, the MMPIs have been used as a way of screening for personality problems in nonclinical situations. Colleges, the military, businesses, and even the original Soviet space program have based personnel decisions on the test. But although the MMPI's computer printouts give a sense of objectivity and accuracy, otherwise normal people sometimes score abnormally high on one of the test's ten behavior scales. These documented cases prove that the MMPI is capable of misdiagnosing an otherwise well-adjusted person.

Ethical questions regarding misuse of the MMPI and other personality tests have been raised, much as the improper use of intelligence tests has been criticized. Of particular concern has been the growing use of integrity tests by employers. A job applicant who scores below the cutoff point on one of these pencil-and-paper tests will be "selected out" as a potential shirker or thief. Although many psychometrists question the validity of simple integrity tests (a typical test contains only 33 questions), a number of major retail chains believe their use has sharply reduced employee theft.

PROJECTIVE PERSONALITY TESTS. Many psychologists believe that projective tests tell more about a subject's personality than do objective tests. The theory behind such tests is that people will "project" their innermost thoughts, anxieties, and conflicts on the "screen" provided by the test. When Audrey D. takes a projective test, the examiner's instructions will be brief. The test is designed to let Audrey's imagination operate freely, so that unconscious feelings can emerge.

Without a doubt, the most famous of all projective tests is the Rorschach Inkblot Test. Designed by Hermann Rorschach, a Swiss psychiatrist, the test simply asks the subject to look at and describe a set of ten inkblots (see Figure 11.9). If Audrey takes the test, she'll tell Dr. Olcina what she sees in each inkblot. The psychologist will write down exactly what Audrey says, including her incidental remarks, expressions of emotion, and even the position in which she holds the cards.

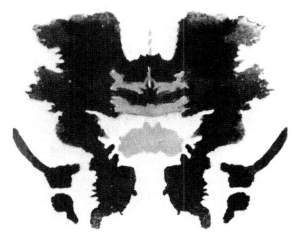

FIGURE 11.9 ■ Here is an inkblot used in the Rorschach test. What does the shape suggest to you?

Next, Dr. Olcina will question Audrey about her responses. If Audrey described one ink-blot as looking like two boys on a seesaw, the therapist would ask about the location of the seesaw, whether it was in motion, the age of the boys, and other related details.

Scoring scales for the Rorschach test have been developed on the basis of responses typical of known personality types. Certain descriptions, for example, are thought to point to specific forms of disturbed behavior. Using these scoring scales requires consider-able experience, and their interpretation is quite subjective. Rorschach specialists some-times call on a computer program called Ror-Scan as a way of increasing scoring objectivity. Other therapists have tackled the problem by switching to the newer Holtzman Inkblot Test and its 45 inkblots. The Holtz-man cuts down on the complexity of the ther-apist's task by allowing only one response per card.

Some people look on the inkblots as a chal-lenge to their own security. They may play it safe, giving only simple, obvious responses. Psychologists who like the Rorschach, how-ever, point out that no one knows what a specific description means, so people can't really "hide" what they're feeling.

In contrast to the Rorschach, the Thematic Apperception Test (TAT) consists of 20 cards. The examiner uses one set of cards for men and a second set for women. Each card shows a rather vague scene in which people's ac-tions and motives can be interpreted in a nearly infinite number of ways (see Figure 11.10). A TAT examiner would ask Audrey to make up a story based on each scene. She'll be asked to talk about the events that led up to the scene, what the people are doing and thinking, and what the outcome will be. The psychologist who interprets TAT stories looks at what they reveal about the subject's basic needs and the forces that are apparently keeping the client from satisfying those needs.

Imaginative test makers have produced an

FIGURE 11.10 ▓ What do you see in this pic-ture from the Thematic Apperception Test? Show it to several people and see how each story differs according to the varying personali-ties and experiences of your subjects.

impressive variety of projective tests. One rel-atively simple test relies on a number of in-complete sentences, which the subject completes as he or she wishes. Typical sen-tence completion items include:

1. I like _____ .
2. My greatest worry _____ .
3. Men _____ .
4. Women _____ .
5. This test _____ .

Other tests, particularly useful with chil-dren, use toys and art materials. Four-year-old Eva, for example, cannot respond in a meaningful way to inkblots or TAT scenes, but she will play happily with a troupe of dolls and a well-furnished dollhouse. The therapist would encourage Eva to talk about the dolls as she plays with them. Perhaps Eva cannot talk about her abusive home environment, but the truth will break through when "mommy doll" burns "baby doll" with a pretend cigarette.

In the Draw-a-Person and House-Tree-Person tests, children and adults use paper and felt-tip pens to draw themselves, their homes, and other familiar people and objects. The nonverbal, nonthreatening activity of drawing seems to open up feelings that would otherwise be repressed. If young Leo, for example, draws a father who towers over

everyone else, the therapist will begin to probe for further evidence that the boy feels overwhelmed by a dominating male parent.

■ SECTION CHECKUP

1 What is the difference between an interest inventory and a clinical personality test?

2 Why is ability no guarantee of success on a job?

3 Contrast objective and projective personality tests. What are the strengths and weaknesses of each?

LOOKING BACK: A SUMMARY

1 Psychological tests are designed to measure intelligence, achievement, aptitude, interests, and personality. When properly constructed, these tests meet four well-defined criteria: (a) They can be scored objectively. (b) They are standardized to norms representative of the general population. (c) They can be relied on to give consistent results. (d) They measure what they say they will measure. Whatever the type of test used, its value depends on proper administration and interpretation by trained psychologists, psychometrists, and counselors.

2 The concept of intelligence has never been defined to everyone's satisfaction. According to a generally accepted definition, intelligence is the total of all the mental abilities that allow an individual to solve whatever problems seem worth working on. Most psychologists today believe that intelligence is actually a number of related mental abilities, including memory, reasoning ability, perception, numerical skills, and verbal abilities. The traditional concept of IQ can be defined more precisely. IQ is the ratio of a person's mental age (as measured by an intelligence test) to the chronological age multiplied by 100. Modern psychometrists prefer to measure in-

telligence in units called standard deviations or standard age scores. By whatever name, IQ is an indication of a person's potential, not a judgment regarding that person's value.

3 In an individual intelligence test, an examiner administers the test directly to a single subject. Although they are expensive, individual tests generally provide a more accurate measurement than group tests. When large numbers of people must be tested, psychologists use the less expensive group tests. While most intelligence tests emphasize vocabulary and reading comprehension, nonverbal tests have been developed that measure intelligence without depending on language skills or cultural variables.

4 Because of increasing doubts about the validity and usefulness of intelligence tests, school boards and courts have limited their use. The debate hinges on several arguments. Since no firm definition of intelligence exists, how can it be properly tested? Also, some studies show that intelligence, at least as measured by the tests, can be "taught," using extra doses of nurturing and stimulation, beginning in infancy. Critics of intelligence testing have pointed out that most intelligence tests have a built-in cultural bias. That tendency of the tests to favor the majority culture, along with the effects of discrimination, seem sufficient to explain the apparent differences in IQ scores among racial and ethnic groups.

5 Achievement tests look backward to measure a person's accomplishments in mastering a specific subject or skill. Most achievement tests emphasize school-related skills—vocabulary, reading comprehension, word usage, and mastery of numbers. Achievement tests are also used to screen people for jobs or entry into special programs.

6 Aptitude tests look ahead to measure the possibility that an individual will succeed in learning a subject or skill. Multiple aptitude batteries can help people discover whether or not they have the abilities needed to enter various occupations. Psychologists caution, however, that having an aptitude does not guarantee success in a related career. Motivation and training are also necessary.

7 Personality tests attempt to measure an individual's emotions, motivations, and attitudes. Because of the subjective nature of such tests, the results must be interepreted with great care. Interest inventories help people take stock of their preferences regarding work, leisure-time activities, and friends. A subject's test profiles can be compared with those of successful people in a particular field to see if their interests match. Interest plus ability usually leads to success, but interest without ability or ability without interest does not make for productive careers.

8 Objective personality tests such as the Minnesota Multiphasic Personality Inventory ask the subject to make forced responses to hundreds of questions covering a variety of personal feelings and attitudes. The results give the psychologist some insight into possible problem areas in that subject's personality. Projective personality tests probe the unconscious by asking the subject to respond freely to unstructured material—inkblots, pictures, and unfinished sentences—or to "play" with toys and art materials. Both types of personality test measure specific personality traits such as conformity, neurotic tendencies, aggression, depression, and strength of personal beliefs.

ANSWERS TO TEST ITEMS

THURSTONE'S SEVEN BASIC MENTAL ABILITIES (pages 361–362)

1. Give yourself credit for any word that meets the rule, including *dear, deer, door, dour, daughter, disaster, despair,* and *Dover.*
2. *azbycxd*—w. *mmmlllkkk*—jjj. *acegik*—m.
3. 8264=male. 264=ale. 468=elm.
4. c.
5. Row b: face number 2. Row c: face number 1.
6. a. (a) 47.647211. b. (b) 10.263858.
7. b and e.

ANSWERS TO UNFAIR TEST ITEMS
(page 369)

1. Answer: *M,* because all the others are made with only three lines, but an *M* is made with four lines. You could also make a case for *A,* the only vowel, or *F,* the only letter not made with a diagonal line.
2. Answer: the knife (b), because all other objects begin with the letter *S.* Knife begins with the letter *K.* You could also have chosen the spoon (c), the only item without a cutting edge, or the scissors (e), which have two parts.

SAMPLE QUESTIONS FROM THE WAIS
(page 371)

1. Labor Day is celebrated on the first Monday of September.
2. 64 cents.

3. Give yourself credit if you repeat the sequence exactly as given.

4. The calendar tells you the month, but not the year.

5. You would need the actual blocks to complete this test item.

SAMPLE ITEM FROM THE PROGRESSIVE MATRICES TEST
(page 372)

The correct answer is (c).

SAMPLE ITEMS FROM THE COGNITIVE ABILITIES TEST (page 373)

1. c.
2. c.
3. e.
4. d.
5. e.

SAMPLE ITEMS FROM A TYPICAL ACHIEVEMENT TEST (page 381)

Vocabulary: 1. d. 2. c. 3. a.
Reading ability: d.
Mastery of numbers: 1. d. 2. a. 3. d.

SAMPLE ITEMS FROM THE DAT
(pages 382–383)

1. e.
2. d.
3. b.
4. You would mark cB and 44 on the answer sheet.
5. B
6. (d)
7. A. W.   B. R.   C. R.   D. R.
8. (a)

PUTTING YOUR KNOWLEDGE TO WORK

■ TERMS YOU SHOULD KNOW

achievement test	interest inventory	performance test
aptitude test	mental age	projective personality test
chronological age	multiple-aptitude battery	psychometrist
clinical personality test	normal curve of distribution	reliability
cultural bias	norms	standard age score
culture-free test	objective personality test	standard deviation
intelligence	objectivity	standardization
intelligence quotient (IQ)	percentile ranking	validity

■ CHAPTER CHECKUP

1 A useful definition of intelligence says that it is (*a*) a quality people are born with that never changes (*b*) a quality that is completely the result of environmental influences (*c*) a measure of the ability to solve the problems people face in building a successful life (*d*) the ability to achieve economic success.

2 According to the traditional IQ formula, six-year-old Gail, who tested at a mental age of eight, has an IQ of (*a*) 75 (*b*) 100 (*c*) 133 (*d*) 180.

3 A psychological test that does *not* measure the trait or behavior it claims to measure could not be called (*a*) objective (*b*) standardized (*c*) reliable (*d*) valid.

4 If the studies that show that IQ scores of young children can be increased are valid, (*a*) the dominant role of heredity in determining intelligence would be increased (*b*) the role of environmental influences would be increased (*c*) the role of both heredity and environmental influences would be decreased (*d*) the role of both heredity and environmental influences would be increased.

5 Cultural bias in an IQ test means that (*a*) the test makers are prejudiced (*b*) the test is not valid for any group taking it (*c*) anyone from a minority group who takes the test should automatically receive 15 extra points (*d*) the test contains items outside the experience of some minority groups, who earn lower scores as a result.

6 A simple way to distinguish between achievement and aptitude tests would be to remember that (*a*) achievement tests measure inborn traits while aptitude tests measure personality (*b*) an achievement test looks back at what you've learned, while an aptitude test looks ahead at what you could learn (*c*) achievement tests measure your IQ, while aptitude tests measure your interests (*d*) achievement tests measure general vocational skills, while aptitude tests measure what you've learned in specific subject areas.

7 If Sally's test profile on the Strong-Campbell Interest Inventory matches that of astronauts who have taken the test, (*a*) she's certain to be successful in that vocation (*b*) her interests are similar to those of astronauts, but she also must have aptitude, motivation, and education if she is to be successful in that field (*c*) she should ignore the results since scores on interest inventories have little correlation with vocational success (*d*) it means that she has an unconscious wish to become an astronaut.

8 The insights gained from a clinical personality test would not benefit (*a*) an adolescent who is having trouble keeping up with the demands of schoolwork and social adjustment (*b*) a man who cannot seem to keep a job, even though his skills fit the occupation (*c*) a woman who has been accused of repeated incidents of shoplifting (*d*) someone who gave false answers while taking the test.

9 Clinical personality tests (*a*) are useful only for those people with severe emotional problems (*b*) have been known to cause psychotic episodes in people who don't have any apparent emotional problems (*c*) offer useful insights to anyone who wants to learn more about his or her own abilities, interests, and needs (*d*) have such low validity that most states have outlawed their use.

10 When taking a group test, particularly of intelligence or achievement, it is a good idea to (*a*) work as quickly as possible and then rest if you have time left (*b*) never ask for help or to have directions repeated (*c*) get a good night's sleep and eat a balanced breakfast to ensure adequate energy and alertness (*d*) leave all questions blank that you aren't sure you can answer.

▪ EXPLORING CONCEPTS

1 Write a definition of intelligence that makes sense to you. Why do you think your definition is a good one?

2 As you're reading the newspaper, you see an article about a woman whose IQ tested out at 67 when she entered a mental hospital. Two years later, the report says, she was retested and found to have an IQ of 118. How can you explain the difference in the two IQ scores?

3 What advantages would be gained by administering a clinical personality test to an emotionally healthy person?

4 Distinguish among the uses of intelligence, achievement, aptitude, interest, and personality tests. Describe a situation in which each one would be useful.

5 Think back to the last time you took a standardized group test. Describe your feelings before, during, and after taking the test. List some techniques that you can use next time to decrease the tension of the test experience.

6 Some people maintain that personality tests are an invasion of privacy. Do you agree or disagree? Tell why. Under what circumstances should schools and employers be allowed to give personality tests?

▪ HANDS-ON ACTIVITIES

1 Make an appointment to see your guidance counselor for the purpose of better understanding the test results that have found a home in your cumulative record over the years. Prepare for the interview by jotting down some appropriate questions. As the interview progresses, look for elements of consistency or inconsistency in your scores, particularly in IQ and achievement results. Do you think your test scores accurately reflect your future school and career plans?

2 Invite a school psychologist or guidance counselor to visit your class to talk about the school's testing program. Ask the speaker to describe the various tests given, the ways in which the scores are recorded and used, and the programs of evaluation and follow-up that have been developed to ensure validity.

3 Use the *Readers' Guide* or your library's computer to track down several articles that discuss current research in the field of testing. Read the articles and write a critical analysis of one of them. Turn in your paper to your psychology teacher for evaluation.

4 Although the psychology profession maintains strict security on its standardized tests, you can find general purpose intelligence tests in bookstores and libraries. One of the best known is H. J. Eysenck's *Test Your IQ*. After taking the test and scoring your results, how would you rate the test? Does it provide information on standardization and validity? What mental abilities does it seem to emphasize? If your teacher is willing, share the test with other students in your class. *Remember, however, that the very fact that the test is available "over-the-counter" suggests that it may not meet proper standards. High or low, do not take your score too seriously.*

5 You can learn something about test construction by making up your own "friendship test." This is an interest inventory that asks people to respond to questions about their likes and dislikes in music, sports, food, school, books, and other areas that are important to you. First, write the test, using questions that you think reveal important attitudes and interests. Objective questions that you can score on a point basis are best. For example, "Rate these leisure activities from 1 to 5 (5 being the highest in interest for you): (*a*) watching TV (*b*) playing an outdoor sport (*c*) cruising in a car (*d*) going to a dance." When you have finished, make eight copies of your test. To "standardize" your test, try it out on three close friends. Their scores will give you your norms for judging the scores of your other subjects. (Remember, how-

ever, that it takes thousands of subjects to standardize a test properly.) Next, give the test to five persons you don't know very well. Did they score higher or lower than your friends did? What do you think their scores mean? Do you think you've written a valid test? Why or why not? You may even end up with several new friends at the same time that you're learning something about the complex art of test construction!

FOR FURTHER READING

Chafetz, Michael. *Smart for Life; How to Improve Your Brain Power at Any Age.* New York: Penguin Books, 1992. Chafetz draws on the latest research in neuropsychology to recommend what might be called a "brain fitness regimen." As with physical fitness programs, diet and exercise both play a role. The payoff, Chafetz says, will be in a more tenacious memory, heightened creativity, and faster problem solving.

Fixx, James. *Games for the Superintelligent.* New York: Barnes & Noble Books, 2003. Don't let the title put you off. The fun and beauty of the puzzles printed in this exasperating book are that they depend more on logic than mathematical wizardry.

Mensh, Elaine and Harry. *The IQ Mythology; Class, Race, Gender, and Inequality.* Carbondale, IL: Southern Illinois University Press, 1991. The Menshes will never be mistaken for supporters of IQ testing. Intelligence tests, they argue in this well-documented book, have always been biased. The authors are particularly effective when they tackle the old argument that IQ test results confirm the existence of genetically based race and gender differences.

Shurkin, Joel. *Terman's Kids; the Groundbreaking Study of How the Gifted Grow Up.* Boston: Little, Brown, 1992. Lewis Terman, the father of the Stanford-Binet, was convinced that the nation's future depended on its high-IQ children. In 1921 that near-obsession led him to begin a study of the lives of gifted children that continues to this day. Shurkin's book tells the compelling story of the 643 youngsters (they called themselves "Termites") chosen for the project. Some lived up to their early promise; others died young or drifted into dead-end jobs. All have something to teach us.

Gleick, James. *Genius: The Life and Science of Richard Feynman*. New York: Random House Value Publishing, 1994. Without a doubt, Nobel Prize winner Richard Feynman qualifies as one of the twentieth century's authentic intellectual heroes. Any account of the renowned physicist's life can be expected to describe his landmark contributions to quantum theory and the atomic bomb project, but Gleick also gives equal time to an exploration of Feynman's exuberant and many-faceted personality. Reading this book will leave you with a far greater appreciation of what the term "genius" really means.

Janda, Louis. *The Psychologist's Book of Personality Tests: 24 Revealing Tests to Identify and Overcome Your Personal Barriers to a Better Life*. New York: John Wiley & Sons, 2000. One of the truisms taught in any beginning psych class is that all of us are bumping up against psychological barriers that keep us from living a fully productive and satisfying life. The first step in breaking through those barriers is to identify them, and Dr. Janda's tests will help you assemble the data you need to make the breakthrough. Better still, you'll find expert advice at the end of each test that will help you make use of the insights that you've gained.

THE INDIVIDUAL AND SOCIETY

- BEHAVIOR IN GROUPS
- SEX ROLES, SEXISM, AND SEXUALITY

Chapter

12 BEHAVIOR IN GROUPS

Livia, a 15-year-old Puerto Rican, was brought to her high school principal's office. The note she carried said that she was suspected of smoking on campus. Although the girl didn't have any previous record of troublemaking, the principal decided to suspend her.

"It wasn't what she said," he reported later. "It was simply her attitude. There was something sly and suspicious about her. She just wouldn't meet my eyes. She wouldn't look at me."

Why did the principal jump to that conclusion? A social psychologist could probably tell you quite a lot about how people make up their minds. Unlike the psychologists who focus on individual behavior, social psychologists are more interested in the way people interact with others. After all, much of your behavior grows out of the fact that you were born into a particular culture. And no matter how independent you are, your every thought and action has been conditioned to some degree by your family, your community, your school, and the other groups to which you belong.

What would a social psychologist say about Livia's interview with her principal? Research shows that the messages sent through posture, movement, facial expression, and other physical actions often reveal what people are thinking or feeling. This type of *nonverbal communication* is often called *body*

language. Once you know the "vocabulary," you can interpret a wide range of messages without hearing a single spoken word.

It's easy to forget, however, that cultural differences can change the meaning of body language. By his standards, the principal was on firm ground. Livia stared at the floor during her interview, apparently unable to meet the principal's gaze. Her attitude, his experience told him, pointed to a guilty conscience. To make matters worse, Livia's mother complained to her neighbors instead of asking for a meeting with school officials. As a result, a group of Puerto Rican parents gathered at the school the next morning to demonstrate against Livia's suspension.

Body-language expert Julius Fast tells the rest of the story:

> Fortunately, John Flores taught Spanish literature at the school, and John lived only a few doors from Livia and her family. Summoning his own courage, John asked for an interview with the principal.
>
> "I know Livia and her parents," he told the principal. "And she's a good girl. I am sure there has been some mistake in this whole matter."
>
> "If there was a mistake," the principal said uneasily, "I'll be glad to rectify it. There are thirty mothers outside yelling for my blood. But I

questioned the child myself, and if ever I saw guilt written on a face—she wouldn't even meet my eyes!"

John drew a sigh of relief, and then very carefully, for he was too new in the school to want to tread on toes, he explained some basic facts of Puerto Rican culture to the principal.

"In Puerto Rico a nice girl, a good girl," he explained, "does not meet the eyes of an adult. Refusing to do so is a sign of respect and obedience. It would be as difficult for Livia to look you in the eye as it would be for her to misbehave or for her mother to come to you with a complaint. In our culture, this is just not accepted behavior for a respectable family."

Fortunately the principal was a man who knew how to admit that he was wrong. He called Livia and her parents and the most vocal neighbors in and once again discussed the problem. In the light of John Flores' explanation, it became obvious to him that Livia was avoiding his eyes not out of defiance but out of a basic demureness. Her slyness, he now saw, was shyness. In fact, as the conference progressed and the parents relaxed, he realized that Livia was indeed a gentle and sweet girl.

The outcome of the entire incident was a deeper, more meaningful relationship between the school and the community. . . . What is of particular interest in this story is the strange confusion of the principal. How did he so obviously misinterpret all the signals of Livia's behavior?

Livia was using body language to say, "I am a good girl. I respect you and the school. I respect you too much to answer your questions, too much to meet your eyes with shameless boldness, too much to defend myself. But surely my very attitude tells you all this."

How could such a clear-cut message be interpreted as, "I defy you. I will not answer your questions. I will not look

FIGURE 12.1 ▧ Can you read the body-language conversation going on between this couple? For example, who has just made a suggestion? Is the other person responsive? What clues told you how to "read" this bit of non-verbal communication?

you in the eyes because I am a deceitful child. . . ."

The answer of course is a cultural one. Different cultures have different customs and, of course, different body language. They also have different looks and different meanings to the same looks.

In America, for instance, a man is not supposed to look at a woman for any length of time unless she gives him her permission with a body-language signal, a smile, a backward glance, a direct meeting of his eye. . . . In other countries different rules apply.

In Latin countries, though freer body movements are permissible, such a look might be a direct invitation to a physical "pass." It becomes obvious then why a girl like Livia would not look the principal in the eye.

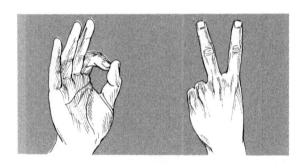

FIGURE 12.2 ▓ Hand gestures provide us with a simple, universal form of nonverbal communication—or do they? Consider the two common gestures shown at the left. Most Americans would agree that the thumb-and-forefinger circle means "A-OK," a friendly confirmation that everything is going well. If you use the gesture in some parts of Europe, however, be ready to fight. In France and Belgium, it means "you're worth nothing." A Greek would view it as a vulgar sexual invitation. Now, what about the palm-in V-sign? Americans use it as a shorthand for "victory," or as a quick way to order two soft drinks in a noisy cafe. If you're traveling in Great Britain, however, be sure to turn the palm *out* when you use the V-sign. Otherwise, you'll insult onlookers with the British equivalent of "the finger."

Studies in body language and cultural differences are only two of the many areas that attract the attention of social psychologists. As society grows more complicated and stressful, these studies become even more important. Before Americans can change *what* people are doing to each other, they need to know *why* they're doing it. In that context, this chapter will examine the following aspects of social psychology:

12.1 How do groups influence your behavior?

12.2. What effect do social pressures have on behavior?

12.3 What causes aggression? What can be done about it?

12.4 What causes prejudice? What can be done about it?

12.5 What can psychology tell you about suicide, aging, and death?

12.1 ▓ HOW DO GROUPS INFLUENCE YOUR BEHAVIOR?

Lord Chesterfield, an English writer, once advised his son that true knowledge of the world can be obtained only by studying people. The record doesn't show whether the younger Chesterfield took that counsel to heart, but social psychologists have certainly done so. Using all the tools of the social scientist, from research and experimentation to observation and surveys, these psychologists study individual and group behaviors within a social setting.

Does your family have an uncle like Tim? Normally, he's a mild-mannered, quiet fellow. But whenever the family gets together, he seems to go out of his way to argue with his siblings. Why does this usually gentle man turn so bitter and aggressive? Is he remembering ancient grudges left over from childhood? Is he reacting to the knowledge that he's been less successful than his brothers and sisters?

Tim is an excellent example of how family dynamics can upset the equilibrium of an otherwise well-adjusted person. How did he learn his responses to family pressures? What does he feel about his place in the family?

The Lure (and Danger) of Gangs

Youth gangs have long been a part of life in the inner city. Today, these violence-prone groups have spread to well-to-do suburban communities as well. Parents, politicians, and the police look with horror on this phenomenon and seek ways to combat it. Some counsel social programs to wean young people away from the gang culture. Others demand stricter laws and tougher enforcement.

Why do teenagers risk their lives and freedom by joining gangs? First, like most adults, teenagers tend to act in what they see as their own self-interest. In interviews, young men and women speak freely about gang membership:

Gangs offer a sense of belonging.
Lacking a coherent family life of their own, many members find a substitute family in the gang, complete with siblings and older role models. They are drawn to the gang's distinctive clothing and colors, its willingness to fight for its territory, and its access to drugs and alcohol. Knowing the gang's signs and secrets gives them a much-needed sense of identity.

Gangs offer a sense of power.
Gang members enjoy the feelings of fear they inspire in outsiders. In communities ruled by fear, they walk the streets with a swaggering sense of security. If they have a tendency toward violence, the gang culture encourages and rewards it.

Gangs offer financial rewards.
In poverty-stricken neighborhoods, gang members often wear gold chains and drive fast cars. Drug dealing, robbery, and other crimes provide financial rewards as well as the thrill of challenging adult authority.

Contrary to their public image, gang members are quite aware of the hazards of their way of life. They know that belonging to a gang involves a number of risks.

Gangs are schools for crime.
Joining a gang means embarking on a life of violence and lawlessness. Even though many gang members do not think of themselves as criminals, they are drawn inexorably into drug use and drug dealing, robbery, extortion, and (all too often) murder.

Gang members live with danger and death.
Gang members live in a constant state of warfare with the police and with other gangs. Many die in drive-by shootings that often claim innocent lives as well. A large number of gang members who escape death or injury on the streets spend time in prison for gang-related crimes.

Gang members are trapped.
The twin lures of security and easy money are addictive. Some gangs threaten members who try to resign with violence or exposure and arrest. Those who make the break after starting their own families may later be dismayed to find that their children are growing up to become second-generation gang members.

Given the chance, the social psychologist would study Uncle Tim in all his social roles: as a family member, as a worker, as a citizen, as a member of the bowling team, and as a church deacon. In learning more about Tim, they would also gain insight into the behavior of other people as well.

GROUP BEHAVIOR

Most people are surprised to discover how many groups they belong to (see Figure 12.3). Take yourself, for example. Any time you join with other people who share common goals and who feel a sense of interdependence, you've become part of a group. You probably belong to a family group, a religious group, a group of students called a psychology class, an athletic team, a social club, and so on. If you examined these varied groups carefully, you'd find that they have two basic functions. Some groups, such as a committee set up to plan the homecoming dance, are *task oriented*. *Socially oriented groups,* by contrast, have the primary purpose of providing social interactions for their members. If your school is at all typical, the daily bulletin will announce meetings of the art club, the foreign languages club, and other special-interest groups. Some groups combine both functions, as when a task-oriented soccer team puts on a pancake breakfast to raise money for a summer trip to Europe.

Most groups change over the years. Even within the family, people grow up and move away, marriages and divorces take place, and feuds sometimes develop. But studies show that the basic rules of group behavior remain fairly constant.

1. Group size greatly affects the manner in which group members interact. As groups grow larger, opportunities for taking leadership roles decrease. A growing sense of frustration can splinter the group into warring factions. Knowing this, youth groups such as the Boy Scouts and Camp Fire Girls keep their units small in order to encourage interaction.

2. Group behavior can be conditioned by reward and punishment, just as individual behavior can be changed. When teachers punish an entire class for the misbehavior of a few, they are using this principle. This policy will backfire, however, if the group bands together to support its transgressors.

3. The ability of a group to reach its goals depends largely on how well its members work as a unit. A basketball team that turns a deaf ear to the coach's pleas for team play will not win many championships, no matter how skilled the players are as individuals.

4. In most groups, both participation and distribution of rewards tend to be unequal. You've probably noticed how often a few people do most of the work. In a similar way, rewards are often given out to only a handful of the members—and not always to those who most deserve them. All-American awards, for example, often go to a few highly publicized athletes. Meanwhile, the team members who made their victories possible must content themselves with a little reflected glory.

5. People are more likely to stay with groups they join voluntarily if joining requires a sacrifice of some sort. Social groups such as fraternities and sororities, for example, bind their members tightly to the organization by making initiations both difficult and painful. Similarly, the military academies make the first year of school so demanding that most of those who survive develop deep loyalties to their branch of the service. Communes, which bring their members together for religious, political, or economic reasons, work best when new members are required to give all they own to the common community. The rule seems clear: if you make personal sacrifices to join, you're more likely to stay with the group.

FIGURE 12.3 ▪ Although American society values individual freedom and responsibility, people spend much of their time in groups. What does group membership contribute to the individual? How many groups do you belong to?

ROLES WITHIN GROUPS

Every group assigns roles to its members. A *role* is the pattern of behavior that allows the group to fulfill its functions. Your family, for example, expects certain behaviors from you in your roles as son or daughter, brother or sister, cousin, part-time household worker, student, and so on. If you don't play these roles according to the family's rules, you'll probably feel pressure to change. Psychologists call these rules for role playing in a particular situation the *social norms* of the group. In your role as son or daughter, for example, you run into situations in which the social norms vary. At an everyday family meal, you

can feel relaxed about your dress, speech, and table manners. When Aunt Alice invites everyone to an expensive restaurant, the rules change. Along with dressing and behaving differently, you'll *feel* different as well.

INFLUENCE OF SOCIAL NORMS. Learning social norms for the groups you belong to (a process called *socialization*) is one of your most demanding tasks. Roles in recreational and work groups are the easiest to learn. If you're a tennis player or a short-order cook, you'll quickly learn the social norms of the tennis court or the restaurant kitchen. Even so, the sports pages in recent years have been full of stories about tennis players who shout obscenities at officials and opponents alike. Much of the shock tennis fans feel over such antics stems from the unconscious fear that the very foundations of the sport will crack if players are allowed to violate its norms.

Family roles and social roles are more challenging and differ from person to person. Think of your own roles. Outside the family, you must learn the social norms that go with belonging to clubs, teams, work crews, political organizations, and the like. As a friend, you will be expected to be loyal, affectionate, and ready to share new experiences. A friend who breaks these social norms usually destroys the friendship.

At an obvious level, your roles require that you learn different ways of dressing, speaking, and behaving. At a deeper and more important level, you must develop the emotional values that attach to certain roles. Jarvis C., for example, left home at 18 and severed all connections with his family. Now, 20 years later, is he still a son to that family? In a genetic sense, yes. But in a social sense, by abandoning his role as son, he "resigned" from the family group.

LEADERSHIP. Every group has a leader. Sometimes leadership is shared; sometimes it is exercised in a dictatorial fashion. Whatever the style of leadership, someone must make decisions, give orders, settle conflicts, and keep the group moving toward its goal. Psychologically, the forces that create a leader instead of a follower cannot be pinned down exactly. Many people seem to enjoy the challenge of taking over and getting things done. Their abilities and personalities fit them for this role. Others would prefer not to take a leadership role but accept it when necessary. Less positively, a smaller group of people seek power as a way of compensating for their own inadequacies.

Many leaders are chosen on the basis of their ability to do a job. If you were going to climb Mt. Everest, you'd want an expedition leader who knows how to make the climb safely and efficiently. In politics, leaders are often selected on the basis of their powerful personalities. This personal appeal, a quality known as charisma, sometimes overwhelms more objective measures of ability. The election of popular entertainers to public office, for example, may depend more on looks and style than on ability. Other leaders gain control because their jobs give them the power to do so. Popular state governors and U.S. senators, for example, have a better chance of being elected president than do equally qualified candidates who lack national name recognition. Finally, there are leaders who use underhanded tactics to gain power. These manipulators will do whatever they think is necessary to consolidate their authority over the group.

No single style of leadership guarantees success for a group. Sometimes democratic processes work best, with everyone sharing in the decision making. With other groups, discipline and efficiency may require a strong leadership hand. Generally, groups work best when the members freely choose their leaders and agree on the group's goals.

■ SECTION CHECKUP

1 Why are psychologists interested in group behavior?

2 What is the difference between a task-oriented group and a socially oriented group? Give several examples of each.

3 Name some of the roles you play in the groups to which you belong. List some social norms for one of those roles. Under what conditions do these rules change?

4 List four ways in which a person can gain a leadership position in a group. Give an example of each.

5 Why do most groups follow democratic processes when choosing their leaders?

12.2 ▧ WHAT EFFECT DO SOCIAL PRESSURES HAVE ON BEHAVIOR?

You are walking with a group of friends through the zoo. Just as you pass a "Keep off the grass" sign, Rex says, "Let's cut across right here." He hops over the railing, and the others follow. What do you do?

Most people would ignore the sign and go with their friends. Social psychologists call this *conformity,* the willingness to accept the social norms of a particular group. The opposite of conformity, of course, is *nonconformity.* What if Rex said, "Let's throw rocks at the elephants so we can see them stampede." At that point, you would almost certainly choose to be a nonconformist. The desire to protect the animals would be stronger than your need to keep the approval of your friends. Psychologists try not to make judgments about whether conformity is right or wrong. Instead, they're more interested in *why* people tend to conform.

Research shows, for example, that group pressure can cause people to deny the evidence of their own senses. One of psychologist Solomon Asch's experiments proves this point. Asch starts by seating his subject in a room with five or six other so-called subjects. Actually, these other five are "stooges" who already have been given their instructions. After Randy, the actual subject, sits down at the end of the table, Asch holds up a card with an eight-inch line drawn on it. He calls it the standard line. Next, Asch picks up a second card that shows three lines of various lengths. The task, he says, is to match the standard line to the proper comparison line on a series of cards. In control tests, subjects pick the correct line 99 percent of the time. In the experiment, Randy and the stooges begin by guessing the first two cards correctly. But on the third trial the stooges pick the longest line, even though it is clearly longer than the standard line. This puts Randy in a bind. He

can see that line *A* is wrong. Should he trust his own eyes, even though that means going against the judgment of the others?

If Randy is typical, he'll stick to his own decision, but he'll show a high degree of nervousness as he does so. About one third of Asch's subjects, however, conform to the group choice. When asked about it later, some subjects rationalize by saying they didn't want to upset the group or that they felt it was all a trick. But others insist that they really thought the two lines were identical. Unconsciously, they solved their conflict by denying its very existence!

What other factors influence conformity? Self-confident people stand up to group demands for conformity better than those who have low self-esteem. The degree of authority behind the pressure for conformity also plays a major role. Imagine a situation in which high school seniors have littered their lunch area. Whose request to clean up would they be most likely to honor—one from a ninth grader, a student council leader, or the

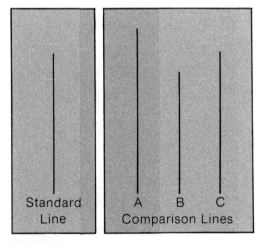

FIGURE 12.4

principal? Finally, conformity also varies according to the rewards or punishments it brings. Most people pride themselves on their independence, but they readily sacrifice that pride if conformity will win social approval. That's probably the reason why some of Asch's subjects picked the wrong lines. In fact, as soon as someone else disagreed with the majority's choice, most subjects in Asch's experiments felt free to select the correct line.

TYPES OF CONFORMITY

Social psychologists have identified three types of conformity: compliance, identification, and internalization.

COMPLIANCE.   When you conform only long enough to gain a reward or avoid a punishment, your behavior can be called *compliance.* Elementary school classrooms are good places to watch this type of conformity. Normally noisy, restless youngsters surrender to the discipline of schoolwork and class routine in order to earn grades and approval. But watch them as they burst out of their classrooms at the end of the day. Most of them throw compliance to the winds as soon as they're dismissed.

IDENTIFICATION.   You've probably noticed that some teenagers copy the style and man-

nerisms of their favorite entertainers or sports stars. If the lead singer in a popular rock group appears in a new hairstyle, it won't be long before her fans begin copying the cut themselves. This type of conformity, known as *identification,* helps people feel as though they are part of a glamorous, exciting world that they admire. Sharing the identity of a successful person provides only a limited amount of satisfaction, however. By middle and late adolescence, most young people have switched much of their energy to the task of developing their own identities.

INTERNALIZATION.   The process of integrating a set of values into your own thinking and behavior is called *internalization.* You brush your teeth and comb your hair each day because you've made the values of society part of your own personality. Start the day without combing your hair and brushing your teeth and see how uncomfortable you feel! Values relating to honesty, trust, patriotism, and other important aspects of life are also internalized. Once a value becomes part of you, it will probably stay with you, even when you leave the original group associations behind. Adults who move to another country, for example, almost always retain some of the customs and values of their native land.

REASONS WHY PEOPLE CONFORM

By now, you've probably wondered about your own degree of conformity. Some people conform more than others, and each person has different reasons for accepting the restrictions on independence that conformity imposes. Five reasons for conformity can be seen in the following listing.

FIGURE 12.5 ▪ Fashions in clothing often reflect the type of conformity that psychologists call identification. What evidence of this kind of conformity do you see here?

SHARED VALUES. If you decide to join an organized group, it's probably because you like something about it. As a member, you understand that the group's success depends upon working together and sharing common goals. But what happens when group values conflict with an individual's other needs? Belinda joined the drill team, for example, because she wanted to perform at football games. Now she realizes that the practices and performances interfere with her homework. If the drill team is important enough to her, she will conform to its demands and accept lower grades. Or she can drop out of the group and concentrate on winning a scholarship.

DESIRE TO BE LIKED. The need to be accepted by a peer group is a powerful force for compliance. This seems especially true during adolescence when young people need to know that other teenagers find them attractive and interesting. When Lloyd moved into a new school, he felt lonely and left out. Anxious to gain acceptance, he went out for the cross-country team. In truth, Lloyd was out of shape, and the practice runs almost killed him. In addition, his father laughed at him for spending all that time running when he could have been making money at a part-time job. But Lloyd refused to give up. The chance to make new friends was worth the pain of practice and the disapproval of his family.

NEED TO MAINTAIN RELATIONSHIPS. People will often conform to maintain an important relationship. Thus, a husband will take up tennis in order to be with his wife, even though he'd rather spend his free time on the golf course. Similar compromises are common in sports and business. Some baseball managers, for example, insist that their players shave off beards and mustaches as a condition for playing on the team. And if your job depends upon exchanging a T-shirt and blue jeans for a three-piece suit, you'll very likely conform. For employees who work in an office run by a conservative boss, the price of nonconformity might well be measured by dismissal notices.

ACCEPTANCE OF AUTHORITY. Obedience to authority represents a special type of conformity. Experiments have shown just how deeply embedded respect for authority is in most Americans (see pages 409–410). Conforming to the wishes of those who have power over you begins in infancy. The baby's demands for attention and unlimited freedom slowly bend to the socializing process. This inner respect for authority lasts a lifetime. You can confirm that statement by talking to anyone who has ever looked up to see a flashing red light in the rearview mirror. Even if the individual was driving safely and sanely, that old childish reaction to authority probably caused a momentary surge of doubt and guilt.

GUILT FEELINGS OVER PAST ACTIONS. At some point in your life, you've probably felt the sense of guilt that accompanies the breaking of a social norm. Even if you weren't caught, the inner voice of conscience still speaks up when similar situations arise. For example, Elsa and Tony once took money from their family's grocery funds to buy treats for their friends. They were never caught, but 20 years later they still remember the terrible guilt feelings they experienced. Both Elsa and Tony now enforce stricter standards of honesty in their own families than those they were taught as children.

COGNITIVE DISSONANCE

Meet Walt Adams and Laura Vickers. They're going to demonstrate a special kind of response to pressure.

Walt smokes like a steam locomotive, three packs a day. Like just about everyone else these days, Walt knows that cigarettes can cause lung cancer. A social psychologist would call the conflict between what Walt

FIGURE 12.6 ■ Performing in a marching group demands long hours of practice. Why do these marchers sacrifice individual freedom and accept the constraints of group discipline?

does (smoke heavily) and what he knows to be true (the cigarette-cancer link) a *cognitive dissonance*. Listen as Walt tells his friend Laura how he resolves this inner conflict.

LAURA: Hey, Walt. I thought you were giving up smoking!

WALT: Yeah, I thought about it. But, you know, old Henry Peters is 90 years old, and he still smokes a pack a day. I'm beginning to think those cancer stories were made up by a bunch of health nuts.

LAURA: The statistics look pretty scary to me. Smoking cigarettes is almost as dangerous as working in a coal mine.

WALT: Besides, I've switched to a low-tar brand. And if I stopped smoking, the stress from my job would kill me in three months. My smokes are really lifesavers!

Can you see what Walt is doing? Lacking the will to kick his addiction, he must justify that decision *to himself*. No one can live comfortably with a heavy load of cognitive disso-

nance. The unresolved conflict will not give you peace until it's resolved.

When she's not arguing with Walt, Laura is an active member of a group that protests the generation of nuclear power. Given her strong views, is there any way to moderate her position? One way would be to talk her into taking the pro-nuclear side in a debate. Afterward, win or lose, you'll find that her feelings about nuclear power very likely will have softened. In order to uphold her side of the debate, Laura will have been forced to research the positive aspects of nuclear plants. As she does so, she will unconsciously modify her more extreme views in order to reduce the resulting cognitive dissonance. Otherwise, she couldn't have carried on the debate.

The lesson is that you'll often find yourself in a position in which your actions won't square with your beliefs. In order to reduce dissonance, you'll find some way to justify your behavior. Sometimes you can do it by citing facts you've heard or read about, as Walt did by citing "evidence" that heavy smoking won't really cause cancer. Or you can find reasons you had previously ignored, as Laura did by "discovering" unexpected values in nuclear-power plants.

Let's say that you believe profanity is wrong. But your new friends use four-letter words rather freely. You feel pressured to talk like the others, and before long you're using these formerly taboo words. Your dissonance is clear. You can either soften your anti-profanity position or give up friends who are important to you. Many people would unconsciously modify their attitude toward profanity, perhaps on the grounds that "everybody talks like that these days." But reducing dissonance without examining the decision may leave you open to more compromises in the future. In time, people who take this "easy" route may not be able to admit to making mistakes at all, as the following experiment reveals.

SOCIAL DANGERS OF CONFORMITY

Psychologist Stanley Milgram upset a lot of people with his experiments. He upset himself as well. Milgram started with the hypothesis that German citizens obeyed the orders of their Nazi rulers during World War II because they were conditioned to obedience. In contrast, he reasoned, Americans would never follow orders that would result in harm to other human beings. To test this part of his theory, Milgram ran an experiment that is still being discussed.

Imagine that you're living in New Haven, Connecticut, in the early 1960s. You have answered an ad offering $4.50 to take part in a learning experiment. Upon entering the laboratory, you meet an experimenter dressed in a lab coat and a second subject. You learn that the experiment deals with the effect of punishment on learning. Your partner, an older man, tells you that he has a mild heart condition. The experimenter conducts a drawing to see who will be the teacher and who will be the learner. You draw a slip that assigns you to be the teacher. You watch as the learner is strapped into an "electric chair," with electrodes attached to his wrists. In a

second room, the experimenter seats you in front of an impressive-looking shock generator (see Figure 12.7). You count 30 switches, ranging from 15 volts to 450 volts. The warning signs above the switches warn of "Slight shock" for the low-level voltages up to "Danger—severe shock" for the higher voltages.

The experimenter touches your arm with an electrode. The shock hurts! Clearly, this experiment is for real. In your role as teacher, you're told to read a test to the learner. When he responds correctly, you go on to the next item. If he answers incorrectly, you are ordered to give him an electric shock. The first shock is set at 15 volts; each additional mistake adds another 15 volts. You can't see the learner, but an intercom lets you talk to each other.

Now, you're ready. You read a word, and the learner answers. One right. Two right. Then he makes an error. You reach for the switch. You know it hurts. You remember the shock you received. What about his heart condition? As you hesitate, you look at the experimenter. He's watching you, clipboard in hand. Your hand is on the switch. Do you flip it?

Almost all of the subjects did; not until the

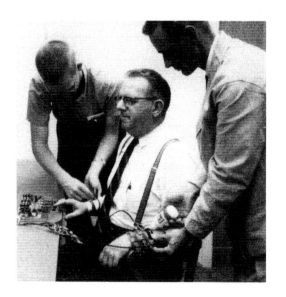

FIGURE 12.7 ■ The Milgram experiment on obedience to authority puts you in front of a "shock generator." The "learner" is strapped in and hooked up to electrodes. When the "learner" makes his first mistake, would you give him the shock as instructed? (Copyright 1965 by Stanley Milgram. From the film *Obedience,* distributed by The Pennsylvania State University, Audio Visual Services.)

409

voltage level reached 285 did some subjects refuse to continue. They stood up and left the room. But Milgram found that about 65 percent of his subjects do not stop with the first switch; they go on to the 450-volt level. As they do so, they hear the learner moan, complain, and finally scream. In the end, the learner lapses into silence. Is he unconscious? Even so, at the urging of the experimenter, some subjects continue to administer heavier and heavier shocks. They break into a sweat and their hands tremble, but they keep on flipping the switches.

You've probably guessed by now that the learner is an actor. He knows when the switches are thrown so he can time his screams properly. Sitting at the control panel, the subjects can't help but believe that the older man is receiving a series of shocks, each more painful than the last. Their responses tell us that a majority of American men ages 20 to 50 will obey authority even when it means harming another person. Milgram concluded:

> With numbing regularity good people were seen to knuckle under the demands of authority and perform actions that were callous and severe. . . . The kind of character produced in American democratic society cannot be counted on to insulate

its citizens from brutality and inhumane treatment at the direction of malevolent authority.

You'll often run into less extreme situations in which the social pressure to conform runs counter to your personal values. To be a nonconformist simply to be different is a kind of game. To be a nonconformist when it costs you acceptance, financial gain, or personal pleasure is another matter.

A popular sign in business offices reads, "Examine the turtle. It makes progress only when it is willing to stick its neck out." The best time to decide on the values you'll stick your neck out for is now. If you wait until you confront the actual situations, it may be too late.

■ SECTION CHECKUP

1 What does the psychologist mean by conformity and nonconformity? Give a sample of each based on something you have experienced personally.

2 What are some of the reasons why people conform?

3 What is the significance of Stanley Milgram's experiment on obedience to authority? Why did he think Americans wouldn't accept orders to hurt another person?

12.3 ■ WHAT CAUSES AGGRESSION? WHAT CAN BE DONE ABOUT IT?

Almost any day's headlines tell the story:

> TERRORISTS KILL 47 IN BOMB ATTACK
> STRIKERS BURN FACTORY TRUCKS
> LOVERS' LANE KILLER STRIKES AGAIN
> DRIVE-BY SHOOTINGS TERRORIZE
> NEIGHBORHOOD

And so it goes. Incidents of *aggression,* in which one person inflicts physical or emo-

tional injury on another, seem to dominate the news. You don't need a psychologist to tell you that violence can dominate personal relationships just as surely as it sometimes dominates relationships between ethnic and national groups.

Despite extensive research, psychologists do not agree on the causes of aggression in humans. According to the simplest explanation, aggression is an instinctive behavior that appears when the proper stimulus occurs. Naturalist Konrad Lorenz, for example, found this pattern in the attack behavior of the male stickleback fish. When the stickleback sees a red spot on the belly of a second male, he attacks. If a researcher moves the spot to the other fish's head, the aggressive male remains calm. Driven by that same instinct, stickle-backs will attack a red-spotted wooden fish just as fiercely as they do a live rival. Although a few scientists have tried to apply this theory of inborn and uncontrollable aggression to humans, the bulk of the evidence does not support the theory.

A related viewpoint suggests that people are "wired" for aggression at conception. Each person has an inborn capacity for vio-lence, the theory says. But violent behavior is activated only when something blocks the in-dividual's ability to satisfy his or her needs. Frustration, therefore, emerges as the trigger-ing mechanism for aggression. If you're standing in line for concert tickets, for exam-ple, you probably feel relaxed and happy as you look forward to hearing your favorite group. Then, just as you get to the ticket win-dow, it slams shut. A sold-out sign appears. You feel frustrated—and with the frustration comes anger and a desire to get even. Unlike the stickleback, however, you're not pro-grammed to be blindly aggressive. You can shout and pound on the gates with the rest of the crowd—or you can shrug and walk away.

Many modern psychologists prefer a the-ory that describes aggression as a learned re-sponse to frustration. Human beings, they say, become aggressive when inner tensions become unbearable. If those tensions can be relieved before you reach the bursting point, you probably will not act aggressively. Men-tally healthy people have no natural instinct for violence. If society could solve such deep-rooted problems as poverty, discrimination, pollution, and the like, aggressive behavior would be greatly reduced. In the meantime,

parents and teachers must take the lead in teaching children to use nonviolent methods of coping with the inevitable frustrations of daily life.

SOCIAL CAUSES OF AGGRESSION

Aggression takes many forms. Angry, frus-trated parents may abuse their children. Teenagers vandalize schools that do not meet their needs. Mobs loot neighborhood stores during a power blackout. A recently fired em-ployee grabs a rifle and starts shooting co-workers.

A number of factors may be involved in such violent behavior.

REWARDS TO BE GAINED.   Some parents un-knowingly reward aggression in their chil-dren. Children who gain attention by fighting, truancy, or other disruptive acts may carry their aggressive behavior into later life. It's the same principle that applies to any learned behavior: If the behavior is rewarded, the be-havior will be repeated. In time, it will be generalized to other situations. Imagine that Roy has grown up with a father who tells him to stick up for his rights by "smacking the other kids when they get in your way." Now that he's a teenager, is it any surprise that Roy reacts to conflict by "smacking people"?

MODELS OF AGGRESSION.   Critics charge that television, comic books, and professional sports all seem to teach the same lesson: Ag-gression solves problems and pays off in prestige, money, and self-esteem. A study by psychologist Albert Bandura showed how children model their behavior on that of adults. After preschool children were frus-trated in a task, they were allowed to see an adult punch, kick, and shout at a Bobo clown doll. Afterward, both boys and girls copied the adult aggression against the doll. When the adult remained calm, the children also handled their frustration more peacefully.

Social psychologists find abundant evidence that TV provides a similar model for aggression. Heavy TV viewing by younger children, research shows, produces the same modeling effect demonstrated by Bandura. Violence on the screen, for example, apparently has triggered real-life "copycat" crimes by children and adults. TV's defenders dispute this charge. The link between television watching and aggression has not been proved, they say.

PROTECTION OF TERRITORY.   Many animals are born with an instinctive need to protect their territory. Rats in a closed colony live peacefully together until their high birth rate leads to overcrowding. At that point, fighting breaks out over living space, and the social order breaks down. Some social critics fear that similar forces may be affecting the millions of people who live in crowded cities. As traffic congestion increases drive time and frays tempers, motorists begin to take their frustrations out on each other.

Psychologist Jonathan Freedman, however, disputes the close parallels that some researchers find between animals and people. "Small animals," he says, "have a very small social structure. They have one way of life. If anything interferes, they have no way of coping with it. . . . Human beings, by contrast, are terribly adaptable. They . . . are amazingly gregarious, so it is natural for us to live in very dense communities." Freedman's research tells him that crowding has no direct relation to the crime rate, delinquency, mental illness, and other social problems. He concludes, "If the cities can be made healthy, pleasant places to live in, the high density will enhance the positive aspects of city living, and the cities can continue to be what they have been in the past—dynamic, vital forces."

LACK OF POWER.   Poverty, prejudice, old age, and illness can cause people to feel as though they have lost control of their lives. They feel "invisible," their needs ignored by the rest of the society. Lacking hope, they may turn to aggression as a means of protest. Similar feelings develop when one group believes that another group is taking advantage. Workers on strike, for example, may turn their frustration into violence when employers refuse to negotiate demands for higher pay or improved health benefits. Such violence was once a common outgrowth of management-labor confrontations. Today, it is usually confined to lengthy strikes or strikes in which a company hires nonunion strikebreakers.

REDUCING AGGRESSION

One way to reduce aggression is to do away with the frustrations that cause it. Elimination of overcrowding, unemployment, pollution, and racial discrimination would help. But even if local, state, and national governments could find enough money in their budgets to mend the tattered social fabric, aggression wouldn't disappear. Hostility between groups is often based on learned dislike of people outside one's own group (see Figure 12.8). At a simple level, this shared group identity helps explain the hostility of sports fans who support rival teams. At a more serious level, it accounts for the continuing hostility between different political, religious, and economic groups. The calamitous conflicts triggered by the collapse of the old Soviet Union in 1991, for example, testify to the survival of age-old ethnic hatreds in the Balkan states of Serbia, Bosnia, and Herzegovina.

BREAK DOWN BARRIERS TO COOPERATION. Some of the problems caused by shared group identities surfaced in the Robber's Cave experiment run during the 1950s by social psychologist Muzafer Sherif. For several years, Sherif and his assistants ran a summer camp for 11- and 12-year-old boys. All the

A Prison Simulation Taps Into an Unexpected Reaction

Social psychologist Philip Zimbardo's experiment in group behavior under prison conditions lasted only six days. Zimbardo had signed up a group of Stanford University men for a two-week simulation. Some of the men were assigned to play the role of prison guards while others took the role of prisoners. But, Zimbardo reports, the students almost immediately overstepped the line between role and reality. The guards, who had been chosen by random drawings, began to treat prisoners "as if they were despicable animals, taking pleasure in cruelty." The prisoners, on the other hand, became "servile, dehumanized robots who thought only of escape, of their own individual survival, and of their mounting hatred for the guards."

Zimbardo concluded that people kid themselves about their ability to control aggression. Violence lurks within, he says, ready to surface when prompted by the right triggering mechanism. Another group of psychologists disagree with this analysis. They do not believe that the subjects were acting out inborn behaviors. Instead, they say, a lifetime of watching television and movies taught the men how guards and prisoners are supposed to behave. When placed in an unfamiliar situation, they simply acted out the roles they had learned.

campers were healthy, well-adjusted children from middle-class homes. Once there, the boys were divided into two groups and housed in isolated cabins. Sherif then assigned tasks that required close cooperation among the boys in each group. As they prepared for campouts and hikes, the groups developed their own names (Rattlers and Eagles, for example), jokes, rules, and leadership. The boys within each group formed close bonds, but they knew almost nothing about the other group.

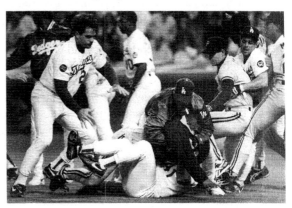

FIGURE 12.8 ▨ When a fight starts on the baseball field, both dugouts empty as players rush to help their teammates. What do you think causes this group solidarity? How could umpires prevent such mass brawls?

At this point, the experiment introduced competition between the two groups. These activities, which included tugs-of-war and ball games, offered highly desirable prizes. Almost immediately, the Rattlers took an intense dislike to the Eagles. The Eagles responded with an equally ferocious dislike of the Rattlers. At first, the groups contented themselves with name calling. Then they stepped up hostilities by raiding the opposition's cabin. The formerly peaceful camp was soon teetering on the edge of violence.

Sherif found that it was easier to put the groups at each other's throats than to restore harmony. Only when he set up tasks that required intergroup cooperation did tempers begin to cool. When the food truck was rigged to break down, for example, the boys had to join forces to haul their dinner into camp. After several days of joint efforts, friendships began to form across group lines. The fighting died out.

MODIFY PUNISHMENT. Society has traditionally used punishment as a way of dealing with criminal aggression. Psychologists point out, however, that punishment itself is a form of aggression. The public feels safer when criminals go to jail and serve long sentences. But all too often, the only lesson the prisoner learns in jail is how to be more violent the next time. Paradoxically, many of the adults who take a hard line on punishing criminals know that punishing a child is effective only within a loving parent-child relationship. In a similar fashion, modern methods of dealing with lawbreakers combine punishment with programs that teach new ways of coping with frustration. Therapy and counseling, combined with vocational training, have helped turn many felons into productive law-abiding citizens.

ELIMINATE MODELS FOR AGGRESSION. When society rejects aggression as a model for be-

havior, people soon reduce the level of individual violence. A typical proposal centers on controlling America's passion for firearms. Countries such as Great Britain and Japan, which have strict gun control laws, report far fewer murders in relation to their population than does the United States. Japan, for example, reported only 1.1 murders per 100,000 people in 2002. The United States, by contrast, recorded five times that number—5.6 murders per 100,000 people during the same period. Another plan aims at reducing violence on television and in the movies. The film rating system and the TV "family hour" attempt to resolve this issue without requiring strict censorship of what Americans see on the screen.

REWARD ACCEPTABLE BEHAVIOR. Experiments with children have reduced aggression by ignoring violent acts and rewarding more peaceful behavior. When Brad throws a tantrum in the supermarket because he's been denied a treat, he's certain that his parents will respond. If they do, and buy his silence with a toy, Brad will use the technique again and again. But if his mother says quietly, "Bradley, when you're finished, I'll be over at the meat counter," he'll soon learn that tantrums don't pay.

The inevitable frustrations of married life often yield to constructive fair-fight techniques. In one popular method of fair fighting, husband and wife are armed with foam rubber bats. A referee gives them permission to whack each other on the back, shoulders, arms, and legs. No blows to the head or midriff are allowed. A few minutes of vigorous battle with such bats can work off tensions and frustrations to a remarkable degree (see Figure 12.9). Afterward the two combatants can sit down in relaxed camaraderie, ready to tackle the real problems in their relationship.

BUILD UNDERSTANDING OF OTHERS. People are more likely to commit aggression against victims they don't see as human beings. If the other person is a symbol for frustration, as is sometimes the case with the police or another ethnic group, the aggressor can more easily rationalize his or her crime. Judges sometimes try to break down these walls by ordering convicted criminals to visit the families of their victims in order to see the consequences of their crime. The sharing of common experiences among racial and ethnic groups makes school integration a worthwhile social goal. Once they've worked with, eaten with, and played with members of another group, most people discard long-held prejudices.

ASSERTIVE BEHAVIOR

Hitting someone with a baseball bat is aggression. Using every possible means to convince that person of the justice of your position is *assertive behavior*. Whereas society generally penalizes aggression, it often rewards assertive behavior. Businesses, sports teams, and political parties, among others, encourage employees and members to be assertive. Assertive people have the energy, commitment, and skills needed to cope with frustration.

It's not hard to see the difference between slugging people and working to change their minds. Not all assertive behavior can be identified as readily, however. Here are the ways social psychologists describe what assertive behavior is.

1. Assertive behavior is directed against a real opponent, usually the cause of your frustrations. It does not strike out blindly against anyone or anything within reach.

2. Assertive behavior does not produce guilt feelings. Those who use it feel their actions are justified—and the person on the receiving end of the assertive behavior does not feel threatened or violated.

3. Assertive behavior does not go too far.

FIGURE 12.9 ▓ Nonviolent fighting with foam rubber bats can reduce frustrations and relieve tensions. Why is this technique a better means of resolving conflicts than the usual verbal battles between two people?

It uses only the pressure required to resolve the specific problem—and no more.

4. Assertive behavior is aimed at specific goals. It is not used to displace personal frustrations, nor is it easily provoked.

5. Assertive behavior is called for when you are working to advance a cause. Success comes most often when you are also ready to invest your time, money, and energy in the project.

The U.S. civil-rights movement provides a clear-cut contrast between aggression and assertive behavior. In the 1960s, organizations such as the Black Panthers took to the streets to promote black power. Worthwhile goals were thrown away in violent clashes with police, and a number of lives were lost. By contrast, Dr. Martin Luther King, Jr., relied on nonviolent marches and demonstrations to promote the African American cause (see Figure 12.10). If King had relied on aggression, the majority society would probably have refused to listen to his demands. Nonviolence and civil disobedience, however, spoke to the conscience of America. The movement

▓ **PRO & CON:**

Is the United States Declining
Or Only Changing?

For a long time now, doomsayers have warned: "Beware! The United States will collapse if the values that made it great continue to decline." The social behavior that concerns the critics is plain to see: changes in family life, loss of respect for the law, collapse of the work ethic, and a diminished faith in the goodness of the American way of life.

Social psychologists have tried to measure the effect of rapid social change on the individual. From one point of view, uncontrolled change is equal to decay. From another, change is seen as a force for positive growth. Here are some of the arguments that have grown out of this debate:

PRO

1 Morality of every kind has declined to the point that no standards of behavior are left. Honesty, trust, and respect for one's fellow citizens are vanishing rapidly.

2 Laws should protect law-abiding people, not criminals. But too many citizens live in a climate of fear because criminals do not fear capture or punishment. Even when criminals do go to jail, sentences are too short and parole too easy to obtain.

3 Every institution that upholds the law is under attack, whether it is the family, the church, or the state. If America's institutions collapse, society will enter a chaotic period that could well result in the rise to power of a charismatic dictator.

4 Today's permissive attitudes encourage people to avoid responsibility for their actions. Like children, many Americans seem to forget about tomorrow in a frantic quest for pleasure.

CON

1 Morality now reflects the basic nature of humanity, rather than artificial and impossible standards. When a new moral code emerges, it will be rooted in the realities of human nature.

2 Everyone accused of a crime deserves the full protection of the law. Moreover, hard proof exists to show that punishment alone doesn't reduce crime. Only when everyone has a fair share of the good things of life will crime begin to decrease.

3 People make institutions, and people have the right to change their institutions. Most U.S. institutions are out of date. New systems of family organization, new rules of behavior, and a new sharing of political power are long overdue.

4 Old ideals of self-denial and hard work tended to conceal the fact that only a privileged few enjoyed the good things of life. Today's values tell us that everyone has a right to a fair share of the nation's resources.

Do you believe that U.S. society is sliding toward disaster? If you were the president, what changes would you want to make in the way Americans think and in the way they act?

FIGURE 12.10 ■ Dr. Martin Luther King, Jr., leading a rally in support of civil rights for America's African American citizens. What might have happened if King had chosen aggressive instead of assertive means to obtain his goals?

King led eventually helped pass federal laws that affected civil rights, housing, education, and job opportunities. Although King's protests did touch off some violence by people outside his movement, he helped to defuse tensions that could have exploded into a much wider conflict.

■ SECTION CHECKUP

1 Discuss the three theories that explain the process of aggression in human behavior.

2 What are some of the causes of aggression? How can some of these causes be reduced or eliminated?

3 What does the Robber's Cave experiment suggest as a way of reducing aggression between hostile racial groups in a community?

4 How does assertive behavior differ from aggression? Give some examples of assertive behavior.

12.4 ■ WHAT CAUSES PREJUDICE?
WHAT CAN BE DONE ABOUT IT?

A picture similar to Figure 12.11 has been used in an experiment to demonstrate prejudice. Psychologists define *prejudice* as the unthinking attitudes or biases people hold about other individuals or groups. In the experiment, a group of white subjects is told they are taking part in a study of communication. All subjects leave the room except one, who studies the picture carefully. The experimenter then removes the picture and instructs the first "wit-

FIGURE 12.11

ness" to describe it in as much detail as possible to a second person. In turn, the second subject calls in the third and tries to repeat the description, and so on. As you might guess, each witness loses some detail along the way—and often adds something new. By the third or fourth repetition, the knife will very likely end up in the black man's hand!

What role does prejudice play in this unconscious transfer? Social psychologists explain that the world is too complicated to think about in every detail. People, therefore, tend to reduce complex social relationships to greatly simplified views of how they expect other racial, ethnic, or social groups to behave. These shorthand ways of judging people are called *stereotypes*. Most prejudices have been built up on the basis of limited and poorly evaluated information. Many white subjects start out the "communication" experiment with a prejudiced belief that young black men carry knives. Challenged by the task of trying to remember details, it's easy for the unconscious to switch the weapon from the white hand to the black one.

CAUSES OF PREJUDICE

You can be prejudiced in favor of someone or something, but most prejudices tend to be negative. When a negative prejudice leads someone to take action against another person, that act is known as *discrimination*. At one level, prejudice may simply lead like-minded people to band together as a way of reinforcing their mutual dislikes and fears. At an ultimate level, these same prejudices can lead one group to attack another, as Europe's skinheads have demonstrated in recent years. Whatever the level of prejudice and discrimination, however, the causes of this distorted thinking stem from a number of sources.

CAUSES OUTSIDE THE INDIVIDUAL. Historically, prejudice has roots in several realities of human existence. As people form a group, they tend to emphasize the similarities of skin color, religious belief, language, or customs that bind their group together. From there, it's an easy step to consider people who differ in belief or physical appearance as inferior. Slave owners, for example, found it easier to justify harsh treatment of their laborers if the enslaved peoples were thought to be less human than their masters.

The pressures of life in today's urban societies also tend to create hostility between groups. Great Britain, for example, has always prided itself on a broadminded attitude toward nonwhites. In recent years, however, competition for jobs and living space in London and other British cities has created an explosive hostility toward West Indians, Pakistanis, and other people of "colour."

In addition, like arithmetic and reading, prejudice can be "taught." Children are born without any feelings of prejudice. But parents, teachers, and their peer group soon instruct them in the "right" views. Young Bess may not know why her new playmate has earned Dad's disapproval, but she can read his reaction quite clearly. Because her position within the family would be endangered if she did not share its prejudices, she will learn them just as surely as she learns the more positive family attitudes. All too often, by the time she's an adult, Bess will no longer

wonder why she doesn't like this race or that religion. Her prejudices will have become part of her world view, and she'll very likely pass them along to her own children.

Governments also make—and sometimes unmake—prejudices among their citizens. U.S. relations with the Soviet Union offer a good example. During World War II, the official policy built up American respect and admiration for the Russians and their valiant fight against the common enemy, Nazi Germany. After 1945, however, as the Soviet Union competed with the United States for world influence, old prejudices against the Communist system revived. The cold war, as it was called, set off a wave of anti-Russian feeling. Then, as the cold war gave way to more peaceful coexistence, attitudes toward the Soviet Union moderated. Most Americans again saw the Russians as a basically friendly and energetic people who were misused by a government dedicated to world domination. Americans were ready to cheer, therefore, when Russia's Communist government collapsed and the new government took its first halting steps toward democracy.

CAUSES INSIDE THE INDIVIDUAL. Psychological forces also affect the development of prejudices. Social psychologists explain individual prejudices as a way of discharging hostilities built up by frustration.

The effect of frustration can be seen in the use of minority groups as convenient scapegoats for feelings of despair, anger, or hopelessness. Let's say that you're a farmer. Times are tough. Your crops are suffering from drought, the bank is demanding its mortgage money, and wheat prices are falling to new lows. Just then a neighbor stops by with news that a Vietnamese family has moved in nearby. You can't do much about the weather or the local banker, but here's a readily available target. You lash out at these "foreigners" as a symbol for all that's going wrong in your world. The fact that you don't know the

"Don't Bother Me With Facts. My Mind Is Already Made Up!"

If Martians landed today, by tomorrow some people would be prejudiced against them. Once such stereotyped thinking takes hold, it is hard to change. Perhaps the following dialogue will give you a taste of how prejudice works. Ms. Block is arguing with Mr. Glass about his anti-Martian prejudice.

MR. G.: Those Martians! They landed only yesterday and they already think they own the planet. Who do they think they are, anyway?

MS. B.: Is that fair? They've given us an anti-gravity device that will solve our energy crisis. And all they've asked is a chance to live here and become part of our culture.

MR. G.: I don't believe that for a minute. Those three-eyed greenies are just trying to lull us to sleep. When our backs are turned, they'll kill us all with their secret death rays.

MS. B.: CNN says our military has investigated them, and they don't have any weapons. So far, they haven't broken a single one of our laws.

MR. G.: Yeah, but I heard they're buying up good American farmland. How will our farmers be able to make a living if ugly green Martians spread out and grab off half of Kansas and Iowa? Next thing, they'll be wanting to move in next door and send their spores to school with my kids.

Mr. G. is just getting warmed up. As you can see, he refuses to examine his tightly held prejudices. Since Ms. Block's facts can't really be denied, he simply ignores them and heads off in a new direction. Such thinking (or nonthinking) is all too typical of prejudiced people.

Dinhs as individuals makes it easy to dehumanize them.

THE POWER OF PREJUDICE

It's not uncommon for racial and ethnic groups to work together to defeat a common enemy, whether it's a flood, fire, or unwanted government action. Once the threat passes, personal needs and fears return. Feelings of isolation, frustration, and fear provide fertile soil for the growth of prejudice. Members of the in-group begin to assume that all members of the out-group behave according to accepted stereotypes. Once established, these simplistic ideas are hard to kill. Too many people "know" that Italians are lovers, Germans obey orders, Mexicans are lazy, the Irish drink too much. As prejudice grows, it also feeds on humanity's tendency to ignore what it doesn't want to see (see Figure 12.12).

Many studies have proved the harmful effects of prejudice and discrimination. Author Richard Wright described its impact in *Black Boy,* his novel about growing up in Mississippi in the 1920s. After being forced to leave a job because the white workers wouldn't accept him as an apprentice, Wright's hero said he "felt drenched in shame, naked to my soul. The whole of my being felt violated, and I knew that my own fear had helped to violate it."

Until leaders such as Martin Luther King, Jr., and Malcolm X helped create a new sense

"I can see that the Smiths are having some real troubles. Maybe I can round up a neighborhood work crew and give them a hand."

"Just as I predicted, the Garcias aren't keeping up their property. When people like that move in, the neighborhood goes downhill."

FIGURE 12.12 ▓ How do you account for the jogger's different reactions? What could you do to change his attitude toward the Garcias?

of self-worth among African Americans, black children always preferred to play with white dolls. They said that black dolls weren't as pretty. Psychiatrist Robert Coles found that six-year-old Ruby, an African American girl, revealed the same pattern of thinking in her drawings. She drew white people larger and more lifelike than she drew African Americans. Ruby's self-portraits often lacked a feature or two, but her white girls always had the proper number of fingers and toes.

Similarly, before the feminist movement increased their pride in being female, women tended to see men as more powerful and successful. In one study, two groups of women read an identical article in which only the name of the author was changed. As a result, one group thought the article had been written by a man, while the second group believed its author was a woman. The group reading the "Patrick N. Thomas article" rated it better in every respect than the group that read the "Patricia N. Thomas article." Only when girls began to grow up without the crippling effects of sexist prejudice did large numbers of women feel free to choose careers other than homemaking.

Other results of prejudice can be equally damaging.

1. When given a choice, some minority or outgroup members deny kinship with their group. At one time, light-skinned African Americans sometimes chose to "pass" as whites because they knew they would have better opportunities that way. Similarly, im-

migrants often changed their names when they came to the United States so that they could blend more easily into the majority society. People who leave their group to join the majority, however, often feel guilty about their decision. The civil rights movement and increased emphasis on ethnic pride have lessened this tendency of minorities to leave their group.

2. Historically, many minority members passively accepted their inferior position. Gays and lesbians, for example, stayed "in the closet" rather than risk discrimination by the straight population. In this era of civil rights and protest movements, such attitudes have become less common. Most minority groups now use demonstrations, political campaigns, and self-pride campaigns to fight for full rights and opportunities.

3. Stereotypes can become self-fulfilling prophecies. If a minority group is thought of as lazy, cunning, or incompetent, some of its members will adopt those traits. Such behavior can cause the minority group to develop feelings of self-hatred. Children, who feel the sting of prejudice most keenly, may refuse to learn their parents' language, follow their religion, or practice their customs.

4. People who are discriminated against often compensate by developing a prejudice against some other out-group. Perhaps this helps explain why blacks and Hispanic Americans have found it difficult to combine forces. Each sees the other as an opponent in the struggle to gain a stronger voice in the American political and economic system.

5. Out-group members who suffer prejudice and discrimination show increased symptoms of physical and emotional illness. Stress-related illnesses such as ulcers, high blood pressure, and heart disease hit hard at minority populations. Drug abuse, alcoholism, depression, and other mental problems go hand in hand with the lack of opportunity and sense of hopelessness that often affect members of minority groups.

ELIMINATING DISCRIMINATION

Since the 1960s, the United States has tried to reduce prejudice and eliminate discrimination based on race, religion, sex, or any other factor. On the positive side, schools have been integrated, job opportunities have opened up, and better housing has been made available. But a negative side exists as well. Laws, speeches, and good will cannot undo overnight the built-up prejudices of centuries. For every advance in reducing prejudice, a sorry example of new or renewed discrimination can be found. Legal efforts can go only so far. Community programs that help people cross the boundaries between groups must also be encouraged.

1. Despite the problems school integration has created, children who learn to work together in the classroom graduate from school with less prejudice. Even the parents who resist integration find that their attitudes change after school starts. Psychologists explain this by reminding us that people can't hold two conflicting feelings at once. It's easy to hate Group X when they're somewhere else. But if your children are sharing a classroom with Group X children, you're faced with a cognitive dissonance. Maybe, you say to yourself, those other kids aren't so bad after all. And in fact, experience usually shows that they're pretty much like your own kids. Communities that reinforce integration plans with study groups, cultural exhibits, festivals and fairs, films, and counseling programs find that much of the resistance to school integration can be overcome (see Figure 12.13).

2. Personal contacts can be encouraged at the neighborhood level. Groups that meet and work together on common projects gain feelings of mutual respect. Block parties, clean-up campaigns, youth groups, athletics, and similar activities help people see that old stereotypes aren't true. Such projects cannot be forced on people, however. Impetus must come from the people involved, perhaps with

quiet, behind-the-scenes leadership from government, school, and religious leaders.

3. Encounter groups have a good record of reducing prejudiced thinking. Role playing, psychodrama, and other self-awareness techniques can help people "get into someone else's shoes." These programs work best when the participants come together voluntarily. As with all group therapy, the effectiveness of an encounter group depends largely on the skills of its leader.

In the final analysis, nothing works better to reduce prejudice and eliminate discrimination than putting people in touch with their own feelings. When each American takes personal responsibility for recognizing his or her own prejudices and overcoming them, the battle may finally be won.

▓ SECTION CHECKUP

1 Name some of the reasons why almost everyone is prejudiced in some way toward people who are of a different race, religion, or ethnic origin.

2 Why are prejudice and discrimination so damaging to those who suffer their effects? Give some examples of these effects.

FIGURE 12.13 ▓ Members of a multi-ethnic, multi-racial dance company pose for a group photograph. What can audiences learn from watching this group perform that will help break down old prejudices? What can the members of the group learn from each other?

3 What can be done to reduce prejudice in this country? Why isn't it enough to pass tough antidiscrimination laws?

12.5 ▓ WHAT CAN PSYCHOLOGY TELL YOU ABOUT SUICIDE, AGING, AND DEATH?

If you're anything like the typical psychology student, your attitudes about suicide, aging, and death are still being formed. Indeed, you may be a kindred soul to the teenager who learned that her piano teacher had just turned 30. "Thirty!" the girl gasped. "I hope I never live to be *thirty!*" Social psychologists understand this attitude, but they know it's important that everyone think about old age, death, and dying. If you can build up a logical and positive attitude toward these facts of life,

you'll be that much better prepared to deal with them when chance or the natural life processes bring you face to face with the unthinkable.

SUICIDE, THE "DECISION TO END ALL DECISIONS"

About 150 years ago, public officials in London ordered the hanging of a man who had "come back from the dead." His crime? He had attempted suicide.

Men and women who try to kill themselves are no longer thought of as criminals. Social psychologists, in fact, see them as people who can no longer cope with the frustrations of life. In their depression, suicide becomes their "decision to end all decisions."

FACTS REGARDING SUICIDE. Any event as emotionally disturbing as suicide creates its own mythology. Most people believe, for example, that more women commit suicide than men—but the reverse is actually true. A group known as the Suicide Prevention Coalition is doing its best to set the record straight with some basic truths about suicide:

1. Suicide rates increase with age, but the suicide statistics for young people are especially worrisome. One in eight suicides in the United States falls into the 15-to-24 age range. Translation: more teenagers and young adults will kill themselves this year than will die from cancer, heart disease, AIDS, birth defects, stroke, pneumonia, and chronic lung disease combined. Suicide, the record shows, is the third leading cause of death in the 15-to-24 age group and the fourth leading cause in the 10-to-14 age group. Researchers blame a variety of factors for these deaths, including dysfunctional families, drug and alcohol abuse, peer pressure, and the stress of growing up.

2. Suicide statistics vary from country to country, with the industrialized nations reporting the highest rates. In any country, suicides increase with age, and men are four times more likely than women to take their own lives. According to the World Health Organization, the number of suicides per 100,000 population vary from a high of 39.4 in the Russian Federation to a low of 0.1 in Egypt. The United States has a rate of 10.7 per 100,000, relatively low for an industrial society. Our neighbors, however, vary considerably. Canada's rate of 12.2 is close to that of the U.S., but Mexico's rate of 3.1 is significantly lower.

3. Anyone who threatens suicide should be taken seriously. Mental health experts believe that suicide threats are actually cries for help based on real feelings of despair, loneliness, or rejection. Suicide threats that are ignored can easily turn into the real thing. Perhaps Pat didn't really mean to swallow those pills, but a lack of response from her friends and family pushed her over the brink.

4. Once a person attempts suicide, the chances are good that he or she will try again. This is particularly true when the life situation causing the emotional distress doesn't change. A pattern of repeated attempts is often ignored by relatives, who hush up the failed suicide as a family embarrassment.

5. Suicide statistics provide a strong argument for gun control. Of those who use a gun in a suicide attempt, 92 percent succeed. Any policy that hopes to lower the suicide rate, therefore, must aim at taking guns out of circulation. In Canada, where owners must register their firearms, the suicide-by-gun risk to a family that chooses to keep guns in the home shows a nearly five-fold increase.

PREVENTING SUICIDE. Few people go all through life without thinking at one time or another of taking their own lives. Failure, loneliness, chronic health problems, long-term depression, and a sense of being trapped in an unhappy life situation often lead to thoughts of suicide. The odds are good, therefore, that you'll someday come into contact with someone who is thinking seriously about killing himself or herself. If you do, check for these danger signs:

1. Has the person attempted suicide before? (About 75 percent of those who kill themselves have made at least one previous attempt.)

2. Has he or she been unusually depressed or withdrawn for a long period of time?

3. Does the person's family have a history of suicide or suicide attempts?

4. Has the individual recently suffered a severe blow, such as a death in the family, the collapse of a love affair, the loss of a job, or a severe illness?

5. Is he or she a loner who lacks friends and family who are able to provide close and loving support?

6. Does the person talk frequently about death?

7. Has the individual been putting his or her affairs in order (writing a will, giving away prized possessions, withdrawing from normal activities)?

If the answer to two or more of these questions is "yes," you should enlist the help of a responsible person who can help you evaluate the problem and obtain assistance. Circumstances vary, but you can usually turn to a relative, a counselor, a member of the clergy, or a doctor. Suicide-prevention clinics and "suicide hot lines"—24-hour-a-day emergency numbers for people who feel suicidal—can also be found in many towns and cities. The counselors there will tell you how to help a potential suicide find help.

AGEISM, THE NEWEST PREJUDICE

In the 1700s, people wore white wigs to make themselves look older. By contrast, a recent research study could find only one child in ten who had anything positive to say about growing old.

Social scientists speak of this negative attitude toward aging and older people as a new form of prejudice. Some writers have called it *ageism*, the tendency to exclude the elderly from any important role in U.S. society. This trend has developed even though the number of people over 65 now has grown to over 35 million, a 12-fold increase since 1900. As life expectancy inches upward, that rapid increase can be expected to continue. In 1900,

FIGURE 12.14 ▪ Growing old in a society that seems to worship youth can be depressing and lonely. This woman feels useful and appreciated as she shares her knitting skills with students in an art class.

the average person lived for 47 years. By comparison, boys born in 2000 can expect to live to 74.1, and girls to 79.5. By the year 2030, one American in five will be over 65.

CAUSES OF AGEISM. Why do children carry a stereotype of the elderly as "old, wrinkled geezers, feeble and crippled by arthritis"? After all, to be prejudiced against old age is to be prejudiced against yourself, for barring accident or illness, you will someday be old, too (see Figure 12.14). The answer seems to come from social patterns that no one designed deliberately, but each contributes to ageism.

1. In a mobile society, many children seldom see their grandparents. Families move away, often to communities where everyone seems to be the same age. Without regular contact with older people, children may develop stereotyped views of age as a time of decay and unhappiness.

2. Until a turnabout began in the late 1980s, the mass media added greatly to the

prejudice against aging. The occasional seniors who appeared in TV sitcoms were often portrayed as cranky old fools or helpless incompetents. Commercials added to the one-sided picture by assuring viewers that the young have all the fun. The beautiful people who cavorted through countless ads seldom looked older than their mid-twenties. Some balance was restored when television executives realized that aging Americans have money to spend, too. Programs such as *Frasier* and advertisers such as McDonald's and Pepsi began to feature vigorous elders who could play tennis, give sage advice, and (wonder of wonders!) fall in love.

3. As people grow old, many are caught in a self-fulfilling prophecy: "Old people are sick, senile, sexless, spent, or sessile [immobile]." Expecting the worst, the elderly sometimes let themselves sink into isolation and despair. Because many people view their jobs as an essential part of their identity, mandatory retirement practices have contributed to this expectation. It wasn't until 1987, for example, that the federal government passed a law ending mandatory retirement for most federal employees.

4. The financial hardships caused by a weak economy and inadequate pensions place an additional burden on old people. The occasional article about the old couple who supplement their meager diet with canned dog food underlines that fact that 9.7 percent of all Americans who are over 65 live in poverty.

5. "Granny-bashing" is no joke for many of America's elderly. Family members and caregivers who see their elderly charges as useless burdens are more likely to abuse them, both physically and emotionally.

FACTS ABOUT THE ELDERLY. AARP, an association devoted to the needs and interests of its 35 million aging members, believes that the unfair and deadly prejudice of ageism need not exist at all. Throughout history, most cultures have treasured elderly people for their wisdom, experience, and hard-won skills. A culture that throws away the capabilities of one fifth of its people is discarding a national treasure. Perhaps your own attitude toward aging might change if you understood these facts about old age.

1. No one can set a specific age as the point at which a person becomes old. Sixty-five is no more a magic gateway than is 21. Try to think of age as a measure of individual capacity for continued growth as a person. By that yardstick, some people are old at 18; others are young at 87.

2. Old age need not be a drawn out period of illness and inactivity. In fact, older people tend to have fewer illnesses than the average population. Teenagers are more likely to be depressed than their grandparents (they're under more stress). As for life expectancy, scientists are making rapid progress in their search for the secrets of aging. Molecular biologist Thomas Johnson, for example, has bred a strain of nematodes (translucent worms the size of a comma) that live 70 percent longer than the species' average three-week life span. The difference, he believes, lies in a single gene. Based on these findings, Johnson speculates that manipulating similar genes in humans might well extend the life span to 120 years and beyond.

3. Less than five percent of the over-65 population live in nursing homes. Most elderly men and women can take care of themselves, particularly in those communities that provide in-home nursing and housekeeping help. The senile dementia associated with conditions such as Alzheimer's disease strikes only a relative few. What society mistakenly calls senility often can be traced to two causes. Some old people act senile because they have been taught that the elderly are supposed to act that way. Others display the memory dysfunction and loss of mobility associated with senility because of poor nutrition, lack of exercise, and inadequate health

care. When their diet is improved and their health problems treated, they tend to snap back rather quickly.

4. Old age does not rob us of our intelligence or our capacity to perform complex tasks. Some old people do slow down, but if they are given enough time they do as well as younger people on intelligence and achievement tests. Alex Comfort, an expert on aging, writes that old people who are physically fit are the least dangerous drivers on the road. "By seventy-plus," Comfort notes, "you have experience, and the accident-prone fraction of the population is dead or disqualified." Matilda Ray, a pioneer in the field of social gerontology, wants to trash the old career timetable that called for people to train, work, and rest. There's no reason, she believes, why a fit and capable 70-year-old shouldn't be working—or why a 40-year-old shouldn't be given a generous slice of free time to fight burnout or to launch a new career.

Young people benefit when they make room for older relatives and friends in their lives. Of course, no one claims that all old people are saints. Like people of all ages, some are difficult, cantankerous, and self-involved. But the hard-won wisdom that comes with age can also create sensitive, helpful human beings. Once you understand this, you can begin to view old age as a natural extension of youth and middle age. You'll also realize that people who lead healthy, productive lives have an excellent chance of staying healthy and productive to the end.

COPING WITH DEATH

Of all the earth's creatures, only the human species lives with the knowledge of eventual death. Yet most Americans do their best to ignore the fact that they will die. They speak of friends and relatives who "pass away," or go on to their "eternal rest." In funeral homes, families visit the "deceased" in a "slumber room" with recorded music playing softly in the background.

The idea is spreading, however, that death can be an individual's last creative act. After a lifetime spent loving, working, growing, and building, death can give dignity and meaning to one's accomplishments. Psychiatrist Arnold Beisser, confined to a wheelchair by polio, has written extensively about this concept. "Death is one of the wonders of life," Beisser says, "and like the other significant life events should be celebrated, not hidden away. Unfortunately, we are influenced to expect that life is going to continue indefinitely. Life is often treated like a competitive sport, as though dying were the equivalent of losing. That . . . dooms us all to be losers eventually."

Dr. Elisabeth Kübler-Ross, another renowned expert in this field, believes that the first step we should take is to allow the dying to keep their dignity and humanity. When people come face to face with approaching death, Dr. Kübler-Ross explains, they need support while they learn to accept the end of life. With time and loving care, shock and denial eventually give way to a readiness to put one's life in order. As an example of how death practices in an earlier rural society differ from those of today, read Dr. Kübler-Ross's story of a European farmer's death (BioBox, pages 428–429).

MAKING DEATH LESS TERRIFYING. Psychologists and other experts on death recommend that several specific steps be taken to ensure that each of us has a chance to die with a sense of dignity.

1. Although many people find thoughts of death upsetting, high school and college curricula should be modified to include units on death and dying. Stripping away the mystery that presently surrounds death would make it less frightening and thus easier to face. Those schools which have added such elective courses report that students leave the program

Elisabeth Kübler-Ross:
The Dying Teach Us to Live

Swiss-born Dr. Elisabeth Kübler-Ross (1926–2004) spent most of her life helping people overcome the old taboo that kept death out of sight and out of mind. In 1969, Dr. Kübler-Ross's best-settler, *On Death and Dying,* brought her ideas before the public.

Dr. Kübler-Ross first came in contact with people's reactions to death when she worked with the survivors of World War II concentration camps. After medical school she trained as a psychiatrist and treated both the retarded and the schizophrenic. It was during these years that she began to recognize the psychological steps that the dying person goes through. Understanding this progression, which begins with denial and moves through rage, bargaining, depression, and on to final acceptance, has greatly increased people's ability to cope with death and dying.

Dr. Kübler-Ross spent much of her time trying to arrange more human care for the dying. She described a death with dignity that she witnessed as a child in Switzerland:

much better equipped to handle both the business of dying (insurance, wills, mortuaries, cemeteries) and the emotional side (grieving, comforting survivors, working through to acceptance).

2. Dying patients should receive as much information about their condition as possible. Many doctors now believe that the tradition of withholding bad news from the patient does more harm than good for all but the most immature people. As patients move from denial of their approaching death to acceptance, they feel less helpless. Not only do they face death with greater calm, but their improved emotional state makes them better patients. Their doctors find it easier to monitor their condition and to control their pain.

3. The hospice concept should be expanded. Hospices are special nursing homes where people go to die in a humane way. Trained staff members provide companionship, counseling, and relief from pain. In the homelike setting, family members can visit often. Hospice staff members have the time to offer the time-consuming services that busy hospital staffs cannot provide.

4. Families should be encouraged to allow children from age nine or ten onward to participate in funerals and other death rituals. Psychologists say that allowing a youngster to express grief along with the adults of the family gives the child a chance to accept death as a necessary part of life. Hiding the death of a close relative or friend from chil-

I remember as a child the death of a farmer. He fell from a tree and was not expected to live. He asked simply to die at home, a wish that was granted without questioning. He called his daughters into the bedroom and spoke with each one of them alone for a few minutes. He arranged his affairs quietly, though he was in great pain, and distributed his belongings and his land. . . . He also asked each of his children to share in the work, duties, and tasks that he had carried on until the time of the accident. He asked his friends to visit him once more, to bid good-bye to them. Although I was a small child at the time, he did not exclude me or my siblings. We were allowed to share in the preparations of the family just as we were permitted to grieve with them until he died. When he did die, he was left at home, in his own beloved home which he had built, and among his friends and neighbors who went to take a last look at him where he lay in the midst of flowers in the place he had lived in and loved so much.

Why do some people grieve more deeply than others? Grieving, Dr. Kübler-Ross said, "is an expression of unfinished business, hurts never healed, love unexpressed, regrets unre-solved. . . . Dying people teach how to live. That's all. I mean, if I die today after having told my family 'I love you,' I've said it. If I got home and found that a loved one had died, I'd say, 'thank heavens I've said all those things I've always wanted to say.' "

As a summary of what she has learned from her patients, Dr. Kübler-Ross repeated a poem by Richard Allen:

> . . . as you face your death,
> it is only the love
> you have given
> and received
> which will count . . .
> if you have loved well
> then it will have been worth it . . .
> but if you have not
> death will always come too soon
> and be too terrible to face.

Do any of Kübler-Ross's insights regarding death strike a responsive feeling born of your own experience? Why was she so concerned that people "say all the things they've always wanted to say"?

---

dren only confuses them and makes death seem doubly frightening and mysterious.

5. People should prepare for their own deaths, including their funerals, ahead of time. This practice provides for a memorial service that truly expresses the individual's wishes and personality. Making prior arrangements also keeps funeral directors from selling a more expensive service and casket to grieving relatives than they may want or can afford.

THE "RIGHT TO DIE."   As medical science develops better ways of keeping critically ill patients alive, new practical and moral questions arise to complicate the natural process of dying. At what point, for example, should a terminally ill patient be allowed to die without further suffering? In their rush to save lives, doctors and nurses sometimes forget that they're dealing with human beings. The patient becomes "the heart attack in 204A," and in the flurry of high-tech treatment all dignity and opportunities for peaceful reflection are lost.

Doctors have always believed that they have no choice when treating critically ill patients. Their job, they say, is to do everything possible to save lives. But "everything possible" can mean long days of pain for the patient and mounting expenses for the family, with no hope that the patient can ever return to a productive life. The courts have sometimes been called upon to decide at what point life-support systems should be turned off. Unfortunately, no universal standard has been established. Several states have passed laws that allow terminally ill patients to request the removal of life-support machines. People who take the opposing position, however, also make a strong case. No one should be put in a position of "playing God," they say, with responsibility for deciding who should live and who should die. Furthermore, they continue, medical miracles happen almost every day. Apparently hopeless cases recover and live for years—years they would not have had if someone had decided to let them die.

This life-or-death issue has aroused a controversy that is compounded by each advance in medical technology. Perhaps the answer lies in rephrasing the question. Instead of asking, "Do people have the right to die?" maybe we should be asking, "Do people have the right to decide?" As a voter and family member who will someday face such decisions yourself, your opinions will count in this debate.

■ SECTION CHECKUP

1 List at least five signals that should alert you to the possibility that a friend may be planning to commit suicide. What can you do to help your friend?

2 What arguments could you use to convince someone that old age need not be a time of decay and despair?

3 What advantage can be found in helping people develop more positive attitudes toward death and dying? List some of the ways this can be accomplished.

LOOKING BACK: A SUMMARY

1 Social psychologists study individual and group behaviors in a social setting. The field is concerned primarily with socialization, the process by which people learn the rules of behavior for their culture and for the groups they join. Group behavior is affected by the size of the group, the type of rewards it offers its members, the way members cooperate in order to achieve group goals, and the way group tasks are distributed.

2 All groups assign roles to their members so that each person will know how to behave. The rules for playing roles properly are called social norms. Learning the proper roles and social norms for group membership is one of the challenges of growing up. Group leadership grows out of the need to make decisions and to move the group toward its goals. Leaders may be chosen on the basis of ability, personality, control of rewards and punishments, or through manipulation.

3 Conformity is a measure of the extent to which people meet social norms. The degree to which people conform depends upon their self-image, whether or not they find someone else to support their position, the group's authority, and the desire to gain approval and avoid punishment. When people conform only long enough to gain a reward or escape some sort of discomfort, the behavior is called *compliance*. Identification is a form of conformity in which people copy the behavior or life-style of someone they idolize. Internalization refers to the process of making a set of values part of one's own inner system of thinking and behaving.

4 People conform for several reasons. Those who share common goals with other group members conform in order to ensure the group's success; others conform as a way of gaining favor. People also conform in order to maintain important relationships and to relieve feelings of guilt. Obedience to authority tends to be drilled into children and is often carried over into adult life. Although nonconformity can be costly in terms of group cohesion, a democratic society needs citizens who are willing to challenge the established order.

5 Cognitive dissonance is the internal conflict that arises when people believe one thing but do another. People reduce dissonance by unconsciously altering their thinking to conform to their behavior. Reducing dissonance without clearly examining the compromise it requires can lead people to abandon beliefs that are important to their self-esteem.

6 Aggression is the act of deliberately harming someone else. Most social psychologists believe that aggression grows out of frustration rather than out of instinctive behavior. In their view, incidents of aggression multiply when society rewards violence and provides numerous models for violent behavior. Other factors that trigger aggression include the need to protect one's living space and to overcome feelings of hopelessness. Studies show that aggression can be reduced when frustrating conditions are changed, when criminals are rehabilitated, when models for aggression are eliminated, and when nonviolent behavior is rewarded. Social scientists believe that aggression should be replaced with nonviolent, assertive behavior. Assertive people know how to achieve their personal and professional goals without resorting to aggression.

7 Prejudice is an unthinking, biased attitude held by one group about another. When prejudice leads to unfair acts against members of another group, it is known as discrimination. Prejudice gives people an excuse for looking down on those who are different or who threaten their security. The psychological forces that cause prejudice grow out of the need to blame one's failures and frustrations on something or someone.

8 Prejudice has a powerful hold on people because it forms a basic part of their identity. To reject a prejudice often means going against long-held beliefs and old friends. Left unchallenged, prejudice has a harmful effect on those who feel its sting. Group stereotypes can become self-fulfilling prophecies for minority-group members. Out-group members also suffer higher rates of physical and emotional illnesses. Before prejudices can be eliminated, people must be taught to regard all human beings as worthy of respect.

9 People attempt suicide when depression, loneliness, or frustration overwhelms their ability to cope with these problems. All suicide threats must be taken seriously, particularly when other danger signs are present. These signals include long-term depression, a recent emotional shock, lack of family support, and a previous history of suicide attempts.

10 American society's tendency to worship youth and to reject old age has condemned many of the elderly to lives of social and economic privation. Ageism results from age segregation, the general neglect of the elderly in the mass media, and a tendency of both young and old people to assume that age automatically means becoming sick, feeble, and incompetent. This unfortunate prejudice can be overturned when people understand that old age can be a healthy and productive extension of one's earlier life.

11 Efforts are being made to help people see death as a positive part of living. These programs include teaching about death in the schools, giving people a chance to die in a humane way, and asking people to help plan their own funerals. "Right-to-die" laws are also giving seriously ill patients an opportunity to decide that they do not want to be kept alive when there is no chance that they will recover.

PUTTING YOUR KNOWLEDGE TO WORK

▪ TERMS YOU SHOULD KNOW

ageism	group	prejudice
aggression	identification	role
assertive behavior	in-group	socialization
body language	internalization	socially oriented
cognitive dissonance	nonconformity	social norm
compliance	nonverbal communication	stereotype
conformity	out-group	task oriented
discrimination		

▪ CHAPTER CHECKUP

1 The information conveyed by a person's posture or movement is called (*a*) personal insight (*b*) body language (*c*) verbalization (*d*) socialization.

2 Which of the following is *not* a basic rule of group behavior? (*a*) Group size greatly affects the way group members react to one another. (*b*) Group behavior can be changed by rewards or punishment. (*c*) Rewards given to group members are usually given out equally. (*d*) People are more likely to stay with groups that were difficult to join.

3 Stanley Milgram's experiment on obedience to authority proved that (*a*) everyone obeys orders without question (*b*) Americans will not follow orders if doing so means harming other people (*c*) many men will obey orders even when it means inflicting harm on a fellow human being (*d*) people are less likely to harm strangers than people they know.

4 Which of the following is an example of assertive behavior as opposed to aggression? (*a*) Susan leads a student delegation to protest the principal's cancellation of the Senior Prom. (*b*) Tom throws a brick through a restaurant window after the owner refuses to serve him. (*c*) Debbie cuts off another driver after he refuses to give her room to make a lane change. (*d*) Bill steals a turkey from the supermarket to give to a hungry family at Thanksgiving.

5 A social scientist would say that the best way to cut down on aggression in U.S. society would be to (*a*) take away all guns and knives owned by U.S. citizens (*b*) condition children to be passive and nonaggressive (*c*) punish all acts of aggression with long jail sentences (*d*) improve the social conditions that seem to trigger many incidents of hostility and violence.

6 Which of these is *not* a reaction to prejudice found in a minority group? (*a*) Many minority group members develop prejudices against some other minority group. (*b*) Minority group members often adopt the stereotyped behaviors expected of them. (*c*) With little to prove, minority group members seldom develop neurotic symptoms. (*d*) Some minority group members actively deny their own heritage.

7 Social psychologists agree that (*a*) old age begins at 65 for everyone (*b*) old people almost always become senile if they live past 70 (*c*) the elderly do not show any marked decrease in intelligence (*d*) a person's personality in old age has little to do with earlier stages of life.

8 Suppose some UFO fanatics sold all their belongings in preparation for being carried off to another planet. According to the theory of cognitive dissonance, what would group members be most likely to say after the flying saucers didn't come on the appointed day? (*a*) "The Air Force probably intercepted our saucer. It will surely come next week." (*b*) "We'll never believe in flying saucers again." (*c*) "Well, we were wrong that time." (*d*) "The joke's on us, isn't it?"

9 Which of the following is a *true* statement about suicide? (*a*) Those who talk about suicide never do anything about it. (*b*) More women commit suicide than men. (*c*) A person who tries to commit suicide but fails will very likely try again. (*d*) Suicide attempts can never be predicted in advance.

10 Teaching people to deal openly with death and dying (*a*) can only create neurotic behavior (*b*) isn't needed since American society has always done a good job of preparing people to cope with death (*c*) means that people will begin to look forward to death (*d*) will help people accept death as a natural part of life.

■ EXPLORING CONCEPTS

1 Try to name all of the groups to which you belong. How much do you think each of these groups affects your behavior?

2 What are the dangers of too much conformity in a society? From your own knowledge of history and from your own experience, give some examples of useful nonconformity. When, if ever, is nonconformity dangerous?

3 What would you do to reduce aggression in our society if you had the power? Would you also try to eliminate assertive behavior? Why or why not?

4 How does prejudice get started among the members of a majority group? Why is it so hard to get rid of once it is established?

5 Suppose you were planning a curriculum for elementary school children and you wanted to eliminate racial, age, and ethnic prejudices. What studies and experiences would you want the children to have?

6 How would you raise your children so that they would not respond, as Milgram's subjects did, to orders to harm another person?

■ HANDS-ON ACTIVITIES

1 Invite a panel of elderly people to talk to your psychology class about their views on aging. You and your classmates will probably be pleasantly surprised at how much you have in common with these elderly men and women. You can obtain more information about programs aimed at building positive attitudes toward aging by contacting AARP at 601 E St. NW, Washington, DC, 20049 <Web: *www.aarp.org*>. Another assertive group, the Gray Panthers, can be reached at 733 15th St. NW, Suite 437, Washington, DC 20005 <Web: *www.graypanthers.org*>.

2 Do you know an otherwise healthy retire person who seems to be withdrawing from contact with others? You might be able to do that person (and your community) a service by encouraging him or her to volunteer to help others. Some elderly people find satisfaction caring for premature infants at a hospital. Others work in literacy programs or dish up meals for the homeless. One of the most creative volunteer organizations is the Make-a-Wish Foundation, which helps make dreams come true for children suffering from life-threatening illnesses. Whether the child dreams of a visit to a space center or a ride on an elephant, the foundation's volunteers make it happen. For more information, contact Make-a-Wish Foundation, 3550 N. Central Ave., Suite 300, Phoenix, AZ 85012 <Web: *www.wish.org*>. If you'd rather stay closer to home, check the Community Services section of your phone book.

3 Cigarette smokers can provide you with an excellent way of demonstrating cognitive dissonance. Find a copy of an article warning about the dangers of smoking. Show it to several smokers who are willing to discuss their addiction with you. Then ask the smokers why they haven't quit when the danger to their health has been clearly proved. You should end up with an imposing list of poorly reasoned answers and a better understanding of how far people will go to reduce a dissonance.

4 Try to arrange for a speaker from a local suicide-prevention clinic or hot line to visit your psychology class. Since our society tries to ignore the fact that people commit suicide, you and your classmates will probably be amazed at the seriousness of the problem. Ask the speaker to pay particular attention to the incidence of suicide among teenagers and young adults.

5 Write across the top of a piece of paper the names of five racial, religious, or ethnic groups different from your own. Under each name, as quickly as possible, write as many descriptive words as you can. When you're finished, examine the results. Is it possible that you have repeated a number of stereotypes that you've never examined very closely? How well do your descriptions apply to actual people you know from each of the groups? Perhaps the exercise will help you think more clearly about the nature of prejudice and its effects on people's thinking.

6 Run the Asch experiment on conformity (see page 405) to see if you obtain similar results. You'll need to make several sets of cards with the standard and comparison lines. Be sure to coach your "stooges" carefully so as not to give the experiment away. Also, debrief your actual subjects afterward, so that they will understand what has happened. That's a tough position you'll be putting them in, and those who caved in to group pressure will need to be reassured that most people respond as they did.

FOR FURTHER READING

Aronson, Elliot. *The Social Animal.* New York: W. H. Freeman & Co., 2003. Dr. Aronson writes about social psychology with wit and insight in this new edition of his popular textbook. As he states in the introduction, "I nurse the secret belief that social psychologists are in a unique position to have a profound and beneficial impact on our lives by providing an increased understanding of such important phenomena as conformity, persuasion, prejudice, love, and aggression."

Baron, Robert, and Donn Byrne. *Social Psychology.* Boston: Allyn & Bacon, 2002. Now in its tenth edition, this lively text draws on both classic and current research. Along with coverage of topics such as prejudice and aggression, the authors have added discussions of nonverbal cues, volunteer work, bullying, and other social issues. Another new feature, "Beyond the Headlines," examines news events from the viewpoint of the social psychologist.

Garrod, Andrew, et al. *Souls Looking Back: Portraits of Growing Up Black.* New York: Routledge, 1999. This collection of autobiographical essays by black and biracial college students offers a hopeful portrait of minority adolescents. As you might expect, the young authors write passionately about poverty, prejudice, loneliness, and anger. Their well-balanced essays also give equal attention, however, to such topics as positive role models, spirituality, and racial pride.

Gonzales, Laurence. *Deep Survival: Who Lives, Who Dies, and Why.* New York: W. W. Norton, 2003. When faced with a life-threatening situation, nine out of ten people freeze or panic—but a hardy few stay focused . . . and alive. The survivors tend to share traits that include know-how, training, and the ability to stay calm. The bottom line: whether you're climbing Mt. Everest or driving in rush-hour traffic, you're more likely to survive if you stay cool, act decisively, and never, never give up.

Kohn, Alfie. *The Brighter Side of Human Nature: Altruism and Empathy in Everyday Life.* New York: Basic Books, 1992. The author makes a strong case for his belief that caring and generosity are as natural to human nature as are selfishness and aggression. Unlike animals, he points out, humans can (and do) take time to see the world through another's eyes. The book ends by proposing a morality of caring designed to transcend our culture's tendency to promote competition and individualism.

Morris, Desmond. *Peoplewatching: the Desmond Morris Guide to Body Language.* Toronto: Random House of Canada, 2002. Anthropologist Morris has been watching people all his life. In this richly illustrated book, he shows you how humans, consciously and unconsciously, signal attitudes, desires, and feelings with their bodies. One useful lesson teaches you how to interpret emotion by watching the other person's eyes. The more the pupils dilate, he says, the more excitement that person is feeling.

Wright, Richard. *Black Boy.* New York: Harper & Row, 1937. Richard Wright's classic autobiography vividly describes the terrible weight of prejudice that African Americans were forced to endure in the South of the 1930s. Perceptive readers will be left with a deeper appreciation for the accomplishments of the civil rights movement—and for the distance our society still must travel to ensure equal rights for all.

York, Pat. *Going Strong.* Boston: Little, Brown & Co., 1991. Do you dread the thought of growing old? This provocative book will remind you that the elderly can—and do—live active, fulfilling lives. York uses photos and short biographical sketches to introduce you to 70 senior citizens, all of whom are still "going strong."

Chapter

13 SEX ROLES, SEXISM, AND SEXUALITY

Revolutions change the way people think, feel, and behave. Some revolutions are fought with guns, while others involve changes in science or technology.

A revolution of a different sort has been taking place in this country. Before it's over, this revolution will have given us sweeping new definitions of what it means to be a man or a woman in U.S. society.

As in all revolutions, many men and women are unhappy about the changes they see around them. But a major social movement cannot be ignored. Its influence can be seen in the lives of people everywhere. Here is what three of them have to say.

Beth Durango, age 45. I grew up in a traditional family, the kind you see on reruns of old sitcoms. My parents never said it in so many words, but I knew I was supposed to marry, keep house, have kids, and bake chocolate chip cookies, just like Mom. So that's what I did. I married Tom, moved into a nice house in the suburbs, and gave birth to two fine babies. It was a pretty good life, by most standards. So, I kept asking myself, why did I feel so depressed?

Tom was so wrapped up in his work that he hardly noticed. Whenever I tried to talk to him about my feelings, he looked real uncomfortable and tried to change the subject. Finally, I decided to do what my friends in the women's movement had been urging me to do. I arranged child care for Sonny and Nell and went back to school. It was time to get a life of my own.

After a while, Tom stopped grumbling about late meals and dust on the bookshelves. He and the kids pitched in and took over more of the chores. I think they all could see that I was happier than I had been for a long time. When I graduated, Tom rather hoped I would settle down again, but I went out and found a job with a small, fast-growing company. The money wasn't great, but I hit the ground running and worked my way into a management position right away. Now, everything's rosy, right? It would be, except that I'm bumping up against PowerTek's glass ceiling.

Three times in the past year I've been passed over for promotion to department manager. Each time, my CEO smiled sadly and told me how close I had come to beating out the man who was chosen. He knows and I know that I'm better qualified than two of those turkeys, and I have more seniority than the third. What it comes down to is the very

FIGURE 13.1 ■ Entering the business world, whether you are just starting out or making a new start later in life, presents enormous challenges. What can women do when they bump into the infamous glass ceiling?

simple fact that those smug suits who run this company aren't anxious to share their power with a woman. Tom thinks I should move on, but I hate to walk away from what I've built here.

Emma Prescott, age 23. Am I a feminist? Don't be silly! Sure, I guess you might get that idea because I'm a firefighter, and that's supposed to be a man's job, right? Well, the way I see it, firefighting's a job—period! When I applied to take the exams, I wasn't trying to prove anything except that women should have the same chance as men to wear this uniform. You probably heard about the problem I had with the physical tests. I can see where you have to be able to climb walls and carry heavy loads, but the old tests weren't fair—for men or women. One of the women's groups helped me take my case to court, and the judge ruled that the tests had to be changed.

Then, after I finished training and was assigned to this station, some of the men's wives signed a petition about me. I guess they thought my big goal in life was to steal their husbands. My own boyfriend wasn't too happy about my sleeping here, but that's part of the job. At first the other firefighters thought they'd have to risk their lives to take care of me, but they cooled down when I showed them I could do the job.

A couple of the guys call me "Libber," but that's crazy. I'm not marching for women's rights or making speeches. I guess most girls dream about being models or flight attendants, but I always wanted to fight fires. That's not such a big deal, is it?

Brad Grant, age 26. Hey, I can see by the surprised look on your face that you're wondering why I brought Stephanie into the men's rest room. I guess it does look a little strange, but you wouldn't want me to change her diaper out in the restaurant, would you? Sure, some people think this is woman's work, but in my marriage it's just a job that needs doing. Besides, Anita's away on a business trip, so it's only fair. When I work overtime on my job, she pitches in and does what's necessary. That's how we work everything out.

You see, before we got married, Anita and I talked a lot about things like this. Neither of us wanted to repeat the mistakes our families made. I still remember seeing my folks drag in after their shifts at the plant. Dad would plop down to watch TV, but Mom just kept on going. She still had all the cooking, cleaning, laundry, and child care to do.

So Anita and I worked out a marriage contract. It's got a lot of personal stuff in it, but the important thing is that we agreed on how we'd divide up the work. And we do a lot of things together, like cooking and cleaning. Most of all, we share the child-raising tasks. Anita hasn't forgotten that she hardly ever

FIGURE 13.2 ▪ As women and men take on new roles in the workplace and at home, they may be subject to criticism, harassment, and ridicule. Even after years of performing competently as firefighters, women are often not given full respect by their male colleagues. Men who take on child care and household responsibilities on a regular basis are still the exception rather than the norm.

saw her father when she was growing up. That's not going to happen to our kids. We may never make a ton of money, but I'm not going to be the kind of father whose kids run and hide when he slams the front door after a hard day at the office. And just look at Stephanie kick! I'm not going to push her into athletics, but if she wants to play sports she'll have the same encouragement I plan to give my boys.

You might not agree with all of the ideas expressed by Beth, Emma, and Brad. But the decisions people like them are making about marriage, children, and jobs will undoubtedly affect your life in the years to come. This chapter will give you some insights into this nonviolent revolution.

13.1 How do people learn masculine and feminine sex roles?

13.2 What are the effects of sexism on women?

13.3 What are the goals of the women's movement?

13.4 What effect is the women's movement having on men?

13.5 How do changing patterns of sexuality affect the individual?

13.1 ■ HOW DO PEOPLE LEARN MASCULINE AND FEMININE SEX ROLES?

What does it mean to be male? What does it mean to be female?

Throughout most of history, people thought they knew how to answer these questions. Men were expected to be skilled hunters and farmers, brave warriors, and stern but loving fathers. Women were supposed to be loving wives and mothers, keepers of the home, and guardians of the softer human virtues. Many people never did fit these stereotyped *sex roles*, of course, but they were either ignored or dismissed as "abnormals."

Only in recent decades has psychology begun to study the biological and environmental forces that create male and female behavior. The studies have reached two major conclusions: (1) The physical differences between men and women do affect behavior but not to the degree once supposed. (2) Culture, not biology, plays the major part in determining sex-role behavior.

MALE-FEMALE DIFFERENCES

A star basketball player soars high for a rebound, then turns to throw in a 20-footer as the game ends. The crowd surges onto the floor to greet the new national champions.

A two-year-old child, chasing a puppy across the lawn, falls and begins to cry. A neighbor quickly picks up the child, hugs it, and kisses away the tears.

Can you guess the sexes of the victorious basketball player and the kindly neighbor? Many people would assume that the basketball player is a man and the kindly neighbor a woman. Is that what you thought? If so, you were caught up in old stereotypes relating to sex roles. But in this time of increased opportunities for women in sports, college women now play for national championships. And why shouldn't a man comfort a crying child with a hug and a kiss?

Despite these changing patterns, real differences still exist between men and women. Some differences are related to physical traits, others to behavior. Three theories have been advanced to explain these differences: the hereditary view, the environmental view, and a combined view.

FIGURE 13.3 ■ Cartoonists like Cathy Guisewite are alert to the problems that crop up whenever men and women try to communicate. Do these misfired messages grow out of our genetic inheritance or do adults teach us how to misunderstand each other? That argument has never been fully resolved, but current research suggests that male/female differences are a product of nature *and* nurture.

CATHY By Cathy Guisewite

For Every Woman . . . and Every Man

Feminists believe that success for their movement will benefit men as surely as it will improve the lives of America's women. Here is how Nancy R. Smith describes the changes a nonsexist future will bring:

- For every woman who is tired of acting weak when she knows she is strong, there is a man who is tired of appearing strong when he feels vulnerable.

- For every woman who is tired of acting dumb, there is a man who is burdened with the constant expectations of "knowing everything."

- For every woman who is tired of being called "an emotional female," there is a man who is denied the right to weep and to be gentle.

- For every woman who feels "tied down" by her children, there is a man who is denied the full pleasures of shared parenthood.

- For every woman who is denied meaningful employment or equal pay, there is a man who must bear the full financial responsibility for at least one other human being.

- For every woman who takes a step toward her own liberation, there is a male who finds the way to freedom has been made a little easier.

THE HEREDITARY VIEW. Supporters of the *hereditary view* believe that biological inheritance determines sex roles. This theory uses history as a kind of proof. Look, the argument says, man's superior size, strength, and logical mind have made him the naturally dominant sex. And just as men once excelled as hunters and tribal chieftains, they now surpass women as engineers, doctors, and political leaders. Similarly, women's role has been conditioned by biology. As the bearers of children, women fit naturally into their traditional task of caring for husbands and children. Their softer physique, gentler nature, and lesser strength are linked to hereditary factors, the argument concludes.

A careful look at human heredity, however, suggests that women may well be the superior sex. Women generally live longer than men. A woman born in 2000 will live longer, by five years, than a man born in the same year. Males also experience more colorblindness, autism, speech problems, reading disabilities, and infant mortality. Although men have heavier and stronger muscles, women generally have greater stamina. Individual differences among males are also greater than among females. While these differences mean that society will produce more male geniuses, they also mean that more male idiots will be born.

Where, then, did the pattern of male dominance begin? If heredity plays any part in determining sex-role differences, it probably relates to women's role as childbearers. To carry, give birth to, and nurture a child to adulthood requires an enormous investment of energy, both physical and emotional. Traditional sex roles probably started with this basic fact of life. Since women were occupied with caring for the children, men took on the task of finding food. Although hunting was difficult and dangerous, it was also exciting. Even when better weapons and better food-producing methods became available, men continued to monopolize the higher prestige jobs.

THE ENVIRONMENTAL VIEW. Supporters of the *environmental view* believe that sex roles are shaped mainly by cultural pressures. The famous anthropologist Margaret Mead (1901–

FIGURE 13.4 ▪ Anthropologist Margaret Mead refused to let traditional ideas about women's roles keep her from doing the field studies that made her famous. She also found evidence that male/female sex roles are conditioned more by culture than by biology.

1978) singled out three tribes from the South Pacific island of New Guinea as proof of this theory. Among the Arapesh, she found in her landmark 1930s study, both men and women were nonaggressive. Cooperative and gentle, these people shared those traits that modern society has often labeled as "feminine." Unlike the Arapesh, Mundugumor men and women behaved in equally aggressive, competitive ways. Mundugumor women would be considered "unfeminine" in many cultures, but their fierce behavior was encouraged within their society. Finally, the Tchambuli reversed the usual sex roles. Tchambuli men took pride in caring for children and in producing beautiful artwork. Tchambuli women turned Western expectations upside down by growing up to be independent and domineering. The women fished, traded, and took charge of producing the goods needed for survival.

Critics have pointed out that Mead based her conclusions on three small, isolated cultures. Other studies have found that most tribal societies follow the traditional division of labor, with men as hunters and women as homemakers and food gatherers. Dr. Mead, however, insisted that the social environment, not heredity, dictates sex roles. In the United States, for example, only 26.6 percent of the doctors and 19.8 percent of the dentists are women. These 1998 statistics might suggest that only men have the qualities necessary to be doctors and dentists—except that in Russia, those percentages are almost exactly reversed. Mead seemed to be on safe ground, therefore, when she concluded that personality differences between the sexes are "cultural creations to which each generation is trained to conform."

THE COMBINED VIEW.   As you might have already guessed, many psychologists occupy the middle ground in this debate. Male/female differences, they suggest, develop as a result of inborn sex differences interacting with the environment.

An example of this interaction between "nature and nurture" can be seen in the sleep patterns of infants. Because baby boys sleep one to two hours less per day than do baby girls, the boys are generally more active during the day and tend to demand more attention. As a consequence, mothers spend more time holding baby boys and are more likely to encourage them to reach, grasp, pull, and stand. In this way, the biologically more active boy draws a more active response from his environment.

Similarly, women's superior verbal skills begin in the cradle. Studies show that baby girls make more of the babbling and cooing noises typical of infants. This verbal activity encourages parents to talk more to baby girls. The resulting feedback conditions girls to rely on their verbal abilities to obtain rewards, just as their brothers gain approval through physical activity. In this way, cultural forces seize on an inborn trait and turn it into an integral part of the adult personality.

Like many psychological "rules," this principle applies only to the population in general. You probably know a number of girls whose athletic talents would stand out in any company. Similarly, the classroom spotlight often shines on boys whose verbal abilities surpass those of their female classmates. Eleanor Maccoby, an expert in sex differences, believes that people perform best when they possess both male and female qualities. As proof, you probably have noted already that society often rewards the man who develops superior verbal abilities. Today, moreover, rewards are increasing for women who demonstrate superior physical abilities. If this means that U.S. society is learning to respect both men and women for their accomplishments, without regard to stereotyped sex roles, the United States will have taken a giant step forward toward a more enlightened future.

COMMUNICATION OF SEX ROLES

Because children are not born with blueprints for male or female behavior, they must look to the people around them for information on sex roles. In primitive societies, in which sex roles are often clear-cut, the process causes little confusion. Boys identify with their fathers and from childhood practice the skills of the hunter, herder, farmer, or craftsman. Girls copy the nurturing behavior of their mothers and slip quietly into the traditional role as family caregiver.

Today's children have a more difficult time figuring out male and female roles. In a society that no longer requires sheer muscle power for most jobs, the distinctions between men-only and women-only jobs are blurred (see Figure 13.5). Despite numerous exceptions, the majority of American parents now say they expect their children to learn "human" roles that transcend outmoded male and female roles.

ROLE OF PARENTS.   One theory on the learning of sex roles suggests that parents and other adults have always shaped desired behavior through reward and punishment. This process includes such parental behaviors as applauding Keith's rough-and-tumble play—while scolding Gloria for being "unladylike" when she wrestles with her playmates. Similarly, you may have heard a parent react to a boy's tears with the order, "Stop that! Big boys don't cry!" Repeated incidents of this type carry over into adult life, leaving men unable to cry, no matter how deep their grief.

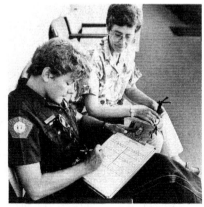

FIGURE 13.5 ▓ Thanks to the women's movement, most formerly male-only jobs have been opened up to qualified women. Why did it take so long for the army and police departments to admit women as regular soldiers and patrol officers?

An angry look or a smile can communicate as much information about "proper" behavior as a spanking or a gift. If Gloria returns home covered with mud, her parents don't have to punish her to let her know they disapprove. By withholding love for a little while, they'll soon convince Gloria that "nice girls" don't get dirty.

Children also learn sex roles by imitating the behavior of their parents. This *modeling behavior*, as it is known, seems to be a natural part of growing up. Each child tends to model on the parent of the same sex, although boys and girls do not follow the same process. Very young boys identify strongly with their fathers. At the same time, they learn about feminine behavior from their mothers and their female caregivers. Girls are more likely to adopt mixed male and female roles during early childhood. This weaker role identification does not last, however. Although they're surrounded by strong male models, girls model themselves more closely on women as they grow older.

Today's sex roles allow girls to play active sports, dress in jeans, and generally forget about being "ladylike." Not long ago, girls who enjoyed vigorous outdoor activities were derided for being "tomboys." Now, most girls can participate in athletics without being labeled in any way. Much to the surprise of many parents, their daughters have proven to be just as competitive as their sons—and just as athletic.

ROLE OF THE COMMUNITY. The community also influences the development of male/female behavior. Even though parental messages make the strongest impression on children, family influences can be weakened by exposure to conflicting messages from religious institutions, school, or the media. Keith's parents, for example, may encourage him to play with dolls at home. Their message is one of approval, since they want him to develop nurturing qualities. But if other children laugh at Keith for being a "sissy" or if his nursery school teacher shows disapproval, he'll probably lose interest in his dolls.

In the same way, the community's standards of male/female behavior can become a self-fulfilling prophecy. In the 1950s, for instance, society defined long hair as a feminine characteristic. Boys and men, therefore, wore their hair short as part of their masculine identity. In the 1960s, however, young men began experimenting with long hairstyles. Men who chose to wear shoulder-length hair had to endure reactions that ranged from suspicious stares to outright rejection. In time, the "rules" about hair length changed. Today, a more relaxed attitude about hair encourages men to wear whatever style pleases them—from sculptured crew cuts to long ponytails.

■ SECTION CHECKUP

1 How do heredity and environment interact to determine male and female behavior? Give several examples.

2 How would you explain the historic tendency of men to take over the more energetic jobs, such as hunting, fishing, building, and the like?

3 How do parents and community "teach" sex roles to children?

13.2 ■ WHAT ARE THE EFFECTS OF SEXISM ON WOMEN?

Newborn babies look pretty much alike. Unless the first one you see is your own, you probably won't be much impressed. One look will tell you that no one could honestly see masculine or feminine qualities in such tiny, wrinkled creatures.

No one, that is, except parents. T. Berry Brazelton, renowned "baby doctor," agrees with numerous studies showing that parents of newborn girls describe them as "softer, smaller, finer-featured, and less alert" than boys. In another experiment, women were asked to play with cross-dressed baby boys. As predicted, the women played more gently and soothingly with the boys than they did with cross-dressed baby girls. If parents "see" girls as being different from boys right from the first days of life, it's not hard to predict that they will also treat girls differently in the months to come.

As the previous section demonstrated, that's exactly what does happen. Maybe that fact would not alarm us if the differences in treatment added up to a rough sort of equality. But such is not the case. By locking infants into categories labeled "boy" and "girl," parents open the door to a form of discrimination known as *sexism*. Social psychologists define sexism as the social and economic domination of one sex by the other. Until recently, this practice meant that most men *and* women grew up believing that women are the inferior sex. As a consequence, women were forced to accept a secondary role in political, economic, and family life. Studies show that women trapped in dependent roles are more likely to become depressed. During therapy, one woman dramatized her feelings by sketching herself as weighted down by huge lead boots.

EFFECT OF SEXISM ON SELF-ESTEEM

Has this long history of sexism had an effect on women's self-esteem? One of many studies answering that question with a firm "yes" comes from Matina Horner, of the University of Michigan. Horner first conducted her "fear of success" study in 1968. The test was simple enough. Horner asked college-age women to finish a story about a young woman named Anne, who has just learned that she received the highest grade in her class at the end of the first semester of medical school. Men write about an identical situation—except that their story substitutes John for Anne.

Horner's 1968 study found that a high percentage of her women subjects predicted a dim future for Anne. The men described a bright career ahead for John. A typical response for Anne often centered on the pressures of competing with men. By contrast, the men who wrote about John usually described him as reaping the rewards of work well done. As the women's movement slowly rebuilt women's self-esteem, Horner found that Anne's positive writeups began to increase. Today, men and women tend to write equally positive responses for Anne and John (see the box on page 444). If only about one college-age woman in four saw Anne in positive terms in 1968, you can assume that the other three women felt inferior when it came to competing with men. This conclusion is supported by an older study. When asked what sex they wanted their first child to be, two-thirds of the women surveyed said they wanted a boy. The researchers interpreted this response to mean that the women were convinced that boys had more opportunities, more fun, more freedom. A similar survey today would reach a different conclusion. Most young women now believe their daughters have as much chance as their sons to live a productive and satisfying life.

The women might be more optimistic if ongoing studies didn't regularly uncover evidence of deep-rooted sexist (and racist) attitudes. In a 1991 experiment, Ian Ayres of Northwestern University School of Law sent six volunteers to "buy" a new car from Chicago dealers. Although all followed an identical script, the white women were charged $150 more per car than were the white men. Black women were asked to pay *$900 more.*

LOST WOMEN OF HISTORY

Until recently, the stories of great achievements—whether in law, religion, science, philosophy, or the arts—were mainly the stories of men. Many *male chauvinists* (people who have an exaggerated notion of male superiority) have used this fact as a way of

John v. Anne: A Test of Attitudes

Do women view the costs of success different from men? The John/Anne test, originally created by Matina Horner of the University of Michigan, shows that attitudes have changed dramatically in recent years. Where women once wrote that Anne's success had compromised her chances for married happiness, women today see her success in much more positive terms. Here are some typical responses, written by high school seniors:

	MEN WRITE FOR JOHN	**WOMEN WRITE FOR ANNE**
The script	Finish this brief story about John: *After graduating from high school and college, John was accepted by a first-rate medical school. When first semester exams were over, John joined the crowd that had gathered around the showcase where the grades were posted. Someone was reading the class rankings aloud, and John was listed as the Number One student in the class. Everyone turned to look at John . . .*	Finish this brief story about Anne: *After graduating from high school and college, Anne was accepted by a first-rate medical school. When first semester exams were over, Anne joined the crowd that had gathered around the showcase where the grades were posted. Someone was reading the class rankings aloud, and Anne was listed as the Number One student in the class. Everyone turned to look at Anne . . .*
A typical negative response	Suddenly, someone shouted, "You're a cheater, you used cheat notes on all of the tests." Everyone gasped in astonishment. This was a bold statement and all ears turned to hear John's denial. Amazingly, John broke down and said, "You're right, I cheated. The work was just too tough for me. I don't deserve to be at the top of the class. I should be at the very bottom."	Anne blushed and turned bright red. She felt proud, but scared, too. What would Steve say? She looked around to see him staring at her. Oh God, she thought, I should have been content with an average grade. Steve will never marry me if he thinks I'm brighter than he is. As she pushed her way through the crowd, she reminded herself that good grades wouldn't keep her warm at night.
A typical positive response	"John who?" everyone asked. It turned out that no one knew John. He never went out at night, never had a girlfriend, and kept strictly to himself. Quietly and efficiently, he had set out to earn the top ranking in the class. Now that he's succeeded, everyone looks up to him. Some envy him, but most people admire his dedication and invite him to their parties. "Best of all," says John, "all the girls are calling me for help. I love being smart."	Anne felt a little embarrassed, but then she realized that most of her classmates were happy for her. Well, if they're happy for me, I should be, too, she decided. As people crowded around to congratulate her, she told herself that even though she now had a reputation to uphold, she must not become obsessive about grades. Smiling, she took advantage of the moment to get to know her classmates better.

"proving" that women are inferior. *Feminists* (men and women who work to achieve political, social, and economic equality for women) have been quick to point out two major flaws in this reasoning. First, the feminists argue, history books have always emphasized male accomplishments because men wrote most of them. Women's achievements were often overlooked. In the 1950s, for example, anthropologists reported from Australia that male aborigines kept their women at arm's length with "dazzling displays of magic they said came from the gods." Thirty years later, a female anthropologist took the time to do what her male predecessors had failed to do—she talked to the women. The aboriginal women, she learned, had always known the "magic" was a hoax. They pretended to believe in the men's power but laughed at the men behind their backs.

Further, the feminists add, sexist attitudes have kept women locked in a position of inferiority. Without equal education and equal encouragement, women generally have not been given the same opportunities as men. As proof, the feminists point to the fields of literature and politics. In the 19th century, when publishers began to welcome manuscripts from women authors, women were soon competing on even terms with men. And when politics opened up to women in the final decades of the 1900s, Great Britain, India, Israel, and Pakistan elected women to lead their governments. Closer to home, 14 women senators joined 86 male colleagues when the U.S. Senate convened in January 2003. The new makeup of the chamber meant that women had more than tripled their representation since 1993.

SEXISM ON THE JOB

Sexism's most obvious penalty is imposed in the workplace. Even though women make up 47 percent of the workforce, they take home only 78 percent of what men earn. In

FIGURE 13.6 ■ These women are determined to work at jobs that challenge them and that pay well. What problems do you think they had to overcome before they were allowed to work on construction sites?

2002, for example, male workers were paid an average salary of $35,360 a year—and the women who worked alongside them averaged $27,560. A college degree improves everyone's earnings, but male college grads have an even greater edge on their female coworkers, $50,730 to $33,662.

Barbara J., age 24, learned about job discrimination at first hand. A talented and ambitious young woman, she hired on as a maintenance worker with a major chemical company. Her pleasure with her new job faded quickly when she learned that company policy kept women from pursuing career paths that led to higher-paying production line jobs. Unwilling to accept this injustice, she cornered her supervisor during a lunch break and demanded an explanation.

Terry Hopkins stared at her, half amused and half annoyed. "This company has your best interests at heart," he said. "If we put you on the production line, you'd be exposed to all kinds of dangerous chemicals, including lead compounds."

Barbara didn't try to conceal her impatience. "If lead's so bad, what about the men who work on the line?" she demanded.

■ PRO & CON:
The Debate Never Seems to End

The debate over the proper role for women in society has been going on for thousands of years. A quick look through the pages of history, ancient and contemporary, yields these conflicting points of view.

ISSUE	THE CHAUVINISTS SPEAK	THE FEMINISTS RESPOND
Women's rights	In childhood a woman must be subject to her father; in youth to her husband; when her husband is dead, to her sons. A woman must never be free. *Hindu Code of Manu, V (ca. 100 B.C.)* These [extreme feminists] are the ... man-hating "FemiNazis" ... who claim to speak for all women and use their legitimate grievances as a path to power. *Rush Limbaugh (2003)*	Remember, all men would be tyrants if they could. If particular care and attention is not paid to the ladies, we are determined to [stir up] a rebellion and will not hold ourselves bound by any law in which we have no voice or representation. *Abigail Adams, in a letter to John Adams (1776)*
Husbands and wives	Wives, submit yourselves unto your own husbands as unto the Lord. For the husband is the head of the wife, even as Christ is the head of the Church. *New Testament, Ephesians 5:22–23 (ca. A.D. 100)* They have a right to work whenever they want to—as long as they have dinner ready when you get home. *John Wayne (ca. 1970)*	The prolonged slavery of women is the darkest page in human history. *Elizabeth Cady Stanton (1881)* Those women who glom on to men so that they can ... spend the rest of their days shining up their status symbol, and figure they never have to reach, stretch, learn, grow, face dragons or make a living again are the ones to be pitied. *Helen Gurley Brown (1963)*

Terry played his trump card. "We can't put you on the line because lead is a hazard to your unborn babies," he said with a knowing smile. "Some day, when your babies are born with all their fingers and toes, you'll be happy the company's fetal policy was there to protect them."

"Even if I do get married, I'm not sure I want children," Barbara argued. "You can't treat me like some sort of flower pot full of unfertilized seeds! If and when I conceive a child, that's the time to worry about lead exposure."

Terry shrugged and looked at his watch. "Break's over," he said. As a parting shot he added, "There's nothing more to say. The Su-

ISSUE	THE CHAUVINISTS SPEAK	THE FEMINISTS RESPOND
Women in politics	Sensible . . . women do not want to vote. The relative positions to be assumed by man and woman in the working out of our civilization were assigned long ago by a higher intelligence than ours. *Grover Cleveland (1905)*	I believe a woman's place not only is in the home, but in the House and Senate and throughout the government. One thing we are insisting on is that we not have this stag government. *President Lyndon Johnson (1964)*
Childbearing	The best prescription for a discontented female is to have a child. *Pablo Picasso (ca. 1960)* Most women would rather cuddle a baby than a typewriter or a machine. *Phyllis Schlafly (ca. 1970)*	Women have childbearing equipment. For them to choose not to use the equipment is no more blocking what is instinctive than it is for a man who, muscles or no, chooses not to be a weightlifter. *Betty Rollin (ca. 1970)*
Achievement	The shattering truth is that men outshine women in every field of endeavor. *Wallace Reyborn (1972)* It would be terribly naive to suggest that a B.A. can be made as attractive to girls as a marriage license. *Grayson Kirk (ca. 1960)*	If I have to, I can do anything. I am strong; I am invincible; I am woman. *Helen Reddy (ca. 1970)* Since 1982, women have earned more bachelor's degrees than men, and they have earned more master's degrees since 1981. *AFL-CIO (2002)*

Do these arguments give you a clearer idea of the long-running debate over women's rights and roles in modern society? You might find it interesting to state your feelings about these issues in your own words.

preme Court may be on your side in cases involving reproductive safety, but I'd think twice before I took this to court. You're just a small fish in a very big pond."

Bewildered by oppression that seemed too big and remote to fight, Barbara could take little comfort in media reports of women who work as police officers, sportswriters, steve-

dores, and coal miners. She realized that she was one of the women whose jobs are still defined by sexist stereotypes. Social pressure and limited opportunities tend to push women into low-paying positions as domestic workers, secretaries, retail clerks, waitresses, and the like. Even in fields dominated by women, such as library science and elementary school teaching, the top jobs are often held by men. Primary-care nurses stand out as a notable exception to this rule. A severe shortage of registered nurses in the late 1980s and early 1990s forced hospital administrators to improve the nurses' pay and working conditions.

THE HOMEMAKER'S DOUBLE BIND

The changing definition of sex roles has left some women uncertain about their future. At one time, women were conditioned to believe that a career as a wife and mother was the finest ambition a woman could have. Many women still find that role to be a deeply satisfying one, particularly while their children are young. But today's homemaker often faces scornful remarks from her working sisters. After a 12-hour day of cooking, cleaning, shopping, gardening, caring for children, doing volunteer work, and driving car pools, she runs up against the comment, "Oh, you're a housewife! How lovely it must be to have all that free time with nothing important to do." (See the table on page 449 for one study of a homeworker's "free time.")

Psychologists know that women who stay home to care for their families can lose their sense of self in a world limited to kitchens, kids, and car pools. In a culture that defines people by what they "do," homemakers are often identified with the achievements of their husbands and children. Women who see themselves only as wives and mothers may also suffer a severe emotional shock if they lose either of these roles. Divorce, the husband's death, or children leaving home can trigger a period of severe depression. Suddenly cut off from the old role and anxious to find a new one, such women may find that the qualities that made them superior wives and mothers do not pay off in the job market.

Many young adults are resolving this problem by combining careers and home life. Some delay marriage and children until they have established themselves in their careers. Later, they arrange their schedules so that both husband and wife share equally in child care and housework. Even when these self-aware women choose to stay home with their young children, they do not cut themselves off from the outside world. They see full-time motherhood as a highly satisfying, temporary role in a long and active life.

THE COSTS OF SEXISM

The price women have paid for generations of sexist discrimination can be counted in lost wages, lost opportunities, and lost identities. But society also has paid a heavy price for keeping women in a secondary role. How many potential female scientists, artists, political leaders, inventors, composers, and explorers have lived and died with their talents unrecognized? Novelist Virginia Woolf illustrated this misuse of human resources in her book *A Room of One's Own* by imagining that the great dramatist William Shakespeare had a sister. The 1500s, she reminded us, were not ready to accept a woman's talents.

> She was as adventurous, as imaginative, as agog to see the world as he was. But she was not sent to school. . . . She picked up a book now and then, one of her brother's perhaps, and read a few pages. But then her parents came in and told her to mend the stockings or mind the stew and not moon about with books and papers. . . . [To avoid an unwanted marriage] She made up a small parcel of her belongings, let herself down by a rope one summer's night and took the road to London. She was not seventeen. The birds that sang in the hedge were not more musical than she was. She had the quickest fancy, a gift like her brother's, for the tune of words. Like him, she had a taste

What's a Homemaker Worth?

Most people take the work a woman does around the house for granted "John is *working* on the car," we say, "while Alice is *fixing* dinner." But when the American Council of Life Insurance added up the hours typical homemakers *work* on each of their separate jobs, the council came up with some surprising figures. How many hours would you guess? Forty hours, after all, is a normal workweek.

Assuming that the family has small children, the homemaker's week looks like this:

Child care	45.1 hours
Meal planning	1.2
Meal preparation	13.1
Food buying	3.3
Dishwashing	6.2
Housekeeping	17.5
Laundry	5.9
Sewing	1.3
Maintenance	1.7
Gardening	2.3
Transportation	2.0
	99.6 hours

That 99.6-hour workweek is over twice the number of hours that most workers put in on their jobs. And if you had to pay for these services on an hourly basis (figuring the U.S. Labor Department's recommended wage of $11.94 an hour for housekeepers), be prepared to write out a check for $1,189.22 each week—or $1,545.04 if you pay time and a half for overtime.

---

for the theater. She stood at the stage door; she wanted to act, she said. Men laughed in her face. . . . She could get no training in her craft. Could she even seek her dinner in a tavern or roam the streets at midnight? Yet her genius was for fiction and lusted to feed abundantly upon the lives of men and women and the study of their ways.

In time, Woolf wrote, the young woman commits suicide, her "poet's heart caught and tangled in a woman's body." Perhaps now, with doors opening for women of talent and determination, the story would have a happier ending.

■ SECTION CHECKUP

1 What is meant by the term *sexism?* Give several examples of sexism that you have seen, experienced, or read about.

2 How would a feminist explain the failure of women to match the achievements of men in such fields as science, art, and politics?

3 How has sexism affected women on the job?

4 Why is today's housewife caught in a double bind? What can be done to ease the strain of this problem?

13.3 ■ WHAT ARE THE GOALS OF THE WOMEN'S MOVEMENT?

In 411 B.C., the Greek playwright Aristophanes wrote a play called *Lysistrata*. Even though Aristophanes was a man, he gave Lysistrata, the play's hero, one of the most telling lines. "How is it, husband," Lysistrata asks, "that you men manage these affairs so foolishly?" She believes that the long and senseless war with Sparta could be ended if the men would substitute reason for emotion. To hasten that process, she persuades the women of Athens to banish their husbands from their beds until the men make peace.

In the play, Lysistrata's strategy brings peace to the city. In today's real world, many women are still bound by sexist customs. These women lack property rights, a voice in public affairs, and even the right to choose their own husbands. In these societies, women must endure what they have no power to change. The custom of *purdah*, for example, where it is still practiced in the Middle East, restricts the Muslim woman's freedom of movement, expression, and choice. These veiled women, along with their sisters in similar cultures, are still waiting for rights guaranteed to most Western women.

That progress toward equality has not come easily. In this country, the modern struggle for women's rights dates back at least to the 1800s, when feminists such as Susan B. Anthony and Elizabeth Cady Stanton fought for suffrage (the right to vote). As Anthony, honored in 1979 as the first real-life woman to appear on a United States coin, put it: "Men, their rights and nothing more; women, their rights and nothing less." That first feminist goal was not fulfilled until 1920, when the Nineteenth Amendment sent American women to voting booths alongside men. Afterward, the Great Depression and World War II delayed the pursuit of additional feminist objectives.

In the 1960s, a new generation of feminists revived the movement. Some seemed willing to work within the system to bring about change; others demanded that the system itself be changed. But a number of goals are common to almost all feminists.

EQUALITY UNDER THE LAW

During the 1970s and the early 1980s, the women's movement made the passage of the *Equal Rights Amendment (ERA)* its top priority. If it had passed, this amendment to the U.S. Constitution would have banned all discrimination based on sex. For a while, it looked as though the ERA would become law. It died when male-dominated legislatures in the last few states needed for ratification refused to approve it.

The fight to ratify the ERA was led by the largest of all feminist groups, the *National Organization for Women (NOW)*. Since its founding in 1966, NOW has focused its energies on winning legal equality for women. Originally led by Betty Friedan (See BioBox, page 451), NOW teaches that sexism is as great an evil as racism. Its philosophy calls for women to participate fully "in the mainstream of American society now, exercising all the privileges and responsibilities thereof in truly equal partnership with men."

NOW's approach to feminist issues does not receive universal support among women. The organization's call for the abolition of all limits on access to birth control information and the repeal of all laws governing abortion alienated a number of its members. During the drive to ratify the ERA, a Stop-ERA movement, led by author and housewife Phyllis Schlafly, emerged to battle the amendment. Her organization, the Eagle Forum, felt that existing laws did an adequate job of protect-

Betty Friedan:
Explorer of "The Feminine Mystique"

Betty Friedan (1921–) didn't begin the modern feminist movement in the United States. But when portions of her book *The Feminine Mystique* first appeared in magazines in 1962, she caught the attention of the nation. Friedan's scholarship and criticism provided the spark the women's movement needed.

Betty Friedan graduated *summa cum laude* from Smith College. After working with the well-known psychologists Kurt Koffka and Kurt Lewin, she married, had three children, and lived the life of a suburban housewife. Publication of *The Feminine Mystique*, however, changed the course of her life. Now separated from her husband, she lectures, writes, teaches, and serves as a spokeswoman for feminist causes. One of the founders of the National Organization for Women, she served as its president until 1970.

If you asked Friedan to sum up her criticism of the role of the traditional American housewife, she'd tell you that the myth of the happy homemaker is just that—a myth. In *The Feminine Mystique*, she wrote:

> If a woman had a problem in the 1950s and 1960s, she knew that something must be wrong with her marriage, or with herself. Other women were satisfied with their lives, she thought. What kind of a woman was she if she did not feel this mysterious fulfillment waxing the kitchen floor? She was so ashamed to admit her dissatisfaction that she never knew how many other women shared it. If she tried to tell her husband, he didn't understand what she was talking about. . . . When a woman went to a psychiatrist for help, as many women did, she would say, "I'm so ashamed," or "I must be hopelessly neurotic." . . .

> Just what was this problem that has no name? What were the words women used when they tried to express it? Sometimes a woman would say "I feel empty somehow . . . incomplete." Or she would say, "I feel as if I don't exist." Sometimes she blotted out the feeling with a tranquilizer. . . .

> If I am right, the problem that has no name stirring in the minds of so many American women today is not a matter of loss of feminity or too much education, or the demands of domesticity. It is far more important than anyone recognizes. . . . It may well be the key to our future as a nation and a culture. We can no longer ignore that voice within women that says: "I want something more than my husband and my children and my home."

Betty Friedan wrote these words in the 1960s. She is still speaking out. In what she calls the Second Stage of the women's movement, she sees the need for new approaches to divorce, abortion reform, housing, and education. To achieve these goals, she says, feminists must learn to cooperate with men, not to engage in a class struggle against them. Friedan is also turning her attention to the problem of ageism. "This is the next revolution," she tells enthusiastic audiences of senior citizens. "New values will come from new pioneers of aging."

ing women's job, credit, and educational opportunities. Under ERA, Schlafly said, women would be forced to serve in the military and would lose the protection of laws that prevent employers from assigning women to jobs beyond their strength and endurance.

Another major feminist goal aims at ending all remaining discrimination in areas such as credit, housing, and employment. Title VII of the Civil Rights Act of 1964 firmly established the principle of legal equality, but laws passed in Washington do not always change what happens in the nation's schools, factories, or offices. Despite the Equal Credit Law, for example, Pat W. was turned down when she applied for an oil-company credit card. Angered, she rewrote her application, concealing only her sex. Based on the same job record and income, the company sent her the card by return mail. Pat took her complaint to court and won. Her success reflects the growing willingness on the part of feminists to file lawsuits when women's rights are violated.

In 1992, for example, NOW's lawyers sued Cal State Fullerton after the college disbanded its women's volleyball team. The suit led to a settlement in which Fullerton agreed to reinstate volleyball and to adopt a ten-year gender equity plan for its sports teams. Individual cases like this are contributing to a growing body of case law that defines women's rights in such areas as education, pensions, survivor's benefits, unemployment, and welfare benefits. When cases reach the Supreme Court, the nation's highest court has thrown out a number of state laws that discriminate against women.

EQUALITY IN EMPLOYMENT

The feminist goal of equal pay for equal work has not yet been met, although the future for women at work looks brighter. The number of employers who think of women as temporary workers ("As soon as she gets pregnant, she'll quit") or as people who cannot handle heavy or dirty jobs ("I can't have my drivers stopping to powder their noses") is decreasing. With federal and state fair-employment laws on their side, women are entering construction work, law enforcement, skilled crafts, and other fields once closed to them. When the Alaska pipeline was started in the 1970s, for example, the contractors hired only 21 women for heavy construction jobs. After the U.S. Department of the Interior threatened legal action, the number of women working on the pipeline shot up to 1,700.

If you check the classified ads in a local newspaper, you'll find that help-wanted ads are no longer sex-segregated into "help wanted—male" and "help wanted—female." NOW won that victory in 1968 and went on to end sex discrimination in one of the country's largest companies, American Telephone and Telegraph Company (AT&T). In all, AT&T paid out $60 million to women and minority men to settle discrimination complaints. Women who receive equal treatment when they apply for loans or credit cards can thank the Equal Credit bill of 1974. Other feminist successes have come in improved maternity rights for working women and in revised labor laws that once kept women from taking well-paid but strenuous factory jobs.

Women have also begun to make their way into jobs that have high prestige, pay, and power. In the past, such positions belonged almost entirely to men. A new generation of professional women is challenging men for a share of society's economic and political power. More women are running for public office—and being elected. Women are taking their places as mayors, judges, professors, executives, and members of the president's cabinet. Beginning in the late 1970s, female sailors joined the crews of U.S. Navy ships, the military academies admitted their first female cadets, and space officials selected the first women astronauts. In 1981, Sandra Day

O'Connor became the first woman to sit on the U.S. Supreme Court.

Feminist leaders point out, however, that progress is not equality. Women make up 51 percent of the population and over 47 percent of the work force. But fewer than 30 percent of the nation's doctors, lawyers, legislators, and company presidents are women.

EQUALITY MEANS ENDING ALL VESTIGES OF SEXISM

Women will never be free to take their rightful places alongside men as long as sexism is condoned in America's schools, homes, and workplaces, the feminists say. To achieve that goal, they ask for improvements and changes in several areas of our lives.

ELIMINATING SEXISM IN EDUCATION. Feminists believe that equality in education must take two directions. First, women must be given equal access to all courses of study from elementary school to graduate school. With some prodding from the federal government, most of the old barriers have fallen. If they can endure the teasing and occasional harassment inflicted by male teachers and classmates, young women are now free to enroll in courses as varied as auto mechanics, bodybuilding, and computer science. Second, textbooks and courses of study must be rewritten to give credit to women's contributions to society and to avoid sexist stereotyping. A number of schools have added courses in women's studies as a way of helping people learn more about women's role in building American culture.

One measure of progress in education can be seen in the number of women who qualify for jobs in occupations that were once dominated by men. In 1970 one lawyer in 20 was a woman. In 1998 the ratio had grown to three in ten. During those years, the percentage of women physicians increased from 9.7 to 26.6; women airline pilots rose

FIGURE 13.7 ▪ Lisa Olson, a *Boston Herald* sports reporter, made headlines of her own in 1990 by insisting on her right to conduct locker room interviews. A national debate arose after players from the New England Patriots exposed themselves to her and made lewd remarks. In another era, the uproar might have been enough to force Olson and her counterparts to limit themselves to reporting women's sports. In the 1990s, it resulted in new rules that guaranteed Olson's right to do her job while also ensuring a reasonable degree of privacy for the men.

from zero to 3.4. Women made similar progress in the corporate world, although the much-publicized "glass ceiling" kept all but a handful from climbing into the ranks of upper management positions.

SEXISM AND BODY IMAGE. Doctors and psychologists worry about the numbers. Feminists do their best to change them. The problem? Women don't like what they see in their mirrors. They watch supermodels strut down the runway, envy superfit actresses

The Struggle to Discard Sexist Language

One of the less publicized struggles for equality involves the use of sexist language. Standard usage, critics say, tends to reinforce the culture's unconscious bias against women. The changes needed to end old usages have forced writers (including the authors of this textbook) to rethink the words they use. Here are some of the results:

PUBLICATION	OLD USAGE	NEW USAGE
Newspapers, magazines, and nonfiction books, including textbooks	Man, mankind (when referring to the human species)	Humans, humankind, humanity, people, *Homo sapiens*
	One man, one vote	One person, one vote
	Actress, heroine, stewardess	Actor, hero, flight attendant
	Trashman, workman, chairman, watchman, postman	Trash collector, worker, chair or chairperson, guard, letter carrier

Can you spot biased language in your own speech? If you're not careful, you'll find yourself writing or saying things like, "An athlete must watch his diet." Hey, the feminists say, women athletes watch their diets, too. To correct the error, switch to the plural. It's just as easy to say, "Athletes must watch their diets."

and athletes, and wail, "I'm fat!" A Minnesota study showed that teenage girls were three times more likely than boys to have negative body images. In another study, 90 percent of the women surveyed said they wanted to lose weight. Doctors, however, say that only about one-fourth of those women exceed weight guidelines for height, build, and age.

The reason for this obsession with weight isn't hard to find. From childhood onward, young women are taught that their self-worth depends on "looking good." In pursuit of that elusive goal, some develop eating disorders. Women who suffer from anorexia nervosa (AN) cut down on their calorie intake to the point of near-starvation. Even when they look like living skeletons, anorexics continue to argue that they're "fat." Bulimia's victims, by contrast, go on eating binges followed by bouts of guilt-induced vomiting. Both of these life-threatening illnesses require medical intervention.

Thanks to pressure from feminist groups, a more realistic model of what it means to be beautiful is emerging. More women who look like real people are showing up on television and in films. Even the advertising industry, long a bastion of sexist thinking, has responded to women's concerns with a more evenhanded approach.

A related goal of the women's movement is teaching children to accept less restrictive sex roles. This goal could lead to a world in which children have *human* models to imitate, not male or female models. The fiction that women are inferior and that sex roles are biologically determined would be abolished.

THE RIGHT TO CHOOSE. Another major feminist goal can be summed up as the "right to choose." In practice, this includes such choices as having or not having children; going out to work or staying home with the children; and having a free choice of lifestyle.

This goal has led to great controversy, particularly when "the right to choose" is interpreted as the right to birth control and abortion. Many feminists believe that without this right, all other women's rights become unimportant, for having children almost automatically limits a woman's freedom of choice. Other women have joined groups such as Operation Rescue to fight for more restrictive abortion laws. Abortion legislation has thus become a national political issue. Neither side seems likely to give in on what it sees as a bedrock principle.

Budget deficits and conservative government policies have sidetracked the goal of establishing a national system of government-supported child care centers. As matters now stand, working mothers are often forced to choose between leaving their preschool children with inexperienced babysitters or paying for expensive nursery schools. Many school-age children are left without supervision by mothers who must work if the family is to survive.

A growing number of employers are stepping in to fill this need by setting up alternative day-care programs. These programs include on-site child care, extra pay to help pay for private day-care, and flexible work schedules. In Charlotte, North Carolina, five major employers teamed up to open a 194-child day-care center. During holidays and school breaks, John Hancock Mutual Life sponsors all-day field trips for the children of its workers. A few companies pay for full-time babysitters when they send an employee on overnight trips. In what may be the most innovative program of all, Stride Rite Corporation of Cambridge, Massachusetts, established an intergenerational day-care center. Workers can leave children and elderly parents there with the security of knowing that both age groups will receive proper care.

ELIMINATING SEXUAL HARASSMENT. "Boys will be boys," adults used to say when little girls complained that they were the targets of such indignities as spitballs, name-calling, and (in a Montana elementary school) "Friday flip-up day." That was a weekly tradition in which boys competed to see how many girls' skirts they could lift. Today, those not-so-endearing behaviors are labeled *sexual harassment.* Susan Webb, a specialist in such issues, defines sexual harassment as "deliberate and/or repeated sexual or sex-based behavior that is not welcome, not asked for or returned." Reduced to bedrock basics, Webb says, sexual harassment is really about power—the power of one sex to demonstrate its superiority over the other.

Recent studies confirm that sexual harassment is a widespread problem. One frequently quoted survey revealed that 40 to 70 percent of women (and 10 to 20 percent of men) have experienced some form of sexu-

SALLY FORTH By Greg Howard

FIGURE 13.8

al harassment at work. Nor is the problem confined to offices and factories. A second study found that 10 percent of middle school and high school girls had been forced to perform a sexual act other than kissing. Sixty-five percent said they had been grabbed or pinched, and 76 percent had been subjected to unwelcome sexual remarks, gestures, or looks at school.

Backed by tougher federal anti-discrimination laws and court decisions, women have been fighting back. Students (male or female) can sue for harassment and collect damages. In the workplace, victims of sexual harassment can sue for damages ranging from $50,000 to $300,000, depending on the company's size. As a result of this new awareness of women's rights, many schools and companies have organized seminars and training programs designed to sensitize students and workers to their mutual responsibilities.

ELIMINATING VIOLENCE AGAINST WOMEN. These are not isolated instances:

- "I thought there was no way out but death," says Laurie, an Oregon college student. Laurie used to hide in the closet to escape further battering by her live-in boyfriend.
- Sue, an Iowa homemaker, shows up at a shelter for battered women with her two children. Her face is bruised and she has a broken rib. Her husband beat her this time, Sue says, because she burned the pork chops.
- Jean, a college freshman, walks back to the dorm with a man who lives on the floor below hers. They talk for a while in her room—and then the casual encounter turns ugly. The man asks her to have sex with him. Jean says "no" and tells him to leave, but he forces her to submit. The media calls this "date rape"—forced sexual intercourse by someone the woman thinks of as a friend or acquaintance. During his subsequent appearance before a hearing board, the man says, "Sure, I heard her say 'no,' but I thought she was playing hard to get." The all-male board finds him guilty of sexual assault but limits his

punishment to a reprimand and a few hours of community service.

The women's movement charges that violence against women is too often seen as the victim's fault. Why didn't she just say no? Why didn't she leave? Social psychologist Carol Tavris explains, "Like prisoners of war, abused women come to believe . . . that they have no exit. They know that their husbands will track them down and murder them if they leave, . . . if indeed leaving were even economically feasible." The law, Sheila James Kuehl of the Southern California Women's Law Center observes, has generally been interpreted only from the male experience. Perhaps that helps explain why law enforcement agencies often subject victims of rape, battering, and incest to grueling, personal investigations.

As in other areas of concern to the women's movement, the courts are slowly extending the protection of the law to women. In 1991, for example, the U.S. Ninth Circuit Court of Appeals adopted a "reasonable woman" standard in finding for a woman in a sexual harassment case. Judge Robert Beezer wrote, "We believe that a sex-blind reasonable-person standard tends to be male-biased and tends to systematically ignore the experiences of women." Since then, cases involving domestic violence and *date rape* tried under that standard have produced verdicts far different from those of an earlier era.

MEASURING THE PROGRESS

Has the women's movement achieved any of its goals? On the down side, more women are endangering their health by smoking and hitting the bottle. On the plus side, more women are earning college degrees, more women are becoming doctors and lawyers, and more television shows are spotlighting strong female characters. Most significantly, more women than ever say they're happy with their lives.

You can also see the change in the stories

of individual women. A few years ago, Adrienne would have joined the pep squad to cheer for the boys' basketball team; today she's a hard-driving forward on her own winning team. Yesterday, Hope would have felt herself a failure if she weren't married by her mid-20s; today, she's so involved in her business career that she's not even thinking of marriage for at least five more years. A year or two ago, Clare would have felt empty and useless when her last child left home; today, she's taking computer training as the first step in a new career. Rhonda, meanwhile, has just given birth to her first child. Rhonda likes her job with an aerospace firm, but she's going to take several years off to stay home with her daughter. She feels free to make that choice, just as other women feel free to go out to work.

■ SECTION CHECKUP

1 What did Susan B. Anthony mean when she said, "Men, their rights and nothing more; women, their rights and nothing less"? Do you think modern feminists would still agree with her statement? Tell why or why not.

2 Name some of the techniques feminist groups use to achieve their goals.

3 What are the basic goals of the women's movement? Which goals do you think are closest to fulfillment?

13.4 ■ WHAT EFFECT IS THE WOMEN'S MOVEMENT HAVING ON MEN?

Many men have experienced the same mild shock as that felt by Ted in Greg Howard's cartoon strip (see Figure 13.8). Behaviors that were once taken for granted are now being called into question as U.S. society takes a hard look at the problem of sexual harassment. Whether they work in a corporate office or on an auto assembly line, men are finding (sometimes the hard way) that the old rules no longer apply.

As you learned earlier in this chapter, people are learning new male and female roles. Most of the publicity has gone to women. But men have also been forced to examine their own concepts of appropriate masculine behavior. To the surprise of many people (but not to psychologists), they are discovering that women can be winners in the struggle for equality without turning men into abject losers.

THE HIGH PRICE OF MACHO

You've probably heard the term *macho* used to describe male behavior. The term comes from the Spanish word for "masculine" and has come to mean the state of mind that insists on male superiority. Even though Jess E. doesn't like the term, he subscribes to the code of macho: a "real" man is tough, aggressive, ambitious, fearless. To live up to this ideal, Jess must conceal his all-too-human emotions. Showing tenderness, understanding, and affection for others might expose him as something less than the macho ideal.

Listen to Jess as he talks to Kate, the young woman he's been dating.

JESS: What do you mean, you're going out tonight with your girlfriends? Friday night is our night! Call Elsa and Mira and tell them you can't make it.

KATE: Jess, get serious. If you ask me about Friday night before I've made other plans, I enjoy going out with you. But you don't own me. Elsa and Mira are my friends, and I want to spend some time with them.

JESS: Hey, I figured you knew I was coming over. Look, I've got the van all polished up. Put on something sexy, and we'll try out that new dance club.

KATE: No way, Jess! Maybe next week.

JESS: OK, be that way. I'll call Delia! She hasn't been spoiled by all this feminist garbage.

You can see why Jess looks on the women's movement as a threat. Because he defines masculinity in terms of dominant male/submissive female, he can't cope with Kate's independence. And if Kate should choose a career over marriage, he'll be even more bewildered. Poor Jess! He wants a woman "just like the girl that married dear old granddad." He can't grasp the fact that women no longer feel obligated to cater to the whims of their boyfriends and husbands.

For Jess, success means making money and enjoying the prestige that goes with it. Like his father, he's already channeling his energies into his career, certain that long hours and hard work will pay off. Political scientist Marc Fasteau thinks that playing this macho role creates a one-dimensional human being he calls the "male machine":

> The male machine is a special kind of being, different from women, children, and men who don't measure up. He is functional, designed mainly for work. He is programmed to tackle jobs, override obstacles, attack problems, overcome difficulties, and always seize the offensive. . . .
>
> He has armor plating which is virtually impregnable. His circuits are never scrambled or overrun by irrelevant personal signals. He dominates and outperforms his fellows, . . . In fact, his internal circuitry is something of a mystery to him and is maintained primarily by humans of the opposite sex.

According to Fasteau, men who bury the emotions they think of as feminine are actually mutilating their personalities. Robert Bly, a poet who has emerged as a leader in the movement to help men redefine themselves, puts it this way in his book *Iron John*:

> It is clear to men that the images of adult manhood given by the popular culture are worn out; a man can no longer depend on them. By the time a man is thirty-five he knows that the images of the right man, the tough man, the true man which he received in high school do not work in life.

Macho males, both critics agree, are compelled to believe that self expression or displays of so-called softer emotions are indications of weakness. But many stress-related illnesses may stem from repressed emotions. Like powerful acids eating away at inner gears, these buried feelings can cause a physical or emotional breakdown. The doctors will very likely bring in a diagnosis of ulcers, heart attack, or severe depression. In reality, the human body wasn't designed to hold up under the stresses that go with maintaining the macho personality.

HOW A MAN'S ROLE MIGHT CHANGE

Psychologists believe that the women's movement is also leading to the liberation of men. Once men liberate themselves from macho thinking, they are free to develop more fully as human beings. As 60-year-old Terry H. says:

> I never got to know my children. When they were young, I was so busy building my business I never had any time for them. And now that I have the time, they're grown up and left to live their own lives. I look at the wonderful relationship my son Sean has with his kids and I know I'd give up all the money I've made if I could go back and really be a father to my kids.

Sharing fully in the experience of raising children is a splendid goal, but it is only one of the differences that "male liberation" can make in men's lives.

SHARED RESPONSIBILITIES. In the old system, men assumed responsibility for making most of the decisions. Women are too emotional, the macho thinking said, to make tough choices. Under the new concept of shared responsibilities, the energy that once went into maintaining a macho image can be put into creative and productive work. People can be judged on their abilities and on their performance. Many men feel threatened, for example, when asked to work for a woman. Those doubts and fears usually subside when the men discover that their new boss earned her job the old-fashioned way—through talent and hard work. New attitudes toward sex roles are also easing the feeling that a man's masculinity is diminished if he can't always have his own way.

At home, shared responsibilities mean that men can enter into a true partnership with their wives. Caring for children will be a task for both parents to share. If this means that more men will be changing diapers, it also means that more women will be called on to administer the heavy discipline. As more women work outside the home, men will also lay down the burden of serving as the family's sole breadwinner. No longer will men look to their jobs as the sole source of their identity.

FINDING NEW ROLES. A few years ago, a handful of men made headlines by choosing to work at home as "househusbands" (see the box on page 460). Perhaps that option will never become widespread, but having the freedom to make life choices is what sex-role liberation is all about. Feeling trapped in jobs they no longer enjoy, middle-aged men are switching to more rewarding occupations. Engineers have taken up farming, dentists have turned into artists, and mechanics have become elementary school teachers. Even though these job switchers often work harder and make less money, most report a liberating sense of fulfillment.

Role reversals are becoming common in career fields that were once restricted to one sex only. Americans aren't surprised these days when they meet women pilots, engineers, and naval officers—but neither are they surprised to see men working as telephone operators, nurses, secretaries and in other "female" jobs. Real progress is being made in turning work into a human choice, not a male or female choice.

RAISING CHILDREN AFTER A DIVORCE. Divorce once meant that custody of the children was always awarded to the mother. Fathers, no matter how loving, were not considered capable of raising children. Social workers, judges, and women in general, men complained, were guilty of "father bashing." Denied visitation rights and hit by costly divorce settlements, many men refused to make child care payments. Single mothers, in turn, were left to cope as best they could. Many fell into poverty.

Slowly, the courts are recognizing the fact that men make competent and caring single parents, too. When a marriage falls apart, judges and parents are free to choose what is best for the children. The issue of nonpayment of child support has not been solved, but fathers who stay involved with their children are more likely to keep up their child support obligations.

BALANCING THE ACCOUNT

You've probably heard people say that opportunities and freedom for women can come only at the expense of men. In the short run, there's some truth to that remark. If Veronica is accepted at dental school, her seat is no longer open to a man. Girls who make formerly all-male athletic teams eliminate less talented boys from those positions. On a strictly "what's-in-it-for-me" basis, the women's movement asks that men give up some of the privileges they once claimed by birthright—including the princely role of watching their mothers, girlfriends, and wives do the cooking, scrubbing, ironing, dusting, and mending.

Confessions of a Househusband

Joel Roache found out firsthand what it means to take on the duties of a "house-husband." Here he describes what happened after he and his wife, Jan, agreed to share equally in the housekeeping and child care chores:

There was something of a shock for me in discovering the sheer quantity of the housework, and my standards of acceptable cleanliness fell rapidly. It became much easier to see my insistence on neatness as an inherited middle-class hang-up now that I had to do so much of the work myself. One of the long-standing sources of tension between Jan and me was almost immediately understood and resolved. What's more, I enjoyed it, at first.

But within a few weeks that satisfaction and that enthusiasm began to erode a little more each time I woke up or walked into the house, only to find that it all needed to be done again. . . . I became lethargic, with the result that I worked less efficiently; so that even when I did "finish," it took longer and was done less well, rendering still less satisfaction. . . .

I can pinpoint the place in time when we saw the necessity for a more careful adjustment of responsibilities. It was at a moment when it became clear that Jan's work was beginning to pay off and her group scored a definite and apparently unqualified success. I went around the house for a full day feeling very self-satisfied, proud of her achievement, as *if it were my own*, which was fine until I realized, somewhere near the end of the day, that much of that sense of achievement resulted from the fact that I had no achievement of my own. I was getting my sense of fulfillment, of self-esteem, *through her*, while she was getting it *through her work*. It had happened: I was a full-fledged househusband.

If Roache came to this conclusion in just eight weeks, what effect do you think years of housework and child care have on women?

Joel Roache, "Men: Confessions of a Househusband," *Ms. Magazine,* November 1972. Reprinted by permission of *Ms. Magazine,* © 1972.

Social scientists promise that, in time, temporary dislocations will balance out. More women working means more paychecks to buy more products. Increased sales mean more jobs. Tapping the creativity of one-half of the population will lead to new ideas and techniques that will benefit everyone. Freed from the fierce competition created by macho rules, men will have more time to enjoy leisure-time pursuits and closer family ties.

In general, the new sex roles leave both men and women free to make the choices they feel will make them happy. Jenny D. likes mechanical work, so she takes responsibility for the upkeep of the family car. Her husband, Dexter, does the gardening because he takes special pleasure in working with plants. Jenny and Dexter also have a special arrangement with the company that employs them. When they have children later on, they plan to share a single job, so that one of them can always be with the children. By sharing both work and household responsibilities, they will have a chance to grow to their full potential as parents and as individuals.

■ SECTION CHECKUP

1 What is meant by macho behavior?

2 What price do women pay when the men in their lives are bound by macho rules? What price do macho men pay?

3 If the women's movement succeeds, what will men be giving up? What will they be gaining?

13.5 ▪ HOW DO CHANGING PATTERNS OF SEXUALITY AFFECT THE INDIVIDUAL?

Adolescents and young adults have always faced the task of coming to terms with their own sexuality. The confusing messages that hit them from every side today make rational decisions even more difficult. On the one hand, many Americans seem to regard sexual freedom as an important expression of personal freedom. On the other hand, psychologists, parents, religious leaders, and other concerned observers warn that sex without affection and respect can be empty and self-destructive. As Walt Z. put it:

> I thought that when I got to be eighteen, I'd know what's going on. But I'm more confused than ever. I've got my head on pretty straight about most things. But sex confuses me. My parents tell me one thing, my church another, and the messages I get from magazines and movies seem exactly opposite. Should I follow my instincts, or should I try to live by the rules? And just what are the rules anyway?

Walt's not the only one who's confused. You might have experienced some of the same feelings. Perhaps the following section will help you make some sense out of society's changing patterns of sexuality.

CHARTING A COURSE

Social psychologists hesitate to deal in terms like right or wrong. They prefer to leave such questions to philosophers, politicians, and theologians. But psychologists do worry that too much rapid change can threaten emotional health.

DO NEW PATTERNS OF SEXUALITY INCREASE FEELINGS OF ANXIETY AND GUILT? Casual sex once carried with it the stigma of social disapproval. Today, casual sex carries with it the danger of AIDS, herpes, syphilis, and other sexually transmitted diseases. But even for partners who practice safe sex, the act itself creates a new problems. Peggy R., for example, drifted into a sexual relationship with her boyfriend. Even though she enjoyed the physical part of it, Peggy often felt guilty. She worried about pregnancy, and she worried that her parents might find out. At times, she felt used. Spence seemed to want sex all the time, but Peggy sometimes preferred unhurried interludes of quiet talk and physical closeness that didn't end in "going all the way." She finally broke off the relationship because it was causing her more pain than pleasure.

While individual cases vary greatly, Peggy's experience turns out to be rather typical. Repressed sexual drives can cause emotional trouble, as Freud discovered. But engaging in sex without strong bonds of love and commitment can also leave people feeling lonely and anxious.

IS THE NEW SEXUALITY FORCING YOUNG PEOPLE INTO EXPERIMENTATION THEY'RE NOT READY FOR? Freud described the powerful sexual forces that help shape the personality in childhood. But this childhood sexuality is largely unconscious. Today, however, young people have sex forced upon their consciousness even before they reach puberty. Television programs and films freely portray scenes of lovemaking, rape, incest, nudity, and perversion. Magazines featuring sexually explicit stories and photos can be found on many newsstands. It seems that no matter where children go, they come into contact with a consistent message: How can anything that feels so good be bad for you?

Sex education has become an accepted part of the curriculum in most schools, and a number of big-city school districts now issue condoms to their students. Although the schools would prefer to discourage teenage

FIGURE 13.9 ▓ Young people today face many new anxieties as they try to build romantic relationships. What should this couple—or any couple—try to learn about each other before they become involved? How might their relationship be affected by the new patterns of sexuality?

sexual activity, they have accepted the responsibility of encouraging safe sex among those students who are unwilling to practice abstinence.

Almost all psychologists agree that adults should be the judges of their own sexual choices. But they worry that exposure to sexually stimulating material may push children into becoming sexually active before they are physically or emotionally ready. Casual, "recreational" sex ignores the deep feelings created when two people become physically intimate. In a way, the experts say, pushing a young person into sex before he or she is ready is like handing a loaded pistol to a four-year-old. Someone is going to get hurt.

In the final analysis, parents must take the responsibility for helping their children develop a healthy attitude toward their own sexuality. Parents can begin by protecting children from exposure to experiences beyond their level of maturity. Second, parents can give their children a proper sex education. This responsibility, of course, requires that the parents themselves know how to explain the "facts of life" in a clear, honest, and unemotional way. Because many parents can't or won't do the explaining, schools have developed sex-education programs. In the best of these schools, trained teachers at each grade level present carefully prepared information about sex as it relates to children of that age.

Controversy surrounds such efforts, however. Many communities refuse to allow sex education—perhaps on the theory that "the kids won't do it if they don't know about it." If someone tries this argument on you, you don't have to argue. Just point to the statistics. Over 600,000 unwanted teenage pregnancies each year, along with uncounted cases of AIDS and assorted STDs, will make the point for you.

IS HOMOSEXUAL BEHAVIOR A THREAT TO SOCIETY? Scientists believe that human beings are born with a hormone balance that tilts the individual toward heterosexual behavior (attraction to members of the opposite sex). Between 2 and 10 percent of the population, however, grow up physically and emotionally attracted to people of the same sex. This sexual preference, called *homosexuality*, alarms many people. They consider homosexual behavior a danger to social stability, particularly family life. As more homosexuals have come "out of the closet" and begun to participate actively in community life, this fear has increased.

The majority of psychologists no longer consider homosexuality as a mental disorder. Instead, they view it as an alternate life-style that puts extra emotional pressure on the individual man or woman. Sigmund Freud wrote, "homosexuality . . . is nothing to be ashamed of, no vice, no degradation. . . . We consider it to be a variation of the sexual function produced by a certain arrest of sexual development." In 1973, the American Psychiatric Association officially removed homosexuality from its list of mental disorders. Only those homosexuals who actively seek treatment should be considered disturbed, the APA concluded.

This nonjudgmental approach to homosexual behavior has enabled psychologists to clear up a number of misunderstandings regarding *gay* behavior (as homosexuals prefer to have their life-style described). The classic studies that began with Freud agreed that the roots of homosexual behavior could be found in childhood. According to this theory, a boy raised by a possessive, clinging mother and a weak or absent father may grow up frightened of intimate, loving relations with women. Similarly, girls who become overly attached to immature, passive fathers may never develop their full feminine identity. Exposure to strong homosexual influences at a vulnerable age is also thought by some to lead to homosexuality. Research shows, however, that many children who grow up with mixed messages regarding their sexual orientation develop into fully heterosexual adults.

A new perspective emerged in the early 1990s, when neuroscientists reported that homosexual behavior may be, as a popular T-shirt exclaimed, "a brain thing." The researchers released studies showing that an important brain structure connecting the left and right sides of the brain is larger in women than in men—and larger still in male homosexuals. That finding followed an earlier study that revealed that another part of the brain is smaller in gay men than in heterosexual men. The researchers cautioned that further study is needed before anyone can say with certainty that homosexual behavior is determined by genetics.

Research has also enabled psychologists to clear up some mistaken ideas about homosexuality. Children and adolescents may have isolated homosexual experiences without becoming gay. The famous 1948 Kinsey study of American sex life found that almost 40 percent of the men surveyed reported at least one homosexual experience. In the same way, physical appearance or mannerisms do not provide proof of homosexual tendencies. Girls who appear masculine or boys who seem overly feminine may, however, fall victim to a self-fulfilling prophecy. Teased and scorned by their peers, these young people may turn to homosexual contacts out of confusion and anxiety. Finally, forced psychotherapy cannot change homosexual behavior. Aversion therapy, hormone treatments, psychoanalysis, and group therapy have been tried with little long-term success. Therapy works only when the individual is totally committed to changing his or her sexual preferences and way of life.

CHANGING CONCEPTS OF MARRIAGE

Until the 1960s, men and women who didn't marry and have children were often thought of as failures. Most people believed that unqualified love, personal growth, and true happiness could only be found in a " 'til-death-do-us-part" marriage. Perhaps that romantic ideal never existed in real life. In any event, the high divorce rates of recent years have led to a search for new ways to satisfy the human need for companionship, security, and the care of children.

THE CASE FOR MARRIAGE. Despite the rise and fall of alternate life-styles, many people still choose marriage as the best way to join two lives together. Even though single parents often do a good job of raising children, most experts feel that a stable marriage provides the optimum environment for raising children. Along with such factors as companionship and the sharing of work, married people generally enjoy better physical health than single people. The specter of AIDS has also strengthened the appeal of an exclusive sexual relationship within the framework of a traditional marriage. Emotionally, married men and women score higher on mental health tests and experience fewer mental breakdowns. Perhaps these factors will change with time, but even divorced people usually try again. In many cases, the second marriage works quite well.

MEN & WOMEN   by Calman

I want a wife, mistress, mother, friend, nurse, housekeeper and someone who will worship me...

Can you afford seven women?

© Mel Calman, 1978
Dist. Field Newspaper Syndicate

MARRIAGE BROKER

calman   7-26

FIGURE 13.10

LIVING TOGETHER. Many young couples live together without going through a marriage ceremony. Supporters of this arrangement believe that it gives them a chance to try out a relationship without the "until-death-do-us-part" pressures of marriage. If the arrangement doesn't work out, the partners are spared the expense and trauma of a divorce. People who choose to live together often invest as much love and commitment as others do in a traditional marriage.

Opponents of living together feel that the arrangement often exploits the female. In effect, the man receives sexual and housekeeping services without giving up his option of walking out when the arrangement no longer pleases him. Some couples solve this problem by signing a contract that spells out mutual obligations and makes arrangements for sharing income and community property.

CHILDLESS MARRIAGES. A couple like Mae and Howard J. probably live in your neighborhood. You may even envy them. They vacation in Hawaii, buy expensive cars and stereo gear, throw lavish parties, and dress in the latest fashions. What makes Mae and Howard stand out in a crowd is their decision not to have children. Ask them why, and they'll mention fears of overpopulation, concern over the environment, and the time, money, and energy that raising children requires. They believe that by not having children, they can live a happy, fulfilling life balanced between work and pleasure. As they grow older and as their values change, Mae and Howard may decide to rethink their decision. Right now a growing number of young couples share their commitment to a childless marriage.

COMMUNAL LIVING AND COMMUNAL MARRIAGE. Experiments in *communal (group) living* date back to the dawn of the human race. The idea reached its modern peak in the 1960s and early 1970s but has not disappeared. Most modern communal arrangements are built on the concept of the extended family—the idea that everyone benefits when there are a number of nurturing people around to provide love and support. In most communes, children have many "parents" to turn to for comfort, advice, and companionship. By sharing living expenses and household tasks, the commune members believe that everyone's life is enriched. In spite of sensational media accounts of "free love" arrangements, most communes have found that one-to-one relationships between individual men and women still work best.

SAME-SEX UNIONS. In June 2003, a Canadian couple made headlines when they celebrated their marriage. The wedding, which united two men in a same-sex union, fanned the flames of a growing debate about homosexual marriages. Critics charge that these unions violate the traditional definition of marriage. Supporters argue that committed same-sex couples should not be denied the rights granted to couples in a conventional marriage. After Vermont took the lead in recognizing same-sex unions, a July 2003 Gallup poll found that only 40 percent of the people surveyed favored such unions. Nine months later, just as same-sex unions were becoming legal in Massachusetts, another poll found 48 percent in favor and 49 percent opposed. Clearly, the public is still making up its mind.

BENEFITS TO CHILDREN

Generations of parents have told their offspring to "do as we say, not as we do." And generations of children have continued to imitate the behaviors they *see*, rather than the words they hear. When parents share cooking, shopping, and cleaning chores, children will learn that these are tasks that simply need doing—not menial jobs for women only. Similarly, when children see their mothers replace a faucet washer or change an automobile tire, they will understand that mechanical skills need not remain a mystery to girls. Being nurtured by both parents will encourage all children to express their joy and sorrow, love and anger.

Children raised in a nonsexist environment will enjoy toys and reading materials without regard to what's for boys and what's for girls. Both sexes will grow up knowing that gender does not limit their vocational choices. Girls will freely choose a career or marriage—or a combination of both. Boys will no longer fear parental rejection if they choose to be dancers, nurses, or hairdressers. Best of all, children raised in a nonsexist home will bring those same positive attitudes to their adult relationships with other people.

■ SECTION CHECKUP

1 Why do changing patterns of sexuality confuse and upset people? List some of the positive and some of the negative aspects of the changes discussed in this section.

2 Why should children be protected from excessive sexual stimulation?

3 Discuss how changing social attitudes affect marriage choices.

4 What effect will nonsexist attitudes have on children?

LOOKING BACK: A SUMMARY

1 Researchers have come up with three theories to explain the differences in male and female sex roles. In the hereditary view, biology determines sex roles; since men are stronger, they "naturally" dominate women. Research shows, however, that male dominance developed for cultural reasons, not biological ones. According to the environmental view, sex roles develop primarily as a result of cultural influences. Most psychologists today conclude that both heredity and environment contribute to sex roles. Genetic differences in physical and verbal activity between male and female infants are strengthened by the way parents respond to these sex-related behaviors.

2 Children learn sex roles when adults reward desired behaviors and punish or ignore unwanted behaviors. Children also learn through modeling their behavior on what they see older children and adults doing. Boys and girls receive their primary influence regarding sex-role modeling from same-sex adults. Society's standards of male or female behavior often establish the norms by which all behavior is judged. Thus, the community in which children live also affects sex roles.

3 The effect of sexism (the social and economic domination of one sex by the other) can be measured in many ways. As the usual victims of sexist discrimination, many women have had lower self-esteem than men. The achievements of the women's movement (the drive to achieve political, social, and economic equality for women) have greatly improved women's self-images. Because of sexism, female accomplishments have been largely overlooked and female opportunities have been curtailed. When encouraged to develop to their full potential, women match men in intelligence, endurance, and accomplishment.

4 Sexism shows up most clearly at work. On the average, women make only 78 percent of what men earn. Many women still find themselves locked into low-paid jobs as domestic workers, secretaries, and salesclerks. No one knows how many potential female scientists, artists, inventors, and other productive individuals never had a chance to develop because of sexist discrimination.

5 Housewives sometimes feel that they lose their identities in the daily round of housework and child care. Self-aware women have learned to maintain control of their own lives. They work outside the home, do volunteer service, or delay the birth of their children until they're well established in their careers.

6 The feminist movement has roots deep in the past, but its greatest successes have come since the early 1960s. Voices of the movement include mainstream organizations such as the National Organization for Women (NOW). Feminists were unable to pass the Equal Rights Amendment (ERA) to the Constitution, but passage and enforcement of laws designed to end all remaining forms of sexism is still a major goal of the movement. Many former men-only jobs are now held by women, but highly qualified women still find it difficult to enter upper-level jobs for which pay and prestige are highest.

7 Schools have opened doors to women in both academics and in athletics. Textbooks are being written and courses are being taught that give proper attention to women's achievements. Sexism in the media has been more difficult to control. The goal for future generations is to help children learn sex roles that will allow them to fulfill their potential regardless of gender.

8 Feminists also want the right to choose. This includes such decisions as having or not having children. Since this goal often includes the right to birth control and abortion, it has led to fierce political battles. Because mothers are not free to pursue their careers if they do not have proper child care facilities, enlightened companies are supplementing the private child care industry with on-site nursery schools for their workers. The women's movement is also working to eliminate sexual harassment and violence against women from America's homes, schools, and workplaces. Recent court decisions have made it easier for women to file and win suits when their rights are violated.

9 The macho male is conditioned to repress the tender, "feminine" side of his personality. Macho behavior not only makes it difficult for men to relate to other people but also leads to stress-related illness. Given a more balanced male role, men will learn to share responsibilities with the women in their lives. They will feel free to change roles and jobs without losing their feelings of masculinity and self-worth.

10 Changing patterns of sexuality leave many people confused and troubled. Some worry that liberal divorce laws and newly defined sex roles will disrupt family life. Others find that sexual freedom without love and commitment can lead to feelings of loneliness and guilt. The epidemic of AIDS and other STDs has added a new and forceful argument to the trend toward long-term single-partner relationships. Psychologists warn that too much sexual stimulation can harm young children. They advise parents to help their children learn to deal with sex in a mature and balanced way.

11 Psychologists believe that homosexual behavior may result when parents provide poor role models, but neuroscientists have found evidence that genetics may play a role as well. Isolated homosexual experiences during childhood do not always lead to adult homosexual behavior. Because gay behavior is no longer considered to be a mental disorder, psychotherapy is given only when the stress associated with the homosexual life-style leads the individual to seek help.

12 Although a stable nuclear marriage is still considered the best environment in which to raise children, people are experimenting with alternate forms of marriage. More people are living together, hoping to avoid the expense and trauma of divorce if the arrangement doesn't work. More couples are also choosing to remain childless in order to concentrate on the pleasures of adult life. Others join communal living groups because they provide much-needed companionship and emotional support. When the issue of same-sex unions arises, opinions differ sharply. Critics charge that allowing gays to marry violates the sanctity of traditional marriages. Supporters believe that same-sex couples should enjoy the same privileges as those granted to heterosexual couples.

13 Nonsexist family life will allow children to grow up without the limitations of traditional sex roles. Girls will learn that women can do mechanical things; boys will not be afraid to express their feelings. Both sexes will be encouraged to choose jobs and a life-style that make them happy and productive individuals.

PUTTING YOUR KNOWLEDGE TO WORK

■ TERMS YOU SHOULD KNOW

anorexia nervosa	feminist	modeling behavior
battered women	gay	same-sex unions
bulimia	hereditary view	sexism
communal living	homosexuality	sex roles
date rape	macho	sexual harassment
environmental view	male chauvinist	women's movement

▪ CHAPTER CHECKUP

1 Most sex-role behavior results from social conditioning. One difference between men and women that seems to be definitely linked to heredity, however, is that boys show more (*a*) affection (*b*) physical activity (*c*) intelligence (*d*) emotional response to stress.

2 Which of the following has the strongest influence on the development of a child's sex role? (*a*) peer pressure (*b*) community standards (*c*) parental models (*d*) biological inheritance.

3 If children are raised in a nonsexist culture, they will probably grow up believing that (*a*) women are superior to men (*b*) men are superior to women (*c*) women should be housekeepers and mothers, and men should be breadwinners (*d*) all men and women deserve an equal opportunity to develop their talents and abilities.

4 When a male chauvinist puts women down by saying that their achievements don't match those of men, a feminist would reply that (*a*) male historians have largely ignored women's achievements (*b*) women have been denied the opportunity to compete on equal terms with men (*c*) women have been conditioned to think of themselves as unable to deal with high-level abstract thought (*d*) all of these reasons help explain the historic differences in male-female achievement.

5 Feminists believe that when a woman goes to work, she (*a*) is entitled to the same pay as a man doing the same job, if both have equal experience (*b*) deserves special treatment because she is a woman (*c*) neglects her responsibilities to her family (*d*) will have to act like "one of the boys" if she is to be successful.

6 The Equal Rights Amendment was intended to guarantee that (*a*) women will have the right to work (*b*) men will not be obligated to support their families (*c*) women will become the dominant sex (*d*) both sexes will receive equal treatment under the law.

7 Which of the following plots for a children's book would a feminist say is a step in the right direction? (*a*) A brave and intelligent girl rescues her family from a gang of kidnappers. (*b*) A girl spends all her time playing active outdoor games while her brother stays indoors to cook and do

housework. (*c*) A teenage girl drops out of high school to marry her boyfriend. (*d*) A teenage boy solves a spy case by using his girl friend's good looks to trap the enemy agent.

8 The top priority of the women's movement is to (*a*) establish women as dominant over men (*b*) establish equal rights as the legal and moral law of the land (*c*) remove sexist language from books and magazines (*d*) guarantee admission to graduate school for any woman who wants to go.

9 Which of the following situations best fits the definition of sexual harassment? (*a*) A teenage boy spends an entire class period staring at a girl who sits two rows away. (*b*) A store manager tells a female clerk that if she has dinner with him, he'll approve her request for a promotion. (*c*) A female college student tells her professor that if he doesn't give her an *A* she'll tell the administration that he tried to force her to have sex with him. (*d*) All are examples of sexual harassment.

10 Children raised in non-sexist homes are likely to (*a*) embrace time-honored gender roles (*b*) look to their moms for comfort and their dads for discipline (*c*) grow up knowing that gender does not limit their career choices (*d*) divide home chores on traditional lines—boys cut the grass; girls wash the dishes.

▪ EXPLORING CONCEPTS

1 Why do many writers describe the women's movement as a social revolution? Describe some of the changes this nonviolent revolution has caused in American life and culture.

2 In the past, women were considered the "inferior" sex. How do you explain that? What penalties have both sexes paid for the long acceptance of sexism in this society?

3 Discuss the major goals of the feminist movement. Which goals do you support? Which goals do you oppose? Explain the reasons for your decisions.

4 What effect might the success of the women's movement have on men? Why is a nonsexist way of life so difficult for some men and women to accept?

5 Suppose you are thinking about getting married. What important agreements would you want to have with your future partner before you decide to go ahead with the wedding?

6 Would you vote for a woman as president of the United States? As vice president? As governor of your state? Discuss the reasons for your answers.

7 Why is it important that every young woman, whether she plans to marry or not, has job skills that will enable her to support herself?

■ HANDS-ON ACTIVITIES

1 Contact one of the women's organizations in your community and invite a speaker to discuss the current status of the movement. By checking the phone book, you can probably locate a nearby chapter of the National Organization for Women. Your local college may have a women's group that will supply speakers. If there is an antifeminist group such as the Eagle Forum in your community, ask for a representative to join in a debate on feminist goals.

2 You can obtain an interesting collection of feminist literature by contacting national organizations. Here are three useful sources:

National Network for Women's Employment
1625 K Street NW, Suite 300
Washington, DC 20006 <*www.womenwork.org*>

National Organization for Women
733 15th Street NW
Washington, DC 20005 <*www.now.org*>

National Women's Political Caucus
1634 Eye Street NW, Suite 310
Washington, DC 20006 <*www.nwpc.org/contact.html*>

After you've read the literature, share it with your classmates. It will probably lead to some interesting discussions.

3 Start a collection of anecdotes gathered from interviews with men and women who feel that they have run into sexual discrimination or harassment. If you find that such incidents are common, you might want to put together a booklet for everyone in your school describing job, credit, and educational rights. The Equal Employment Opportunity

Commission, 1801 L Street NW, Washington, DC 20507 <*www.eeoc.gov*> can furnish the data.

4 On your own, or with a task force of friends, survey the textbooks used in your local elementary and secondary schools for sexist stereotypes. Your librarian can help you find guidelines for judging the books you review. It will help to look at some textbooks and children's picture books published before 1970.

5 Make a collection of pictures from magazines and newspapers that portray stereotyped sex roles for men and women. Label each clipping according to the particular stereotype it represents. Display your collection on a bulletin board or poster.

6 Do males really do better in mathematics, and do females really have higher verbal abilities? Ask your counseling office to help you survey achievement- and aptitude-test scores to see if the scores back up these generalizations. Your teachers can help you organize the study so as to ensure a valid sampling.

7 Does your school sponsor a club or group dedicated to the goals of the women's movement? If so, and you're not a member, you will find it interesting to sit in on a meeting or two. If a group of this type doesn't exist, you might want to start one. First, find a faculty sponsor who shares your interests and start building your organization. Along with guest speakers and general discussions of feminist goals, your group can take on some of the following activities:

(a) Interview women in your community who have made successful careers for themselves. Find out what it took for them to succeed and what it means to compete with men for jobs and power. Ask those who are married whether or not they experience conflicts between their two roles.

(b) Has the women's movement affected the plans of your school's seniors? Survey the class members to find out what they're planning to do with their lives. For example, how many men and how many women are planning careers in fields once thought to be gender-specific (the military, police work, nursing, elementary school teaching, and the like)? How many expect to marry within the next four years? How many plan to combine child raising with a career? Add your own questions, conduct the survey, and write up the results for your school newspaper.

(c) Run your own John-Anne study (see page 444).

(d) Survey current TV programs for examples of sex stereotyping. Are women being portrayed in a nonsexist manner? Do women receive a fair number of important roles?

FOR FURTHER READING

Archer, Jules. *Breaking Barriers: The Feminist Revolution from Susan B. Anthony to Margaret Sanger to Betty Friedan.* New York: Viking, 1991. Historian Jules Archer believes that the lives and achievements of these remarkable feminists encompass the past, present, and future of the women's movement in the United States. The short biographies bring each woman to life within the context of the era in which she lived and the challenges she faced.

Bly, Robert. *Iron John: A Book About Men.* Reading, MA: Addison-Wesley Publishing Co., 1990. Bly, a poet by trade, turns to ancient stories and legends to help men rediscover the truths about "a vigorous masculinity that is both protective and emotionally centered." His book is built around the tale of Iron John, an ancient "hairy man" who becomes mentor to a young boy. Their adventures serve as instructive guideposts to the stages of male growth.

Cole, Joni, B. K. Rakha, and Rebecca Joffrey, eds. *This Day: Diaries from American Women.* Hillsboro, OR: Beyond Words Publishing, 2003. The authors started with a question: "What is a day in the life really like for today's woman?" To find out, they invited a diverse group of America women to create a "day diary" of a single, ordinary Tuesday. The entries that made it into the book are intimate, revealing, and surprisingly funny. By the time you turn the last page, you'll have a far greater appreciation of what it means to be a modern woman.

Friedan, Betty. *The Feminine Mystique.* New York: Norton, 2001. Although it dates back to 1963, Friedan's feminist call-to-arms still bristles with power and authority. The introduction to this reprint spotlights some of the progress women

are making and some of the battles still to be won. On the plus side, working women are winning better wages and promotion opportunities. On the debit side, they're still fighting for affordable health insurance and better enforcement of sexual harassment policies.

Moir, Anne, and David Jessel. *Brain Sex: The Real Difference Between Men and Women.* New York: Carol Publishing Group, 1992. Moir and Jessel draw on the latest research in brain physiology as they attempt to answer the old question, "Why can't a woman be more like a man?" Their conclusion: Women can't be like men because their brains are constructed differently. Acceptance of these differences, they argue, will enable men *and* women to exploit and enjoy complementary qualities.

Ms. Magazine. This readable magazine serves as a forum for feminist voices. Month after month, *Ms.* demonstrates that a market for nonsexist thinking exists in this country.

Sternberg, Robert J. *Cupid's Arrow: The Course of Love Through Time.* New York: Cambridge University Press, 2000. Sternberg, who teaches at Yale, draws on fields ranging from history and folklore to cognitive psychology to take you on a guided tour through the history and intricacies of humanity's most perplexing emotion. The book focuses on love's three main components—intimacy, passion, and commitment—and explores each in a way that invites you to apply the lessons to your own life.

Tannen, Deborah, *You Just Don't Understand: Women and Men in Conversation.* New York: Quill, 2001. Tannen's provocative and anecdote-filled book confirms that men and women speak to each other from vastly different world views. From early childhood, she says, girls use language to seek confirmation and reinforce intimacy. Boys, on the other had, use language to protect their independence and to negotiate status in large-group activities. Learning to "translate" these conflicting styles of conversation will help both sexes find a common language of love and understanding.

UNIT VII

NEW DIRECTIONS IN PSYCHOLOGY

- EXPLORING UNKNOWN WORLDS
- SEARCHING FOR NEW WAYS TO GROW
- STRATEGIES FOR COPING

Chapter

14 EXPLORING UNKNOWN WORLDS

"Watch closely, ladies and gentlemen! The Great Bamboozle is about to defy the laws of nature."

As you watch spellbound, the smooth-talking stage magician pulls rabbits out of hats and levitates his pretty assistant. But even as you marvel at the performance, you know beyond doubt that Bamboozle's art is based on clever deception.

No one, scientists agree, can violate physical laws. But what about the claims that some gifted individuals do have extraordinary powers? Can these people actually "read" someone else's mind or move objects without touching them? Skeptics warn that such performances are usually done through sleight of hand or by illusions. Others, however, believe that some men and women do possess *psychic powers* (abilities that lie outside known physical laws). As proof, they point to everyday people who report events that defy rational explanation. What do you make of these stories?

The Kellers are watching television in their living room. All seems normal on this spring evening—until a picture falls off the wall and crashes to the floor. Before anyone can move, the family is further startled by the sound of an unseen hand rapping on the coffee table.

In the next instant, the cup Mrs. Keller is holding flies out of her hand and smashes against the wall. The Kellers stare at 13-year-old Tim.

"I didn't do anything," Tim says. He looks ready to cry.

Mr. Keller sighs and puts his arm around his son. "The *poltergeist* only throws things when you're upset," he says gently. "What is it this time?"

"My teacher sent me to the principal's office again," the boy blurts out. "He hates me. All the teachers hate me."

Legend says that *poltergeists* (from the German for "mischievous spirits") cause the sudden, destructive storms that send books flying, shatter dishes, and generally wreak havoc in otherwise peaceful households. A more modern explanation suggests that angry, upset children and pre-adolescents are the cause. If so, Tim's rage is tapping the power of the unconscious to move objects without touching them, a phenomenon known as *psychokinesis (PK)*.

Many accounts of psychic events originate in India. Consider this report, taken from the work of a respected researcher named Ian Stevenson.

Young Jasbir Jat appeared to have died of smallpox and was being prepared for burial.

FIGURE 14.1 ▪ Rema Stone, billed as a psychic healer, consults a polished obsidean stone to help her predict this woman's future. A surprising number of Americans flock to "Psychic Fairs" to watch people like Stone demonstrate what they claim are paranormal powers.

To his family's joy and amazement the boy suddenly showed signs of life. After three weeks of recuperation, Jasbir abruptly announced that his name was Sobha Ram, not Jasbir Jat. My father, he said, is Shankar Tyagi of the village of Vehedi. Jasbir further claimed that he was of the Brahmin caste and refused to eat his family's modest diet.

A few years later, the Jats received a visit from the family of Sobha Ram. Jasbir called them all by name, even though he had never seen them before. He went on to describe intimate details about the family that also proved to be accurate. Sobha, he said, had died in a fall from a carriage. After Shankar Tyagi confirmed these facts, the two families compared notes. Sobha's death, they found, coincided with Jasbir's near-fatal illness. As time went on, Jasbir sometimes visited the Tyagis in Vehedi. He said he was much happier there.

Stories of death and rebirth are common in India, where a belief in reincarnation is basic to the Hindu and Buddhist religions. Was Sobha Ram actually reborn in the body of Jasbir Jat? You'll have to decide for yourself.

A woman who claims psychic powers relaxes in a California laboratory. A researcher watches her every move. Ten miles away, a volunteer "sender" picks a sealed envelope from a stack of five similar envelopes. The directions inside send him to a lakeside restaurant. Promptly at the stroke of noon, he pulls into the restaurant parking lot. For the next 15 minutes he observes every detail of the scene before him.

Back in the lab, the psychic begins to sketch the scene that she is receiving on her mental vision screen. As she sketches, she records her impressions on tape for later playback. "I see a body of water," she says. "Not the ocean, smaller . . . more like a lake." She goes on to describe a wooden building with many windows, a grove of trees, and a playground. Each of them appear in her sketch, forming a crude but recognizable landscape.

When the sender returns, the researcher

473

compares the sketch with his Polaroid photos of the place he visited. All of the major elements match. The experiment in remote viewing is an apparent success. What the researcher cannot explain is how the information was conveyed from the sender to the receiver.

Research into psychic forces has drawn increasing public attention. Researchers have adopted the terms *parapsychology* and *psi* to describe the study of events that cannot be explained by natural law. At the same time, other religious and supernatural beliefs have captured the imagination of millions of people around the globe. Some Eastern religions, for example, report that skilled practitioners can control their minds and bodies in seemingly impossible ways. Followers of New Age philosophies claim the ability to communicate with "entities" from other worlds. Another large group puts its faith in *pseudosciences* (literally, false sciences, such as astrology and palmistry) because they promise quick and easy answers to difficult questions.

Although most psychologists remain skeptical, some are intrigued by evidence that appears to support some parapsychological claims. Psychologists also study meditation, yoga, and other offshoots of Eastern religions because these practices add to our understanding of the mind's powers and potential. They accept the fact that belief in the pseudosciences influences human behavior. The questions explored in this chapter will give you a chance to make up your own mind about the value of exploring unknown worlds.

14.1 Why do people believe in the supernatural?

14.2 Do the pseudosciences offer any useful insights?

14.3 What do Eastern religions teach about the powers of the mind?

14.4 What is parapsychology?

14.5 How can research in parapsychology be controlled?

14.1 ■ WHY DO PEOPLE BELIEVE IN THE SUPERNATURAL?

If a demand exists, U.S. free enterprise will soon fill it. And a demand exists today for the supernatural.

Do you doubt that? Look at any big-city newspaper. You'll find a column of horoscopes—an astrologer's advice on what the day will bring you, based on your birth sign. The classified ads will probably announce the services of a psychic adviser or a palm reader, and you might even spot an article about a meeting of local witches. Turn the page and chances are good that you'll find a review of the latest best-seller on UFOs. Finally, check the film listings. You'll surely see ads for movies about vampires, poltergeists, werewolves, ghosts, and other supernatural forces.

BELIEF IN MAGICAL FORCES

For most of human history, in spite of efforts by organized religions to eliminate such beliefs, people have continued to believe that their lives are ruled by magical, supernatural forces. Even though most people today rely on science and the scientific method, belief in the supernatural still finds popular support. Why is this so? Psychologists list several reasons why people hold so tightly to magical beliefs.

A SEARCH FOR FULFILLMENT. Many people find little satisfaction in their personal lives.

By turning to such mysterious forces as witchcraft or magic, believers convince themselves that they're powerful and successful.

A SEARCH FOR ANSWERS. Most of us feel anxious when we are called on to make an important decision. To relieve this anxiety, some people put their trust in magical, supernatural forces. If "it's written in the stars" or in a "magic" number, how can we go wrong? Adolf Hitler, dictator of Nazi Germany during World War II, relied on astrology. Hitler scheduled important battles on "lucky days" that were determined by the positions of the stars, sun, moon, and planets.

A SEARCH FOR COMFORT. Some people turn to magical forces when they cannot find comfort in their religion. Unable to accept the loss of a loved one, for example, parents may ask a spiritualist to help them contact their dead child.

A SEARCH FOR "KICKS." People who have no serious belief in the supernatural still find it exciting to consult the tarot cards or to read about mysterious "trips" through time and space. Experimenting with the supernatural adds spice to their lives.

A SEARCH FOR BELONGING. Believers in the supernatural enjoy a natural bond with those who share their beliefs. "In-groups" that focus on such interests as witchcraft, UFOs or out-of-body experiences provide otherwise lonely people with a needed sense of belonging.

A SEARCH FOR PROFIT. Both the well-meaning and the less-than-honest turn a profit on the public's interest in the supernatural. If believers are demanding horoscopes, palm readings, lucky-number charts, and past-life regressions, you can be sure someone will provide them—at a good price.

DANGERS OF RELYING ON PSEUDOSCIENCE

A surprisingly large number of Americans believe that they have had telepathic experiences. Others report psychic adventures involving spirits, dreams that predict the future, or mysterious runs of luck. Millions more buy horoscopes, lucky charms, tea-leaf readings, healing crystals, and so on. If you question them about their beliefs, they'll probably reply, "Sure it sounds crazy—but it works. I wouldn't dream of making a big decision without consulting my psychic adviser."

The danger, psychologists believe, is not in spending money for a few words of psychic advice. The real risk arises when individuals abdicate their responsibility for decision making. These people can easily develop what some psychologists have described as a "loser's personality." Losers, they say, tend to view themselves as victims. When they put their faith in mystical forces, they lose control of their own lives. They sit back and hope, instead of working to make good things happen.

People who make their own decisions, by the same token, can be "winners." You already know how hard it is to take responsibility for important choices. When you do, you sometimes make mistakes. Some of the emotional bruises last for a long time. But you learn from your mistakes. You grow stronger because you take responsibility for the choices you make.

■ SECTION CHECKUP

1 What proof exists that many people still rely on magical ideas to help them run their lives?

2 How would a psychologist explain an individual's reliance on magical beliefs?

3 What is the danger of depending on the pseudosciences to help make important life decisions?

14.2 ▓ DO THE PSEUDOSCIENCES OFFER ANY USEFUL INSIGHTS?

SECOND WITCH: Eye of newt, and toe of frog,
Wool of bat, and tongue of dog,
Adder's fork, and blind-worm's sting,
Lizard's leg, and howlet's wing:
For a charm of powerful trouble,
Like a hell-broth boil and bubble,

ALL WITCHES: Double, double toil and trouble;
Fire, burn, and caldron, bubble.

Macbeth, Act IV, Scene i

Like most citizens of his day, Shakespeare was aware of magic and the supernatural. He spiced his plays with ghosts, magical spells, prophecy, and witchcraft. What was common belief in the 1500s, moreover, has not totally disappeared. The pseudosciences still attract both casual participants and dedicated followers. The promise that one can peek into the future exerts a powerful attraction.

PREDICTING THE FUTURE

Divination is the magical art that tries to foretell events or discover hidden knowledge.

Over the centuries, diviners have used almost every natural event you can imagine to obtain information about the future. Some claimed that the gods sent messages in the livers of freshly killed animals. Others watched the stamping of horses' hooves or studied the smoke as it rose from a fire. Some diviners still read tea leaves and look for visions in crystal balls. Two other enduringly popular methods of divination are the tarot cards and the *I Ching*.

THE TAROT. The 78 cards of the *tarot* deck date back to at least the 1300s. Fifty-six of the cards make up the four suits, similar to a modern deck. The other 22 cards (the major Arcana) picture colorful medieval symbols that are said to have special meanings (see Figure 14.2). Among these picture cards are such universal figures as the fool, the lovers, justice, death, the sun, and the hanged man. Each card stands for several related meanings. The fool, for example, represents foolishness, lack of discipline, or excess. The sun signifies more positive qualities, such as triumph, success, and happiness.

In telling the tarot, the diviner lays out the cards after the questioner has thought about his or her question. The entire deck can be used, but many diviners prefer to work only with the picture cards. As each card is turned up, the diviner relates the card to the questioner. Since each card has several meanings, the diviner can adjust the reading to the ques-

The Hanged Man   The Lovers

FIGURE 14.2 ▓ The meaning of the colorful picture cards used in the tarot depends on the position in which they appear. The Hanged Man often represents frustration and obstacles to success. The Lovers, as you might guess, signify beauty, temptation, and the possibility of romance.

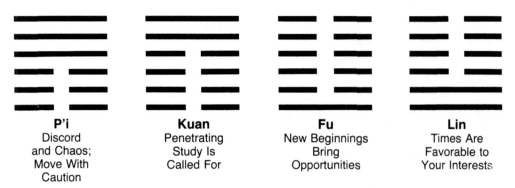

P'i	Kuan	Fu	Lin
Discord and Chaos; Move With Caution	Penetrating Study Is Called For	New Beginnings Bring Opportunities	Times Are Favorable to Your Interests

FIGURE 14.3 ▪ P'i, Kuan, Fu, and Lin are four of the *I Ching*'s most important hexagrams. Consultation with any book of the *I Ching* will yield further explanation and interpretation of the basic meanings printed below the name of each hexagram.

tioner's reactions. This "intuitive" response by the diviner plays a major role in the success or failure of the reading.

Tradition tells us that the Emperor Napoleon saw his defeat at the Battle of Waterloo (1815) foreshadowed in the tarot. The military genius who led the French armies to so many victories may well have suffered a fatal loss of confidence when the Tower, symbol of defeat, turned up next to the emperor. That combination told him that he would lose the battle and his crown in the coming showdown with the Duke of Wellington.

I CHING. More than 3,000 years ago, Chinese diviners began writing a book of prophecy called the *I Ching*. To use this ancient book, the diviner asks the questioner to create a hexagram by tossing three coins six times. If a toss produces all heads or all tails, the questioner draws a solid line. A mixed toss of heads and tails creates a broken line. The various combinations of solid and broken lines yield one of 64 possible hexagrams. After a hexagram is created, the diviner consults the *I Ching*, which describes the various meanings ascribed to each figure. As in the tarot, the diviner chooses the interpretation that seems to fit the questioner best. The

hexagram P'i (see Figure 14.3) signifies discord and chaos. If a young man asked the *I Ching* for advice about a love affair, P'i would warn him of pitfalls ahead. The diviner would probably say, "Your slightest word or deed is likely to be misunderstood. Rely on your inner strength to help you endure this chaotic period."

THE SEARCH FOR PERSONAL INSIGHTS

Three popular pseudosciences promise personal insights to those who accept the idea that their lives are shaped by natural forces that operate outside the laws of physics. Like the tarot and *I Ching*, astrology, palmistry, and numerology date back to the earliest civilizations.

ASTROLOGY. Astronomy is a science that studies the movements of the sun, moon, stars, and planets and tries to understand the workings of the universe. *Astrology* (see also Chapter 6, pages 174–175) is a pseudoscience with practitioners who assert that these same movements dramatically influence human affairs. Astrologers divide the sky into 12 equal segments called the zodiac. The astrologers

THE SIGNS OF THE ZODIAC

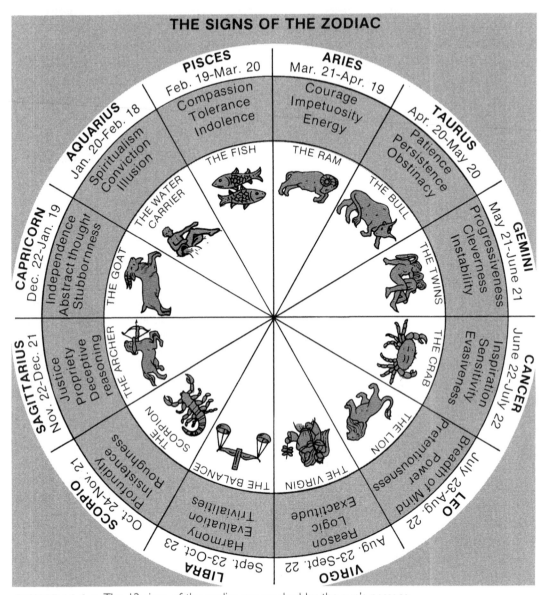

FIGURE 14.4 ▪ The 12 signs of the zodiac are marked by the sun's passage across the major constellations. How well do you match the behavior traits assigned to your birth sign by this traditional astrological chart?

believe that the zodiac sign under which a person is born determines that individual's personality (see Figure 14.4). Using an individual's time and place of birth, astrologers prepare a horoscope. The horoscope describes the subject's character, abilities, and appearance. Some charts go so far as to say that Pisceans (Pisces is the fish) often stand with feet crossed—like a fish's tail. A horoscope also gives advice on how to deal with money, romance, school, family relationships, and other matters.

Detailed horoscopes take time to prepare and cost more money than most people want to invest. Their accuracy, moreover, is open to question. In one study, each subject was shown a number of horoscopes. One of the horoscopes had been prepared for the subject by a well-known astrologer. The others were similar in style and format, but were filled with statements that could apply to anyone. "Find the horoscope that fits you exactly," the researcher told the subjects. The subjects tried—and guessed wrong far more often than they guessed correctly.

Newspaper readers often turn to a daily table of astrological advice called "Your Horoscope" or "Astrological Forecast." These tidbits of advice might tell Virgos that "It's a good day for making new friends," or warn Scorpios that "An opponent will try to make trouble for you." If you think about it, you could write such vague predictions yourself. Isn't every day a good day for making friends?

PALMISTRY.   Medical research shows that a number of diseases and genetic disorders (liver disease and Down syndrome, for example) can be diagnosed by studying the lines in the palm of the hand. The same doctors who study the hand as a "blueprint" to the body's health, however, reject palmistry as a valid way of interpreting personality and divining a person's future. Even so, in cities everywhere, palmists dressed in traditional gypsy costume "read" the hand's distinctive lines, mounts, and finger shapes (see Figure 14.5).

Palmists study the hand for clues to the individual's mental and emotional states. Breaks in the "life line," for example, are seen as predictions of future illnesses or accidents. A person with a strong "heart line" may be told to expect a happy love life. Skillful palmists adjust their reading to the questioner's reactions. Slight facial movements and hints dropped in conversation are often enough to ensure a successful reading.

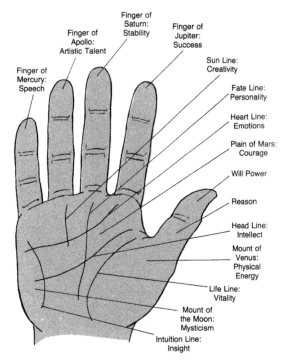

FIGURE 14.5 ▓ Palm readers say they can analyze character and predict a person's future from the lines and mounts of the hand. Why do people believe in this pseudoscientific tradition?

NUMEROLOGY. Believers in the pseudoscience of *numerology* calculate their "magic number" according to a table that assigns values to each letter of a person's name. If your magic number turns out to be seven, for example, the numerologist would describe you as a "mysterious, withdrawn, scholarly person." Threes, by contrast, are supposed to be "lucky, lively, and charming." Skeptics point out that these so-called magic numbers seldom fit the subject's actual personality. Believers in numerology, however, claim that the universe "vibrates" to precise numerical relationships, such as can be found in planetary orbits and the structure of atoms. Numerology, they say, applies these same relationships to human affairs.

SPIRITUALISM

Spiritualism is based on a belief that the living can communicate with the dead. If Benjamin wants to speak to his late Uncle Ted, for example, he would consult a *medium* (someone who claims to be able to contact the spirits of the dead). The actual attempt at contact takes place during a seance, which is usually held in a darkened room. The medium asks Benjamin and his fellow petitioners to join hands. Then the medium seems to fall into a trance. Soon the ghostly voice of Uncle Ted, or a messenger spirit, appears to answer Benjamin's questions. Most seances also feature table rapping, flickering candle flames, and ghostly objects that fly around the room.

"Ghostbusters" have found that mediums, despite their fervent denials, rely on special props, projectors, and hidden helpers to achieve their ghostly effects. The famous escape artist Harry Houdini (see Figure 14.6) offered a $10,000 prize to any spiritualist he could not prove to be a fake. Houdini sat through a number of impressive seances but never had to pay off on his offer. Despite the proven fakery, grieving men and women still turn to spiritualists in hopes of regaining contact with loved ones who have died. Psychologists warn that such efforts lead only to continued unhappiness. It's better, they say, to nurture relationships while the people you love are still alive.

NEW AGE MOVEMENT

Followers and practitioners of New Age philosophies share the belief that New Age mysticism holds the key to the healing of such personal and cultural ills as disease, war, poverty, ethnic and racial hatreds, and ecological destruction. Agreement breaks down, however, when New Agers try to define the specific methods, materials, and techniques that will lead humanity to a peaceful, harmonious future. As a result, the movement has no single leader, no central organization, and no firm agenda. Here are three examples of the pathways chosen by today's New Agers:

CHANNELING. Soon after the channeler goes into a trance, a spectral voice speaks to the waiting questioners. The voice identifies itself as Roth, a disembodied spirit who resides on Alpha Centauri. Speaking through the channeler, Roth offers advice that ranges from the spiritual to the commonplace. Interest in channeling dates back to the late 1960s, when Jane Roberts published the first of a series of books about a visiting entity known as Seth. Skeptics argue that a channeling session is simply a New Age variation on the largely discredited art of the seance.

FIGURE 14.6 ▓ Escape artist Harry Houdini (seated at left) used his knowledge of stage magic to expose fake spiritualists. Here he demonstrates the tricks of the trade. Can you spot any of the props used to simulate the appearance of spirits during a seance?

The Yoga Way to the Perfect Tennis Serve

In his fascinating book *Powers of the Mind*, Adam Smith describes how the principles of Zen and yoga improve sports skills. Here Smith describes what happened when he went to a tennis pro who taught Zen techniques.

I went back to my tennis guru. My requirements were simple: I wanted a serve, that's all, with the power of a rocket, accurate to within six inches.

We went out to the court with a basket of balls. I hit a couple. The Zen master didn't say anything. Some went in, some went out. The Zen master didn't say anything. I hit some more.

"Okay," he said. "Breathe in with your racket back, and out when it moves."

That was easy.

"Okay, now, where should the ball go over the net? And where should it land?"

I pointed.

"Okay, ask your body to send it there, and get out of the way."

"Please, body, send it there."

A miss.

"It's not listening."

"Slow it down. Visualize the whole shot before you hit it. Listen to the sound the ball makes against the string."

It's amazing, but if you really visualize, and you really listen to the sound, you can't go racheta racheta with your mind. . . .

We set up an empty tennis ball can in the corner of the service court. . . .

"Slow it down more. More. Please, body, send the ball—

"Slower, body, send the ball—

"Slower, slower. Make time stand still. No time.

"Please body, send the ball—"

Zank! The empty tennis ball can went up into the air and bounced metallically.

"Who did that?" I said.

The tennis guru said nothing. He handed me another ball. It went into the corner of the service court, on roughly the same spot. So did the next one.

I began to giggle wildly. I danced around a little, the scarecrow had a brain, the cowardly lion had courage. I had a serve. "I did it! I did it!" I said.

Immediately it went away.

"Visualize. Don't use words. Don't think. Use images. In between shots, count your breath."

Adam Smith admits that he never mastered his Zen serve—but, he says, it does come back now and then. If you'd like to apply the same principle to your own tennis, try Tim Gallwey's book *The Inner Game of Tennis*. And good luck!

CRYSTALS. Wearing crystal amulets to ward off evil is an ancient custom that New Agers have revived and updated. Every New Age shop sells these polished stones, which are said to have healing, psychic, or magical properties. A properly programmed crystal, New Agers believe, can reduce stress, enhance creativity, and awaken the psychic senses. Although scientific evidence is lacking, wearers claim that the crystals emit vibrations that cannot be detected by today's instruments.

HEALING. Many New Age beliefs focus on techniques for healing the mind and body. Actress Shirley MacLaine, a widely read author of New Age books, holds sessions that teach meditation, past-life regression therapy, and sound and color healing. Healing power, she says, comes from meditating on the body's *chakras*, or energy points. Greg Schelkun learned the art of therapeutic touch in the Philippines. He says that he can relieve pain simply by touching his patients. Surgeon Bernie Siegel believes that "all disease is ul-

FIGURE 14.7 ■ The sun's first rays strike fire in a quartz crystal held aloft at a sacred site in the Black Hills of South Dakota. This was a moment in time—August 16, 1987—known to the New Age movement as the Harmonic Convergence. The date was said to mark the end of the materialistic world and the beginning of the next phase in humanity's spiritual evolution. New Agers were certain that exposing crystals to the sunrise on that special day would recharge their healing energy.

timately related to a lack of love, . . . for the exhaustion of the immune system thus created leads to physical vulnerability." Psychologists argue that New Age patients improve because (a) they learn to relax and (b) their belief in the treatment frees the mind to eliminate symptoms that are often psychosomatic in origin.

MODERN PSEUDOSCIENCES

Two pseudosciences combine ancient beliefs with modern research and experimentation. Believers in pyramidology and graphology try to apply scientific principles to the age-old search for self-knowledge and control of the natural world.

PYRAMIDOLOGY. In 1959, the patent office in Prague, Czechoslovakia, issued a patent to Karel Drbal for a device that sharpened razor blades. That wasn't so unusual, except that the "sharpener" was a small pyramid. Place a dull blade inside the pyramid, engineer Drbal claimed, and it becomes sharp again. Fans believe that pyramids work their "miracles" by focusing the energy of the cosmic rays that constantly bombard the earth.

True believers use their pyramids to purify water, invigorate seeds, and to give new life to ailing plants. Some sleep and meditate inside or under pyramid shapes. Used in this way, they claim, pyramids cure headaches, speed the healing of wounds, and provide a refreshing sleep. John Onan, of Wadsworth, Illinois, went a step further. After building several smaller pyramids that convinced him of their value, he built a five-story, gold-plated, pyramid-shaped home for himself and his family. He completed his pyramid in the mid-1980s and now opens it to the public. (You can try your own pyramid experiments by following the instructions in the box on page 483.)

GRAPHOLOGY. Handwriting experts believe that graphology—the analysis of individual variations in handwriting—provides a nearly foolproof key to the personality. Think about your own handwriting. You shape each letter almost unconsciously while your mind concentrates on choosing the words. Using the written word as a sort of Rorschach test, the graphologist analyzes slant and spacing, the shape of loops and crossbars, end strokes, and punctuation. Each element is then correlated with common personality traits.

The letter "t," for example, is thought to reveal over 100 specific traits, including procrastination, efficiency, and sarcasm. Handwriting that slants upward reveals an optimistic frame of mind. Erik Rees, a well-known graphologist who does consulting work for major British corporations, claims

Do Pyramids Have Special Powers? Find Out for Yourself

Humanity's fascination with the powers of the pyramid may have begun in ancient Egypt. Since you probably lack the 13-acre vacant lot and the 2,300,000 stone blocks it would take to create your own Great Pyramid, you will have to make do with something smaller if you want to experiment with pyramid power.

Begin by making your own mini-pyramid out of poster board, using the dimensions given below. Tape the sides together, but tape the base to one side only. This will allow you to put objects inside the pyramid. When your pyramid is finished, set it on a two-inch wooden block (one-third the height of the pyramid itself). Locate your pyramid at a reasonable distance from electrical appliances, radios, windows, and heaters. Use a compass to find magnetic north, and line up the pyramid precisely on the north-south axis.

What should you put inside the pyramid? Try anything organic—dead insects, a chunk of beef, or fresh-cut flowers. If pyramid power works as advertised, the test pieces should "mummify" (dehydrate), while a control piece placed in a nearby box decays. For a second experiment, buy a packet of radish seeds. Put half of the seeds inside the pyramid for a few days; leave the remainder in the packet. Then plant the two sets of seeds in side-by-side pots filled with the same planting soil. Give both pots the same amount of water and sunshine. If pyramid power works, the treated seeds will grow faster and more vigorously than the untreated seeds.

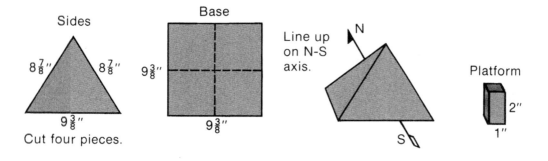

that "you can soon see if a person's a liar. A liar's letters are ambiguous—an 'e' could be an 'a,' an 'o' could be an 'a,' an 'l' could be a 't' and so on."

The growing tendency by big companies to rely on the recommendations of a graphologist when hiring executives has alarmed many psychologists. Psychometrist Roy Hammand advises his clients to ignore the claims of the graphologists. "It has totally failed to predict even the easiest characteristics like extroversion," he says. Skeptics also note that graphologists do not always agree on the meaning of such basic handwriting quirks as the dot over the "i." Some say an undotted "i" reveals laziness or weakness. Others are just as certain that the missing dot signifies a rebellion against the need to conform. (Figure

14.8 on this page shows a typical analysis of two celebrity signatures.)

■ SECTION CHECKUP

1 Describe several ways in which people try to foretell the future. Why are such pseudo-sciences attractive to those who believe in them?

2 If forced to make a choice, why would a scientist put more faith in graphology than in astrology or palmistry?

3 Why do pyramidology and graphology attract people who otherwise would refuse to believe in the pseudosciences?

FIGURE 14.8 ▓ Graphologist Hariette Surovell believes that signatures reveal a personality as surely as does a standardized personality test. Famed rock star Bruce Springsteen's "small, somewhat illegible middle zone," she writes, "might indicate that despite his innumerable successes, The Boss is still a bit insecure." She goes on to say that "the double valentine formed in the capital B" shows that Springsteen "is so romantic that we can assume his touching love lyrics are truly 'heartfelt.'" Actress Whoopi Goldberg's signature, by contrast, "shows strong discipline. Roundedness shows strong sensuality, but the extreme regularity also reveals high standards." From this, Surovell concludes that "Whoopi is very selective and choosy about picking partners."

14.3 ▓ WHAT DO EASTERN RELIGIONS TEACH ABOUT THE POWERS OF THE MIND?

At first glance, the town of Fairfield, Iowa, (population 10,000) seems much like its neighboring farming communities in the heartland of the Middle West. It is Fairfield's exotic neighbor that sets it apart. Nestled among the rolling hills on the northern edge of town is Maharishi International University. Founded in 1974, the school emphasizes meditation and the development of creativity.

Guru and founder Maharishi Mahesh Yogi believes that if enough people meditate they can bring about world harmony. To achieve peace in the Middle East, he says, would require 7,000 meditators (a number based on the square root of one percent of the world's population). In October 1990, thousands of out-of-town meditators descended on Fair-

field to test the Maharishi's theory. Peace did not come to the Middle East that day, perhaps because the crowd assembled in the college's two amphitheaters numbered only 4,500. David Orme-Johnson, chairman of the psychology department, was not dismayed. "Even with less than 7,000, we should be able to have an effect," he said. After all, meditators had already claimed credit for the peaceful reunification of East and West Germany in 1988–1989.

Transcendental Meditation (TM), the system taught by the Maharishi, represents an Eastern approach to problem solving. Typically, Eastern thought emphasizes inner calm as a counterbalance to Western society's harshly competitive spirit. Supporters believe

The Relaxation Response: A Simple Guide to Meditation

Cardiologist Herbert Benson recommends meditation as a convenient, natural means of reducing stress and relieving the tensions of everyday life. A regular program of meditation—the "relaxation response"—can also provide a valuable health benefit. The secret, Benson says, is to combine meditation with a belief in a healing power that lies either inside yourself or out. Those who do so find relief from such stress-related conditions as headaches, high blood pressure, and chronic back pain.

Benson lists three basic requirements for successful meditation: (1) Meditate in a quiet environment, where you will be free from distraction. (2) During meditation, adopt a passive attitude, a state of mind in which you ignore distractions and cultivate a "let-it-happen" feeling. Don't worry about intrusive thoughts, and don't ask yourself how well you are "doing." (3) Sit in a comfortable position, one that requires no unnecessary muscular tension. The cross-legged yoga position is fine, but do what feels best for you. Don't lie down, however, or you may fall asleep.

With these principles in mind, you're ready to try the Relaxation Response:

1 Sit quietly in a comfortable position.

2 Close your eyes.

3 Relax your muscles, beginning at your feet and working up to your head. If tension returns, repeat the process. Do not grasp your legs or clasp your hands together.

4 Breathe through your nose. As you breathe out, silently repeat a single word or phrase. Keep your breathing easy and natural. Repeat your "mantra" each time you breathe out. It's best to pick a word or phrase that reflects your personal beliefs. Many people turn to a

favorite prayer, poem, or quotation for inspiration. If you can't think of a word or phrase that feels right, simply say "one" over and over.

5 Continue this process for 10 to 20 minutes. It's okay to look at a clock, but don't set an alarm. When you finish, sit quietly for a few minutes with your eyes closed. Let your mind and body return to normal activities slowly and gently.

6 Learning to meditate takes time. With practice, the response will come more and more easily. Meditate twice daily, but not within two hours of eating a meal.

Most people finish a period of meditation feeling calm and relaxed. Others report feelings of pleasure and a heightened sense of well-being. How will you react? You won't know until you give the relaxation response a fair trial. This is a gift that only you can give yourself.

that a union of East and West will free everyone to find a personal, peaceful relationship with the universe.

CONCEPTS OF EASTERN PHILOSOPHY

By using Eastern philosophy, religious leaders (often known as gurus, or teachers) hope to show people how to use more of their mental and physical potential. Believers in Eastern concepts claim that most people limit themselves to a narrow range of thought that the culture defines as "normal." They believe that once the barriers of this artificial mind-state are broken the mind can move into a wider field of consciousness.

Although Westerners once scoffed at Eastern ideas of meditation and inner harmony, millions of Americans now study them seriously. Famed psychologist Carl Jung believed that Western thought and Eastern religions were meant to work together, much as the left and right hands cooperate to play the guitar. The search for a more satisfying life has taken people along a path familiar to followers of Zen Buddhism, yoga, and Transcendental Meditation.

ZEN. *Zen Buddhism*, or Zen, began in India. After reaching Japan in the 12th century, it has now traveled to the United States. Zen teaches that human beings can use *meditation* (a period of quiet, focused thought) to reach true self-knowledge and a sense of unity with Ultimate Reality. This state, sometimes known as enlightenment, can be reached only through strict discipline. Zen teaches that the details of everyday life must be ignored. Intuitive knowledge, the knowledge that comes through meditation, will lead the Zen follower to the deepest and most important truths.

Sitting meditation, known as *zazen*, lies at the heart of Zen. Zen teachers instruct their students in the proper posture, hand positions, and breathing. Without these techniques, the mind cannot be properly quieted.

Rituals also include prayer, chanting, and stories called *koans*. Typical koans challenge the student to think about questions such as "What is the sound of one hand clapping?" and "Is it the flag or the wind that is moving?" If beginners practice these lessons faithfully, Zen Buddhists say, their worries will drop away and life will acquire new meaning.

The lengthy inward search for meaning in Zen does not always appeal to the Western mind's desire for quick results. True followers of Zen must be willing to make it a way of life. Reading about Zen or asking questions, the Zen masters say, isn't enough. You can read a book on horseback riding, they say, but you can never fully know the reality of the experience until you climb into the saddle.

YOGA. Most Westerners think of *yoga* as a complicated form of exercise. But the true yogi (one who practices yoga) believes that you can liberate yourself from the prison of your body through exercise and meditation. Yoga attempts to promote the growth of physical, mental, moral, and spiritual forces. According to yoga teachings, students who follow the proper course of instruction will have a molecular change in their bodies. After about six months, personal tastes and habits will also change. Yogis claim that students stop being lonely, their fears vanish, and they experience true happiness.

Most Westerners limit themselves to the practice of yoga postures, deep breathing, and relaxation exercises. Sometimes known as *Hatha yoga*, this practice involves stretching the entire body and holding difficult postures. Yogis believe that correct posture and a flexible body help achieve a state of inner balance. Unlike more familiar exercises such as sit-ups or jogging, yoga does not require great strength nor does it strain the body. Yoga diets call for fresh fruits and raw vegetables, milk, rice, and nuts. Yogis avoid meat, coffee, onions, tobacco, alcohol, and drugs of any kind.

TRANSCENDENTAL MEDITATION. The techniques of *Transcendental Meditation* (TM) are anything but new. TM began at least 2,500 years ago in India but gained its widest popularity in the 1960s when Maharishi Mahesh Yogi set up training centers in the United States. The Maharishi claims that TM can improve people's health and emotional stability, and strengthen their ability to handle daily tasks. Lab studies have proved that TM does reduce stress and apparently increases people's ability to enjoy life—but so have other, simpler meditation techniques (see the box on page 485).

If you were interested in TM, you would first visit a training center or attend a lecture. Next comes a personal interview, followed by eight hours of individual and group training in TM meditation techniques. You will also receive your personal *mantra*, a special sound used to focus your thoughts during meditation. Twice-daily meditation sessions usually last about 20 minutes each. A final group ceremony completes your training. If you wish, you can return to the TM center to have your progress checked and to receive guidance in applying TM principles to your life.

Conflict has marked TM's history in the United States. Fearful that TM promotes Hindu religious teachings, parents have filed court suits to prevent its being taught in the public schools. The TM organization denies any religious intent, claiming that its only goal is to help people find a higher awareness. After its initial period of rapid growth, TM's popularity waned. In part, this stemmed from publicity about the Maharishi's tax problems. TM's problems also reflect the widespread skepticism that greeted the unveiling of a controversial program of advanced TM thought involving paranormal feats such as levitation. Well-meaning projects such as Maharishi's Program to Create World Peace also have aroused doubts because TM's supporters tend to claim results that cannot be verified by independent research.

■ SECTION CHECKUP

1 What new ideas do Eastern religious teachings add to Western thought?

2 Describe the basic techniques used by followers of Zen, yoga, and TM to achieve greater self-fulfillment.

3 List the basic steps you would take to start meditating. Why does a person who is meditating repeat the same sound over and over?

14.4 ▓ WHAT IS PARAPSYCHOLOGY?

Find a felt pen and 25 3″ × 5″ cards. Draw a circle on five of the cards. Then repeat the process for each of the designs shown in Figure 14.9 (page 488). Take care that the ink does not show through from the back. When you finish the task, you'll have created a deck of Zener cards. Decks like this are often used for experiments in *parapsychology*. This field of study concerns itself with the mysterious and intriguing world that lies just beyond the boundaries of everyday reality. Ready to test your powers of telepathy? Shuffle the cards and look for a willing subject.

What happens next? Conceal the cards from your subject. Turn them over one at a time, concentrating on each figure as you (the sender) reveal it. Ask your subject (the receiver) to write down the name of the card you are looking at. After you've gone through all 25 cards, check the results. A score of five "hits" is no better than random chance. Scores above ten suggest that you or your

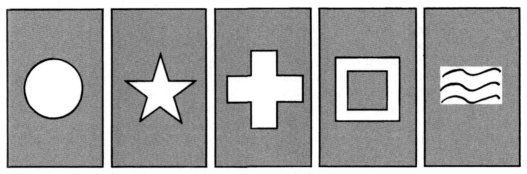

FIGURE 14.9

subject may have telepathic powers, particularly if you can repeat the high scores.

At one time, most scientists scoffed at ideas such as telepathy and busied themselves with studies of "real" events. But reports kept coming in. In the 1880s, the Society for Psychical Research in London began looking into a number of apparently genuine claims involving parapsychology. Modern studies began in 1927, when Duke University opened a Department of Parapsychology to carry on scientific studies. Pioneer researcher J. B. Rhine headed the new department, which attracted widespread attention from supporters and skeptics alike.

EXTRASENSORY PERCEPTION (ESP)

Parapsychologists define *ESP* as the ability to send or receive information in ways that would be impossible under the known laws of physics. *Psychokinesis* (PK) is the paranormal ability to move or otherwise affect objects without touching them. Let's say that your favorite rock group is playing a concert in London. If you're in the United States and "hear" the concert, is that ESP? No, not if you've tuned in your radio to pick up the broadcast. Yes, if you hear the music inside your head without benefit of a radio or television receiver. To demonstrate PK, you'd be asked to make a pencil roll across a table simply by staring at it. Some parapsychologists believe that gamblers who hit a "hot

streak" at the craps table are actually using PK to influence each roll of the dice.

Surveys show that 49 percent of the American people believe in ESP (defined as the paranormal powers of telepathy, clairvoyance, and precognition). PK is thought to involve separate mind powers, but all may be related in ways yet to be explained. Researchers have designed a number of complex techniques and instruments to study these mystifying phenomena. For every successful demonstration of ESP or PK in a research lab, however, a dozen failures have been reported.

TELEPATHY. Twins, lovers, and close relatives sometimes seem to know exactly what is happening to the other person, even over great distances. When two people communicate their thoughts and feelings without using the normal senses, the phenomenon is known as *telepathy*. The Zenner card experiment is often used to test for this ability. (See the feature on page 489 for a description of an unusual experiment that combines telepathy and dream research.)

In studies at Duke and at other centers, researchers have concluded: (1) Telepathy seems to be a function of the unconscious. Like all unconscious processes, telepathy is normally blocked off from the conscious mind. (2) Telepathy seems to be associated with alpha brain waves. Telepaths emit an

ESP and Dreams: A Rock Audience "Sends" a Telepathic Message

Start with two psychics, add a rock group, and stir in an audience of 2,000 rock fans. This unusual recipe produced an experiment in dream telepathy for Drs. Stanley Krippner and Montague Ullman of the Maimonides Dream Laboratory in Brooklyn.

At exactly 11:30 each night for six nights, the audience at a Grateful Dead concert in Port Chester, New York, was asked to send a mental image to psychic Malcolm Bessent. At that moment, Bessent was already asleep in the dream lab 45 miles away. Psychic Felicia Parise, who served as the control, slept at her home in Manhattan. While the Grateful Dead performed, the audience concentrated on a randomly selected slide that was projected on a screen along with Bessent's name.

Each morning, Bessent and Parise handed in their dream reports to Krippner and Ullman. According to Krippner, Bessent described four of the six slides with reasonable accuracy. Parise had only one "hit," on the final night. Since Bessent did not know what slides would be projected, the experiment was counted as a successful demonstration of dream telepathy.

---

increased volume of alpha waves during telepathic experiences. (3) Distance and physical barriers do not seem to block transmission of telepathic messages. (4) Bad news tends to be communicated more easily than good news. Perhaps this explains the classic cases in which people claim to have telepathically sensed the death or injury of a loved one.

CLAIRVOYANCE. Parapsychologists define *clairvoyance* as the power to perceive objects or events outside the range of one's normal senses. For example, you'd be using telepathy if you correctly called the Zener card your sender was concentrating on. If you correctly named the *next* card in the stack before it was turned over, that would be clairvoyance. Controlled studies of clairvoyance are difficult to design. In a well-run experiment, no one else (including the experimenter) is allowed to know what the clairvoyant person is trying to describe. Unless those conditions are met, the "hits" could be the result of telepathy, not clairvoyance.

Peter Hurkos, a Dutch clairvoyant, has been called a "psychic detective." Asked to help solve a murder, Hurkos first asked to hold the victim's coat. Guided by the "aura" the killer left on the coat, he described the man in detail, down to his mustache and wooden leg. Clairvoyant John Edward, star of a popular television show called *Crossing Over,* claims that he can communicate with the dead. Ask him how Grandpa is doing, answer some leading questions, and he'll dazzle you with names and facts that no one outside the family could have known. Strip away the hype, however, and you'll find that Hurkos and Edward chalk up more misses than hits.

PRECOGNITION. How many stories have you heard about people who change their minds at the last moment before boarding a plane—and escape death when the plane crashes? In parapsychology, predicting events that have not yet happened is called *precognition.* Psychic Jeane Dixon, for example, predicted in 1956 that "the election will

Did Uri Geller Use Psychic Powers to Bend Nitinol Wire?

Uri Geller has long reigned as one of the psychic world's superstars. Keys, spoons, and other metal objects seem to bend as if by magic when he touches them. In 1973, Geller was challenged to bend a piece of nitinol wire. The test seemed an easy one for the Israeli psychic, but nitinol wire has an unusual property: It "remembers" the shape in which it was manufactured. You can bend, twist, or crumple nitinol, but it always springs back to its original shape when heated. Reports of the experiment, which seemed to carry the endorsement of the U.S. Navy, appeared to verify Geller's psychic powers.

Careful study of the test procedures, however, revealed that the facts may not have been fully reported. In this Pro & Con, the description of the experiment will appear in the Pro column. On the Con side, Geller's critics will point out the faults they found in the design and conduct of the experiment.

PRO: GELLER'S NITINOL EXPERIMENT

1 Uri Geller performed the nitinol experiment under the supervision of physical scientist Eldon Byrd in October 1973.

2 The test took place at the Isis Center of the Naval Surface Weapons Center, Silver Spring. Maryland.

3 Nitinol at that time was not available to the general public. After Geller failed in his attempts to alter larger pieces of nitinol, Byrd held a smaller diameter (0.5 mm) piece of nitinol between his fingers. Geller stroked the middle of the wire.

CON: A CRITIQUE OF THE EXPERIMENT

1 Eldon Byrd has a long history of involvement in parapsychological research. He further compromised his objectivity by stating that "Geller is basically honest."

2 The Isis Center has no direct connection with the Navy. It's actually a meeting place for believers in the supernatural.

3 Geller could not "perform" his trick on the heavier pieces of nitinol. He explains that he cannot always control his powers—but he seems to do much better with objects that are easily bent.

be won by a Democrat, but he will be assassinated or die in office." President John F. Kennedy, a Democrat, was elected in 1960. Three days before he was assassinated in 1963, Dixon "saw" him dying of a head wound.

Parapsychologists are quick to remind the public that true precognitive experiences are rare. If you study a collection of predictions made by well-known psychics, you'll find that only a handful come true—about the same percentage as any well-informed student of world affairs might achieve. In one

study, 27 psychics predicted the date and location of 240 earthquakes. Matched against a control group that made its own random guesses, the guessers outscored the psychics.

Most precognitive experiences probably relate to the work of the unconscious. Let's suppose that you have a dream in which your father falls off a ladder. A day later he actually does fall. Was this a precognitive dream? It's more probable that the dream was based on unconscious observation: You know the ladder is old and shaky. You know that Dad tends to be careless when he's painting. You

PRO: GELLER'S NITINOL EXPERIMENT

After 20 seconds a bump formed at the center of the wire. Byrd placed the wire in boiling water, which should have removed the bump. Instead, the wire bent itself into a right angle.

4 Byrd later gave Geller other nitinol wires to touch, with similar results. He writes that the changes Geller made in the nitinol normally would require a temperature of 900° F and a pair of pliers.

5 Because Byrd could not detect any marks on the surface of the wire, he concluded that Geller was using some sort of psychic power.

6 Byrd also noted that he was once an amateur magician. He does not believe that Geller used sleight-of-hand or any other tricks.

7 Byrd's article ends with a statement of "official approval" by authorities of the Naval Surface Weapons Center.

CON: A CRITIQUE OF THE EXPERIMENT

4 Byrd cut the smaller diameter nitinol into several pieces. He does not appear to have kept these extra pieces under tight security.

5 Conditions at the Isis were quite disorganized. Geller's assistant, Shipi Shtrang, could have substituted previously prepared wires or could have secretly bent the ones Geller eventually handled.

6 Professional magicians cannot always detect sleight-of-hand tricks performed by other magicians—and Geller started his career as a stage performer.

7 The endorsement by the Navy applied only to the accuracy of statements about the properties of nitinol. The Navy neither confirmed nor denied the parapsychological part of the study.

As you can see, it is difficult to test psychic performers. Even so, many people still believe that Geller bent the nitinol exactly as Byrd reported. Until better tests are run, however, science cannot accept such clouded results. What's your opinion? Is Geller a clever performer or a talented psyhic? You can read more about Geller and his career on his Website, <*www.uri-geller.com*>—but perhaps it would be best to withhold judgment until all the research is in and the scientists have had the last word.

heard him say that he was planning to paint the garage on Saturday. Using that data, your unconscious composed a warning dream that only seemed to be precognitive.

PSYCHOKINESIS (PK). Uri Geller, a well-known Israeli psychic, once made a good living by causing spoons and keys to bend as he stroked them. If his power was real (skeptics say any accomplished stage magician can duplicate the trick), he was demonstrating psychokinesis. More often, PK seems to be

related to crisis situations such as death or disaster. There are many stories, for example, about clocks that "stopped dead" at the moment a family member died. As in Geller's case, many psychics claim an even greater power. They deflect compass needles, move small objects, and influence the flip of a coin. Nelya Mikhailova, a Russian woman, once demonstrated what appeared to be an exceptional psychokinetic talent. Nelya didn't stop with moving cigarettes, matches, and glasses. She separated a raw egg yolk from the white—from a distance of six feet!

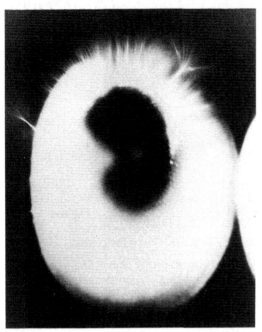 

FIGURE 14.10 ▪ Kirlian photography provides a look at the energy field, or aura, that surrounds all living things. Kirlian photos show the energy changes that seem to go with different moods. The subject's finger (left) is deeply relaxed, compared to the finger of a strongly aroused person (right).

THE BODY'S ENERGY FIELDS

Spiritualists and mystics have long insisted that the human body is surrounded by an energy field, or *aura*. In the early 1970s, a Russian research team developed a technique that appears to capture the aura on film. Kirlian photography, as the process is called, reveals that living bodies are surrounded by a sparkling energy field (see Figure 14.10). These photos have led to the suggestion that old paintings of saints and angels, which often show the holy figure surrounded by a halo of light, may have had a basis in fact.

Auras have some unusual properties that scientists are only now beginning to investigate. The aura of a sick person, for example, shows noticeable changes around the area of the illness. Psychic healers, who claim to cure illness by touching the sick, show a brighter than usual aura in Kirlian photos. This aura grows dimmer when they make contact with a patient. Similarly, psychics show greatly increased energy flows during psychokinetic demonstrations, particularly around the eyes.

EXPLORING OTHER MYSTERIES

How far can you go in trusting the stories of parapsychological events that appear in books and newspapers and on TV? In many cases, the accounts are supported by what seems to be solid evidence. Here are a few examples of paranormal mystery stories:

1. Ted Serios, a psychic treasure hunter, stares into the lens of a Polaroid camera. When the unexposed film is developed, it shows a fuzzy image of building shot from a strange angle. The building turns out to be a

hotel located a hundred miles away. Serios has somehow projected a mental image onto the film while it is still in the camera.

2. Rock star Ronnie Hawkins was diagnosed with terminal cancer in 2002. A year later he was cancer free, thanks to a sixteen-year-old miracle worker. The teenager, known simply as Adam, says that his X-ray vision allows him to look "into" a sick person and see "blockages." He then "tears those energies apart and pushes them outside the skin to die." Hawkins marvels at his recovery, and says he's glad the Big Rocker put Adam on his case.

3. A woman is seated in a college office, her eyes closed. A psychologist generates some random numbers on a computer and places the printout on a high shelf without looking at it. The woman slips into a self-induced trance. Ten minutes later she opens her eyes and reports that her "astral body" has moved around the room in spirit form and looked at the numbers written on the paper. To the psychologist's amazement, she correctly recites the five numbers he concealed from her. The odds against her guessing them correctly are 100,000 to 1.

4. Holding only a Y-shaped hazel branch, a man walks back and forth across a rough, wild patch of land. Suddenly the branch begins to twist in his hands, the long leg of the Y pointing downward. When workers drill a well at the spot, fresh water gushes forth. The man is a dowser, and his skill has been practiced for centuries. Major oil and water companies keep dowsers on their payrolls, even though science doesn't fully understand how the process works. One guess is that dowsers somehow sense the electromagnetic fields that can be found in the presence of water, oil, or mineral deposits.

It is tempting to write off paranormal events as not worth investigating. But what if science had never explored the mysteries of gravity or radiation? Ignoring data that doesn't seem to fit known facts adds nothing to the fund of scientific knowledge. Perhaps the best thing to do is to subject parapsychology to the same rigorous tests that are presently used in chemistry and physics labs. You'll read about attempts to do just that in Section 14.5.

▪ SECTION CHECKUP

1 Define the three types of ESP generally included in the study of parapsychology: telepathy, clairvoyance, and precognition. How is psychokinesis different?

2 A friend has a dream that appears to be precognitive. Explain the dream-come-true in terms of what we know about the unconscious.

3 What does the parapsychologist mean by an aura? What possible uses could auras have?

14.5 ▪ HOW CAN RESEARCH IN PARAPSYCHOLOGY BE CONTROLLED?

Try as they might, skeptics cannot explain away the immense body of paranormal data. If pressed to do so, scientists explain the possible existence of ESP and PK as (1) resulting from the unexpected application of known scientific principles or (2) resulting from previously unexplored powers of the natural world and the human mind.

ASKING THE RIGHT QUESTIONS

Believers in parapsychology often demand that people suspend all critical judgments. After all, they say, the possibility that human beings possess psychic powers promises a new and exciting future. Skeptical observers, however, start with a list of questions that should be asked whenever psychic events are studied.

DOES THE EVENT SEEM VALID ONLY BECAUSE PEOPLE WANT TO BELIEVE IN IT?

The everyday world often seems dull and limited. People should ask themselves if the appeal of psychic mysteries doesn't tempt belief simply because it's novel and exciting. Children accept fairy tales and monster movies as true. Critics charge that parapsychology has become an adult fairy tale, dressed up for a scientific age.

WHO SAYS IT'S SO?

Conducting ESP and PK experiments and evaluating the resulting data requires an unusually high level of skill and adherence to scientific method. In a field already marked by inconsistency and inflated claims, some of the scientists who study parapsychology are working outside their own fields. Others may have, consciously or unconsciously, lost their objectivity. To further complicate matters, many psychics cannot or will not perform under tight laboratory controls. Telepaths and clairvoyants, for example, often see their scores fall sharply when they are tested under strict protocols.

WHAT DO THE DATA REALLY MEAN?

Writing up experiments and calling them valid doesn't make them so. Critics who look at the data raise such questions as, "What controls were set up? Have data been collected over a large number of trials? Has the statistical analysis been done properly? Did the study prevent the experimenter's own biases from influencing the results? Pyramidologists can treat any number of razor blades with pyramid power, but until they can answer these questions, their results must be classed as unproven.

DOES A CAUSE-AND-EFFECT RELATIONSHIP REALLY EXIST?

True believers in parapsychology deny the possibility that coincidence can play a role in so-called psychic events. If Charlie is thinking about a friend and the friend calls him on the phone, Charlie shouts, "Telepathy!" Baseball fan Stella has a hunch that the Red Sox will win the pennant—and they do. Has she had a precognitive experience—or has coincidence (coupled with her knowledge of baseball) ruled her choice? Parapsychologists go by a simple rule to separate chance or coincidence from statistically valid proof. They demand that a psychic performance meet the test of *95 percent confidence*. That is, the experimenter must prove that there is only 1 chance in 20 that the results could have happened by chance.

Imagine, for example, that you've been tested for clairvoyance. In the test, you were asked to guess the contents of sealed envelopes without actually looking at them. Inside each envelope is either a black or a white card. If you have 100 guesses, the odds are that you'll get 50 right. A score of 50, therefore, would not meet the "95 percent confidence" test. A look at a special table of statistics, however, will tell you that a score of 65 or better meets the standard.

Finally, those who study psychic happenings should ask themselves a final question:

DOES IT MAKE SENSE?

After all the statistics and descriptions have been analyzed, the data should fit into a rational, logical universe. If the data do not fit, wait for better evidence. The scientific study of parapsychology is still a young field. You can have fun with ESP and PK—or even the pseudosciences—without relying on them to make your life decisions.

RUNNING A CONTROLLED EXPERIMENT IN PARAPSYCHOLOGY

Controlled parapsychological experiments should be double-blind whenever possible. Neither the experimenter nor the subjects should have prior knowledge about the con-

James Randi:
The Psychic's Nemesis

James "the Amazing" Randi (1929–) is an internationally known magician and escape artist. But Randi is much more than an entertainer. For the past 20 years, he has devoted much of his time to investigating the psychic world. Anyone who claims paranormal powers, from dowsers to psychic surgeons to tarot readers, is almost certain to draw Randi's attention. His job, the Canadian-born Randi says, is to help the public understand the difference between genuine scientific research in parapsychology and the pseudoscientific nonsense promoted by fakes and charlatans.

Randi first came to public attention in his role as the psychic's nemesis when he called Uri Geller a fraud in the early 1970s. His 1975 book, *The Magic of Uri Geller*, showed readers how to duplicate Geller's metal-bending tricks without using PK. Geller tried to sue Randi for slander, but the courts dismissed his suit. Randi later traveled to the Philippines to expose the "psychic surgeons" who flourished there. These fakers used sleight-of-hand tricks to create the illusion that they were inserting their hands into the body cavities of their patients to remove tumors. The MacArthur Foundation noted these exploits and awarded Randi one of its "genius grants" in 1986.

In 1976 Randi became one of the founding members of the Committee for the Scientific Investigation of Claims of the Paranormal (CSICOP). The organization, which has debunked numerous paranormal claims, takes a "show-me" attitude toward any claim of psychic powers. In 1988 Randi headed a CSICOP team that looked into reports of psychic phenomena in China. One set of claims involved "psychic children" who could "read" written messages by sitting on them or stuffing them into their ears. All of the claims collapsed under the team's investigation.

What is the purpose of his work? Randi writes:

> Parapsychology is a farce and a delusion, along with other claims of wonders and powers that assail us every day of our lives. Knowing what I do, and holding the opinions I do, has not made this world any the less exciting and wonderful and challenging for me, nor should it for you. Throw away the tarot deck and ignore the astrology column. They are products offered you by charlatans who think you are not the marvelous, capable, independent being you are. Nonsense has reigned too long as Emperor of the Mind. Take a good look. The Emperor has no clothes!

For more than 20 years, Randi has offered $10,000 to anyone who can demonstrate a parapsychological happening under controlled conditions. Seventy-five self-proclaimed psychics have tried for the money. None have come close, Randi says.

Do you think James Randi makes a good case against parapsychology? You might want to read some other sources before making up your mind. But whatever your final conclusion, you'll probably agree that he's a convincing voice for what he believes.

tent of the actual test. The following experiment in clairvoyance demonstrates these precautions. The test took place at Duke University under the supervision of J. B. Rhine, using the standard Zener deck described on pages 487–488.

PREPARATION.   The cards were shuffled and cut under controlled conditions. Neither Hubert Pearce, the test taker, nor J. G. Pratt, the test giver, was present. Neither of the two young men could possibly have known the sequence of the cards ahead of time.

SETTING.   Pearce and Pratt met in Pratt's room to begin the experiment. After the men synchronized their watches, Pearce walked to another room 340 feet away. As he did so, Pratt shuffled and cut the cards. At no time did he look at the face side of the cards.

THE TEST.   At the zero hour, Pratt took the top card from the deck and laid it on the table face downward. One minute later he laid another card down, and so on through the deck. In his own room, 30 seconds after Pratt laid down the first card, Pearce wrote down his first guess. The process continued through two decks, with Pearce writing down his guesses every 60 seconds. Afterward, Pratt looked at the cards for the first time while he

made two copies of the results. He sealed one copy and sent it to Dr. Rhine. At the same time, Pearce was sealing a duplicate copy of his guesses for delivery to Dr. Rhine. All records were later photographed.

RESULTS.   Altogether, Pratt and Pearce carried out 1,850 trials. If only chance had been at work, Pearce's score would have been 370 hits (1 out of 5). Pearce, however, ran up a score of 558 hits, 188 better than chance. The odds against such a score happening accidentally have been figured at better than a hundred billion to one.

Since the results far exceeded the "95 percent confidence" test, Dr. Rhine's experiment appeared to confirm that Pearce has clairvoyant abilities. Until science can explain the "how" of Pearce's feat, clairvoyance will remain only a fascinating mystery.

■ SECTION CHECKUP

1 What questions would a skeptical scientist ask someone who claimed to have psychokinetic powers?

2 What is meant by the "95 percent confidence" test in parapsychological research?

3 Describe the controls used in a double-blind test of a subject's clairvoyant powers.

LOOKING BACK: A SUMMARY

1   People who put their faith in divination, ESP, channeling, and other parapsychological powers come from all walks of life. The following reasons help explain their beliefs: (1) People are searching for fulfillment in a cold, impersonal world they feel powerless to control. (2) People are looking for easy answers to hard questions. (3) People turn to magical beliefs as a way of seeking

reassurance. (4) There are profits to be made from the ongoing interest in the supernatural.

2   Dependence on mystical, psychic beliefs can lead people to forfeit responsibility for their own lives. A search for answers written "in the stars" or elsewhere can lead to development of a "loser's personality." Losers depend on luck and magic and often end up as victims. People who make their own decisions and take responsibility for their failures and successes have a good chance to become winners.

3 Pseudosciences (beliefs that claim to have a factual foundation for their existence) have existed since the dawn of human cultures. Divination, the art of foretelling the future, still attracts followers eager to know what lies ahead. Two popular methods of divination are the tarot cards and the *I Ching*. The symbols on the tarot cards are believed to represent the basic life forces, and the fall of the cards is said to forecast the questioner's fortune. The *I Ching*, an ancient Chinese book of proverbs and advice, bases its divinatory wisdom on the random selection of one of 64 hexagrams. As with most forms of divination, the success of the reading usually depends upon the diviner's ability to interpret the reactions of the questioner.

4 Other pseudosciences attempt to provide personal insights. According to believers in astrology, each person's life is influenced by the position of the heavenly bodies at the moment of birth. In palmistry, the shape, lines, and mounts of the hand are thought to give clues to a person's past, present, and future life. Numerologists use "magic numbers" based on names and birthdates to identify personality traits and provide guidance for making decisions.

5 Spiritualists claim they can communicate with the dead. Once contact has been established, they believe that messages can be exchanged with the spirit world. Despite the total lack of evidence supporting such beliefs, some people still turn to spiritualism when they cannot cope with the death of loved ones. Some followers of New Age philosophies seek advice from entities from other worlds who communicate through psychics known as channelers. The New Age movement itself embraces a wide variety of beliefs, each of which promises to help the individual achieve some sort of personal transformation.

6 Several pseudosciences have attempted to apply scientific principles to the age-old quest for knowledge and power. Believers in pyramidology use the pyramid shape to sharpen razor blades, mummify raw meat, and generally improve their lives. Graphologists study handwriting as a way of gaining insight into an individual's personality and emotional states. Alone among the pseudosciences, graphology has gained some status for its apparent ability to analyze the writer's personal strengths and weaknesses.

7 The search for self-fulfillment has led many people to Eastern (Asian) beliefs. These philosophies stress meditation and inner harmony. Zen Buddhism, for example, teaches that human beings can reach true self-knowledge and peace (enlightenment) through strict mental discipline. Serious followers of Zen must devote their lives to practicing its teachings, but anyone who is capable of self-discipline can learn and use its basic principles.

8 Yoga promotes physical, mental, and spiritual growth through exercise and meditation. Most Westerners practice only the yoga exercises, which help develop good posture and body control. Transcendental Meditation (TM) concentrates on meditation techniques. TM claims to reduce stress, improve health, and increase enjoyment. The religious and commercial aspects of TM have caused controversy, but the movement still has many adherents.

9 Parapsychology, which includes ESP and PK, is the scientific study of forces outside the boundaries of natural law. Research in this field has grown rapidly since it first began in the 1800s. Telepathy is the ability to exchange ideas with another person without using the normal methods of communication. Clairvoyance is the ability to "see" objects or events outside the range of one's own senses. A psychic who "reads" the thoughts of a person in another room is using telepathy. But if the same psychic identifies a criminal by touching the victim's clothing, that's clairvoyance.

10 Precognition is the ability to look into the future to predict events that have not yet happened. Psychologists believe that most precognitive experiences are really messages from the unconscious. Psychokinesis, unlike the three ESP abilities, works on physical objects. Someone with psychokinetic power would be able to move or influence such things as dice, pencils, compass needles, and the like. As with all paranormal powers, PK seems to fail more frequently than it works.

11 The human body is surrounded by an energy field that is known as the *aura*. The aura has long been described by psychics, but today a technique known as Kirlian pho-tography can take pictures of it. Little is known about the aura, except that it seems to reflect the health of the individual and is found only around living matter.

12 Research in parapsychology often fails to meet the test of scientific validity because results are inconsistent and experiments poorly run. Observers should ask such questions as: (a) Does the event seem valid because people want to believe it? (b) Can the researchers be trusted? (c) Have the data been properly handled and interpreted? (d) Does a cause-and-effect relationship really exist? Before any psychic event can be considered valid, it must meet the test of "95 percent confidence." This test means that the odds are better than 20 to 1 that it could not have happened accidentally or by chance. (e) Finally, does the event make sense when examined in the light of known information about the universe?

PUTTING YOUR KNOWLEDGE TO WORK

■ TERMS YOU SHOULD KNOW

astrology	*I Ching*	pseudosciences
aura	meditation	psychic powers
channeler	medium	psychokinesis (PK)
clairvoyance	New Age movement	pyramidology
crystal	95 percent confidence	spiritualism
divination	numerology	tarot cards
dowser	palmistry	telepathy
extrasensory perception (ESP)	parapsychology	Transcendental Meditation (TM)
graphology	poltergeist	yoga
healing	precognition	Zen Buddhism

■ CHAPTER CHECKUP

1 A psychic's ability to reproduce pictures drawn by someone in another room is called (*a*) precognition (*b*) psychokinesis (*c*) telepathy (*d*) divination.

2 Roxy C. never makes a major decision without first consulting a palm reader. Which of the following reasons best explains Roxy's dependence on palmistry? (*a*) The accuracy and dependability of palmistry have been scientifically proved. (*b*) Depending on a palm reader is much the same as asking a psychologist or minister for advice. (*c*) Everyone believes in some form of magical power.

(*d*) People who rely on a magical power outside themselves feel that they don't have to take responsibility for their decisions.

3 John G. believes in psychic powers. If he wants to find out what his girlfriend will say when he asks her to marry him, he would most likely consult a (*a*) dowser (*b*) person with psychokinetic powers (*c*) tarot reader (*d*) pyramidologist.

4 Amos wants to make contact with his dead father so he can ask forgiveness for not visiting him before he died. He'll be tempted to visit (*a*) a spiritualist (*b*) an astrologer (*c*) a graphologist (*d*) a psychic with clairvoyant powers.

5 A New Ager who believes in crystal power would *not* program a crystal to (*a*) reduce stress (*b*) cast a horoscope (*c*) enhance creativity (*d*) awaken the psychic senses.

6 Research in parapsychology is complicated by the fact that (*a*) no capable scientists are working in the field (*b*) psychics cannot control their powers, and experiments cannot always be duplicated (*c*) the public has no interest in paranormal happenings (*d*) research in parapsychology did not start until the 1980s.

7 A psychic who tells police where to find a lost child after touching the youngster's favorite toys is practicing (*a*) telepathy (*b*) precognition (*c*) clairvoyance (*d*) spiritualism.

8 If Sara tells you she has forgotten her mantra, you know that she has been learning (*a*) the *I Ching* (*b*) astrology (*c*) yoga (*d*) Transcendental Meditation.

9 If an experiment in telepathy scored 200 "hits" out of 1,000 trials with the Zener cards, the results would be called (*a*) a successful proof of possible telepathic powers (*b*) incredible, since no one has ever scored that high (*c*) a failure, since the score did not exceed that expected under the laws of chance (*d*) certain proof that telepathy doesn't exist; no further tests should be made.

10 Which of the following steps would invalidate an experiment in clairvoyance? (*a*) The test giver stays in a room well separated from the test taker. (*b*) The Zener cards are randomly shuffled and sealed by a machine. (*c*) The test giver turns each card over and records the symbol during the test. (*d*) All results are delivered to the experimenter before the test giver and the test taker meet to check scores.

■ EXPLORING CONCEPTS

1 Why do psychologists say that reliance on supernatural beliefs can lead to the development of negative personality characteristics?

2 Describe the differences among the tarot, astrology, and graphology. Which comes closest to providing valid insights into personality? Why?

3 Why do the fields of parapsychology and the pseudosciences attract so many fakes? If you were introduced to someone who claimed psychic powers, what questions would you ask to prove or disprove those claims?

4 Why is meditation so important to Eastern beliefs? What can Eastern philosophies add to Western life-styles?

5 Assume that your psychology teacher has asked you to set up an experiment in telepathy. Describe the steps you would take in designing an experiment that provides proper safeguards against cheating, either deliberate or inadvertent.

■ HANDS-ON ACTIVITIES

1 How common is belief in parapsychology and the supernatural in your community? Survey a cross section of people to find out. Ask them about their beliefs in any form of parapsychology or the supernatural and whether or not they have had any personal psychic experiences. Write up the results in a paper to share with your psychology class.

2 Use the directions printed on page 487 at the beginning of Section 14.4 to make a set of Zener cards. Test a number of people for telepathic powers. Ask a friend to be the sender so that you can monitor the test and keep records. Most scores will cluster around 5 right guesses out of 25, but you may get a few who exceed 8 or 10. If you do, retest those people to see if they can demonstrate their "power" consistently. When you've finished, examine your data and draw a conclusion from the results.

3 If you're interested in carrying your psychic experiments a little further, here are some other tests you can run:

(a) Test the claims of pyramidology. Make a pyramid (see the feature on page 483) and run controlled experiments with razor blades, seeds, raw meat, or whatever.

(b) Check out a book about numerology from the library. After reading the simple instructions, calculate the "name numbers" for some of your friends. Do the personality characteristics attributed to each number correlate with what you know of their personalities? How accurate is your own number?

(c) If you find someone in your neighborhood who does tarot readings, *I Ching*, or any other form of divination, ask for a test reading. Be prepared with specific questions the diviner could not possibly answer based on prior knowledge of you and your family. Remember that there's a tendency to forget the wrong guesses and to remember only those insights that seem accurate. Evaluate the reading in a report to your psychology class.

(d) Pick up a book on handwriting analysis and study the basic techniques. Ask a friend to gather some handwriting samples and to code them so as to conceal the names of the writers. Analyze the samples. Then check with your friend to determine how well your readings match the actual personalities of the subjects.

4 Watch a current TV program (*Crossing Over,* perhaps) that features psychic phenomena. Could the program stand up to rigorous scientific investigation? Why or why not?

5 If you've never meditated, why not give it a try? You don't have to join TM. Just use the meditation techniques described on page 485. If you want more detailed instructions, check out Herbert Benson's updated guidebook, *The Relaxation Response* (2000). Don't expect instant results— it may take a week or two to learn how to screen out the distracting "noise" that hovers around and inside your head.

FOR FURTHER READING

Alcock, James, et al. *Psi Wars: Getting to Grips with the Paranormal.* Exeter, UK: Imprint Academic, 2003. Like the public, the scientific world divides into skeptics and true believers when called on to evaluate the claims made for parapsychology (*psi* for short). This collection of essays gives both sides a fair hearing, although Alcock's own essay, "Reasons to Remain Doubtful," suggests that the authors take their stand with psi's skeptics.

Broughton, Richard S. *Parapsychology: The Controversial Science.* New York: Ballantine Books, 1991. Dr. Broughton's highly readable and well-documented book "maps the territory" for anyone interested in the scientific study of parapsychology. He describes the personalities who work in this field and the experiments they conduct. Despite our inability to explain the "how" of paranormal experience, he concludes, researchers are obtaining results that cannot be ignored.

Eysenck, Hans, and Carl Sargent. *Are You Psychic? Tests and Games to Measure Your Powers.* London: Prion Books, 1997. Best known for his writings on intelligence, Eysenck's interests also extend to the paranormal. You don't have to be hooked on psychic phenomena to have fun measuring your ESP powers (or lack of same) with this collection of over 30 tests, games, and experiments.

Guiley, Rosemary Ellen. *Harper's Encyclopedia of Mystical & Paranormal Experience.* New York: HarperCollins, 1994. This 666-page paperback may well be the best single-volume reference book available on parapsychology and mysticism. All of the major personalities, movements, beliefs, and phenomena appear in over 500 cross-referenced entries.

Randles, Jenny, and Peter Hough. *Psychic Detectives: The Mysterious Use of Paranormal Phenomena in Solving True Crimes.* Pleasantville, NY: Reader's Digest, 2001. This fascinating book explores the work of psychic detectives—clairvoyants who use their paranormal powers to help the police catch criminals who might otherwise go unpunished. As a bonus, the authors discuss such puzzling phenomena as poltergeists and spontaneous combustion.

Whitworth, Belinda. *New Age Encyclopedia: A Mind-Body-Spirit Reference Guide.* Franklin Lakes, NJ: Career Press, 2003. This homey guide puts everything you might want to know about the New Age movement at your fingertips. You'll find coverage of topics as diverse as herbal medicine, acupuncture, numerology, spirit guides, and alternative childbirth. If you want to dig further into a topic, Whitworth also provides lists of addresses, Websites, and suggestions for further reading.

Chapter
15 SEARCHING FOR NEW WAYS TO GROW

Almost every industry sponsors weekend "shows" as a way of introducing new products to the public. Perhaps you've been to a boat show or a home fair. Now, how about spending an afternoon at a psychology fair? Step right this way. The banner over the arena entrance spells outs the theme: PSYCHOLOGY— NEW DIRECTIONS FOR A NEW MILLENNIUM.

There's the main exhibit hall on the right. Banners wave above row upon row of colorful booths. Salespeople greet you with big, sincere smiles and stuff your carryall with their literature. If this were a county fair, they'd be selling hot tubs and stain removers. Instead, they're pushing new life-styles. They're convinced that they know how to make you a healthier, happier, and more productive individual.

Here's a promising looking booth, sponsored by the Institute of Core Energetics. The pitch gets right to the point: the institute will help you resolve emotional problems by using creative self-expression and the uncovering of your Life Task to bring love and joy into your life. "Change your energy, change your life," CE's brochure advises. Moving on, you pass signs for a number of self-help groups. One offers a parenting workshop, a second invites you to join Overeaters Anonymous, and a third teaches life-management skills.

Across the aisle, a white-haired woman waves a friendly greeting. "Please join us at our mountain retreat for our Spring Celebration of the Inner Self," she says. "We'll cleanse our systems with herbal remedies and sleep under the stars on Japanese futons." She waves a brochure under your nose. "Our instructors will help you overcome the psychic barriers that keep you from enjoying life to the fullest," she promises.

You escape to a booth that features a flight simulator. A young man wearing a flight helmet is seated in the cockpit. An image of an enemy fighter plane appears on the television screen in front of him. As you watch, the simulator banks sharply to the left, levels off, and then banks to the right. What's going on? The pilot isn't touching the controls! An elderly man steps forward to explain. "Todd doesn't have to touch the joystick," he says. "He's flying the simulator by mind control—a technique called biofeedback. Electrodes inside the helmet feed his brain waves into a light display. To 'fly' the simulator, he simply changes the strength of his brain waves."

Flying a plane by mind control sounds like something out of *Star Wars*. You're still thinking about science fiction when you stop to read a hand-lettered sign. "Have you been abducted by aliens?" the sign asks. "Do you

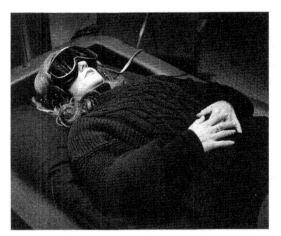

FIGURE 15.1 ■ Technology has made possible the creation of new devices to help one relax—controlled movement of waterbeds, electronically produced sounds, and engineered color galaxies. All of these devices are designed to blot out the stresses of modern life. What is your favorite way to soothe your jangling nerves?

despair that no one believes you? Join our support group." A middle-aged couple offer to show you the scars left by the instruments of the aliens who kidnapped them. "Isn't this a very small group?" you ask. "Oh no," the man assures you. "UFO abductions and sightings occur every night all over the globe. You don't hear much about it because most people are afraid to talk about their experiences."

The auditorium is filling up for the day's lectures. You study the schedule. A well-known radio psychologist is going to speak on the value of summer camps that teach skills such as yoga and aikido. At a Cosmi-Kids camp, incense floats in the air as a boy recites a Hawaiian chant. Instead of playing rough-and-tumble sports, campers pursue inner peace by meditating. Next up is a cancer specialist who uses guided imagery to control pain. She teaches her patients to "give" their pain to fantasy animals that "live" in their heads. As she steps down, a certified

Life Coach takes her place. Life coaches, he explains, "coach" their clients through everyday challenges, whether it's coping with anxiety, losing weight, or finding a prom date.

Ready for a snack? While you're enjoying a glass of organically grown grape juice, a fast-talking teenager gives you an acupressure demonstration. Pressing hard at the proper spot at the top of the thigh, you learn, can relieve backache pain. Tension headaches yield to pressure on a point that lies at the center of the eyebrow.

Anxious to complete your tour, you wander to a booth that has a banner inviting you to transform your energy with VibraSound. A friendly young man talks you into lying down on what looks like a high-tech waterbed. As he fits you with headphones and goggles, he talks about finding health, inner peace, and personal growth with this "potent healing technology." You lie back as soothing music fills your ears and the goggles flash a galaxy of colored lights before your eyes. The waterbed thrums and vibrates with the music. The effect is soothing and energizing at the same time.

When the VibraSound session ends, you inquire about the cost—and walk quickly on. You pass booths inviting you to learn about feng shui, ecopsychology, holistic healing, and Transactional Analysis. The names begin to run together. It's time to leave. But before you go, you buy a pair of highly polished Ying-Yang Health Spheres. A Chinese man with a wispy white beard tells you that rotating the metal balls in the palm of your hand will stimulate the acupuncture points.

Later, as you walk home, you try to make sense of it all. What would Freud and Jung think of these highly nontraditional approaches to solving emotional problems? The answer comes to you in the click of your Ying-Yang Spheres. If far-out ideas like MindGyms and UFO support groups can help people cope with the challenges of life in the new millennium, why not let a thousand flowers bloom? You find tht you're looking forward to learning more about these "new ways to grow."

15.1 Why are so many people searching for new ways to grow?

15.2 How do bodywork techniques help people?

15.3 Can people attain personal growth through control of their minds and bodies?

15.4 Which therapies combine self-realization techniques with traditional psychotherapy?

15.5 How can Transactional Analysis help people stay in the "OK" position?

15.1 ■ WHY ARE SO MANY PEOPLE SEARCHING FOR NEW WAYS TO GROW?

You don't have to visit a psychology fair to realize that people are searching for the missing pieces of their lives. Almost everywhere you turn you'll find a new self-help book, a recovery group, or a self-realization experience that promises improved emotional health. Each is focused on the fact that our communities are littered with the walking wounded—people of all ages and ethnic groups, whose ability to enjoy life has been short-circuited by emotional hangups.

Scientists, psychologists, doctors, religious leaders, and other experts on human behavior have been trying to help. When traditional therapies proved too slow and too expensive, they experimented with shortcuts or developed new systems. This attempt to help people take control of their lives is sometimes called the *self-realization movement (SRM)*. To be sure, the movement receives little support from mainstream therapists. It survives and prospers because people tell their friends that someone or something has restored their ability to feel good about their lives. In an age of increasing anxiety, the promise of self-actualization finds ever more willing listeners.

THE LONELINESS OF THE TIMES

Many people who join a self-realization program are like 20-year-old Sam M. Sam's not emotionally ill. Most of the time he functions quite well. More and more, however, he's been feeling vaguely depressed and anxious. He isn't sure his life has any meaning, and he feels cut off from his family and friends. Sam believes that he should be able to enjoy life more, to feel self-fulfilled. As he complains to his girlfriend, "I know it's a Kodacolor world out there, but all I can see are shades of gray."

No two people seek out a self-realization experience for the same reason. Sam wants self-fulfillment, but Jean A. is trying to overcome angry feelings about her divorce. Here's a list of the reasons people give for joining an SRM program.

1. "I can cope with a tornado or an earthquake, but I fall apart when the kids spill their milk." Small annoyances and everyday conflicts leave some people upset or depressed. Life turns into an endless struggle against overwhelming odds.

2. "No matter how hard I try, I can't build a lasting relationship." People who feel this way are lonely much of the time. They have never learned how to build a friendship or how to experience love. In many cases, the family structure that once insulated people from this type of loneliness cannot survive long-distance moves, divorce, and the other ills of modern society.

3. "I'm bored with my life. Nothing exciting ever happens to me." The small pleasures

Berry's World

"Quick! Where are the self-help books?"

FIGURE 15.2 ▧ Many self-help books promise instant "cures" for emotional problems. What advice do you think the salesclerk should give this man?

of life escape many people. They may find temporary release in sexual promiscuity, drugs, or high-risk sports, but the excitement usually turns out to be both short-lived and unhealthy.

4. "Even when my life is going well, I feel as though it can't last. I know I'm doomed." Anxiety and stress overshadow every relationship and activity these fear-driven people attempt.

5. "Suddenly I'm afraid to go outside. I never felt like that before." Phobic fears cripple some people's ability to enjoy life. As the fears increase, these people may lose their ability to carry on normal activities.

6. "I fail at everything I try. At the feast of life, I end up with the turkey neck." A lack of self-esteem can make it impossible for people to take charge of their lives. Because they doubt their abilities, they cannot stand up for their rights.

7. "I'm obsessed by thoughts of food (or exercise, or guns, or . . .)." People suffering from an enormous variety of obsessive or addictive behaviors need help in learning to treat their bodies with respect. There's even a Trichotillomania Support Network (for people who pull their hair out, strand by strand).

8. "My life is pretty solid, but it could be better. I want to develop new abilities and resources." These people sense that even a good life can be improved. They see the self-realization movement as a step to help them move in that direction.

BASIC PRINCIPLES OF SELF-REALIZATION

The self-realization movement grew out of the chaotic decades of the Sixties and Seventies. Rebellions against the "establishment" in politics, the arts, and education led to a similar revolt against traditional psychotherapy. A new generation of Americans insisted that psychology focus on growth and self-awareness. In response, groups sprang to life on every side. Whatever their names or however outlandish their theories, self-realization programs tend to share a common set of beliefs. They are:

1. You *can* make contact with your true inner self. In doing so, you will discard the artificial social roles you've been conditioned to play.

2. You *can* learn to communicate honestly, openly, and intimately with others.

3. You *can* develop your full potential for growth.

4. You *can* benefit from taking part in self-realization experiences.

5. You *will* be happier and more productive as you rid yourself of old, self-defeating behaviors.

POSSIBLE DANGERS OF SRMS

What could be wrong with a system that promises you better health, vitality, and improved creativity? Such come-ons are common in the ads for some self-realization groups (see Figure 15.3). Most SRM programs will cost you money, and a few can do great damage to your mental or physical health. Poorly trained leaders can—and do—lose control of the powerful emotional forces set loose during group sessions.

Even for a basically healthy person, the SRM experience can backfire. Thirty-eight-year-old Reggie R., for example, was bored and restless. His success as a real estate salesman no longer gave him much satisfaction. On impulse, he joined an SRM group he heard about through a friend. The group leader believed that everyone should learn to express his or her "inner rage." At each group meeting, the members took turns shouting, screaming, and punching a foam-rubber dummy "to get the anger out." Reggie felt better, but his job still frustrated him. It seemed natural to release his tension by telling his clients and coworkers exactly what he thought of them. After a violent shouting match with his boss, Reggie was fired. The group had encouraged him to express his anger, but the leaders had failed to teach him to use it constructively.

Other people become chronic whiners, lose hope, and "drop out" of normal activities because their SRM program couldn't deliver its advertised miracles. Self-realization "junkies" move from one group to another, constantly searching for fresh experiences and easy answers. Perhaps all self-help and self-realization groups should carry a warning label: "Use with caution! If pain persists, see a therapist."

MIND CONTROL NOW!

Improve your mind, ensure success, and transform your life by using

PSI

Mind-Energy, Inc. presents a program of lessons to help you handle:

- Job Problems
- Marriage
- Creativity
- Vitality
- Bad Habits
- Sleep
- Drugs
- Smoking
- Weight
- Headaches

Learn to harness your mental and spiritual powers by using amazing mind-control techniques. Scientific research proves that these methods can work for YOU!

FREE INTRODUCTORY LECTURE

7:00 P.M. Friday, Feb. 6th
713 West 59th Street

Call 123-6673 for further information

FIGURE 15.3 ■ Do you think a PSI lecture can really accomplish all it promises? Why would people fall for such an obvious come-on?

■ SECTION CHECKUP

1 What are the basic goals of the self-realization movement?

2 List some of the reasons people give for turning to the SRM for help. Why would a basically healthy, well-adjusted person join an SRM program?

3 Can SRM programs cause harm? Give some examples.

15.2 ■ HOW DO BODYWORK TECHNIQUES HELP PEOPLE?

You already know that what happens in your mind can affect your body. If a friend breaks a promise, you're likely to feel a surge of anger. Angry feelings begin in your brain, but they also trigger changes in your heart rate, stomach activity, skin temperature, and metabolic rate.

Studies have shown that emotionally disturbed people often respond to misleading messages from their bodies. Poor sleep habits, tense muscles, and high metabolic rates can turn minor anxieties into crippling neurotic reactions. The same principle applies to otherwise healthy people. Janie M., for example, tenses her neck and shoulder muscles whenever her boss treats her unfairly. After a few months of this, Janie's muscles stay rigid much of the time. As a result, she *feels* upset even when she's on vacation.

Dr. Wilhelm Reich would have explained Janie's problem as a physical-emotional conflict that has lodged itself in her muscular tissue. He called this process the creation of "body armor." Although he was trained in Freud's "talking therapy," Reich turned to breathing exercises and physical manipulation to break down that armor. As in Asian medicine, his approach stressed that mind and body are one. Mental well-being and physical well-being, he taught, cannot be separated.

Reich's theories led to the development of therapies that treat emotional problems through bodywork—body movement and manipulation. After the individual does some exercises or receives a special massage, the "emotional knots" are supposed to disappear. To some degree, you can think of these bodywork therapies as working backward. They calm and relax the mind by tending to the needs of the body.

FELDENKRAIS METHOD

Moshe Feldenkrais, an Israeli physicist, taught a self-realization technique that dismisses traditional psychotherapy. In its place, the Feldenkrais method substitutes a thousand intricate movements and exercises, each with some 40 variations. All ages, including the elderly, seem to enjoy the movements. Many are taken from yoga, Eastern martial arts such as aikido and jujitsu, and the dances of India. Feldenkrais believed that his slow, intricate movements allow you to tap the power inside you by altering basic patterns of thinking and feeling.

Feldenkrais practitioners claim that their method is the least stressful of all types of bodywork. In the process known as Functional Integration, a practitioner creates awareness of the smallest units of movement by gently bending, twisting, or pushing the

FIGURE 15.4 ■ Reflexology, which originated in China, is growing in popularity despite the lack of hard evidence to support the claims of its practitioners. A reflexologist treats illness by massaging the feet. The massage is said to keep the life force in balance by unblocking the body's "clogged channels." Working on the big toe, for example, is said to relieve headaches.

■ **PRO & CON:**

Can Self-Realization Be Learned From a Book?

Americans are great on "do-it-yourself" projects. Look in any bookstore, and you'll find titles promising to teach you how to do everything from furniture refinishing to handling your own divorce. What about self-realization and self-help? Take your pick from hundreds of titles. But can these "pop psychology" texts really help you?

PRO

1 Psychotherapists have limited time and can see only a few patients. Self-help books make their insights available to the general public.

2 Self-help books provide valuable insights. When people read these works, they realize they are not alone and that help is available.

3 Reading a self-help book can lead disturbed people to admit that they need help. The easy-to-follow advice given in most books is almost certain to lead to some psychological growth.

4 Most people cannot afford the services of a therapist or cannot bring themselves to ask for help. Reading a book may not be a perfect solution, but self-knowledge gained in this way can be a useful step toward building a better life.

CON

1 The most important therapists seldom write for the general public. Many of the pop psych books are written by people with limited qualifications.

2 The people who most need help will not or cannot profit from reading self-help books. Without the guidance of a therapist, the few insights they gain are quickly lost.

3 Most self-help books don't deliver what they promise. Too many offer shortcuts that leave a person's deeper emotional problems untouched. Readers seldom make the life-changing commitments necessary for true growth.

4 Mental health care is available to everyone. Public agencies provide help for those who cannot afford private therapy. People who won't admit that they need therapy are unlikely to change because a self-help book says they should.

The popularity of self-help books suggests that many people agree with the Pro side of this argument. What do you think? If you've never looked at a book of this type, here are several useful titles: John-Roger and Peter McWilliams, *Life 101;* David Niven, *100 Simple Secrets of Great Relationships;* John Powell, *Why Am I Afraid to Tell You Who I Am?;* Michael Westham, *Self-Psyching.*

various parts of the body. The movements help make the individual aware of the body's resistances and limitations. Feldenkrais groups are more likely to be seen practicing Awareness Through Movement. These are the intricate, slow-moving exercises that reproduce and reinforce the hands-on work performed during Functional Integration.

"The body only executes what the nervous system makes it do," Feldenkrais told his students. He warned that people are prisoners of bad habits learned while they are growing up. His exercises are designed to break those habits. His followers claim that as their posture and flexibility improve, their personal awareness and contentment also increase. Therapists have used the Feldenkrais method to treat diseases of the nervous system such as multiple sclerosis and to combat the effects of aging.

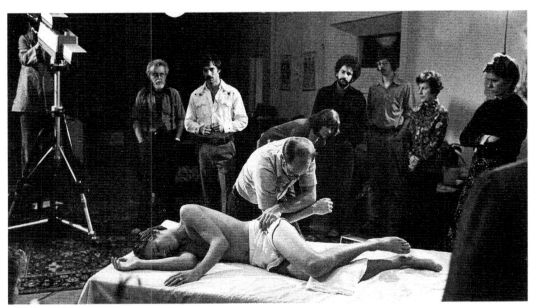

FIGURE 15.5 ▪ A demonstration of rolfing, deep muscular manipulation and massage, is being filmed. Would you be willing to undergo a fair amount of pain in order to "feel physically lighter and emotionally stronger"?

STRUCTURAL INTEGRATION (ROLFING)

Dr. Ida Rolf, a biochemist and physiologist, believed that people's bodies are damaged and thrown out of alignment by painful emotional experiences. Like a car that has been rear-ended, the body still moves, but in a draggy, awkward way. To counter this condition, Dr. Rolf designed a program of deep muscular manipulation and massage that she called *structural integration. Rolfing*, as it is more commonly known, calls for the therapist to use fingers, knuckles, and elbows to probe deeply into the patient's rigid, contracted muscles.

Rolfing theory states that the ten one-hour sessions release damaging emotional memories by relaxing and stretching muscles and tendons. The rolfing experience itself can be quite painful, for the rolfer-therapist's fingers dig into the body's soft tissue without mercy. Dr. Rolf felt that the pain is a necessary part of the process of overcoming resistance from tense, knotted muscles. The final three sessions concentrate on revising the body's posture so that it again moves in tune with the natural forces of gravity.

As they complete their bodywork, rolfing patients say they feel physically lighter and emotionally stronger. As Leslie D. reports, "I can't deny that it was painful, but I can't dispute the fact that I felt a release of a lot of my tensions after the first four sessions." Other patients claim better posture, increased sensations of happiness, and improved confidence in dealing with problems. Because rolfing apparently produces more fluid physical movements, athletes sometimes "get rolfed" in hopes of improving their performance during a competition.

Like most bodywork techniques, rolfing has drawn its share of criticism. Traditional psychologists fault the method for being too passive. By focusing on the purely physical, they say, emotional hangups go unattended. As a result, the positive changes reported by rolfing clients tend to disappear over time.

The Rolf Institute challenged that assumption with a study conducted by two university doctors. The study showed that rolfing does produce a definite improvement in muscular functioning. Its ability to provide long-term emotional improvement is still a question that has not been fully answered.

BIOENERGETIC ANALYSIS

Almost everyone has something to "kick about," says Dr. Alexander Lowen, a former psychoanalyst. In his approach to therapy, called *bioenergetic analysis*, Dr. Lowen encourages his patients to come to grips with repressed feelings by literally kicking and punching them into the open. Bioenergetic sessions also include exercises that alert people to their rigid body postures and help them release repressed feelings. Dr. Lowen believes that increased ease of movement and muscle control will increase one's self-awareness.

At a bioenergetic session, people stretch, twist, move, kick, and even scream. As patients lose themselves in these movements and postures, they say they sometimes feel intense sensations of release, "like a balloon suddenly cut loose from its anchor." Some people vividly relive the moments when they adopted the stooped, crooked body postures that Dr. Lowen thinks cover up strong, honest emotions. You may have seen a child, for example, cower in fear when scolded by an angry parent. Dr. Lowen feels that such postures become part of a person's body armor. As he tells his patients, "You are your body—let it express itself freely and openly."

Lowen is not the only practitioner in this field. Trained in music, bodywork, and Gestalt psychology, Ilana Rubenfeld conducts workshops that combine bioenergetic-like techniques with methods and movements she learned from Fritz Perls and Moshe Feldenkrais. "I treat the psychophysical problems people carry around in their beings," she says. "The physical body is highly sensitive to all kinds of feelings which create distress and often manifest as disease. If you deal with the emotional body, then symptoms often abate."

Along with gentle touch and movement, Rubenfeld leads participants through exercises in visualization, breathing, humor, and Gestalt verbal expression. She expects her students to leave with two gifts: an enhanced physical and emotional well-being, coupled with the ability to release and resolve emotional conflicts in their daily lives. This active awareness, she says, is the cornerstone of self-healing.

USEFULNESS OF BODY THERAPY

You've probably discovered for yourself that vigorous physical activity can make you feel better when you're tense or upset. Some people jog, while others punch a pillow or slam a tennis ball as hard as they can. Moshe Feldenkrais, Ida Rolf, Alexander Lowen, and Ilana Rubenfeld based their therapies on that insight. They saw emotional stress reflected in the way people sit, stand, walk, and run. Why not remove that stress by releasing the individual's creative energies in a natural, physical way? Bodywork's critics do not disagree with these insights, but they caution that all emotional ills cannot be treated alike. Releasing repressed emotions feels wonderful, they agree. It's how the system teaches the client to deal with those newly released emotions that makes for lasting growth.

▪ SECTION CHECKUP

1 What is the basic theory behind the bodywork therapies?

2 Contrast the Feldenkrais method with structural integration (rolfing).

3 Why does bioenergetic analysis require patients to kick, stretch, twist, move, and scream? What seems to happen when patients "free" themselves of the emotions they have kept bottled up?

15.3 ▪ CAN PEOPLE ATTAIN PERSONAL GROWTH THROUGH CONTROL OF THEIR MINDS AND BODIES?

As a member of today's human race, you can expect to grow taller and live longer than did your ancestors. Human mental processes, however, haven't changed very much. Perception, observation, and logical thought work pretty much as they did 80,000 generations ago. More and more scientists, psychologists, and other experts, however, believe that the powers of the mind can be greatly expanded.

These researchers ask that people open their eyes to evidence that traditional scientific attitudes tend to ignore. Why dismiss as a "trick," for example, the Amazon native who walks unharmed across a bed of broken glass? A related "trick" called biofeedback lets college students control their natural anxiety before a big exam.

Another behavioral technique, assertiveness training, can turn a shy, timid person into a strong-willed individual without months of costly therapy. And then there's the softball player who uses a mental "trick" called psychocybernetics to "pitch" a complete game without leaving the living room. Does that have anything to do with her championship performance the next day?

All of these cases have one thing in common: According to the laws of traditional psychology, they shouldn't happen. But they do.

BIOFEEDBACK

Would you like to be able to control your blood pressure? Stop the pain of a headache? Cure insomnia? *Biofeedback* training can accomplish these apparent miracles.

Yogis and other mystics long ago proved that the mind can control almost any involuntary body function. Yogis, for example, can reduce their heart rate and other autonomic body processes to almost zero. This ability allows them to stay alive for hours in sealed coffins. Biofeedback, however, shortcuts the years of meditation and study required by Eastern disciplines. The process involves three steps.

1. Biofeedback devices have been developed that can monitor any specific biological system, from brain waves to muscle tension. Let's assume that you have developed high blood pressure. As part of your treatment a biofeedback therapist will hook you to a machine that monitors changes in blood pressure. The machine's job is to display the data sent by the pressure cuff on your arm as flashing red and green lights on a control panel.

2. The therapist asks you to sit in a relaxed position, watching the lights. A red light means your blood pressure is too high; a green light signals that the pressure has decreased. Your job is quite simple: keep the green light on as much of the time as possible. Biofeedback experts can't describe exactly how this process works. They do know if you are given exact data on what's happening to a particular body function, your mind can learn to control that function. Some researchers use a basketball analogy to explain biofeedback. It would be almost impossible, they say, to learn to shoot free throws blindfolded. Except for the general sounds of the ball hitting the rim and backboard, you'd have no feedback to help you correct your aim. But what if someone stood next to you and told you exactly where your shots were going? Armed with that feedback, you could begin to make the necessary adjustments.

Now, how are you doing with your blood pressure? After you've worked with the feedback device a few times, you should be able to keep the green light on most of the time.

3. Once you've mastered the technique, you'll be able to control your blood pressure without the feedback from the machine. True, you won't be able to tell someone else *how* to do it, but *you* can do it. In biofeedback, it's the results that count.

CONTROL OF BRAIN WAVES. Early biofeedback experiments centered on the control of brain waves. These waves result from the electrical activity of the brain during wakefulness. The basic waves, as measured on an EEG machine, are called alpha, beta, and

BRAIN WAVES AND EMOTION: THE ELECTRICAL ACTIVITY OF THE BRAIN RELATES TO HOW YOU FEEL

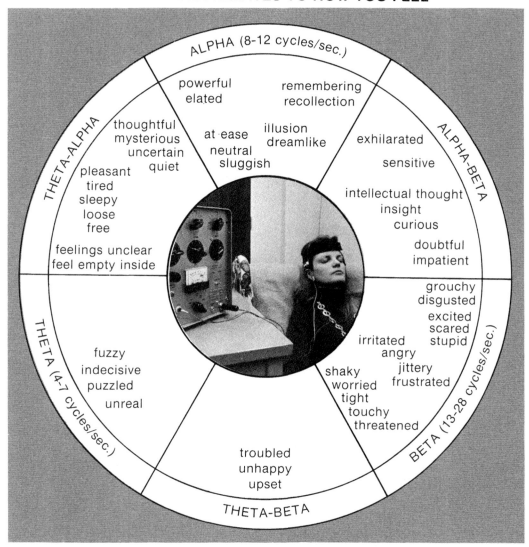

FIGURE 15.6 ▓ Feeling states can be related to specific brain-wave activity. What type of brain wave do you think you're producing right now? How does biofeedback train you to produce alpha waves on command?

theta. (Delta waves occur only during deep sleep.) All three brain waves are present during your waking moments, but what you're doing or thinking generally determines which wave type dominates (see Figure 15.6). Biofeedback-trained subjects quickly learn to produce alpha waves—the same type of brain waves produced by Zen monks during meditation. Researchers believe that switching into an alpha state helps you relax and prepare for a period of creative thought.

MEDICAL USES OF BIOFEEDBACK. Doctors now use biofeedback to treat chronic illnesses such as asthma, lower-back pain, migraine headaches, epilepsy, and high blood pressure. Migraine sufferers, for example, are trained to raise the temperature of their hands at the first sign of an approaching migraine. Diverting a heavy flow of blood into the hands seems to prevent or ease the excruciating pain. The same technique works well with amputees who suffer from "phantom limb" pain. Teenagers who suffer from scoliosis were once forced to wear a bulky harness designed to straighten their curved spines. Enrique's scoliosis, however, is being treated with a new device called Micro Straight. Instead of the harness, he straps a web of wires around his back. Whenever he slouches, Micro Straight beeps softly, reminding Enrique to stand up straight.

Much of this medical therapy is based on the estimate that up to 75 percent of the problems a doctor sees relate back to the patient's emotional state. If the mind can make you ill, the reasoning goes, why shouldn't biofeedback be used to help the mind cure what it originally caused? Perhaps one day the lights and buzzers of biofeedback trainers will replace tranquilizers, painkillers, and other medications. Doctors and patients alike would consider that a fair trade. After treating her frequent migraines with biofeedback training, 12-year-old Katie K. agrees that the technique has reduced the frequency and se-verity of the headaches. She has only one complaint. The training sessions, she says, are boring.

ASSERTIVENESS TRAINING (AT)

How often have you backed down when someone—a parent, friend, teacher, or sales-clerk—refused to give you what you felt was rightfully yours? It might have been only a promised favor or a place in line, but you probably felt frustrated when it happened. Many people run into such problems, back away from them, and gradually learn to think of themselves as inadequate. Psychologists call such reactions *nonassertive behavior.* They know that along with feelings of depression and inadequacy, nonassertive behavior can lead to an actual physical illness, such as ulcers.

Assertiveness training (AT) starts with the idea that everyone has the capacity to change nonassertive behavior. Many people, however, have never learned the skills that an assertive person seems to use instinctively: persistence, reasonable compromise, rejection of unreal fears, and the ability to communicate needs to others. Assertiveness should not be confused with aggressiveness. Aggressive people impose their will on others, often for selfish reasons. Assertive people know how to deal with frustration without losing either their temper or their self-respect.

USING AT IN CONSUMER SITUATIONS. Imagine for a moment that you have returned a defective CD to a music store. The clerk, however, refuses to give you a refund. Four basic AT skills will help you assert your rights as a customer.

1. *Broken record:* calm, persistent repetition of your position. The nonassertive person asks for something once, then gives up.

CLERK: It's not our policy to give refunds on discounted CDs.

YOU: I understand, but the disk is defective, and I want my money back.

CLERK: I can't do that. It's against policy. See the sign over there on the wall?

YOU: Yes, but I want my money back. [You will repeat this without anger or impatience until the clerk makes the refund or calls for someone who has the authority to do so.]

2. *Fogging:* acceptance of criticism without becoming anxious or defensive. Criticism usually deflects people from their goal. AT teaches you to guard against that.

CLERK: Look, the packaging is torn.

YOU: That's right, it is.

CLERK: And you're holding up the other customers.

YOU: Yes, I know. As soon as you give me my money back, I'll be out of their way.

3. *Negative assertion:* acceptance of one's faults or errors through agreement with the criticism.

CLERK: Where's your receipt?

YOU: I didn't save it.

CLERK: Well! How can you expect a refund when you don't have a receipt!

YOU: You're right, that was a dumb thing to do. But I still want my money back.

4. *Workable compromise:* bargaining for a reasonable solution to a disagreement (but only when your own self-worth is not directly involved).

CLERK: Don't you understand? We never give cash refunds!

YOU: Well, I'd rather have my money back, but I'll settle for a new CD of equal value.

CLERK: All right! Go pick one out.

YOU: Thanks for your help.

SINGLE SLICES By Peter Kohlsaat

When the going gets tough, the tough get going!

For $80 an hour Bernie expected more.

FIGURE 15.7 ▓ Bernie, it appears, could profit from some assertiveness training. AT would equip him with the nonconfrontational techniques he needs to keep his counselor focused on the task at hand.

USING AT IN SOCIAL SITUATIONS. Other AT skills lend themselves more readily to social situations. Many conversations die because neither person works hard enough to keep communication going. To prevent this, you can use the AT technique of *free information.* You keep the conversational ball bouncing by throwing interesting items into the discussion that you know will appeal to the other person. Another AT technique for improving a relationship is called *self-disclosure.* Most people wait for others to guess how they feel. AT helps you move quickly into deeper areas of communication by expressing your feelings openly and with honesty.

Finally, *negative inquiry* requires that you encourage others to criticize you. This gives you a chance to take advantage of the criticism (if helpful) or to exhaust it (if negative). AT experts believe that practicing these techniques will quickly improve your ability to deal with whomever you meet—whether you're at home, at school, at work, or at a party.

PSYCHOCYBERNETICS

Dr. Maxwell Maltz started his career as a plastic surgeon. He soon realized that his surgery opened up new lives for some patients but left others just as unhappy as before. Maltz concluded that people make their own success or failure. He invented the term *psychocybernetics* to describe the mechanism that creates this positive or negative self-image. In psychocybernetics, the subconscious controls an integrated system made up of the brain, the nervous system, and the mind. This "creative mechanism," as Dr. Maltz calls it, takes in information, processes it, and acts upon it. If you feed negative information into your creative mechanism, you will be geared for failure. "I'm going to fail; I can't do algebra," moans Perry—and promptly fails his test. But feed in positive information and your creative mechanism will ensure success. "I know I can win this race," thinks Angela—and she goes out and runs her opponents into the ground.

Research studies later showed that psychocybernetics depends on the powers of the right hemisphere of the brain (see pages 67– 68). Lacking that insight, Dr. Maltz put his faith in "the power of positive thinking." His book suggests that you set a goal for every day and do everything you can to reach that goal. If you fail, get a good night's sleep and set a new goal tomorrow. Self-doubt, lack of faith, and destructive behaviors (mainly left-brain thinking) must be set aside. A key exercise directs you to spend 30 minutes alone every day. During this time you are told to concentrate on building a better self-image by visualizing yourself succeeding in whatever is important to you.

Imagine that you're about to go out on a job interview, for example. Dr. Maltz would tell you to "rehearse" the interview in your mind, moment by moment. Imagine what questions you might be asked, and practice answering them. Visualize the way you'll walk into the office, how you'll greet the interviewer, and what you'll do with your hands. This rehearsal will give you the self-confidence you need to convince your future boss that the business can't do without you!

If psychocybernetics sounds too good to be true, Dr. Maltz asks that you give his system three weeks to show results. In that time, he believes, you will experience improvement in your self-awareness and in the quality of your life. Therapists who teach an updated version of psychocybernetics called *creative visualization* use it to help clients relieve pain, overcome shyness, achieve goals, improve memory, and increase energy levels. Sports psychologists use a similar technique to help athletes improve by having them mentally rehearse every step of a successful performance.

Think of psychocybernetics as a simple, well-tested self-awareness mechanism. Saying to yourself each morning, "I am beginning this day in a new and better way," can't hurt—and it might do you a world of good.

▪ SECTION CHECKUP

1 How does biofeedback control body processes that normally can't be influenced by the conscious mind? What uses have been found for biofeedback?

2 What is assertiveness training? Describe the AT techniques you could use when your little brother demands that you change the channel during your favorite TV show.

3 Describe the basic theory of psychocybernetics. How could athletes use the system to prepare themselves for tomorrow's marathon race?

15.4 ■ WHICH THERAPIES COMBINE SELF-REALIZATION TECHNIQUES WITH TRADITIONAL PSYCHOTHERAPY?

A number of psychotherapy systems that combine traditional practices with new and experimental methods have emerged in recent years. Most have attracted as much criticism as acceptance. As with all new approaches in psychology, the critics counsel a "go-slow" approach—even as enthusiastic patients shout that they've found the perfect solution to their emotional problems.

These new therapies have little in common except that they all try to help disturbed people find healthier ways of coping with life. In this section, you'll learn about primal therapy, reality therapy, family therapy, and past lives therapy.

PRIMAL THERAPY

The floor and walls of the room are padded. A number of adults, young and old, are crawling on their hands and knees. Two of them raise their heads and scream, a terrifying blend of pain and rage. Their fellow crawlers respond by pounding their fists on the floor and walls. Therapists move among them, encouraging their patients to allow long-buried feelings to come to the surface (see Figure 15.8).

Dr. Arthur Janov, a psychologist and psychiatric social worker, refers to this unique process as *primal therapy*. Along with Freud and other psychoanalysts, Janov believes that neurotic behavior develops out of the unmet needs of childhood. Most adults, he feels, build up defenses against the pain. Repressed memories, an inability to feel deeply, and dependence on tobacco, drugs, and alcohol are common defense mechanisms. Some otherwise healthy adults sometimes express their "unending neediness," Dr. Janov observes, by joining religious cults. There they exchange blind obedience for the sense of being loved and needed. Unlike most traditional therapists, Dr. Janov insists that these defenses can be broken down and "primal pain" released only through screaming.

Talking about past experience in the Freudian style, the primal therapist explains, widens the gulf between thought and feeling. Primal therapy thus begins with a three-week period of almost constant therapy. Patients are asked to give up smoking, drinking, drugs, and other habits that Janov believes grow out of built-up tension. Primal therapists teach patients how to relax and also how to deepen their breathing. At the same time, patients learn to "primal"—to scream out the pain of the past. After this intensive therapy, patients join primal groups that meet two or three times a week for several months.

Primal therapy grew out of an experience Janov had with two of his patients when he

FIGURE 15.8 ■ Primal therapy as formulated by Dr. Arthur Janov encourages patients to relive painful early-childhood experiences as a way of resolving their neuroses. How does screaming out the pain of a "primal experience" contribute to that goal?

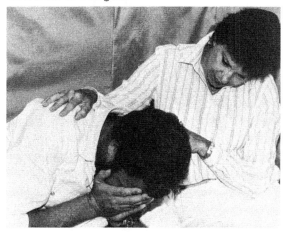

was working in a Freudian clinic. When he told these patients to call out to their parents one day, they repeatedly shouted, "Mommy! Daddy!" Then they broke into an eerie scream. Afterward, they said that although the experience had been intensely painful, it had enabled them to "see" the reality of their own lives.

Dr. Janov tries to help each of his patients experience that primal moment. After they have had their "primal experience," Janov says, his patients lose their anxiety, depression, and nervous habits. Because they are free at last of the chains of the past, problems become more manageable.

Janov admits that neurotic behaviors built up over a lifetime cannot be eliminated overnight, but he holds fast to his belief that "primal therapy offers the only cure for neurosis." Traditional therapists, who hesitate to talk about "cures" with any system, are outraged by his claims. To defend his theory, Janov points to evidence showing that primal therapy relieves many serious medical and emotional problems. He lists depression, anxiety, sleep disorders, addictions, phobias, obsessions, migraines, high blood pressure, and ulcers as some of the conditions that respond. Studies by medical researchers have confirmed at least one aspect of Janov's claims. Patients who have gone through primal therapy display lower heart rates and improved vital signs—key measures of good mental and physical adjustment.

REALITY THERAPY

It's all right with Dr. William Glasser that Chris is a junkie and a car thief—as long as he is willing to accept the consequences of those choices. But, Dr. Glasser would be quick to add, "Chris, there must be a better way of taking care of your needs."

Dr. Glasser, a practicing psychiatrist, refers to this low-key way of helping patients as *reality therapy*. He doesn't think much of tra-

ditional psychotherapy, with its emphasis on past experiences. What's done can't be changed, he says. Instead, Dr. Glasser concentrates on improving his patients' awareness of the here and now. He refers to his formula for reality therapy as the three *R*s: reality, responsibility, and right-and-wrong.

Reality therapists begin by building a close personal relationship with their patients. Once Chris learns to trust his therapist, the two can work together to identify the unhealthy behaviors that dominate Chris's existence. The payoff starts when Chris makes a commitment to act more responsibly in one small area of his life.

Dr. Glasser makes no grand promises for reality therapy. He doesn't even claim that his therapy will make people happy. All anyone can do, Dr. Glasser explains, is to give people a fair chance of finding happiness for themselves. Even with such modest claims, reality therapy has helped many neurotics, delinquents, drug addicts, and other difficult-to-treat patients return to productive lives.

Reality therapists also promote a self-realization technique that everyone can practice. Addiction is great, Dr. Glasser says, if people become addicted to things that are good for them. Dr. Glasser defines this *positive addiction (PA)* as any relaxing activity that makes you feel good. To qualify as an addict under Glasser's rules, you must set aside 30 minutes a day for "doing your thing." Depending on your skills and interests, you can choose from any number of sports or hobbies: square dancing, painting, sewing, meditation, gardening, bicycling, model building, jogging, and so on.

It's not hard to become positively addicted. Choose an activity that you can do by yourself, so you won't have to worry about looking for a partner every day. You'll also want to choose a PA that has some physical, spiritual, or emotional value for you. Never criticize yourself for your performance and don't set goals. The idea of PA is to let the mind

FIGURE 15.9 ▪ What's your PA? Dr. William Glasser believes that everyone needs a totally absorbing activity that will relieve the tensions of daily life.

relax and escape from the day's pressures. Many people depend on alcohol, television, cigarettes, or other negative addictions to relieve tension. PA, Dr. Glasser insists, will get you hooked on healthy habits. You'll have fun, and you'll also gain awareness of your own potential for positive growth.

Dr. William Rader, a specialist in the treatment of compulsive behaviors, cautions that positive addictions can be carried too far. An addiction to exercise, for example, can be just as damaging as an addiction to alcohol. Compulsive exercisers no longer gain pleasure from their five-times-a-week aerobics classes and late-night sessions on the Stairmaster—but they can't stop. The once-healthy behavior has turned into a mechanism for repressing painful feelings.

At what point does a PA turn destructive? Rader gives his patients this checklist:

1. Does the behavior take precedence over family, friends, school, church, and job?

2. Is the behavior being used as a way of avoiding feelings or problems?

3. Is the behavior continuing even though the individual wants to stop?

One or more "yes" answers should be seen as a sign that counseling may be needed. A PA should add to a person's joy in life, not subtract from it.

FAMILY THERAPY

Family therapists break many of the rules set by traditional therapy systems. Although not all family therapists agree on methods, many share the ideas developed by therapist and teacher Virginia Satir. Therapists who follow Satir's methods insist on treating an entire family rather than a single individual. While exploring a particular situation, they often hold therapy sessions in the family home. Occasionally, they invite the family dog to a group session. After all, the way a family treats its pets says a lot about the way they treat each other. Over a number of sessions the therapist will try any technique that seems appropriate: psychodrama, encounter tactics, or even a game of musical chairs (to see who ends up sitting in daddy's chair).

With American families more dysfunctional than ever, family therapy has grown in importance. It may be Belle's withdrawn behavior at school that brings the family to the attention of a therapist. But family therapists believe that Belle cannot be evaluated or treated outside her home environment. One major task is to persuade Belle's father that he should join the group. Many men resist, but once the family begins seeing a therapist, they usually join in to find out what's going on. If Belle's case is typical, her problem is

▓ **BIOBOX**

Michael Murphy:
Esalen's Founder Predicts an Extraordinary Future

Back in the 1960s, people searching for self-awareness and realization of their potential flocked to Michael Murphy's Esalen Institute. Located on the wild California coast at Big Sur, Esalen hosted all of the influential movements of the day: humanistic and transpersonal psychology, Transactional Analysis, Gestalt therapy, encounter therapy, and a phalanx of body-awareness techniques. Celebrity visitors included actress Jane Fonda, author Aldous Huxley, scientist Linus Pauling, futurist Buckminster Fuller, physiotherapist Ida Rolf, and psychologist Fritz Perls.

With the 1980s came a renewed national interest in moneymaking. The "touchy-feelie" days were over, the media reported. Murphy (1930–) and his partner, Richard Price, responded by transforming Esalen into a more businesslike enterprise. They attracted top-flight workshop leaders and emphasized personal transformation and social change. As a result, the institute still attracts 800 paying guests a month from all over the globe. Many are professional people who come hoping to find the joy, passion, and love that seem to be missing from their lives.

likely to relate to conflicts within the home—often between her parents. In other cases, the therapist may discover that the members of the family haven't learned to value one another as people worthy of love and capable of change.

According to family therapists, everyone in the household shares in the responsibility when a family member is disturbed. Group discussions open up new lines of communication and spotlight the roles that each member plays in the family structure. To bring about change, the therapist tries to get one person started in a new and healthier direction. Then, like a line of dominoes, the other family members will be forced to fall into new ways of dealing with that one member. As tensions decrease and both adults and children learn to be honest and loving with each other, the family begins to heal itself.

In her book *Peoplemaking*, Virginia Satir offers some useful advice to family members everywhere: "If you discover that something is going wrong in your family, treat it as you would when the red light goes on in your car, indicating that the engine is overheating. . . . Stop—investigate—and see what you can do. If you can't change it, find someone who can. Whatever you do, don't waste your time moaning about 'poor me' and 'bad you.' "

The smooth-running operation gives Murphy time to focus his energies and intellect on a life-long interest—the future of the human race. His 800-page book, *The Future of the Body* (Tarcher, 1992), is the result of over seven years of study, research, and serious thinking. Each of us, he says, has an extraordinary potential (he calls it metanormality) that is not fully utilized. After all, he notes, two-thirds of the population has reported some sort of ESP experience. He explains his thinking this way:

> One human attribute, as an example, is the ability to perceive external events. . . . A bacterium can perceive a change in the chemical content of the fluid in which it swims. Animals and humans, which evolved from the same single-celled organisms, can perceive their surroundings with much more precision and range. Some humans have gone beyond this ability . . . and can recognize objects and events at a greater distance still. There are other types of extraordinary perception, including the deliberate use of clairvoyance.

> Sometimes metanormality pops up where you least expect it. . . . In emergencies, people perform feats of strength that defy scientific explanation. Patients under anesthesia sometimes report events in the operating room they couldn't possibly have perceived through their ordinary senses. The extraordinary comes as a gift, a grace, even when we don't seek or expect it.

Murphy believes that there are 37 types of metanormal experience—with more yet to be identified. Almost everyone, he says, has experienced a few of them.

> If we can surrender to their spontaneous arising in us, and if there's enough cultural support for them, there's no telling how far their realization might go. Someday, perhaps, the cultivation of the metanormal will lead to forms of love, joy, and embodiment beyond our present abilities to conceive. And if enough of us cultivate them instead of turning to drugs, violence, and trivial, life-deadening activities, this world will be a better place for us all.

Is Murphy stepping outside the boundaries of hard science? No, he says. Even though ESP events are difficult to replicate in the lab, thousands of experiments by reliable investigators have produced statistically significant results. Have you or someone you know experienced anything that could be classified as a metanormal event? You might want to pick up Michael Murphy's book to learn more about the event (or lack of it).

PAST LIVES THERAPY (PLT)

Sigmund Freud pioneered the theory that emotional problems are rooted in the deeply buried fears, trauma, and pain of early childhood. A therapy system developed by psychologist Helen Wambach reaches even further back. Wambach believed that the origins of some phobic fears, compulsions, depression, and other destructive behaviors could be found in her patients' past lives. She called the system *past lives therapy* (PLT).

When Nikita Y.'s hydrophobia became so severe that he panicked at the thought of taking a bath, he sought help from a past lives therapist. Using hypnosis, Dr. Parker regressed Nikita back to childhood. When no clues as to the origins of the phobic fear showed up there, she asked him to go back even further. Soon Nikita was describing a life spent as a New York seamstress at the turn of the century. Then he went back even further. As a cowboy in the 1870s, he reported, he had fallen into a river during a cattle drive. Reliving the terror of his drowning helped Nikita come to terms with his fear of water in this life. "Maybe now I can take swimming lessons," he said with a smile.

Is PLT just another New Age fad? Does the illusion of reliving past lives depend on hypnotized patients telling therapists what they want to hear? Critics charge that past life regressions are really fantasies based on subconscious memories of long-forgotten books, articles, and films.

Wambach trusted her patients and their detailed reports. Over a ten-year period, she regressed over a thousand patients, some of whom talked about lives that reached as far back as 2000 B.C. When checked against historical records, their descriptions of clothing, coins, and household tools proved accurate down to the number of tines on the forks they used. Most importantly, patients who be-

lieve in PLT do regain control of their lives. Perhaps that's all that really matters.

■ SECTION CHECKUP

1 Why do primal therapists insist that their patients scream?

2 How does reality therapy differ from both psychoanalysis and from primal therapy? What is the value of a positive addiction?

3 Why does the family therapist insist that all members of the family take part in the therapy sessions?

15.5 ▓ HOW CAN TRANSACTIONAL ANALYSIS HELP PEOPLE STAY IN THE "OK" POSITION?

Psychoanalyst Eric Berne didn't think that psychology should belong only to people with doctor's degrees and a tendency to talk psychobabble. When Berne talked about behavior, he used terms everyone can understand. Even the name of his system, which he called *Transactional Analysis*, has been shortened to *TA*. Another TA psychologist, Tom Harris, added the concept of "OK" and "not-OK." To be OK means to feel good about yourself and others; to be not-OK means that you feel bad about yourself and others. TA, in brief, gives people a nontechnical way of understanding their behavior and changing it if they want to do so.

THE THREE EGO STATES

Have you ever noticed how the same person can shift from one personality to another in a flash? For example, Mom is just sitting down to dinner with the family. Listen to her tone of voice.

"Jimmy, get your elbows off the table!" (Spoken like a true *parent*, right? You recognize the old shape-up-your-table-manners

routine, spoken in a stern, commanding voice.)

Dad interrupts to ask her to describe what happened when she went to pay the water bill. "The people there were very helpful," she replies. "They found the error right away, and I wrote them a check for what we owed." (Can you spot the switch? She had information to give, and she gave it in a calm, *adult* voice.)

Finally, the meal is over and Dad tells the kids to wash the dishes. He's going to take Mom to a movie. "That's great!" she beams. "I'll be ready in a minute!" (Another change. She sounds just like a *child*, bubbling over at the thought of having fun.)

The different personalities Mom displayed during those few minutes illustrate one of Eric Berne's key insights. He said that everyone has three *ego states*—three distinct ways of behaving and thinking. He called them the Parent, the Adult, and the Child (P-A-C). Each ego state can be recognized by what you say and how you act while you're in that ego state (see Figure 15.10). A newborn infant starts life with only a Child ego state, but the

Once you recognize the signals, you can spot ego states in yourself and in others.
The chart below shows you what to look and listen for.

	EGO STATE	TYPICAL STATEMENTS	TONE OF VOICE	TYPICAL ATTITUDE
PARENT	 CRITICAL PARENT	"Don't do that." "You should..." "You must..." "You always..." "You'd better..." "Behave yourself."	Critical Loud Disgusted Scheming Whining Superior	Judgmental Moralistic Dictatorial Rigid Comparing Demanding respect Demanding love
	 NURTURING PARENT	"I love you." "Take care." "Be happy." (and other words that are consoling, comforting, reassuring)	Soft Comforting Concerned Loving	Caring Understanding Giving Supportive
ADULT	 ADULT	"How, what, where, who, why?" "It seems to me..." "Let's get on with it." "Will it work?" "Here's what I think..."	Appropriate to situation and feeling. Calm Controlled Businesslike	Flexible Confident Supportive Realistic Practical Alert Open
CHILD	 FREE CHILD	"Wow!" "I hope..." "I wish..." "I can't..." "I want..." "I don't want to..." "What fun!"	Emotional Laughing Crying Loud	Impulsive Uninhibited Any feeling: happy sad, mad, scared
	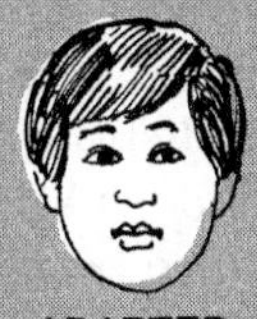 ADAPTED CHILD	"If you want..." "I guess I'll have to." "If you say so." "Is this OK?" "Do I have to?" (and other words that show compliance)	Sweet Placating Repetitive Annoying	Complaining Demanding Jealous Ashamed Seeking attention
	 REBEL CHILD	"I won't..." "Make me!" "Aw, nobody will care..." (and other defiant, rebellious words)	Angry Defiant Rebellious	Seeking power Seeking revenge Demanding own way

FIGURE 15.10

Parent and Adult states begin to develop almost immediately.

PARENT EGO STATE. Your Parent state is made up of all the messages you received from your parents and other adults when you were a kid. These messages are mostly instructions, advice, and commands. Children also learn Parent behavior by watching what grown-ups do. Much of your Parent information is of the "how-to" variety: how to get dressed, how to behave in church, how to change a tire. But imagine that the cashier has given you too much change. What will you do next? Your Parent voice will probably say, "Give it back. Only bad people keep money that's not theirs." You are free to ignore that instruction, but your Parent will make sure you feel guilty if you do. The Parent speaks for the moral values you learned as a child.

If you listen carefully, you'll discover that your Parent has a dual personality. It can be a *Nurturing Parent* one minute and a *Critical Parent* the next. Your Nurturing Parent takes care of people. When you say to a friend, "I know you're busy today. I'll mail those packages for you," you're in your Nurturing Parent state. By contrast, your Critical Parent's job is to criticize, command, and make judgments. If you've ever raised your voice and said something like "Sherry, don't play with that muddy puppy!" you've heard your own Critical Parent speaking.

ADULT EGO STATE. Think of your Adult ego state as your own private computer. The Adult gathers information, tests it, and files it away for later use. Your Adult also checks out the information stored away in the Parent and Child. When you were little, you were told that fires are hot—but your Adult had to test that fact to make sure.

You make your best decisions when you're in your Adult state. Perhaps you've had your eye on a new computer game. Your Parent would likely say, "Save your money; you might need it later." Then your Child would jump in with, "Buy it now! I want it!" But your Adult will analyze the purchase from all angles before making a decision. Whether you buy the game or not, your Adult decision will be made rationally.

CHILD EGO STATE. If a child has an Adult, does an adult have a Child ego state? Most definitely! Your Child is made up of all the impulses natural to children plus your childhood memories. TA says that this *Free Child* is the source of your joy, excitement, creativity, and zest for living. Everyone has a Free Child, but many adults have forgotten how to let theirs out. Unable to make contact with their Free Child, they become grumpy, joyless individuals. When you're in your Free Child, you smile and laugh and have fun. Games, dances, being with good friends, and plunging into creative activities give your Free Child a chance to take over.

Along with your Free Child, parental influences and restrictions may have given you an *Adapted Child* or a *Rebel Child*. The Adapted Child wants so desperately to gain approval that it gives up its own needs to satisfy others. An Adapted Child does what it's told, minds its manners, and speaks only when spoken to. If you hear Jeff say, "I'll do that if you want me to," when he really means, "I don't want to do that," you've heard the voice of the Adapted Child. Because the Rebel Child decided early in life that adults don't know anything, he or she refuses to live by the rules. You've possibly seen the Rebel Child in other students, as when Sara tells her teacher, "No, I won't do that assignment, and you can't make me!" Carried to an extreme, an out-of-control Rebel Child can lead his or her owner to oppose all authority—whether it means running red lights or starting revolutions.

TRANSACTIONS

When you were a baby, you needed food, warmth, dry clothes, and a great deal of love.

FIGURE 15.11 ▪ The overwhelming power of parents often leaves children in what TA calls a "not-OK" position. This child will now be forced to learn unhealthy behaviors to earn the strokes so necessary to life.

TA refers to the love and good feelings people give each other as *strokes*. When you rub a baby's back, that's an obvious stroke. But saying something pleasant to another person ("Hey, your new haircut looks good!") is also a stroke. Interactions with other people while in search of strokes lead to transactions. A transaction consists of a stimulus (you say something) and a response (the other person replies). When you don't get enough strokes, you start feeling "not-OK." (Figure 15.11 shows how easily a child can be pushed into a "not-OK" position.)

TA analyzes two main types of transactions.

COMPLEMENTARY TRANSACTIONS. When a transaction can be diagrammed to show that each speaker's ego state is talking directly to the other, it is a *complementary transaction*. Complementary transactions make it possible for people to get on with business. Typical transactions involve Adult-Adult exchanges of information (Figure 15.12a), Parent-Child arguments (Figure 15.12b), and Child-Child invitations to have fun (Figure 15.12c).

CROSSED TRANSACTIONS. How many times have you said something only to get back a response that throws the transaction off track? In TA, such breakdowns are *crossed transactions* (Figure 15.13). You may start out speaking to Paula's Adult, but when her Child answers back, your Parent tends to take over. At that point, useful communication stops until someone switches ego states.

As you gain experience in recognizing ego states, you'll be better prepared to cope with crossed transactions. The TA rule is to go into or stay in your Adult ego state when you encounter a crossed transaction. In most cases, this step will bring the other person into his or her Adult as well. If that doesn't work, break off the transaction. If you don't, you're probably going to be hooked into a game.

GAMES ANALYSIS

If a friend asks you to play a game, you'll probably answer, "Sure, I like games." But Eric Berne wasn't talking about tennis or Monopoly when he described "the games peo-

FIGURE 15.12

COMPLEMENTARY TRANSACTIONS

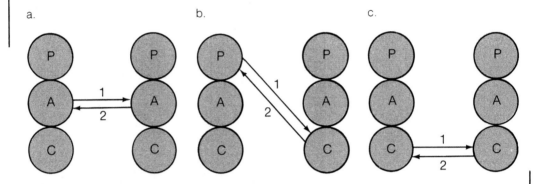

a.

1 *Adult:* What time is it?

2 *Adult:* It's half past two.

b.

1 *Critical Parent:* Eat your spinach.

2 *Rebel Child:* Ycch! I hate spinach.

c.

1 *Free Child:* Let's dance!

2 *Adapted Child:* Do you think we should?

ple play" in his best-selling book of the same name. When Dr. Berne speaks of *games*, he's talking about psychological games, the kind no one plays for fun.

The person who starts the game is seeking a payoff. If everyone plays according to the rules, the game player can collect a prize. Unlike a Super Bowl win, psychological games pay off in negative strokes. Even worse, game playing prevents the development of honest communication.

Most people learn to play psychological games during childhood. As they grow up, they get better at carrying their games through to a payoff. Dr. Berne thought that game playing conceals real feelings, particularly those that cause guilt. In a TA game, many of the actual transactions are hidden. In a game called "Ain't It Awful" (Figure 15.14), what sounds like a complementary Adult-Adult exchange between two older people

(solid lines) conceals the actual transaction. The dotted lines tell you that the real transaction is taking place between two Critical Parents who feel threatened by the rapid pace of social change. Good "Ain't It Awful" players can keep a game going for a long time.

Once you catch on to the idea, you can easily spot any number of games. People play these games over and over, like a child who never gets tired of playing patty cake. In "Uproar," for example, husband and wife pick fights with each other so that they won't have to deal with the deeper problems of their marriage. "Kick Me" players, on the other hand, deliberately forget assignments or make mistakes so that someone will scold or punish them. This confirms their negative self-image and gives them an excuse for feeling sorry for themselves. Talented "Yes But" players set up a problem and ask for help in solving it. But no matter what solutions you

(Text continues on page 527.)

FIGURE 15.13

CROSSED TRANSACTIONS

a.

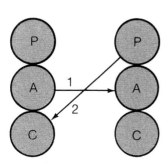

b.

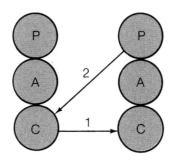

c.

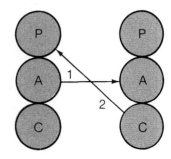

1 *Adult:* Dad, can I use the car Friday night?

2 *Critical Parent:* What's wrong with your feet? Walk! I did when I was your age.

1 *Free Child:* I can't wait 'til Christmas gets here!

2 *Nurturing Parent:* You've been so good Santa is sure to bring you lots of presents.

1 *Adult:* That cake looks lovely, but I'm on a diet.

2 *Rebel Child:* Diets are for dummies. If you don't eat it, I will.

FIGURE 15.14

A GAME CALLED "AIN'T IT AWFUL"

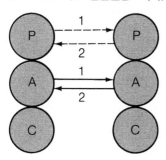

1 *Harry:* Ain't it awful how those kids listen to such terrible music?

2 *Joyce:* Yes, whatever happened to the good music we enjoyed when we were growing up?

TA CONTRACT

Contract written by *Pat Garibaldi*   Date *10/7*

1. Describe the behavior pattern or attitude you wish to change:

I'd like to get more involved in my psych class. But I feel too shy, and I never do.

2. State exactly what the new behavior will be:

When I complete this contract, I'll feel confident enough to join in class discussions or activities at least once a day.

3. List three specific steps you will take to fulfill the contract:

(a) *I will study harder so I'll know what I'm talking about*

(b) *I'll get to know the teacher better so I won't feel so shy.*

(c) *I'll raise my hand every day until I'm called on.*

Set a date for completing each step: (a) *10/11* (b) *10/14* (c) *10/18*

4. How will you know that you've fulfilled the contract? *I'll be joining in without making it a specific thing to do. I'll also be more involved in my other classes. It will feel natural.*

5. Set a target date for completion of the contract: *10/28*

6. All contracts include a payoff. How will you reward yourself for completing your contract?

I'll reward myself with a special night out with my friends.

Pat Garibaldi   Signed   *10/7*   Date

Mrs. Jane Carson-Smith Witness   *10/8*   Date

FIGURE 15.15

offer, the response always comes back, "Yes, but . . ." Skilled players really want attention and sympathy, not answers.

It's useful to remember that game players are addicted to the negative feelings that games provide. As a consequence, games will never make anyone happy or healthy. When someone starts a game, you have three choices: You can play the game; you can walk away from it; or you can try to help the person understand what he or she is doing. Don't expect anyone to appreciate your efforts to stop a game once it's started. Game players have been programmed since childhood to repeat the same behaviors over and over.

SCRIPT ANALYSIS

Imagine for a moment that you have a tiny tape recorder inside your head. You were born with it, and it's been recording everything that's happened to you ever since. Today, whenever you face a problem, that tape recorder plays back a childhood message that tells you what to do. TA refers to those messages as your *life script*. Most of your script messages were recorded during transactions with your parents and caregivers. As a child, for example, you might have been told over and over that you were clumsy. As a result, your script now calls for you to *be* clumsy whenever agility is called for.

The first step in rewriting a poor life script is to understand just how you've been scripted in the first place. You may discover that your Parent has convinced your Adult that you really are a clumsy person. Backed into that not-OK position, your Adult makes sure that you follow the script. Every time you stumble or hit your thumb with a hammer you're saying to the world, "See, I really am clumsy. Don't you feel sorry for me?" TA teaches that you *can* write yourself a more rewarding life script. Some people can do so on their own; others need to seek the help of a therapist.

TA AS THERAPY

TA's simplicity has made it a popular part of the self-awareness movement. Eric Berne's ideas have been applied to emotional difficulties ranging from simple adjustment problems to serious neuroses. Young and old alike seem to respond well to TA's nontechnical way of explaining the causes of their self-defeating behavior. Therapists who work with disturbed teenagers in hospitals and detention homes report particularly good results with TA.

One common technique used in TA groups is the TA contract. A TA contract singles out a specific negative behavior and sets up a step-by-step plan to change it. Assume, for example, that Pat Garibaldi wants to overcome her shyness. If Pat really wants to become more outgoing, a TA contract can show her the way.

First, she must zero in on a specific situation in which her shyness keeps her from doing something she badly wants to do. In this case, Pat decides that she wants to take a more active role in her psychology class. Using her Adult ego state, she states her goal in clear, simple language. She must be in her Adult because her Parent will promise almost anything to satisfy her Child. Pat's Child loves to make resolutions it never intends to keep. Only the Adult can write a successful TA contract.

As you can see on page 526, Pat's contract spells out every step of her battle against shyness. Following through on the contract won't be easy, but success will give her enough self-confidence to tackle another area in which her shyness interferes with her life.

▪ SECTION CHECKUP

1 What are the three basic ego states identified by TA? What role does each ego state play in the personality?

2 What is meant by a complementary transaction? A crossed transaction? What can you do when you run into a crossed transaction?

3 Why does TA consider game playing a negative behavior? Give two examples of "games people play."

4 Define the TA concept of a life script. How can a TA contract be used to change a negative script?

LOOKING BACK: A SUMMARY

1 People young and old are turning to the self-realization movement (SRM) in an effort to improve the quality of their lives. Most of these people aren't emotionally disturbed, but they are troubled by feelings of loneliness, anxiety, and insecurity. They hope that one or another of the SRM programs can make their lives much happier and more productive.

2 For the most part, the self-realization movement offers growth and self-discovery rather than treatment for neurotic disorders. People are encouraged to look honestly at themselves, communicate openly with others, develop their potential for growth, and leave self-defeating behaviors behind. Seeking self-realization also carries risks, however. Some people have been hurt by groups whose leaders do not have proper training. Others are disappointed when a group fails to live up to its promises.

3 One segment of the self-realization movement treats emotional problems through bodywork—body movement and manipulation. These groups believe that repressed emotions are released when body armor (rigid, contracted muscles) is broken down. The Feldenkrais method uses intricate dance movements and exercises to improve posture and flexibility. Structural integration (rolfing) uses deep, painful massage to free the body and to release repressed emotions. In bioenergetic analysis, participants stretch, twist, kick, and scream as they "get in touch with their bodies." Followers of these body-oriented therapies believe they promote self-healing and release natural creative energies.

4 Research shows that the mind is capable of expanding beyond its present limits. Biofeedback teaches people how to control involuntary body processes (heart rate, temperature, brain waves, blood pressure, and the like). Special biofeedback machines provide data on what's happening inside the body. After a few sessions, the subject is usually able to control the body function that the machine is monitoring. Biofeedback training has been used to control asthma, scoliosis, migraine headaches, high blood pressure, and other chronic conditions.

5 Assertiveness training (AT) teaches people to stand up for their rights. Specific techniques include fogging, broken record, negative assertion, and self-disclosure. These and other AT methods help nonassertive people develop better communication skills and a nonviolent way of dealing with others. Psychocybernetics uses positive thinking and creative visualization to program the mind for success. Daily practice of this technique aims at removing self-doubt and prepares people to work to their full potential.

6 Several new therapies combine self-realization ideas with conventional treatment methods. Primal therapy attempts to change neurotic behavior by forcing people to relive the pain experienced during infancy and early childhood. These repressed memories are released by screaming, a process called the *primal experience*. By contrast, reality therapy ignores the past and concentrates on building a sense of responsibility and a positive self-image. Reality therapy doesn't claim to make people happy. Instead, it tries to give them a chance to find happiness for themselves. Reality therapists also promote positive addictions—those relaxing hobbies and sports that leave people more aware of their ability to achieve positive growth. People whose positive addictions have taken over their lives may need counseling help.

7 Family therapists believe that even if only one person in the family is disturbed, everyone shares in the problem. To bring about change, the therapist tries to get at least one family member started in a new direction. Family therapists will try any technique that seems capable of breaking down the barriers that prevent close, loving communication among family members. A much more controversial therapy system relies on past life regressions to help patients overcome neurotic behaviors. Because past life therapists believe that each human being has lived many lives, they seek the roots of today's problems in lives "remembered" from other times and places.

8 Eric Berne's Transactional Analysis (TA) uses simple language to explain human behavior. According to the concept of ego states, every person has a Parent, an Adult, and a Child inside. People switch from one ego state to another, depending on the situations they find themselves in. Transactional Analysis shows how communication breaks down when the wrong ego state responds to a statement or question. Games analysis describes the psychological games people play. These games, which always involve a negative payoff, grow out of the individual's inability to gain positive reinforcement (strokes).

9 Script analysis looks at the life-shaping messages people are given during childhood. Negative scripts can be rewritten once people figure out the script that is controlling their lives. A common script puts people in the not-OK position, which means that they do not feel good about themselves. TA's goal is to help them move into the OK position. TA has proved effective as a therapy because of its ability to eliminate self-defeating behaviors in a simple, direct, and nonthreatening way.

PUTTING YOUR KNOWLEDGE TO WORK

■ TERMS YOU SHOULD KNOW

Adapted Child	family therapy	positive addiction (PA)
Adult ego state	Feldenkrais method	primal therapy
assertiveness training (AT)	fogging	psychocybernetics
bioenergetic analysis	Free Child	reality therapy
biofeedback	free information	Rebel Child
body armor	games	rolfing
bodywork	life script	self-disclosure
broken record	negative assertion	self-realization movement (SRM)
Child ego state	negative inquiry	strokes
complementary transaction	Nurturing Parent	structural integration
creative visualization	Parent ego state	Transactional Analysis (TA)
Critical Parent	past lives therapy (PLT)	workable compromise
crossed transaction		

■ CHAPTER CHECKUP

1 The major goal of the self-realization movement is to (*a*) develop people's ESP abilities (*b*) cure psychotic behavior (*c*) help people make their lives happier and more productive (*d*) improve the body's posture and flexibility.

2 If you join a self-realization group, choose one that (*a*) promises quick and easy answers to difficult emotional problems (*b*) does not have a licensed or well-trained leader (*c*) requires investment of large sums of money without any guarantee of refund (*d*) is recommended by a mental health professional.

3 You just walked into a room where people of all ages were going through a series of slow, intricate exercises designed to break bad emotional habits. You know you're watching (*a*) a rolfing session (*b*) Feldenkrais method (*c*) primal therapy (*d*) biofeedback training.

4 If you go in for a rolfing session, be prepared to (*a*) receive deep, painful muscle manipulation (*b*) learn how to meditate (*c*) crawl around screaming (*d*) learn about brain waves.

5 The technique most directly useful for treating migraine headaches would be (*a*) psychocybernetics (*b*) assertiveness training (*c*) Transactional Analysis (*d*) biofeedback.

6 According to assertiveness training, when a waiter in a restaurant brings you a badly cooked steak, you should (*a*) eat the steak but don't leave a tip (*b*) angrily demand to see the manager (*c*) calmly but firmly insist that a second, properly cooked steak be brought to you (*d*) get up and storm out of the restaurant.

7 Primal therapy requires that patients scream out their pain in order to (*a*) achieve an alpha state (*b*) create a positive addiction (*c*) relax tense, knotted-up muscles (*d*) release the repressed pain of early life experiences.

8 Which of the following therapists would be most likely to say, "Before I can treat Tommy's neurotic behavior, I must set up a meeting that includes Tommy, his parents, and his sister"? (*a*) a family therapist (*b*) a reality therapist (*c*) a primal therapist (*d*) a past lives therapist.

9 If you hear a mother say to her child, "Come on, let's run on the beach and let the waves try to catch us," she's most likely in the ego state known as (*a*) Critical Parent (*b*) Adult (*c*) Free Child (*d*) Rebel Child.

10 In TA terms, you should avoid games because (*a*) game players always end up in the "I'm OK, You're OK" position (*b*) games prevent honest communication (*c*) game players never earn strokes of any kind (*d*) playing games is a sure sign of mental illness.

■ EXPLORING CONCEPTS

1 Why have so many people been attracted to the self-realization movement in recent years? Are there any possible dangers in this search for self-fulfillment?

2 What would you say to someone who claims to have discovered the "only certain cure" for a troubled personality?

3 Contrast the treatment for neurotic behavior found in primal therapy with that used in reality therapy.

4 Describe how you could use biofeedback to control your heart rate. What other uses can you think of for biofeedback techniques?

5 What do psychologists mean by "the power of positive thinking"? Describe how psychocybernetics and assertiveness training make use of this principle.

6 What if you read tomorrow that a psychologist had started a new self-realization program based on marathon running and weight lifting? Could such a program help troubled people? Why or why not?

■ HANDS-ON ACTIVITIES

1 With the help of your psychology teacher, arrange to visit a self-realization or self-help group. Look for notices of meetings on supermarket and library bulletin boards, in the newspaper, and at free clinics and mental health agencies. One way of speeding up the search would be to ask for help from the National Self-Help Clearinghouse, 365 5th Avenue, Suite 3300, New York, NY 10016 <Web: *www.selfhelpweb.org*> or phone: 212-817-1822). Prepare for your visit by researching the group's philosophy and methods. After the meeting, write a report of your impressions to share with your class.

2 Do you have a behavior pattern or an attitude that you'd like to change? Perhaps you want to improve your grades in a particular class. Or you may feel that you lose your temper too easily whenever you discuss anything with your parents. Whatever the behavior, once you've recognized the need to change, a TA contract can help you. Use the sample contract on page 526 as a model. Copy the six steps on a sheet of paper, and then fill in the blanks in your own words. With the help of the contract, you may discover that you can change negative behaviors in a relatively short time.

3 If you're not already familiar with assertiveness training, you can get up to speed by reading Dr. Manuel Smith's book, *When I Say No, I Feel Guilty,* or by checking out the useful AT Website *<www.uvm.edu/~uvmeap/stress8.html>*. After you practice AT techniques for a while, you'll enjoy the good feeling that comes when you stand up for your rights in a nonaggressive, assertive way.

4 The self-realization movement often uses simple exercises to help you gain self-insight. Try the following exercise, both for the experience and as a chance to learn something about yourself. First, write the names of three people you actively dislike or avoid. Then, without hesitating or blocking out anything, write five descriptive words or phrases that come to mind when you think of each person. When you're finished, compare the lists. Do you find any similarities? Do you tend to classify people as types rather than as individuals? Do your descriptions reflect any prejudices against a particular age group, ethnic group, sex, or religion? After analyzing your lists and answering the questions as honestly as possible, sum up the results in a single sentence that also includes a statement of responsibility. For example, "I seem to have trouble getting along with older people, but I'm going to make an effort to understand them better."

5 Here's another useful self-realization exercise. Share this one with someone you feel close to. Begin by sitting quietly together. Each of you should let your mind drift. Then pick a color that fits the way you feel right now. Choose a second color that fits your partner. Share your choices. Why do you think each of you picked the colors you did? Talk about it. You can go on to choose animals, flowers, even songs or TV characters in the same way. Fantasy exercises give your Free Child a chance to express your creativity—and you'll also find that sharing such experiences can make a relationship deeper and stronger.

FOR FURTHER READING

Alberti, Robert, and Michael Emmons. *Your Perfect Right.* Atascadero, CA: Impact Publishers, 2001. The authors must be doing something right—this is the eighth edition of their pioneering self-help book on how to bring assertiveness and quality to your life and relationships. Their easy-to-use text is crammed full of procedures, case studies, and exercises that you can use to learn how to stand up for your rights without triggering anger and resentment in others.

Benson, Herbert, and William Proctor. *The Break-Out Principle.* New York: Scribner, 2003. The authors believe they can help you "activate the natural trigger that maximizes creativity, athletic performance, productivity, and personal well-being." Using their four-step method, they promise, will allow you to spend more time in that state of heightened awareness athletes call "the zone." Benson's well-researched break-out principle isn't a cure-all, but it is a useful tool for anyone seeking a manageable path to self-awareness.

Browne, Joy. *Getting Unstuck: 8 Simple Steps to Solving Any Problem.* Carlsbad, CA: Hay House, 2002. Best known for her popular radio and television shows, Dr. Browne has packaged her problem-solving advice into a system that can help you "become your own best friend, mentor, and shrink." She illustrates her eight steps with easy-to-follow scenarios that mimic calls to her radio show, and reminds you that "today is what you've got . . . and all you really need."

Harris, Thomas A. *I'm OK, You're OK: A Practical Guide to Transactional Analysis.* New York: BBS Pub., 1999. TA cuts to the heart of interpersonal relationships by helping people analyze their life positions in terms of easy-to-understand concepts—feeling okay or not okay, the competing needs of the child, adult, and parent ego states. When communication breaks down, whether it's with a parent, teacher, friend, or sales clerk, TA's simple tools can help you analyze and fix the problem.

Kaminer, Wendy. *I'm Dysfunctional, You're Dysfunctional*. Reading, MA: Addison-Wesley, 1992. Kaminer believes that the popularity of self-help and recovery groups is creating a nation that encourages people to view themselves as victims. She sees a danger to both individual self-reliance and to American democracy in this orgy of self-revelation and public confession ("Hi, I'm Wendy, and I'm a recovering Chocoholic"). You may not agree with everything in this book, but it does provide a useful counterbalance to the self-help books that currently occupy the bestseller lists.

McGraw, Phillip C. *Life Strategies: Doing What Works, Doing What Matters*. New York: Hyperion Books, 2000. Just as you wouldn't start out on a long road trip without a map, Dr. McGraw (television viewers know him as "Dr. Phil") believes you shouldn't start life's journey without a strategy that can guide you toward success and fulfillment. Whether you're trying to fix a bad relationship, break a harmful habit, or move on to a more productive phase of your life, you can use McGraw's life laws, strategies, and assignments to help you reach your destination.

Shone, Ronald. *Creative Visualization: How to Use Imagery and Imagination for Self-Improvement*. Rochester, VT: Destiny Books, 1998. With Maxwell Maltz's books on psychocybernetics largely out of print, this book helps fill the gap. The publisher describes it as a "guide to recovering and tapping your inherent powers of imagination and using them for positive change in your life." After teaching the basic principles of visualization, Shone describes how they can be applied to business situations, athletic performance, overcoming illness, and improving memory.

16 STRATEGIES FOR COPING

CATHY   **by Cathy Guisewite**

FIGURE 16.1

Cathy's problem is pretty funny, isn't it?

Or is it? Sometimes a cartoon strip can zero in on feelings you'd rather ignore. Unfortunately, pretending that a negative emotion doesn't exist won't make it go away.

Take a moment to think about what you've read in this book. You've probably learned a number of useful facts about people and behavior you didn't know before. But psychology has more to offer than interesting bits of information. You can use your knowledge to help people find ways to cope with their problems. That means people like Cathy . . . and like you.

Psychologists know with considerable certainty that sometime in your life you'll have to deal with depression, loneliness, frustration, or grief. Maybe you'll be in a position to help a friend or relative through a bad time—or maybe you'll be the one who needs help.

The problem doesn't have to carry a clinical diagnosis. Finding your way through the thickets of this complex, fast-changing world is a challenge for everyone, even for those who seem most self-actualizing.

What can psychology do to help someone who isn't coping very well? That's what this chapter will teach you. You'll meet eight real persons, each with a painful emotional problem. They'll tell you about themselves and their feelings in their own words. Then a psychologist will step forward to explain what's gone wrong and how the behavior can be changed for the better. Finally, you'll be asked to try a self-awareness exercise related to each case history.

Ready? It's time to meet Marjorie, Jim, Rosa, Martin, Tammy, Ralph, Judy, and Eric. You're almost certain to recognize the problems that are defying their coping skills.

Case History I ■ MARJORIE: OVERCOMING LONELINESS

Marjorie grew up in a close, loving family. On her own now, she lives in a well-furnished apartment. Her job as a research biologist pays well enough to keep her dressed in the latest styles. Her friends agree that she's an intelligent, responsible person.

Recently turned 27, Marjorie has become increasingly moody of late. When asked to describe her feelings, she takes a few moments to collect her thoughts. Then she begins by talking about her parents.

"I've always been very close to Mom and Dad," she says. "They gave me a truly happy childhood. I never had any chores to do. In college I wrote home every day. I still talk to my Mom every day on the telephone. My ambition is to have the same happy married life she has enjoyed.

"I need to have someone to do things for," she continues. "I'm always happiest when I

FIGURE 16.2 ■ Will Marjorie be able to overcome her feelings of loneliness and depression?

have a goal. I worked hard for my *A*s, for instance, to please my folks.

"Last year I had a steady boyfriend, and I was sure our relationship would lead to marriage. I was so happy I was walking on air." Marjorie's eyes glisten with tears, but she goes on. "Maybe I scared him by coming on too strong. Anyway, he broke off the relationship. Now, I feel really depressed. My life is fine in every other way, except that I don't have a man of my own. I know the feminists say that a woman doesn't need a man to feel complete, but being alone seems to take the fun out of everything I do."

Marjorie sinks back into the chair. Her voice sounds drained of energy. "In the evenings, I fantasize a lot about having someone around. I've taught myself how to keep busy when I'm alone. But there's nothing to look forward to on the weekends."

Her tears are falling freely now. "Look," she says, "how easily I cry. Most people think I'm strong, but these days I fall apart at the least little pressure."

THE PROBLEM

Marjorie doesn't seem to suffer from the sense of rejection that sometimes triggers feelings of loneliness. On the plus side, she has an on-going, loving relationship with her family. She grew up knowing that she was loved, that she was someone "special." Her career is on track and she has a circle of supportive friends. Despite that, she's lonely, and she admits to feeling depressed.

An analysis of Marjorie's problem must begin by focusing on her relationship with her parents. Perhaps she was allowed to stay a child too long. How many young adults write or call their parents every day? She seems to be quite limited in the number of people she feels close to—and also in the manner of her closeness. Marjorie gives you the feeling that she lives in a state of eternal girlhood. She shows adequate intellectual development but little emotional growth.

Clearly, Marjorie needs someone to set goals for her. She learned from her mother that a woman's role is to build her life around one special man. Because Marjorie hasn't been able to follow this pattern, she feels that her life doesn't have much meaning. When she did have a boyfriend, she smothered him with attention. As she admits, that's probably what drove him away. It might be accurate to say that she's seeking another parent—in the form of a husband—so that she can live through him.

From a psychologist's point of view, Marjorie might be described as a friendly, intelligent, loving . . . nonperson. She believes that she cannot be complete without a man in her life. Doing things on her own or with her women friends doesn't satisfy her. As she says, "There's nothing to look forward to on weekends." Mature people know that good things don't happen unless they make them happen. As long as Marjorie keeps on waiting for a handsome prince to sweep her off her feet, she'll go on being lonely and unhappy.

SOLUTIONS

Before she can change, Marjorie must understand that she's been following a life script written by someone else. Despite her obvious intelligence, she has never questioned the rules that she learned during childhood. According to her script, she's supposed to bubble over with good spirits, remain close to her parents, marry a good man, and devote the rest of her life to him. Those aren't totally negative goals, but pursuing them has kept Marjorie from finding out who she really is. She needs to give herself permission to explore her own interests and needs without constantly feeling pressured to please others.

After she understands why she feels so desperately unhappy, Marjorie can begin a step-by-step journey of self-exploration. A short period of therapy can help her speed up the process. Her therapist will assure her that she is bright, loving, healthy, and free of serious neurotic behaviors. During her search for self-identity, she will be encouraged to redefine many of her attitudes about men, marriage, and her purpose in life. If she does marry with her present attitudes unchanged, she may be in for a painful awakening.

A SELF-AWARENESS EXERCISE FOR FINDING YOUR IDENTITY

Marjorie's problem isn't unique. Many people reach adulthood without developing a strong sense of self. A psychologist would approach this issue by asking you to respond to four questions: Who am I? What do I want out of life? What kind of person am I? What kind of person do I want to be?

Those aren't easy questions to answer. You can make a start by tackling some of the more

---

LISTEN

If you are in conflict within your self, have the different parts talk out loud to one another.

Listen to what they have to say to each other.

Feel/find out what they/ you really want to do.

BERNARD GUNTHER

specific ones. Write out your responses to the following:*

1. What activities and experiences do I find the most satisfying and enjoyable?
2. How do I know when a decision or action is right or wrong?
3. What are my religious beliefs? How important are they to me?
4. What are my beliefs concerning love and sex?
5. What kind of career do I really want?
6. Do I want to marry? To what kind of person? When?
7. Do I want to have children? How many? When?
8. Where do I want to live?
9. What do I enjoy doing with my free time?
10. What kind of image do I try to project to others?
11. What kind of people do I enjoy being with, and why?
12. What do I hope to be doing five years from now? Ten years from now? Twenty years from now?
13. What changes do I need to make in order to achieve my personal goals? My career goals?
14. What can I do to improve the quality of my life? The lives of others?
15. What are my thoughts about death and dying?

Your answers to these questions add up to your own sense of self—your identity. You may not be ready to answer all of them now; when you do, you'll be in a position to make better decisions about your future. Better yet, you'll be free to rewrite your life script according to goals you've set for yourself. If she's willing to try, it's not too late for Marjorie to do the same.

Case History 2 ▓ JIM: MAKING CHOICES FOR THE FUTURE

Jim is a pleasant, soft-spoken young man. At 17, he's anxious to make a success of his life. His friends envy the freedom his parents have given him to make his own decisions. Lately, though, Jim has been suffering from severe headaches. At times they're painful enough to cause him to miss school and soccer practice with the team.

The headaches become worse each time Jim's school counselor calls him in to talk about next semester's courses or about his future. Today the counselor has been prodding him to make some choices. Jim looks angry for a moment. Then his expression softens.

"Maybe you're right," he says. "I dread

* Charles Zastrow, Dae H. Chang, *The Personal Problem Solver* © 1977, pp. 368–369. Published by permission of the publisher Prentice-Hall/a Division of Simon & Schuster.

making choices, because I don't know what I want to do after high school. Most of my friends have already made up their minds. They're the lucky ones! I look at all the different courses, and I feel totally confused. I worry that if I make the wrong choices now, I'll never catch up."

Jim sighs. "When I started high school I thought I wanted to be a carpenter. I'm pretty good with my hands, you know, and I liked the shop courses I took. My folks are still using the coffee table I made. After a while, though, I realized I could do more with my life than build kitchen cabinets. I decided that I wanted a career where I could spend more time with people.

"That's when I decided I wanted to be a nurse. I like helping people, and I've always been interested in how the body works. I took biology in my sophomore year, and now I'm struggling through physiology. My supervisor at the hospital where I do volunteer work says I should take chemistry, too. But my aunt has been warning me about nursing. First, there's too much hard work for too little money. What's worse, nurses don't seem to have any real power to make decisions about their patients. So, I thought about becoming a doctor. That's when my dad warned me how hard it is to get into medical school, and I got discouraged all over again.

"As you know, I switched to a computer science major last semester. My friend Angelo convinced me that computer skills will always come in handy. Computer work isn't very people oriented, but a good programmer can always find a job. And I could work my way through college if my folks can't pay my way."

Jim smiles wryly. "The trouble is, it's hard to see myself chained to a computer eight hours a day." He raises his hands in mock surrender. "I just don't know what I want to do, and the days are slipping by. I guess you and Doc Choi are right. Trying to make up my mind is probably causing me all these headaches."

THE PROBLEM

Jim has already made some progress. He's beginning to realize that his physical symptoms are probably caused by anxiety over making career decisions. This realization doesn't mean that his headaches aren't painful or that they won't recur. But in being honest with himself, Jim has taken the first step toward solving his problem.

Because Jim isn't clear about his life goals, he can't choose a path that will lead to personal and career satisfaction. Other people—his aunt, his father, his friends—push him one way and then another. Without a foundation of self-insight to build on, he cannot make a decision. The opposite extreme would be to

FIGURE 16.3 ▓ Jim has some difficult decisions to make about his future.

make a hasty decision born of desperation. His switch to a computer science major seems to fall into that category.

To his credit, Jim seems aware of the difference between talent and training. Once he makes up his mind, he seems willing to invest the time and energy it takes to reach a goal. Caught up in the drama of making life choices, however, he worries too much about making a mistake. In time, he'll learn that no choice is perfect. All anyone can do is to find the best alternative among all the imperfect choices. Luckily, no one need be stuck forever with the wrong career. Even if Jim chooses medicine now, he can still change to another field later on.

Jim also seems to be hoping that someone or something will "turn him on." This passive approach might well keep him from reaching his full potential. Even so, Jim has eliminated several choices, and his attitude toward work seems realistic enough. His next step should be to evaluate his interests, his abilities, and his long-range goals. Until he does, he'll remain paralyzed by his fear of making a mistake. And that would be the biggest mistake of all.

SOLUTIONS

Once Jim understands that his problems are self-inflicted, he'll probably be ready to accept some advice. His counselor might suggest that he begin by setting aside a block of time when he can be by himself. Then he should focus his thinking on four concepts: money, love, ego food, and health. After he writes these four headings on a piece of paper, he should fill in the columns as honestly as he can.

MONEY.   When Jim thinks about money, he should make a realistic estimate of what his adult needs will be. Many young people leave home without knowing how expensive it is to rent an apartment, buy a car, travel, and keep food on the table. Jim should also try to project his money needs five and ten years into the future. If he's responsible for educating a younger sister, for example, his job will have to provide that level of income. At the same time, Jim should not ignore the costs of his own education and training. He's already inclined to choose a career in medicine over a job as a computer programmer because of the higher pay and greater job satisfaction. Those advantages, however, must be balanced against medicine's long and expensive training period.

LOVE.   Thinking about love gives Jim a chance to consider what he needs from the other people in his life. He already knows that he'll want to marry when he meets the right woman. Jim should also remember that after he leaves his family he will be welcoming a new set of friends into his life. The challenge of building adult relationships is to accept their closeness without losing his own identity.

EGO FOOD.   Ego food is a shorthand way of describing the satisfaction Jim will need from his work. In this category, he should list (1) his genuine interests, (2) what he would take pride in doing with his life, (3) his present

LIFE IS NOW

There is no future outside of us; it lies within us, and we make it for ourselves. Rarely do we have large blocks of time in which, uninterrupted, we can start and complete a task. And so novels are read on the bus to and from work, or paintings are dabbled at in bits of time evenings. Life is now.
IRA TANNER

abilities and training, and (4) the steps he must take to reach his goals. If he hasn't already done so, he should take a standardized vocational aptitude test. Far too many people choose careers that are attractive only because they offer a quick return for a minimum investment of effort.

Jim's friend Richie, for example, left school to work full time at a gas station. At age 17, he felt that the money was marvelous and the work more exciting than going to school. Five years from now, Richie may discover that he's caught in a dead-end job that no longer gives him much satisfaction. If helping people is really a central goal in Jim's life, he should make sure that his future career provides that opportunity.

HEALTH.   Because of his headaches, Jim should evaluate his health right now. With the help of his doctor, he can isolate the cause and decide on a treatment. If he smokes or drinks, is overweight or underweight, has trouble sleeping or other symptoms of potential illness, this is a good time to adopt a healthier life-style. The chances are good, however, that his headaches will disappear when he ends his chronic indecision.

A SELF-AWARENESS EXERCISE FOR CHOOSING A CAREER

Perhaps you've been going through some of these same uncertainties. If so, the following exercise will help you clarify your thinking.

1. If you were free to do any kind of work you wanted, what would it be? Ignore reality for a moment, and write down what you *really* want to do. Be as specific as possible.

2. *Close your eyes for a few minutes.* Imagine that you are in the situation you named—doctor, engineer, farmer, secretary, homemaker, pilot, baseball player, social worker, teacher, carpenter, musician, mechanic, accountant, or whatever. Where are you? Describe the setting.

3. What are you doing? What other people are there with you? What are they doing?

4. Did you need any special training to get where you are? What skills or abilities were required?

5. What does this occupation allow you to do that's especially important to you?

6. *Now come back to the present.* How much do you really know about this occupation?

7. What values, abilities, and interests do you have that relate to this type of work?

8. Are there any related occupations that you would consider?

9. What new information do you need before actually choosing this occupation?

10. Is what you want still a dream, or is it a realistic possibility?

11. What concrete steps can you take *right now* to turn this dream into a reality?

No one can guarantee that you'll be successful in your career choice. Thoughtful planning and evaluation, however, will point you in the right direction. Twenty years from now, when you look in the mirror and ask yourself who started you in the direction your life has taken, you'll want to be able to answer: "I made my own choices with my eyes open. For better or worse, I take full responsibility." Would you want it any other way?

Case History 3 ▓ ROSA: LEARNING TO EXPRESS ANGER

Rosa is 19 and in search of some answers. Although she's been in encounter groups off and on for a year, she still feels unhappy because she hasn't been able to maintain close relationships. As soon as she does open up with a new friend, Rosa complains, the other person starts to back away.

"I was raised to be honest about my feelings," she says. "In my family, it was okay for us to yell at one another. We slammed doors and threw things. Once my father broke the door of the kitchen cabinet. I mean, isn't that better than hitting somebody? Sure, we said things we didn't always mean, but we got over it."

Rosa clenches her fist, then slowly opens it. "It's good for you to let off steam—better than bottling it up inside. If you don't let go, it's ulcer city. When someone gets in your face, you can bite your tongue and take it, or you can tell the jerk where to get off. That's just being honest.

"Look, if people know you and like you, it shouldn't matter if you snap at them now and then." Rosa smiles. "After all, my friends have the same privilege. I think it's a pretty insecure person who can't face the truth, anyway. If two friends hang out together, one is bound to rub the other the wrong way at times. What I mean is, if something makes me angry, I sound off. It clears the air. It's healthy.

"Suppose a salesclerk tries to high-pressure me. Doesn't it make sense to fight back? Come on strong, and people back down. Lots of people think that to make it in this world you have to be some kind of wimp." Rosa taps her chest. "Not me. Never!"

THE PROBLEM

Rosa is having trouble sorting out the difference between being aggressive and being assertive. She hasn't developed the inner controls that allow most people to handle

FIGURE 16.4 ▨ Rosa hasn't learned how to handle anger in a nonaggressive way.

their natural feelings of anger in a constructive way. Instead, Rosa allows herself the luxury of venting her emotions. Her home environment taught her this behavior pattern, and her experiences in encounter groups may have reinforced it. Encounter groups often teach coping skills by encouraging participants to express repressed feelings.

In time, Rosa will discover that explosive outbursts of anger don't allow much room for emotional growth. Behavior that is barely acceptable in young children cannot be tolerated in adults. Rosa's anger lets her relieve frustration, but it cannot shield her from the secret guilt she feels when she realizes that she's driven the other person away. Her attempt to find help in encounter groups marks a step forward. Despite her self-justifying speeches, she's beginning to realize that her own behavior is preventing her from making and keeping close friends. Rosa can be a loyal and helpful friend, but only a masochist would stay around to serve as a target for her hair-trigger temper.

SOLUTIONS

Anyone who has ever been consumed by anger knows how powerful that feeling can be. If Rosa wants to change her behavior, she must start by developing self-control. This does not mean that she will turn into a doormat. Instead of attacking the other person, she will learn to focus on solving problems in a calm, nonthreatening manner.

Keeping an "anger journal" would be a good starting point for Rosa. In her journal, she would record each day's arguments, insults, and rages. Writing down what happens each day will give her a chance to reflect on her feelings. How often does she give in to her anger? How does she feel about it afterward? When she reviews the journal, she should hold herself to rigid standards of honesty regarding the reasons behind her outbursts. She may spot a tendency to excuse herself because "it was really hot today" or because "Steve knows I don't like being teased." If so, Rosa will learn to recognize such self-serving rationalizations and how to deal with them as they occur.

Along with her journal, Rosa can use behavioral techniques to control her sharp tongue. The next time she gets into an argument, for example, she might try putting herself into the role of a spectator. As she stands back and "watches" the situation, she can ask herself if the incident really deserves such an angry reaction. She can also keep anger from building up by imagining the other person doing something ridiculous. Instead of blowing up when Steve teases her, Rosa could visualize him jumping around in a pink gorilla outfit. Silly fantasies can defuse anger almost instantly.

Another approach would be for Rosa to set a mental timer on herself. She might start by limiting herself to two minutes per outburst. On the second day, she would cut the time to 1:50, on the third day to 1:40, and so on. As an alternative, she could discipline herself to wait for a longer and longer period each day before allowing herself to express her anger openly. Either technique will make Rosa more aware of her own feelings and reactions. After a while, her "anger time" will dwindle to almost nothing. Rosa should also keep count of how many times she *could* have given in to anger during the day. At night, to release bottled-up feelings, she can punch her pillow several times for each incident. Finally, Rosa should watch to see how other people express anger. As she'll find out, angry people aren't very attractive.

At this point, Rosa might reasonably ask if it's ever okay to express anger. After all, if someone shoves ahead of her in line at a concert, she can't ignore it, can she? Rosa has a point. Swallowing your anger doesn't make it go away. Repressed rage eventually reappears, often emerging as aggressive behavior aimed at an innocent third party. Over the long term, the body may also convert repressed anger into physical ailments such as headaches or ulcers.

With assertive behavior, Rosa can handle most of the problems that once sparked her anger (see Chapter 15, pages 512–514). Instead of shouting at the concert goer who shoves ahead of her in line, she can say, "Look, we all waited our turn. Go back and get in line like everyone else." If necessary, she can repeat her request several more times. This broken-record technique will cause most people to back down. If the technique doesn't work, Rosa can call for a guard

---

ON UNDERSTANDING YOUR ANGER

The world is not necessarily just. Being good often does not pay off and there is no compensation for misfortune.

You have a responsibility to do your best nonetheless.

SHELDON KOPP

---

or an usher to take care of the situation. Even if she doesn't win the argument, she can feel as though she handled it properly. Best of all, she won't be left choked up with rage, unable to enjoy the evening.

A SELF-AWARENESS EXERCISE FOR EXPRESSING ANGER

Learning to cope with anger doesn't mean that you can't express what you're feeling. Psychologists believe that you can learn to "fight fair." For example, if you can get hold of two light, foam-covered bats, you and your partner can release a tremendous amount of anger by whacking each other (harmlessly) for several minutes. Such fights have rules, of course. No hitting is allowed around the face or in the genital areas. Even a mild-mannered and repressed person can learn to fight with foam bats—and feel good about it afterward.

Another fair-fight technique is known as the Hurt Museum. This exercise refers to the collection of little injuries and resentments people accumulate from day to day. Playing the Hurt Museum game gives you a chance to defuse that time bomb before it goes off. The exercise works as well with parents as with partners your own age. Here are the rules.

1. Both partners must agree to take part in the exercise. Each must play according to the rules.

2. No personal attacks or insults are permitted. You must stick to specific incidents which caused pain and anger. It's okay to write, "I was angry when you didn't call me last night," but not, "You have the time sense of a banana slug."

3. To start the game, separate for ten minutes and write down all the hurts you've collected from the other person. Concentrate on those you haven't talked about before. You'll probably be surprised at how many little grievances you've been storing in your personal Hurt Museum.

4. One person then reads his or her list while the other person remains silent. The listener cannot question, defend, or attack what the reader is saying. When the reader finishes, the two change roles. Neither person may discuss any item on either list until both have finished.

5. You now have several options for dealing with the collection of "hurts" the two of you have uncovered:

(a) "Bury" certain items on each list by agreeing that you'll both erase them from your thinking.

(b) Trade off some items. For example, you might say, "I'll forget about the time you didn't call me if you'll forget about the

time I pushed you off the diving board at the lake."

(c) Agree that a few items deserve to be discussed in a fair and constructive way. These are the problem areas that could damage a relationship if they're not resolved. If one person continually breaks promises, for example, that shouldn't be ignored.

Once you've resolved all the "hurts," don't look back. That's the time to move on to a happier, more open relationship. Like Rosa, you'll have learned that anger—whether uncontrolled or repressed—is one of humanity's most destructive emotions.

Case History 4 ▨ MARTIN: ADJUSTING TO CHANGE

Martin has been called into the office to talk about his grades. He sits on the edge of his chair, tugs nervously at his collar, and refuses to meet his counselor's gaze.

Mr. Johnson opens a folder. "Martin," he says, "you came to this high school with a B-plus average, but all I see on this report are C's and D's. On top of that, several of your teachers have asked me to talk to you about the way you've been dressing. Can you help me understand what's going on?"

Martin looks down at his black shirt, jeans, shoes, and socks and grins nervously. "Yeah, I guess it does look a bit Goth," he says, "but don't get me wrong. I don't worship Satan or sleep in a coffin. I know about those two trench-coat mafia guys who went on a shooting spree at Columbine High School. I could never do anything like that!"

Mr. Johnson smiles reassuringly. "Okay, I'll buy that, especially since your parents assured me there aren't any guns in your house, and that you go to church every

Sunday. Still, you're clearly not the same 16-year-old I enrolled in September."

"It's this school!" Martin snaps, his eyes flashing. "Back at my old school, I was involved in lots of activities and I knew everybody. Here, everyone belongs to a clique, whether it's the jocks or the nerds or the party crowd. Where I come from, most of the kids like the same things I like—horses, country music, hunting and fishing. These city guys are always bragging about their wild parties and how they're going to make tons of money some day. And the girls? I had lots of dates back at my old school. Here, the girls just laugh when I ask them out."

"Moving from a small town to a big city can be a shock." Mr. Johnson says with a nod. "I can see how you might feel a bit lost—but does that explain the poor grades and the all-black outfits?"

"What's the use of studying?" Martin says with a sigh. "Most nights, I just go online to chat with my friends back home. I started wearing these clothes as a kind of rebellion, I guess. I felt as though I was invisible, so I dressed the part. I never guessed people would worry that I'd come to school some day and shoot up the place. I know my dad's new job will keep me here until I graduate. But the day I get my diploma, I'm heading back to where I belong!"

THE PROBLEM

Martin has reacted more emotionally than most people to a fairly common event in today's mobile society. Uprooted from a secure environment, he's having difficulty adjusting to a new one. Martin shows good insight when he analyzes the difference between the two communities, but his conclusions aren't always realistic. Whether he likes it or not, change is a constant in most modern lives. He will often face the challenge of adjusting to new situations.

For someone who was so active in his former community, Martin's attitude is surprisingly passive. Except for a half-hearted attempt to make friends, he hasn't taken any positive steps to develop new relationships. To make matters worse, he is resisting the reality of his family's move. If Martin really looked, he would find that opportunities for friendship and growth exist wherever he goes. Martin also needs to understand that his dreams of returning to his old home are equally unrealistic. If he went back, he would find changes there, too. People refuse to stand still, no matter how much we want them to stay the same.

Martin's low grades are a symptom of his unconscious decision to reject his new situation. His earlier involvement in school and social activities shows that he has the skills he needs to repeat those successes. As for Martin's statement that the kids are different at the new school, he's probably referring to

FIGURE 16.5 ▪ Can Martin learn to cope with the problems caused by his family's move to a new community?

surface appearances, such as dress styles and mannerisms. People are much the same wherever you go, but you have to dig beneath the surface to contact the real personalities underneath.

SOLUTIONS

Once Martin decides to make an effort to become part of his new community, he has several options. First, along with dressing in a less provocative way, he must become an *accepting* person. People don't need ESP to sense that they are being measured and rejected. When Martin sincerely reaches out to others, they will respond to him. Second, he needs to map out an action program. He can begin by checking out the groups that are open to him, such as school clubs, religious groups, athletic teams, Explorer Scouts, 4-H, and the like. When he finds a likely group, he

YOU CAN NEVER HAVE "ENOUGH"

The outside world can never give you "enough" if you are programmed always to want something you don't already have or more of what you do have. If you always want "more," you will never have "enough."
KEN KEYES, JR., AND BRUCE BURKAN

should immerse himself in its activities. Every group treasures members who volunteer to do the time-consuming chores that keep the group going. As soon as he reaches out to others, Martin's social life will improve almost overnight.

Close friendships usually happen without too much planning. Martin will find that the activities he enjoys will attract the kind of people to whom he can relate. Adopting a more mature attitude about winning friends will help. He must be assertive enough to make the first efforts, but he can't push too hard. If he looks too needy, the girls he wants to date will reject him.

In time, Martin will find that his new environment isn't as alien as he thought. If he is serious about a career in ranching or farming, he will have plenty of time after graduation to complete his training. But he should also consider the career opportunities offered by his new community. As he makes friends and joins in new activities, he'll discover that he has much in common with the same people who now seem so different.

A SELF-AWARENESS EXERCISE FOR EVALUATING FRIENDSHIPS

For most young people, friends are as important as eating and sleeping. The growth and sharing possible in a solid friendship help us make the transition from family attachments to the commitments of adult life. Even the best of friendships has its ups and downs, however. Perhaps you're having nagging doubts about the way things are going with a particular friend. If you're ready to take an honest look at the relationship, try the following exercise.*

Directions: Select the word in each statement that *most accurately* describes your friendship. The letter *X* has been used here so that you can substitute the name of your friend whenever it appears.

1. When I see *X*, I feel (a) happy, (b) indifferent, (c) nervous.
2. My conversations with *X* are usually (a) exciting, (b) impersonal, (c) boring.
3. When I talk about a success of my own, *X* usually responds with (a) pleasure, (b) indifference, (c) envy.
4. When I think of *X*, I often feel (a) happy, (b) annoyed, (c) depressed.
5. When I disagree with *X*, it usually leads to a (a) discussion, (b) fight, (c) temporary breakup.
6. When I'm with *X*, we generally have (a) fun, (b) nothing to do, (c) emotional upsets.
7. When I leave *X*, I usually feel (a) happy, (b) tired, (c) confused.
8. When I'm working, *X* usually feels (a) free to let me finish, (b) irritated, (c) rejected.
9. When I'm with *X* and the conversation stops, *X* seems to feel (a) at ease with silence, (b) uncomfortable, (c) nervously talkative.
10. When I seem unusually quiet, *X* (a) asks me what's the matter, (b) tries to get my mind off my troubles, (c) takes my silence personally and gets upset.

* Adapted from Howard M. Newburger and Marjorie Lee, *Winners and Losers: The Art of Self-Image Modification* (New York: David McKay, 1974), copyright Howard M. Newburger and Marjorie Lee, pp. 88–89 and 155–156. The numerical point score in the last paragraph of the exercise (page 545) has been added to the original exercise created by Newburger and Lee.

11. When I'm supposed to go somewhere with X, I tend to (a) look forward to it, (b) worry about whether it will work out, (c) forget the arrangements we made.

12. When I meet X's other friends, I usually find them to be (a) good company, (b) boring, (c) unpleasant.

13. When we have plans to do something together, X tends to arrive (a) on time, (b) late, (c) with other friends I didn't know were coming.

14. When I give a gift to X, X says (a) "Thank you," (b) "You shouldn't have," (c) "When is your birthday?"

15. Regarding personal interests, X and I (a) have exactly the same ones, (b) have several in common, (c) don't like the same things at all.

16. I sometimes think that I'd like to (a) be just like X, (b) borrow some of X's traits, (c) never be like X.

17. In most ways I feel that X is my (a) equal, (b) superior, (c) inferior.

18. If I have special news to share, X is the person I (a) think of first, (b) tell the next time we meet, (c) tell only when absolutely necessary.

19. If I tell X a secret, I'm sure the secret will be (a) kept, (b) told to a few of X's friends, (c) blabbed to everyone X meets.

20. Whenever I get into an argument with someone, X (a) takes my side, (b) stays neutral, (c) tells me I'm in the wrong.

When you've finished the exercise, look at your answers. Score three points for each *a*, two for each *b*, and one for each *c*. A score of 50 or better means that you have a great relationship! Anything from 35–49 suggests that your relationship is like most friendships—you have your differences, but the friendship is worth keeping. If the score is under 35, it's time to face the fact that the friendship is causing you more pain than pleasure. Talk to X about your feelings and look for ways to resolve your differences. X will very likely welcome your candor.

Case History 5 ▮ TAMMY: COPING WITH DIVORCE

Tammy slips quietly into the counselor's office at the Free Clinic. She looks embarrassed, but she has made up her mind to talk to someone about her problem. Her parents' divorce became final three months ago. Tammy, a much-loved only child, is having a difficult time adjusting to the breakup of her family. After a couple of false starts, she pushes her hair back off her forehead and plunges in.

"I knew the divorce was coming," she says. "Last year, on my 16th birthday, I called a family council and tried to talk them out of filing the papers. Instead of working to save their marriage, though, they just gave up. They threw away 22 years of marriage, just like that. Now I can see that both of them are unhappy. My mother won't admit it, but I'm pretty sure she'd take my father back if he asked."

Tammy brushes away a tear. "They think of divorce as a way of solving problems, but the problems are still there. In fact, they used to argue a lot about money, but now there's less money than ever. The biggest laugh is they said we'd still be a family. They even told me I'd be closer to my father because when I saw him, I'd have him all to myself. Big deal! I hardly ever see him, and when I do, we don't have anything to say to each other."

The counselor asks Tammy to narrow her complaints down to the problem bothering her the most.

FIGURE 16.6 ▨ Tammy believes that her parents' divorce is the cause of her own unhappiness.

"That's easy," Tammy replies. "I've had to grow up overnight. It's like things have turned upside down. I used to depend on my mother for everything, but now she leans on me. And she's so unhappy I don't feel that I can tell her my problems. She cries on my shoulder, and I keep my feelings to myself.

"And to make it worse, my father is already living with another woman. She's younger than he is, and she's a terrible housekeeper. Instead of solving his problems, he made them worse." Tammy takes a deep breath. "How can adults be so stupid! I'd never do anything like this to my kids."

THE PROBLEM

The Free Clinic counselor describes Tammy as "an honest, mature young woman who sees life in realistic terms." Tammy's description of the effect the divorce has had on her family seems accurate enough—although Tammy's own biases should also be taken into account. Talking about her feelings with a sympathetic listener will probably help her put the changes in her life into perspective.

Fortunately, a counselor can do more for Tammy than listen. Tammy needs to understand that it's self-defeating to blame her unhappiness on others. She should consider the possibility that her negative feelings about the

divorce come (at least in part) from her inability to see the conflict through her parents' eyes. She hasn't tried to find out if they honestly believe the divorce has solved anything. At the same time, Tammy should ask herself whether she was ever close to her father, divorce or not. It might be that the separation only finalized a loveless situation that already existed.

Tammy also says that she resents being forced into a position of independence and responsibility. She might want to look more closely at that statement. Maybe it's time for her to repay some of the nurturing she's received from her mother. At 17 she can't remain a child much longer. It would make sense for her to look at her new role as a chance to grow.

In a similar way, Tammy should examine her attitude toward her father's new companion. Does the woman really deserve Tammy's scorn, or does Tammy dislike her simply because she appears to have "stolen" her father? Tammy should give the new relationship time to prove itself before she decides that her father has made a terrible mistake.

SOLUTIONS

Tammy can learn to cope with her problems concerning the divorce if she first divides

WE CAN ALL HELP OURSELVES

You have a right to your feelings, your painful feelings just as much as your happier ones. To feel all that you can feel is to be truly human. But too often people cling to unpleasant feelings; they even court them. Without fully realizing what they are doing, they actually bring them about. They do things that make them feel bad, and then they say, "I couldn't help myself." What most people mean when they say that is, "I didn't help myself." But we can all help ourselves.
MILDRED NEWMAN AND BERNARD BERKOWITZ

them into two categories: her feelings about the new situation in which she finds herself, and the three new relationships.

Tammy should begin by thinking about why people get married and why their marriages fail. Reading a book or two about family relationships and continuing her talks with the counselor will help. She should also meet with other young people whose parents are divorced. She can locate a group through a hot line, free clinic, or other helping agency.

It would also help if Tammy thought honestly about her own reasons for opposing the divorce. After a while, she might begin to accept the fact that, for some people, divorce is a painful but necessary way of resolving an intolerable situation. If nothing else, Tammy should accept the finality of the divorce. She apparently harbors hopes of reconciling her parents, but that is probably wishful thinking.

When Tammy examines the new family relationships, she should focus first on herself. Thus far, she seems to have seen herself only as an extension of her parents. As a young adult, however, she has her own independence to consider. A useful step for her would be to sit down with each parent for a "gut-level" discussion of feelings. With her mother, Tammy might begin by telling her how happy she is that they can still be close. She should also say that she needs to know that her mother is still interested in Tammy's own feelings and problems. When she talks to her father, she might ask for time to work out her feelings about her new relationship. Right now, he probably feels hurt and confused by Tammy's coldness.

Finally, Tammy should realize that her relationship with her parents has been changing ever since she became a teenager. The divorce came at a difficult time, just as she was nearing the end of adolescence. She feels resentful at having this separation forced upon her too soon. But as she matures, Tammy will learn that no relationship stays the same forever. Although coping with the divorce has been difficult, it does give her a chance to accelerate her own emotional growth.

A SELF-AWARENESS EXERCISE FOR COPING WITH DIVORCE

Everyone daydreams once in a while. These fantasies do no harm and sometimes do some good. Psychologists have learned how to put fantasies to work in an organized way. Through such an exercise, anyone whose parents are involved in a divorce can use creative fantasies to work through the problems that develop when a home breaks up. In fact, you can adopt this technique to tackle any problem involving human relationships.

In this exercise, you will practice saying the right things *before* you run into a painful situation. Imagine yourself responding in a definite, positive way. Try to avoid saying things calculated to make people feel guilty, such as the classic, "It's your fault that I'm not happy!"

Play all the parts in your fantasy inside your own head. If necessary, go over it several times until you get it right.

Situation 1: It's your birthday. For the first time since their divorce, your parents have both agreed to attend the celebration. During the party, you have a chance to talk to each of them privately. *I would say . . .*

RESPECT

A son should respect his father
He should not have to be taught to respect his father
It is something that is natural
That's how I've brought up my son anyway.

Of course a father must be worthy of respect
He can forfeit a son's respect
But I hope at least that my son will respect me, if only for
leaving him free to respect me or not.
R. D. Laing

Situation 2: You walk into your mother's room several months after the divorce. Before you can say anything, you notice that she's been crying. It's not the first time. *I would say . . .*

Situation 3: At a picnic with several friends from school, the topic of divorce comes up. You're the only one in the group who's been in the middle of a family breakup. Everyone turns to you for an opinion. *I would say . . .*

Situation 4: Every time you see your dad, he wants to talk about the terrible things your mother did to him during their marriage. *I would say . . .*

Situation 5: You're having dinner with your father and his new wife. When your father leaves to run an errand, an awkward silence develops. Your stepmother looks as uncomfortable as you feel. *I would say . . .*

Situation 6: All at once, your family has doubled in size. Your mother has remarried, and you now have two stepbrothers and a stepsister. Because bedroom space is limited, you'll have to share your room. Your new sibling has just walked in and is looking around the room that used to be yours alone. *I would say . . .*

Make up as many real-life situations as you wish. The value of this exercise is that it gives you a chance to work through your feelings before you're put on the spot. Creative fantasies are dress rehearsals for the real thing.

Case History 6 ▨ RALPH: RESOLVING PROBLEMS WITH PARENTS

A guard catches Ralph drinking on campus. That comes as a surprise because Ralph has never been in serious trouble before. When he walks into the principal's office, Ralph is wearing a cocky grin. He breaks into a tirade before the principal can speak.

"So now you'll kick me out of school," he challenges. "Big deal! My old man is always telling me I'll end up in the gutter. He'll be pleased to find out that you agree with him."

Ralph slouches lower in his chair. "You know, it really bugs him that I'm not just like him. He works all day in that crummy store, selling support hose to old ladies. And he expects me to follow in his footsteps!"

The principal interrupts to ask Ralph about his drinking. The teenager shrugs. "Sure, I've been taking a few drinks to get me through the day," he says. "Getting high makes me feel better, at least for a while." For the first time, he looks directly at the principal. "Believe me, I'll get my act together as soon as I finish school and start earning my own way.

"You want to know what really started this? My old man hates the fact that I want to be a mechanic. He practically blew a gasket when I signed up for advanced auto mechanics this year instead of those dumb business courses he's always pushing. I keep telling him that in two years I'll be making more money than he does. But all he can talk about is grease—grease on my pants, grease under my fingernails."

He holds up his hands for inspection. "See that? I'm proud of that grease. It's honest. And since I won't change, Dad is always on me about little things. Can you guess the last four major crimes he blasted me for? Tearing an elbow out of my jacket. Getting a ticket for running a red light. Coming in late—well, it was 2:30—from a date. And forgetting to buy him a card for his birthday. Does that sound like a federal case?"

Ralph looks at the principal, pleading mixed with the defiance in his voice. "It doesn't have to be this way, does it? Why can't my old man let me alone? Boy, life would be a lot easier if kids could only pick their own parents!"

THE PROBLEM

Ralph's problem belongs to his entire family. At this point, however, only Ralph's point of view has been heard. If he goes into counseling, a psychologist would want to talk to both of Ralph's parents. But certain facts seem obvious.

First, the problem doesn't have much to do with Ralph's drinking on campus. His drinking can't be ignored, but it can be handled separately. More basic is the conflict between Ralph and his father. A no-win battle has developed over the question of Ralph's future. That disagreement is compounded by the father's refusal to accept the fact that his son is no longer a child.

Ralph's father thinks of his small business as a step upward from his family's blue-collar origins. He takes pride in what he has accomplished. But a wise father would not insist that his son carry on the tradition. Ralph is trying to find his own identity, but he's hemmed in by his father's expectations.

Second, Ralph doesn't seem to have thought about his future very carefully. Before he jumps into any career, he should think about job satisfaction, income, opportunities for advancement, and social rewards. Working as a mechanic could well be the right choice for him—or it could be a dead-end job that will ultimately leave him unhappy and unfulfilled.

SOLUTIONS

Family counseling seems called for in Ralph's case. The therapist's first job will be to ask all members of the family for a commitment to seek help. If that hurdle can be overcome, the odds are good that harmony can be restored to the household.

FIGURE 16.7 ▓ Ralph is reacting to pressure from his parents by rebelling against all authority.

Ralph thinks of himself as the injured party, but he has some work to do, too. He needs to realize that even though he has the right to reject his father's values, those values are the foundation on which his father's life is built. With the therapist's help, Ralph may once again be able to see his father as a human being who wants the best for his son.

Ralph's father has two major adjustments to make. First, he must accept his son's growing independence. The rules and expectations that worked when Ralph was young are no longer appropriate. Second, he must face the fact that Ralph is determined to make his own vocational choices. In time, he may discover that having a mechanic in the family can be a blessing. On paper these may look like easy changes, but modifying beliefs built up over a lifetime will take skillful counseling.

Ralph and his father both seem immature in their reaction to father-son conflict. Because Ralph chose to drink on campus as his gesture of rebellion, a psychologist would guess that Ralph expected (or even hoped)

PERSONAL INVENTORY FOR _____	TRUE	FALSE	NEEDS CHANGE
1 Gets along with adults	☐	☐	☐
2 Relates well to children	☐	☐	☐
3 Has a good sense of humor	☐	☐	☐
4 Is interested in the outside world	☐	☐	☐
5 Is rarely sick with minor illnesses	☐	☐	☐
6 Expresses appreciation for gifts and favors	☐	☐	☐
7 Expresses anger openly but rationally	☐	☐	☐
8 Is able to ask for help	☐	☐	☐
9 Does well in school or on the job	☐	☐	☐
10 Is adaptable to new locations or a change in status	☐	☐	☐
11 Respects the possessions of others	☐	☐	☐
12 Keeps surroundings reasonably neat	☐	☐	☐
13 Isn't afraid to express personal opinions	☐	☐	☐
14 Works toward goals despite frustrations	☐	☐	☐
15 Is proud of physical and emotional growth	☐	☐	☐
16 Accepts others who are different	☐	☐	☐
17 Is fun to be with	☐	☐	☐
18 Respects the parent-child relationship	☐	☐	☐
19 Recognizes faults and works to change them	☐	☐	☐
20 Is willing to listen to advice but makes own decisions	☐	☐	☐

SOURCE: Howard M. Newburger and Marjorie Lee, *Winners and Losers: The Art of Self-Image Modification* (New York: David McKay, 1974).

he'd be caught. Perhaps he figured (at some deeper level of consciousness) that if he were thrown out of school, he wouldn't have any choice but to go to work as a mechanic. It also seems unreasonable that a father would insist on a career for his son that matches neither his interests nor his abilities. Both father and son have some emotional growing up to do.

A SELF-AWARENESS EXERCISE IN PARENT-CHILD UNDERSTANDING

If you'd like to open up some useful dialogue within your family, participating in this exercise is a good way to start. First, rate yourself on the personal inventory on this page. Be as honest as possible. Then give blank copies to your parents or guardians and ask each to fill in the inventory *as he/she/they see you*. When you sit down to compare your answers with theirs, you'll have the makings of a thought-provoking discussion. Later, you can reverse the procedure. As other family members rate themselves in turn, they can compare the results with the evaluations the rest of you have made.

Directions: Prepare a separate personal inventory sheet for each person. If a statement is true, check column one. If it is false, check column two. If you also think that the person being rated should change his or her behavior, check column three, "Needs Change." Do not check column three unless you feel strongly about the need to change that particular behavior.

Don't be surprised if you find that your own ratings don't match the evaluations others make of you. Once you get over the initial shock, you'll find that the exercise gives you and your family some useful data to think about—and to act on, if you sincerely want to change.

Case History 7 ▦ JUDY: OVERCOMING SHYNESS

Judy has ignored two requests from the counseling office to come in and plan her courses for the fall semester. Finally, in mid-August, her mother calls for an appointment. When the teenager and her mother arrive at the office, Judy refuses to return the counselor's friendly smile. Her mother settles herself into a chair and launches into a well-rehearsed speech.

"Judy has turned into a couch potato this summer," she complains. "When she gets up in the morning, she has three cups of coffee before she gets moving. Then she figures out her day from an astrology book. At noon she fixes herself a sandwich for lunch, then watches soap operas on TV. She does help me fix supper, I'll say that for her, and she does the dishes without being asked. But in the evening she plops herself down in front of the TV set again. What kind of day is that for a girl as bright and pretty as she is?"

The counselor turns to Judy and asks about her friends and hobbies. In the silence that follows, the mother speaks up again. "Judy goes out shopping once in a while, and every other week she has her nails done. Aside from that, she doesn't do anything. I've tried to talk her into inviting her friends over for a party or joining a dance group at the YWCA, but she always finds an excuse." The older woman throws up her hands in despair.

Judy is sitting very still, her shoulders hunched as if in self-protection. When it becomes obvious that she won't speak with her mother there, the counselor suggests that the older woman wait outside. When the door closes, Judy takes a deep breath and meets the counselor's gaze for the first time.

"I'm content with the way I live," she says softly. "Mom thinks I should get a job, but what's the use? My dad makes enough money to take care of us. He's not pushing me. Besides, no one would hire me without any experience. As for friends, why should I try? The other kids don't care whether I'm alive or dead. My best friend moved away this spring, and I'll never find anybody else like her."

She tosses her neatly brushed hair defiantly. "Look, maybe I'm not the happiest person in the world, but I get by. My brother and sister are both married, and they're killing themselves to take care of their families. Who needs that?"

Judy's voice falters. "Besides, why would anyone want me hanging around? My teeth are crooked, my voice is all wrong, and the

551

new styles look terrible on me. When a guy does talk to me, I blush so badly I want to run and hide. After I finish school, things might be different. That's time enough to look for a job and to make some new friends. For now, I'll just have to be content with my life the way it is."

THE PROBLEM

About 40 percent of the people surveyed in one study identified themselves as suffering from shyness and lack of self-esteem. Only 7 percent of the survey group said they had never experienced shyness. Few people are as intensely shy as Judy, but Judy has better reasons than most. Her mother reminds her constantly that she is weak, yet she doesn't give Judy the responsibilities she needs to improve her self-image. Judy's father, busy with his own career, leaves all the decision making to his wife. To Judy, his hands-off attitude simply confirms her low opinion of herself. Her basic need to grow by accepting new challenges is overruled by her fear of facing situations in which she might fail.

FIGURE 16.8 ▓ Judy's withdrawn behavior has its roots in her extreme shyness.

With her parents' approval, Judy has become a passive, dependent person. She says she enjoys her predictable, repetitive life. Variety and new situations are scary, and must be avoided. Left unchecked, this withdrawal could develop into a neurosis with anxiety symptoms, depression, or phobias. Her father says, "Leave her alone; she'll grow out of it," but Judy's shyness isn't a "phase" she's going through. Perhaps it won't lead to neurotic symptoms, but it can turn her life into a self-imposed prison.

At some level, Judy probably recognizes that her shyness keeps her from embracing change and growth. She rationalizes that failure by hiding behind her imagined physical deficiencies and the loss of her one close friend. To Judy's fragile ego, these defenses are both logical and important. They make it possible for her to get out of bed to face each new day.

WHY AM I AFRAID?

I am afraid to tell you who I am, because, if I tell you who I am, you may not like who I am, and it's all that I have.
JOHN POWELL, S.J.

SOLUTIONS

With added maturity and insight, Judy might be able to break out of her self-imposed prison. Normally, however, extreme shyness cannot be overcome through self-help techniques. A poor self-image and stubborn habits of withdrawal need professional assistance. When she goes into therapy, Judy must first admit to the need for change. She will then be encouraged to set new goals for herself, along with a strategy for reaching her objectives.

Once Judy understands that the therapist accepts her and likes her just as she is, she will feel safe enough to lower her defenses.

Perhaps for the first time, she will be able to look closely at her own emotions. This process is often painful. But if she sticks to her resolve, Judy will find that self-examination can be a rewarding experience. Once she begins to understand the insecurities that have caused her shyness, Judy can regain control of her life. She'll stop letting things happen *to* her.

As her self-insight increases, Judy will be able to program herself to take a series of small steps. She will set realistic social and career goals for herself, and she will take risks in her personal life. As she reaches out to new friends and tries out new social roles, her fears will decrease. Her family and her friends will marvel at the changes they see in her. She will actually look prettier, livelier, and more approachable.

One of the therapist's strategies will be to ask Judy to act as if she has great self-confidence. As Judy involves herself in more and more difficult social situations, her new attitude will become a self-fulfilling prophecy: Each successful experience will create greater self-esteem. Although Judy will probably never be a life-of-the-party person, she can learn to stand alone, secure in her own pride and independence. Her newly found warmth and joy in living will make her a prized and supportive friend to those close to her.

A SELF-AWARENESS EXERCISE FOR OVERCOMING SHYNESS

For anyone who has suffered the pounding heart, moist hands, and sinking feeling of being truly shy, Jonathan Cheek's book will come as an eye-opener. In *Shyness: Conquering the Battle Anyone Can Win* (G. P. Putnam's Sons, 1989), he points out that well-known personalities such as Johnny Carson, Barbara Walters, Kim Basinger, Henry Winkler, and Carol Burnett have also had to fight to overcome shyness. Their success proves that the problem can be overcome.

The two exercises* that follow are designed to help shy people cope with their feelings. Like most awareness experiences, the exercises are useful for anyone who wants to work on his or her own self-image.

Exercise 1. Costs and benefits. Prepare charts similar to the ones on page 554. The idea is to list the cost of what you've given up or lost because of shyness. In the middle column, describe a valued event, action, or opportunity that you lost or saw diminished because of shyness. An example has been filled in to give you the idea. Add as many items as you wish. In the last column, describe what happened to you and how you felt.

Now, think about what you've *gained* by being shy. If that sounds strange, remember that people don't adopt a behavior unless it has some sort of payoff. Examples of the benefits gained from shyness include avoiding criticism, preventing emotional tangles, avoiding rejection, and escaping responsibility. In the second column, set down a specific experience that came about because of your shyness. Then describe the benefit of your action. In the last column, note the result. Add as many items to the list as you wish.

When you analyze your two charts, you'll understand immediately what your costs and payoffs are. Then you can ask yourself, "Is this the way I want to keep on living my life?" If your answer is "No," try the next exercise.

Exercise 2. Taking risks. Start out by listing all the important risks (chances that you have taken in your life—whether it was learning to drive, trying out for the school play, or

* *Shyness: What It Is; What to Do About It* (pp. 143–146), © 1977 by Philip Zimbardo, Inc. Reprinted by permission of Addison-Wesley Publishing Company, Inc.

Shyness Liabilities

DATE	SITUATION/ACTION TAKEN OR REFUSED	RESULTING LOSS
1. May 7	I wanted to ask Pat to the prom but couldn't get up enough nerve.	I stayed home from the prom even though all my friends were going. I felt miserable.
2.		
3.		

Shyness Benefits

DATE	SITUATION/ACTION TAKEN OR REFUSED	RESULTING BENEFIT	RESULTING LONG-TERM LIABILITY (IF ANY)
1. May 2	I saw Pat walking toward me at lunch. I buried my nose in a book.	I didn't have to take a chance that Pat would ignore me.	At this rate, Pat and I will never get together.
2.			
3.			

asking someone for a date). Decide whether each risk was wise or foolish. Complete this step before you go on to the next one.

Ready? *Now go out and take a risk.* Do something "scary" that you have wanted to do but have been avoiding. Take one such risk every day this week, but first write down what you're going to do and why it's scary. Remember, this step does *not* include fool-

hardy things like jumping off the pier or picking a fight with someone who holds a black belt in karate. Your risks should center on social challenges: speaking up in class, joining a new group at lunch, making a new friend, and so on. Day by day, enjoy your successes and learn from your failures. After a while, you'll find resources and strengths inside yourself that you didn't know existed.

Case History 8 ▓ ERIC: FINDING HAPPINESS

Eric has missed a month of school. When he returns, he is reluctant to talk about the reasons for his absence. Finally, a week later, he makes an appointment to talk to his psychology teacher. At three o'clock, he slips into the classroom. He looks as if the slightest move will send him running.

"Nobody else at school knows this," he says, "but I was out of your class so long because I had a breakdown. Can you believe that? I thought only old people had breakdowns."

The teacher tells Eric that emotional problems can happen to anyone, regardless of age. That reassurance seems to make the teenager feel a little better, and he begins to tell about his experience. His voice trembles slightly, despite his best efforts to control it.

"I guess you could say I've lost control of my emotions. Almost any little thing upsets me, and then I start to feel all choked up. When this last episode started, I felt as though my lungs were full of cotton wool. I've had what my dad calls an 'asthma condition' as long as I can remember, but this was much worse. My folks rushed me to the hospital, and the nurses gave me oxygen to help me breathe. The doctors ran all kinds of tests, but they couldn't find anything physically wrong. They thought the news would make me feel better, but it didn't. I felt so ashamed! Here I was causing everyone so much trouble, and the problem was all in my head.

"The doctor asked me if anything had happened to upset me, something emotional. The only thing I could think of was the time a few weeks ago when my dad missed some money from his bedroom. He accused me of taking it. I swore on my mother's honor that I didn't take it, but he didn't believe me. My mother says she has faith in me, but deep inside I think she still has some doubts.

"I've been depressed ever since that night at the emergency room. My father says I can snap out of it any time I want. He thinks I'm using my shortness of breath as a way of escaping from my problems. And man, do I ever have my share." Eric's smile is mocking. "I only feel really good when I have a steady girl friend. Sara and I broke up four months ago, and I haven't had a date since. Lately, I've given up asking girls out. What's the use? They always turn me down."

The psychology teacher points out that Senior Ditch Day is coming up. That seems like a good time for Eric to be with his friends. It's always easier to talk to people in a group situation, especially if everyone's relaxed and having fun.

"I don't know if I'll go on Ditch Day," Eric says, shaking his head. "I don't really get a kick out of anything I do. Life seems so pointless right now. I've always needed something to look forward to, like Christmas or a ski trip. But whenever I get what I've waited and hoped for, I'm usually disappointed. Something always spoils it."

Eric buries his face in his hands. "I'm beginning to wonder if life is worth all the trouble," he says, his voice muffled and close to tears. "What do I have to do to feel happy again?"

HAPPINESS IS "DOING"

You can paralyze yourself with perfectionistic do-your-best nonsense. Perhaps you can give yourself some significant areas in your life in which you truly want to do your best. But in the vast majority of activities, having to do your best, or even to do well, is an obstacle to doing.... Try changing "Do your best" to simply "Do."
Wayne Dyer

FIGURE 16.9 ▪ Eric believes that something will always interfere with his hopes of finding happiness.

THE PROBLEM

Eric has done a good job of diagnosing his own condition. He's unhappy with himself and with life in general. His attitude has carried him close to the point of neurosis, as evidenced by his inability to cope with any part of his life. Instead of feeling relief when the doctors told him his illness is psychosomatic, for example, Eric felt even more anxious. At this point, he probably cannot pull himself out of his depression without professional help.

Somehow, Eric has managed to position himself as a bench warmer in the game of life. Add that to his negative outlook, and his unhappiness becomes understandable. He says that he's capable of enthusiasm but that things always go wrong. This attitude tells us that Eric doesn't know himself very well. He has the mistaken notion that life should be fair—but life isn't fair or unfair; it just is. The possibility must also be considered that Eric unconsciously makes things go wrong so that his negative expectations will be fulfilled.

Eric's desire to find happiness is genuine, but happiness doesn't just happen to people. It grows out of a sense of purpose and accomplishment. Because Eric hasn't established goals for himself, he doesn't really know what makes him happy. Once he analyzes his needs, he can work with a therapist to find ways of achieving them. His father's mistrust, for example, can be overcome by setting up a series of situations in which Eric has a chance to demonstrate that he can be trusted. Right now his father may not have much reason to give his withdrawn, unhappy son the benefit of the doubt.

A complete psychiatric review would also check out the possibility that Eric's depression has physical causes. If psychotherapy is called for, he might profit from treatment with one of the antidepressant medications. Whatever medical help he receives, however, Eric must still find contentment within himself. As he finds out every year when he celebrates his birthday, happiness is not something you can expect other people to give you.

SOLUTIONS

Eric needs immediate help before his downward spiral of anxiety and depression carries him beyond the point of no return. The case histories of some suicides show a similar pattern. Short-term, client-centered psychotherapy can help him sort out his tangled emotions. Most of all, Eric needs to have his own value as a human being reinforced. Reality therapy, or an existentialist approach might also be helpful.

Once Eric and his therapist have established a good relationship, the therapist will ask Eric to talk about his own feelings and needs. When Eric sees that happiness is a byproduct of an active, productive life, he will feel less pressured to "be happy." He will also feel better when he understands that his "breakdown" is not unique. Gradually, the therapist will encourage Eric to take a more active part in his own life. His asthma-like attacks may not disappear immediately. Their intensity will decrease, however, as he learns to cope with failure and to enjoy success.

At present, Eric doesn't understand why he isn't as happy as the sitcom characters he watches on television. Trapped in the quicksand of his depression, he has forgotten that only one person is responsible for Eric's life—Eric himself. Once he learns to live according to his own values and needs, he'll have a chance to find the happiness he's seeking.

A SELF-AWARENESS EXERCISE FOR IDENTIFYING PERSONAL VALUES

All human beings, young and old, feel a sense of inner peace and contentment when their personal values and needs are fulfilled. But what makes someone else happy might very well leave you utterly miserable. Do you know what your own values are? Some people do; many have never stopped to think about what's really important in their lives. This exercise will help you compile your own list.

The exercise will work only if you complete each of the following items quickly and honestly. Don't pause to think about "right" answers or what others would expect you to say. On a separate sheet of paper, write the first four things that pop into your mind in each category.

1. Happiness is _____
2. Unhappiness is _____
3. I would really like to _____
4. I hate to _____
5. I am proud of _____
6. The biggest lessons about life I learned this year are _____

When you're finished, look back at your answers. Do you find any recurring ideas, themes, or connections? Perhaps you'll discover that your values revolve around making other people happy. There's nothing wrong with that, as long as it makes you happy, too. But some people spend so much time taking care of others that they never tend to their own needs. If you want to continue the exercise, try some different lead-ins:

"A value I really admire is . . ."
"My worst faults are . . ."
"This year I learned that men/women . . ."

Now, rate your responses. Put a *C* next to those that you would like to change. Writing "I hate to get up in the morning" may be how you feel, but it's also something you may want to change—especially if your first period class or your job requires early rising. Mark a *W* by those items that are wishes for the future. For example, you may have written, "Happiness is graduating from college," even though that great day is still years away. Finally, put a *T* next to those statements that stand out as expressions of your bedrock values and needs.

Clarifying your values in exercises like this lets you see exactly where you stand. The process frees you to discard the emotional baggage that no longer makes sense in your life.

AFTERWORD: ON DEVELOPING A BEAUTIFUL SOUL

Few of us can duplicate Irwin the Troll's feat of flower diving. But wouldn't it be lovely if we could? In a world that too often turns its back on crime, hunger, poverty, illness, and discrimination, beautiful souls are in short supply.

Can psychology do anything to help? Certainly the lessons that psychology teaches weren't meant to be confined within the covers of a book. In less than a hundred years, psychology has emerged as a living, working tool. It teaches a lesson worth repeating: *People can improve the quality of their lives.*

Okay, you're probably saying, that *sounds* good. Now *prove* it. If Skinner can't agree with Freud, and if Maslow doesn't see eye to eye with Horney, how can the poor amateur

hope to find a path through all the confusion? If one person's Oedipus complex is another's conditioned response, what's the point of continuing the debate?

If this entire text could be boiled down to its most important concepts, four key ideas would emerge. Each speaks to the importance of psychology in a world where the bad days regularly outnumber the good.

YOU HAVE THE POWER TO CHANGE YOUR LIFE

Many aspects of your life lie beyond your personal control. You can't do much to change your age, height, foot size, and so on.

At one time psychologists also thought that your emotional life was determined by forces that lay outside your control.

Today, that negative outlook has been greatly modified. To a degree, you are your parents' child. The person you are today has been shaped by the random chance of genetic inheritance and by childhood. *But you also have the power to change*. Most psychologists now think that it's a cop-out for a person to say, "I can't help it. That's the way I am." You *can* help yourself—if you will. Through your own efforts or with the help of a counselor or therapist, you can overcome almost any childhood trauma.

That's not to suggest that it's easy to change behavior patterns built up over many years. You may be carrying parental messages in your head that tell you not to succeed, not to love, never to take chances, and so on. Once you recognize these messages for what they are, psychology can help you replace them with healthier rules for living. Think of that effort as an investment in your future. Positive change will pay dividends in your own life, of course, but it will also be multiplied a hundred times through the effect you have on other people.

YOU ARE A SPECIAL PERSON

Look at the tip of your index finger for a moment. The delicate pattern of lines and loops you see there has never been duplicated on another human being. And just like your fingerprint, *you* are unique. No other person shares your exact genetic and environmental heritage. After all, even identical twins have different life experiences. So stand a little straighter, and give yourself a high five. You're one of a kind!

True, we all have our share of the faults, traumas, frustrations, fears, anxieties, compulsions, and all the other negative behavior patterns that psychologists have identified. But you also have abilities, strengths, intelli-gence, love, and a hundred other positive qualities. If you owned a rare orchid or a classic Rolls-Royce, you'd treat it with the care it deserves. Why not accept the help that psychology can give you in recognizing and developing your own special qualities and potential? The powers of the mind can be used to change behavior and improve the quality of your life. Are you willing to accept that responsibility? A special person like you deserves the very best!

PROBLEMS ARE FOR SOLVING

Living a carefree existence on a South Seas island would be paradise—for a month or two. But after a hundred identical days of sleeping, eating, and snorkeling, wouldn't you begin to long for a storm, a shipwreck, a visitor—anything to break the routine? Before you knew it, you'd be inventing problems just for the fun of solving them.

Life being what it is, you will seldom be called on to invent problems. They'll come knocking on your door. Many will be minor, but others will challenge every ounce of intelligence, courage, and love you possess. If you know something about human behavior, you won't have to tackle the difficult times blindly. Some day, for example, you'll have to cope with the overwhelming grief that people experience when death comes to someone they love. Psychology can't prevent that grief, nor should it. But it can prepare you to accept your feelings as a necessary part of saying "good-bye." By accepting your grief and working through it, you'll more quickly be free to go on with your own life.

PEOPLE ARE FOR LOVING

In an age whose theme song often seems to be, "What's in it for me?," psychology reminds us that we share our lives with others. If we ignore that message, our inborn selfishness restricts our vision. More than that, some people have misread psychology. They claim that they should be allowed to say and do whatever "feels good," regardless of how their behavior affects others. Husbands and wives leave home to "find themselves"; drug and alcohol abusers excuse their self-destructive behavior by repeating the mantra, "I have the right to do what I want with my body"; and too many young people "go with the flow" because they believe that work, discipline, and ambition somehow prevent the full flowering of human nature.

Perhaps a grain of truth exists within each of these attitudes. But consider a greater truth. The happiest and most productive people find joy in relating to others. This won't happen if you use people for your own selfish purposes. Nor can it happen if you close yourself off to the needs and interests of those people with whom you share your life.

Try a simple experiment, if you will. Ours is not a "touching" society. You've probably noticed how careful most people are not to touch others. For a week, make a point of touching the people to whom you feel close. You don't have to hug or grab or stroke them. A light, quick pressure on the hand or arm or shoulder will do. Try it in greeting, during conversation, or when saying good-bye. This extra touching is almost sure to improve your relationships with your family and friends.

THIS BOOK IS ONLY A STARTING PLACE

Now that you've come to the final page of the final chapter, you may feel that you've "learned" psychology. In fact, after 500 or so pages, you can be forgiven for thinking that you've exhausted the subject. As it turns out, you've only scratched the surface. For proof, check the psychology section of any library. You'll find dozens of titles dealing with every topic covered in these pages, as well as with others that lack of space prevented us from exploring.

We hope that your study of psychology is only beginning. A few of you may be planning to go on to careers in this field. If you do, your professional training will take you into the challenging world of the university, the research laboratory, and the clinic. For those who go on to separate careers and lives far removed from the formal study of psychology, we send a sightly different message: *Stay involved.* Psychology can't answer all your questions, nor will it solve all your problems. Even so, it's the best means we have of understanding the how and why of human behavior.

Finally, we invite you to share your reactions to this book. Since we're human, we'd be pleased to hear positive things about your experiences with *Psychology: A Way to Grow.* But if you think something should be added or changed or deleted, we want to know that, too. Write to us in care of Amsco School Publications, 315 Hudson Street, New York, NY 10013. We want to make this book a living text that will grow with this young and vigorous science. That can't happen without your help.

Take good care of yourself. You deserve it.

CARL R. GREEN
WILLIAM R. SANFORD

INDEX

A

Abell, Richard, 298
Abnormal behavior, degrees of, 240–242
Abnormal psychology, 19–20
Accident trauma, 249
Achievement tests, 379–382
Acne, 141–142
ACT (American College Testing Program), 380
Adams, Abigail, 446
Adapted Child, 522
Adler, Alfred, 209–212, 287
Adolescence, 99, 134–163
  alcohol and, 160–161
  categorizing personality in, 147
  contrasting views of, 139
  defined, 136–137
  developmental tasks of, 150–157
  drugs and, 160–161
  early or late maturation in, 143
  emotional challenges in, 144–149
  external changes in, 140
  family breakup and, 158
  group pressures in, 155–157
  growth spurts in, 141
  impulse control in, 150–151
  internal changes in, 140–141
  physical appearance in, 150
  physical changes during, 139–143
  rapid growth in, 142–143
  self-identity in, 152
  shifting emotional ties in, 148–149
  special problems in, 157–163
  stages of, 137–138
Adrenal glands, 71, 73
Adult ego state, 520–522
Adulthood, 99, 138–139
Affective reactions, 262
Afterimage, 76
Age regressions, 30

Ageism, 425–427
Aggression, 410–417
  eliminating models for, 414
  models of, 411–412
  reducing, 412–415
  social causes of, 411–412
Aggressive antisocial personality, 265
AIDS, 106, 145
"Ain't It Awful" game, 524, 525
Al-Anon, 305
Alateen, 305
Alcohol, use of, 49–51, 54, 160–161
Alcoholics Anonymous (AA), 304–305
Alter ego, 296
Altered states of consciousness (ASC), 37–38
Alvarez, Alfred, 424
Alzheimer's disease (AD), 258–259
American College Testing Program (ACT), 380
Amnesia, 253
Amphetamines, 49, 54
Amyl nitrite, 54
Anal stage, 193
Analytic psychology, 220, 228
Anger, self-awareness exercise for expressing, 541–542
Anima and animus, 222
Animal rights, 18–19
Anna O., 170–171
Anorexia nervosa, 454
Anthony, Susan B., 450
Antidepressant drugs, 310
Antipsychotic drugs, 309
Antisocial personality disorder, 263, 265–266
Anxiety, 146, 148, 245
Anxiety disorders, 255
Aptitude tests, 379, 382–383
Archetypes, 220–221
Aristophanes, 450

Aristotle, 175
Artificial intelligence, 366
Artificial life programs, 366
Asch, Solomon, 405
Assertive behavior, 415, 417
Assertiveness training (AT), 510, 512–514
Assimilation, 334
Astrology, 175, 477–479
AT (assertiveness training), 510, 512–514
Attention deficit disorder, 271
Auditory canal, 77
Auditory nerve, 78
Aura, 492
Autism, 271–273
Autonomic nervous system, 34
Autonomy versus doubt, 215
Aveyron, Wild Boy of, 118
Axons, 68

B

Bahrick, Harry, 326, 328
Barbiturates, 54
Barnes, Mary, 290
Basic anxiety, 212–213
Basic needs, 224–225
Beezer, Robert, 456
Behavior
  abnormal, degrees of, 240–242
  brain and, 61–89
  emotional, 119–120
  in groups, 398–431
  hearing and, 77–80
  normal, defining, 240
  psychology as study of, 2–27
  skin senses and, 83–86
  social pressures and, 405–410
  vision and, 73–76
Behavior development, theories of, 99–101

Behavior-learning theory, 99–100
Behavior modification, 208, 292
Behavior therapy, 292–294
Behaviorism, 8, 228
Behaviorist model, 283
Behaviorist theory, 205–207
Behaviorists, personality and, 204–207
Being and becoming, 229
Beisser, Arnold, 427
Benson, Herbert, 485
Berne, Eric, 520, 523–524
Bernstein, Morey, 30
Bessent, Malcolm, 489
Bettelheim, Bruno, 94–95
Binet, Alfred, 360, 365, 367
Biochemical imbalances, 248–249
Bioenergetic analysis, 509
Biofeedback, 510–512
Biological view, 8
Birth order, effect of, on intelligence, 114
Birth trauma, 97
Blind spot, 75
Body language, 398–400
Bodywork techniques, 506–509
Boring, Edwin, 359–360
Brain, 63
    behavior and, 61–89
    left versus right, 67–68
Brain development, imperfect, 268
Brain dysfunction, 270–273
Brain function, research into, 32–33
Brain trauma, 269
Brain waves, control of, 511–512
Brainstorming, 347
Brazelton, T. Berry, 442
Breuer, Joseph, 170–171
Bridey Murphy, 30–32
Broca, Paul, 33
Broken record, 512–513
Bronfenbrenner, Urie, 123
Brown, Helen Gurley, 446
Bruner, Jerome, 99
Bruner, Jerome, 99
Bulimia, 454
Butyl nitrate, 54
Byrd, Eldon, 490–491

C

Caesar, Julius, 270
Caffeine, 50, 54
CAI (computer-assisted instruction), 326, 327
Careers
    in psychology, 23–25
    self-awareness exercise for choosing, 538–539
Castration complex, 193
Catatonic schizophrenia, 259–260

Catharsis, 284–285, 287
Cattell's rating scale, 179
Cell body, 68
Central nervous system, 65
Cerebellum, 64
Cerebral cortex, 66–67
Cerebrum, 66–67
Chakras, 481
Channeling, 480
Cheek, Jonathan, 553
Chesterfield, Lord, 400
Child ego state, 520–522
Child neglect and abuse, 128–129
Childhood phase, 97, 99
Childhood sexuality, 192
Childless marriages, 464
Chlamydia, 145
Chromosomal abnormalities, 105–106
Chromosomes, 103
Chronological age (CA), 363
Circadian rhythms, 87–88
Clairvoyance, 489
Cleveland, Grover, 447
Client-centered therapy, 290–292
Clinical personality tests, 385–390
Cocaine, 52, 53, 54
Cochlea, 78
Codeine, 53, 55
Coffee, 50
Cognition, 325
Cognitive Abilities Test, 373
Cognitive development, Piaget's four stages of, 113–115
Cognitive dissonance, 407–408
Cognitive processes, 113
Cognitive theory, 325
Cognitive therapy, 292
Coles, Robert, 421
Collective unconscious, 220
Color blindness, 75
Communal living, 464–465
Communal marriage, 464–465
Community mental health centers, 306
Community resources, 306–308
Comparative psychology, 20
Compensation, 210
Complementary transactions, 523, 524
Compliance, 406
Compulsions, 251, 261
Computer-assisted instruction (CAI), 326, 327
Concept formation, 117–119
Concepts, 337
Concrete operations stage, 115
Conditioning, 7, 207
Cones, in eye, 75
Conformity, 405
    reasons for, 406–407

social dangers of, 409–410
    types of, 406
Confrontation groups, 298
Conscience, 187
Conscious mind, 34, 181, 182
Consciousness, 30–58
Conservation, 115, 116
Control groups, 15
Controlled variables, 13–14
Conventional group therapies, 295
Conventionalists, 147
Conversion hysteria, 252–253, 254
Convulsive disorder, 270
Coping, strategies for, 533–560
Cornea, 74
Corpus callosum, 68
Correlations, 16, 17
Counseling services, 307
Countertransference, 195–196
Cousins, Norman, 61–62
Crack, 53, 54
Creative self, 209
Creative visualization, 514
Creativity
    elements of, 349–350
    improving, 348–349
    teaching, 349
Cretinism, 73
Crisis intervention, 306–307
Critical Parent, 522
Crossed transactions, 523, 525
Crystals, 481, 482
Cultural bias, 376
Culture, language and, 340
Culture-free tests, 376
Cumulative learning, 326, 328

D

DAT (Differential Aptitude Tests), 382–383, 384
Date rape, 456
Daytop Village, 304
de Bono, Edward, 345, 346
Death, coping with, 427–430
Death force, 184
DeCasper, Anthony, 113
Decay through disuse, 334–335
Decibel scale, 78–80
Deductive reasoning, 343
Defense mechanisms, 187–191
Deficiency needs, 225
Delgado, José, 72
Delinquency, 161–163
Delirium tremens (D.T.'s), 257–258, 260
Delusions, 257, 260
Demonological model, 280
Dendrites, 68
Dependent variables, 13–14

Depressants, 53, 54
Depression, 249–250, 261
Despair versus ego integrity, 219
Developmental calendar, 109
Developmental psychology, 20–21
Developmental tasks, 150–157
Dewey, John, 6
Diet, adequate, 123–124
Differential Aptitude Tests (DAT), 382–383, 384
Differential psychology, 21
Disabilities, people with, 110–111
Directed thinking, 339
Discipline, 125
Discrimination, 419
    effects of, 377–378
    eliminating, 422–423
Diseases, and behavior, 249
Displacement, 188
Dissociative reactions, 253
Distortion of memory patterns, 334
Divination, 476
Divorce
    children of, 128
    raising children after, 459
    self-awareness exercise for coping with, 547–548
Dix, Dorothea, 284
Dixon, Jeane, 489–490
Dominant genes, 103–104
Donaldson, Kenneth, 308
Double-blind experiments, 15
Doubt versus autonomy, 215
Down syndrome, 105, 268
Draw-a-Person test, 390
Dream symbols, 45
Dreams, 38–39
    analyzing, 42–44
    catching, 43
    Freud's theory of, 40
    lucid, 44
Drug babies, 127–128
Drug culture, 160
Drug therapy, 309–310
Drugs
    and adolescence, 160–161
    antidepressant, 310
    antipsychotic, 309
    during pregnancy, 106–108
    psychoactive, 49–56
    psychotropic, 309–310
D.T.'s (delirium tremens), 257–258, 260

E

Ear, mechanism of, 77–78
Eardrum, 77
Eastern philosophy, 486–487

Economic independence, preparing for, 151–152
ECT (electroconvulsive therapy), 250, 262, 264
Ectomorphs, 176–178
Education, eliminating sexism in, 453
Educational Testing Service (ETS), 374
EEG (electroencephalograph) machine, 38
Ego, 184
Ego ideal, 187
Ego integrity versus despair, 219
Ego states, 520–522
Eidetic recall, 334
Einstein, Albert, 174, 360
Electroconvulsive therapy (ECT), 250, 262, 264
Electroencephalograph (EEG) machine, 38
Ellis, Albert, 292
Emotional behavior, 119–120
Emotional challenges in adolescence, 144–149
Emotional environment, 110
Emotional independence, achieving, from family, 153–155
Emotional ties, shifting, in adolescence, 148–149
Emotions, 326
    brain waves and, 511
    defining, 119
Encounter groups, 298–303
Endocrine and metabolic disorders, 269–270
Endocrine glands, 69, 71, 73
Endomorphs, 176–178
Environment, and personality, 173
Environmental causes of mental illness, 244–248
Environmental variables, 102
Environmental view, 439–440
Epilepsy, 270–271
Epileptic seizures, 69
Equal Rights Amendment (ERA), 450, 452
Equilibratory sense, 86–87
Erikson, Erik, 213, 215, 219
Erikson's eight stages of development, 217
Eros, 184
ESP (extrasensory perception), 488–491
Ethics in gathering data, 18–19
Ethnic diversity, role of, 231
ETS (Educational Testing Service), 374
Evolved-primate theory, 100
Existential approach to psychotherapy, 288–290
Existential psychology, 229–230

Existential view of neurotic behavior, 230
Expectations and "seeing," 37
Experimental groups, 15
Extrasensory perception (ESP), 488–491
Extroversion, 222
Eye, 74–75, 76
Eysenck, H. J., 177

F

Family
    achieving emotional independence from, 153–155
    functioning within, 245–247
Family breakup and adolescence, 158
Family size, effect of, on intelligence, 114
Family systems theory, 230–231
Family therapy, 303, 517–518
Faraday, Ann, 41
Fasteau, Marc, 458
Feedback, 326
Feldenkrais, Moshe, 506
Feldenkrais method, 506–507
Female-male differences, 438–441
Feminists, 445
    jobs and, 452–453
    and Sigmund Freud, 186
Fictional finalism, 211
Flexibility and creativity, 349–350
Fogging, 513
Forebrain, 65–67
Forgetting, 334
Formal operations stage, 115
Frank, Anne, 148
Frankl, Viktor, 229, 230, 288
Frederick II, 110
Free association, 195, 287
Free Child, 522
Free information technique, 513
Freedman, Jonathan, 412
Frequency (sound), 77
Freud, Anna, 180, 213
Freud, Sigmund, 7, 30, 96, 170–172, 179–181
    feminists and, 186
    neo-Freudians versus, 212
    personality theory since, 202–232
Freud's psychosexual stages, 216
Freud's theory of dreams, 40
Freud's theory of personality, 170–198
Friedan, Betty, 451
Friendships, self-awareness exercise for evaluating, 544–545
Fritsch, Gustav, 33
Fromm, Erich, 159, 211
Frontal lobe, 67

Frustration, 244–245
Functional fixedness, 344
Functional psychoses, 259–263
Functioning
    within family, 245–247
    on job, 247
    in society, 247–248

G

Gage, Phineas, 269
Gall, Franz Joseph, 175
Games analysis, 523–525, 527
Gangs, 401
Gardner, Howard, 362
Garfield, Patricia, 44
GATB (General Aptitude Test
    Battery), 382
Gay behavior, 422, 463
Geller, Uri, 490–491, 495
Gender, role of, 231
General Aptitude Test Battery
    (GATB), 382
Generation gap, 149
Generativity versus stagnation, 219
Genes, 102–106
Genetic screening, 112
Genital stage, 194
Genital warts, 145
Gesell, Arnold, 115
Gestalt therapy groups, 300, 302
Gestalts, 35–36
GHB, 54
Glands, 69–73
Glasser, William, 516–517
Golding, William, 101
Gonads, 73
Gonorrhea, 145
Graphology, 482–484
Group behavior, 402
Group intelligence tests, 372–373
Group pressures in adolescence,
    155–157
Group therapy, 294–305
Grouping, 115
Groups
    behavior in, 398–431
    roles within, 403–404
Growth
    rapid, in adolescence, 142–143
    stages of, 96–99
Growth spurts, in adolescence, 141
Guidance, 326
Guilford, J. P., 362
Guilt versus initiative, 215

H

Halfway houses, 310
Hall, G. Stanley, 139

Hallucinations, 256–257
Hallucinogens, 49, 53, 55
Hammond, Roy, 483
Hand gestures, 400
Handicapped people, 110–111
Happiness, in existentialism, 230
Harris, Tom, 520
Hashish, 55
Hatha yoga, 486
Healing, 481–482
Hearing
    art of, 78
    behavior and, 77–80
Hebephrenic schizophrenia,
    261–262
Hedonists, 147
Hereditary view, 439
Heredity, 101–108
    contributions of, to personality,
    173
    genes, in, 102–106
Hermann, Ned, 328
Heroin, 52, 53, 55
Herpes, 145
Hindbrain, 63–65
Hindu Code of Manu, 446
Hippocampus, 329
Hippocrates, 33, 176, 280
Histrionic personality disorder,
    266–267
Hitzig, Eduard, 33
Hobson, Allan J., 42
Homeless mentally ill, 310–311
Homemaker's double bind, 448, 449
Homosexuality, society and, 422,
    462–463
Hormones, 69
Horner, Matina, 443, 444
Horney, Karen, 212–213, 214
Horoscope, 478–479
Hospices, 428
Hot lines, 306
Houdini, Harry, 480
House-Tree-Person test, 390
Househusbands, 459, 460
Howe, Julia Ward, 350
Human-potential groups, 298
Human-relations groups, 298
Humanist psychology, 8, 223–226
Humors, 176
Hurkos, Peter, 489
Hyperactivity, 271
Hypnosis, 45–49
Hypothalamus, 65–66
Hypotheses, 11–13

I

I Ching, 476, 477
Id, 184
Idealists, 147

Identification, 406
Identity
    role confusion versus, 215
    self-awareness exercise for
    finding, 535–536
Illness, term, 244
Images, 337
Impulse control in adolescence,
    150–151
Inadequate antisocial personality,
    265
Independence, 154
Independent variables, 13–14
Individual psychology, 287
Individual therapy, 286
Inductive reasoning, 342–343
Industrial psychology, 21
Industry versus inferiority, 215
Infant mortality, 127
Infant phase, 97
Inferiority
    feelings of, 209–210
    industry versus, 215
Initiative versus guilt, 215
Insight, 343, 350
Intellectual development, 113–119
Intelligence, 326
    birth order and family size effect
    on, 114
    defined, 360–362
    race and, 376–379
    "teaching," 375–376
Intelligence quotient (IQ), 362–364
Interest inventories, 385
Interference, 334
Internalization, 406
Interpersonal relationships, 9
Interpersonal therapy, 287–288
Intimacy versus isolation, 219
Introspection, 6
Introversion, 222
Iowa Tests of Educational
    Development (ITED), 380
IQ (intelligence quotient), 362–364
Iris, in eye, 74
Isolation tanks, 56
Isolation versus intimacy, 219
Itard, Jean-Marc, 118
ITED (Iowa Tests of Educational
    Development), 380

J

James, William, 6
Janov, Arthur, 515–516
Jayson, L. M., 239
Job(s)
    feminists and, 452–453
    functioning on, 247
    sexism on, 445–448

Johnson, Lyndon, 447
Jung, Carl, 219–222, 486
Jungian unconscious, 220–222

K

Kennedy, John F., 490
Kinesthesis, 86
King, Martin Luther, Jr., 415, 417, 420
Kirk, Grayson, 447
Kirlian photography, 492
Koans, 486
Köchler, Wolfgang, 343
Koko, 318–320
Kopp, Sheldon, 154
Krippner, Stanley, 489
Kübler-Ross, Elisabeth, 427–429
Kuehl, Sheila James 456

L

Laing, R. D., 288–290
Laird, Eleanor and Donald, 336
Language
    culture and, 340
    mastery of, 115–117
    sexist, 454
    in thinking process, 339–340
Lashley, Karl, 329
Latency period, 194
Latent content of dreams, 42
Lateral thinking, 345–347
Leadership, 404
Learning
    defined, 321
    factors influencing, 325–328
    improving, 335–337
    improving ability for, 341–342
Learning psychology, 21
Learning styles, 328
Leboyer, Frederick, 98
Left brain versus right brain, 67–68
Lens, in eye, 74
Leveling, 334
Lewin, Kurt, 299
Libido, 184
Life, power for changing, 558–559
Life force, 184
Life script, 527
Lilly, John, 56
Listening skills, 342
Living together, 464
Lobes of cerebral cortex, 66–67
Logotherapy, 288
Long-term memory, 331, 332
Lorenz, Konrad, 411
Lowen, Alexander, 509
LSD, 49, 53, 55
Lucid dreams, 44

M

MA (mental age) score, 363
Macho, term, 457–458
MacLaine, Shirley, 481
Magical forces, belief in, 474–475
Magnus, Albertus, 175
Maharishi Mahesh Yogi, 484, 487
Maladjusted people, 240, 241
Malcolm X, 420
Male chauvinists, 443, 445
Male-female differences, 438–441
Maltz, Maxwell, 514
Manic-depressive psychosis, 262
Manifest content of dreams, 42
Marathon groups, 302–303
Marijuana, 51–52, 55
Marriage
    changing concepts of, 463–465
    early, 157
Martin, Joseph, 305
Maslow, Abraham, 223–226
Maturation, 108–109
    in adolescence, early or late, 143
    sexual, 144–146
May, Rollo, 227, 230
McConnell, James, 330
McMillan, Robert, 342
MDMA, 54
Mead, Margaret, 139, 439–440
Media, eliminating sexism in,
    453–454
Meditation, 485, 486
Medium, 480
Medulla, 63–64
Meecham, William, 80
Memory, 329–337, 361
    as electrochemical process, 330
    improving, 335–337
    physical basis for, 329–330
    process of, 331
    types of, 330, 332
Men
    changing roles of, 458–459
    women's movement and, 457–460
Menninger, Karl A., 243
Mental age (MA) score, 363
Mental health-illness scale, 245
Mental health problems in American
    society, 242
Mental hospitals, 308–310
Mental illness
    causes of, 244–250, 282
    environmental causes of, 244–248
    among homeless, 310–311
    physical factors that cause,
    248–249
    treatment of, 283–284
Meperidine, 55
Mesomorphs, 176–178
Messages, transmittal of, 68–69

Metaneeds, 225
Methadone, 55
Methamphetamine, 54
Mikhailova, Nelya, 491
Milgram, Stanley, 409–410
Milieu therapy, 309
Mind-altering (psychoactive) drugs,
    49–56
Mind set, 343–344
Minnesota Multiphasic Personality
    Inventory (MMPI), 386–388
Mistrust versus trust, 215
MMPI (Minnesota Multiphasic
    Personality Inventory), 386–388
Mnemonic devices, 333
Modeling behavior, 442
Morality, development of, 120–121
Moreno, J. L., 295
Morphine, 53, 55
Motivation, 125–126, 326
Mozart, Wolfgang, 350
Multiple aptitude batteries, 382
Multiple personalities, 253, 255
Murphy, Michael, 518–519
Mutual aid groups, 303–305

N

Napoleon, 210–211, 446, 477
Narcissistic personality disorder, 267
Narcotics, 53, 55
National Organization for Women
    (NOW), 450, 452
Nature versus nurture debate, 101
Negative assertion, 513
Negative conditions, removing, 341
Negative correlation, 16
Negative inquiry, 513–514
Negative reinforcement, 205
Neo-Freudians, 209, 228, 287–288
    Freud versus, 212
    personality theory and, 209–219
Nervous system, 65
Neural pathway, 68
Neurasthenia, 255
Neurons, 63, 68–69
Neuropathological model, 281
Neuroses, 250–255
Neurotic behavior, existential view
    of, 230
Neurotic needs, 213
Neurotransmitters, 69
New Age movement, 480–482
New Testament, 446
Newborn phase, 97
Newhart, Bob, 285
Newton, Isaac, 63
Nicotine, 49–51, 55
95 percent confidence, 494
Nociceptors, 84

Noise pollution, 78–80
Nonassertive behavior, 512
Nonconformity, 405
Nondirected thinking, 339
Nondirective therapy, 291
Nonverbal communication, 398
Normal behavior, defining, 240
Normal curve of distribution, 363, 364
Norms, 368
Novelty, 326
NOW (National Organization for Women), 450, 452
Numbers, mastery of, in tests, 381
Numerical skills, 361–362
Numerology, 479
Nurture, 101
Nurturing, 123
Nurturing Parent, 522

O

Obesity, 124
Objective personality tests, 386–388
Objectivity, 366
Obsessions, 251, 261
Occipital lobe, 66
Occupational and recreational activities, 310
O'Connor, Sandra Day, 452–453
Oedipus complex, 193
Olfactory bulbs, 81
Olfactory patches, 81
Operant behaviors, 205–206, 323
Operant conditioning, 322–323
Operant conditioning theories, 292
Opium, 53
Optic nerve, 75
Oral stage, 192–193
Organic psychoses, 257–259
Outer ear, 77
Overlearning, 341

P

PA (positive addiction), 516–517
Pain receptors, 84
Palmistry, 479
Pappenheim, Bertha, 170–171
Paranoid reactions, 262–263
Paranoid schizophrenia, 260
Parapsychology, 474, 486–496
Parent-child understanding, self-awareness exercise in, 550–551
Parent ego state, 520–522
Parental pressure, 129
Parents, role of, 441–442
Paresis, 257

Parietal lobe, 67
Parise, Filicia, 489
Passive-aggressive personality disorder, 267
Past lives therapy (PLT), 519–520
Patterson, Penny, 318–320
Pavlov, Ivan, 7, 204
PCP, 49, 50, 55
Peak experiences, 226
Pearce, Hubert, 496
Penfield, Wilder, 33
Percentile ratings, 368
Perception, 35
Perceptual ability, 361
Perceptual inference, 36
Performance tests, 381–382
Peripheral nervous system, 65
Perls, Frederick ("Fritz"), 300, 301, 302
Persistence and creativity, 350
Persona, 221–222
Personal-growth groups, 298
Personal unconscious, 220
Personal values, self-awareness exercise for identifying, 557
Personality
    behaviorists and, 204–207
    categorizing adolescent, 147
    contributions of heredity and environment to, 173
    defined by traits, 178–179
    defining, 172–173
    explaining, 174–181
    Freud's theory of, 170–198
    physical attributes and, 175–176
    psychosocial theory of, 179, 181
    supernatural forces and, 174–175
    troubled. See Troubled personality.
    typologies explaining, 176–178
Personality testing, 383–385
Personality theory, 21
    key, comparing, 228–229
    neo-Freudians and, 209–219
    since Freud, 202–231
Peyote, 55
Phallic stage, 193
Phencyclidine, 55
Phobias, 251–252
Phrenology, 175
Physical appearance in adolescence, 150
Physical attributes and personality, 175–176
Physical changes during adolescence, 139–143
Physical defects, 110–111
Physical factors that cause mental illness, 248–249
Physiological psychology, 21–22
Piaget, Jean, 100, 113, 116–117

Piaget's four stages of cognitive development, 113–115
Picasso, Pablo, 447
Pinel, Philippe, 284
Pituitary gland, 71
PK (psychokinesis), 472, 488, 491
Placebo, 15
Placebo effect, 61
Plath, Sylvia, 238
Plato, 6
Pleasure center, 66
Pleasure principle, 184
PLT (past lives therapy), 519–520
Poltergeists, 472
Positive addiction (PA), 516–517
Positive correlation, 16
Positive reinforcement, 205, 210–211, 323
Post-traumatic stress disorder (PTSD), 249
Posthypnotic suggestion, 47
Poverty, and children, 128
Powelson, Harvey, 52
Power
    for changing life, 558–559
    lack of, 412
Pratt, J. G., 496
Preadolescence, 137–138
Precognition, 489–490
Preconscious, 181, 182
Pregnancy
    drugs during, 106–108
    unwanted, 157, 159–160
Prejudice, 417–423
    causes of, 418–420
    power of, 420–422
Prenatal phase, 97
Preoperational stage, 113–115
Pressure receptors, 83–84
Price, Richard, 518
Primal therapy, 515–516
Private psychotherapists and clinics, 307–308
Problem solving
    improving ability for, 344–347
    types of, 342–343
Procrastination, 191
Projection, 189
Projective personality tests, 386, 388–390
Pseudosciences, 474
    dangers of relying on, 475
    modern, 482–484
Psi, 474
Psychoactive (mind-altering) drugs, 49–56
Psychoanalysis, 7, 172, 194–196, 286–287
Psychoanalytical model, 281
Psychocybernetics, 514
Psychodrama, 295–298

Psychodynamic theory, 100–101
Psychohistory, 213, 215
Psychokinesis (PK), 472, 488, 491
Psychological dependency, 51, 161
Psychological testing, 358–391
Psychology
  basic areas of study in, 19–22
  careers in, 23–25
  defined, 5–6
  getting started in, 24
  history of, 6–8
  reasons for studying, 8–9
  as study of behavior, 2–27
  undergraduate requirements for
    major in, 23
Psychometrist, 358
Psychopoetry, 297
Psychoses, 256–263
Psychosexual stages, Freud's, 216
Psychosocial development, theory
  of, 215, 219
Psychosocial model, 281
Psychosocial stages, 215
Psychosocial theory of personality,
  179, 181
Psychosomatic illness, 188
Psychosurgery, 70
Psychotherapists, 12–13
Psychotherapy
  choosing type of, 284–285
  defined, 280–285
  effects of, 293
  existential approach to, 288–290
  historical approaches to, 280–
    283
  individual, strengths and
    weaknesses of, 285
  radio, 289
  types of, 286–294
Psychotropic drugs, 309–310
PTSD (post-traumatic stress
  disorder), 249
Puberty, 138
Puharich, Andrija, 45
Punishment, 206, 323, 326
  modifying, 414
Pupil, in eye, 74
Purdah, 450
Pyramidology, 482, 483

R

Race, intelligence and, 376–379
Rader, William, 517
Radical model, 283
Radical psychiatrist, 283
Radical psychiatry, 288–290
Radio psychotherapy, 289
Randi, James, 495
Rank, Otto, 98

Rapid eye movement (REM) sleep,
  38–39
RAS (reticular activating system),
  64–65
Rational Emotive Therapy (RET),
  292
Rationalization, 190–191
Reaction formation, 190
Reading ability, and tests, 381
Reality principle, 184
Reality therapy, 516–517
Reasoning ability, 361
Rebel Child, 522
Recall, 331
Recessive genes, 103–104
Recognition, 334
Recollection, 331
Reddy, Helen, 447
Rees, Erik, 482
Reflexology, 506
Regression, 189–190
Rehearsal, 331
Reich, Wilhelm, 506
Reinforcement, 205, 323, 324
Relationships, maintaining, 407
Reliability, 368
Religious model, 280
REM (rapid eye movement) sleep,
  38–39
Remembering, 332–334
Repressed material, 334
Repression, 181, 187–188
Research psychology, 22
Resistances, 196, 287
Respondent behaviors, 205, 322
Response, 321
Restlessness, in adolescence, 146
RET (Rational Emotive Therapy),
  292
Reticular activating system (RAS),
  64–65
Retina, 74–75
Rewards, 323, 326
Reyborn, Wallace, 447
Rhine, J. B., 488, 496
Right brain versus left brain, 67–68
"Right to choose," 454–455
"Right to die," 429–430
Rigidity, 344
Rites of passage, 138
Rods, in eyes, 75
Rogers, Carl, 8, 223, 290–291
Rohypnol, 54
Role confusion versus identity, 215
Roles, 403–404
Rolf, Ida, 508
Rolfing, 508–509
Rollin, Betty, 447
Roosevelt, Theodore, 210
Rorschach, Hermann, 388
Rorschach Inkblot Test, 388–389

Roth, Lillian, 305
Rubenfeld, Ilana, 509
Rubin, Theodore Isaac, 238
Rules, 337
Rush, Benjamin, 284

S

Same-sex unions, 465
SAS (standard age scores), 370
SAT, 379
Satir, Virginia, 517–518
Scatterplots, 17
Schedules of reinforcement, 324
Schizophrenia, 248, 259–262
Schlafly, Phyllis, 447, 450, 452
Schlessinger, Laura, 289
Schloss, Gilbert, 297
Schreiber, Flora, 255
Scientific method, 11–12
SCII (Strong-Campbell Interest
  Inventory), 385
Searching for new ways to grow,
  501–505
Séguin, Edouard, 6
Self, 222
Self-actualization, 10, 226
Self-actualizing person, 224, 225
Self-awareness exercise
  for choosing career, 538–539
  for coping with divorce, 547–548
  for evaluating friendships,
    544–545
  for expressing anger, 541–542
  for finding identity, 535–536
  for identifying personal values,
    557
  for overcoming shyness, 553–554
  in parent-child understanding,
    550–551
Self-disclosure, 513
Self-esteem, sexism and, 443
Self-fulfilling prophecy, 126
Self-identity in adolescence, 152
Self-realization,
  basic principles of, 504–505
  through books, 507
Self-realization movement (SRM),
  503–505
Semicircular canals, 87
Senility, 258–259
Senses. See specific names.
Senses, additional, 86–88
Sensitivity groups, 298
Sensory adaptation, 83
Sensory-awareness games, 298
Sensory experience, 35
Sensory memory, 330–332
Sensory-motor stage, 113

Sensory stimulation, 124–125
Serios, Ted, 492
Sex determination, 105
Sex education, 461–462
Sex glands, 73
Sex roles, 438
  communication of, 441–442
  development of, 121
Sexism, 443
  body image and, 453–454
  costs of, 448–449
  in education, eliminating, 453
  ending, 453–456
  on job, 445–448
  self-esteem and, 443
  women and, 442–449
Sexist language, 454
Sexual drives, influence of, 192
Sexual harassment, 455–456
Sexual maturation, 144–146
Sexuality, 435–467
  changing patterns of, 461–465
  childhood, 192
Sexually transmitted diseases
  (STDs), 144–146
Shadow, 222
Shakespeare's seven ages of man,
  217
Shaping behavior, 206–207
Shared values, 407
Sharpening, 334
Sheldon, William, 176–178
Shepard, Martin, 286
Sherif, Muzafer, 412–414
Short-term memory, 331, 332
Shtrang, Shipi, 491
Shyness, self-awareness exercise for
  overcoming, 553–554
Signals, 324
Simon, Theodore, 360, 365
Simple schizophrenia, 259
Single-blind experiments, 15
Size constancy, 76
Skeels, H. M., 375
Skin senses, 83–86
Skinner, B. F., 100, 202–204, 205,
  211
Skinner, Eve, 203
Sleep stages, 38–39
Smell, sense of, 80–81
Smith, Adam, 481
Smith, Nancy R., 439
Social causes of aggression, 411–412
Social dangers of conformity,
  409–410
Social interest, 211–212
Social norms, 403
Social pressures, behavior and,
  405–410
Social psychology, 22
Social urges, 209

Socialization, 120, 403
Socially oriented groups, 402
Society, 9
  functioning in, 247–248
  homosexuality and, 462–463
Sociobiology, 175–176
Sociopaths, 147
Somatotypes, 176–178
Sophocles, 193
Sound, 77
Spatial perception, 361
Sphinx, riddle of, 216
Spinal cord, 65
Spiritualism, 480
Sports psychology, 22
SRM (self-realization movement),
  503–505
Stagnation versus generativity, 219
Standard age scores (SAS), 370
Standardization, 368
Stanford-Binet Intelligence Scale,
  369–371
Stanton, Elizabeth Cady, 446, 450
Statistical significance, 16
Statistics, 15–16
STDs (sexually transmitted
  diseases), 144–146
Stereotypes, 418
Stern, Daniel, 102
Stevenson, Robert Louis, 255
Stimoceiver, 72
Stimulants, 49, 53, 54
Stimulus, 35, 321
Stimulus-response theory, 321–325
Stimulus-response units, 205
"Storm-and-stress" theory, 139
STP, 55
Strategies for coping, 533–560
Stress, 244
Stringers, 328
Strong-Campbell Interest Inventory
  (SCII), 385
Structural integration, 508–509
Sublimation, 188–189
Suicide, 423–425
Sullivan, Harry Stack, 287–288
Superego, 184–185, 187
Supernatural, belief in, 474–475
Supernatural forces and personality,
  174–175
Symbols, 337
Symptom substitution, 294
Synapses, 69
Syphilis, 145
Systematic desensitization, 207

T

T-groups, 299
TA contract, 526, 527

TA (Transactional Analysis),
  520–527
Talk-oriented groups, 402
Tarot cards, 476–477
Taste, sense of, 80, 81–83
TAT (Thematic Apperception Test),
  389
Tavris, Carol, 456
"Teaching" intelligence, 375–376
Telepathy, 488–489
Temporal lobe, 66–67
Terman, L. M., 365, 370
Territory, protection of, 412
Tetrahydrocannabinol (THC), 51
Thalamus, 65
Thanatos, 184
THC (tetrahydrocannabinol),
  51
Thematic Apperception Test (TAT),
  389
Thermoreceptors, 84–85
Thinking, 337–340
  directed, 339
  language in, 339–340
  logical, pitfalls in, 338
  nondirected, 339
Thorndike, Edward L., 321–322
Thurstone, L. L., 361
Thyroid gland, 73
Tillich, Paul, 214
TM (Transcendental Meditation),
  484, 487
Tobacco, 50–51
Tolman, E. C., 325
Touching, importance of, 85–86
Toxin model, 281
Traits, personality defined by,
  178–179
Tranquilizers, 309–310
Transactional Analysis (TA),
  520–527
Transactions, 522–523
Transcendental Meditation (TM),
  484, 487
Transfer of attention, 347
Transference, 195, 287
Trauma
  accident, 249
  brain, 269
Trial-and-error learning, 322
Trial-and-error methods, 342
Troubled personality, 240, 241
  defining, 240–243
  double bind of, 290
  getting help for, 306–311
  helping, 278–313
  understanding, 238–274
Trust versus mistrust, 215
Twelve Steps, 305
Typologies explaining personality,
  176–178

U

Ullman, Montague, 489
Unconditional positive regard, 291
Unconscious, 34, 171
   Jungian, 220–222
   power of, 181–184
Undergraduate requirements for
   major in psychology, 23
U.S. society, problems in, 242, 416

V

Validity, 368
van Gogh, Vincent, 270
Variable-interval reinforcement, 324
Variables, 13–14
Verbal relationships, 362
Verbalization, 342
Vertical thinking, 344–345
Viscott, David, 254, 278
Vision, 73–76
Vision adaptation, 75–76
Vocabulary, and tests, 380–381

W

Wambach, Helen, 519–520
Watson, John, 8, 204–205
Wayne, John, 446
Webb, Susan, 455
Wechsler, David, 360, 371
Wechsler scales, 371–372
Well-adjusted people, 240, 241
Wilson, Edward O., 176
Wolfe, Thomas, 137
Women
   eliminating violence against,
   456
   sexism and, 442–449
Women's movement, men and,
   457–460
Woolf, Virginia, 448–449
Word association test, 222,
   223
Word fluency, 361
Workable compromise, 513
Working through, 287
Wright, Richard, 420
Wundt, Wilhelm, 6, 204

X

X-chromosomes, 105

Y

Y-chromosomes, 105
Yoga, 486
Young adulthood, 138–139

Z

Zajonc, Robert, 114
Zangwill, Oliver, 68
Zazen, 486
Zen Buddhism, 486
Zener cards, 487–488, 496
Zero correlation, 16
Zimbardo, Philip, 413
Zodiac signs, 477–478